# POLICYMAKING
# UNDER ADVERSITY

# POLICYMAKING UNDER ADVERSITY

## YEHEZKEL DROR

Transaction Books
New Brunswick (U.S.A.) and Oxford (U.K.)

First paperback edition © 1988
Copyright © 1986 by Transaction, Inc.
New Brunswick, New Jersey 08903

All rights reserved under International and Pan-American Copyright Conventions. No part of this book may be reproduced or transmitted in any form or by any means, electronic or mechanical, including photocopy, recording, or any information storage and retrieval system, without prior permission in writing from the publisher. All inquiries should be addressed to Transaction Books, Rutgers—The State University, New Brunswick, New Jersey 08903.

Library of Congress Catalog Number: 84-24119
ISBN: **0-88738-721-7** (paper)
Printed in the United States of America

**Library of Congress Cataloging in Publication Data**

Dror, Yehezkel, 1928-
  Policymaking under adversity.

  Bibliography: p.
  Includes indexes.
  1. Policy sciences.   I. Title.
H97.D758  1986              361.6′1                    84-24119
**ISBN 0-88738-721-7**

To Bracha and Zvi Elboim,
my unusual parents-in-law

# Contents

# Preface

This book deals with the theory and practice of policymaking under adversity, with some historic inputs and a forward look. Focusing on what I propose to call metaphorically *maze policy-behavior*, and applying my general policy sciences approaches to conditions of adversity, I make an effort to advance general theory, on one hand, and to design applicable improvement approaches, on the other hand. Thus, this book is quite different in focus from my recently republished *Public Policymaking Reexamined* (Transaction, 1983), as supplemented with a new introduction.

I continue working on a third volume, titled *Policy-Gambling*, which develops a theory of policymaking as coping with uncertainty and ignorance. Each one of the trilogy volumes adopts a different perspective and stands by itself. It is my hope that when the trilogy is finished, it will add up to a comprehensive and multidimensional treatise on policymaking theory, reality, and improvement as a main part of a general theory of societal command and control.

This book could not have been written without a three-year research leave granted to me by the Hebrew University of Jerusalem. For this I am grateful to my colleagues at the Department of Political Science, who willingly accepted additional burdens to enable me to engage in my studies.

I am also deeply indebted to a number of institutions and their devoted staffs, who supported and aided this study, as well as to senior policymakers in many countries, including my own, who made me a partner to their Herculean labor and endless adventure (Oliver 1931). In particular, I would like to thank the Samuel Neaman Institute for Advanced Studies in Science and Technology, Technion—Israel Institute of Technology, Haifa, for sponsoring a study on the improvements of policymaking in Israel, which I headed; the United Nations Development Program, for opportunities to work on policymaking problems in some Third World countries, broadening my perspectives and providing some tough pilot-testing of ideas; and the Technical Co-operation Service of the Organization for Economic Co-operation and Development (OECD), for outstanding insights deep into governance.

Different, but not smaller, is my gratitude to the Woodrow Wilson International Center for Scholars, Washington, DC, and the Science Center Berlin for providing very stimulating environments. Special appreciation is due to the Institute for Advanced Study Berlin and the Russell Sage Foundation, New York, where this book slowly took shape.

Last, but not least, let me thank Transaction, Inc., and especially its president Irving Louis Horowitz and his colleagues, for willingly undertaking and carefully implementing a double publication venture.

One feature of this book that needs some explanation is the extensive, though incomplete, list of mainly recent references integrated into the text. These references are provided neither as scholastic support for propositions nor to demonstrate erudition. Their purpose is to help readers to look into subjects that they find interesting. Bibliographic aid is all the more necessary because of the breadth of multidisciplinary literature salient to the study of public policymaking, combined with lack of suitable comprehensive annotated bibliographies (as provided by D.E. Wilson 1979 for parts of the subject. Invaluable and amazingly underutilized are the *Future Survey* monthly and annuals edited by Michael Marien; see Marien 1980; Marien 1982; Marien 1983. Nagel 1983b is an important literature guide to policy studies as is Robey 1984).

Rather than prepare a bibliographic essay, as in other books of mine, I share with readers, in the form of references in the text, some of the fruits of an extensive literature examination that consumed large parts of the three-year research leave. At the very least, this may save the time and effort of colleagues and students. Some German literature that has no equivalents I know of in English and single essential items in French are also included. The policy of this book not to belabor subjects adequately covered in the literature and to refer to them only succinctly makes extensive references to the relied-upon writings all the more necessary.

The study of policymaking being an endless venture, not less so than the practice of policymaking, comments, suggestions, and enlightenments by readers are solicited. These can be of much help to the author in his continuous concerns with the problematics of governance. All inputs will be appreciated.

# 1

# Scope, Concepts, Methods

## Leitmotif

The overall problematics at which this book is directed is well put by a simile used by a historian in evaluating belated Roman response to financial crisis (MacMullen 1976, 116): "Government . . . reacted like a frightened child at the controls of a runaway express train, pushing all sorts of levers and knobs."

The main questions to be probed in this book are whether and when such a simile presents a correct picture of policymaking, perhaps now with a jet plane, loaded with nuclear bombs, to be substituted for express train; what are the main features and causes of such "maze policy-behavior"; what can be done to improve it; and what consequences are to be expected from it.

Moving from pictorial images to the book as a scientific and professional endeavor, one needs to explore its scope, concepts, and methods somewhat before moving into the matter itself.

## Need for Theoretic Perspective

Policy sciences (a concept I write in the plural, to recognize multiple contents, but treat grammatically in the singular, to underline basic unity) continues to lack adequate concept packages and significant theoretic conjectures. Although this book does not presume to arrive at an integrated general theory of policymaking, nevertheless an effort is made to put dispersed and disparate findings and ideas into a meaningful theoretic framework and to revise some widely accepted premises, with the help of adversity used both as a theoretic construct and as a pervasive feature of policymaking realities.

Most of the book looks at adversity as facing policymaking at present and in the foreseeable future. But this is only one situation out of a larger set, even if one of particular concern at present. Adversity in different forms has conditioned policymaking in nearly all historic situations and will do so in the future. Therefore, examination of policymaking as shaped by adversity and as trying to face up to adversity exposes universal characteristics of policymaking.

Because most of modern public policy research has developed during a unique period of economic growth between 1948 and 1973, the overwhelming importance of adversity in shaping policymaking has received inadequate attention. Recent economic problems may open up thinking and research to more realistic views and make the approach of this book more relevant to pressing concerns, but, in principle, the perspective proffered in this book does not depend on short-term economic upswings or downturns: Adversity in different forms being endemic to policymaking situations, studying policymaking under adversity does provide a needed theoretic perspective of broad applicability.

## Adversity as a Prevailing Policymaking Condition

To repeat the crucial point made above: This book deals with actual features and required characteristics of policymaking as conditioned by adversity. All policymaking faces adversity, sometimes less and usually more so, but many policymaking studies have adopted a rather optimistic perspective, neglecting till recently the impacts of adversity. At present, under the influence of manifest realities, more attention is being paid to features of policymaking related to adversity (C. Campbell 1983; C. Carter and Pinder 1982; Chazan 1983; Cox 1981; Hood and Wright 1981; A.G. Jordan and Richardson 1979; Richardson 1982). Still, the subject is very undertreated, especially on a broad theoretical level.

One way to proceed is to design a pure-type construct, or set of constructs, of policymaking under serious adversity. Within such an approach, at least three pure-type constructs are needed: One, of policymaking under prosperity; a second, of policymaking under serious adversity; and a third, of policymaking in situations of acute calamity. The difference between policymaking under adversity, including serious adversity, and policymaking in situations of acute calamity needs attention: Serious adversity can include a propensity toward situations of calamity, but policymaking in situations of acute calamity follows different patterns and raises separate issues, as touched upon in part in some of the studies dealing with crisis management. (An extreme case is decision making by the Jewish councils put in charge by the Nazis of Ghettos, the so-called "Judenrat," who faced the most extreme adversity one can imagine. See Trunk 1972).

Another way to approach the subject is a historic-comparative one, with examination of the central minds of governments at various periods and locations of serious adversity.

This book adopts a third approach, with some supplements from the first and second ones: Contemporary policymaking is treated as policymaking under adversity, with some revealing features all the more visible because of the transition from growing prosperity and rosy assessments of the future to worsening conditions and dark assessment of things to come. Concomitantly, some historic inputs are utilized and some elements of a pure type of policymaking under serious adversity are explored.

In dealing with adversity, main attention is paid to specific features of contemporary and emerging situations, as considered in chapter 2. Conceptually, the term *crisis* is reserved for situations of time-compressed and sudden imposing events up to calamity that require rapid decision making; the term *adversity*, as qualified and elaborated by various adjectives when necessary, refers to all forms of massive difficulties facing policymaking, other than crisis, as defined above. In this way, it is hoped that some of the ambiguity of the term *crisis* as used in the literature is avoided.

Responses of governance to adversity constitute an important subject scientifically, and a crucial subject applicatively. From a scientific perspective, periods of pressure and stress expose basic features of governance, inaccessible under relatively stable or incrementally changing conditions. In this sense, hard cases make indeed good science. Within a prescriptive orientation, periods of pressure and stress pose a supreme need for help: If applied social sciences in general and policy sciences in particular are of use only when the sun is shining or, at most, partly clouded, then their significance as aids to societal and governmental problem handling is very low indeed. This is a challenge taken up in the present book, all of which is oriented toward adversity-related features of policymaking.

## "Central Mind of Government" as Focal Subject

A few studies on societies and governance under pressure exist, ranging from historic investigations of particular polities (Bois 1984; MacMullen 1976; Manning 1983; Pocock 1975; Salmon 1975; C. Starr 1982) and types of societies (Eisenstadt 1963), to contemporary investigations of governance under stress (Jänicke 1973a; Jänicke 1973b; Preisl and Mohler 1979), up to breaking points of democracy (Erdmann and Schulze 1980; E. Kaufman 1979; Linz and Stepan 1978). Attempts at adversity-related theory building also occur: on crisis (in the sense of waves of difficulties) as inbuilt in accelerated development (Almond, Flanagan, and Mundt 1973; Binder et al. 1971; Grew 1978); on decline as endemic to societal dynamics (M. Olson 1982) or as related to some historic processes (Rüstow 1981); on crisis (mainly in the sense of breakdowns in legitimacy) and its political outcomes (Zimmermann 1979); and more.

This book is different from most such treatments in its already-mentioned interests in a broad and theoretic approach to policymaking under adversity. Another main specific feature is its concentration on the *central mind of government,* a subject rarely studied in historic treatments of governance under adversity (MacMullen 1976, 48) and often handled as a black box in treatments of historic processes (Faber and Meier 1978) in modern political sociology and in much of political science.

The catchy term *governability* demonstrates the preoccupation of contemporary writings with the environments within which governments operate, neglecting another essential side of the problem, namely, the *capacity to govern.* In this book the emphasis is different, with high-level policymaking by central government, as a core dimension of the capacity to govern (a concept used by G. Graham 1960, but otherwise neglected), serving as the main object for investigation. In particular, the "central brain" of government, in the sense of top-level policymaking units and processes, serves as the focus of attention (as pioneered, in different forms, by Stafford Beer 1981, and Deutsch 1969). This perspective is related to the concept of "state" but is not sensitive to different traditions and perceptions of the role of the state in societal problem handling (Dyson 1980, esp. 270ff.), other than in specific settings, to be considered when salient to the subject under discussion.

The term *central mind of government* implies no individualistic-psychological or organistic connotations. *Central mind of government* is used interchangeably with the concept of "central policymaking process-system," both clustering around top-level decision making configurations in governments. Alternatively, one can speak about the higher echelons of the societal command and control system-process, or about the *raison d'état* (in a clinical and not pejorative sense, Meinecke 1957; modern treatments, such as Donelan 1978, are weak) of managing central components of governance. To avoid conceptual overload, the book sticks to the terms *central mind of government* and *central policymaking process-system* as denoting its main subject.

The central mind of government, or central policymaking process-system, is partly handled as a black box and partly opened up (as done in part in Goldwin 1980) with separate treatment of its main components and their interrelations, as necessary for the ongoing inquiry. It is recognized that in different countries and at different periods, various institutions and roles partake in the central mind of government. Thus, in the United States, some parts of Congress and the Supreme Court should be regarded as sometimes included in the central mind of government—depending on the policy issues under consideration and the period taken up (Sundquist 1981). Despite such complexities, used heuristically and subject to specification as needed in particular contexts, the concepts of central mind of government or central policymaking process-system serve adequately the limited purposes of this book. At the same time, the main findings, conjectures, and recommendations of this book are in no way derived from these concepts and stand independent from preferred terminology.

## Embedment in Politics and Society as a Whole

There is need for comprehensive treatments of "politics under adversity" and, indeed, "societies under adversity," beyond the growing number of available partial examinations and sweeping historic grand theories. In many respects, the present book can be looked at as part of an endeavor to investigate polities under much pressure and as a corridor into the broader issues of societies under adversity. But, there is a difference between "policymaking" under adversity and "politics" under adversity, however difficult to draw. While interactions between politics and policymaking are considered as far as necessary, the treatment of this book focuses more on formation of central political will, with accent on decisional aspects, though not exclusively so. Wider political and social processes are taken up as inputs, targets, constraints, and infrastructure but do not constitute main objects for inquiry by themselves. No claim is made that this is a valid distinction between distinct features of reality; sufficient that it is a pragmatically useful one for the world of discourse of this book (following a pragmatical approach to definitions, Ogden and Richards 1938).

## Contemporary Study and Historic Perspectives

The study of contemporary and emerging situations is useful at most for narrowly understanding current realities and providing tinkering help. It carries serious shortcomings: short time spans prevent recognition of basic patterns; contemporaneity keeps perceptions captive to time-bound conceptions; myopia produces "fatal remedies" (Sieber 1981); and emotional attachments bias findings and treatments beyond the unavoidable.

This book tries to reduce such damages by following some deliberate strategies: To move beyond dangers of simple historicism in dealing with present realities (Meinecke 1965; Popper 1961; Troeltsch 1977), an attempt to develop broad and combinational theoretic frameworks characterizes the book. To contain perception constraints, historic perspectives and comparative materials are utilized, at least as heuristic aids and for inference by analogy. Methodological difficulties (Andreski 1965; Bonnell 1980; Przeworski and Teune 1970) are reduced by the limited ambitions of comparisons and, when dealing with the present, by converging use of contemporary history methods and some "interpretative" approaches (Rabinow and Sullivan 1979), together with examination of secondary material and some original field study, as mentioned later. And, to minimize biases consequent upon emotional involvement, a value-free stance of clinical concern is adopted as ideal, even though beyond reach. (For a theoretic-philosophic justification of this stance, see Dror 1983a, new introduction. Recent writings on this issue add little to its clarification; e.g. see Callahan and Jennings 1983.) Iterative movement between empiric findings, inductive and deductive analysis, theoretic generalizations, and prescriptive conclusions and recommendations may help to limit damage of errors, as does some compartmentalization between different dimensions of this book, despite intense interdependence.

With all such attempts to control weaknesses inherent in contemporary treatments of present situations, this book cannot presume to jump over its own shadow. Particularly vexing in attempts to move beyond the limits of contemporary phenomena is the fundamental question, whether present and emerging adversities and policymaking responses to them are similar in basic features to realities in other periods of strenuous pressures exerted on governance; or, whether contemporary situations are unique in crucial features, making any comparison with other periods a metaphor at best and posing strict boundaries to diachronic generalizations.

Strong arguments can be made in either direction. Thus, there is a world of difference between the equipment of the weakest contemporary government on one hand, and of the most successful historic polities, on the other hand. For instance, the Roman emperor at the climax of his achievements (Millar 1977) lagged behind present rulers in the most underdeveloped countries by order of magnitudes in information, in realistic tacit theories on social phenomena, and in policy instruments. This is true much more so in comparison to earlier forms of rulership (Frankfort 1958). But, policymaking then as now depends largely on the same or similar UR-components of governance, such as individual top decision makers, small groups, hierarchical organizations, and policy theologies of much doubtfulness (despite the absence of political ideologies in the modern sense, which developed in the sixteenth century. See D. Kelley 1982).

Preliminary study of historic material tends to lead to the provisional proposition that fundamental features of governmental decision making have demonstrated many constants since the emergence of states, going back in part to earlier forms of collective action. This seems to hold true also when governmental decision making did not take forms similar to modern policymaking patterns; and despite radical differences in internal and external conditions between then and now. Therefore, historic studies may have much to contribute to the understanding of policymaking and are essential for building up well-founded general theory (e.g. S. Checkland 1983 demonstrates potentials of historical approaches for public policy studies). *Inter alia,* historic-comparative study of the responses of the central minds of governments to adversity can provide knowledge far beyond the possible in studies limited to a very thin slice of time-space.

Further examination of such issues, including underlying problems of the philosophy of social sciences, such as nominalism versus essentialism, are beyond the scope of this book. But, a main connection with the present endeavor needs pointing out: One of the significant contributions of the study of contemporary policymaking under adversity to social sciences theory may lie in sensitization to deeply rooted causes of incapacities and in generation of concept packages and hypotheses sets that can serve for reprocessing historic data in theory-relevant ways. Such reprocessing (which requires also additional historic detection work, in line with J. Davidson and Lytle 1982), in turn, may help the construction of a general theory of societal command and control, sorely missing at present (D. Bell 1982, 7). Hopes and aspirations of this kind make it all the more necessary to base the study of contemporary policymaking under adversity on explicated concepts and propositions.

Recognition of the inherent weaknesses of contemporary studies leads to an additional conclusion: Any and all propositions on complex sociopolitical processes based on their examination within thin slices of time-space must be regarded as rather weak conjectures, till subjected to the falsification tests of historic material. (As the reader notices, some basic ideas of Karl Popper are adopted as parts of an appropriate philosophy of knowledge for policy sciences. See especially Popper 1972b; Popper 1972c; and further discourse in Albert 1978; Albert 1980).

### "System" versus "Historic Process"

Time frames condition appropriate methods of investigation and permissible trust in conjectures, and determine preferable concept packages. Conversely, various concepts can easily and unintendedly introduce assumptions and axioms that may sometimes be useful for a limited study but otherwise are quite misleading. Thus, the contemporary perspective of this book can misleadingly produce an equilibrium view of "normal" policymaking, with adversity being identified with external disturbances to the balance of stable "systems" (even sophisticated systems thinkers have difficulties in getting away from such worldviews inbuilt in the "systems" concept, e.g. J.G. Miller 1978. Overinterpretations to preserve the "systems" concept against "process" thinking is not an economical way to handle the problem, despite Luhmann 1978).

Following, for instance, Norbert Elias (Elias 1977, introduction), it seems that the concept of process is superior for handling many subjects, especially when longitudinal dynamics are to be considered. Accepting the concept of process, especially in the sense of sociohistoric processes (itself not an easy term, see Faber and Meier 1978) as appropriate for analyzing unfolding realities, and combining it with the advantages of the concept of "system" as emphasizing interactions, I use a neologism in this book, namely, *process-system,* in the meaning of "a system of processes."

A dynamic process view supplies a quite different perspective on happenings from quasi-static "system" images, with rejection of simple "functional" terminology (Demerath and Peterson 1967), with search for nonsmooth and step-level change periods, with acceptance of many unpredictable consequences as inherent in policymaking at its best, and more. These are perspectives central to the treatment of policymaking under adversity in this book.

It is tempting to press on with speculation, with metaphoric application of evolutionary thinking to societal change (accepting the critical position of Elster 1979, sec. 1.1, against taking such applications too seriously). In such a view, periods of concentrated adversity partake more of *punctuationalism,* in the sense of episodical evolution (Stanley 1981), than of disturbances to be eliminated. In this book, such speculations are not taken up, with some exceptions. But, a view of policymaking as a process-system embedded within evolving societal-cultural processes and constituting an existential expression of them is essential for counterbalancing simplistic views of adversity, of policymaking, and of the relations between those two.

Adversity and policymaking can be regarded as inbuilt, dynamic, and variable interacting social processes evolving within changing and active environmental fields. Such a perspective can view familiar phenomena in quite strange ways. Just to provide one illustration: one can speculate on the importance of serious adversities as upgrading societal adjustment capacities, in part by stimulating policymaking improvements. In turn, such environment-stimulated semievolutionary progress in societal adversity-handling capacities, up to possible upgradings of mental abilities (see Lumsden and Wilson 1983, to be compared with Konner 1982 and Stanley 1981; see also H. Simon 1983, ch. 3), may be essential to prepare humanity for periodic catastrophes caused by cosmic forces (Clube and Napier 1982).

This book does not pursue such speculative thinking, with a few exceptions. But a number of daring propositions may be quite useful antidotes to overly conventional political science frames of appreciation, within which the main body of this book remains located.

## Pointillism of Select Features

Additional features should be mentioned in sketching the scope, concepts, and methods of the book.

### Western Bias

While trying to deal with policymaking under adversity in the contemporary world as a whole, this book shares the widespread weakness of being overinfluenced by Western thinking and being oriented more toward Western democracies than to Third World countries (which is an incorrect category, Pletsch 1981) and communist states. A main reason for this bias is the inadequacies of the literature dealing with policymaking in non-Western countries: Despite some relevant writings on communist countries (Beck and Meso-Lago 1975; Breslauer 1982; Burg 1983; Cocks, Daniels, and Heer 1976; Holmes 1981; Juviler and Morton 1967; Lowenhardt 1981; Gordon Smith 1980; Triska and Cocks 1977), on developing countries (Ballard 1981; Barkan and Okumo 1983; Brewer and Brunner 1975; Clapham 1979; Clapham and Wallace 1977; Dietz 1980; G. Grant 1979; Grindle 1980; R. Jackson and Roseberg 1982; Lindenberg and Crosby 1981; Quandt 1982, passim; Rothschild and Curry 1978; Somjee 1982), on the very special case of Japan (J. C. Campbell 1977; Hofheinz and Calder 1982; C. Johnson 1982; Pempel 1977; Pempel 1978; Pempel 1982; Vogel 1975; Vogel 1979) and China (Bobrow et al. 1979; Greenblatt et. al. 1981; Harding 1981; Morse 1983; Schurmann 1968), and more, the literature is quantitatively much smaller than comparable work on Western democracies. And, qualitatively, much of the literature is mistaken in applying Western theories and concepts to very different realities. (This is illuminated by comparing Morishima 1982 with most of the above-quoted and other multiple books on Japan. Morishima explains Japanese realities in terms of Japanese Confucianism, while the others in the main stick to Western schemata, even while dealing with Japanese peculiarities.)

Exposure of the author to some of the realities of policymaking in a few developing countries did serve to underline the misleading features of much of the available literature, but it was inadequate to improve much upon the handling of the subject of policymaking in non-Western countries. An effort is made in this book to point out a few main features of policymaking under adversity in non-Western countries, but on an insufficient basis and in an unsystematic way. (It should be added that, with some distinguished exceptions, writings by non-Westerners on politics and policymaking in developing countries suffer from serious biases of their own, either by adopting standard political science schemata, liberal as well as neo-Marxist, or by moving into a number of postures that can be explained in terms of sociology and psychology of knowledge but are not acceptable on their merits. Romanticism about precolonial sociopolitical situations, and conspiracy theories to explain governance failures after independence illustrate dominant biases in some indigenous professional literature in many countries.)

## Validity Level

This book presents some of the outcomes of subjective processing of a mixed set of data and materials. Main inputted data and materials include:

1. Extensive processing of literature, as reflected in the references dispersed throughout the book.
2. A number of years of action-observation within the central policymaking process-system, in two countries.
3. Extensive stays in three additional countries, with close observation of their policymaking and politics, including much interviewing of knowledgeable persons and main actors.
4. Systematic local surveys of some particular policymaking features in more than thirty countries, such as recent innovations in central policymaking institutions and methods.

Such inputs have been transformed heuristically into the analysis, findings, theorems, and recommendations of this book. This, under the combined and somewhat contradictory impacts of scholarly research and study on one hand and personal observation as a kind of "policymaker-ethnographer" (Hayano 1982, app. A, esp. 147-54) on the other hand. Let me add that experiences and observations in and near central minds of governments (as discussed in Dror 1983a, new introduction) have been very influential for this book and intensely shape perceptions of policymaking in general, and policymaking under adversity in particular, as presented in this book.

It follows that main findings, propositions, and proposals are proffered as "conjectures," with a somewhat more solid or more tentative claim for validity, as the case may be.

## Movement Between Analysis and Theory, and Prescription

The book moves between analysis and theory on one hand and prescription on the other hand. As in all of my policy sciences endeavors (Dror 1971a; Dror 1971b), the search for theoretic understanding and some attempts at prediction proceed in tandem with development of improvement proposals. In this book, these integrated efforts of mine are pushed ahead, with the working out of a systematic approach to policymaking improvement in chapter 9. Thus, more of an explicit bridge between nomographic theory and operational prescriptions is provided.

*Underlying Worldviews*

Despite my striving for the value-free ideal of the social sciences, it is unavoidable that my underlying worldviews influence problem formulation, data perception, conjecture formulation, and prescription development.

Having dealt with main problems of values in policy sciences elsewhere (Dror 1983a, new introduction), I acknowledge here such tacit bindings. Their concrete expressions will become clear throughout the book. It is hoped that possibly idiosyncratic worldviews held by the author are not taken as the main cause for the substantial matters in which conclusions of the book deviate from many accepted views. Rather, the special "adversity" angle from which policymaking is reviewed in this study may produce conjectures that cast some doubt on parts of present political science and policy sciences "public knowledge" (Ziman 1968), whether consensual or divided into a few main schools.

# 2

# Policy Predicaments

## Policy Travelogue

To take a short break before difficult theoretic issues and baneful policy predicaments, parts of a policy-issues cartography can be sketched in the form of a travel guide for policy scientists bored by the problems of their own countries and looking for some real excitement on distant shores. Based on personal exploration, the following policy-predicament tour includes some of the choice places to try one's brains and skills on policy-challenges impossible.

A good place to start is the Republic of South Africa, the policy plight of which defies imagination, once we drop dogmatics and make-believe panaceas. To express opinions from far away is easy, but to show a realistic way from apartheid to a viable multirace state or state-system, without inviting genocide, is the most difficult policy abyss anywhere (G. Carter 1980; Giliomee 1982; Nolutshungu 1982; Rotberg 1980; Slabbert and Welsh 1979; Study Commission on U.S. Policy towards Southern Africa 1981; L. Thompson and Prior 1982. An important historical and comparative perspective for understanding segregation is provided by Cell 1983, to be supplemented by P. Rich 1984. A good description of public reactions to the pressures is provided in G. Frankel 1984).

From South Africa, Australia is within direct reach for those who like airplanes. Here, problems can be expected to be relatively easy, with a resources boom around some corner and many miles of deep blue water providing a barrier from old-type global conflicts (Blainey 1966). But, the economy is depressed; politics is far from sanguine (Hawker, Smith, and Weller 1979; Theophanous 1983, for a radical view); choices are difficult (Kahn and Pepper 1980); and, looking a little into the future, the security problems of a rich and empty country temptingly facing multiplying masses of overpopulated and impoverished nations loaded with potential energy and prone to look for enemies should cause policy nightmares (Babbage 1980).

13

Not far away is Papua New Guinea, in many respects one of the most interesting concentrations of policy problems existing nowadays. Trying to run a democracy, after recently emerging from the Stone Age, with more than seven hundred languages, with excellent telecommunications instead of nonexisting roads, and with a culture very different from those of all other democratic countries (as best reflected in local literature, such as Beier 1980; or autobiographic writings, such as Somare 1975) produces unique problems (Ballard 1981; to be compared with the radical views of Amarshu et al. 1979). Just to mention a small but fascinating example: Can one hope to preserve traditional artistic creativity, and with what policies, when the religious meanings of art are lost and modernization takes place?

Our next stop is Hong Kong. This unique territory lives by a sandglass, with a predetermined date of possible extinction as an autonomous entity. Escape into economic-rationality assumptions, with the People's Republic of China being expected to somehow maintain a situation that is economically advantageous for it, while fear increases and everyone who can do so prepares a safe nest in Zurich and buys real estate in New Zealand, characterizes the elites and growing parts of the population. At the same time, public management more or less as usual, with gyrating attention to the approaching termination date, characterizes government and administration (Miners 1975; Siu-Kai 1983).

From Hong Kong, a number of countries of interest to the policy scientist are within easy reach: Taiwan is quite a policy spectacle, trying to fuse a thriving economy with an impossible political dream and reliance on a departing partner. The Philippines combine a European language and religion, resulting from a unique occupation experience (S.C. Miller 1982), with a quite different social tradition hard to mold into stable political institutions. And the People's Republic of China is a real trove of singular, massive policy problems, ranging from fitting modern science into an ancient tradition and language, to managing and developing more than 20 percent of humanity through unstable mixtures of tradition and revolution (Bloodsworth 1982; J. Gardner 1982, in addition to already mentioned literature), not to speak of demographic breaking points (well reflected in medical policies, Lampton 1977, but see also G. Henderson 1984, compared to foreign policy decisions, Bobrow et al. 1979). But time is running short, so let us proceed to Japan.

Japan is a real enigma, despite all scholarly and popular literature. Japan's alternative futures aside (Kahn and Pepper 1978; a very interesting study on Japan in the next century was sponsored by the Japanese National Institute for Research Advancement [NIRA] and done by a group of Japanese think tanks, but the English summary is unrepresentative of the material as a whole, see Nira 1979), a major theory shock is provided for the policy scientist by the main patterns of policymaking, such as slow consensus building from the middle level up, instead of multiple advocacy and competing options to be chosen from at the top (Vogel 1975). The fact that Japan is highly successful with decision modes quite different from those regarded as optimal in Western thinking is very sobering. As already mentioned, experts differ on how far Japanese reality is unique to local traditions and culture or can serve as a basis for generalizations and learning (e.g. Morishima 1982 and Gibney 1983 versus Vogel 1979). The resilience and adequacy of present Japanese policymaking patterns under the pressures of possible economic dilapidation are an open question.

Japanese policymaking capacity is an issue not only of profound theoretic importance but also of great significance for the future of Western societies and their ability to compete, or integrate, with East Asian economic performance (Hofheinz and Calder 1982).

By now, the touring policy scientist is probably tired of strange policy predicaments and eager to return to the Old World. A short stop in Asian Russia on the way is enough to demonstrate what may well be the most fundamental long-term policy problem of the USSR, namely the accelerating shift in demographic balance from European to Asian Russia, which in the longer run may have far-reaching consequences for the very fabric of the state (d'Encausse 1981; Feshbach 1982; Simes 1977; Wimbush and Alexiev 1982), changing the whole context of policymaking (Gelman 1981).

Hopes to relax at the next station, in Sweden, are soon disappointed. Viewed just a few years ago as a paragon of policy achievements, the frailty of the compasses by which grand policies were developed and countries were steered in Western Europe is demonstrated by Sweden, all the more starkly because of rapid transition from success to cul-de-sac. This indicates perhaps that some policies, such as social security, have an exhaustion point or asymptotic values, beyond which their progression becomes impossible (Childs 1980; Dilnot and Morris 1984; Guldimann 1976; Dorothy Wilson 1979; on policymaking in Sweden, see Ruin 1982). Sweden also illustrates semispontaneous policy mutations as a possible response mode to new predicaments, such as redistribution of available jobs which evolved without a deliberate national choice into a potential alternative to unemployment or to attempts at job creation (Johannesson and Schmid 1980; Scharpf 1981. The situation in Sweden should be appreciated within the Nordic context, see N. Elder, Thomas, and Apter 1983, and B. Turner and Nordquist 1982).

Before returning to the familiar predicaments of the policy scientists' own countries, the policy tour concludes with a detour to a very hopeful country, say, Venezuela, expecting oil money with democracy to quiet the waves of policy storms. This may have been the first impression up till

1983. But, a little digging hits harsh policy plights. In short, even assuming that the economy is put in order, few good ideas are around anywhere about how to transform huge amounts of money into accelerated social progress without calling up the demons of revolution and turmoil. All known alternatives for societal architecture rapidly demonstrate inadequacies, exposing the paucity of policy ideas and shattering the illusion that we know what to do if only money were less of a constraint. The shock of disappointments from oil-generated hopes, exacerbated by expectable but unprepared-for fluctuations in oil prices and mismanagement of foreign currency flows, may yet endanger the very fabric of democratic politics in Venezuela.

A short side trip to Mexico provides a really disturbing experience, with huge amounts of money and an apparently stable political system having mixed badly, producing socioeconomic-political crises (Hellman 1983), the longer-term outcomes of which are shrouded in doubts with possible destabilization resulting from oil-price fluctuations and revolutions in neighboring countries (some roots are exposed in Grindle 1977, to be compared with Peter Smith 1979).

By now, the policy-explorer is probably too weary to take up the tempting policy sights and to visit the bewitching policy labyrinths advertised in the tour booklet and waiting in the very poor countries of Central Africa, among multiplying masses of India, in the fanaticism-prone Middle East— indeed, in all directions of the wind. But beware, by the time you return to your own country, probably its policy predicaments have aggravated, giving little pause to the exhausted policy scientist.

If England is sweet home, short episodes of euphoria, thanks to "enemies," and oil money do little to hide predicaments deeply rooted in social change and long-term decline, with no in-depth solution striking the eye (Alt 1979; Ashford 1981; S.H. Beer 1982; Dahrendorf 1982b; Halsey 1978; A. King 1976; Keegan 1984; Kramnick 1979; Sampson 1983; Geoffrey, Smith, and Polsby 1981; M. Wiener 1980). To be noted are predicaments not fully related to economic difficulties, such as bad race relations (C. Brown 1984), sport hooliganism (J. Williams and Murphy 1984), and political strikes (Jeffery and Hennesey 1983).

If the United States is your habitat, you are relatively well off; indeed, you must be very careful to avoid a mirror approach to other countries, seeing them in light of your own experiences. Still, you do not lack harsh predicaments, which may easily aggravate in the foreseeable future. The spectacle of deep policy cleavages on foreign and security policy, without real ideological parties, testifies to the intricacy of problems. Collisions among many needs, strong wills, and rigid constraints produce failure-pregnant policy mazes (J. Palmer and Sawhill 1982; W. Williams 1983), with policy theologies and so-called common sense competing in policy misdirection. The spectacle of many policymaking having seriously considered constitutional limitations on one of their most important policy instruments, namely the budget (Ellwood 1981), provided an unusual exhibition of ostensible self-denial, to be explained, metaphorically, as a depressive form of maze policy-behavior, in reaction to sensing oneself caught in a policy *aporie*—a very useful Greek concept meaning a policy corner with no visible way out. (Overall treatments are illustrated by Fawcett and Thomas 1982; Phillips 1982. Essential social-historic perspectives are supplied by Hays 1980. An unusual comprehensive treatment, with predictive elements, is Oxford Analytica 1984.)

If your home beat is somewhere else, some other predicaments are awaiting you, with some bigger adversity avalanches slowly but surely building up. Thus, to pick up just one illustration out of many, in Western countries demographic changes assure a growing number, absolutely and proportionally, of elderly and very old persons, producing qualitatively different social situations fraught with possibly explosive problems (Binstock and Shanas 1976; Butz et al. 1982; Calhoun 1978; Crystal 1982; Eversley and Köllmann 1982; Graebner 1980; Guillemard 1983; G. King and P. Stearns 1981; W. Lammers 1983; Kraft and Schneider 1978; Montgomery et al. 1979; L. Olson 1982; Phillipson 1982; Pratt 1977; Roebuck 1979; J. Schulz 1979; Stearns 1981). This is a relatively reliable, predictable monumental issue, all the more so if the opinion that populations shape the generation and diffusion of technology has some grains of truth in it (Boserup 1982). The fact that an extensive search failed to identify any government seriously girding for a different population composition is all the more disturbing, while being typical of inherent policymaking incapacities, as discussed in chapter 6.

Maybe there are somewhere oases of policy tranquility, but I have failed to find them outside the illusions of those blind to see the shapes of predicaments with us and to come. It is possible that shifts for the better are approaching, but few hopeful omens can be discerned. The impressions and findings are not dependent on short-range economic upturns or downturns. Much more basic factors are at work producing what is later called an epoch of grave adversity.

If we had a time capsule and would travel into the past, a quite different conclusion would surely be reached—with many (though not all) present predicaments looking more like utopia to inhabitants of earlier periods. But, in terms of present consciousness and aspirations, the aggravation of policy predicaments, both current and expected, is very pronounced, accelerating, and becoming increasingly visible, with important consequences for actual and preferable policymaking.

## Some Models of Adversity

Coherent survey and analysis of "adversity" pose serious difficulties, once one moves beyond enumeration of some external manifestations. Some situations are easy to discern. Thus, diagnosing a situation of economic difficulties within given cultural perspectives is not very difficult in terms of obvious symptoms, such as negative growth, balance of trade deficits, inflation, and unemployment—even if most of the statistics are not very reliable and ignore important factors, such as gray economies. Moving from visible symptoms to comprehensive conceptualization and in-depth understanding is quite a different matter. Coherent and meaningful statements are hard to make in the absence of trustworthy theories. Thus, as long as Keynesian economics was accepted as correct, economic malaise symptoms could be attributed to a coherent set of courses. But once Keynesian models are no longer trusted, movement from some symptoms of economic difficulties into deeper layers of economic adversity is controversial and doubtful. For instance, whether the concept of "deindustrialization" is a meaningful describer and partial explainer of economic malaise or is more of a misleading misnomer is in debate (Bacon and Eltis 1978; Blackaby 1979; Bluestone and Harrison 1982).

All the more speculative are conceptualization and analysis of variform adversity in social, political, and cultural domains—where comprehensive relevant theories are absent, with different cognitive maps, dogmas, and theologies dominating instead the debate. As illustrated by the shortcomings of much less ambitious efforts at "social indicators" in the absence of strong and comprehensive social theories, societal diagnostics is unavoidably shallow, fad dominated, and disparate. When the inherent fallacies of taking a contemporary look at thin slices of historic processes are added to the difficulties, then the barriers to comprehending present adversity loom very large indeed. Thus, easy and simple-looking descriptions and pseudo-explanations must be rejected out of hand, such as "decadence" (an issue interestingly taken up but shallowly treated in R. Adams 1983). It may even be that what looks like "adversity" is but some shifts in human attitudes toward the natural world (as discussed in the context of England 1500-1800 in K. Thomas 1983) and changes in feelings about "luxury" (comparable to shifts in the eighteenth century, as discussed in Sekora 1977). However speculative, such perspectives can be arrived at only within a longitudinal view of culture and society as well as politics (e.g. Finley 1983 is a good introductory text to politics in the ancient worlds), while being essential for pinpointing basic features of what is called here policymaking "adversity."

Luckily some relaxations of the requirements of acceptable analysis of adversity are permissible in the world of inquiry into policymaking as taken up in this book. Trying to examine the images of adversity as held in the central minds of governments, comparing such policymaking-subjective views of adversity with some of the more obvious "objective" features of adversity, and searching for ways to improve the adversity-handling capacity of policymaking, within the limited potentials of that process-system—these are much narrower tasks than presuming to move toward an overall diagnosis of societal predicaments. Still, the broader problematics must be kept in mind, adding a strong mental reservation against pragmatic treatments of adversity, even if the latter are all that can perhaps be done before social science theories advance by orders of magnitude.

For the main purposes of this book, even less of an effort to analyze adversity may suffice: with reliance on the profusion of literature dealing with multiple aspects of "adversity," a present and expected situation of much adversity could be taken as postulated, without much further treatment. The main body of the book is quite insensitive to detailed specifications of adversity, for it deals with policymaking under "adversity" as an aggregate concept, without much fixation on particular features of discrete predicaments. Nevertheless, the subject of adversity is too important, this book is too much predicated on the concept of adversity, and most of the available treatments are too limited not to explore the subject somewhat further.

Given the limited task of exploratory analysis of adversity in relation to policymaking, a relatively doable first step is the development of a facet design or concept package for looking at adversity. A minimum facet design for describing and analyzing adversity in the abstract, and specific situations of adversity in particular, includes the following polar concepts: simple or complex; handleable or intractable; short or epochal; endogenous to governance or exogenous up to extrasocietal; and all these, as perceived within policymaking and by various policy influentials, as compared to "objective" reality, that is, findings by external researchers.

Put into pure type form, the above dichotomies can be explained briefly, as follows:

Simple adversity is one that is related to a definite and understandable cause, such as an "enemy"; complex adversity is one that is caused by multiple and often uncomprehensible causes.

Handleable adversity can be treated with known and feasible policies; intractable adversity is not susceptible to any known treatment.

Short adversity is limited to a small bit of time, with the polar case of "crisis" situations as defined earlier; epochal adversity is endemic to basic structural features and continues for long periods, either in acute form or as a pandemic, with recurrent outbreaks.

Adversity can be endogenous to governance, in the sense of being inherent in features of the political system itself; or can be exogenous, being related to phenomena external to the political system, up to extrasocietal, in the sense of being caused by variables external to the considered society and its territory.

All the above facets can be policymaking-subjective, in the sense of characterizing images of adversity as held by different components of the central mind of government; and/or characteristic of adversity as analyzed by independent specified investigators (care to be taken not to call the latter "objective," especially because adversity is a subject on which little consensus among investigators exists, negating use of even that relatively weak criterion of "scientific" knowledge; compare Popper 1972a with Ziman 1968). This is an area where professionals are especially prone to what has been called "reflection-in-action," rather than "expert knowledge." (See Schön 1983.)

These and additional dimensions form an N-dimensional matrix, permitting classification and analysis of situations of "adversity," with many combinations and in-between situations.

Various questions on empiric-analytic and theoretic levels can be formulated with the help of the above categories, such as: What are the main features of present adversities and their dynamics? What are their probable futures in foreseeable time spans? How do different features of various adversity items aggregate into overall policy predicaments? In respect to these and related questions, what are the main relations between subjective images and "objective" realities? And, how far do the answers to such questions fit present (and historic?) states, and are they specific to certain state-types or polities?

Such categorization leads to the distinction between different layers of adversity, including manifest symptoms, direct causes, remote causes, and underlying forces and processes. However speculative some of the conjectured parameters and however soft the evidence, some penetration beyond manifest expressions of adversity is essential for trying to explain them; and for taking up, however gingerly, some prediction attempts. Policymaking can hardly be effective if limited to the handling of manifest symptoms, even if in-depth treatment of the roots of adversity is usually impossible, both because these roots are unknown and often nontouchable in their very nature, and because of the lack of suitable policy instruments. But, in moving into underlying layers of adversity, one runs quickly into the logical problematics of infinite reduction and search for primary causes; and the very differentiation between layers and between symptoms and causes may be inappropriate in respect to what may better be considered in terms of different facets of a multipattern configuration. Indeed, a view of society within its environment as kaleidoscopic may be appropriate, "interspersing its moments or intervals of order, assurance and beauty with sudden disintegration and a cascade into a new pattern" (Shackle 1972, 76).

All these explorations and speculative thoughts are but antecedents to major theoretic issues, which are of cardinal importance for policymaking. First and foremost among the theoretic issues is the nature of adversity aggregation effects: A central query is, whether, when, and how different adversities add up to a conjuncture, a meeting place where adversity reaches thresholds and brings about step-level effects, such as systems transformations. Internal synergy between different adversities, reinforcement of adversity by counterproductive intervention efforts, and large-scale effects of multiple coterminous adversities—these may perhaps produce quantum jumps in adversity status, with parallel quantum effects on societies.

To ponder such issues, a number of points must be kept in mind.

1. It is worth repeating that contemporaneity does not permit reasonable conjectures on processes that take a long time. Thus, the short, cyclic, pandemic or epochal nature of adversity may become clear in restrospect, but is hard to recognize during initial visible phases of changing waves in the adversity processes themselves. To take a relatively simple country illustration, it is quite clear that the Netherlands is in a period of serious adversity, with so-called consociational politics breaking down and the "Dutch Malaise" taking over (compare, consecutively, Lijphart 1968 and Lijphart 1977; then Daalder 1974 and Daalder 1979; then Putten 1982 and Moerings 1983. A broader treatment is Obler et al. 1977.) But, it is impossible to tell whether this is a temporary situation that will dissipate, more or less on its own, within a few years, with most of Dutch policymaking returning to its usual patterns (Eldersveld et al. 1981), even if the economic situation remains difficult; or whether Dutch society will move into an epoch of serious malaise, with unknown features, even if the economy should improve. The historic fact that the Netherlands easily readjusted after the decolonization trauma (Lijphart 1966) is no indication of what will happen under quite different kinds and levels of adversity. The fact that the Netherlands was unique in the post-World War II period in maintaining consensus-based salary and income controls, but that this was due in part to the accidental shared experiences of leaders of all the main parties during the Nazi occupation (as was the case in Austria, with similar results for postwar domestic politics) adds the complication of chance at work, shaping reality and policymaking-capacities substantively in the past. This may happen in the future, too, raising major issues of uncertainty, to be taken up later.

2. A long-range historic-process perspective should be kept in mind, with adversities being perhaps best comprehensible, as mentioned, as expressions of inherent antinomies of societal unfoldings, taking place in active fields. Such a perspective brings out sharply the difficulties of meaningfully conceptualizing and correctly analyzing adversities from within a short time slice, and it adds the important point that the negative and undesirable connotations of the term *adversity* may stem from a very narrow value and time base. True, adversity involves human sufferings, but so does life itself. In the longer run, as already speculated about, adversity may constitute a challenge essential for human progress (on a different scale, the position of Hirschman 1958 is relevant), if not an unavoidable condition of human evolution (and even progression?).

Some minor conceptual issues are more conveniently raised later while considering pertinent features of specific adversities, such as windfall benefits (e.g. the sudden influx of oil money) as subsumed under the term *adversity* as used in this book; and special situations that constitute adversity from an overall societal perspective but may be regarded from the narrow perspective of the central mind of government as more of an advantage, such as having visible but not very dangerous enemies.

To put present adversity into some proportion, before looking at it from close up, a quote from sixteenth-century poet John Donne will serve to redress overfixation on immedite concerns (taken from Lockyer 1982):

> *The sun is lost, and th'earth, and no man's wit*
> *Can well direct him where to look for it . . .*
> *'Tis all in pieces, all coherence gone.*

Much shorter looks backward (e.g. Middlemas 1979) can provide a corrected view of present predicaments, too.

### Main Predicament Features

To avoid too ethereal a treatment of the idea of adversity and to provide some concrete environmental context for the body of this book, a few main features of present and foreseeable policy predicaments need exploration. For the purposes of this book, a rather cursory look at main predicament features will do on an aggregate level. This involves some overgeneralization and loss of important details. For other purposes, comprehensive policy-issues taxonomies and cartographies are urgently needed such as on the lines of the world handbook of political and social indicators (C. Taylor and Jodice 1983), but on more sophisticated a level, to meet the complexities of the matter; this with due care not to freeze perceptions and not to channelize analysis by narrow problem formulations, closed concepts, and rigid catalogues. But for the limited world of discourse of this book, much less will do: Some generalized features of main policy adversities are summed up, with a few illustrations, so as to serve as a basis for sharpened propositions and to serve as background for a few theoretic conjectures. These characterizations of adversity will later serve for examination of main policymaking responses, deficits, and requirements.

Particularly to be considered are shifts and jumps in policy issues; erosion of political bases; and absence of reliable policy compasses. To bring out special features of contemporary adversities, present and foreseeable predicaments are then put into a historic perspective.

## Shifts and Jumps in Policy Issues

Shifts and time-compressed turns in the nature of issues make traditional policy paradigms, policy assumptions, policy habits, policy "grammars," and grand policies increasingly doubtful. Recent, present, and foreseeable shifts and jumps in policy issues include transformations in expectations, aspirations, and beliefs; inflections of the internal dynamics of policies, which make their linear continuation with only incremental changes impossible or counterproductive; jumps in the material features of policy issues; and emergence of new and unprecedented problems. Some illustrations serve to concretize these aggregate characteristics:

- The reversal of twenty-five years of historically unprecedented economic growth, on a global scale and in the Western democracies (OECD 1979b, esp. 65ff.), with a shift from what has been called a "golden age" (Maddison 1983) to a period of economic stagnation and high endemic unemployment. The downturn of the economy is the single most pronounced predicament aggravation since 1973, throwing its darkening shadow on all issues. If countries move into a lengthy epoch of economic troubles, including in the form of a pandemic with recurring declines and some recovery in between, the whole context of policymaking—taken for granted, perhaps rashly, not long ago—is overturned. Policymaking in most countries is not yet facing squarely this intimidating specter. Ideas for radical policy innovations to handle such a possibility are just beginning to be taken seriously, such as reindustrialization (Netherlands Scientific Council for Government Policy 1980), revamping of the welfare state (Matzner 1982; Netherlands Scientific Council for Government Policy 1983; New Zealand Planning Council 1979; OECD 1981a), and radical turns in public expenditure (Grauhan and Hickel 1978; M. Wright 1980). The changing economic outlook (Boltho 1982; Dahrendorf 1982a; A. Frank 1981) constitutes the most dramatic turn in policy situations, producing much of the visible adversity and conditioning all of it (Häfele 1981; Parikh and Rabár 1981; Yergin and Hillebrand 1982), *inter alia* requiring novel policy-alternatives.

The basic picture does not change if some economic uplifts occur. Improved economic performance does ameliorate adversity. But, even if some of the more optimistic predictions should prove correct (e.g. Kahn 1979 despite its admitted dependence on "absence of bad luck and bad management," which is a doubtful assumption, and its explicit exclusion of conflict) economic growth will not achieve its 1948-73 levels, 10 percent and higher unemployment levels will become endemic in the highly industrialized countries (Eiu 1984), and recurrent economic crises will aggravate adversity. A number of countries may enter an epoch of continuous relative economic decline, which may also become absolute with negative economic growth.

- Escalating problems of relations between rich and poor countries, with no mitigating realistic scenario in sight (P. Bauer, 1981; Brandt 1980; Brandt Commission 1983; Cline 1979; R. Feinberg 1983; R. Hansen 1979; Leontief et al. 1977; Pauker 1977; D. Smith 1982; Tinbergen et al. 1976; World Bank 1982; World Bank 1983). Changes in the income distribution among countries take place, with new industrial nations catching up rapidly and, perhaps, the very poor countries also improving their economic performance. But trickle-down effects will not meet rising expectations and relative deprivation will become less and less acceptable and, therefore, more and more of a predicament, up to various acute crises possibilities. (For a relevant sociopolitical fiction see W. Clark 1984).
- In the Third World itself, a number of countries may advance significantly their capacity to govern. But, in many countries, abysses between resources and aspirations, cultural-social turmoil, absence of any viable "state" traditions, and additional factors inhibit effective policymaking. Parts of Africa are especially prone to this adversity, but other countries are not immune to it either (Abrahamian 1982; Ajami 1981; A. Frank 1980; R. Jackson and Roseberg 1982; D. Lamb 1982; Loup 1982).
- The international debt problem illustrates a serious issue, easily predictable but not anticipated, demonstrating combined effects of economic problems, rich-poor country relations, and Third World issues—producing a difficult predicament (Cline 1983; Dale and Mattione 1983; Delamaide 1984; Moffitt 1984). No solution is in sight, despite many proposals (such as calls for "statemenship," Kissinger 1984). A historical perspective is necessary to see this predicament in correct proportions (Kindelberger 1984).
- Escalating problems with the proliferation of mass-lethal weapons building up catastrophic potentials, quite irreducible with present grand policies (D. Baker 1982; Bull 1977; Canan 1982; Dror 1980b; Fallows 1981; Glucksmann 1984; Harvard Nuclear Study Group 1983; Inde-

pendent Commission on Disarmament and Security Issues 1982; Amos Jordan and Taylor 1981; Kennan 1982; Kuppermann and Trent 1979; Leontief and Duchin 1983; Rohety 1980; Schell 1982; Weizsäcker 1976; Wieseltier 1983).

- Local and perhaps global scarcities and crises, such as in food and energy (Lester Brown and Eckholm 1974; Ion 1980; Murdock 1983; Nussbaum 1983. But see Parikh and Rabár 1981; and International Energy Agency 1982). and other natural resources (Welch and Miewald 1983), up to possible disturbances of essential ecological balances by human action, such as the so-called greenhouse effect with the warming up of the atmosphere (H. Bernard 1981; Floher 1980).
- Implications of new technologies, such as microchip-based technologies (Friedrichs and Schaaf 1982), with robots and "network societies"; and biotechnologies, as well as other trend-shifting scientific and technological inventions and applications (Adkins 1984; Blank 1984; Commission of the European Communities 1984).
- Radicalization in belief systems, as illustrated by Islam fundamentalism; and lesser, but still very significant, value shifts, also in Western societies (Inglehart 1977a; Klages and Kmiecieak 1979).
- Changes in the very fundaments of society, such as the already-mentioned population size and age distribution (see also Salk and Salk 1981; World Bank 1984). Some other changes may be slow and take a long time but can move inexorably toward overpowering situations, such as possible climatic shifts that are neither made by humans nor stoppable by human policies (*Journal of Interdisciplinary History* 1980; World Meteorological Organization 1978). But, this is hardly the realistic policy-relevant period under consideration here (H. Lamb 1982).

This list includes but a few samples of shifts and jumps in policy issues, as experienced increasingly by country after country and partly discussed in the literature, often with some exaggeration (Blaney III and Clay 1979; Lester Brown 1984; Camilleri 1976; Fritsch 1981; Geze et al. 1982; Gruhl 1975; Hallowell 1976; Heilbroner 1975; Heilbroner 1978; Hull 1981, to be put into perspective by Mannheim 1951b; Kerr 1983; Vickers 1973). These illustrations make concrete the nature of transformations in policy issues constituting adversity. By making relatively easy policymaking modes, such as segmented incrementalism and disjointed mutual adjustment more and more inadequate, such shifts pose very heavy demands upon policymaking.

It strains language to regard all shifts and jumps of reality as policy "predicaments." Many sudden, radical, and/or rapid changes in reality require transincremental policymaking and impose strain on policymaking, but some such shifts include very positive aspects, for societies and for governance. This applies, for instance, to advances in knowledge, which in part pose difficult problems and also dangers, but as a whole do not fit the concept of "adversity" in its usual annotations and connotations. More complex is the acquisition of sudden riches, as in oil-producing countries. Such windfalls produce serious policy problems, but can be regarded as "adversity" only by stretching the term.

Subjective evaluation enters the picture again here. Thus, whether to regard rapid population increases as a "predicament" or a blessing or both is more a question of basic pronatalistic or antinatalistic postures, conditioned *inter alia* by cultures and religions, than of a clinical finding (Eversley and Kollman 1982. But see World Development Report 1984).

Most of the analysis in this book is insensitive to such distinctions, applying largely to all policy strains, whether strictly "adversity" or not. Therefore, such differentiations will not be pursued, unless pertinent to particular subjects. In general, the term *adversity* will, by extension, also cover policymaking strains consequent upon shifts with positive features, *mutatis mutandis.*

## Erosion of Political Base

Concomitantly with the above-discussed material aggravations in challenges facing policymaking, and often in synergistic interaction with them, many of the bases of policymaking itself erode. Essential political foundations of effective policymaking contract, with no substitution in sight. Parts of this phenomenon are covered in political science and general literature under a variety of terms, such as *ungovernability* (Crozier, Huntington, and Watanuki 1975; Hennis, Kielmansegg, and Math 1977 and 1979; Isensee and Meyer 1979; Lieberam 1977; Noack 1981; D. Yates 1977); *overload* (A.G. Jordan and Richardson 1979; Rose 1980; Rose 1981; as well as the 1983 Royal Australian Institute of Public Administration Papers, e.g. R. Howard 1983); *limits on capacity to govern* (G. Graham 1960; Lehner 1979; Sundquist 1980); *alienation* (J. Wright 1976); *legitimation crisis* (Denitch 1979; J. Freedman 1978; Habermas 1976; Heidorn 1982; Kielmansegg 1976; Kielmansegg 1977); *governance in crisis* (Jänicke 1973a; Jänicke 1973b; Wittrock 1983); and so on (Graubard 1981), up to possible new class conflicts (Roemer 1982). Leaving consideration of the power requisites of high-quality policymaking for later, and detailed treatment of overall incapacity-to-govern problems to another occasion, the author here selects some features of the erosion of the political base of policymaking in Western democracies for attention. Other types of regimes suffer in part from similar phenomena, and/or suffer from other forms of erosion of the political base (the communist countries, see e.g. Drewnowski 1983), or/and move in gnostic directions and search for enemies.

*Elimination of Transcendental Justification.* Nowadays in most demo-cratic countries, and in many of the nondemocratic too, governments lack any transcendental justification (T. Eschenburg 1976; Flathman 1980). Not only have religious bases of government nearly disappeared but "pa-triotism," "national mission," and similar creedal supports of governments are on a steep decline in highly developed countries (but this is not the case in parts of the Third World, producing quite different situations). Util-itarian, concordantial, and similar "rational" justifications of democratic regimes (Rogowski 1974; Rogowski 1978) and collective action (Hardin 1983) operate in effect as a restraint and limitation on government rather than as a supportive base for policymaking.

*Scarcity of Enemies.* Without going to the extreme of putting "enemies" into the center of politics and government (Schmitt 1963; criticized in Fijalkowski 1958 and Laufer 1962, discussed in English in Bendersky 1983 and briefly in Poggi 1978, and further developed in Schmitt 1975; for a different treatment see Finlay et al. 1967.), there is convincing historic and analytical support for the proposition that images of the existence of active enemies constitute a strong base for governance. They serve to mobilize support, to justify inadequate governmental performance, and to depress demands and expectations. The absence of consensually recognized "en-emies" in the large majority of Western democracies thus eliminates one of the historic political bases for policymaking.

This is an important illustration of contradictions between societal and private benefits on one hand; and political and policymaking advantages on the other hand. The absence of recognized enemies, if fitting reality, is desirable from a humanistic perspective and usually a benefit for society as a whole. But, from the narrower perspectives of politics and policymaking, having an enemy who is neither so weak as to be contemptible nor so strong as to be terrifying is quite an asset (as well put, in literarily exagge-rated form, both in L. Lewin 1967 and in Orwell 1954). Such antinomies are inbuilt weaknesses of all known forms of governance, raising funda-mental problems beyond the scope of this book.

The antinomy between "enemies" as a societal adversity and, at the same time, a convenience for governments serves to illustrate a point of much theoretic importance and, also, of relevance to policymaking: There is no necessary identity between policymaking adversity and societal adversities, though often these situations will overlap to various degrees. The logic of democratic forms of regimes is directed, *inter alia,* at increasing overlap between what is "good" for society (itself a difficult concept) and what is "good" for governments (another difficult concept, quite different from the first one; I avoid at this point use of the concept of "state," which would complicate terminology without enlightening the presently considered issue.) Full success in overcoming such governance-society differences and antinomies is far from being achieved by any historic or contemporary regime and seems beyond the potentials of any currently conceived form of governance, other than reality-distant utopias.

*Reduced Force Monopoly.* As elaborated by Max Weber and repeated in similar formulations since, a main characteristic of government is an effective monopoly over force. This postulate needs expansion to include an ability and will by government to use its monopoly of force to enforce its decisions, if necessary. Significant recent weakenings in meeting this requirement include: (a) the reduced will and capability of Western democratic goverments to use force to enforce duly promulgated decisions because of values opposing such action; (b) the more diffuse, but nevertheless pronounced, hesitations by governments to make decisions, even when supported by democratic majorities, if their implementation may require the threat or the actual use of force; (c) against such restraints in government, the growing acceptance of militant minority action as a permissible mode of political behavior (Efron 1984; E. Muller 1979; E. Muller and Jukam 1983; Nelkin and Pollak 1981; Touraine 1983), up to some support for terrorism in some democracies, such as in ethnic conflicts (Esman 1977). These changes, in the aggregate, transform a main historic feature and base of government that is very important for policymaking.

*Diminished Trust.* Trust (on the difficulties of the concept, see B. Barber 1983) in government's living up to its promises and being able to deliver desired goods is diminishing (Lipset and Schneider 1983; A. Miller 1974), with some ups (A. Miller 1983. Again, a historic perspective is needed. Thus, the decline of trust in Julius Caesar [Yavetz 1983] needs another explanation, adding an essential dimension to a general theory of trust in government). This is the result, *inter alia,* of three main developments:

- The specter of nuclear war as a possibility about which most governments can do nothing meaningful reduces the credibility of government by making it irrelevant to an issue about which populations are very anxious.
- Governmental failures to handle relative economic decline in most Western democracies, coupled with very visible unemployment, is another important trust-diminishing variable. Its effects are exacerbated by the lack of accepted dogma for handling the situation, which in turn causes most democracies to oscillate in their politics and thus to become even more uncreditable.
- On a quite different level, growing exposure of the innermost processes of governments to the public eye, thanks to right-to-know legislation and the mass media, breaks the myth that "those up there know what

they are doing." Far-reaching demystification and demythologization of government and popularized diffusion of information on some realities of top-level decision making thus further diminish trust in government. (A striking illustration is provided by the British TV series *Yes Minister,* unimaginable 20 or even 10 years earlier. See J. Lynn and Jay 1981-83.)

*Political Resources Fragmentation.* Political fragmentation is relatively fully discussed in political science literature: disconsensus, single-interest groups, local overcrowding, multiple groupings of political activists, dealignment and growing voter vocality, political action committees, resurgence of ethnic politics, various forms of policy movements, and more (Barnes and Kaase 1979; S. Berger 1981; Burg 1983; Crewe et al. 1977; Crouch and Pizzorno 1978; Dahl 1982; Esman 1977; Huntington 1981; Kelso 1979; A. King 1978; Klion and Waterman 1983; Kornberg and Clarke 1983; Lijphart 1977; Lowe and Goyder 1983; Narr and Offe 1975; Nelkin and Pollak 1981; Paddison 1983; Ra'anan 1980; Ramsay 1983; Rokkan and Urwin 1982). Breakdowns in traditional parties and changes in their dynamics are an important contributor (Castles 1982; Kavanagh 1982). The situation is not shared equally by all Western democracies. Thus, Austria still enjoys a quite coherent sociopolitical structure enabling consensual policymaking on many, though not all (nuclear energy being a main exception), issues (H. Fischer 1977; OECD 1981b). The overall trend seems to move in the direction of further political fragmentation, with very important consequences for policy predicaments and policymaking quality.

Changes in politics are very salient to this book, closely related as they are to policymaking, as a base and resource, as a constraint, and as a target. Later in this chapter, some deeper underlying possible causes of political transformations will be speculated about. Here, some additional features need mentioning. In particular, the following cluster of trends deserves attention:

- Increasing disagreements, reaching second-order disagreement, that is, disagreement on what is disagreed on; and what can be called third-order disagreement, namely, disagreement on how to try to reach agreement (on related consensus-conflict theories, see T. Bernard 1983).
- Intensified political romanticism and theologies (in the senses of Schmitt 1970; Schmitt 1979; Schmitt 1982, more or less). Thus, conflict between materialistic and so-called postmaterialistic values (a doubtful term, especially in its temporal and, as it were, "inevitability" connotations) and around nuclear policies, in energy as well as defense, increasingly take on the features of creedal conflicts—this in countries with very strong democratic traditions (Cotgrove, 1982). The psychol-

ogy of "cults" (Appel 1983) may become increasingly important in a reemerging period of ideology (Bracher 1982) and reenchantment (Gellner 1979), *inter alia* with possible dismal consequences for tolerance in the future, up to a new "politics of cultural despair" (Stern 1961).

- Growing tendencies toward protest and expressive as well as accusative politics (Barnes and Kaase 1979; A. Marsh 1977), including in countries where political discourse was very solid, such as Sweden (compare Anton 1980 and Lundquist 1980 with Ruin 1982), with potentials for "revolt" (Gurr 1979). The defeats of the whole political establishment by public referenda in Austria, on nuclear energy, and in Norway, on joining the EEC, are significant here. Trends toward "litigious societies" (Lieberman 1983) may be correlated with such phenomena.
- Tendencies toward reduced political participation by large parts of the population (as illustrated by declining participation in referenda and elections in Switzerland, Riklin and Kley 1982) and intensified activity by small groups may combine in the direction of what has been called "Zealocracy" (Tivey 1978, 129).
- Related to the above-considered variables, and in addition to them, political support for governments is decreasing (Easton 1976), public authority is becoming increasingly problematic (Diggins and Kann 1982), procedural agreement is more and more inadequate and eroding—in short, the political bases of policymaking are declining.

Many of these changes can be summed up in the statement that the power of the state is diminishing in Western democracies, undermining an essential basis of policymaking. I recognize the many problems raised by this statement, such as the use of the term *state* and the multidimensionality of the verbal symbol *power* (only partly brought out in Galbraith 1983 and in Wrong 1979, for instance; for quite different a treatment see Margolis, in preparation); nevertheless, it serves to present one of the main adversities faced by central minds of government in their own societies.

To avoid a one-sided picture, it is necessary to take into account that countervailing forces are also operative and that some fragmentation trends may be short-lived. Thus, movements may exhaust themselves (Pertschuk 1982); tax revolts may be short-lived (Hibbs and Madsen 1981; A. Lewis 1982) and may be less radical in their implications than supposed (Kirlin 1982; Rabushka and Ryan 1982; Sears and Citrin 1982; Woodside 1982); voting behavior may be relatively stable (Himmelweit et al. 1981) and less influenced by individual circumstances than by national perspectives (Kiewiet 1983); political tolerance is still strong in main democracies, though some strains begin to show (Corgett 1982; McClosky and Brill 1983; J. Sullivan et al. 1982); moderate and socialist nonradical conservative parties do well in many countries (R. Morgan and Silvestri 1982);

and findings on rather conventional political participation (Verba et al. 1978) may continue to hold true, with only temporary ups and downs.

Also, new forms of political configurations become more important and may compensate for fragmentation, such as corporative politics and tripartite structures (R. Harrison 1980; Goldthorpe 1984; Schmitter 1977; Schmitter 1981; T. Smith 1979; Wilensky 1976), concertation (Ionescu 1973; Ionescu 1975), patronage politics (Clapham 1982), and more. In some respects, larger numbers of policy actors and growing policy circuits can also increase policymaking leeway by providing alternative supporters (Fritschler 1983). Even in divided societies, such as Ireland, cooperation goes on (Rea 1982). Nevertheless, fragmentation of political bases for policymaking in Western democracies is a main policy predicament, resulting in lack of power-political policymaking resources essential for main policy tasks, as will be discussed more fully later in the book.

Leaving aside the special political predicaments of development countries, often related to absence of a continuous state tradition and to perhaps unavoidable upheavals related to accelerated social change (Heilbroner 1963, 134-35), and the special political predicaments of communist countries, partly related to the oligarchic features of governance (Goldman 1983), the continuous and increasingly costly fragmentation of global politics needs mentioning. On the global scene, political resources fragmentation continues unabated, despite hopes to the contrary and irrespective of increasingly recognized escalating needs for global policymaking. Some progress in regional political consolidation, mainly in the European Economic Community, is helpful but limited (S. George 1984; Ludlow 1982). It does not adequately compensate for fragmentation trends. Possible upsurges in nationalism, especially in the Third World (Gellner 1983; Sathyamurthy 1982), may well aggravate the situation.

The growing antinomy between a global regime (on this term, see Krasner 1983; for a somewhat different use Coate 1982) of political fragmentation and possible decay (Haas 1983) on one hand and increasing interdependences and emergence of a "world system" (on this term, see Bergesen 1980; Wallerstein 1974; Wallerstein 1980) on the other hand, constitutes one of the unique features of contemporary and foreseeable adversities, as compared to other periods.

*Political-Economic Syndrome.* This syndrome is important in effects and reveals some of the dynamics producing aggravating policy predicaments. Main factors in this syndrome include:

• The use of economic tools to gain support, especially before elections in democracies, providing a main cause for policy-electoral cycles (Keegan and Pennant-Rea 1979; and Tufte 1978). Similar phenomena on a local level are interesting (P. McClelland and Magdovitz 1981).

- On a deeper structural level, strong antinomies exist between capitalism, liberalism, and mass democracy. Thus, capitalism permits and even encourages and requires capital accumulation, economic power concentrations, and income differences of large magnitude; liberalism supports economic freedom on one hand and public critique of the economic order on the other hand; and mass democracy can move into demands and expectations that ruin the economy and build up support for economic changes unacceptable to economic power. (Best and Connolly 1982; Brittan 1975, as elaborated in Brittan 1979; Crouch 1979; O'Connor 1984; Offe 1972; Usher 1981). More fundamental antinomies are at work on the cultural level, such as contradictions between basic values and basic social institutions, as a growing sense of "entitlement" versus work ethics (Daniel Bell 1979; for a Marxist view, see O'Connor 1973).

It must be remembered that contradictions and antinomies are inherent in society and in historic processes, with political-economic expressions (e.g. for a history of inflation, see Schmukler and Marcus 1983). Other types of regimes have antinomies and contradictions of their own, such as between traditionalism and modernization in all of the Third World; and between political rigidities (Casals 1980) and desires for economic advancement in the communist countries. The question of what governance types have antinomies and contradictions that carry more benefits/costs under given historic conditions is of major theoretic importance and of some, though very difficult, applied significance. Some limited segments of the above issues are taken up later. Here, this comment serves to put examination of antinomies and contradictions of modern democracies into a comparative framework, a need neglected in much of the "critical" literature (e.g. Offe 1972; Wolfe 1977 and Wolfe 1981—which are among the better books of this genus).

- Such latent tensions and pressures can be managed in democracies without recognized enemies, as long as rapid and stable economic growth provide sufficient new resources to meet growing and contradictory demands. When economic growth declines (whether more as a result of external factors or more as a result of inbuilt dynamics and policy weaknesses), a first consequence is erosion of a main policymaking and political resource, namely, benefits that can be distributed. From plus-game politics, in which conflict is focused on the question of who gets more and who gets much more, politics moves to a zero-sum and minus-sum situation, where some get nothing and some must give up benefits that are regarded as semisacred in many countries (Hirsch and Goldthorpe 1978; M. Olson and Landsberg 1973; Thurow 1980. An interesting application to social security is provided in Rosa 1982; on related "Politics of Inflation"; see also Medley 1982).

- The accepted guides for handling economic problems are discredited, as illustrated by problems in applying Keynesian economics to economic realities (Daniel Bell and Kristol 1981; J. Buchanan and Wagner 1977; Cairncross 1981; J. Hicks 1974; Hutchison 1979; McCloskey 1983; McKenzie 1982; O'Driscoll and Rizzo 1983; Stigler 1983; Wilber and Jameson 1983), and the related rise and decline of economists in the inner council of policymaking (the few writings on economic advice in governments pay more attention to the rise than to the decline. (see Coats 1981; Peacock 1979, pt. 4; R. Porter 1980; and Thirlwall 1982; on economic advisors in development countries see Currie 1981). Such shattering of policy compasses, in turn further reduces policymaking quality and its power-political support, as well as trust.

These four factors interact with more diffuse societal processes, such as long-range impacts of economic abundance (Potter 1954), structural adjustments to changing economic situations (Leveson and Wheeler 1980), already-mentioned value changes (Inglehart 1977a), and more—producing a syndrome that, once it starts to get malignant, can have far-reaching consequences. Thus, to take a relatively clear though very complex issue, the implications of large and permanent unemployment for societies and governments are a very ominous unknown, requiring *inter alia* reconsideration of the very concept of *work* (for contradictory views compare Handy 1984 with Macarov 1980). To expect economic decline to find its nadir in public apathy (Rose and Peters 1978) and growing self-sufficiency (Gershuny 1978a) is a very tame prediction with little support in the history of societies and regimes.

*Absence of Reliable Policy Compasses*

Related to shifts in policy issues, but going beyond them, is the just-illustrated scarcity of reliable policy compasses. The shattering effects of novel situations on the utility and credibility of accepted policy doctrines is well illustrated by the mentioned crisis in Keynesian economics, as well as in other economic doctrines. (For an outstanding critique of contemporary economics, in addition to other literature quoted above, see McClosky 1983; for an illustration of well-intended but lame recommendations based on contemporary economic thinking, see United Nations Committee on Development Planning 1982.) The lack of good ideas on what to do with the international economy as an embedment in the gaps between countries—with many of the loans being of doubtful impact (R. Ayres 1982) and the New International Economic Order (as summed up in Agarwala 1983) and other available alternatives (Cline 1979) being promising in neither development-theory assumptions (Bauer 1983) nor feasibility—illustrates further the paucity in policy compasses. It is illuminating to compare the situation with the breakdown of Victorian economic doctrines after World War I (Silverman 1982), as well as the earlier irrelevance of much of English economic thinking to pressing problems of the British Empire (Wood 1983).

Related illustrations are supplied by efforts at industrial policies, with all the modes of handling structural industrial problems tried in Western societies being inadequate (R. French 1980; W. Grant 1982; somewhat different, Pinder 1982); the demise of the "Danegeld" welfare state ideas (Gellner 1979) as a reliable policy-guiding star; and the scarcity of ideas of what to do about youth unemployment (Lenhardt 1979). In many countries of the Third World, the lack of alternatives on how to prevent a growing labor surplus while building up the economy illustrates another grave compass failure.

Economic stagnation is only one dramatic instance out of a great bundle of Gordian policy knots, the knives for the cutting of which prove blunter and blunter. Thus, without going to the extremes of simplistic egalitarianism (W. Feinberg 1978, passim), the failure of education in reducing many social inequalities (Boudon 1974) serves as another illustration of a widely accepted policy compass whose misleading bearings are only slowly being recognized. In respect to many aggravating policy predicaments, it is not lack of money and absence of political power that prevent adequate response but also, and often mainly, the scarcity of good policy ideas.

An interesting different illustration is provided by the aggravated tasks of "risk management" that must be undertaken in policymaking (Conrad 1980). Changing cultural attitudes toward risk (Aharoni 1981; Dierkes et al. 1980; Douglas and Wildavsky 1982; a good literature survey on perception of technological risks is provided in Covello 1983), on one hand, and unavoidable fuzzy-betting needs inbuilt increasingly in policymaking on important issues, on the other hand, create problems for which no compasses are available, going far beyond traditional hazard management (G. White 1974). Such problems are just beginning to be faced by systematic policy-oriented thinking (Ascher and Overholt 1983; Fischhoff et al. 1981; Lind et al. 1982; Kobrin 1982), not to speak of needed innovations in politics (Rossi et al. 1983).

To go one step further, it is interesting to consider the idea of *Angst* (which goes beyond the English term *anxiety*; see the important examination in Bergenholtz 1979) as expressing an important, though diffuse and ambiguous, predicament—with *Angstabwehr*, i.e. protection and defense against *Angst*, becoming an increasingly important function of governments. Here, no ideas at all are available, once economic safety nets are inadequate, and "soulcraft" (Will 1983) becomes required.

To move for a moment to global problematics, most of the ideas put forth for handling them are either utopian or mundane, and often both (to cite some of the relatively better writings: Cornish 1984; Didsbury 1984; Okita Owen and Brzezinski 1984).

The negative effects of suddenly and visibly misleading policy compasses, or the absence of any relevant compasses on policymaking patterns, must be added, such as retreat into dogma, search for "strong leaders," and, sometimes, most dangerous of all, looking for scapegoats and enemies to blame. Positive feedback between decreasing problem-handling capacity, more disconsensus, increasing mass *Angst,* less trust in government, and, as a combined result, further reduced problem-handling ability can easily produce predicament escalation and spirals of declining policymaking qualities.

## Historic Uniqueness

Putting present policy predicaments into a historic perspective brings out the paradoxical contemporary combination between living under conditions superior in material achievements, human rights, and knowledge to any historic period (spiritual achievements and degrees of "happiness" cannot be meaningfully compared; and "human needs" is too protean and ideologized a concept to permit meaningful discussions of comparative "need satisfaction"; see Springborg 1981), and, at the same time, suffering from serious and dangerous policy predicaments, objectively and subjectively. A historic perspective puts problems and aspirations into correct proportions, and brings out the relative time- and culture-bound nature of policy "achievement" and "predicament" images and perceptions.

On a more concrete level, macrocomparison with past situations puts into stark relief some unique features of present and foreseeable adversities:

1. The emergence of a "world system" that constitutes a very dense environment for national policymaking (as compared to earlier periods of empty space surrounding human decisionmaking, Simon 1983, 20; and later periods in which large parts of the world were inferior objects for national policymaking by hegemonic states). The world system is not only a dense policymaking environment but an active one, influencing national policymaking in multiple ways, quite separate from the nation-states that constitute the dominant discrete actors (Bertsch 1982; J. Meyer and Hannan 1979).
2. An accepted cosmology that regards adversities as mainly made by humans and as susceptible to human treatment, rather than as acts of God to be accepted with fatalism or prayer-like responses.

3. Partly related to the above characteristics, but going beyond them: a rise of collectivism (Greenleaf 1983), with the size and scope of modern government being unprecedented (Dyson 1980; Fry 1979. This is not necessarily true also in comparison with classical bureaucratic empires: Eisenstadt 1963; Wittfogel 1957) and governments being expected to take care of all main predicaments.
4. Mass reactions to images of adversity carry more political weight and are themselves a component of policymaking predicaments. Such phenomena now take a form quite different from the role of masses in Rome, for instance, or in classical Greece (Meier 1980a; Meier 1980c; Yavetz 1969; and Staveley 1972).
5. The available policy instruments are incomparably more powerful than those wielded by any historic polity. This is largely a result of science and technologies. Hardly less important is the very structure of modern mass states and the very idea of deliberate extensive policymaking as a way to influence future realities. These put policymaking into a quite different situation with much more potency, for better and for worse.
6. The production and utilization of knowledge play a much larger role in shaping policy issues and conditioning their handling.
7. The whole culture of policymaking seems different, with the central minds of modern government combining UR-components of decision making going back to the early beginnings of human societies with advanced rational-scientific elements, all within a unique "modern" world view.

Despite these and other pronounced special features of present adversity, historic comparisons provide revealing analogues and help the derivation of generalized propositions, *inter alia* by confirming or falsifying inference. In particular, comparisons with various periods of ultrachange (that is, change in the patterns of change itself) are illuminating. For instance, much can be learned about the nature of policy adversity and about patterns of response to adversity from the histories of Rome at the end of the Republic (Blits 1983; Meier 1980a; Meier 1980b), Rome during the late Empire (MacMullen 1976; C. Starr 1982), and the Italian city-states during the Renaissance (F. Gilbert 1965; Pocock 1975). The experiences of the 1929-39 depression are directly relevant to present predicaments (Kindleberger 1973; Romasco 1983). To provide an example of possible conclusions from the reprocessing of historic material, discussed later in this book: the inherent inability of societies and governments to perceive correctly fundamental changes and to estimate correctly the time cycles of adversities emerges as a main finding from historic comparisons and can be better explained with the help of historic materials. Historic experiences serve from time to time in this book to bring out some main constant and time-variant features of adversities and their handling, when applicable.

A prime lesson from history is that prediction of policy predicaments is a very doubtful matter, with most predictions in the past, especially during periods of change, being soon proven completely wrong. The present understanding of reality, thanks partly to more of an awareness of history, is much superior to that of Roman times and, on lesser a scale, to that of the Italian city-states. Attempts to refine prediction methods abound. Nevertheless, fundamental limits on the ability to transgress current cultural perceptions and to grasp ultrachange remain rigid and strong. The following attempt to comment on *futuribles* (in the sense of alternative possible futures, Jouvenel 1967) of adversity must, therefore, be taken with strong reservations. But, first, the partial survey of some adversity features needs reprocessing in the form of some generalized conjectures and some attempts at explanation. Such attempts are a precondition for any thinking on the future, which must be based on at least some understanding of the present and its underlying longer-term processes.

## Generalized Propositions

Moving from fragmentary description of select policy predicament features to generalizations, and utilizing the concept package presented earlier, a number of propositions on present adversity seem justified:

1. Policy adversities are very complex, in the sense of including a large number of interacting and dynamic factors not reducible to a few clear-cut causes.
2. In terms of currently available policy alternatives, most policy predicaments seem to be intractable. It is an open question whether this is unavoidable, with policy predicaments being inherently "unsolvable," and/or how far this is a matter of permanent or transient policymaking weaknesses.
3. Policy predicaments are, in part, exogenous to governance, belonging to social, technological, economic, and cultural facets of society. In part they are endogenous to governance, related to main features of politics, for instance. And, in part, they are external to societies, being multinational and global in character.
4. Present categorization of situations as "predicaments" or "adversity" is inexorably conditioned by contemporary culture and Weltanschauung. This is well illustrated by the discontinuous history of "poverty" as a policy issue and nonissue (Katz 1983). In a historic perspective, humanity is much better off now than ever before in most respects, with the exception of dangers inherent in novel, very powerful policy instruments wielded by governments. How our period will be seen by future generations, in turn, is beyond our minds.

There remain major issues of "objectivity" and various "subjectivities" of adversity images. In many respects, the very formation of images of adversity also constitutes a major response to adversity. Therefore, it is more convenient to consider problems of the correctness and distortion of images of adversity as a form of response by central minds of governments to adversity, closely related to policymaking responses, in the next chapter.

## Theoretic Speculations

Theoretic speculations on underlying forces and processes resulting in present and foreseeable policy adversities overlap metaphysics and Weltanschauungen (e.g. see the discussion of Toynbee's position in Perry 1982). Yet, a look at some relevant speculative conjectures serves to provide some sense of the kind of factors that may be at work, even if they are hard to conceptualize and impossible to prove or refute (and, therefore, in some views are beyond the domain of "science").

To glance into the doubtful, first some speculative views on jumps in predicaments in general are mentioned. Then, somewhat more specific contemplations on possible causes for political predicaments, on the level of fundamental forces and factors, are looked at.

### On Predicament Shifts in General

The most abstract approach to predicament shifts is to view historic processes as unfolding in terms of dialectic jumps, "catastrophe" transformations, S-curves, L-curves or U-curves, spike curves, and waves. Apparent statistical support for some forms of wave or cycle schemata in respect to innovation (A. Graham and Senge 1980; Marchetti 1980), global politics (Modelski 1978), and the economy (Duijn 1983; C. Freeman 1983; Kondratieff 1936; Rostow 1978) is interesting but should not be mistaken for reliable empiric support for what are, with present modes of scientific thinking, at best speculative conjectures. This caveat also applies to the interesting proposition of Albert O. Hirschman on periodic shifts between private interests and public action as main modes of societal behavior (Hirschman 1981).

Shifts resulting from accumulated contradictions are a subcategory of the above type of explanation. An important case is constituted by situations where extrapolation of trends clearly indicates an emerging impossibility situation. The Club of Rome report, *The Limits of Growth* (Dennis Meadows et al. 1972, based methodologically on the works of Forrester, especially Forrester 1969. More recent work of this type is discussed in Donella Meadows et al. 1982), is the most famous illustration of such predictions. Without going into the weaknesses here of this or other particular attempts (Cole 1973; Walter 1981, especially part 2), this approach is the technically most developed one for explaining fundamental processes resulting in shifts, usually associated with acute adversity. But multiple computer runs do not necessarily produce knowledge. Many underlying models at best are doubtful, with historic processes not fitting any such simple schemata.

More specific but also on a speculative level are explanations of contemporary predicament accumulations in terms of the following factors:

1. The combined effect of multiple shocks to which Occidental culture and society are subjected, including World Wars I and II, decolonization, economic ascendance of non-Western societies with Japan in the lead, the West-East cleavage, becoming a minority among sovereign nations, and the specter of nuclear war.
2. Results of mistaken grand policies, such as vast expansion of collective responsibilities for individual needs, encouragement of migrant labor, export of advanced technologies, and more. Some of the development policies followed in a number of Third World countries, together with some of the aid policies of Western countries, serve as good illustrations of grand policies which resulted in harsher predicaments in quite a number of societies (Cuny 1983).
3. The transition phase to a different form of society, such as various images of "postindustrialism" (e.g. Gershuny and Miles 1983), together with adjustment frictions while absorbing radically new technologies and responding to new kinds of global situations. (Huntington 1969 is still relevant.)
4. Transformations of the international system, in part related to differential modernization and industrialization phases of different countries and to clustered distribution of natural resources, and, in part, to emergence of a "world system" as mentioned above.
5. Changes in culture viewed as a semiautonomous variable, ranging from lifestyles to "modernity." This variable will be illustrated below, in the context of political predicaments. To be noted again is the need for care in considering cultural variables as causing policy predicaments because of intense susceptibility to catchwords and irrelevant moral judgments. Thus, the term *decadence* should be avoided unless strictly defined and circumscribed (R. Adams 1983). Attempts at what can be called psychoanalysis of society and culture (e.g. Harrington 1983; Deleuze and Guattari 1977) are interesting as long as they are taken as literary speculations.

In various combinations, processes, factors, and events as mentioned above can reasonably be included in any attempt to explain present predicaments and their shifts. Infinite reduction in the search for "ultimate causes" can lead to seeking deeper forces and factors, returning specula-tions to square one if not square zero. But, on the level of a social change grand theory attached to a process view of history, consideration of factors such as the above pushes present knowledge to its limits.

Crosscutting such variables and pervasive in any consideration of his-toric processes is the question whether factors such as those mentioned above operate in a more deterministic or more stochastic or indeterminate mode in producing present adversity. Take the 1973 oil price rise as an example. It makes quite a difference in our perception of present economic difficulties and their treatment if they are seen as largely due to the price rise, which in turn is explained in terms of the Yom Kippur War as a historic accident; or whether the oil price rise is viewed as inevitable in the longer run, accidental factors serving as a timing device; or whether it is believed the economic difficulties would have occurred in any case and at more or less the same time, with or without the Yom Kippur War—which too can be viewed as accidental or unavoidable.

This is a cardinal issue for considering the potentials of policymaking to influence the future. As will be elaborated in chapter 4 and further dis-cussed in later chapters, this book is predicated upon a mixed view of historic process dynamics, with significant trends and events being seen as partly deterministic, partly stochastic, and partly accidental. Without nec-essarily accepting the particular instance of the 1973 oil price rise as a main cause of present predicaments, the importance of accidental variables is quite obvious in the short term and is probably also important in the longer term, within unknown ranges. It is enough for present purposes to mention what has been called a "fortuitous gatekeeper" theory of social development that was shared to some extent by Karl Wittfogel and by Max Weber (Gellner 1983; this view is shared by Ernest Gellner himself, Gellner 1979; see also D. Landes 1969), and that is also, interestingly enough, a part of some modern Soviet thinking on the "Asian mode of production" so-cietal type (Bailey and Llobera 1981; S.P. Dunn 1982) to illustrate the importance and potentials of stochastic and indeterminate explanations of historic processes as an alternative to deterministic views. In other words, present adversities can be seen as partly a chance product of factors that could also have resulted in quite different situations. It is possible to pro-duce after the fact explanations for such "tides of politics" (Schlesinger 1949, ch. 4), but chance must be allocated some role in such explanations and imponderable factors must be recognized as significant.

For the purposes of this book, it is unnecessary to take up such issues, including their implications for the very possibilities of valid social science generalizations (e.g. Boudon 1983, to be read in the context of Boudon 1981). Within the limited world of discourse of understanding and improving policymaking, it makes little difference whether present predicaments are viewed more as historically unavoidable or more as a result of chance factors. But, as will be made clear later on, for collective goal-directed action in the form of policymaking, an underlying Weltanschauung accepting significant roles of chance in shaping historic processes has cardinal implications, leading to a gambling view of policymaking, as taken up later.

## On Shifts in Political Predicaments

In the domain of politics, various views of inherent cyclic process patterns have been profferred since Aristotle and Polybius. On a less a priori level, fundamental factors helping to explain, at least in part, present shifts in political predicaments (and *mutatis mutandi,* shifts in other societal domains) include:

1. Antinomies and contradictions inherent in contemporary political process-systems, such as between economic capitalism, political liberalism, and mass democracy, as already mentioned, and additional ones (e.g. see Sandel 1982). Partly different built-in antinomies and contradictions operate in communist regimes and in developing countries. Such antinomies and contradictions can operate on their own, and/or are aggravated by extrapolitical phenomena, such as economic stagnation, and pushed up to threshold levels of dramatic impacts.
2. Direct effects of politics-exogenous processes, independent from antinomies and contradictions built into politics. Illustrations include postindustrial developments (Daniel Bell, 1973; Huntington 1974; Kumar 1978), modern mass education, shifts in subjective time applied to political impatience (Renshon 1977), and modern mass communication together with already-mentioned "ungovernability" factors. (Constantly changing research findings on the impact/nonimpact of TV on main features of politics demonstrate the difficulty of empirically proving or refuting conjectures on such subjects, even when formulated in operationalized middle-range theory and, in principle, researchable. Compare Pearl 1982 and T. Cook et al. 1983; Milavsky et al. 1983; and National Institute of Mental Health 1982).
3. Direct effects of politics-endogenous processes, such as politicization of the economy, growing scope and complexity of governance, and failure to produce "alternatives" for gross and visible inadequacies of present political institutions. For instance, the already-mentioned conjecture by Hirschman on the inherent pendulum-like swings between more private and more public action, based on a permanent tendency to be disappointed is interesting (Hirschman 1981, esp. chs. 2, 6, 7). To expand his conjectures, if populations become disappointed with both private and public modes of available actions, jumps into different action modalities

can be expected, as demonstrated by some features of political adversity discussed above.

4. Diffuse changes in culture and society, in their projections on politics. In addition to already-mentioned phenomena, such as reduction of transcendental legitimation of the state and government, the impacts on politics of a number of sociocultural factors are interesting to speculate on. These include the already-mentioned *Angst,* weakening of traditional religions, lack of ready social roles for personality types tending to "sainthood," and the absence of realistic political visions in Western democracies. (The situation in these respects is different in a number of Third World countries and, less so, in some of the communist countries.) All these factors together can combine and result in a tendency toward new political theologies propagated by true believers. The political arena may take over functions fulfilled historically by religious and other domains, with resulting mutations in the nature of Western democratic political cultures. Suggestive is literature on religious beliefs as an answer to *Angst* (Jaspers 1960, passim; Pfister 1944); on religion as a way to make sense out of the world, a need that may be projected onto politics (Jonathan Smith 1982); on the functions of saints, which is now a nonexisting role that may move into politics (Weinstein and R.M. Bell 1982; and, differently, Billington 1980); on the politics of utopia (Goodwin and Taylor 1982; Kelley and Bakunin 1983); on the need for political myth and epic (Cuthbertson 1975); and more. I do not need here to consider possible emergence of a new chiliastic eschatology of a mainly political character as a possible *futuribles* of politics (but see N. Cohen 1970; and, within a particular culture context, Sarkisyanz 1955; partly relevant are Mendel and Bakunin 1983; Mühlmann 1964; Wagar 1983), but such radical cultural impacts on politics must not be ignored as a distinct possibility.

Theoretic speculations add a dimension to trying to understand adversity and its underlying forces but they are not a reliable basis for predictions. Nevertheless, for short-term prediction, speculative conjectures may provide some help for deriving *futuribles,* for rejecting naive extrapolations, and for throwing doubts on simplistic Delphic exercises on very complex processes. A minimum conclusion from a first look at processes possibly underlying adversity is to be wary about predictions and always to consider the future in terms of alternative possible futures, that is *futuribles,* with acknowledged uncertainties and unknowables. With all these hedgings, some prediction of possible and perhaps probable *futuribles* of policy adversity is essential as a basis for future-oriented evaluation of policymaking under adversity.

## Lookout for Adversity Futuribles

Analysis of main predicament factors leads to a tentative conclusion that adversity will become worse in the foreseeable future, say the next twenty to thirty years at least, and probably longer into the second half of the twenty-first century. Contrary views, as presented in some literature, border in part on ignorance of present facts, reality-distorting wishful thinking (Toffler 1981; somewhat more careful, for instance in recognizing political difficulties, is Toffler 1983, esp. ch. 6), or neglect of crucial variables (Kahn 1979; Kahn 1982; Naisbitt 1983; L. Simon 1980, to be compared with Mensch 1979; and Stavrianos 1976). Long-range predictions of more than, say, fifty years belong to the domain of pure speculation. Such contemplation may sometimes be interesting (as Kahn, Brown, and Martel 1976) but, on principle, should be regarded as incorrect, *inter alia* because of the inherent impossibility of predicting ultrachange (Dror 1975) and some crucial factors, such as future human knowledge (Popper 1972a).

A useful metaphor for thinking on some of the more serious policy predicaments, if not taken too literally, is provided by catastrophe models (Isnard and Zeeman 1976; Woodcock and Davis 1980). These mathematical and topological models deal with jumps and mutations, as discontinuous alternatives to smooth curves, for describing some types of phenomena. Relations between the North and the South, some scenarios of the global arms race, welfare policies under conditions of economic decline, global population growth together with diffusing high energy use— these are domains in which, as already mentioned, continuation of present curves leads to impossibilities, with potentials for catastrophes, in the sense of jumps and mutations that will be very unpleasant and, in part, very dangerous. Without pushing the catastrophe-models metaphor too far and without taking up philosophy-of-history questions of possible long-range adjustive effects of disasters (e.g. as postulated by Malthus), catastrophe curves indicate qualitative features of policy predicaments and the innovative policy responses essential for handling them.

This guesstimation of futures of policymaking adversity does not assume "doomsday" scenarios but fits most of the serious attempts at predicting probable middle-range world futures. The latter indicate very serious predicaments with grave dangers but not disaster (C. Freeman and Jahoda 1978; Institute of Social Studies 1979; E.T. Jones 1980; Kotharu 1974; McHale 1981; OECD 1979b; U.S. Council on Environmental Quality and Department of State 1980). Neither does the guesstimation ignore the very pertinent, already-mentioned fact that in many respects most of humanity is today better off than ever in history, such as in life expectancy and living conditions. This fact must not be forgotten in all the outcries about policy predicaments. Neither can predictions of aggravating circumstances be fully relied upon, lacking as we do real understanding of the present and a sound basis for exploring, not to say predicting, futures. Such considerations do not diminish the seriousness and anguish of prevailing adversity or the dismal possibilities of the future but recalibrate them.

To sum up, recognizing the fallibility of predictions, as far as present indicators can serve to explore the near future, policy adversity seems to be epochal, with a high probability of getting worse during the next thirty-year span and beyond. This conjecture can be overturned by ultrachange in favorable directions, but, taking into account the lead time of such turns, the probability of main policy predicaments dissipating within one generation seems low.

At the same time, images of a clear-cut crossroad between large achievements or rapid decline and even catastrophe, as sometimes presented in simplistic treatments (e.g. Curtis 1982), are overstatements. Similarly exaggerated are proposals for radical shifts in global regimes and policy cultures (e.g. Fuller 1978; Laszlo 1983; B. Ward and Dubos 1983; M. Wiener 1978), which even if desirable in some sense are definitely not open options, at least without the intervention of catastrophes that dissolve present policymaking realities. In this book such extreme possibilities are left aside, with attention focusing on less extreme, though still quite radical, predicaments and improvement possibilities.

A large variety of possible *futuribles* can be constructed for a more specific prediction concerning adversity features, as is done in some of the literature cited above. Different combinations of various forms of economic, social, political, cultural, security, and other features add up to endless scenarios, some of which can be graded as more or less probable for specified groups of countries. Such variations are not important for our concerns here. Focusing on adversity in a generic sense, the analysis and proposals developed in this book apply in the main to a wide range of *futuribles,* with the exception of very optimistic ones and very pessimistic ones: If pressures on policymaking decrease a lot, thanks to a turn for the better in most features of adversity and/or a downturn in demands upon governance, then the applied aspects of *Policymaking Under Adversity* are less relevant, though academic interests and theoretic significance may be untouched. If Armageddon occurs, radically different rules apply to survivors, requiring separate treatment as *Decisionmaking Under and After Calamity.* But, at present both harbingers of catastrophe and signs of propitious upturns are scarce.

The author's tendency is to recommend preparations for the bad and even some for the worst. This is not a matter of temperament but can be justified in terms of a "minimization-of-possible-regret" posture: With the accepting of doubts about the futures of adversity, it seems prudent to recommend preparing policymaking for an extended period of adversity, for a strong case can be built for such a period. And even if the expectation is in error, it is better to have prepared policymaking for grave adversity than not to be ready if adversity continues and worsens. If the massiveness of involved factors is taken into account, there is little danger of self-fulfilling prophecy effects, as if preparing for an epoch of adversity will bring it about, as long as preparations are on the level of the central policymaking process-system. But, care must be taken to avoid runaway chain reactions, for instance in expectancy-shaped economic behavior.

# 3

# Policymaking Responses

## Conceptual and Methodological Issues

Quite independent from the tremendous achievements of modern states in historic perspective (Deutsch 1981) and from past and continuous successes in handling acute problems (Levitan and Taggart 1976; Romasco 1983; J. Schwarz 1983), such as terrorism (B. Bell 1978; Dror 1983b; E. Evans 1979; J. Lodge 1981), a main feature of contemporary policymaking is growing awareness of bleak problems, though often superficially perceived and deficiently diagnosed, both in establishments (Pollard 1981) and in academic work (as illustrated by parts of Amin et al. 1982; Bourne and Levin 1983; Cornford 1975; Cotgrove 1982; Goerner 1971; Inglehart 1977b, and in most of the so-called social problems texts, e.g. DeFleur 1983; not to speak about dogmatic misperceptions in doctrinaire writings, such as Chomsky and E. Herman 1979). Adversity is somehow perceived and a variety of responses do take place.

Consideration of main policymaking response patterns to adversity raises a number of thorny conceptual and methodological issues. Thus, distinction between policymaking dynamics that occurs independent from adversity and that which constitutes a response to adversity is difficult; it is very hard to construct a useful taxonomy of main response patterns that does not lose too much of the richness of reality; and generalizations on response patterns are hard to justify empirically, depending as they do in part on specific adversity features, on national cultures, on policymaking traditions, and on accidents such as the presence and the preferences of strong leaders.

Methodological and conceptual difficulties are further illustrated by the necessity to select appropriate levels of discourse. The choice is between four main "pure-type" levels for considering responses to adversity.

1. The social-process level. On this level, human and societal evolutions and processes are contemplated in terms of "challenge and response," "social processes" or related schemata, leading to various grand views of

history, as illustrated differently by Norbert Elias, Alexander Rüstow, Arnold J. Toynbee, Oswald Spengler, and more; up to catastrophe theories of human evolution and progress (Clube and Napier 1982).
2. The macroresponse level. Here, the subjects of investigation are somewhat more limited, with attention focusing on broad societal responses to defined adversity, such as invading immigration (Diesner 1982), war (McNeill 1982), or pestilence (Gottfried 1983; Ziegler 1969; and, more generalized, McNeill 1977).
3. The mezzoresponse level. On the mezzoresponse level, medium- or short-term reactions of parts of a social system to various ranges of adversity are investigated. An already-quoted illustration very relevant to this book is provided by *Roman Government's Response to Crisis* (MacMullen 1976), which focuses on a period of about one century and on the responses of the "mind of government" to a broad but defined set of adversities.
4. The microresponse level. Finally, on the microresponse level, specific reactions in terms of discrete decisions or behavior by concrete entities serve as objects for attention. Thus, the reactions to adversity of business corporations (e.g. see Boswell 1983; and B. Yates 1983); of parties; of unions (P. Lange et al. 1982); and so on are interesting and understudied. All too few, also, are studies of particular policies adopted and implemented under adversity, though some such studies do exist (e.g. Mitroff, Mason, and Barabba 1983), such as in the domain of energy (e.g. Grainger and Gibson 1981, which is prescriptive in basic orientation), and on local disasters (e.g. Wettenhall 1975).

Various shades and shading between these pure-type distinctions are possible, and studies can adopt different mixes to fit their interests. It is also possible to try to develop a combinational, integrated, or comprehensive theory of responses to adversity in its multiple forms (e.g. on calamities, Sorokin 1942), but with present scarce knowledge this is a very heroic endeavor.

Applying these distinctions to the more limited subject of policymaking responses to adversity, an optimal method would combine a large number of microresponse studies leading to aggregate findings with direct investigation of higher-level behavior, arriving together at reliable findings on the mezzoresponse level. Put into a historic perspective with heuristic comparisons, mezzoresponse findings can perhaps stimulate propositions on a macroresponse level, up to propositions about policymaking within historical processes. For instance, it may be possible to arrive at speculative conjectures on the significance of weaknesses in central minds of governments and their responses to adversity as a factor in the decline of nations.

Yet, the knowledge infrastructure for adopting such an approach is lacking. Thus, not many investigations have considered specific responses in concrete policy domains to present adversity, though interest in some aspects of this subject is growing rapidly, such as in "cutback management" (e.g. Ellwood 1981; Wynne 1983). Very few studies deal with the behavior of senior political decision makers and of policymaking organizations under conditions of adversity (but see Holsti and George 1975). Psychological studies dealing with individual and group decision making under stress (Janis 1982; Janis and Mann 1977) are suggestive, but their applicability to senior decision makers under sustained pressures of adversity is doubtful. Even less has been done to consider organizational behavior under sustained pressure, the few studies touching upon parts of the subject (e.g. March and Olsen 1976) being one-sided in their conclusions (e.g. see Greene 1982; and, for a case study of successful organizational handling of adversity, C. Johnson 1982, to be compared with B. Yates 1983).

Symptomatic of the present preoccupations of political science in general and policy sciences in particular, systematic studies of the responses of governments to war are absent. Some lessons of war economies have been looked at (e.g. Chester 1951); adjustments of the machinery of governments to the challenges of managing a war have sometimes been explored (e.g. Burk 1982; F. Johnson 1980; J. Turner 1980); and handling of specific issues has been investigated (e.g. Doughty 1983), but the subject as a whole has been sorely neglected. Similarly, only disparate investigations deal with the adjustment of machineries of government to the Great Depression (e.g. Howson and Winch 1977).

Thus comparative-historic studies are sorely lacking. This omission is all the more disturbing, for main responses to contemporary adversity are just in their beginnings. This is a major difficulty because response patterns must be viewed dynamically, as a continuous multifarious process, evolving with time under the impacts of further changes in the states of adversity; of internal developments in the central minds of governments; and of feedback, such as from politically effective publics.

To handle such limitations while taking up the essential subject of policymaking-responses to adversity, the following strategies are pursued in this chapter:

1. A distinction is made between primary response patterns and continuous dynamics. Primary response patterns include initial policymaking responses to newly cognized adversity. Continuous dynamics includes consequent processes, such as further evolution of adversity, feedbacks to policymaking, and later patterns of policymaking responses. This is an artificial breaking up of one and the same process but, by analytically differentiating between various response phases, some of the dynamics of the response process can be more easily exposed.

2. In addition to main policymaking response patterns to adversity, some reactions of political publics (that is, politically effective segments of the public, as active in various polities) to adversity are also touched upon—this to consider the main dynamics of evolving policymaking response patterns.

3. Policymaking response patterns are aggregated, with neglect of important differences between distinct components of the central policymaking process system, and of diverse responses in various adversity domains. Similarly, very important differences in response patterns of policymaking to adversity between countries and types of regimes are mentioned only in passing, though this is a very important subject in need of systematic investigation. Despite some attempts in such directions (e.g. Richardson 1982) and the existence of country studies that can help in such an endeavor (e.g. compare Cerny and Schain 1980 with Ellman 1979), present adversity syndromes are too recent and relevant studies too scarce to permit derivation of refined and differential conjectures.

4. With the exception of a survey of adjustments in policymaking as a response pattern to adversity, based largely on a field study by the author, findings are based on subjective observation, augmented by dispersed interviewing and extended stays in a number of countries, together with processing of the little relevant literature. Therefore, findings are presented as impressionistic conjectures and as hypotheses for systematic investigation.

5. In line with the remarks above, no attempt is made to tie specific primary and consequent response patterns to diverse political, social, and cultural variables. Theories doing so are necessary but require massive historic-comparative study and can be undertaken only after more time has passed to provide a better perspective (though suitably designed longitudinal studies should be started now).

6. One specific response pattern especially salient to the central subject of this book is subjected to more detailed treatment, on the basis of an already-mentioned survey done by the author, namely, attempts to improve policymaking so as better to handle adversity.

7. After main findings and conjectures on present response patterns are presented, some theoretic conjectures are developed, relating some primary and consequent response patterns to exploration of different outcomes in terms of alternative futures of political systems and of policymaking. This leads into ignorance-shrouded problems of societal destabilization, political transformation, and regime-breaking loads, as well as of governmental mutation potentials, which will be partly identified but not considered in any depth.

8. Policymaking realities, as considered later in chapters 6 and 7, serve to explain policymaking responses to adversity, as explored in the present chapter. Thus, combined reading of chapters 6 and 7 provides an en-

hanced picture of policymaking realities, policymaking dynamics, and some of their underlying variables.

## Main Primary Response Patterns of Policymaking to Adversity

Responses of policymaking to adversity take various shapes and appear in different mixes. Some patterns contradict others, while some tend to reinforce one another and often appear in clusters. Leaving such interdependencies aside, eleven main primary response patterns of policymaking to adversity can be identified in the contemporary scenery.

### Adversity Image Formation in the Mind of Governments: Denial, Simplification, Externalization, Cognitive Map Consistency Preservation

Images of adversity in the minds of governments are a heterogeneous and amorphous phenomenon, hard to study. Such images are only partly reflected in overt policymaking behavior. Direct investigation is possible, but available studies are outdated and incomplete (relevant are parts of the University of Michigan Comparative Elites Project. See, for instance, Aberbach et al. 1981; Anton 1980; Eldersveld et al. 1981). Also, images held in the central minds of government are heterogeneous, different images being formed at different times in various components of the central policymaking process-system, with large variations between countries and regime types. Processes of image formation and reformation themselves are diverse and closely related to broader reality cognition and assessment capacities, as considered later in the book.

Despite all these difficulties, the subject cannot be put aside because of inadequate bases for conjectures. Images of adversity are not only a response to adversity but a main factor in shaping responses to adversity. Therefore, speculative conjectures are preferable to leaving this crucial response pattern unconsidered.

Impressionistically, on the basis of the little relevant literature and of unrepresentative but extensive interviewing of policymakers in a variety of countries, some of the main image formation responses to adversity seem to include the following:

- Denial of harsher aspects of adversity, such as its possibly pandemic and epochal nature. Thus, tendencies to regard economic stagnation as temporary and recovery as just around the corner are very pronounced. Many economic advisors have testified to intense pressures on them by senior policymakers not to produce studies and predictions contradicting such pious hopes, even on a "for-your-eyes-only" basis. Still, adversity does have impacts on world pictures; few policymakers are showing signs of Victorian-type (Bradley 1980) optimism.

- Simplification of the nature and causes of adversity, with frequent reduction to a few factors. The tendency of top policymakers to remain riveted to very simplistic reality pictures is very pronounced and comes through in most interviews, even when the politicians try to answer in a sophisticated way. Top civil servants also admit to serious perplexity, oscillating between clinging to simple explanations and withdrawing into semiapathy.

  The response pattern of clinging to some policy theology that is considered later is closely related to the one now being discussed, with dogmas supporting closed minds that are attached to simple explanations of predicaments.

- Externalization and transference of the causes of adversity. A strong tendency can be discerned to explain adversity in terms of some modern "act-of-God" factors, such as the "international monetary system." In some countries, quasienemies, or at least former other-party governments, are blamed for main adversities. There is a strong tendency to pick external causes about which one can do nothing. Only in single cases have senior policymakers related adversity to mistakes of their own in the past.

- Strong cognitive-map consistency maintenance seems to be the rule. Few top policymakers indicate any material changes in their basic assumptions and their worldviews because of the adversity. While few claimed to have foreseen adversity, the causes for prediction failure are put as "unpredictable accidents," ignorant experts, and so on—not faults in the worldviews of the top policymakers themselves.

None of these tentative findings on the perception of adversity in the central minds of governments is surprising, fitting as they do main psychological and related investigations, as considered later in this book. Nevertheless, the persistence of grossly distorted adversity images in the central minds of governments must be emphasized. This is not only a matter of individual, group, and organizational cognition processes but also of self-reinforcing dynamics. Thus, when more realistic images of reality may reveal situations for which no known treatment is at hand, tendencies to overinterpret facts so as to fit wrong but manageable or acceptable diagnoses are reinforced. As yet not enough time has passed for incorrect adversity images to be clearly refuted by reality, though increasing doubts appear. Some learning does take place, as was illustrated in the French government in 1984. But this is more an exception than the rule. What will happen to the central minds of governments if and when reality shocks utterly shatter cognitive maps that are now clung to?—this is another question.

*Attempts to Shape Adversity Images Held by Political Publics:*
*Expectation Reduction, Self-Blame, Externalization*

Shaping public images of realities, partly through symbolic policies, is a principal function of the political system as a whole and of top politicians in particular (Bennett 1983; Cockerell et al. 1984; Edelman 1971; C. Elder and Cobb 1983; Goodin 1980; Schelsky 1984; Weissberg 1976). What is new, within contemporary perspectives, are some directions of adversity image shaping being adopted increasingly by the central minds of governments, including:

- Reduction in expectation, efforts being made by top politicians to decrease demands on government and to get political publics to accept an extended period of trouble. For instance, strong efforts are made in a number of Western European countries to reduce expectations of constant expansion in social welfare entitlements.
- At various historical periods of harsh adversity, moral degeneration of the public was proffered as a leading explanation and conveyed to political publics, while also often believed in by top politicians themselves. Some elements of such explanations can be found in contemporary image-shaping endeavors, with an accent sometimes on lack of work effort. It seems that this is an important motif in the USSR but less so in the democracies. Perhaps top politicians hesitate to blame the electorate, in any case in public. In interviews a number of them did blame permissiveness, ruined work ethics, "decadence," overmaterialism, etc. as causes of adversity, but most of them admitted frankly that they cannot publicly attack a public on which they depend for support. (Here, images of voting behavior came into play; they may be incorrect but they are held by policymakers.)
- Externalization and transference are main modalities of the efforts to shape public images of adversity. In Western democracies, a shift has occurred in comparison with the past, more blame being put—within the central minds of governments, as mentioned, as well—on impersonal and Kafka-like forces, such as the "international monetary system," than on specific scapegoats and enemies, internal or external. Some handling of the Japanese economic performance includes strong traces of identifying a quasienemy, but as yet this is kept under control. Here, senior policymakers express awareness of a difficult dilemma: On one hand, quite a number of them tend to blame Japanese economic behavior for some painful adversity. At the same time, they support the doctrine of free international trade and open economic competition. They have difficulties in reconciling these elements in their own thinking and seem to be aware of the dangers to free trade if the public adopts a view of Japanese economic competition as a main cause of unemployment.

The situation is quite different in a number of Third World countries, where enemies ranging from "imperialists" to multinational corporations and sometimes internal dissidents are often blamed for harsh adversity.

The effectiveness of such image-shaping efforts is hard to evaluate. For many countries no reliable public opinion data are available; also, the impacts of image-shaping efforts by top politicians, as compared with other variables, are hard to isolate. The role of the mass media is especially complex. In Western countries, where relevant data are available and are being processed (Inglehart 1977a; Klages and Kmiecieak 1979), public images of adversity move somewhat in directions similar to those aimed at by central political image-shaping endeavors.

*Adversity Routinization*

A special form of response to adversity, which belongs to shaping its images but goes beyond it, is adversity routinization. Handling of terrorism has achieved its already-mentioned successes in a number of countries partly through the routinization of terrorism images, in the sense of acceptance of some terrorism as part of the normal situation rather than as an acute "adversity" (Horowitz 1983; a good literati treatment of this phenomenon is Böll 1982. Very relevant is Alon 1980, dealing with Israeli responses to terrorism, with a tendency to overestimate the threat on one hand and successful routinization, in the sense of "living with terrorism," on the other.) Attempts in highly developed countries to routinize a high level of unemployment illustrate such a policymaking response to a harsh predicament.

*Adversity Ennobling*

Historically, the ennobling of adversity as an expression of the will of God, as a prelude to the Millennium, or as an ordeal sure to harden and strengthen society and the state has constituted the main mode of handling adversity. To ennoble adversity, acceptance of transcendental meanings for adversity, or of some sense of national mission to which adversity can be related, is essential. This is absent in contemporary Western democracies, with the unique exception of Israel. Israel is faced by many conditions that would be regarded as extreme adversity in other countries but has "unadversitized" them, to coin a verb, through a mixture of routinization and acceptance of the predicaments as an integral part of the challenges of Zionism.

In a number of Third World countries, the ennobling of adversity plays an important role. Apparent decreases in continuous acceptance of adversity as justified by national development missions seems to be a leading cause of growing failures in politics and policy in a number of developing countries. (These, in turn, are caused by a number of factors beyond the scope of this book, such as elite behavior, international diffusion of expectations, and more.)

## Nominal and/or Visible Activism

Tacitus noted "when the Republic is maximally corrupted, there are most laws." Nominal activism—in the sense of "placebo policies" (Gustafsson and Richardson 1979) and attempts to handle adversity through many laws, declarations, and demostrative activities (Rose 1983c) up to a kind of "policymaking stampede"—seems to constitute one of the prime possible response patterns to adversity. Analytically distinct from symbolic and image-shaping activities as considered earlier, though often overlapping them, nominal activism is a pronounced phenomenon in many contemporary situations. Intense needs to show that something is being done, both to gain political support and to meet psychological needs of top decision makers, result from general acceptance of the idea of the "active society" (Etzioni 1968), lack of visible governmental response to adversity being unacceptable in most polities. Some forms of activism are a policy charade having no impact whatsoever on reality, such as a great amount of legislation, which creates a programmatic blockage. Other forms of activism have very visible short-term effects but only seldom contribute to handling adversity. Stylized treatments of adversity, ritualistic policymaking, conduct-oriented rather than result-directed behavior by central minds of governments—all these are among the main policymaking responses to adversity.

Attempts to face adversity through a few dramatic acts characterize some types of polities that, *inter alia*, have strong power centers and erratic decision-making propensities. In democracies, the tendency is more toward nominal activism, fitting fragmented politics. But, visible activism can be discerned in some democracies too, and may increase with aggravating and persisting adversity.

One can speculate on the possible functioning of some nominal policymaking as political theatre, recognized by all as such and, nevertheless or perhaps therefore, fulfilling anodynic functions compensating in part for failures to handle adversity and compensating for public ennui (on the subject of ennui, see R. Kuhn 1905. Application to politics and public life in Western societies awaits treatment). In this, as well as other effects, modern polities may be more of "Theatre States" (Geertz 1980) and fulfill more "theatricality" (E. Burns 1972) functions than meets the eye (J. Combs 1980), with adversity making this modality of politics all the more important. This might be a subject to be studied, but the present unavailability of relevant data permits no more than tentative mention of this speculative conjecture.

## Policymaking Responsibility Reallocation

A very interesting response pattern by the central policymaking process-system to adversity is to try to reallocate responsibility and share risks. Moving into real or imagined tripartism (D. March and Grant 1977), heaving off functions to central banks, the devolution of authority, the multiplication of summit meetings on adversity, block grants leaving to recipients determination of negative priorities—these characterize conditions of adversity (without being unique to them). The growing willingness in the United Kingdom, the United States, and Sweden to allocate functions to local authorities, and reluctance by the latter to take them over under conditions of adversity illustrate this reponse pattern in democracies (compare Ellwood 1982), as do changes in the roles of legislatures (compare Kornberg 1973 with Schwarz 1980).

In nondemocracies, and in some democracies too, a contrary direction can also be identified, with more concentration of authority being sought by the central policymaking units so as to have powers deemed essential for handling adversity. Some trends in Switzerland interestingly illustrate this direction in a country extreme in its devolution of decisionmaking powers.

Within the central policymaking institutions, responsibility reallocations again play a role as a response pattern to adversity. Thus, in many countries a clear trend toward more powerful rulers can be discerned. This tendency, especially striking in Western European countries lacking a tradition of strong heads of governments, has multiple causes, as considered later in this book, but it also constitutes, in part, a response pattern to adversity. Public psychological needs under conditions of adversity may also have something to do with the trend toward more powerful leaders.

## Incrementalism, with Sporadic Jumps.

A main response, or nonresponse, to adversity has been continuing incrementalism, with policymaking following its traditional patterns. The strength of policy orthodoxies (Dearlove 1979, esp. 3) often results in a tendency "not to think in the correct order of magnitude" (Tinbergen 1981, 149) even when transincremental policy alternatives are adopted. All in all, incrementalism continues to be very strong in actual policymaking responses to adversity.

With time, when adversity becomes manifest and incrementalism clearly inadequate, a number of sporadic jumps in policies enter the response pattern, not only as visible activism as discussed above but as a bona fide adversity-directed mode of policymaking. This, not in the form of "mixed scanning" (Etzioni 1968, ch. 12), or selective radicalism, as discussed later in this book, or any similar deliberate strategy, but as a semiconvulsive response to overwhelming stimuli that have been permitted to build up for a long time without treatment; or as a result of dogmatization, as discussed soon. Devaluations in a number of countries serve as striking illustrations of incrementalism plus sporadic jumps. A somewhat different way to look at this response pattern is to view it as extemporization or improvisation under stress, with jumps from what are in the main minor variations on "grooved" policies occurring from time to time, when the latter are clearly thrown out of gear. No theory of political improvisation being available as yet, perhaps some ideas from improvisation in music may be heuristically relevant (D. Bailey 1981; Sudnow 1979; Sudnow 1981).

### Attempts at Great Administrative Reforms

A very widespread response pattern to adversity has been attempts at great administrative reforms, to make government more effective, with special attention to central machineries of government (C. Campbell 1983; an important historic perspective is supplied by Skowronek 1982). This response pattern was taken up in a number of countries before adversity became very pronounced, as illustrated by the "quiet revolution" in government in the United Kingdom and its follow-ups (Bruce-Gardyne 1974; Fry 1981; Pollitt 1980; Stacey 1975; Thornhill 1975) and a parallel planning euphoria in the Federal Republic of Germany (Mayntz and Scharpf 1973; Murswieck 1975). Some comparable waves also occurred in the United States, such as in the Carter civil service reform attempts. In a number of Third World countries and some Western democracies, great administrative reforms still play an important role in policymaking responses to adversity (Hammergren 1983).

As already noted, efforts to improve policymaking itself are sometimes an important ingredient of great administrative reform projects, for instance in the United Kingdom report *The Reorganization of Central Government* in 1970 (United Kingdom 1970). But such efforts also take place in tandem with other response patterns. Because of their special salience to this book, they are considered in greater detail later in this chapter.

### Cutting Public Expenditure

The prime response to the dominating economic dimensions of contemporary adversity in most countries is determined efforts to cut public expenditure (Hood and Wright 1981; Tarschys 1982). In some countries, this response takes on the features of a quasi idol, beyond instrumental meanings. This latter phenomenon is better considered in relation to policy theologies, a broader response pattern, next.

*Renewed or New Policy Theologies*

Harsh predicaments together with disappointment from traditional policy compasses lead to the main response pattern of adoption of one or another policy theology as a trusted guide for action. In Western countries, policy theologies embraced by central minds of governments, with strong political support in the population, are renewed versions of classical doctrines, either in a neoconservative or a socialist direction. In a number of Third World countries, some "third way" is searched for. As yet unusual are new and extreme creeds, of the Iranian Islamic Republic Type.

A major shift occurs in a number of countries in the direction of reducing the scope of governmental activities, especially in the social welfare domain. This shift is partly related to efforts to cut public expenditures and partly overlaps with an ideological commitment to some version of neoconservatism as a policy theology (well illustrated by Heatherly 1981, to be compared with J. Palmer and Sawhill 1982, and with Netherlands Scientific Council for Government Policy 1983).

*Nondogmatic Grand-Policy Innovations*

Distinction between innovations resulting from new policy theologies and significant innovations that are nondogmatic in base is both difficult and essential. Without assuming that nondogmatic innovations have ipso facto a higher success probability and without ignoring their often axiomatic and axiologic premises, one can see a clear difference between innovations directly expressing one kind or another of social or political "theology" (Schmitt 1970; Schmitt 1979) and innovations resulting from rational-creative policy development, based on values and visions (as elaborated later in this book, and in Dror 1983a, esp. new introduction and pt. 4). To take an illustration, parts of science and technology policy, as also tied in to efforts to encourage high-technology industries in Western Europe, partake of nondogmatic policy innovation—whether effective or not is another question.

Impressions must be hedged by conceptual and methodological difficulties in identifying more-or-less "nondogmatic policy innovations," as well as by misgivings about looking at so diffuse and broad an arena as policy innovations as a whole. Nevertheless, as a main tentative finding, it seems that nondogmatic grand-policy innovations dealing with main issues posed by adversity or underlying the latter are very scarce, though this may change (e.g. Commission of the European Communites 1984). Policymaking capacity deficits, as examined in chapters 6 and 7, fully account for this finding.

*Some Lacking Responses*

To complete the picture, a few possible response patterns that might have been expected but that are not pronounced in most countries should be mentioned. Thus:

- Few top policymakers willingly abandon their positions of power or adopt a whistle-blowing posture. "Exit and voice" (Hirschman 1970, as reconsidered in Hirschman 1981, 203 ff.) plays a role among the clients of policymaking, so to speak, but not resignation and whistling-blowing among the top policymakers. Individual statesmen leave the scene, but as yet insufficient cases have accumulated to constitute a trend of withdrawing from what can well be described as increasingly "joyless policymaking" (on Helmut Schmidt, for instance, see Bölling 1982).
- Emergency regimes have not been adopted in democracies; few augmentations in the legal authorities of governments have been sought to face growing adversity (Preisl and Mohler 1979). In many Third World countries, the situation is different, with extreme emergency regimes being widespread. The latter are more often the results of political instabilities than of surges in other adversities. Few economic emergency measures, beyond rather mild foreign exchange controls etc., have been adopted in Third World countries, though they are inherent in communist regimes in economic trouble. Differences in responses to economic crises in Mexico and Poland illustrate dissimilarities in policymaking propensities that are in need of research and theorizing.
- In democracies, and also in many nondemocracies, the search for scapegoats has been rather restrained, as already mentioned. It is interesting to speculate on the influence of the history of Nazism on making scapegoat responses to adversity disreputable and avoided. Such possible lessons from history should be compared, for instance, to the slight efforts being made to reduce unemployment, despite bitter historic memories in this matter too.
  Whether these nonresponses to adversity are temporary delays in response patterns that will occur with increasing frequency in the future, if adversities aggravate, or whether some such historic response patterns go against present policymaking grains and have low probabilities of frequent occurrences, even if adversity aggravates—these are among the many open questions.
- Historically, a main response by governments to demands by the population has been to expand the scope of activity and the size of government in all its layers (e.g. from a growing literature, Fratianni and Soinelli 1982; Fry 1979; C. Taylor 1983. Other factors influencing growth of governments are illustrated by interaction with the World System, e.g. Boli-Bennett 1979; G. Thomas and Meyer 1980). In most

Western democracies this response pattern is now foreclosed, with growth in government also being inhibited in countries depending on Western thinking, as imposed by the International Monetary Fund and the World Bank, for instance. In many Third World countries, the number of state employees continues to grow, not only as a main response pattern to adversity (Duvall and Freeman 1983), including the special case of providing employment, but also as a general adversity-independent trend. Whether new waves of expanded scope of governmental activities, with or without increasing state employment, will occur as a response to continuing adversity remains to be seen.

## Policymaking Improvement Attempts

One segment of policymaking responses to adversity, which is of special importance for the main subject of this book, is attempts to improve policymaking itself. Usually, but not always, such efforts take place within a broad administrative reform response pattern, as mentioned above, but considerable policymaking improvements have been introduced separately, and many survived the demise of great administrative reforms.

Whatever their history, some policymaking improvements have been added to governmental equipment in a number of countries (Baehr and Wittrock 1981; R. Levine 1981; Prince 1983), and all attempts in that direction are important for drawing lessons cardinal to this book. A select list of such improvement attempts serves to introduce some later discourse and does provide a more concrete picture of this particular response to adversity. A survey by the author covering about thirty countries identified the following interesting main attempts, some of which have failed and even been closed down, many of which are still in the balance, and a few of which are clear successes:

- Approaches in the direction of "national planning" as illustrated, *inter alia,* by the French Planning Commission, the United Kingdom experiments with a "National Plan," the Norwegian Long-Range Planning Unit and, in most Third World countries, by special planning ministries.
- Special units, quite independent but part of the governmental structure or closely related to it, engage in long-range outlook and futures thinking, as illustrated by the Swedish Secretariat for Futures Studies and the New Zealand Commission on the Future.
- Policy planning and policy analysis units for the prime minister or president and the cabinet as a whole, as illustrated by the White House staffs in the United States, parts of the Prime Minister Department in the Republic of South Africa, the Central Policy Review Staff in the United Kingdom, the planning units in the Office of the Chancellor of the

Federal German Republic, and "presidential general staffs" in a number of Latin American countries and in the Philippines. (Again, a historic perspective is essential, e.g. the tortuous history of cabinet reform in the United Kingdom. See Daalder 1963; Mackintosh 1981).

- "Mirror structures" for heads of governments, with large staffs paralleling main ministries and designed to supervise and partly duplicate the operations of the latter. The Cabinet and Prime Minister Department in Australia was for some years a highly developed illustration of a large mirror structure.
- Follow-up and decision-management units near heads of governments, to try to manage the decision making process and monitor implementation in select areas. The staff of the National Security Council in the United States during some parts of its history and a special decision monitoring unit in the Republic of China (Taiwan) illustrate such arrangements.
- Departmental planning units, as illustrated by the attempts to set up Departmental policy planning staffs in the United Kingdom and basic issues units in ministries in the Federal Republic of Germany.
- Encouragement and establishment of think tanks, in the sense of policy research, analysis, and design organizations (for a different terminology, see Polsby 1983a), to work on main policy problems for the benefit of government directly, as illustrated mainly in the United States by RAND Corporation-type organizations, such as RAND itself, the Urban Institute, the Hudson Institute, and the Institute for Defense Analysis. The Presidential Center for Special Studies, in the Philippines, illustrates comparable bodies in Third World countries, though very scarce. The Japanese National Institute for Research Advancement, set up by the government in 1974 to encourage think-tank work for government, such as by the Nomura Research Institute, the Mitsubishi Research Institute, and the Institute for Policy Sciences, is interesting.
- Encouragement and establishment of think tanks to improve the quality of policymaking through publication of material for enlightened public debate, such as the Canadian Institute for Public Policy Research, the United Kingdom Institute for Policy Studies, the Centre for European Policy Studies, the Science Center Berlin, the New Zealand Planning Council, and the Netherlands Scientific Council for Government Policy. The Brookings Institution, the American Enterprise Institute for Public Policy Research, the Heritage Foundation, and the Institute for Policy Studies illustrate such types of policy research organizations, partly with political trends, in the United States. In the United States, the format of small think tanks is becoming widespread as an organizational frame for nonprofit policy study endeavors, as illustrated by the Roosevelt Center for American Policy Studies and the Institute for East-West Security Studies, both set up in 1982. The International Institute for Applied Systems Analysis pioneers international think tanks, working on shared

and global issues. The Woodrow Wilson International Center for Scholars, which is more of an institute-for-advanced-study type organization, is different; it is oriented toward policy-relevant but not directly policy-related knowledge.

- Institutionalization of special interdepartmental policy review procedures, is illustrated by the United Kindom Policy Analysis and Review (PAR), as it operated for a number of years (Gray and Jenkins 1982).
- Superministries and ministries of state, as in the United Kingdom and, till 1984, in Canada, respectively, to provide better integration between related ministries, with the help of a hierarchical superstructure.
- Budgeting reforms, so as to increase linkages with policy planning and priority decisions. Many countries tried their hand at budgetary reforms, main illustrations being provided by United States Planning-Programming-Budgeting-Systems (PPBS) and its successors; the United Kingdom Public Expenditure Survey procedures, as changing with time; Swedish multiyear budgeting patterns, in defense and science; and Canadian policy and expenditure management system (Privy Council Office 1981; Treasure Board 1980). Such approaches, and others, including various public expediture control procedures, illustrate in part policymaking innovations under the pressure of resources reductions.
- Efforts to change the higher civil service, in part so as to improve its performance in policymaking. Intensive training, such as at the French National School of Administration (ENA), and new ranking and motivation, such as in the Carter administration's civil service reform, illustrate such efforts.
- Equipping top politicians with political-professional advisors of their own, to permit them to have better and more impact on actual decisions, as illustrated by the special political policy staffs of the prime ministers in Canada and Australia, large parts of the White House staff in the United States, and the introduction of "special advisors" to ministers in the United Kingdom.
- Public resources for policy research equipment of the main parties, including opposition leaders, as illustrated by the Political Academies in Austria and the Caucus Research Units in New Zealand.
- Institutionalization of the evaluation of policy results and policy learning, often in relation to the legislature, as in the United States. And, attempts to move ahead with social experimentation as a tool to improve policymaking.
- Policy audit, as a development of efficiency audit, oriented toward considering the effectiveness of policies. The General Accounting Office in the United States well illustrates efforts in this direction (Mosher 1979; for some comparative material see Geist 1980).
- Equipping legislatures with professional staffs and policy research units up to special budget offices, as most developed in the United States, but

slowly being introduced in a number of countries. Also, other changes in legislatures, such as in the committee structure in the United Kingdom and in Australia, to permit in-depth consideration of policy matters.

This by no means complete list illustrates main features of attempts to improve policymaking: useful, but fragmented and circumscribed in impact. The fact that the United States pioneered many, though by no means all, of such innovations while a goodly number of its policies remain problematic demonstrates the limited effects of such improvements and their dependence on multiple additional variables. This raises problems of central concern to this book, to be discussed later. In the meantime, attempts at policymaking improvements are diagnosed as a significant, though as yet minor, response pattern to adversity.

To complete the picture, it should be added that quite a number of policymaking improvements have been abandoned, while others have been downgraded. Thus:

- National planning has been on the retreat, failing quite clearly in most Third World countries and partly in the communist countries (Nove 1983, esp. pt. 3) and having declined in France (Estrin and Holmes 1983).
- Units devoted to future thinking have been closed down, as in New Zealand, or pushed down in the government hierarchy, as in Sweden.
- Some staffs for heads of governments have been closed down, including the Central Policy Review Staff in the United Kingdom, or much reduced in scope.
- Think tanks as a whole are in trouble, with some exceptions (Dror 1984a).
- Interdepartmental reviews have often not survived, with PAR in the United Kingdom having been closed down, for instance.
- Budget reforms have often failed (Grafton and Permaloff 1983).
- Budgets for various other policymaking improvements have been cut in many countries, such as for party research units in the Netherlands.
- And so on.

A number of reasons explain such fates of policymaking improvement efforts, ranging from their irrelevance to "hot" politics and policy theologies, up to lack of patience by senior politicians under pressure with letting the new processes slowly unfold their potentials. Inherent weaknesses in many of the improvements, which prevented them from making any real contributions to policymaking under adversity, have also been an important factor in their demise. These are issues that will be taken up again, in different contexts, in this book.

## Continuous Dynamics of Policymaking Response Patterns to Adversity

Consideration of the continuous dynamics of policymaking responses to adversity, beyond the enumeration of some main response patterns as presented above, faces many difficulties. Particularly vexing are the complexities of interactions among adversities, policymaking responses, and attitudes and behavior of political publics; the timing rhythm of policymaking responses and its relations to adversity; and the possibility of regularities in response sequences of policymaking to adversity, quite independent from external circumstances, caused by features of central policymaking process systems.

A perspective of at least twenty to thirty years is necessary for the dynamics of policymaking response patterns to adversity to unfold and become visible, as has been pointed out several times. The present syndromes of adversity being much younger in some central dimensions, such a perspective is unavailable. Therefore, observations on the continuous dynamics of policymaking responses are preliminary propositions at best. It should be noted that the weaknesses of theoretic propositions are inherent in their timing in relation to the time scales of the phenomena up for investigation. Therefore, no improvement in empiric research methods can hope to upgrade the validity of conjectures in this matter, in the absence of sufficient time slices for investigation. Indeed, improving the exactness of observations on details of current events may disturb pattern recognition beyond a certain point, though of course mistaken fact images must be avoided. Subject to such hedgings, three main issues of the continuous dynamics of policymaking responses to adversity can now be taken up for preliminary exploration.

### Interaction among Adversity, Policymaking, and Political Publics

Policymaking responses must be looked at within a triangle of strongly interacting clusters, with intense interfaces with adversity on one side and with political publics on the other side, these two in turn also intensely interfacing. Interactions within this basic triangle of policymaking are not symmetric. Thus:

1. Policymaking often has little impact on the principal features of adversity, while adversity has much impact on policymaking. This asymmetry may change with the passage of sufficient time for policies to have effect or, more probable, if and when more effective policies evolve. Also, with time, policymaking may become desensitized to some features of adversity. At present, the principal features of adversity seem insensitive to policymaking, while strongly influencing the latter.

2. Adversity has strong impacts on political publics, as has policymaking. Policymaking influences the public in two ways: first, when directly aimed at influencing the political public and its reactions to adversity, as considered earlier; and second, indirectly, when the political public reacts to governmental attempts to handle adversity. The direct impacts of adversity on political publics are hard to differentiate from the impacts on the same political publics of governments and their visible handling of adversity. Also, main impacts of adversity on political publics may take a long time to crystallize. Thus, unemployment has as yet in most countries only limited impacts on political publics, but long-standing nuclear conflict dangers cause waves of intense action by parts of the political public, triggered in various and partly unclear ways.

An important response to adversity by parts of the political public, especially academics, professionals, and the intelligentsia, is to develop new ideas, including policy proposals. This is not a new phenomenon; troubled times often stimulate thinking, as illustrated in the political domain by Bodin and Machiavelli, to pick two cases out of many. This happens also in closed societies, as illustrated by upsurges in proposals for economic reforms in the USSR whenever the leadership admits economic troubles. But, one of the advantages of open society is the freedom to innovate policy ideas, which in turn can significantly improve governmental policymaking, though this may take a long time.

The capacity of a society to innovate policy ideas in the face of adversity is an important dimension of societal problem-handling capacities, about which not much is known. Thus, it seems that some countries produce more policy theologies, while others produce much nondogmatic policy thinking—as illustrated by differences in some of the adversity-stimulated policy literature of the Federal Republic of Germany and the United States. The United States is distinguished by a very large amount of writings on policy problems, with great increases since economic problems became acute (as illustrated, to pick just a small subset from the books being published every week, by Abernathy et al. 1983; Barker 1982; Bowles et al. 1983; Calleo 1982; Carnoy 1983; Choate and Walter 1983; Cornuelle 1983; F. Davidson 1983; J.M. Davis 1983; Etzioni 1982; Heeman 1983; S. Levy and D. Levy 1983; Magaziner and Reich 1983; S.M. Miller and Tomaskovic-Devey 1983; A. Mitchell 1983; Phillips 1982; Ramo 1983; R. Reich 1983; Roosevelt 1983; Rostow 1983; Schram 1982; Sloma 1983; Sullivan et al. 1982; Thurow 1983; Trezise 1982; Wolfe 1981. The German literature of this type, much smaller in size and more controversial in tone, is illustrated by Eppler 1981.) This should be contrasted, for instance, with Israel, where many more books are published on the history of Israel, in Biblical times and in prestate periods, than on present pressing adversities.

In any case, the impact of adversity on the societal production of new policy ideas, and in turn the influence of the latter on the policymaking response to adversity constitute a most important modality of adversity-political publics-policymaking interactions, which may be critical in determining the adequacy of policymaking under adversity in the longer run. Here societal problem-handling capacities strongly condition governmental adversity-handling capacities, leading to many complex issues about which very little is known. Some related problems and their implications for policymaking-improvement possibilities are taken up in later parts of this book.

3. In many respects, policymaking is more sensitive to political publics than to nonpolitical aspects of adversity, more so in democracies, but also in other types of regimes. The tendency for policymaking responses to adversity to be more oriented toward political publics than toward substantive aspects of adversity is not universal in democracies either, depending *inter alia* on the political power of the central mind of government. This raises crucial issues of policymaking leeway and quality, to be considered later in the book.

Additional complications enter the picture. Thus, different political institutions interact in various ways with political publics on one side and the central minds of governments on the other side, with the interaction modes changing with time and differing between various policy issues. Also, some interaction patterns take quite unfamiliar forms, being neglected in research and not obvious to the eye. For instance, the impacts on politics of broadening scales of government and policies have been neglected for long (L. Brown 1983). Nevertheless, the simplified triangle model at least brings out the need for a dynamic interaction analysis to understand and improve policymaking under adversity, while permitting postulation of additional problems.

In the longer run, the triangle of interactions among policymaking, adversity, and political publics determines the effectiveness and viability of different regimes under adversity. At present, in countries with a tradition of stable regimes, changes in political behavior under the impact of continuous adversity and of failures of policymaking visibly to reduce adversity are relatively limited. Some related political phenomena have already been considered in chapter 2, as parts of "adversity" as seen from the perspective of the central minds of governments. Pronounced political changes that can be viewed, largely or partly, as reactions by political publics to adversity and to policymaking failures in handling adversity include, among others:

• Increasing fluidity in political behavior, with more shifts in electoral decisions.
• Growing delegitimation of governments and decreasing trust in them.

- New forms of political activism, including street action, mass movements, and readiness to escalate violence.
- A growing search for "strong leaders."
- Some trends toward political romanticism (comparable to earlier periods, Schmitt 1982).
- Mild trends toward searching for "enemies."
- Continuous expectation for governments to handle adversities, with some reductions in demands and some acceptance of lower entitlements. Apathy and self-help do occur, but are not substituted for fundamental demands upon governments.

In countries without a tradition of stable regimes and governments, adversity results in much more malignant responses by the political public, up to insurgence and revolutions. In Third World countries military responses to policymaking failures by civilian governments often include taking over government (Collier 1980). Interestingly, failures of the military to handle adversity in turn seem to help restoration of democracy (though other factors may be at work, as illustrated by democratization in Spain, see Alba 1978; R. Carr 1982; R. Carr and Fusi 1979; and Maravall 1982). Whether destabilization may be in store for countries with strong governments and/or long traditions of regime viability if adversities aggravate—this is a question to be taken up later on.

*Policymaking Responses Rhythm*

In 1975 Sweden adopted a new constitution well fitted to conditions of economic prosperity and social tranquility but not adversity. This illustrates main problems inherent in the rhythm of policymaking responses and their relation to the life cycles of adversity. A number of major maladjustments between those two seem widespread:

1. Major policies developed during earlier periods and under quite different conditions are carried on after adversity takes visible turns for the worse.
2. Recognition of new circumstances and evolvement of policies adjusted to them take a long time. Once such new policies are adopted, they in turn acquire much inertia and become difficult to adjust to changing adversity.
3. The strong tendency to view adversity as temporary, already identified as a principal response pattern, adds another cause to lags in policymaking after situations change.
4. To persist in policies explicitly adopted to handle adversity but that show no quick impacts is difficult. Here is a major intellectual dilemma in policymaking, namely, should policies that show no rapid impact be abandoned as wrong or persisted in as needing more time to achieve

positive effects. In quite a number of domains, it is preferable to persist in policies for a number of years because of the impossibility of achieving impacts on most of adversity without sustained and consistent effort. The trouble is that such intellectual considerations (to be fully discussed in chapters 5 and 6) carry little weight in real policymaking, with political forces in many countries bringing about policy shifts at a frequency much too high for a chance to achieve positive impacts on adversity. Inbuilt dissonances between policymaking cycles (a concept that needs revisions to fit conditions of adversity, despite interesting treatments, for instance in Hogwood and Peter 1982; and J.V. May and Wildavsky 1978) and the life cycles of adversity constitute a main incapacitator of policymaking under adversity.

## Regularities in Policymaking Responses to Adversity

A question of much theoretic and applied importance is whether relatively constant features of central minds of governments in different periods and countries result in regularities in policymaking responses to adversity. Preliminary examination of historic materials seems to indicate the existence of some such constancy. Thus, to take the late Roman Republic, its decisions and political actions were characterized by entrenchment in traditional "purified" ideas, even when much outdated by changing situations, as long as no significant alternatives were perceived. As put by Christian Meier, "Rigidity produced failure, and failure produced rigidity" (Meier 1982, 160. Successes, too, produce rigidities which, therefore, constitute one of the common societal incapacities, as considered in chapter 6).

This characterization in turn applies to many policymaking responses to adversity in other regimes at different periods, such as in Imperial Spain, Czarist Russia, the Ottoman Empire, and so on, up to contemporary policymaking in quite a number of countries. But such observations can be only a starting point for investigation: Because logically there exists only a limited range of response-pattern categories in terms of degrees of innovation and reliance on tradition versus seach for new options, identifying regularities in policymaking responses to adversity in terms of such alternative patterns may be a result of the taxonomy. To show significant regularities, some constant correlation between specific conditions and specific responses must be identified, or a relatively regular distribution of responses within the range of possibilities must be proven.

The author can identify some initial signs that may indicate some contemporary regularities in policymaking responses to adversity. Thus, a pendulum seems to operate between responding to adversity with great administrative reforms together with expanded governmental activities on one side, and attempts to reduce the scope of governmental activities on the other side. Also, the often observed tendency of policy theologies to become pragmatized when put into action seems to hold true also in policymaking responses to adversity.

If one tries to look deeper into the central minds of governments, such as by interviewing and with the help of ethological observation, as in the study on which this book is in part based, the picture becomes darker: Growing perplexity and tendencies toward despondency; semiconscious escape into denial of increasingly clear realities; hesitations between stubborn entrenchment in policy theologies more and more rejected by all but a few true believers and reactive improvization on an ad hoc basis; repetitive stop-start decision making; and so on—these seem to emerge as characteristics of the second phase of policymaking responses to adversity in many Western democracies and some other polities. The concept of *maze policy-behavior* is proposed for this building-up policymaking syndrome, resulting from failure of primary responses to adversity and growing recognition of the epochal and complex nature of adversity.

An alternative response pattern is movement into more extreme political theologies, of a type that cannot be easily falsified by clear facts. Fixation on major perceived or created enemies and/or chiliastic creeds and messianic national missions—these may become overriding responses to sustained adversity, already pronounced in some nondemocracies. Such speculations on future policymaking response patterns to adversity lead directly to the broader, and even more speculative, question of what continuous and aggravating adversity may do to regimes as a whole, including their central minds of goverments.

### Some Thoughts on Long-Range Consequences of Adversity

Prediction of the consequences of continuous harsh adversity for policymaking and for politics and societies is a major theoretic and applied challenge. Immediately involved are issues of regime resilience, adjustability, and breaking stresses, and the even harder queries, what may cause and what may follow regime breakdowns?

History provides little hope for such predictive endeavors. To take four relatively recent cases: Nazi Germany and Communist Russia were not and, probably, could not have been predicted with knowledge available then and now; the successful rebuilding of French governance in very effective a form was not and could not have been predicted; and Iran illustrates a contemporary situation of indeterminacy.

Even relatively simple questions on the future impact of specific adversities in discrete countries cannot be answered. Thus, the long-range political implications of unemployment for the United Kingdom cannot be reasonably predicted (B. Jordan 1982). It may well be that some structural features such as the party system (Powell 1982) are more determinative of regime stability than adversity. All the more so, efforts to arrive at a general theory of political instability (D. Sanders 1981) are just in their beginning. And it may inherently be impossible to develop a theory of social change of broad applicability, with the very search for such general theories being based on metaphysical creeds inapplicable to social phenomena (Boudon 1983). In any case, with present knowledge, the longer-range consequences of adversity (as of other major changing variables, such as advanced in science and technology) cannot be predicted, even enumeration of alternative possible futures being very doubtful.

Paradoxically, this very unpredictability casts doubts on the convenient and widespread assumption that nothing much can happen to basic features of present regimes, and especially democracy. In principle, every regime should be viewed as having breaking points, which can be breached by accumulating or climactic events. This, in addition to inbuilt tensions, antinomies, and contradictions existing in all regimes and societies, which may produce waves of transformation triggered by adversities. To take two different illustrations, one mentioned above: Both the results of permanent large-scale unemployment, especially among the young, and the effects of another war between the major powers, even if "limited" are hard to predict and may have breaking impacts on the futures of many regimes (Hackett 1982 is much too sanguine in its handling of war scenarios). Such effects may be very slow in coming, creeping or cataclysmic.

Against possibilities of the radical transformation of regimes as a result of sustained adversity, the capacity of states to adjust to changing conditions through slowly changing regimes must not be underrated. Thus, the building up of administrative capacities to handle growing complexities may take time but is possible without much upheaval (Skowronek 1982); the politics of depression does not have to result in regime destabilization (McSeveney 1972); reforms can handle difficult problems and achieve significant change in a modular mode (B. Harrison 1982; Walters 1978); and democracies adjusted well to war, after dismal planning for it (Burk 1982; D. French 1982). It may well be that in some conditions adjustment processes are at work, permitting states to absorb adversities through induced institutional change, as claimed, for instance, by Binswanger and Ruttan in their hypothese 2: "The effect of stagnation or decline in the income flows available to a society is to induce institutional changes that expand the control of the community or the society over the allocation of resources and the partitioning of income flows" (Binswanger and Ruttan 1979, 411).

We return here to societal problem-handling capacities as interacting with governmental policymaking abilities, with various societies and central minds of governments having differing effectiveness in responding to adversity. But, despite some efforts (e.g. Hawrylyshyn 1980) to work on this matter, available knowledge hardly permits formulation of salient questions. Definitely, there exists as yet no basis for formulating reasonable conjectures. The most that can perhaps be done is to try to identify some alternative scenarios to permit better monitoring of unfolding reality and to stimulate relevant research, including especially reprocessing of historic material:

*Very optimistic:* (1) Regimes adjust to sustained adversity, with more self-reliance, new forms of social solidarity, and global cooperation, resulting in changing conceptions of "adversity" itself and the dissipation of acute forms of the latter (e.g. see Galtung 1980). (2) Policymaking improves significantly, handling adversity successfully and leaving regimes to evolve without dramatic adversity impacts. (3) Adversity dissipates on its own and/or thanks to societal, non-governmental processes rather than deliberate policymaking, reestablishing a balance with policymaking capacities and, again, leaving regimes to evolve without dramatic adversity impacts.(It should be noted that in all cases, regimes are subject to evolvement and change processes, quite separate from many forms of adversity.)

*Medium optimistic:* Some weak democracies experience periods of authoritarian regimes and all countries experience some political destabilization, increased global economic conflict, and much misery. But the basic fabric of societies holds, democracy survives as a main form of governance, and no irreparable damage to humanity occurs.

*Medium pessimistic*: A vicious spiral of adversity, policy failures, and political publics under a situation of lack of perceived alternatives takes hold. Escalating interactions among panic policymaking, withdrawal of high-quality persons from politics, and growing public reactions against governments lead to political destabilization and extremism. New forms of populism, "zealocracy" (in the sense of rule by small and extreme groups of activists, see Tivey 1978, 129), aggression against "enemies," and global decline of democracies in their competition with authoritarian regimes are the outcome. In authoritarian regimes, repression becomes harsher, scapegoats are increasingly blamed, and a new kind of rather unpleasant (by present values) stable society is arrived at (comparable, metaphorically, to the Asiatic Mode of Production States, S.P. Dunn 1982), despite technological change.

*Very pessimistic.* Under the impact of sustained adversity and governance failures, extreme political chiliasm takes over in a number of countries (for propensities in such directions in some cultures, see Sarkisyanz 1955), producing "crazy states" (Dror 1980b) and moving the world into some kind of new neobarbarism. Democracy declines and the whole of Occidental civilization moves into decay.

This range of scenarios is no more than a sensitization device to broaden thinking on possible future developments that may be caused or accelerated by mishandled adversities. Quite different realities may materialize if adversities continue; and harsh futures may be in store also if adversities dissipate on their own. Despite their frankly speculative-imaginary base, such scenarios serve to put into stark relief the problematics of policymaking under adversity and the possibly high or very high costs of its inadequacies.

# 4

# Potentials of Policymaking as an Adversity-Handling Mode

## Nature of Problem

The alternative scenarios presented at the end of chapter 3 starkly pose the question, what, if any, are the potentials of policymaking, and especially of central policymaking as considered in this book, even at its hypothetical best, to influence the realization of such and other futures? At stake is not less than the capacity of central minds of governments to influence historic processes and to intervene in historic momentum. This question does not prejudge the importance of studying policymaking under adversity, which may be an interesting, theory-relevant, and illuminating subject independent from any impact potential of decision making on future realities.

Examination of the potentials and limitations of policymaking as a mode of handling adversity is central to the concerns of this book, theoretical and prescriptive. Related questions to be taken up include: What is the degree of free movement of policymaking, in terms of autonomy from society and of feasibility domains? What are the maximum effects, intended and unintended, of policymaking on realities? Can policymaking effectiveness be augmented by combination with other societal problem-handling patterns, such as creation of knowledge? And what are the main relations between policymaking and various modes of social transformations, such as revolutions and value transformations?

A preliminary and broader question, which logically needs to be faced first, is whether human activities make any difference for future realities (which is quite another matter than the psychological and moral meanings of human act). If the answer to this query is in the positive, the next question is whether human decisions and purposeful acts make any difference for future reality (which, again, is an issue distinct from moral and psychological evaluation of conscious and deliberative action). Only if the last inquiry receives a positive reply, do we reach the questions of whether

73

policymaking under adversity, as a subspecies of decisionmaking, makes any difference to future reality and whether this difference is for the better—with distinctions between different conditions and regimes, various issue domains, central and diffuse policymaking, evolving and deliberative policymaking, main and side effects, intended and unintended impacts, positive and negative influences, and additional refinements.

This is not the place to enter the metaphysical dimensions of these issues (as partly touched upon, for instance in Davidson 1980; and Diamond and Teichman 1980), including the underlying and prior problem, whether and how can one try to hope to answer such questions. Readers with a speculative-philosophic bent of mind might like first to ponder the question whether a butterfly or a colony of ants could better their conditions if they had a mind and knowledge equivalent to human beings. In other words, if your mind were somehow transplanted into the body of a fly and if you suspected that the other flies you meet are equally endowed with human minds, given the physical tools and environmental conditions of a fly, what could you do better than flies do at present? This is not an analogue, not even a metaphor, for the issue of the significance of policymaking and its improvement, but it can serve to dampen overenthusiasm on the capacities of human collective action—based on conscious decisions to influence the future according to our wishes (in addition to posing various questions in the philosophy of the mind on one hand, and on evolutionary interaction between species and ecological niches on the other hand—both outside the scope of this book).

To return to the issue at hand, a note on a philosophy of knowledge that fits main concerns of policy sciences is in order. Parts of the philosophy of knowledge (not the political philosophy) of Popper can serve as a good starting point for inquiries that elucidate some of the problematics of considering relevant issues without necessarily providing any compelling answers. (The uninitiated reader may like to start with Kant, as discussed in Broad 1978, going on to Burke 1983, to Popper 1966 and to Schilpp 1974, and then to Watkins 1970 and Watkins 1975, as conveniently collected in a German version in Watkins 1978; and then take up Shackle 1972—which together provide some of the underpinnings for a relevant philosophy of action for policymaking, as later considered in this book). After all is read, one's opinions will be deeper in understanding but still depend on the Weltanschauung we live by (Jaspers 1960). A more active and enthusiastic Weltanschauung will be more associated with allocation of meaning and impact to human intentions and policymaking; a more contemplative and self-reflecting Weltanschauung will be more doubtful about the influences of human intentions and policymaking and their meaningfulness.

The contradictory term *philosophic anthropology* used in some pertinent German literature (e.g. Plessner 1931; Scheler 1974) testifies to human yearning for a reliable answer to questions on the potentials of human decisions on one hand and their intractability on the other hand. It is possible to arrive at conclusions carrying much verisimilitude on the impacts of specific decisions and also of complex policies, and, perhaps, of alternative policymaking process-systems. But, basically, the question whether history has a travel schedule, as proposed by Ernst Bloch, with decisions being but marionettes of *Weltvernunft* as proposed by Hegel, or whether human decisions shape history is a matter of philosophy, with a lot of metaphysics. It may well be that the very way in which this issue is formulated already prevents adequate handling. In this chapter, a certain perspective for looking at the problem is proposed, but it is limited to the world of policymaking discourse.

However looked at, the issues posed in this chapter are abstract, philosophic, and grand theoretic. They can be ignored within pragmatic or positivistic approaches to policymaking, as dominating most of policy sciences literature. But, to arrive at a view of policymaking under adversity that is not narrowly technical and to lay the groundwork for eventual development of a general theory of societal command and control with its essential philosophic foundations, as well as to preserve a sense of balance and self-doubts among policy professionals and researchers, some examination of rather fundamental issues of the potentials of policymaking as a mode of human action is essential, even if no satisfactory answers can be arrived at.

Renaissance thinking, overwhelmed by events beyond comprehension, groped for ways to fathom the enigmatic and to manage the crushing. (F. Gilbert 1965; Pocock 1975, pts. 1, 2). The germane concept package of *fortuna, occasione,* and *virtue,* as developed by thinkers like Guicciardini and Machiavelli, can be applied to contemporary predicaments and the potentials of policymaking: *Fortuna* stands for uncontrollable, largely unpredictable and not really comprehended trends and happenings; *occasione* stands for temporary opportunities to affect trends and influence events; and *virtue* constitutes statecraft and policymaking qualities that can utilize *occasione* fully for the better. The question is whether central policymaking—a concept related to the idea of *Ragione di Stato* as also developed in the Renaissance, such as by Giovanni Della (Meinecke 1957, 55-56; on related developments in France, see Lloyd 1983)—can influence future unfolding of historic processes for the better, or fits more into the schemata of Greek tragedies, as sharpened in Jean Giraudoux's *The Trojan War Will Not Take Place,* where the very efforts to prevent tragic events makes them come about in what can be called "ironies of history."

## Initial Observations

As intimated by the above remarks, the capacity of policymaking under adversity to influence future realities cannot be a simple yes or no. Some initial observations on the issue can be summed up as follows:

1. Though difficult to conceptualize and even harder to guesstimate, not to say to measure, it is possible to study, in the broad sense of that term, some of the impacts of societal steering capacities and policymaking activities on reality. Therefore, to emphasize a point of critical importance for the hopes for and attempts at the improvement of policymaking, it is possible to consider the relative quality of different policymaking systems (CIA 1982; Ellman 1979, ch. 10; Hawrylyshyn 1980; Hayward 1974; Hayward 1976), both in field-invariant and in field-dependent features. (Similar to possible comparative consideration of "governmental productivity," Almond and Powell 1983. For a contrary view, see Granovetter 1979. Bergson 1978 is interesting in another direction. Organizational effectiveness studies, though dealing with simpler situations, are also relevant, e.g. see Goodman and Pennings 1977; and Spray 1976. Cameron and Whetten 1983 is unusual in exposing evaluation difficulties.)
2. The impact of policymaking usually dilutes with time. With the important exception of perhaps preventable catastrophes, the longer the time spans considered, the lesser the impacts of policymaking and the more forces beyond human will and beyond deliberative steering dominate reality.
3. Different phenomena at various periods are more or less malleable by policymaking. Thus, the more target phenomena are in a state of flux with potentials in different directions and the lower the impact thresholds are, the stronger the potential influence of policymaking on future realities. Especially important are so-called explosive systems in which opportunities exist for momentous choices that constitute an irreversible shifting of future history into one of a number of potential directions (Shackel 1972, 384). A good illustration is provided by the decisions to divide Europe after World War II (Backer 1978; Rostow 1982).
4. Present theories do not permit reliable gauging of reality as more malleable or more recalcitrant. Some features of reality may be deeply rooted in fundamental laws of nature, as proposed by some studies of innovation cycles (A. Graham and Senge 1980; Marchetti 1980), or global political cycles (Modelski 1978), or possibly an inbuilt pendulum between exaggerated demands on the state and withdrawal into private activities (Hirschman 1981), and of long-term economic cycles (Rostow 1978). Long-range societal processes and trends may be deeply rooted in fundamental inherent factors, not really susceptible

to change by deliberative policymaking (as claimed by B. Porter 1983 in respect to the decline of the United Kingdom; and, differently, by Daughan et al. 1980 in respect to the social evolution of France). Furthermore, specific types of societies may have inbuilt propensities not susceptible to intervention, unless the society is radically transformed (as claimed by Marxists in respect to capitalism and its inbuilt, in their view, catastrophe propensity; e.g. see Rousseas 1979). While opinions such as the above are in-between speculations and weak conjectures, impressions from the history of policymaking in various contexts indicate that reality changes in its degrees of malleability and recalcitrance in currently unknown patterns. Various combinations of passing circumstances may provide hard-to-discern opportunties for "critical decisions," that is, decisions that coincide with crossroads of history and significantly influence the shape of things to come, up to momentous choices as mentioned above. Conversely, situations that seem easy to influence may prove to be very resilient and absorb policymaking without any traces of impact; or even have a tendency to bring about contraintended results, making the policies into "fatal remedies" (Sieber 1981).

5. The difference that policymaking can make for future realities depends also on the features of policymaking itself. Thus, the more powerful policy instruments are and the more skillfully they are wielded (*inter alia*, in the sense of meeting various policymaking-quality requisites, as elaborated later in this book), the higher (per definition), relatively, are desired impact probabilities on future realities. Therefore, in considering the potentials of policymaking to bring about intended results, a distinction must be made between (1) policymaking as actually practiced, and (2) policymaking at its optimal best. Introducing into discussions of policymaking potentials an adjusted "Carnot cycle" model (taken from engineering, where a Carnot cycle assumes a thermodynamically efficient cycle showing what an ideal engine can do; for an application to economic development, see Kahn 1979, 332) provides an essential analytic tool to explore maximum hypothetical production functions of policymaking. This requires, in turn, construction of optimal (but not ideal or utopian) models of policymaking and their "running," mainly in the form of *Gedankenexperiments,* to explore their potentials qualitatively and conjecturally. However problematic, such an approach does add an essential dimension to consideration of the potentials of policymaking, going beyond inference from actual policymaking effects.

6. Given an optimal policymaking pattern-system, for instance, such as developed in *Public Policymaking Reexamined* (Dror 1983a, esp. pt.3) and later chapters of the present book, it may be possible to engage in considerable "societal architecture" under some prevailing conditions. But, the requisites for doing so successfully go far beyond present

policymaking realities, as surveyed in later chapters. In any case, the maximum that can be achieved with the help of even top-quality policymaking is limited and falls far short of high human aspirations, in their Occidental form.

7. Special problems are posed by the possibility that social development takes place in part through crises and jumps rather than more-or-less smooth curves and regular cycles (Almond, Flanagan, and Mundt 1973; Grew 1978). This may produce opportunities for enhanced policy impacts intermingled with periods when policymaking can have little effect. Also, this raises the possibility of increasing policy impacts by adopting shock strategies (Hirschman 1958 as reconsidered in Hirschman 1980), and throwing surprises at history (Dror 1975b; Handel 1981; and in a different context Betts 1982).

8. It is possible to provide strong evidence for the impact of some grand policies on major situations, sometimes in robust directions aimed at, though with many unexpected and undesired effects, as in Japanese industrialization policy (Johnson 1982); and sometimes in very counterdesired directions, such as in continuous desertification in the sub-Saharan countries (Grainger 1983). Hosts of policy case studies show various mixes of intended and unintended consequences, with many possible disagreements whether the unintended consequences could have been avoided (Boudon 1982). Let us take just two illustrations. The Falkland War can be characterized as historically predestinated (Goebel 1982) and, according to the Franks Committee of Inquiry (Franks 1982), unforeseeable and unpreventable—claims that will be reconsidered later in this book. More significant are studies of the downfall of the Weimar Republic, which disagree on whether the takeover of Germany by the Nazi regime could have been prevented if only top decision makers in the Weimar Republic had been of higher quality in foresight and willpower (e.g. see D. Abraham 1981; Bracher 1978; Erdmann and Schulze 1980; Höhne 1983; Knopp and Wiegmann 1983; O. Mitchell 1983; Schulze 1982; Stachura 1983). In considering such diverse cases with different outcomes, the difficulties of analyzing historic events from a decision-making perspective should be taken into account, such as the view of Collingwood that failures are much harder to explain than successes (as discussed in Donagan 1962 and debated by Watkins 1970).

9. The issue of policymaking effects through the mechanism of self-fulfilling prophecy, with policies creating expectations that in turn influence behavior, is interesting. Such effects are increasingly taken into account in economic "expectation theory" (e.g. in Cragg and Makiel 1982; an early treatment is Shackle 1952), but they have a broad domain (see Henshel 1982) and may play a significant role in policymaking effects. The converse also holds true: evoked countermeasures may render policymaking in vain because of self-defying prophecies, such as in strategic interaction situations.

10. All observations on limited impact-potentials of policymaking may become outdated if and when breakthroughs in knowledge occur. Thus, to take a doubtful but illuminating example: If psychogenic theories of history and society should be proven and would provide operational policy instruments (such as, hypothetically, changes in child rearing substantially altering some kinds of behavior, compare G. Davis 1977), policymaking may acquire deliberate society-meta-morphosing capacities, for better or worse. At present, no such up-surges in knowledge can be discerned and no theories on which such breakthroughs might be based are available. It is necessary to bear in mind that new knowledge may prove that some societal features are beyond human change capacities. Thus, if genetic factors are definitely shown to cause irreversible inequality in important human features that break through equalization policies, this could have very significant consequences for policymaking (Jensen 1969; Meade 1973; Sowell 1983; Tauberman 1978. For different a position see H. Gardner 1983; Lewontin et al. 1984).

11. In the consideration of the impacts of policymaking, their ascertainment must be kept distinct from their appraisal (in the exact meanings of these terms, namely, identification of impacts and evaluation of these impacts, respectively. See Dror 1983a, ch. 3). In particular, impacts of policies on various segments of reality, such as social groupings, may be quite different and their evaluation as "good" or "bad" is largely a value judgment matter (Page 1983; Rule 1978).

## Some Test Cases

To explore further the impact potentials of policymaking, a few thinking experiments with test cases may be illuminating.

A revealing case to start with is taken from a study on global energy policies by the International Institute for Applied System Analysis (IIASA; an East-West think tank financed by a number of countries, located in Laxenburg, near Vienna, Austria). The minimum time cycle for evolving massive new energy sources for humanity lasts more than fifty years. Policy instruments are available that permit reshaping the energy system so as to assure, with very high probability, secure and permanent energy for humanity, though huge investments are needed to realize this goal. A promising long-range dominant policy option can be identified, at least in outline (Häfele 1981), but the policymaking qualities needed for actually moving in this direction and achieving the desired results go far beyond contemporary policymaking realities. Thus, globally authoritative decision makers who adopt long-range policies based on sophisticated analysis and who accept high intermediate costs to take care of future generations are required. More than that, to implement such a policy, global decisions have to be imposed on national decision makers, with allocation of costs and benefits in ways unacceptable to many, however done. (On the logical problems of allocating such costs with efforts to provide solutions that are based on "reasonable" but, in my opinion, often unrealistic assumptions, see H. Young 1980; H. Young, Okada, and Hashimoto 1980; and H. Young, Okada, and Hashimoto 1981).

This illustration shows a situation in which a preferable policy can be specified and is technologically feasible, with strong positive impacts on future reality as a highly reliable expectation, but necessary power-political capacities are lacking. A different way to characterize this situation is to state that no feasible alternatives for significantly influencing future energy realities were identified in the IIASA study, because the absence of suitable power-political capacities makes the IIASA recommendation politically nonfeasible; and, in principle, there is no reason to regard political feasibility constraints as more elastic than technological feasibility constraints (despite Ackoff 1978, 72).

The above case serves to introduce the very important concept of policy latitude or *policy leeway,* referring to the free field of choice for policymaking. Policy leeway, in turn, may significantly influence the amounts and directions of policymaking impacts on future realities. Related issues will be considered later in this chapter, when policymaking autonomy is examined, as well as in further chapters of this book.

Another hypothetical, but illuminating illustration, can be taken up. In *Genus,* Ivan Illich (1982) puts forth the thesis that clear-cut division of labor and functions between male and female has accompanied humanity since appearance as a distinct species, and probably before. For argument's sake, let us accept this proposition and consider some fundamental questions related to the potentials of policymaking that is poses:

1. If some features have accompanied humanity always, can one expect policymaking to change them, or are we dealing with an intractable subject that will bounce back into its basic state after some transitory and short-lived vacillations?
2. Might it be better to meet equality values through designing new divisions of labor between the genders, to achieve equity without confronting basic characteristics of humanity?
3. What are the dangers of interfering with deeply rooted features of humanity? Assuming it is possible to eliminate sex discrimination through enforcing gender-role near-identity, may not side effects cause more damage than the benefits gained?
4. Or, are all the above positions conservative prejudices, policymaking being capable of achieving new aspirations, including metamorphosis of historic features of humanity?

5. Whatever we may think about such rigidities, can we be sure about our diagnoses? Is it not better to admit ignorance, and then proceed to try to do our best, even if success probabilities are unknown and perhaps low? Might not incalculable factors, such as self-fulfilling prophecy, wrest effects from recalcitrant realities?
6. What about moral meanings and the symbolic and cathartic effects of policymaking, not to speak about policymaking as theatre? Might it not be better to express values and aspiration through policymaking, even if hopeless in terms of effects, than to negate human visions?
7. Do all these questions make any sense, or is this a matter for feelings, deep emotions, and an intense sense of justice, which cannot and should not be subjected to such intellectual queries?

Additional test cases for considering the impact potentials of policymaking easily spring to mind: antidiscrimination policies, demographic and natal policies, migration policies, antismoking and antidrug policies—these are just a few illustrations out of many policy domains, the intensive study of which may provide inputs into considering the potentials and limits of policymaking. Weltanschauungen and transscientific assumptions will still dominate overall opinions, but duly designed studies (e.g. on attempts to influence alcohol consumption, see P. Davies and Walsh 1983; on heroine see J. Kaplan 1983) may provide better insights on conditions under which policymaking can have a somewhat larger or smaller impact, within the limited range of up to fifty years at most with which it is concerned. As yet, such studies are scarce, the necessary raw material is dispersed and suitable investigative approaches are underdeveloped. When such studies become available the conjectures developed in this book will have to be reconsidered. Till then, one has to do with what is available, recognizing its provisional if not speculative nature.

## For Better or for Worse?

The question whether it is good or bad for policymaking to have impact on human futures is tantalizing. It also has normative implications, namely, whether efforts to increase the impact potentials of policymaking on future realties are for the better or for the worse. Rhetoric or nonsense questions of the type "Need man prevail?" (Slack 1982) aside, here, again, response depends on Weltanschauung. This can be explicated by presenting a number of alternative simplified assumptions that lead in different combination to quite opposite conclusions, but that cannot be validated or falsified with empiric data:

1. Human history has an inbuilt tendency toward progress.

2. Human history has an inbuilt tendency toward catastrophe.
3. Human history has no inbuilt tendency, but has potentials toward progress or toward catastrophe.
4. Human policymaking mainly influences human history for the better.
5. Human policymaking mainly influences human history for the worse.
6. Human policymaking has no inbuilt tendency, but has potentials toward influencing human history for the better and for the worse.
7. Human policymaking does not influence human history either way.

The following combinations of assumptions favor attempts at augmentation of policymaking influence on reality: assumptions 1 and 4, but here policymaking does not matter very much; assumptions 2 and 4; assumptions 3 and 4, with policymaking being crucial for reducing catastrophe probabilities. Assumptions 2 and 6 also support augmented policymaking impact by providing at least a chance to avoid catastrophe.

The following combinations of assumptions favor policymaking noninfluence on reality and nonaugmentation of that influence: assumptions 1 and 5; assumptions 3 and 5; assumptions 2 and 5, though here it makes little difference; and assumptions 1 and 6, where policymaking at least carries some danger of ruining the trend.

Assumptions 3 and 6 leave the matter moot and depending on one's attitudes toward risk ("lottery values" in professional terminology, Raiffa 1968).

If assumption 7 is accepted, still a number of questions remain open, such as: Is it better to engage in policymaking improvement efforts, even of futile in terms of policy-outputs, as a morale builder and as providing opportunities for moral choices, with awareness of the nonimpact of policymaking not to be pushed? Or is it better to devote scarce human high-quality resources to other endeavors?

If there are doubts about the correctness of assumption 7, a problem of choice under uncertainty is again reached, with the question being whether it is better to devote efforts to policymaking, with the risk of their being wasted, or whether it is better to neglect policymaking, with the risk of abandoning a chance to influence future reality for the better. On this question, the position proposed by the author is to prefer endeavors to improve policymaking without assurance that great results can be achieved over missing a chance for handling threatening adversities. This position is important for the present book, because it justifies strenuous efforts at improving policymaking, even if the positive potentials of policymaking are only a possibility, without known probabilities; this, on conditions that possibilities of policymaking having impact for the worse are assumed to have a lower probability (which is far from obvious.) Thus, a recent historic study tends to Gibbons's view of history as "a register of the crimes, follies and misfortunes of mankind," seeing many policies as causes of misfortune. (See P. Johnson 1983, to be compared with Vaizey 1983).

Two additional positions may lead to a more negative conclusion on the desirability of policymaking improvement: If policymaking is regarded as inherently of low quality and not really improvable, then it can be expected to remain dismal whatever is done, with the possible conclusion to concentrate on other processes such as market mechanism (Nozick 1974, to be supplemented with Eby 1982 and Wolf 1979). This position is discussed and rejected in chapter 6.

A more fundamental position must be recognized, based on the possibility that augmented human capacities to deliberately influence the future may unduly constrain the unfolding of humanity in the longer run (Dror 1984e). To engage in such a *Gedankenexperiment,* if at any historic moment humanity had indeed been able to "program" the future, progress would have been frozen in terms of then prevailing images and beliefs—resulting in a world anathematic to most of us and very different from present aspirations and values. Despite our cocksureness in the superiority of present thinking, there exists no reason to assume that "colonization" of the future in terms of contemporary ideas would look any better to future generations, once they escape from our "programming." Therefore, if policymaking could be perfected up to being able to program the future, this should be rejected. Paradoxically, it is my conclusion that policymaking can be somewhat improved but cannot shape the future, which justifies the prescription to try and improve policymaking. If a more polar position is held, either that policymaking cannot be meaningfully improved or that it can be perfected up to becoming able to shape the future—then policymaking improvement is not worth the effort or much too dangerous, respectively.

The above exploration of alternative assumptions is not an exercise in scholastics, in the negative sense. Once we move a little beyond random data collection (and also there), underlying assumptions serve as essential justifications for concerns, activities, methods, and tools. Policymaking is too fateful and presuming a subject to be abandoned to tacit assumptions never subjected to explication and evaluation (on such dangers, though in a different context, see Higgort 1980). Too many fundamental issues tend to be neglected in the bulk of policymaking studies available at present. Therefore, it is necessary at least to bring into the open and probe some underlying assumptions.

It is far from obvious whether "progress" or "catastrophe" or both or neither are inherent in human history (Nisbet 1969; Nisbet 1980). It is not obvious that policymaking is for the better, or for the worse, or mixed in effects, or indeterminate in effects, or lacking any real effects. The study of policymaking and its improvement, as an academic-professional subject and/or as a life mission depends therefore on a number of assumptions. My own tentative assumptions are that the future has potentials both for the better and for the worse, and that augmented policymaking capacities involve some risks but have a greater potential for the better.

At the same time, I tend to the assumption and indeed finding, that policymaking is of secondary importance in shaping the future of humanity. For instance, technical change is more important in influencing some historic processes (Landes 1969), while itself being only partly influenced by policymaking. A striking illustration is provided by the printing press (Eisenstein 1979). Computers may have similar effects (some inklings are provided in Turkle 1984), though governments do play active roles in pushing their development (Feigenbaum and McCorduck 1983. For an exploration of technological change within a philosophy of knowledge context relevant to our concerns here, see Elster 1983a). Religious renascence may become again another future-shaping factor, independent from deliberate policymaking (as in the past, see Ozment 1980). Individual thinkers too, exert in the longer run much more influence on the future of humanity than central minds of government. But, given all these stronger variables, still public policymaking is a main mode for exerting deliberate influence on collective futures, all the more important as it may be susceptible to conscious improvement and itself operates in part as an intentional process. At least, adequate policymaking may be a necessary, and perhaps also helpful, condition for other future-shaping factors to operate, and may influence their effects.

The proposition that central policymaking has crucial functions that cannot be adequately fulfilled by any other currently known societal mechanisms or "hidden hand" is related. To achieve structural social changes essential for handling adversities, central governmental policymaking is in part essential and in part very helpful (Shonfield 1984)—if of suitably high quality, which is a great "if." As further developed in chapters 5 and 6 there are many problem-handling functions that can better, and in part only, be fulfilled by societal processes other than central policymaking, such as by free markets and by independent intellectuals. But, because of characteristics of adversity, as considered in chapter 2, central policymaking is becoming more essential and its importance will probably increase, with ups and downs, in most Western democracies. (A different position is adopted, for instance, by Duignan and Rabushka 1980; Ferns 1978; Friedmann 1979; Hayek 1979; Heatherly 1981; Mansbridge 1980; M. Margolis 1979; Nozick 1974; and, in part, Tullock 1970. The proposals for participative redesign of societies as an alternative mechanism, in T. Williams 1982 are interesting but utopian.)

## Policymaking Autonomy

Discourse until now has considered the capacities of policymaking to influence unfolding realities and the potentials of policymaking to exert impacts on historic processes and significant events. Assuming some such capacity, the problem of degrees of autonomy of policymaking process-systems from social and political forces and factors is reached. If the central mind of government is strictly constrained by and only reflects social forces, economic interests, or traditional policy orthodoxies, then central policymaking is inherently very limited in its leeway and its consequent impacts on reality, in directions if not in intensities (in the sense that central policymaking may have strong impacts, in directions fitting dominant economic interests, for instance, but no capacity to adopt policies in other directions). Alternatively, if the leeway of policymaking is strictly circumscribed by rigid enviromental factors that cannot be loosened up even by optimal policymaking, then the impact potentials of policymaking are very limited and the improvement of policymaking may be futile (for an unusual exploration of some related issues, see Müller 1981; Aron 1961 is also relevant, on a quite different level of philosophic discourse).

Two related issues illustrate the complexity of these issues: On a macrolevel, problems of policymaking autonomy are related to the state-society dichotomy. On a microlevel, the debate on great individuals in history and their reflection or shaping of historic conditions is parallel to and overlaps some important aspects of the questions surrounding policymaking autonomy.

This is not the place to survey the history of state-society relations (e.g.,Carnoy 1984; Kiernan 1982); or classic literature on the subject (Hintze 1964; Hintze 1967; Hintze 1970, all passim; in part translated into English in F. Gilbert 1975); or its modern forms (Bendix 1968, passim; Böckenförde 1976, 185-220; Bornstein, Held, and Krieger 1984; Crozier and Friedberg 1980; Hayward and Berki 1979; Narr 1975; Nee and Mozingo 1983; Skocpol 1979, 24-33; Stepan 1978); nor the classical literature on the hero in history (Hook 1943; Plechanow 1977) and its modern versions (Rejai and Phillips 1979; Tucker 1981). Neither is much gained by considering extreme positions, such as naive economic materialism, which denies autonomy to the state and policymaking (B. Frankel 1979) and its modern derivations (Gordon Clark and Dear 1984) or modern "conspiracy" theories that—on the lines of the "Protocols of the Elders of Zion" but with new evil masterminds to blame—see reality manipulated completely by economic superinterests (Chomsky and Herman 1979). Rather, a number of propositions patterning relevant situations are presented, as inferred from comparative and historic studies within attempts to look at policymaking in a broad perspective.

1. Radical differences exist among countries in the extent of the idea and the concept of the "state" playing an important role in political culture and policymaking traditions (as discussed in Dyson 1980). Nevertheless, these differences are not central for examination of the policymaking autonomy of central minds of governments in contemporary situations. Thus, the policymaking leeway enjoyed by the president in the United States is not necessarily smaller than that enjoyed by the chancellor and his cabinet in the Federal Republic of Germany, even though the United States has no "etatist" tradition and Germany has a very strong one. And, in France, the large autonomy of the government in the Fifth Republic, compared with that of the Third Republic, stems from differences in constitutional arrangements and political culture, all within the same tradition of a strong "state" concept. Historic examination of policymaking in the United Kingdom also fails to show any policymaking-leeway weaknesses caused by the absence of a "state" philosophy and "state" political tradition (for an unusual history of policymaking in the United Kingdom, which serves as an example for comparable studies that should be done on other countries, see S. Checkland 1983). While historic traditions of "reforms from above" are correlated with a strong conception of the "state's" being accepted in political culture, this historic factor is not a main variable in determining policymaking autonomy under present conditions in most countries. Nevertheless, the concept of the state and the terminology of "state autonomy" is helpful in exploring some main issues of policymaking autonomy (Hamilton 1983; N. Harding 1984; Nordlinger 1981; Solo 1982; Waldo 1983). A revamped sociology of the state, sorely lacking in Anglo-American political science (as contrasted with France, for instance, see Badie and Birnbaum 1983), may provide a preferable disciplinary context for studying some aspects of policymaking leeways and autonomy, within systematic theoretic frameworks.
2. "Reforms from above," with demonstrated autonomy of centralized policymaking from main social forces and structures, are a feature of history, for instance in the seventeenth and eighteenth century in Imperial Russia, France, Austria-Hungary, and parts of Germany, especially Prussia (Beloff 1962; Raeff 1983; Rogger 1984). Japan provides an analogous illustration in a different cultural context (C. Black 1975), as do various historic bureaucratic states. The facts that every government needs supports in society and that reforms from above run into institutional constraints (C. Findley 1980; Orlovsky 1981) do not negate the significant autonomy enjoyed by small ruling groups in their policymaking.

3. An extreme modern case is National Socialist Germany. Despite the debate on the degrees of monocracy or polycracy in Nazi Germany, it is is quite clear in the light of ongoing research, that Hitler and a small group of associates had dominating influence and reshaped society with much autonomy, though with completely counterexpected results (Bracher 1980; Broszat 1969; Buchheim 1967; K. Hildebrand 1980, passim; Matzerath and Volkmann 1977). Revealingly, some recent treatments in English of Nazi Germany neglect this central feature, as well as many others (e.g. Stachura 1978; J.M. Steiner 1975. Herf 1981 is perceptive). The fact that Germany was a highly industrialized country (which the USSR was not) demonstrates the possibilities for a lot of societal architecture also in highly complex and technological countries. True, National Socialist Germany is an extreme case, but this does not reduce theoretical lessons to be drawn from its history.

4. In a completely different form, the Zionist movement and Israel demonstrate potentials to transform realities through revolutionary policymaking. Zionist policymaking approximated societal architecture—with much reshaping of society at some periods—rather than reflected current interests and structures. Even if the special nature of Zionism as a select social movement is taken into account (Laqueur 1976), this constitutes an important illustration of policymaking autonomy from broader societal contexts without an autocratic regime.

5. Accelerated modernization policies in the Third World constitute a main contemporary attempt to achieve significant impacts, approximating societal architecture, through semiautonomous deliberate policies. Libraries have been written on this subject (as illustrated, in addition to elsewhere cited publications, by earlier writings, such as Apter 1965; Apter 1973; Eisenstadt 1966), but it is too early to evaluate viable impacts and to try to identify the roles of deliberate autonomous policymaking in modernization processes. To take one example: Agrarian reforms illustrate deliberate semiautonomous modernization policies; they do have impacts, but their longer-range effects are complex, depend on many intervening variables, and greatly deviate from intended results (Tuma 1979). Often powerful economic interest groups negate any attempts at meaningful agricultural reforms (Janvry 1983, to be compared with a study of postrevolutionary land reforms, namely, Moise 1983). With all such ambiguities, also when diffuse psychological aspects are added to the picture (Lauterbach 1974), accelerated modernization does demonstrate the potentials, limited but real, for autonomous policymaking with impacts (Samoff 1979).

6. In speaking about enforced modernization in developing countries, "explosive" policies pushed through by strong rulers must be mentioned, in addition to the context of revolutions to be taken up later. Comparison, for instance, of Kemal Atatürk and the Pahlavi shahs of Iran, father and son, who adopted radically different societal transfor-

mation policies, with very different outcomes still in the making is fascinating. (A comparative study of the Turkish and Iranian modernization grand strategies within a policymaking perspective is not available, though much could be learned from it. Good starting points for Turkey include Kinross 1978; B. Lewis 1968; and Ozbudun and Kazancigil 1982. And, for Iran, Keddie with Yann 1981; and Lenczowski 1978.) The dominant position of rulers in Africa presents clear cases of policymaking autonomy, sometimes extreme (R. Jackson and Roseberg 1982) though always within strict limits posed by social and other conditions.

7. The autonomy of policymaking is much more constrained in democracies, where the state is supposed to represent society and is closely subordinated to social forces through elections, interest groups, etc. But the history of the modern welfare state (Flora and Heidenheimer 1980), as well as antidiscrimination policies in the United States, illustrates strong impacts on the reality of policymaking, in the form of "reform from above." Emergencies, wars, and postwar situations illustrate other circumstances where policymaking enjoys much autonomy from internal pressures in democracies. Under normal circumstances, policymaking is often a tool of interest groups, a product of force parallelograms, and a result of exchanges and various coalitions, such as the "iron triangles" of some bureaucrats, some politicians, and strong interest groups (S. Berger 1981; C. Black and Burke 1983; Chubb 1983; Dahl 1967, to be compared with Dahl 1982; Greenstone 1982; Latham 1965; Lindblom 1977; Lindblom and Cohen 1979; McQuaid 1982; Truman 1951). To this must be added bureaucratic politics (Allison 1971; Neustadt 1970). The autonomy of policymaking depends on the balance among such limitations (Fritschler 1983, to be compared with Troyer and Markle 1983 and with P. Taylor 1984), their internal interactions (Bauer et al. 1972), and the endogenous features of the policymaking process-system itself (Krasner 1978).

8. At the same time, policymaking is subordinated to strong social forces. There is no need to go to the extremes of neo-Marxism to recognize the strength of economic power in influencing policymaking (Lindberg et al. 1975; Miliband 1982). In democracies, strong tensions exist between economic influences and voting power (Wolfe 1977), with complex impacts on policymaking autonomy (Barry 1976; Narr and Offe 1975). Often, competing influences provide opportunities for significant policymaking autonomy, if will and skills exist. The situation is both more and less constrained in developing countries with oligarchic rule and institutionalized rigidities (Murdoch 1983), with, for instance, military regimes enjoying more autonomy from economic powers than nominally "elected" governments (Horowitz 1982; Janowitz 1977; Trimberger 1978; whose treatment of Peru should be compared with Stepan 1978; with Booth and Sorj 1983; and with McClintock and Lowenthal 1983).

9. Sanguinity about the autonomy of policymaking in democracies is definitely not justified. Features of domestic politics as considered in chapter 2, such as fragmented politics and cleavages in creedal opinions, may reduce policymaking leeway far below the minimum essential for handling adversity and, at least, avoiding accelerating aggravations of situations. What to do when it is necessary to move in directions unacceptable to strong groups and how to arrive at clear and partly radical policies in the face of determined opposition that rejects legitimacy of majority decisions—these are main issues inhibiting policymaking autonomy in democracies. Without overdrawing on the Weimar case, the Weimar government's inability to handle unemployment because of acceptance of various economic constraints (Borchardt 1982, ch. 9, 10, 11) was not irrelevant; the Nazi regime gave primacy to politics over economics and recruited much support by determined handling of unemployment, using plans mainly prepared within the Weimar government but never implemented. This is not to imply that nowadays democracies, like the Weimar Republic, face downfall, but to pinpoint the problematics of the acceptance of various constraints that add up to narrowing greatly policymaking leeway and, consequently, pose the necessity to break through such constraints. A case in point is provided by the growing domestic constraints on defense policymaking in many Western democracies, reducing policy leeways of central minds of governments below what may be essential for handling external predicaments (IISS 1983).

10. The degree of autonomy of policymaking is itself changeable through policymaking, various leeway-increasing strategies being available (Nordlinger 1981, 130ff.). Characteristics of top politicians and their skills are an important variable in this matter (Czudnowski 1982. A relevant comparison between two historic personalities struggling one against another is provided in Elliot 1984). Upgrading of policymaking qualities may therefore result in increasing policymaking leeway, with more effective policies directed at this objective being adopted. In this case, increasing policymaking leeway correlates with better policymaking capacities, making the larger leeway desirable. But, in general, no "hidden hand" operates to constrain policymaking autonomy when the leeway would result in bad policies, or to increase policymaking autonomy when high qualities of the central mind of government make this desirable in terms of probable policy results.

11. Communist regimes suffer different but not lesser limitations on policymaking autonomy—more rooted in the machinery of government, in bureaucratic politics, in the realities of oligarchy, and in doctrines, and less in dependence on popular support and on political competition within wavering consensus. The question whether the limitations on policymaking autonomy in democracies or in communist regimes are more harmful for handling present and emerging adversities

should not be answered by axiomatic value preferences and is not easy to consider otherwise.

12. The increasing importance of the "global system" decreases the policymaking autonomy of countries, independent from the domestic leeway enjoyed by their central minds of governments (Meyer and Hannan 1979). This is illustrated in the economic domain by the International Monetary Fund strictly constraining the economic policy leeway of many countries. "Global-system" limitations on national policy leeways are superimposed on more traditional forms of external influence, pressure, and dominance—adding up to a quite confining field, reducing policymaking leeway for most countries. But, this is not an absolute constraint, breakthroughs being possible at a price. The threat of declaring moratoriums on international debts illustrates choices open to countries that are willing to consider counterconventional options.

13. The above illustration brings out the important distinction between "objective" and "subjective" policy leeway, depending on awareness or lack of awareness of options and limitations. Mistaken perceptions of policymaking leeway by central minds of governments go both ways: objectively available leeway may be ignored, or illusions about actually nonexisting leeway may prevail. Self-fulfilling and self-defying prophecy effects may be strong here. Distorted perceptions of policymaking leeway illustrate a facet of policymaking autonomy where the upgrading of the capacities of central minds of governments may have significant results.

14. In speaking about policymaking autonomy, it is necessary to differentiate among policy domains that may provide different leeway. In some domains, intense interest groups and much politicization reduce policymaking autonomy very much; at the same time and in the same country, other domains may be dominated by central policymaking without much domestic limitation. Foreign policymaking illustrates an area that in some democracies was left for many years to quite autonomous policymaking by governments, with a present trend to reduce radically this autonomy in some countries.

15. Especially vexing are situations where a strong policy momentum has built up but that now needs redirection—a situation well put into metaphorical imagery by a politician speaking about the "maneuverability of a tanker" (Glotz 1982). A good illustration is once more provided by welfare policies, with their historic roots, ideological bases, statutory rigidities, entitlement psychology, interest groups, and clientele (in addition to already cited literature, Castles and McKinlay 1979, to be compared with Castles 1984; Köhler and Zacher 1982; Wilensky 1975). When changing conditions make transincremental shifts in welfare policies necessary, without orthodoxy-shattering dramatic occurrences helping in policy innovation, policymaking autonomy, leeway, and impact potentials are put to a supreme test.

16. In all policymaking, as discussed above, the central mind of governments, and specific rulers as core components of the central policymaking process-system, can play different roles, depending on their
characteristics. Often, it seems that it is up to the central mind of
governments and small ruling groups to break through constraints on
policymaking posed by rigid structures and forces; and, that success in
achieving much policymaking autonomy, especially in innovative directions, depends greatly on the quality of the central mind of governments (a factor neglected in much of the literature on societal
innovation, as surveyed for instance in Röpke 1977) in combination
with various proinnovation elements in society. The emergence of social welfare policies in the United Kingdom provides good illustrations
of such interplay between outside intellectuals and governmental
power centers (Banting 1979, esp. ch. 5), but, in a field of strong pressures, a central policymaking process-system seeking satisficing, incremental in culture and eager for broad consensus, will not achieve
much autonomy. In the same field, a central policymaking process-
system with strong policy entrepreneurs (E. Lewis 1980), with cohesive
elites, and with will and a sense of commitment may achieve much
autonomy. Still, every central mind of government is limited in its
impacts by rigid constraints and the flow of historic processes (an
interesting test question is posed, for instance, by the speculation
whether different behavior by some rulers could have prevented, or
delayed, the downfall of the French Monarchy, or at least changed the
mode of decline. Some relevant material is provided in Vovelle 1984).

Having till now spoken about autonomy as conditioned by environmental fields and the leeway they provide for central minds of governments,
problems of mental-cultural autonomy of policymaking now need attention: when policymaking elites share fully the views of traditional social
classes, then it makes no difference what environmental autonomy policymaking enjoys. In any case, policymaking will be self-regulating in serving the interests of the social classes with which it identifies, however
hypothetically "free" to adopt different policies if the will to do so should
exist.

Often, policies are deeply rooted in accepted values of dominating elites,
which try to perpetuate these values under changing conditions. A historic
illustration is provided by attempts to apply the moral ideals of a village
culture to emerging cities, through negative and positive "environmen-
talism" (Boyer 1978). Complex interactions between cultural features and
socioeconomic variables often condition policymaking. Thus, the origins
of social policies in England and Prussia (W. Mommsen 1981; Thane 1978)
provide different cases for evaluating degrees of autonomy in policymaking. The special role of Bismarck in Prussian welfare policy origination, as

shaped by his background, illustrates well the coexistence of political and administrative policy autonomy, personal entrepreneurship, and bondage to cultural influences (Crankshaw 1981; L. Gall 1980). Revised Marxist theories, such as on the policymaking elite's working to advance the "real" interests of the economic regime, even when main economic power centers oppose such policies (Femia 1981), are relevant.

These issues lead into questions of elite recruitment, elite self-images, elite values, elite cultures, elite identifications, etc. Good studies are available on parts of the subject (Czudnowski 1975; Czudnowski 1982; Eliassen and Pedersen 1978; Putnam 1976. Unusual in proposing a proelite paradigm is Field and Higley 1980 and, in a less-developed form, Higley, Field, and Groholt 1976). Some pertinent issues are covered by the University of Michigan Comparative Elites Project (summed up mainly in Aberback, Putnam, and Rockman 1981; specific country studies are illustrated by Eldersveld, Kooiman, and Tak 1981, on France, for instance, see Howorth and Cerny 1981; Osborne 1983; Suleiman 1974, Suleiman 1978; and, different, Birnbaum 1982; and Kruisel 1981). But clear conclusions are hard to come by, the subject being loaded with internal antinomies, and over-shadowed by value commitments of researchers (Öberndorfer and Jäger 1975).

Difficult problems are posed by the inertia of cultural limitations imprinted into the worldviews and mind-sets of policymakers in periods of rapid transformation of policy predicaments, when innovative policies are needed. In such situations, active steps to overcome cultural overconditioning of policy-shaping elites are necessary, as considered later. Change of large parts of the policymaking elite, usually in conjunction with social power transformations in periods of revolutions, may be essential. Unexpected mechanisms may also bring about useful shifts in parts of policymaking elites, as illustrated by the effects of the sale of offices in the seventeenth and eighteenth centuries (Malettke 1980).

The experience of revolutions shows that changing the professional parts of policymaking elites is very difficult and expensive, especially in highly developed societies. As a result, even very radical revolutions face the dilemma of leaving large parts of policymaking influenced by prerevolutionary policy cultures or ruining the professional quality of policymaking, as illustrated both in the Communist revolution (Sternheimer 1980) and the Nazi takeover (J. Caplan 1974, with some summing-up in J. Caplan 1978; H. Mommsen 1966). This problem, in somewhat different form, also troubles some newly established Third World countries with highly developed civil services trained and shaped in colonial times, such as India (Arora et al. 1978; Avasthi and Arora 1978; Misra 1970. Braibanti and Sprengler 1963, chapters 1 and 2, is still relevant, as contrasted with the welfare rather than development approach of Dwarkadas 1958. An essential context is provided by Lall 1981).

Returning to the problem of policy autonomy, now in the fuller sense of that term including both environmental and policymaking internal dimensions, the situation is much too complex to permit cavalier conclusions on a subject not operationally conceptionalized and even less empirically studied. The special situations of policymaking under revolutionary conditions and the in-between case of "revolutionary policymaking" are soon to be considered. Under more "normal" conditions, the situation as a whole is mixed, with potentials toward more or less autonomous public policymaking within broad but rigid limits.

This overview does not provide detailed answers to specific questions, such as, what is the influence of big corporations or "power elites" on specific policies (Dettling 1976; McQuaid 1982; Useem 1983); why was United States energy policy ruined by pressure groups (Chubb, 1983; Zinberg 1983), while other policies worked quite well in less intense pressure environments (Krasner 1978); what explains the domination of health policymaking by the medical profession in the United States (P. Starr 1982) compared with the relative autonomy of governments in Europe from the medical profession (e.g. R. Klein 1983, 2); what is happening with the influence of the military establishment (Yarmolinsky and Foster 1983)? What about the interplay between ideologies and interests (as illustrated in respect to national forest policy in Alston 1983)? And so on. Each case can be explained in terms of specific variables; and general theories can be profferred with various degrees of assurance. But middle-range theories on the autonomy of policymaking are still missing. Historical studies examining related and similar issues in different contexts are still underdeveloped, and their absence prevents working out a reliable middle-range theory while also making harder refutation or support of general theoretic conjectures. (The usefulness and feasibility of historic studies on policy autonomy are well illustrated by Hammack 1982, esp. pt. 4). Nevertheless, policymaking can reliably be characterized as enjoying significant leeway, the domains of which expand and contract with a large variety of variables, including the quality of policymaking itself.

The picture is similar in respect to the "freedom" of a ruler, if he wants to engage in autonomous policymaking and overcome field constraints. Quite different experiences are available in historic and contemporary material, and the question is much debated. My reading of the situation in the United States, for instance, is that the degrees of policymaking autonomy of the president depend a lot on his will and skills, which can enable him to overcome societal constraints within a quite large space of potential free movement (V. Davis 1980; Goldsmith 1974; Grossman and Kumat 1981;

Light 1983; L. Lynn and Whitman 1981; R. Porter 1980; I go somewhat beyond Neustadt 1980). Reestablishment of relations with the People's Republic of China may have been an unusual instance, but it demonstrates the potentials of determined and well-assisted presidents (Handel 1981, ch. 4). The experiences of President Reagan in the more difficult domestic arena are illuminating, both by demonstrating degrees of policy autonomy going beyond earlier expectations and their limits (Holwill 1983; J. Palmer and Sawhill 1982; W. Williams 1983).

All in all, literature on "governability" tends to overemphasize constraints operating upon governments and policymaking (e.g., Crozier, Huntington, and Watanuki 1975; Hennis, Kielmansegg, Matz 1977 and 1979; Isensee and Meyer 1979; Lehner 1979; D. Yates 1977). Despite many and growing problems of "governability" and, sometimes, because of the visible needs they pose, more policymaking autonomy is not only necessary but also potentially possible through suitable adjustments and redesigns of policymaking qualities. This basic theme will be taken up again when policymaking improvement is discussed in detail.

To return to the potentials of policymaking as an adversity-handling mode, the question of how far policymaking can go in changing societies (Greiffenhagen 1978; Waterkamp 1974) is especially vexing. Factually, much policymaking is directed at systems maintenance, with incrementalism the rule. Much of policymaking engages in changing some minor features of society to conserve its basic features. But what about situations of necessary or desired systems transformations? Policymaking within a society probably cannot achieve systems metamorphosis, which is a matter for radical revolutions. Policymaking is not a "tool for conviviality" (Illich 1973). But, between systems metamorphosis and incremental systems change, there remains a large and open-ended area of systems transformation (Merritt 1980).

Present policy predicaments in many countries do require considerable systems transformation. Therefore, a crucial question is whether policymaking can engage in societal architecture, how far, and under what conditions. With present ignorance on social macrochange (Boudon 1983), most answers to this question are either speculations or dogmas. But, whatever the limits of systems change through policymaking may be, these limits need pushing outward, because of growing needs and desires for systems transformation. If required systems transformation cannot be achieved through policymaking, more painful and more arbitrary processes may take over. This is a main challenge to policymaking capacities, partly related to policymaking autonomy issues, as looked at above.

One way to try to explore some facets of the limits of policymaking autonomy and of policymaking impact potentials, is to examine policymaking in relation to revolutions.

## Policymaking and Revolutions

Neither literature on revolutions nor literature on policymaking has paid adequate attention to some important features of policymaking-revolution interactions, despite much theoretic and applied significance of the latter.

Relatively easy to study, though underinvestigated at present, are special features of policymaking under revolutionary conditions. In particular, the impacts of gnostic politics (in a sense somewhat related to Voeglin 1952) of revolutions necessarily change many "normal" features of policymaking, such as incrementalism, satisficing, and quasicalculation. Also, the usual requisites of prescriptive policymaking models, such as clinical perspectives, "cold" reasoning, and rationality seeking, do not fit revolutions. Revolutions have manifold consequences for their "policymaking" modes, ranging from mobilization of immense change energy and shattering of usual feasibility boundaries, to fixation on single-dimension worldviews and dogmatic alternatives. With luck, in a minority of attempts at revolutions (not of the "uprising" type or early revolutions, as discussed in Zagorin 1982), it is this very single-mindedness that produces successful revolutions in the sense of overthrowing weakening realities, *inter alia*, with the help of self-fulfilling prophecy effects. At the same time, the extrarational and perhaps irrational quintessence of revolutions, which is a main source of their strength, together with their social-metamorphosis ambitions, assures that the results of revolutions are different from hopes, aspirations, and goals (Eckstein 1977; Eisenstadt 1978; J. Kelley and Klein 1982; and Knei-Paz 1984. The opinion of Lewis-Beck 1979 is different). The hypothetical idea of maintaining within revolutionary movements enclaves of high-quality policymaking meeting mental-intellectual requisites, as detailed later in this book, is probably inherently impossible because of too strong antinomies between revolutionary fervor on one hand and clinical, rationality-oriented, and free-thinking policymaking requisites, on the other hand. Some revolutions are also in their contents and ideologies hostile to the cultural and professional characteristics of high-quality policymaking, as illustrated in an extreme form by the Cultural Revolution in China (e.g. see MacFarquhar 1983). On a more mundane but very real level, the daily pressures, excitements, and crises of revolutions, with jumps between depression and elation (Franqui 1980), leave little scope for "rational policymaking" in the usual meanings of that term.

More difficult to evaluate are the comparative potentials of policymaking versus revolutions as modes of bringing about social change (not that in real circumstances deliberate choice between them is open). When policymaking is in fact servile to status-quo interests, then it can as a maximum bring about minor changes, based on enlightened self-interest, in existing main economic-political realities. If earlier propounded views on the possible autonomy of policymaking are accepted, then societal architecture, by semiautonomous elites with power backing or by consensus, can bring about radical changes in society, though still within basic systems features. Radical forms of "revolutionary policymaking" are possible and in fact observable in reality, with compact ruling elites, based on small but forceful infrastructures, such as the military (Gorman 1982; Trimberger 1978) or an occupation force (Montgomery 1957; Nishi 1982), bringing about social transformations. But, this depends on special conditions and has limits too (Perlmutter 1981).

In most societies, the way to bring about far-reaching and rapid shifts in power distribution and basic social features is revolutions, in the full sense of that term (Arendt 1965; Aya 1979; B. Bell 1976; Chaliand 1977; Cohan 1975; J. Dunn 1972; Greene 1983; Hagopian 1974; Skocpol 1979; *Theory and Society* 1979; Wertheim 1974. A different insight is provided by attempts at artistic depiction of revolutions, e.g. Paulson 1983). Slower and smoother shifts in power can be achieved evolutionarily, including with the help of policymaking; and they often happen as a result of social change brought about by other factors, related neither to revolutions nor to deliberate policymaking such as economic shifts and technological innovation. Social metamorphosis, too, can result from multiple factors, such as those mentioned above, or religious movements, for example. Worth remembering in this context is, as already mentioned, that no good theory of social macrochange is available, leaving strong elements of ignorance in every consideration of ways to achieve or steer such change.

Of practical importance for many countries that are in phases of mixed revolutionary policymaking, or in postrevolutionary conditions, especially in the Third World, is the question of how to move rapidly into high-quality policymaking. This is a main "must" in order to utilize the temporarily increased malleability of society for desired societal architecture before revolutions turn into stubborn new realities or devour themselves. Experiences, as in the People's Republic of China (Chu 1983; Harding 1981; Schurmann 1968), demonstrate how difficult rapid movement from deep revolutions to high-quality policymaking is. A preferable approach is rapid establishment of policymaking enclaves and islands of excellence, impossible under fully revolutionary conditions but more feasible under less extreme circumstances. It seems that no revolution has in fact moved in such a direction, leaving open the question whether the above recommendation is inherently impossible or only nearly so. This is an important issue for large parts of humanity, deserving more study, thought, and application efforts. Developments in China in 1984 and 1985 deserve close study from this perspective.

To conclude consideration of policymaking impacts, policymaking autonomy, and revolutions, it is interesting to ponder the hypothesis that decline of states is brought about by increasing structural rigidities, caused for instance by accumulation of seldom-liquidated and constantly added interest organizations (Olson 1982). Revolutions and wars can, from such a perspective, sometimes be viewed as "derigidification," clearing away debris and doing one part of the "constructive destruction" necessary for a new period of effective policymaking (and, from a different perspective, a new period of social creativity, with the help of free market processes if so desired). Such analysis may lead to the proposition that a main mega-goal for policymaking is to preserve scope for policymaking and reduce the need for revolutions, *inter alia,* by from time to time clearing the societal arena of overdense institutional networks. When societal architecture is discussed in later chapters, this idea is taken up for further consideration.

### Integrative Propositions

To tie together the different threats pursued in this chapter, for the world of discourse of this book, and for policy sciences in general, the following integrative propositions on the possible impacts of policymaking are proposed:

1.  Within a time horizon of up to thirty years, which is the maximum span to be considered in most of policymaking, a kaleidoscopic view of the future with a "skein of *potentia*" (Shackle 1972) available for policymaking constitutes a preferable perspective. This perspective implies a significant domain of choice for policymaking, though a limited one. Present impressions about the dynamics of contemporary and foreseeable realities as in flux increase the impact potentials of high-quality policymaking within the given time frame, both in the form of critical decisions and in the form of consistent grand policies. In other words, within the limited horizons circumscribing deliberate societal action, policymaking matters (which is not necessarily the same as claiming that politics matters. See Castles 1981; and Castles and McKinlay 1979).
2.  A probabilistic view of the impact potentials of policymaking seems to fit best whatever is known and surmised. Moving in a gray area between chance and necessity (Monod 1972; Watkins 1975), and an open universe (Popper 1982), policymaking can change the probability of future events and processes. Such changes in probabilities of alternative futures may be in a desired direction or a contrary one and can be large or small, depending on kaleidoscopic combinations of variables and on constant as well as dynamic features of reality and of historic processes, about which very little is known.
3.  This perspective has far-reaching consequences for policymaking, its study, and its improvement: Policymaking becomes an attempt to change the odds of different possible futures—this, through interventions, the chances of which to change probabilities of future events are

often unknown or guesstimated and which, themselves, take stochastic forms. Therefore, policymaking should be viewed as a partly blind gambling activity, conceptualized later in this book as *fuzzy gambling* (not to be mixed up, despite some affinity, with "fuzzy set theory" and its possible applications to decision making. Kickert 1978). Such a perspective has serious consequences for the whole of policymaking and policy sciences. Thus, evaluation by results, as if the latter deterministically follow policymaking quality, is often a fallacy (Dror 1983a, 40ff.), casting doubts on much of policy evaluation methodologies and further complicating the processing of historic experiences and empiric case studies. Prescriptively, a main conclusion is that policymaking improvement can, in large part, be reformulated as gambling-ability upgrading. Grave value problems follow such a view of policymaking, such as the crucial importance of lottery values. Some important actual weaknesses of policymaking are explained under the proposed view as produced by the abyss between human incapacities to handle uncertainty, on one side (Kahneman, Slovic, and Tversky 1982 to be contrasted with R. Schwartz 1983), and the essential nature of policymaking as fuzzy betting, on the other side.

Policymaking as fuzzy betting attempting to influence the probability of future situations—this is a perspective on which this book is largely based. From now on, this perspective is taken as granted without cumbersome constant repetitions.

4. Even top-quality policymaking in the most active form of societal architecture cannot achieve, nor should it try to achieve, the millennium with present human limits. Efforts to work for the millennium can be very inspiring and bring about great and horrible deeds, partly belonging to the subject of "revolutions," as considered above. But, there is no hope to arrive at the millennium with currently known constants of humans and human institutions and with currently given limitations of the potentials of policymaking, even at its hypothetical best. (This, without moving into the impossibilities of defining ideal societies in any meaningful term, as illustrated by the problematic nature of even relatively simple concepts of "human needs" [Springborg 1981, as contrasted with relatively simplicistic Environmental Protection Agency 1973], and without taking up possible antinomies between different desirable goals, such as equality and cultural creativity [G. Clark 1983, chs. 6,7]. It is possible somewhat to improve the human condition, such as in a Pareto Optimum sense, according to prevailing values, in accord with different value systems, and/or as deemed so by legitimate value judges (despite Rule 1978). It is probably possible to reduce somewhat the frequency of grave mistakes, which by itself would constitute quite a change in the history of governance (Pitkin 1932; Tuchman 1984). Especially appealing is the chance to reduce the probability of catastrophes. Also, high-quality policymaking can ameliorate human misery

and realize some aspirations. But, only in conjunction with break-throughs in other domains, such as values, scientific knowledge, and social propensities, has policymaking sometimes achieved transformations in main policy predicaments; and, in those cases, the specific contributions of policymaking are hard to identify. When such conjunctions may happen again is an open question.

5. The role of policymaking is very important in bringing about conditions conducive to progress in more fundamental human endeavors, which in turn are an essential infrastructure for more ambitious policy achievements in the future. Evolvements of new value systems and paradigmatic advancements in science and technology, in addition to directly reshaping societies, can be regarded as partly aided by high-quality policymaking; and, more pronounced, as conditions for achieving better policymaking impacts on basic policy predicaments. In other words, while it is inadequate to limit policymaking to permitting other social forces to handle adversities, nevertheless policymaking is only one out of many modes of societal problem handling. Therefore, a main function of policymaking is to help to build up other dimensions of societal adversity-facing abilities and to work with them in a relationship of maximum synergism.

6. Under some conditions, policymaking has little chance of making significant contributions for the better. Thus, when policymaking is locked into rigid oligarchies and dominated by traditional forces, some loosening up of society is necessary before policymaking can handle adversities. Under such conditions, it is all the more important to improve policymaking as soon as possible after societal transformations and revolutionary upheavals.

7. Policymaking, and policy sciences, must accept a disturbing combination between urgent needs and high aspirations, on one hand, and stubborn limits on the impact potentials of policymaking, even at its hypothetical best, on the other hand. To take up essential tasks of societal architecture with full awareness of policymaking limits even under very optimistic assumptions is a heavy burden upon responsible and sophisticated statespersons (stateswomen and statesmen alike) and advanced policy scientists (as distinct from prophets and fanatical leaders, who have other functions, whether more or less important and whether more for the better or the worse). To achieve even such restrained ambitions for policymaking impacts for the better, radical changes in the quality of policymaking are essential, as discussed in the next chapters. To expect more from policymaking is a self-defying illusion. To demand less from policymaking is a self-fulfilling resignation.

# 5

# Policy Principles for Handling Adversity

## Concept Package

This book concentrates on policymaking without taking up particular issues and proposing specific policies, but complete detachment of policymaking from the substantive contents of policies may result in too ethereal a treatment that loses contact with reality. After all, human and societal processes take place within specific media and in concrete contexts that shape their configurations. A "pure" theory of policymaking is possible and useful and was the main subject matter of *Public Policymaking Reexamined* (Dror 1983a). But, as there is a difference between painting a picture and managing a war, so there are differences in policymaking depending on domains and fields.

Delimiting the investigation to policymaking under adversity already provides some specifications. To explore somewhat more the contents of adversity-facing policies and their modalities, some policy principles for handling adversity are examined in the present chapter. Being on a middle level between discrete policy contents and abstract handling of policymaking under adversity as a process, the policy principles help to provide a setting for later treatment of policymaking characteristics and requisites, as well as taking up some important substantive issues of handling adversity. The policy principles also serve as a convenient bridge between earlier examination of adversity features and of policymaking responses to adversity on one hand, and design of preferable policymaking pattern-systems in the following chapters, on the other hand.

To locate policy principles for policymaking under adversity, clear distinction between a number of aspects of policies and policymaking is necessary. This is not an easy task, policymaking being, as expounded several times, an existential part of unfolding societal reality, itself composed of a multitude of overlapping and interacting threads. Imposition of explicated concepts on amorphous reality carries dangers of falsification, even if the concepts are meaningful on a tacit level (Polanyi 1974). Nevertheless, some partly clarified concepts are necessary tools for the tasks ahead.

A minimum concept package for the proceedings of this book includes the following terms:

*Grand policy*: A comprehensive material policy setting forth broad directives in respect to the contents of dealing with an issue area. For instance, reindustrialization or containment constitute grand policies in the domestic and international domain, respectively. The term is analogous to the concept of "grand strategy" in the security policy domain (e.g. Luttwak 1977; Luttwak 1983; B. Palmer 1979; Sargeaunt and West 1942, ch. 1; somewhat different is the French concept "total strategy," as developed by André Beaufré [Beaufré 1974, ch.1] ).

*Policy principle*: A comprehensive rule on substantive features for policies, not in terms of contents of a particular issue area but of crosscutting dimensions of policies. For instance, degrees of innovation, mixes between incrementalism and comprehensiveness, attitudes toward risks, activism versus passivism—these illustrate policy principles further worked out later in this chapter. (The term *policy strategy* could also be used.)

*Metapolicy*: A policy dealing with the making of policies, that is the processes, institutions, inputs, infrastructure, etc. of the policymaking process-system. A decision to utilize social experimentation in policymaking illustrates a metapolicy.

*Policy paradigm*: A broader concept, covering all main underlying assumptions, principles, grand policies, axiologies, modus operandi, and similar elements of policies and of policymaking, especially when taken for granted and accepted tacitly.

*Policy orthodoxy*: Policy paradigms that are not only accepted as a matter of fact but regarded with attachment and trust, up to semisanctification. Degrees of policy orthodoxy are more susceptible to measurement than, say, the extent of the existence of grand policies, though the latter too can in principle be empirically studied. Policy orthodoxies can be explained in terms of cultural and organizational dynamics and of psychological propensities. Thus, attachment and trust in policy orthodoxies satisfy organizational needs for certainty and can result, for instance, from longstanding policy traditions; semisanctification can result, for instance, from dogmatic beliefs, such as policy theologies and political romanticism. Vested interests in existing policies and professional ideologies, such as among welfare workers or some militaries, illustrate additional reasons for various forms of policy orthodoxy.

To keep the book semantically as lean as possible, these five concepts are used as the main concept package. Thus, the concept of *megapolicy* is seldom used, though it can now be redefined simply as covering both grand policies and policy principles (compare earlier formulations in Dror 1971a and Dror 1971b.)

## Policy Principles in Relation to Main Thrust of Book

The policy principles presented in the present chapter can be considered within a number of different perspectives:

1. As substantive recommendations for handling adversity, emerging from the study underlying the book; or, as alternative policy principle options, up for consideration within policymaking.
2. As illustrating the concept of policy principle as an often-neglected dimension of policies and policymaking. This is important because of the policymaking-improvement requirements to explicate and thoroughly review policy principles, as discussed in the next chapters.
3. As explicating some substantive opinions of the author that probably color other parts of the book and that therefore should be put on the table.
4. As mentioned above, the policy principles introduce policy substance as a basis for the consideration of metapolicymaking, providing some material context for investigated processual and institutional configurations.

To serve the above perspectives, the following policy principles proposed for handling adversity are considered in brief: societal architecture; critical mass; selective radicalism; risk readiness; output-value priority; and active up to compelling. These six principles are closely related and together constitute a proposed policy posture for handling adversity in an increasing number of countries. But, each one of the policy principles has a somewhat different contour, and their separate consideration adds elasticity in permitting custom fitting to concrete circumstances.

It must be borne in mind that in the present book, policy principles are not the main subject but, rather, serve as a context for close examination of other dimensions of policymaking under adversity. Therefore, the policy principles are mentioned and explained, but not treated in detail. The policymaking implications of the various policy principles will be explored in detail in the following chapters, but the substantive problems of alternative policy principles are only in part hinted at.

### Societal Architecture

Societal architecture expresses the necessity to bring about significant structural changes in important societal institutions and processes, guided in part by central policymaking. The need for societal architecture stems from the contradiction between necessary societal adjustments and transformations on one hand, such as in life styles and aspirations, in the economy, and in social policies and strong societal rigidities, on the other hand, that hinder necessary adjustments and make their achievement through spontaneous processes rather unlikely. Therefore, societal architecture on behalf of central governments and/or aided by it is a necessary policy principle for handling adversity, with the extents and intensities of necessary centrally guided societal transformations differing among various societies (and diverse dimensions of the international scene where global societal architecture is needed even more than in many countries, e.g. see Bressand 1983).

Main features of societal architecture as a policy principle include, among others: far-reaching interventions with unfolding realities; dynamic and complex goals, up to realistic visions of alternative futures; massive policy instruments combined to achieve a critical mass; comprehensive and longitudinal decision frameworks; transincremental changes taking often an L-shape (not a U-shape); and, all the above within a constant learning attitude, with adjustments to ultrachange and ignorance.

Societal architecture is very difficult intellectually as well as politically. It requires mental-intellectual policymaking qualities far beyond those available at present, as demonstrated by the dismal failure of "planning" in most societies as a societal architecture mode. Even more disturbing are the problematics of coexistence between significant amounts of societal architecture and democracy, requiring quite some changes in present institutions and ideological trends (e.g. see Benjamin 1980; Parfitt 1983; Sullivan 1982). Despite such difficulties and the unavoidable risks associated with societal architecture, especially in complex societies, the need for it in order to handle adversity is pronounced. Whether and how it is possible to arrive at policymaking qualities able to take up societal architecture without prohibitive costs is a question central to the next chapters. The present poverty of social science thinking on the subject is not a help either. (The little available thinking is reflected in writings such as Golembiewski 1979; Omer 1983; J. Schmidt 1975; Seidman 1983; Sutherland 1975; Sutherland 1978; Warren 1977; Zaltman and Duncan 1977; and in some of the literature on planning, as surveyed in D. Wilson 1980 and D. Wilson 1979, and to be considered in chapter 7.)

A special form of needed societal architecture is reduction of societal rigidities through removal and decomposition of petrified and dense institutions that create networks inhibiting innovative adjustments by societal processes (Olson 1982; as discussed in Mueller 1983). This form of societal architecture is in part appealing because it is not aimed at advancing specific futures but, rather, at providing latitude for societal processes; albeit the breaking up of rigid structures and other forms of "derigidification" are among the most difficult processes, especially in democracies, depending on special opportunities, and/or invention of new modes of action, and/or significant changes in democratic politics. The already-mentioned concept of "constructive destruction," as proffered by Joseph Schumpeter (Schumpeter 1952), expresses the need well, including the difficulties in doing, or letting other forces do, the necessary "destruction" in democracies.

It should be noted that the need for societal architecture often does not depend on particular adjustments to be introduced in main societal processes and institutions. Whether one wants to reinforce a free-market version of capitalism (Gilder 1981), or change the balance between material and social priorities (Hirsch 1976; as further discussed in Ellis and Kumar 1983), or change "life chances" (Dahrendorf 1980), or make socialism work (Nove 1983), or adopt a global policy perspective (Fuller 1978) within an integrated view of mankind (Boulding 1978), or limit oneself to minimum adjustments to permit the system to work more or less as in the past (OECD 1983), significant changes in societal institutions and processes are necessary, involving substantial amounts of societal architecture, never mind if that term is eschewed and even abhorred.

However looked at, societal architecture is an essential policy principle for handling adversity and the most difficult one, bringing up many dilemmas faced by central minds of governments once they drop dogmatism. In particular, democracies may be faced by a number of difficult and even tragic choices in facing up to needs for at least some societal architecture.

## Critical Mass

Adversity features have change thresholds that depend on their dynamics, size and complexity, states of stability or turmoil, specific fields, and more. To achieve impact, policies must reach an appropriate critical mass, sufficient to have the intended effects on their targets. This, either directly, or indirectly through first transforming the thresholds themselves, such as through destabilization. Such policy critical mass can involve the scope of decisions, the amount of instruments brought to bear, the time spans covered (thus amalgamating the important policy principle of adopting sufficiently long-range policies into the critical mass principle, with related problems to be discussed in chapter 7), the spread of issues handled in an integrated way (amalgamating into the critical mass principle the need for sufficiently comprehensive policies, also to be discussed in chapter 7), and other dimensions as fitting particular cases. A paradigmatic illustration of such "large-scale policy" requirements (Schulman 1980; for a different treatment, see Jamshidi 1983) is provided by some of the space programs, which had no chance of success without large minimum sizes of resources, time, organizational base, and more (Webb 1969). The same applies to main predicaments, such as unemployment, North-South relations, demographic shifts, and so on, as surveyed in chapter 2.

A special situation is provided by domains where policy above a certain scale loses its effectiveness, such as in some opinions in cancer reserch (Rettig 1977, to be compared with Chubin and Studer 1978). In some domains, such as art (Mulcahy and Swain 1982), large-scale policies may have very pronounced counter-productive results. Such "maximum thresholds" contrast with more usual "minimum thresholds" and require careful attention because they frequently are counterconventional. The currently discussed policy principle must, therefore, be applied with discrimination, being thus even more demanding on policymaking qualities.

While incrementalism is usually useless for handling adversity, despite its lingering on as a recommended policy principle (e.g. Lindblom 1979; for different treatments see Collingridge 1982; Dempster and Wildavsky 1979; and Mackinnon and Wearing 1982), it at least sometimes has the advantage of not causing great harm (unless microchanges have macroconsequences, in line with Schelling 1978; see also Odum 1982). Large-scale interventions can bring about very desirable impacts, but adverse and even fatal (Sieber 1981) unanticipated consequences can be very serious (Boudon 1982). Therefore, societal architecture with critical masses of decisions and policy instruments is a dangerous, even if essential, treatment requiring novel policymaking modes, as considered in the next chapters.

When large critical masses are required, a major hiatus opens between frequent features of politics and requirements of effective handling of adversity. Thus, the political propensity toward "compromises" as a way to gain acceptance—often seen as morally desirable (perhaps as a misunderstood version of the Greek "golden mean" ideal, which dealt with emotions and not with purposeful action)—contradicts critical mass requisites. It frequently results in policy bags with little chance of meeting any objective other than looking good for a short time. The critical mass principle also contradicts political propensities toward "ambiguity" (D. Hill 1978).

Furthermore, fragmented politics based on very diffuse power and on mutual adjustment as a main decision mechanism, is unable to concentrate sufficient critical mass to bring to bear on high-threshold adversity. Here some policy predicaments demonstrate an internal "impossibility." On one hand, the nature of the problem requires large critical masses to achieve desired impacts, as illustrated by energy, welfare, reindustrialization, defense, and more. In particular, policies approaching societal architecture require usually large critical masses, even if efforts are made to adopt impact-effective strategies, such as "selective radicalism," to be discussed soon. At the same time, field-related features include erosion of political resources, inhibiting achievement of the critical mass essential for achieving impacts.

This brings us squarely to power-political issues. Pertinent for the critical mass policy principle is a pure-type distinction between two power-political bases:

1. *Fragmented power-political base*: Power diffusion, with heterogeneity and adversity among interests, values, and goals of main actors. Intense activity by militant action groups, rejecting the authority of collective decisions. Absence of dominant power centers or "winning" stable coalitions. Mobility, up to volatility, of public opinion, with a tendency to form transient public movements and shifts in voting preferences. Sense of losing control by main political elites and traditional parties. Intense competition for political support in shifting political markets. Incrementalism, disjointedness, support considerations, and immediate pressures dominate, with bargaining among many interests and seeking of consensus on minimum acceptable action reigning supreme. Drifting and stalemate (Crozier 1973) are the rule rather than political-will formation.

   When these features become extreme, the fragmentary pure type changes into a disintegration pure type, with undermining of the very existence of governance and possiblities of arriving at any policies at all.
2. *Compact power-political base*: Power concentration in a small number of entities, such as parties and main economic organizations. Habits of mixed competition-cooperation among these entities, with agreed rules for arriving at binding decisions. Broad public acceptance of the legitimacy of duly made collective decisions. Main political elites have sense of purpose and efficaciousness. Political competition limited to some domains, agreement permeating others. Incrementalism, support considerations, and immediate pressures important but not exclusive or dominant. "Critical" areas are excluded from political marketing, being settled by broad consensus or by dominating stable power blocks, or being delegated to "closed policymaking" by central government, small elite groups, and other enclaves. When these features become extreme, the compact pure form changes into a power monopoly type, with special features of its own.

As is true by definition for "pure types" (Janoska-Bendl 1965; for a pertinent discussion see also Hekmany 1983), reality moves on continuums between these polars. It is important to note the multiple relations between such power-political bases of policymaking and their implications for the critical mass requisite on one hand, and the regime form on the other hand: In democracies, at one and the same time different policy domains can be characterized by more fragmented or more compact power-political bases. In authoritarian and even totalitarian regimes, still quite a number of policy domains are subjected to very fragmented policymaking, as illustrated by some findings on economic and industrial policy in Nazi Germany (W. Fischer 1968; Forstmeier and Volkmann 1975; Forstmeier and Volkmann 1977).

These pure types help to pin down the antinomy between the critical mass policy principle and widespread features of politics: When politics approximates the fragmentary pure type, as is increasingly the case in some Western democracies, then critical mass policies become impossible. Vice versa, when predicaments require large critical mass policies, then compact power-political systems have, in this respect, an advantage over fragmentary ones. (But, in regard to some requisites of high-quality policymaking, fragmentation has advantages. For, example, power-political fragmentation may be conducive to alternative innovations and policy learning).

However difficult to achieve, critical mass is an essential policy principle for facing adversity. If policies do not achieve critical mass in respect to some main predicaments, there often exists no possibility to handle the latter.

## Selective Radicalism

A basic dilemma of handling adversity via policymaking, shared with most of reform approaches (Greiffenhagen 1978), can be summed up as follows: Incremental changes are relatively easily to analyze, adopt, and implement, and sometimes carry small risks of undesirable and unexpected consequences (Lindblom 1979), but the impacts of incremental change on high-threshold realities (Schulman 1980) and on tradition-bound institutions (Shils 1981) are very small. Conversely, overall reality transformation is usually nonfeasible and carries very high costs. Or, under revolutionary conditions, reality metamorphosis, as far as at all feasible, is hard to steer and is sure to have many unexpected and undesired consequences.

There is no need here to dwell any more on this and related well-known controversies. The policy principle proposed as a way out of this dilemma in all but revolutionary, or stable and content that is nonadversity, conditions is one of selective radicalism.

According to this policy principle, a limited number of societal variables are changed radically. These variables are selected so as to achieve significant impact on the more important features of adversity, with an effort to bring about synergistic interaction between the selected intervention modules. The variables selected for radical innovation should have asymmetric coupling with other adversity-related factors, so as to yield significant impacts, unretarded by the inertia of other, unchanged, variables. If possible, the radically changed variables should stimulate other change factors, causing improvements in adversity without need for multiple direct intervention, such as through self-motivated adjustment by various social actors.

Relations between selective radicalism and societal architecture, as two separate but correlated policy principles, should be noted: Under conditions where adversity can be handled through meliorism, without reaching the dimensions of societal architecture, selective radicalism focusing on a small number of variables may do. When societal architecture is the adopted policy principle, it often should also be engaged in via selective radicalism, with selection of a larger but still limited number of variables and different modules, adding up to achievement of the societal architecture impacts aimed at. Only in special situations, such as very undeveloped countries or semirevolutionary situations, can and should overall and comprehensive intervention in the form of radical change in a large number of variables, within a synchronized design, serve as a main policy principle.

A special extreme version of selective radicalism is shock policy, with major and/or dramatic interventions designed to achieve significant impacts on a system. The introduction of the rationing of sugar to make people aware of a serious economic situation and to increase their readiness for a revamping of the economy illustrates a relatively riskless shock policy. Starting a war to mutate a main feature of one's society (we are not concerned here with attempts to influence external societies, which is an interesting but different subject, to which some of our analysis applies with suitable adjustments) illustrates a high-risk shock policy, the outcomes of which cannot be foreseen. In between are a whole range of shock-policy alternatives. In democracies, shock policies are hardly feasible, but they do constitute a mode of intervention as a polar form of the selective-radicalism policy principle, that should be kept in mind for special stituations. Symbolic policies can also serve as shock-option surrogates, such as declarations of national emergencies and dramatic appeal to the population by rulers.

### Risk Readiness with Minimin Avoidance

A crucial, though neglected and usually unexplicated, dimension of policies is their risk propensity. The nature of policies as gambles in the face of uncertainty, as already explored, makes determination of appropriate risk levels a main policy principle issue. In part this is a matter for value judgment, not conditioned by the situation of adversity as examined here.

But, in part, situations of harsh adversity tip the scales in favor of explicit readiness to bear significant risks as an unavoidable policy principle.

The reasoning behind this recommendation is quite simple and has already been presented in other contexts: When adversities are harsh and when they are expected to continue in the absence of determined interventions, then policies that presume not to take significant risks are an illusion because uninterrupted continuation of adversity carries a high risk in any case. Thus, to tie in with an earlier-considered policy principle, incrementalism is often recommended as carrying little risk and low costs. But, under conditions of adversity this in incorrect: A careful incremental and risk-avoiding policy on a sinking curve is surely both very costly and very risky.

As all policies under adversity carry high probabilities of undesired outcomes, an explicit readiness to accept risks does not really increase the risks, only our awareness of them. Therefore, in real terms, the proposed policy principle does not recommend recklessness and a liking for high antes—which are matters for value judgment and not for recommendations presuming to be based on analysis. Rather, risk readiness as a policy principle demolishes the illusion that low-risk policies exist at all in the face of adversity and substitute conscious readiness to accept guesstimated risks and to adopt policy modes accordingly for the chimera of playing it safe.

Recognition of the fuzzy-gambling nature of policymaking under adversity and of the risks involved in all policies, including the most safe looking and traditional ones, is essential. But to serve as a policy principle, some recommended attitude to risk handling needs to be added. This is a matter for value judgment rather than for clear-cut prescriptions. Nevertheless, the policy principle of minimin-avoidance may be attractive to quite a range of lottery values. "Minimin" refers to the minimum of the minimum, that is the worst of all bad outcomes that are within the range of the possible. When minimin situations are very bad, then their prevention—which means in policy-gambling terms the reduction of their probability—may often be a priority policy principle. This has important implications for policymaking, such as the need to work out worse-case and bad-case scenarios which will serve as targets for "avoidance" policies. The idea of minimin-avoidance as a policy principle is here mentioned as a reasonable, though not logically compelling, policy-principle option under adversity.

In applying this principle, care must be taken not to distort the identity of minimin possibilities by mistaking more obvious possibilities for more dangerous ones. Thus, the possibility of a nuclear power plant blow up is not necessarily more of a danger than staying without energy in case of an oil crisis, even if the first danger is more obvious to most people than the second.

## Output-Value Priority

Policymaking in many countries, and especially in democracies, is subject to two different sets of values, goals, and demands: value, goals, and demands in respect to outputs, that is, in terms of the impacts of policies on reality; and values, goals, and demands in respect to the patterns by which policies are made and implemented, such as participation, openness, and agreement by all who are influenced by the considered decisions.

The dilemma is especially acute in respect to policymaking processes, concerning the relative weights to be allocated in them to satisfy pattern-values versus output-values. Therefore, it will be looked at more closely in the context of policymaking-improvement principles. But, the importance of the subject requires its inclusion among policy principles. While judgment on value priorities is basically a matter of subjective preferences, a relevant consideration is that, under conditions of adversity, achievement of output-values directed at the handling of adversity is more pressing, than, under conditions of prosperity, well-being and continuous progress. Therefore, adversity requires allocation of higher priorities to policy outputs, in comparison to better times, when pattern-values can receive most of the weightings. This is all the more the case when serious minimin possibilities are faced, as characterizes some contemporary situations of adversity.

This policy principle needs subjection to a number of hedgings:

1. Value priorities are a matter of degree and relative multidimensional weightings. The proposed policy principle does not recommend far-reaching displacement of pattern-values but some shift in marginal priorities as fitting specific needs and adversity situations.
2. The recommended policy principle of higher priority for output-values is predicated on satisfaction of a minimum of pattern-values, such as basic human rights and, in many but not all countries, main norms of democracy. This, because such values should receive high priority as a matter of value judgment and their nonsatisfaction is itself a serious form of human adversity.
3. If possible, forms of policymaking and policies should be sought that dominate, in the sense of supplying both more output-values and more pattern-values. It must be admitted that often this is impossible.
4. Some additional satisfaction of pattern-values may be important for handling adversity, such as by reducing domestic political adversity and by gaining support essential for policy implementation. But it should be recognized that, for instance, some demands for so-called further democratization (Greiffenhagen 1973) beyond a certain point, such as veto rights for localities that may be touched by policies, may well entail

serious costs in terms of handling adversity and often must be rejected. (Compare Löwenthal 1979, 172-96. Different is the opinion of Nelkin 1978).

5. After all analysis, giving priority to pattern-values or output-values still remains a matter for value judgment. It is legitimate to regard satisfaction of pattern-values as more important than the handling of other aspects of reality, including adversity as perceived in this book. If opportunity costs are realized, then the policy principle of giving priority to output-values as proposed here can legitimately be displaced by other preferences, but if this is done without consideration of opportunity costs in terms of handling adversity, decisions to give priority to pattern-values are based on political theology and not on responsible judgment.

Present tendencies in democracies to enhance pattern-values, as based on experiences during relatively better times, require reconsideration. It may be necessary to allocate priority to improving output-values when adversity is harsher. This issue is looked at from a different perspective when tragic choice is considered in chapters 7 and, differently, in chapter 9.

## Active up to Compelling

The policy principles of societal architectures and critical mass already imply the need for policies handling adversity to be active, up to compelling when necessary. Needs for controlled and guided changes in significant features of society in the face of rigidities and resistances make active policies, which can overcome inertia and nonacceptance of duly collective choices, an unavoidable policy principle.

Here, again, difficult problems for democracies (but also for the USSR, see Yanvey 1983) are confronted. When deep cleavages in opinions combine with rejection of the legitimacy of majority decisions and when, at the same time, handling of adversity requires action according to one or another option on none of which broad consensus can be achieved, under such conditions there is no way out other than reassertion of the authority of political democracy and imposition of duly taken decisions. Therefore, the possibility of policies' taking a compelling nature must be recognized as a principle essential for handling adversity under a range of contemporary and foreseeable conditions.

To use more striking and less roundabout terminology, to handle adversity, the central mind of government must enjoy command authority to make and implement tough policies. The ability of democracies to follow this policy principle can well be critical for their survival; otherwise they may develop a policymaking handicap putting them at a serious disadvantage in handling adversity.

## From Policy Principles to Policymaking Requirements

Further policy principles for handling adversity can be derived from the study underlying this book but would carry us too far from the book's main *leitmotif*, which is the improvement of policymaking under adversity rather than development of specific policy-contents proposals. The above illustrations suffice to convey the tone of the main policy-principles recommendations and to serve the different perspectives, as presented at the beginning of the chapter.

The six policy principles also constitute an avenue into requisites of high-quality policymaking under adversity. As already mentioned, policymaking under adversity must be able to arrive at such and related policy-principle alternatives and to consider them fully. Never mind if one or another of the above policy principles seems more or less reasonable under particular circumstances or with specific values in mind. There can be little doubt that adversity requires policies different in important respects, such as illustrated by the presented policy principles, from those satisfying less-demanding circumstances. This, in turn, imposes heavily on policymaking and requires suitable policymaking qualities. The concept of "heroic" versus humdrum policymaking as developed by Jack Hayward, while unlucky in terminology because of unfortunate associations of the concept "heroic," well expresses in a nutshell some of the consequently needed qualities of policymaking under adversity: "heroic in the dual sense that it would be both an ambitious political exercise in rational decision-making and an ambitious assertion of political will by government leaders" (Hayward 1974, 399. The author weakens his proposed concept in Hayward 1982, 112).

Various other verbal combinations can serve to indicate needed characteristics of high-quality policymaking under adversity. Thus, the semantic space of *sophisticated, creative, and vigorous policymaking* can be contrasted with the earlier-considered concept of *maze policy-behavior*, to bring out associatively and connotatively the abyss between actual and needed policymaking under adversity, but really to get a hold on the subject, a more systematic approach is necessary. The central importance of identification of specifications for high-quality policymaking under adversity for the whole of this book makes more extended treatment of this subject all the more essential.

# 6

# Required Policymaking Qualities versus Incapacities

## Two Pillars of Analysis

Policymaking realities move uneasily between requirements on one hand and incapacities on the other hand. Policymaking under adversity faces demanding requirements to enable it to achieve impacts for the better on realities, while stubborn features of policymaking process-systems, their components and the materials out of which they are made, and of the environments conditioning them produce what can largely be viewed as inbuilt incapacities. As a result of great and growing gaps between requirements on one side and of incapacities on the other, large performance deficits constitute a pronounced feature of policymaking actuality and tend to become larger.

Requirements in respect to policymaking quality and inbuilt barriers to policymaking quality constitute two major pillars of the main body of analysis of this book. Care must be taken to keep in mind the qualitative difference between these pillars: Requirements are in essence prescriptive, tied into reality by an examination of functional requisites of effective policymaking under conditions of adversity. Incapacities are a feature of historic and existing realities inferred from empiric data and generalized on the basis of morphological and behavioral investigations. Subject to this differentiation between the natures of the two sets, their mutual relationships can be considered within a number of schemata. Thus, requirements and incapacities can be seen as thesis and antithesis in a dialectic relationship; as challenge and response inhibitors within a Toynbee-like interaction; and as antinomies inherent in sociopolitical processes, which can take a sharper form under conditions of adversity but are universal in their existential features.

However looked at, for understanding and improving policymaking under adversity, the gap between requirements of high-quality policymaking and policymaking incapacities is crucial. Thus, the gap explains weaknesses of policymaking responses to adversity, as considered in chapter 3; helps to understand the frequency of policymaking failures as a permanent, and often predominant, reality; and clarifies the apparent fact that dismal policy fiascoes are often a product of the policymaking system-process working smoothly within its usual patterns (as brought out well in respect to U.S. policies in Vietnam by Gelb and Betts 1979, as well as the Pentagon Papers, Sheehan 1971. Relevant also are Steinbruner 1974; as applied to specific cases, such as the F-111, in Coulam 1977, and illustrated differently in respect to the SST in Horwitch 1982; illuminatingly accepting policymaking failure as unavoidable is Franks 1982).

The contradiction between inherent incapacities and policymaking requirements is central to this book. Therefore, while full exposition of the theoretic explanation of incapacities in terms of an evolutionary approach to governance is left for another occasion, the main features of the contradiction within the policymaking process-system require relatively extensive treatment. Accordingly, in the present chapter main dimensions of high-quality policymaking requirements are considered and the concept of policymaking incapacity is elucidated. Then, in the next chapter, detailed specifications for high-quality policymaking under adversity are elaborated, incapacities operating on each one of them are examined, and main resulting policymaking-quality deficits are brought out. Together, chapters 6 and 7 are designed to provide some explanations for policymaking realities, to pinpoint main targets for improvement efforts, and to lay the ground for taking up some fundamental issues of policymaking upgrading in later parts of this book.

## High-Quality Policymaking as Essential for Handling Adversity

The preference, or bias, of Western culture—according to which "better" policymaking is nearly always desired as a matter of principle—left aside, adversity as considered in chapter 2 combines with the assumptions of possible impacts of policymaking, as considered in chapter 3, resulting in high demands on policymaking quality as a necessity for handling adversity. It bears repetition that the preferable qualities of policymaking and the importance of realizing these qualities vary with situations. Thus, when societies are on an upswing caused by factors quite independent from central policymaking, then the quality of the central minds of governments in producing policies does not matter very much and "good" policymaking is incremental in its main features. The situation is quite different under conditions of adversity, as considered in this book, resulting in very demanding challenges to policymaking qualities.

To put the above conclusion into correct proportions as a strong con-jecture but not a fully provable finding, some earlier-considered provi-sional propositions on which it is based repay repetition and further elaboration:

1. Adversities have no great probability of dissipating on their own without an extended period of grave costs and serious dangers, though upswings in some facets, such as the economy, may happen. All of our analysis, as well as any treatment of history, will recognize many domains where the Principle of the Hidden Hand (Hirschman 1967, ch.1) cannot work, and even more domains where it cannot be depended upon.
2. High-quality policymaking can have impacts for the better, in a stochastic sense. This potential for the better of high-quality policymak-ing can be assumed to be greater in its expected value than impacts for the worse.
3. Other modes of societal problem handling are essential but (a) inade-quate by themselves and (b) need help from central policymaking to achieve a high probability of significant impacts for the better under adversity. Thus:
- Market mechanisms are inadequate for handling much of adversity and depend in turn on high-quality policymaking to operate well within their important, but limited, domains of usefulness. Not only are public goods in the main excepted from market mechanisms even if operating at their optimum, which seldom happens, but many cardinal personal human wants cannot be handled by the market mechanism (Lane 1978)—a feature that does not necessarily make them appropriate for policymaking either, but at least requires their consideration as potential candidates for public action. (The important potentials as well as limita-tions of market mechanisms need thorough consideration within a gen-eral societal command and control theory. Relevant is Lindblom 1977, which reaches quite different conclusions than the classic Dahl and Lindblom 1953. Richness and limitations of the large literature on vari-ous aspects of the issue are illustrated by Williamson 1975, as criticized in Francis et al. 1982. The subject will be extensively considered in Dror, in work.)
- Breakthroughs in adversity-relevant knowledge and values may occur. But these are slow processes, not sure to happen in the foreseeable future and partly dependent on help from policymaking (such as allocation of large resources for research), and they carry dangers as well as hopes (as illustrated by possibly aggressive creeds, which need inhibition by policymaking).
- Grass-roots initiatives can be very important in handling some aspects of adversity and in stimulating better policymaking. But, even under optimistic assumptions, their potential impacts on adversity in the fore-seeable future are very limited. (For a good but still overoptimistic treat-

ment, see Michael Taylor 1982. Bermback 1973; Kevenhörster 1974; Osterfeld 1983; Vilmar 1973; Ward 1981; and many more are more fantastic. T. Williams 1982 is interesting, though overly optimistic.)
- As will be considered later in more detail, popular movements are a double-edged knife for attempting to cut through policy knots, at best. To rely on the political sense and goodwill of populations at large (e.g. Wolfe 1977) and their political capacities (Somjee 1982) contradicts much of what is known and has been experienced historically and is, therefore, somewhere between premature hopes, wishful thinking, and a neomagic belief. In particular, the potentials of mass movements for undermining democracy must be kept in mind. Therefore, although mass movements may fulfill important positive functions in pressing for policy innovations, they also constitute a serious hindrance to adequate handling of adversity, adding to the problems that require high-quality central policymaking.

Rather then belabor any more the rather obvious need for high-quality policymaking, that concept must be transformed from a vague slogan into an operational set of requisites and qualifications.

## Main Dimensions of High-Quality Policymaking Under Adversity

Policymaking being viewed as an existential aspect of society beyond any simple and inclusive circumscription, it follows that a large variety of facet designs, archeologies of knowledge (Foucault 1976), and perspectives can serve as partial containers for catching segments of needed policymaking qualities. The existence of a large variety of models of and for decision making and policymaking testifies to the variety of useful approaches, each one limited in some important respects (a unique survey of some main models is provided in Bretzke 1980).

Having designed an elaborate process model for policymaking as a basis for a general theory and improvement in *Public Policymaking Reexamined* (Dror 1983a pt. 4), the author believes the special needs of policymaking under adversity are better brought out by an analytical approach, whereby main needed features of high-quality policymaking under adversity are considered in terms of select characteristics of policymaking as a process. These characteristics do not add up to a complete model, but concentrate on items especially pertinent for handling adversity. In other words, a special cut of policymaking serves to bring out main qualitites required for handling adversity, with some items overlapping elements in the model developed earlier but quite different in overall configuration. There is no presumption of presenting another inclusive model of and for policymaking but of highlighting instead facets particularly salient to handling adversity.

Underlying this mode of treatment is a conception of optimal policymaking under adversity as a complex and multidimensional configuration rather than a very ordered process of ratiocination. This conception is not based on empiric models of the "garbage-can" type and their variations, however relevant (Cohen, March, and Olsen 1972; March and Olsen 1976) but, rather, on application to the central policymaking process-system of recent conceptions of the mind and of artificial intelligence (e.g. Dennett 1980; Hofstadter 1979; and Hofstadter, forthcoming. Also relevant is H. Gardner 1983. Hofstadter and Dennett 1981 is too far out) and also of planning (e.g. Krieger 1981), as earlier recognized under the rubric of "extrarational" components in *Public Policymaking Reexamined.* Without in any way adopting an organistic view of the central mind of government (or assuming a shared or collective mentality, as in the use of the term *mind* in respect to a party in Bentley 1977), the author regards a configuration of multicrosscutting processes on various levels as essential for handling adversity, and especially complexity and uncertainty. Different processes take place serially, concurrently, and interruptedly; interaction takes many and changing forms, including strange loops and tangled hierarchies (Hofstadter 1979, 10); and causal relationships are only a part of the interlocking mechanism, with anticipations and random processes also playing important roles. All this, let me reemphasize, are features of the central policymaking process-system operating optimally under adversity, with essential changes needed in actual policymaking realities to achieve higher quality configurations, with consequent necessity to add and transform some main components, and to repattern central interaction modalities, as illustrated in following chapters.

I leave for another opportunity grand-theoretic argumentation for this perspective and examination of its broader implications, such as a critique of the concept of "bounded rationality" as developed by Herbert Simon (H. Simon 1976b; H. Simon 1982, passim; pervading Simon 1983) and similar theories dominating literature, as too narrow in considering only parts of human multidimensional reasoning capacities and incapacities. In the present book the complex configuration view of optimal policymaking leads to pointillistic treatment of some main components and aspects of policymaking under adversity rather than attempts to construct another comprehensive model of preferable policymaking as a whole. The latter task would require presentation in the form of a dynamic graphic computer program, being much too complex for written static symbols. Even such a program would still be oversimplistic, with many essential extrarational components hard to represent in any currently available language, even if clearly imaginable (Gentner and Stevens 1983; Kosslyn 1983; Sheikh 1983). Still, the task of constructing dynamic computer models of central policymaking process-systems is worthwhile and can be very useful in providing heuristic models of preferable policymaking more isomorphic with stipulated optimal realities than the two-dimensional curves and graphs now filling texts. But this project will have to wait till computer models become an integral part of thinking and communication in policy sciences.

In this book select components, processes, and interactions of preferable policymaking under adversity are taken up, with the absence of integrated dynamic models hardly hurting the main investigation. But, further progress in understanding and improving policymaking, up to evolvement of a general societal command and control theory, will require dynamic public policymaking models capable of handling qualitatively (until new measurement scales and languages fitting the subject matter come along) complexity and multidimensionality within stochastic and random processes.

The treatment of preferable policymaking in this book is qualitative, identifying directions for necessary policymaking features but not the degrees to which these features must be realized to meet to various extents diverse levels of requirements. Quantification of high-quality policymaking requirements is impossible in part and unnecessary in part, for the following reasons:

1. Quantitative specification of many requirements goes beyond available concepts and scales. Thus, quantification of needed amounts of creativity is impossible in meaningful terms in the absence of operational definitions of various types of "creativity" and of "creativity deficits" in policymaking under adversity.
2. The probable sizes of policymaking errors and policymaking deficits vary among different policymaking cases, policymaking domains, and policymaking entities. Therefore, even if in a few cases the magnitude of required improvements can be guesstimated, this is impossible on the level of generalization adopted in this book. (It is interesting to ponder attempts to estimate sizes of errors in studies underlying policymaking, such as Henderson 1977. Even when such studies are possible, it is difficult to translate them into quantitative estimates of needed improvements in relevant elements of policymaking, in part because of the lack of appropriate languages and scales.)
3. The total amount of resources available for policymaking improvement in any polity at any time is limited. Therefore, preferable amounts of policymaking-improvement resources (including attention) to be devoted to upgrading different policymaking qualities depend on expected payoffs, on opportunity costs of multiuse improvement resources, and similar "marginal-utility" considerations applied to policymaking im-

provement, at least as a heuristic rule. Conclusions will differ among various polities and domains, theoretically inhibiting widely valid quantification of requirements, even assuming (incorrectly) the existence of suitable multidimensional scaling instruments.

Lighter tasks of allocation of priorities to different improvement directions suffer from comparable, though easier, difficulties. Thus, under different conditions various qualitative improvements may be more or less important, and changing combinations of improvements may interact positively or negatively. Some generalizations on preferable mixes of qualitative improvement directions are possible, with differentiation according to conditions. This task will be taken up within the context of improvement strategies in chapter 9.

Requirements of high-quality policymaking under adversity can be subsumed under seven main dimensions: mental-intellectual qualities; power concentration; visions, goals, and values; implementation management; infrastructure; self-reshaping abilitites; and overall policymaking culture. These seven dimensions permit construction of the central edifice of qualities needed for policymaking under adversity, as further worked out in the form of detailed specifications, in the next chapter.

*Mental-Intellectual Qualities*

In line with the "mind-of-government" metaphor, the concept of "mental-intellectual" qualities is used, but without any organistic implications. An alternative terminology would use the terms *rationality-extrarationality,* or some similar verbal symbols.

The term *intellectual* overlaps more or less with the term *rational* as used in most of decision literature (Barry and Hardin 1982; H. Brown 1978; Brunsson 1982; Elster 1979; Elster 1983; Gershuney 1978b; Gustafsson and Richardson 1979; Ross Harrison 1983; Hartwig 1978; Hennen 1976; Koertge 1979; Machan 1980; Popper 1967; Simon 1982 passim; B. Wilson 1970; and many more), with special attention to processual rationality (March 1978; Simon 1976a; Simon 1979b) and possible expansions of *rationality* beyond its usual meaning (Benn and Motrimoe 1976; Diesing 1962; Elster 1978; P. Hill et al. 1979; Johnson-Laird and Wason 1977; B. Klein, Appendix 1977; Parfit 1983; Pears 1984; Toulmain et al. 1979. But see the quite different approach of Habermas 1984). Cybernetic models are also very relevant, adding elements missing in many rationality models, such as various types of memories and knowledge, different modes of cognition, various computation abilities, and heuristic reasoning. (Compare the differences between Stafford Beer 1966, Stafford Beer 1975, and Stafford Beer 1981. Still valuable is Deutsch 1969.)

The term *mental* leads to essentially extrarational qualities of effective policymaking under adversity, such as tacit pattern recognition, imagination, inspiration, creativity, intuition in a number of forms (Bastick 1982), and additional capacities of the mind, as mentioned earlier in this chapter. Important mental qualities of policymaking are also energy and will, as partly considered later in conjunction with power concentration, and ability to make tragic choices (which is closely related also to values and visions and to power concentrations), up to fantasy and "realms of the unconscious" (Nalimov 1982). But, care must be taken not to let aesthetics and different stylistic preferences, such as legalistic ritualism (as distinct from the substance of the rule of law and related procedures), take over. Mental-intellectual qualities are to be assessed in terms of their contributions to policymaking outputs, not in terms of their innate merits according to various tastes and likings.

Relevant aspects of mental-intellectual qualities need adjustment to the particularities of policymaking under adversity, such as ultrachange, much complexity and uncertainty, futility of incrementalism, unavoidability of many failures and disappointments, and more. *Inter alia,* the special features of adversity require a suitable philosophy of knowledge and action for policymaking as a basis for necessary mental-intellectual qualities, as taken up in the next chapter.

Special problems are raised by the need to assure "cold" reasoning within suitable components of the policymaking process-system, as against the "hot" cognition and argumentation in much of politics. Related needs to protect some parts of the central minds of governments from public pressures and public control raise difficult issues, especially in democracies. The independence of courts, which often engage in important policymaking, well illustrates the possibilities for enclaves of independence within a democracy, as do sometimes central banks. The need for additional enclaves of reduced accountability for handling predicaments in democracies is recognized in some writings (e.g. Brecht 1978; Shonfield 1982), but still is widely ignored and does indeed raise grave problems, leading directly to the next subject of power concentration.

*Power Concentration*

To meet crucial policymaking requisites, a strong power-political base with much power concentration (and political-will amplification) is needed, especially when fragmented politics characterizes the actual situation. But, such power concentrations easily get out of hand, with disastrous consequences for values and society as a whole, in addition to ruinous policymaking. Also, power concentration (and political will amplification) unaccompanied by other major improvements in policymaking quality will often cause more harm than good by bringing about more determined pursuance of wrong policies based on mistaken policy paradigms. Thus, a basic quandary of governance, and policymaking, is posed by the requirement for "strong government" to handle main policy predicaments: without much power concentration, adversities cannot be handled adequately, but "strong government" can also easily aggravate policy predicaments and, much worse, tends to decay into evil and corrupt governance (partly considered in Dobel 1978).

In some respects, this dimension relates to the classical debate, whether power as such is good, as claimed for instance by Pope Gregory the Great; or bad, as concluded for instance by Jacob Burckhardt (Schmitt 1954, 21) and implied by some recent historical writings (P. Johnson 1983). A better formulation of the question is, under what conditions do various degrees and forms of power have diverse probabilities of results that are bad or good according to stipulated values?

Increasingly, powerful policy instruments multiply the potentials of power concentrations for worse and better, while present and expected policy predicaments require stronger power concentrations, without in any way reducing the possibility of such power resulting in worse situations. Hence, a major dilemma, as considered by political philosophy and political science since their beginnings. Debate continues, with diverse authors adopting contrary opinions (as illustrated within perspectives relevant for the concerns of this book by Gross 1982; Hayek 1979; Lowi 1979; Ophuls 1977; Wenk 1979). The limited but potentially potent contribution to this general controversy of the analysis here is the requisite that, for policymaking improvement under emerging conditions, much, though contained, power concentration, and political-will amplification are necessary. This, without necessarily increasing "political poverty" (Martinussen 1977, 183-85), which easily becomes a disruptive force.

Degrees of necessary power concentrations differ with conditions and traditions. Thus, in some Third World countries, military regimes may provide the only chance for essential stability and policymaking quality (Horowitz 1982), and advanced Western democracies might achieve necessary power concentrations with relatively minor and low-risk adjustments in governmental institutions, in part already taking place with the growing importance of presidents and prime ministers (Blondel 1980; Bunce 1981; Crossman 1972; Duverger 1980; Punnett 1977; Rose and Suleiman 1980; Rush 1984).

To repeat the important and unlikeable point: However risky and unpleasant in many respects, the analysis presented in this book leads to the conclusion that handling of present and emerging adversity requires power concentration, and political-will amplification, as essential bases for adequate policymaking. These must be contained through elections, accountability, etc.—both to preserve basic values and to avoid policymaking spoliation. A variety of checks and balances are essential and need further reinforcement to reduce dangers of power concentration, but, in many countries, there exists a clear need for more power concentration (and more political-will amplification). This dimension of high-quality policymaking requirements follows directly, as already indicated, from the needs of policymaking under adversity as also expressed in some of the policy principles considered in chapter 5, such as societal architecture with constructive destruction, and critical mass. On a broader level of analysis, achievement of policymaking autonomy, as considered in chapter 4, depends on power concentration in the central policymaking process-system. The need for power concentration also derives from other requisites, as considered in chapter 6. Thus:

- Achievement of broad perspectives and the overcoming of compartmentalized views requires concentrated superdepartmental power.
- Policy entrepreneurship and support for new options depends largely on central power centers not captured by vested status-quo interests.
- Agenda setting on the basis of overall perspectives, rather than aggregation of sectorial and departmental views within a power parallelogram dynamic, again depends on central power concentrations (and political will).
- Shortcuts through bureaucratic politics to transfigure implementation institutions depend on concentrated power (and strong political will).

And so on. Many of the policymaking-improvement possibilities to be discussed later also depend on support by strong power centers. Thus, to take a relatively simple proposal, establishment and useful operation of professional policy analysis units working on high-level decision problems depend primarily on the existence of strong power centers willing to support such units (Boston 1980; Dror 1985; R. Sanders 1973; W. Williams 1971).

An already-mentioned urgent and special case is posed by global policy predicaments, which require integrated and large-scale critical-mass-achieving policymaking. Nuclear proliferation, extensive and endemic wars, global energy and ecology issues, possible food scarcities—these illustrate adversities hard to handle within the present fragmented-to-anarchical global system. Whether relatively small changes might suffice to achieve adequate cooperation and move on to compact power-political bases for global policymaking or whether radical changes in the global power structure are necessary to meet threatening predicaments is a question on which opinions differ (Bull 1977; Dror 1980b; Falk 1975; Mendlovitz 1975). But, in one way or another, the global arena is in need of power concentration so as to be able to engage in essential policymaking (and implementation) under adversity.

## Visions, Values, and Goals

Leaving aside axiological issues and adopting a stance of seeking a value-free approach within an ethic of responsibility (Dror 1983a, new introduction), the author holds that the dimension of visions, values, and goals is essential for an adequate treatment of policymaking under adversity, despite the difficulties it raises.

Main issues involving visions, values, and goals as essential requisites of high-quality policymaking under adversity include:

1. Some adversities cannot be adequately handled without changes in the main values at present underlying much of actual policymaking. Thus, the dangers of nuclear holocaust cannot be significantly reduced without changes in nationalistic values, which are still far from being understood (Gellner 1983); growing abysses between rich and poor countries cannot be decreased without changes in empathic values in the highly industrialized nations; and possible ecological constraints cannot be accommodated without transformations in consumption and other values (Attfield 1983; Gershuny 1978a; Laszlo 1977a; Laszlo et al. 1977b; Schumacher 1973). Possible needs to "pull back the bounds of economic self-advancement" (Hirsch 1976, 76); to get rid of, or at least contain and redirect, "rugged individualism" (Hsu 1983; Parfit 1983); and move toward a new social ethics illustrate tasks combining societal architecture with policymaking capacities to guide value changes, posing supreme challenges to policymaking qualities, not the least because of the dangers of misuse of such capacities. These dangers, in turn, lead to the issues of the moral values of the minds of governments themselves, as taken up soon.
2. Changes in even deeper layers of society may be needed, reaching down to mass-psychological features (e.g. Badcock 1983). This may be beyond the capacity of policymaking, perhaps luckily so, otherwise misuses would be terrible. But, as far as something for the better can be done, collective visions may be the only practical approach available with present states of knowledge (perhaps in combination with "identity guidelines," "spellbinders," "soulcraft," and "heroes." See E. Erikson 1975, 22; Willner 1983; Will 1983; and Goode 1978 respectively).
3. A shared realistic vision is a main requisite for effective policymaking in a number of ways, such as to increase commitment of policymakers; to mobilize support and participation; and to achieve compact policymaking within a pluralistic political system. The "energizing" effects of

shared visions, their impacts in encouraging efforts and innovation (within the limits of the visions, which also serve as blinders), and their aiding in integrating decisions make shared visions an effective tool of policymaking, in addition to serving as a direction giver (Cerny 1980; Gelman 1981; Wriggins 1969). Therefore, realistic visions are an especially essential policymaking requisite when societal architecture is in order or aspired to.

4. The importance of values and visions in motivating main actors within the central policymaking process-system is especially interesting. Without such values and visions, policymaking is dominated by what has been called "wantons" (Frankfurt 1971), in the sense of quasi-instinctive desires, approximating some surrealistic political science models of actors behaving economically to maximize their egocentric power drives and material desires. Metaphorically, visions and values serve as a "superego" for the central mind of government, with care being taken (a) to understand the concept correctly in psychoanalytical terms (e.g. Bettelheim 1983); (b) to apply it only metaphorically and gingerly to policymaking; and (c) to remember propensities to invent ideologies to justify interests (Starbuck 1982). The next step is to move into a theory of "political will," with special attention not only to the "determining" facets of political will but also to the problem of Akrasia, with much of policymaking being deviated by current pressures and "wantons" from values and goals to which main policymakers and policymaking cultures are committed. (On discourse exploring some related concept on the level of individual intentions and action, see Korner 1974, passim; and Rorty 1980). This raises issues going beyond this book, but the importance of values and visions within the "psychological" dimensions of the central policymaking process-system deserves attention, relating back in part to some earlier remarks in chapter 4 while policymaking autonomy was being explored.

5. In contrast to "visionary" visions, "realistic" visions are needed to avoid self-defying decisionmaking, such as caused by rigid dogmas, and disruptive frustrations, caused by many forms of overexpectations. This, subject to the special needs of revolutionary groups and the particular problems of policymaking in revolutions, discussed earlier; to the roles of ideology in politics (Seliger 1976) and policymaking; and to the social and political functions of utopia (P. Alexander and Gill 1984; Goodwin and Taylor 1982; Manuel and Manuel 1979)—all very important matters with implications for politics beyond the scope of this book.

6. Hardest of all, the contents of the "conscience of the mind of government" (compare use of the concept "conscience of the state" in P. Marsh 1979) needs reconsideration. In particular, to meet adversities, a new period of "quest for policymaking effectiveness" may be necessary (to be compared, as a historic analogue, with periods of quest for national efficiency, see e.g. Brenna 1975; G. Searle 1971). This raises anew issues

in the search for democracy and efficiency (C. Bohret 1971; D. Yates 1982), on the level of policymaking output-values versus policymaking pattern-values, with the harsh necessity to allocate more priority to the first to meet essential needs of policymaking under adversity, as already looked at in chapter 5 and as further elaborated in chapter 7.

7. The question of the morality of the central minds of governments appears in all its nakedness in an aggravated form when the handling of visions, values, and goals by central policymaking is accented as essential for high-quality policymaking under adversity. In the exploration of some components of a philosophy for policymaking in the next chapter, this difficult subject will be looked at from the perspective of the limited stance of this book in value issues. At present, the importance of the matter is acknowledged, while the limits of policy sciences per se as a basis for providing satisfactory and widely acceptable answers is asserted and admitted, subject to later reconsideration.

Not surprisingly, the subject as a whole is fraught with serious dangers and rich in intractable problematics. Thus:

- Value changes and vision creation and diffusion are spontaneous processes. While it might be possible to synthesize limited value systems and planned visions (Luhmann 1968), this is a matter loaded with perils, well brought out in Orwell's *1984* (Orwell 1954).
- Whether a vision moves in the direction of utopia or dystopia is, after all, a matter of subjective and intersubjective judgment. The improvement of the effectiveness of policymaking by supporting it with and enslaving it to a barbarian value system, which policymaking is made to serve, is a dismal possibility, the realities of which have been demonstrated at great cost in history. Less "effective" but also less-fanaticism-prone policymaking may, therefore, be much preferable as a rule.
- Nevertheless, value innovation and realistic visions and even metaphysical beliefs may be necessary for high-aspiration policymaking and, perhaps, for pleasant and responsive governance as a whole (as apparently thought by Mannheim when postulating in his late writings religion as necessary for democracy, Mannheim 1950). High-aspiration policymaking must often advance on a thin razor's edge over the pit of fanaticism and through control on one side and the tomb of nihilism and value relativism on the other side. Such acrobatic dexterity being quite scarce in policymaking reality, the Hobson's choice remains in respect to the value dimension between abandoning high aspirations for policymaking or trying to achieve unprecedented levels of policymaking quality, including value and vision encouragement, with all associated dangers; or waiting for little understood social processes to provide suitable policymaking infrastructures and policymaking-independent answers, including value and vision transformations—which implies putting one's trust on *fortuna* in one version or another.

The problem is well brought out by W. Y. Elliot in a passage dealing with epic, but applicable to the related issue of realistic vision: "It is of extraordinary interest to the student of politics to contemplate what form of modern epic could take that could be a political culture-shaper in times which are being so punished as ours are and which are looking, because of their very hardships and severities of testing of the system, for a rarity that will not be worse than the disease but will cure the disease and put us back in the path of creative public policy" (Cuthbertson 1975, xvii).

Not having any satisfactory solution to these contradictory needs and dangers, and being quite sure that those who think they have a solution are furthest away from having one, the author believes that the vision, value, and goal dimension of high-quality policymaking under adversity must be recognized and diagnosed as very important, very dangerous, but unavoidable, and in need of much thought.

## Implementation Management

Studies of historic cases (e.g. C. Black 1975; Findley 1980; Orlovsky 1981) combine with lessons of contemporary policymaking to indicate the hopelessness of achieving impacts on realities by innovative policy decisions, unless accompanied by careful implementation management (Bardach 1977; Dunsire 1978; Edwards and Sharkansky 1978; Grindle 1980; Hargrove 1975; Pressman and Wildavsky 1973; Radian 1980; James Thompson 1980; W. Williams 1980b; Williams 1982). Therefore, implementation management is an essential dimension of high-quality policymaking under adversity, with care to be taken not to go too deep into details of management and administration, which would overdilute the concept of policymaking. This dimension is quite clear in its main contents, with some subjects to be taken up in the next chapter.

## Infrastructure

The infrastructure dimension leads into deeper issues and greater complexities. It crosscuts the other dimensions, with relevance for all of them. Societal stocks of knowledge with high-quality human resources, widely accepted worldviews, alternative policy ideas floating around, degrees of policy enlightenment of different publics, broad attitudes toward various forms of rationality and openmindedness and some contents of culture itself—these illustrate features and propensities of society that constitute policymaking infrastructure and that strongly condition policymaking under adversity.

The needs of policymaking under adversity in respect to infrastructure are not difficult to formulate in the abstract, such as much and rapidly growing policy-relevant knowledge; innovative policy alternative percolating in society without extreme policy theologies; many high-quality persons eager to take part in policymaking; commitment to basic values of democracy together with openness to much change; propensities toward compact politics, and so on. But, the problem faced within the central minds of governments is quite different from such exhortations, namely, how to build up required policymaking infrastructures and how to utilize them, and/or how to compensate for the absence of important elements of infrastructure. Long-range investments in advanced research and in higher education on one hand and the partial isolation of central policymaking process-system elements from harmful influences by inappropriate aspects of infrastructure on the other hand illustrate possible, but difficult, approaches. The catch is that very high-quality policymaking is necessary for the accelerated building up of relevant infrastructure, while in turn such high-quality policymaking often presupposes the existence of at least parts of a supportive infrastructure. Difficulties in arriving at higher education policies in Western democracies well illustrate the hazards in trying to develop good policymaking-infrastructure policies even in highly developed countries (Daalder and Shils 1982).

Problems of policymaking infrastructure are especially acute in developing countries, where lack of suitable infrastructure imposes *inter alia* in three ways on central policymaking: (a) weak societal problem-handling capacities, increasing loads on central policymaking; (b) counter-high-quality-policymaking contents of infrastructure and lack of infrastructure necessary for upgrading policymaking, depressing the quality of central policymaking; and (c) necessity for central policymaking to build up suitable infrastructure, within its radical societal architecture tasks. When, thus, many of the policymaking infrastructures somehow taken for granted in most of Western-conditioned political science are absent or scant, the problematics of policymaking under adversity take on a much aggravated form, posing additional requirements hardly given realistic treatment in most of Western literature presuming to deal with the Third World.

*Overall Policymaking Culture*

Some needed transformations in policymaking so as adequately to handle adversity can be considered best, however vaguely, in terms of overall central policymaking "style" or "culture" (without taking up some of the fashionable themes of renewed interest in organizational culture, e.g. Jelinek, Smircich, and Hirsch 1983; T. Peters and Waterman 1983). This dimension can also be viewed as partly overlapping the "mental" sub-dimension considered earlier but deserves attention on its own.

However difficult to pin down, and perhaps even abstruse, high-quality policymaking depends on a whole cluster of cultural features and even civilization and *Zeitgeist*. To keep this matter as concrete as possible, the dimension here is limited to policy culture. But, with the exception of cleaved societies where policy culture can be very different from overall culture, or where an "overall" culture does not exist, policy-culture contents are conditioned by broader culture, civilization, and localized *Zeitgeist* features. Thus, affective maps (Osgood, May, and Miron 1975), language (Fishman 1972; M. Halliday 1978; Sebeok 1976) broad value and thinking patterns (Rokeach 1973), and overall cultural configurations (Marx 1964; M. Wiener 1980) can exert dominant influences on policy culture, illustrating earlier-mentioned infrastructure impacts.

Policymaking-culture requirements go far beyond the "civic culture" concept (Almond and Verba 1963; Almond and Verba 1970), though partly in the same direction. Main needs of high-quality policymaking include: tolerance, and some positive support, for clinical attitudes and "cold reasoning" on "red hot" issues; highly developed "rationality" elements; doubts about policy theologies; creativity propensities; contemplative, as well as enthusiastic, attitudes to pressing issues; belief in worth and efficacy of policymaking; high, but not absurd, aspiration levels; commitment to realistic vision, without fanaticism; strong learning ability; high tolerance of ambiguity; and so on—with nearly every requisite discussed in this book having a reflection in policy-culture desiderata.

Little reliable knowledge exists on the factual distribution of relevant policymaking cultural traits and their dynamics. No general trend can be discerned. Thus, there is no theoretical or empiric basis for any assumption on "progress" in the direction of more advanced policy culture contents. Indeed, as considered in chapter 3, persistent and disheartening policy plights may call forth waves of irrationality, in diverse shapes—which also may result from other causes, including culture-endogenous variables.

Policy culture is not an easy target for intervention. Long-range "cultural engineering" (Mazuri 1972) may be possible under totalitarian regimes and/or in undeveloped societies, with often unclear long-term results. In more open societies, schooling and the mass media provide tools that might be used to introduce improvements into policy culture, such as by habituating thinking to uncertainty. But, such attempts lead easily to abuses and their effectiveness is not assured. In any case, little in this direction is attempted in practice (for an interesting experiment, see Bolt Beranek and Newman Inc. 1980) and not much thought is devoted to it. Some specific possibilities and issues are taken up in chapter 7.

There exist possibilities to influence the cultures of central policymakers, especially their more professional strata. This can happen naturally; or by design, through selective recruitment from subcultures with specific policy cultures (Suleiman 1978); and/or through suitable training and development activities, after initial recruitment. How large a differential in cultures between policymaking enclaves and the population at large is feasible and desirable, especially in democracies, is an open question. Simple assumptions and monodimensional participatory values (Benello and Roassopoulos 1971; Kramer 1972) contribute little to clarification of these difficult issues, which also will be looked at in later chapters.

### Self-Reshaping Abilities

The quality deficits of policymaking under adversity and constant changes in its requirements make very good self-reshaping abilities into a main dimension of high-quality policymaking under adversity. In metaphorical language, the central mind of government needs an ability "to change its mind" (Dennet 1980; ch. 16) on itself, to engage in metacognition and to restructure itself.

Putting boundaries on this dimension is not easy. In particular, close interdependencies between central policymaking on one hand and governance and politics as a whole on the other lead toward expanded needs for self-reshaping abilities. Metapolicymaking, in the sense of policymaking on policymaking itself (Dror 1983a; esp. 164ff.), is essential but inadequate. Also needed is a lot of governance redesign, in part as integral to policymaking reshaping and in part as dealing with closely interlocking parts of policymaking infrastructure. The upgrading of self-reshaping abilities is consequently a first step in trying to improve policymaking. *Inter alia,* involved in self-reshaping is a needed capacity by the central mind of government to exit itself and to look at itself critically as if from the outside.

### Policymaking Incapacities: Theoretic Considerations

If requirements of high-quality policymaking under adversity constitute one of the pillars of this book, then policymaking incapacities constitute the second one. There are policymaking incapacities that explain many, including the more serious, failures to meet policymaking requirements and that produce serious policymaking deficits. Moving from explanation to prescription, policymaking incapacities constitute a main barrier to improvement that must be surmounted or bypassed.

The concept of "incapacity" as used here refers to inherent features of policymaking process-systems and the materials out of which they are construed as explaining many policymaking performance inadequacies, but is not identical with the performance inadequacies themselves. To give a simple but illuminating example: Decision makers make many errors in handling uncertainty, constituting performance inadequacies. The underlying cause of many such errors is the incapacities of human thinking in respect to uncertainty, taking the form of specific bias propensities (Kahnemann, Slovic, and Tversky 1982). Differently expressed, the concept of policymaking incapacities goes deeper, by one or two layers, than behavioral policymaking weaknesses, but without reaching ultimate causes through far-reaching regression or reduction,—about which very little is known (comparable to visual illusions, which still defy satisfactory explanation in terms of "ultimate causes"; e.g. see N. Wade 1982).

A classical and well-known illustration of built-in incapacities is the iron law of oligarchy, formulated by Robert Michels (1962). Lighter in vein, but often loaded with insights, are the observed incapacity regularities of Parkinson's Law (Parkinson 1980), Murphy's Laws (Bloch 1977; Bloch 1980; Bloch 1982), the Peter Principle (Peter and Hull 1969), and similar (Dickson 1978; J. Gall 1975) types.

The main types of incapacities salient to policymaking weaknesses include, for instance:

- Inherent inability of diagnostic processes to comprehend new patterns because of dependence on former cognitive maps and doctrines for cognizing changing reality.
- Inbuilt limitations of group decision making, such as seeking of mutual support as a main driving force.
- Congenital features of organizations, such as trends toward incrementalism and satisficing.
- Rigid features of mass behavior, such as tendencies toward emotionalism and susceptibility to symbolic manipulation.
- Internal antinomies and tensions between various structures and processes, such as between politicians and civil servants. Such antinomies and tensions make important positive contributions to policymaking such as related to the advantages of division of labor and specializations, but they also produce unavoidable limitations and frictions, which constitute built-in incapacities.
- Underlying all these and other incapacities, basic features of human thinking and mental-emotional processes.

These and other built-in policymaking incapacities will be examined in respect to specific policymaking processes and components in chapter 7. Here, some more theoretic aspects of the concept and its implications for policymaking are further considered, because of the crucial importance of the idea of "inherent incapacities" for this book as a whole. Broader exploration of the concept and its implications for political science, and social sciences as well as humanities as a whole, are left for another book (Dror, in work).

The concept of built-in (or, metaphorically, "congenital") incapacities, has far-reaching implications for a general theory of societal command and control on one hand and for a general theory of governance on the other hand. Within the limited world of interest of *Policymaking under Adversity*, the idea of policymaking incapacities serves to explore, partly to explain, and to try to overcome policymaking-quality deficits. Specifications of main policymaking incapacities also serve as main targets and constraints for improvement approaches and improvement proposals.

For the above tasks, it is necessary to work out policymaking inadequacies in respect to specific policymaking-quality requirements, as done in the next chapter. Theoretically a framework for doing so is provided by presentation of a main proposition and some examination of its components.

A main proposition on policymaking incapacities can be formulated, for the limited purposes of this book, as follows: *Currently known core policymaking institutions, including structures and processes and their interactions, have limited maximum performance capacities, error propensities, and resulting incapacities. These result partly from inbuilt characteristics of the process-system and of the materials out of which it is made. Therefore, main maximum performance capacities can be raised and main error propensities and incapacities can be overcome only through significant changes in main features of relevant structures, processes and materials.*

The first part of the proposition is a truism. After all, every entity, institution, and material, as well as their interactions and combination have limits; never mind if this fact is expressed in economic terminology as "production function," in systems terminology as "transformation function," in biology as "stress limits and congenital defects," in engineering as "tolerance margins," in information theory as "channel capacity," in anthropology as "functions adjustment ability," and so on. But the idea of maximum performance limits, while floating around, has been underutilized in social sciences, despite its explanatory potentials.

The statement that core policymaking structures, processes, and materials have inbuilt error propensities is more powerful. In addition to serving as a guide to empiric work, it has a nonobvious substantive content. More is claimed here than the logical complement of inbuilt maximum performance capacities, which states that there are necessarily also inbuilt noncapacities domains, namely, those outside the maximum performance capacities. (This is not a sharp dichotomy with a clear dividing line but a matter of degrees with "pure-type" polar positions and many in-between gradations and mixes). The additional positive idea of the concept of error propensities is that active wrong performance is built into the very nature of core policymaking structures, processes, and materials. The accent here is not on an absence of capacities but on the presence of error-producing factors. This distinction has important practical implications, in addition to its theoretic interest: Noncapacities can sometimes be handled by adjusting the scope of policymaking to exclude as far as possible domains of noncapacity. But inbuilt broad-scope error propensities often cannot thus be treated until policymaking as such, or at least the error-propensity core processes, institutions, and materials, wither away or are radically changed.

The distinction between noncapacities and active error propensities is important but complex because of overlaps and functional interdependences. To take a few simple test distinctions: (a) tasks beyond a certain threshold are beyond capacities, that is, they are in the domain of noncapacity; (b) tasks within the threshold are nevertheless subjected to error propensities actively causing mistakes; but, to complicate matters, (c) tasks in the domain of noncapacities nevertheless undertaken by policymaking will be performed with many mistakes, not only because of inbuilt error propensities but also because of noncapacities; and (d) the theoretic possibility that what are called error propensities are the result of more complex dimensions of noncapacities adds a further complicaton to the whole matter.

Further logical, semantic, functional, and empiric analysis of these distinctions is necessary for construction of a general theory of governmental capacities and incapacities. For the limited purpose of the present book, the above pragmatic distinctions are sufficient. In this book the concept of incapacity is used to include both noncapacity and error propensity.

The next two and last parts of the proposition, which can conveniently be handled together, are important. Here, an empiric-theoretic statement is made, namely, that the incapacities are in part inbuilt characteristics of policymaking process-systems. The next and final statement flows in part from the last one and is also empiric-theoretic and susceptible to some testing, namely, that maximum performance capacities and main incapacities cannot be changed through marginal alterations in their process-system procreators.

Exploration of the concept of incapacity and utilization of that concept for explaining policymaking realities and trying to improve them, are one thing; trying to provide a theoretic explanation for the present shape of main incapacities is quite another thing—not strictly necessary operationally, but important to strengthen the prima facie credibility of the concept and to provide a basis for theory building and for derivation of middle-range propositions.

As mentioned, these tasks are taken up in another book within the broader contexts of politics and governance as a whole. Still, preliminary exposition of some relevant speculative conjectures may serve to understand and utilize better the idea of incapacities within the narrower, though still very broad, domain of policymaking under adversity. Three alternative "pure" speculations may serve to explain the existing capacity limits and error propensities of human institutions in general and policymaking-related processes and materials in particular.

1. Biological and biocultural evolution: According to this view, main modes of thinking are the product of natural evolution, with the contents of culture being largely constrained and conditioned by the biological evolution of *Homo sapiens*. Within such a "pure" approach, one might like to start with higher primate "thinking" processes (Premack and Premack 1983; Rajecki 1983; S. Walker 1983) and move through the concept of "human primate" (Passingham 1983; also relevant is Stanley 1981, *passim*); and go on to human biological evolution as imprinting mental processes and cultural artifacts (Dawkins 1984; Humphrey 1983). The earlier versions of biosociology (E. Wilson 1975; E. Wilson 1978, as discussed, for instance, in A. Caplan 1979) and more recent versions of "coevolution" (Lumsden and E. Wilson 1981; Lumsden and E. Wilson 1983, followed by Lopreato 1984) illustrate such approaches. Interestingly, H. Simon also proposed some similar explanations for bounded rationality (H. Simon 1983, ch. 2), though in a quite enigmatic way and with some doubtful arguments, such as lack of distinction between "weak altruism" and "enlightened self-interest" (H. Simon 1983, 58, to be compared with H. Margolis 1982) and an assumption of the continuous "emptyness" of the world (H. Simon 1983, 106).
2. Cultural evolution: Here government is viewed as an artifact integrated into culture, broadly limited but not shaped by genetic evolution. Within such a perspective, the long periods of prehistory must be taken into account, with the development of modern government being a relatively very recent process. Assuming large variations in culture, including government, and relatively rapid change, this speculation holds that adjustment of culture to changing conditions can still take generations and some core components of society, such as rulers, will have some constant features over different societies and periods. Therefore, with changing environments, cultural artifacts may lag behind the new conditions—demonstrating various incapacities. (Some writings in such a direction include Childe 1981; G. Clark 1970; G. Clark 1983; Corning 1983; Festinger 1983; Geertz 1983; M. Harris 1977; Ruse 1974; Service 1971; Service 1975; Swanson 1983; different but relevant are Guha 1982; Richard Nelson and Winter 1983; Peterson 1983. Related issues are discussed in Langton 1979, not to speak of the classical works of Alfred Vierkandt and, much later, William F. Ogburn).

3. Social change: According to this view, while human institutions are limited by genetic endowments and cultural embedment, evolutionary concepts do not apply. Government should be looked at more as part of society, with possibilities for invention and development. Similar to the incapacities of science and technology till recently are the many inadequacies of government at present—but no grand theory of genetic and cultural limits and evolution is necessary or useful for explaining them, even if we lack an adequate theory of social change. Various versions of Marxism and other "lead-factor" speculations can be amalgamated into the social-change perspective, with innovations in one or another facet of society, such as production technology, being regarded as the determining factor in social change as a whole.

It is important to note that if, according to a social-change perspective, policymaking is viewed as determined by one or another infrastructure facet, then little can be done about improving it separately. The question of the changeability of policymaking independent from changing related features of society is open, with strong interpretrations between policymaking and politics, for instance, requiring handling of their improvement partly in tandem.

As just illustrated, hopes for improving policymaking significantly depend on basic views on the factors shaping present realities: The realism of improvement ambitions is low if genetic factors are conditioning main human capacities, such as decisionmaking. If cultural evolution is the dominant factor, then improvement has more of a chance, though it may take a long time and depend on jumps that cannot be predicted. If improvement of governance is a matter for social change depending on human endeavors, similar to scientific research and development, complex and unknown factors still condition success, but there is much scope for concentrated effort.

I am somewhat doubtful whether any one of the positions briefly outlined above is adequate and whether any combination of them is much better. Probably, biogenetic evolution and cultural evolution do play a role, as do various social change processes, including "accidental" ones. But it is doubtful whether currently available paradigms can explain the evolvement of human institutions, much less expose their changeability in the longer run. In the short run, including the periods dealt with in the present book, existing incapacities are a given fact and proposed changes must handle them as stubborn realities. But, in the face of ignorance on the changeability of policymaking qualities, I vote for the position of Austin Ranney: "If the alternative in this case is the resigned acceptance of human impotence and passivity in the face of human misery, then surely political engineering, with all its faults and failures, beats that" (Ranney 1976, 147).

With the adoption of such an activist posture, the contradiction between policymaking-quality requirements and incapacities built into policymaking structures, processes and materials still must be recognized. This poses a great challenge to improvement endeavors, requiring careful and deliberate redesign approaches, as considered in chapter 9. But, before further examination of improvement possibilities, the generalities of the theoretic discourse about policymaking incapacities will be supplemented and worked out in the next chapter by detailed consideration of policymaking specifications, realities, and deficits.

# 7

# Policymaking Specifications, Realities, Deficits

## Nature of Endeavor

Following general consideration of requirements of policymaking under adversity versus incapacities in chapter 6, the present chapter considers twenty-one main specifications for policymaking under adversity. In line with the preview provided in chapter 6, each specification of a requirement of high-quality policymaking under adversity is contrasted with incapacities and realities, leading to identification of some main policymaking deficits.

Most of the twenty-one specifications can be located gravity-centerwise within one of the main dimensions of high-quality policymaking, as developed in chapter 6, but some specifications belong equally to a number of dimensions, and most of the specifications are relevant to more than one dimension. Therefore, no explicit allocation of specifications by dimensions is made. The principal relevance to different dimensions is obvious from the contents of the specifications.

The twenty-one specifications are not a complete set of high-quality policymaking requisites but a selected subset representing main forms and aspects. Other formulations and taxonomies are possible but do not change the overall picture. *Inter alia*, the specifications reflect different levels and aspects of high-quality policymaking requirements, bringing out again the existential features of policymaking and related processes.

As made obvious by the complexity of the specifications, books can and should be written on each one of them (and have been written on many, as illustrated by the provided references). The purpose of this chapter is to present a conspectus of requirements of policymaking under adversity, not detailed treatment of any single specification. A comprehensive view of the problematics of policymaking under adversity being aimed at, a price in terms of inadequate depth of treatment has to be paid in order to arrive at a general perspective without undue protraction.

One main requirement of better policymaking under adversity is the advancement of policy sciences. This subject is treated separately, in chapter 8 building on the more policymaking-inherent requirements and realities, as considered in the present chapter.

In line with the pointillistic approach adopted in this chapter, as explained earlier, no comprehensive model is provided, nor are interdependencies between the different specifications worked out. Accordingly, it does not matter very much if some issues are located in one or another specification, as long as the different specifications and other discourses add up to a coherent though incomplete subset of policymaking requirements, realities, and deficits that is representative of the not fully presented multidimensional set as a whole.

## Integrative Policymaking Philosophy

It may seem strange that examination of high-quality policymaking-under-adversity specifications starts with the need for an integrative policymaking philosophy. Need for an overall philosophic basis for policymaking receives scant recognition within the mainstreams of policy studies literature (recent partial exceptions are illustrated by P. Checkland 1981; Collingridge 1982; Goodin 1982). Even more, the very idea of an integrative policymaking philosophy as an essential requirement of high-quality policymaking is out of tune with contemporary policymaking cultures, if not an anthema to "common-sense" practitioners and narrow professionals. Such attitudes in central minds of governments, together with the scarcity of suitable treatments in the literature, express and constitute main incapacities, hindering development and utilization of an integrative policymaking philosophy.

Without presuming here and now to undertake construction of an integrated policymaking philosophy adjusted to an epoch of adversity, the author can indicate a number of main elements of such a philosophy and of the issues to be handled by such a philosopy.

### Axiology

Value issues are a subject of policymaking philosophy that receives much and growing attention. (Good discussions are provided by F. Fischer 1980 and Homann 1980. Prevailing opinions are represented by Tribe 1972. Ongoing work is reflected in the journals *Social Philosophy and Policy* and *Philosophy and Public Affairs*.) Having discussed the matter and criticized main trends elsewhere (Dror 1983a, New Introduction), I limit myself here to mentioning axiology as a main part of a necessary policymaking philosophy and as one receiving much attention. Dominant trends are open to debate but at least raise many of the important issues.

What is especially missing is help to policymaking as a goal-seeking process, as distinct from normative approaches, which postulate particular values for policymaking, on one hand, and from "effectiveness" approaches, which concentrate on achieving better benefit-cost results with goals assumed as given, often hidden behind terms such as *utilities* or *preference functions*, on the other hand. What is needed is a "philosophy of value-seeking" to serve as a base for approaches, methods, and techniques; and, more important, to provide heuristic guidance to the crucial realistic-vision dimension of policymaking, all the more important under adversity—when values and realistic visions need revision. A basic starting point is to get rid of the simplistic notion still appearing in the literature that science can derive ultimate values (e.g. Sperry 1983).

*Epistemology*

The situation is quite different in respect to epistemology, which constitutes another crucial part of policymaking philosophy. In the absence of careful attention to development of epistemological approaches fitting the needs of policymaking under adversity, "practicalism" dominates and policymaking follows misleading appearances of verisimilitude, while large parts of policy sciences claim allegiance to inapplicable philosophies of science.

Main elements for building a suitable epistimology for policymaking under adversity do exist in literature, including:

- Schemata for perceiving parts of realities in policy-relevant "systems" patterns (e.g. P. Checkland 1981; Churchman 1982), though more attention to "process" perspectives is necessary, as considered in chapter 1.
- Some inklings of recognition of uncertainty as dominating reality, with proposed radical adjustments in policy thinking and in policy-oriented disciplines (Shackle 1961; Shackle 1972). Also relevant is work on multi-value logic. (Rosser and Turquette 1977; rather technical, but still very relevant is Shoesmith and Smiley, especially chapter 15).
- Applications of Popper to policymaking, with decisions being regarded as based on conjectures and as needing constant revision with the help of encouraged refutations. (Albert 1978; Albert 1980; Collingridge 1982. Popper is conveniently discussed in Schilpp 1974, but Popper 1972a, Popper 1972b, and Popper 1972c are essential readings for any serious approaches to policymaking philosophy. I am speaking about Popper's philosophy of scientific knowledge as fitting in the main policymaking, not his "piecemeal social engineering" which I regard as not fitting policymaking under adversity, similar to Braybrooke and

Lindblom 1963. Also doubtful are Popper's political conclusions, as surveyed for instance in Spinner 1978; Spinner 1982; and Vernon 1976. Neither am I discussing Popper's applicability to the physical sciences, which is quite another matter.)

- Some literature on "reason" and "sufficient justification for action," which is very relevant to the cardinal policymaking problem of adequate evidence for preferring one option over another (e.g. Darwall 1983; Falco 1979; McGinn 1983; Shope 1983; Stemmer 1983; Swain 1981).
- Recent interest in additional approaches to *Verstehen* (e.g. hermeneutics, see Baumann 1978; J. Howard 1983; Rabinow and Sullivan 1979; John Thompson 1981) may provide inputs into suitable bases of knowledge for policymaking, but care must be taken not to displace strict, though soft, criteria for judging conjectures as based well enough to serve policymaking, with purely subjective speculations and "interpretations."

Much remains to be done before epistemology that fits policymaking under adversity reaches required levels. Thus, missing are adequate treatments of situations of indeterminacy and quasi chaos, and needed revisions in "justification" for action in the face of far-reaching uncertainty, but enough is available in the literature to permit some progress in constructing an explicit epistemology for policymaking under adversity. Nevertheless, very little has been done in such a direction: With some exceptions, most philosophers working in epistemology are not interested in policymaking; and even the few so interested are quite ignorant about policymaking. Worse, and less justifiable, policy scientists, with no more than a few exceptions, are quite ignorant about relevant work in philosophy and not even aware of the possible relevance of such work for policymaking.

*Philosophy of Action*

In philosophy, work goes on related to a philosophy of action, going back to Kant and continued by contemporary thinkers (such as D. Davidson 1980; and Watkins 1970, Watkins 1975, and Watkins 1978, in addition to Albert 1978 and Albert 1980, mentioned above, and many more). Especially relevant to policymaking are treatments of "goal-directed action" (e.g. Cranach et al. 1982; Cranach and Harré 1982); German work on "action theory" (unusually well collected in the several volumes of Lenk 1977-81); and broad approaches to the logic of decisions (e.g. Jeffrey 1983). Heuristically relevant are also treatments of "intention" (Anscombe 1966; Diamond and Teichman 1980; Searle 1983), of free will (Inwagen 1983), of the mind (Anscombe 1981), of practical reason (Korner 1974), and more.

Relevant, too, is work on "rationality," discussed elsewhere, and related treatments of "having reasons" (Schick 1983), praxeology (Skirbekk 1983), and reprocessing of classical writings, such as by Max Weber, within an action theory perspective (S. Turner 1983).

As against such important concerns that stand in the center of the modern philosophy of action, some issues continue to be neglected. Thus, to return to an already-mentioned issue of cardinal significance for policymaking under adversity, the special features of far-reaching uncertainty receive scant attention and the unique conditions of "decision making as fuzzy gambles" are ignored in most of the philosophy of action, with the exception of some beginnings in "multivalue" and "plural value" logic (Rosser and Turquette 1977; Shoesmith and Smiley 1978).

Also to be mentioned here are "essentialistic" schools, as represented by Heidegger, which need confrontation within a suitable philosophy of policymaking.

All in all, some components of an integrative policymaking philosophy do exist, but (a) much remains to be done to build up an integrative policymaking philosophy; (b) most of policy studies and policy-relevant disciplines ignore available components of policymaking philosophy; and (c) policymaking reality completely ignores such available components and is quite closed to the very idea of being aided by a policymaking philosophy. These three points add up to quite a large policymaking-quality deficit in the central minds of governments and in the knowledge infrastructure of policymaking.

Such quality deficits are related to incapacities that are inherent, or at least deeply rooted, in policymaking realities. Pressures of current events, dominating practical policymaking cultures, and lack of suitably qualified policy professionals explain in part underutilization of available policymaking-philosophy elements. Characteristics of the community of policy researchers, as partly considered in chapter 8, explain some of the underdevelopments of policymaking philosophy and the ignorance of existing policymaking-philosophy elements in contemporary policy sciences.

More fundamental issues are posed by the hypothetical possibility that the very exigencies of decision making preclude application of philosophic insights, even if available. To speculate, it might be that the time pressures, tensions, and stubborn realities of policymaking condition decision making so as to enforce action without justifiable reasons; to make "practicalism" (quite different from "pragmatism" in the correct sense, which is a quite valuable philosophy for policymaking) the only feasible mode; and to displace *vita contemplative* facets of the philosophy of policymaking by quite different modalities of *vita activa*. The little tentative thinking available on the psychology of Weltanschauungen supplies some basis for such speculations (Jaspers 1960), as do life histories of some rulers who combined much power with philosophic inclinations, such as Marcus Aurelius and Friedrich the Great (Gaxotte 1973), but, with present ignorances, this is a matter for speculations rather than conjectures. This is an important subject for political theory, touching upon the consistency and possibility of the important ideal of a philosopher-king.

On a more mundane level, a blind alley of policymaking may be faced here: To improve policymaking, more openness to basically different thinking on policy issues may be necessary, as presented by some elements of a policymaking philosophy, but to be open to such thinking, policymaking must be of high quality already. Similar to the earlier-noted blind alley of much need for policymaking infrastructure by exactly those countries that need high-quality policymaking to build up such an infrastructure, here are closed loops of policymaking inadequacies, posing difficult challenges to improvement efforts. These are special types of incapacity loops that need much attention, conveniently illustrated here.

### Policy Paradigm Reconsideration and Policy Orthodoxy Debunking

Policy-paradigm reconsideration and policy-orthodoxy debunking are closely related to advancement of a policymaking philosophy that discounts observationalism, doubts policy traditions, suspects policy dogmas, and puts critical probabilistic rationalism into the center of policymaking thinking.

Rapid changes in policy predicaments and in policy environments, as characterizing adversity, require reconsideration of policy paradigms, which cannot anymore be left to policy traditions and spontaneous processes subsumed under such slogans as "accumulated wisdom of generations" and "slow learning from trial and error." In many policy domains, excellent superficial policymaking predicated on unexamined policy paradigms is even worse than what has been called "optimizing on a wrong curve" (A. Wohlstetter 1964, 106); it constitutes the wasting of scarce opportunities to try to influence futures while engaging in nonsense and counterproductive efforts to improve incrementally a rapidly sinking curve. A striking, but not unusual, illustration of such "normal" policymaking and its results is provided by France prior to World War II, which was characterized by good incremental decisonmaking instead of needed policy paradigm shifts (R. Young 1978; see also Haraszti 1983).

In many respects, policy-paradigm reconsideration constitutes an iconoclastic process in which dearly held and deeply entrenched policy idols, or phantasm (in the terminology of Francis Bacon), assumptions, rules, postures, etc. are put up for critique and demolishment. During an epoch of rapid change in policy predicaments, policy environments, and policy instruments, the iconoclasm of accepted policy paradigms and, even more, of policy orthodoxies, is an important requisite of policymaking improvement. But, to understate it, this is hardly an easy requisite. Urgent needs for policy-paradigm reconsiderations and policy-orthodoxy debunking are confronted with zero-approximating capacities to engage in such processes. Large parts of policy-paradigm reconsideration and policy-orthodoxy debunking must take place in, or near, the central policymaking process-system, in addition to innovative parts of society, *inter alia* so as to achieve rapid impact. This necessity makes the policy-paradigm reconsideration and policy-orthodoxy debunking requisite all the more nearly impossible.

Pressures of current problems and costs in terms of disconsensus and conflict are among the relatively minor barriers to policy-paradigm reconsideration and policy-orthodoxy debunking, as are scarcities of philosophic bases and of appropriate methods (for some methodological beginners, see Mason and Mitroff 1981; also useful are multiple perspectives, as proposed in Linstone et al. 1984). More basic and more insidious factors are at work on the levels of individuals, small groups, organizations, and overall policymaking constellations. To take up here just one illustration, tendencies to look for verifying rather than falsifying material (Wason and Johnson-Laird 1972; similar in effects is the so-called Pollyanna Principle, see Matlin and Stang 1978) definitely inhibit policy-paradigm reconsideration. To pass on to usual organizational dynamics, as quite well known in modern organization theory, they are usually unable to meet the policy-paradigm reconsideration requisites (Bass 1983; Breton and Wintrobe 1982; R. Hall 1976; R. Hall 1981; Hanf and Scharpf 1978; Inbar 1979; Kickert 1980; Lerner 1976; MacCrimmon and Taylor 1976; Robert Miles 1980; T. Mitchell 1979; Mohr 1982; Pettigrew 1973; D. Taylor 1965; Warner 1977; Weick 1979).

Even if more extreme views of organizational incapacities are rejected (March and Olsen 1976, elaborating M. Cohen, March, and Olsen 1972; reviewed in Morch and Pondy 1977, and Perrow 1977; and reapplied in Padgett 1980; Dixon 1976 is superficial), policy-paradigm reconsideration, like other transtraditional requisites, is unnatural to most of policymaking. Exceptions in organizations do exist, though they are little understood (see T. Peters and Waterman 1982). Accidental features, such as policy en-trepreneurs as considered later, seem to play an important role, as influenced by broader cultural and societal features that are hard to pin down and to change. With few exceptions, the requirements of policy-paradigm reconsideration on one side and policymaking realities on the other side do produce a serious policymaking-quality deficit.

Even harder are barriers to the debunking of policy orthodoxy. Many policy orthodoxies are closely related to ideologies and basic political dogmas, with further entrenchment in them constituting a widespread response pattern to adversity and to policymaking failures, as examined in chapter 3. Here, a vicious policy-spoiling spiral is met, even worse than the earlier-considered policy-inadequacy closed loops: Failing policies exacerbate clinging to policy orthodoxies and "retreat to commitment" (Bartley 1962), which in turn often assure further and even more disappointing policy failures. Linkages between many policy orthodoxies and broader cultural features further aggravate the situation and inhibit the debunking of policy orthodoxy, as do various sanctification processes of inherently instrumental policies (Merton 1949, 157). Also to be noted is the philosophic difficulty of distinguishing between values that can and should be accepted as binding bases for policymaking as an act of moral judgment and dogmas that bind policymaking in its goal-seeking and instrumental senses without any value justification. This is a theoretically difficult distinciton (well analyzed in Homann 1980, without all his conclusions and assumptions, being necessarily accepted) hard to operationalize in concrete policymaking contexts and to apply in the debunking of policy orthodoxy.

Necessary heterodoxy in fundamental policy thinking, as distinct from political differences of opinions within coalitions and within coalitions of coalitions and as distinct from both tactical and incremental disagreements, is very seldom tolerated in and near policymaking cores, with democracies enjoying some advantage in this respect. Lack of suitable heterodoxy by itself is sufficient to reduce the chances of policy-paradigm reconsideration to nearly zero. Barriers to policy-paradigm reconsideration are further illustrated by the tendency of past successes to reinforce policy paradigms, while dismal failures result either in entrenchment and escalated commitment to policy orthodoxies as mentioned or in panic learning, both of which inhibit policy-paradigm reconsideration and the debunking of policy orthodoxy, as needed for high-quality policymaking.

Rapid shifts in policy paradigms and, sometimes in policy orthodoxies, without reconsideration and debunking in the senses proposed here as an integral part of high-quality policymaking, do occur. These happen mainly as a result of jumps from one doctrine to another, of changing predilections of rulers, of panic reactions to overwhelming events, and of social upheavals up to revolution. In an epoch of shifting adversity, jumps in policy paradigms and policy orthodoxies—especially in conjunction with democratic turnovers in rulers and parties in power (Bunce 1981)—are often preferable to policy-paradigm and policy-orthodoxy stasis, by providing some chance of policy adjustment, at least by loosening the hold of outdated fixations. But often such policy-paradigm and policy-orthodoxy jumps may do more harm than good, by resulting in even stronger fixation on new and wrong paradigms; by creating an illusion of updating; and by rapid rotation in paradigms, none of which gets a chance to be proven useful or false. In most cases, such shifts are a poor substitute for high-quality policymaking, though they may sometimes help to set the stage for the latter.

Factors outside the central minds of governments play important and often overwhelming roles in policy-paradigm reconsideration and policy-orthodoxy debunking. New philosophies, innovations in scientific world-views, critical social movements—these are important factors in reshaping policy paradigms and policy orthodoxies. But, these factors take a long time to evolve, are not always for the better (e.g. social movements of a fanatical nature can be much for the worse), and their occurrence is not dictated by the needs of policymaking. In the face of present adversities some signs of suitable policy-paradigm innovations coming from society can be discerned, such as in the already-mentioned flow of innovative literature dealing with main policy issues in Western democracies. But (1) such social inputs are found only in a few societies and may often miss the main paradigms and orthodoxies in need of debunking and iconoclasm and (2) unless accompanied by receptivity in the central minds of governments, such social inputs may have inadequate and too-much-delayed impacts on policymaking. Hence, the necessity to push toward policy-paradigm reconsideration and policy-orthodoxy debunking within the central minds of governments and to encourage societal policy-paradigm innovative and policy-orthodoxy-iconoclastic processes, again in part by appropriate endeavors on behalf of the central minds of governments.

Main policymaking-quality deficits in respect to policy-paradigm reconsideration and policy-orthodoxy debunking are brought out by the above discourse: Policy paradigms are not reconsidered and policy orthodoxies are not debunked. Futhermore, present patterns of policymaking responses to adversity and shifts in policy publics may aggravate the rigidity of policy orthodoxies and bring about the emergence of more irrational policy theologies, further preventing necessary policy-paradigm reconsideration and policy-orthodoxy debunking.

## Diagnostics

The two policymaking specifications discussed above are comprehensive and constitute facets of most of the specifications to be taken up below. Vice versa, the specifications to be taken up now do detail elements involved in policy-paradigm reconsideration and policy-orthodoxy debunking; and, less so, in building up a policymaking philosophy. Thus, diagnostics applies also to diagnosis of prevailing policy theologies while epistemology is a critical base of diagnostics. Thus, diagnostics illustrates crossrelations and partial overlaps between the specifications discussed in this chapter.

"Diagnostics" is logically an appropriate process to start consideration of more specific policymaking requisites and of inherent incapacities barring their satisfaction. It also serves to preview some central features of most of the requisites discussed in this chapter: Diagnostics is a very complex process; it is crucial for policy quality but difficult and, in part, impossible to improve because of inbuilt incapacities; it has some more and some less understood portions; it is often neglected in policy sciences and in social sciences as a whole (e.g. see McCann 1983, on organizational "diagnosis"); and it is seldom considered explicitly and comprehensively within the central policymaking process-systems themselves, with the exception of defense intelligence (e.g. Pfalzgraff, Ra'anan, and Milberg 1981; and the convenient bibliography Constantinides 1983)—all these features are shared in various proportions by many of the requisites looked at in this chapter.

Diagnostics for policymaking is different but not completely dissimilar from diagnostics for other purposes, such as in medicine (Elstein, et al. 1978; Westmeyer 1972) or in chess (Groot 1965). Attempts to build up a "logic of diagnostics" are sorely missing in the literature, though all diagnostic endeavors share some fundamental elements and processes.

Diagnostics, as a policymaking facet, involves perception and initial explanation ("estimation" in defense intelligence terminology, Godson 1980) of relevant realities, their meanings and their alternative futures. This, both as background "worldviews" and as related to identification and exploration respectively of potential or existing policy issues. Especially important for policymaking are diagnostics of discontinuities, of declining or sinking curves, of cross-impacts of different events and of emerging surprise possibilities. Because diagnostics shapes all of policymaking, its crucial importance is hard to exaggerate. Serious diagnostics distortions are very hard to repair once accepted as postulated reality, as policy assumptions, and as policymaking starting lines.

An extended view of diagnostics (Lasswell 1975) includes all of perception and comprehension of unfolding reality, as objectively salient for policymaking. Such a perspective returns to epistemology as a main concern for policymaking understanding and improvement, as already considered. Even if underlying philosophic issues are neglected in favor of more "practical" approaches (a doubtful position, as clarified earlier), the need for metamodels and schemata to structure infinite reality is inescapable. Thus, preferences for explicit and objective knowledge over tacit and subjective knowledge as bases for more "rational" policymaking are not self-obvious (Polanyi 1974; Popper 1972a; Russell 1948) or simple. Wide acceptance of various metamodels, such as "systems," in large parts of policy sciences is not fully convincing either.

The history of defense intelligence provides striking insights into the inbuilt incapacities and error propensities of diagnostics, in a somewhat narrower sense. Despite major attempts to improve defense intelligence in many countries, with no scarcity of money, high-quality professionals, and political power supports, the history of defense intelligence and its utilization in policymaking is more one of failures than of successes (Garthoff 1984; Hinsley 1979; Whaley 1973; R. Wohlstetter 1962; R. Wohlstetter 1979). Exceptional successes are often a result of outsiders and/or of technological achievments, such as decoding and science intelligence during World War II (B. Johnson 1979; R. Jones 1978; R. Lewin 1978; Montagu 1979). Only in part are intelligence failures a result of deliberate disinformation (Bowyer 1982; Gooch and Perlmutter 1982; and other stratagems, Whaley 1969). Much more important are inherent incapacities of diagnostics, as expressed in defense intelligence failures, such as: rigid cognitive maps; organizational doctrines; information distortion inbuilt in bureaucratic politics; hierarchical pressures; emotional and material vested interests in given worldviews; and fundamental limitations of epistemological capacities and perception processes of the human mind (Betts 1978; Betts 1980; Hughes 1976; Jarvis 1957; Jonsson 1982; Mandel 1978; Prados 1982; Steinbrunner 1979; Agranat Report 1974, to be read against the background presented in Herzog 1982; Sylvan and Chan 1984. The Franks report on the Falkland surprise is unusual in concluding that the prediction errors were unavoidable, Franks 1982, as reinforced by Hastings and Jenkins 1982; compare with Dror 1980b, ch. 1. The Parliamentary debates are interesting; K. Morgan 1982). Broader blinders imposed on intelligence by prevailing cultures are neglected (as exceptionally discussed in Lanir 1983; and well illustrated, in respect to the United Kingdom, in Verrier 1983), as are the very misexpectations inherent in asking intelligence to reduce uncertainty and make definite predictions on phenomena that are indeterminate and jumping, in part. The fact that "common sense" too is a cultural system (Geertz 1983, ch. 9) adds to the invisible blinders unavoidably biasing diagnostics. This also applies to historic perspectives, as shaped by the historiography of each culture (Breisach 1983).

In considering explanations of security intelligence failures, it is important to take into account that much more is known on false-negative errors than on false-positive errors—which usually do not result in dramatic and visible omissions that serve as the main subjects for public investigations and scholarly writings. But, for policymaking as a whole, false-positive errors are also very serious, *inter alia* in distorting policymaking agendas and producing possibly counterproductive unwarranted policies, while also increasing the risk of later false-negative errors by reducing the credibility of intelligence warnings.

These same basic diagnostics incapacities are operative in all policy domains, with some adjustments (A. George 1980; Jarvis 1975; Lyles and Mitroff 1980; Rivera 1968; Steinbrunner 1974; Wilensky 1967). The fact that in domains other than defense the life-and-death importance of diagnostics is less recognized and that diagnostics failures are less obvious and, therefore, seldom admitted and studied makes incapacities worse.

Less demanding problems of reliable fact ascertainment in respect to important policy-salient realities also defy present capacities. While the collection of statistics has made much progress, nevertheless much remains unknown. In the highly developed domains of economic data, little is known reliably on gray economics (Rose 1983a) and on real-income distribution. Also in the most developed countries, a strong demonstration of stubborn fact ignorance is provided by the failures of social indicators. After much theoretic work and expressions of great hopes (Bauer 1966; Sheldon and Moore 1968; U.S. Department of Health, Education, and Welfare 1969), little has happened to provide reliable data on important features of social realities (F. Andrews and Withey 1976; OECD 1976; Office of Management and Budget 1974; C. Taylor 1980; Zapf 1975; annotated bibliography in Wilcox 1974; representative articles in *Social Indicators Research: An International and Interdisciplinary Journal for Quality of Life Measurement,* published since 1974; A good summing-up is provided in Social Science Research Council 1983). Lack of adequate methodologies and little demand for more social information in government (N. Caplan et al. 1975; N. Caplan 1976) are among factors explaining this state of affairs. More ambitious ideas to move into reporting on the overall state of society, including structural dimensions (Dokumentation des BDA IW-Symposium 1980), are little more than wishful talk. Even more difficult is the search for indicators of the "subjective" state of a nation (C. Turner and Krauss 1978). Needless to say, absence of reliable fact knowledge cannot but seriously distort and undermine diagnostics.

Difficulties in the sciences to adjust theories to new facts (T. Kuhn 1970; T. Kuhn 1977) and to utilize adequately new, easily available, data sources (Jodice, Taylor, and Deutsch 1980) testify to the strength of diagnostics incapacities. The latter are further reinforced in policymaking domains by the ambiguity and concept-dependent nature of basic issues, such as "disease" (Rothschuh 1975), "poverty" (J.K. Galbraith 1979), or "unemployment," (Garraty 1978) as well as many other "soft" issues (Gross 1964).

Work on information processing (Bettman 1979; Coulam and R. A. Smith 1984; H. Simon 1979a), on psychology of cognition and perception

(Coultner 1983), and on explanation propensities of the human mind (in "attribution psychology," E.E. Jones 1972; H. Kelley and Michela 1980. Convenient introductions are Hewstone 1983, and Richard Nisbett and Ross 1980) permits additional diagnosis of misdiagnosis as inbuilt in mental processes. Leaving for separate consideration findings on group processes and organizational behavior's adding heavy burdens to diagnostics, one finds that dependence on historic metaphors and language images (Demandt 1978; Lakoff and Johnson 1980; E. May 1972; Sacks 1979; relevant in the even broader context of dependence of all goal-oriented thinking on "scripts," within an artificial intelligence setting, is Schank and Abelson 1977) illustrates additional misdiagnosis causes directly related to policymaking. Also, the problem of vigilance is relevant, with difficulties in sustaining alertness necessary for early discernment of signs indicating serious problems (D.R. Davies and Parasuraman 1982, though transfer from the findings on vigilance in simple situations to policy diagnostics is fraught with difficulties).

Studies on diagnosing in medical practice demonstrate that "overinterpretation errors," in the sense of assigning new information to existing hypotheses (Elstein et al. 1978), is endemic even in a highly professionalized activity, with much peer control and with early and frequently visible result feedback. Little wonder that the situation seems to be much worse with politicians, who not only have strong cognitive predispositions (Putnam 1973, 125ff.) but show tendencies to construct myths that are then superficially adjusted to meet new circumstances (F. Gilbert 1977, ch. 12 and passim), without ever breaking out from their mental cocoons.

On a more fundamental level, the problematics of diagnostics is closely related to inherent limits of cognition and perception as individual and collective processes. This book cannot go into the debates surrounding these subjects (as, in part, conveniently presented in Rock 1975), various novel approaches to them (e.g. Margolis, in work), and different attempts to tie perception psychology to policymaking through intermediate concepts, such as "cognitive maps" (Axelrod 1976). But, however much ignorance prevails about some dimensions of perception and cognition, such as on subconscious pattern recognition abilities, a relatively reliable conclusion seems to be that novel reality is very hard to diagnose (for illustrations from a relatively simple and, in principle, foreseeable area, namely, energy, see Greenberger 1983). As adversity is characterized, in part, by jumps of reality beyond well-experienced patterns, basic limitations on cognition and perception constitute an inherent incapacity of policymaking under adversity.

When events may go beyond available concepts, images, and experiences, as has been the case in some already-mentioned historic periods, correct diagnostics depends on the capacity to transcend boundaries of cultural awareness (Laboratory of Comparative Human Cognition 1979; G. Steiner 1975), which approaches the impossible. Difficulties in Western countries correctly to comprehend realities conditioned by different basic cultural and societal features illustrate on a minor scale such awareness limits and their prohibitive effects on diagnostics of what is unknown to one's experiences and ways of thinking. Quantum jumps in situations and predicaments may well transgress diagnostic capacities of contemporary cultures, leading to incorrect social constructs of reality (P. Berger and Luckmann 1980) and to what has been called "loss of reality in modern society" (Schelsky 1965, 391-404, as further developed in respect to political publicity and mass-media-induced misperceptions in Schelsky 1984).

The overall conclusion is typical for the problematics of policymaking: Adopting a robust view of diagnostics and neglecting more sophisticated requirements (such as use of non-Pascalian probabilities to graduate degrees of diagnostic reliability probability, L. Cohen 1977), one can see that many ingrained factors are at work distorting reality images and frustrating basic diagnostics requisites of adequate policymaking.

The main quality deficits of diagnostics, largely explained by incapacities as partly considered above, include among others: perception of new situations as variations of old ones; inadequate diagnosis of jumps, ultrachange, declining slopes; diagnostics that contradicts accepted opinions, organizational traditions, and vested psychological needs is not seriously considered in policymaking; many aspects of reality important for policymaking under adversity are not susceptible to adequate monitoring; great difficulties in handling ambiguity and uncertainty and inputting them into policymaking; and "loss of reality" in respect to phenomena not fitting into main worldviews, based on the past; and many more.

This is a convenient place to repeat an earlier caveat, namely, do not draw from very strong incapacities the exaggerated conclusion that nothing can be done to improve policymaking under adversity. Thus, it is possible to improve diagnostics and to reduce some of the negative consequences of unimprovable diagnostics deficits, as will be illustrated and discussed in later chapters, albeit to improve diagnostics in the face of built-in incapacities is a difficult endeavor and maximum foreseeable achievements are limited. This conjecture applies to all the requisites considered in this chapter, with variations depending on the complexity of requirements, magnitude of quality deficits, nature of underlying incapacities, states of relevant knowledge and understanding, and availability of improvement resources versus improvement constraints.

## Agenda Setting

Agenda setting deals with the inclusion, with priorities, of cognized and preliminarily formulated issues and problems (S. Brown 1983) in decision agendas, ranging from public debate to cabinet and ruler consideration. Being included on a policy agenda is a necessary, though not sufficient, condition for active and explicit policymaking, as contrasted with policy evolvement through aggregation of events and side effects of other decisions.

For understanding and improving policymaking, agenda setting is a crucial process: Agenda setting allocates attention, as one of the scarcest policymaking resources (H. Simon 1978, esp. 13-14); agenda priorities shape consideration of problems and their resolution (M. Levine and Plott 1977; Plott and Levine 1978); problem formulation, as often inherent in agenda setting, predetermines decisions, such as through reverting thinking to explicitly mentioned terms (Wason and Johnson-Laird 1972). Possibly, national senses of agenda also influence election outcomes (Schweitzer 1984).

Much less is known on the realities of agenda setting than on many other features of policymaking. In particular, agenda-setting processes inside government and in related political and public arenas are little investigated, though interest in the subject is on the increase (Cobb and Elder 1983; Cobb, Ross, and Ross 1976; Haendel 1977; Kingdon 1984; Light 1983; Rose 1976; J. Walker 1977; Weaver 1981). Some of the biasing influences that seem to be at work (Downs 1972; to be compared with Vasquez and Mansback 1983) include: overloads; the tendency for acute and very visible *Tagespolitik* (i.e. "politics of the day") issues to drive basic issues out of the agenda; the strong influence of mass media on agenda setting, inside governments too (raising in turn many questions on public and mass media agenda-setting and agenda-influencing dynamics, including the roles of fads and imitation, e.g. see Flickinger 1983); the impact of fashion and interest cycles; the delay of controversial and unpleasant items for as long as possible; accidentalism; the strong influence of "gatekeepers"; and personal idiosyncrasies of senior decision makers and those who influence them and serve as their mindkeepers.

Ambiguity and changing meanings of words add to agenda-setting difficulties. Thus, to return to an already-mentioned relatively easy example: While the distribution of persons according to age is well known, the boundaries of "old age" are moving (Calhoun 1978; Roebuck 1979), with consequent vagueness on inclusion in policy agendas and doubts on proper formulations to adopt. And, the economic malaise of the West can be conceptualized in terms of quite different policy-agenda formulations (e.g. compare Bacon and Eltis 1978; Blackaby 1979; Jenkins and Sherman

1979) with radically disparate action implications. The inherent intractability of societal antinomies underlying "problems" and amorphous profiles of the latter hinder not only diagnostics but transition from diagnostics to agenda, and to agenda formulation.

Such features of actual agenda-setting processes contradict some requisites essential for high-quality policymaking, such as:

- Some correlation between agenda items and main objective problems facing a polity. In particular, the noninclusion of momentous choices posed by reality in the formal agenda of central minds of governments must seriously impair policymaking quality. (Inherent difficulties in identifying "objective" agenda items are illustrated by the problematic nature of the *Setting National Priorities* and *Setting Municipal Priorities* endeavors by highly qualified study units, e.g. see C. Brecher and Horton 1983; and Pechman 1983, which both miss some main priorities. Tisdell 1981 is also relevant in this connection.)
- Differentiation between agenda items according to their impact potentials, so as to assure adequate attention to the more critical decisions.
- Search for critical decision opportunities, to utilize short and rapidly passing occasions to have impacts on realities.
- Timing of decisions, so as to face predicaments while still relatively easy to handle.
- Decision packaging, so as to consider interacting issues as one bundle.
- Some carefully managed decoupling between internal agendas of central minds of governments and public political agendas, so as to increase feasibility domains for issues that become subjected to fragmented and mutually paralyzing forces, once put on public political agendas (well illustrated by nuclear policymaking in the United Kingdom, Gowing 1974).
- Need for multiple and open-ended problem formulations, not to channelize treatment prematurely.
- Prediction of main agenda items to be taken up at the top policymaking levels, so as to permit adequate study and analysis by the staff units of the central minds of governments.

And more. As a result of contradictions between such requisites and actual agenda-shaping factors, improvement of agenda setting is very difficult while determining policymaking quality.

A special case of agenda-setting difficulties and importance is posed by the requisite of policy-paradigm reconsideration. Policy-paradigm reconsideration involves much more than putting policy paradigm and policy orthodoxy items on a decision agenda, but exclusion of such items from explicit policy agendas is a main direct cause for actual nonreconsideration of policy paradigm. A good illustration is provided by the widespread tendency to substitute "tactical" items for strategic issues, as well brought out within a broad historic context by the study of Gerhard Ritter on foreign and defense policymaking in Germany up to 1918 (Ritter 1969-75. The original German title reflects the main thrust of the book: *Staatskunst und Kriegshandwerk,* which can be translated as "statesmanship and warcraft").

Quality deficits in agenda setting are easy to summarize, though difficult to overcome: Needs of high-quality policymaking under adversity in respect to agenda setting, as mentioned above, are not met. In particular, objectively important items are not put on the agenda or are narrowly and misleadingly formulated, with special neglect of policy-paradigm items, policy-orthodoxy contents, and newly emerging problems; formulation of agenda items forecloses adequate policymaking, with exclusion of paradigm-overcoming and orthodoxy-debunking agenda formulations; and agenda priorities do not meet any reasonable priority-setting criteria correlated with the potential impact of decision items on adversity.

## Alternatives Innovation

Conditions under which incrementalism as a main mode of policymaking is adequate differ radically from situations where incremental change is irrelevant and where, instead, alternatives innovation is necessary, ranging from transincrementalism to radical societal architecture and policy-paradigm shifts. A main feature of contemporary and predictable reality in most countries is that incrementalism is less and less adequate for handling problems. The necessity for far-reaching policy innovations in main domains, as a result of shifts in policy predicaments, constitutes an important policymaking requisite in countries that in the past managed, or thought they managed, with a lot of "muddling through." Thus, even if aspirations are limited to maintaining the status quo, in turbulent conditions this still requires innovative policies. The existence of large and increasing innovation deficits in main policy domains makes alternatives innovation all the more urgent. Health policies illustrate well aggravating innovations deficits (Hunter 1980; R. Klein 1983).

Alternatives innovation is a very interesting subject. It involves extrarational creativity and its improvement, on the level of individuals, of organizations, and of societies. The understanding of creativity, of innovation, and of the diffusion of innovation has not grown significantly, despite continuous interest and studies of various kinds (as illustrated, with different foci and approaches, by Amman and Cooper 1982; Arieti 1976; Barron and Harrington 1981; H. Gardner 1982; Leichter 1983; Madigan and Elwood 1984; Perkins 1981; Salk 1983; Schapera 1970; P. Schmidt 1976;

Marcia Taylor 1978; and T. Peters and Waterman 1983). Lack of understanding of innovation processes hinders explanation of deficits and development of improvement proposals.

It seems in most countries that far-reaching option innovation is scarce in governmental organizations, but exceptions exist (P. Jackson 1981; C. Johnson 1982; Policy Studies Institute 1980). Shocks sometimes encourage innovation (not necessarily for the better; also, sometimes shocks reinforce entrenchment in traditional policy paradigms and policy orthodoxies). "Crusading" organizations and policy entrepreneurs, as latter considered, are additional policy-alternative-innovation factors. The variables influencing degrees and directions of policy creativity are unclear, with pluralism in policy thinking and various organizational structures, such as "matrix," being regarded in literature as among innovation-encouraging variables (E. Alexander 1979; E. Alexander 1982; T. Burns and Stalker 1961; G. Downs 1976; G. Downs and Mohr 1976; Gyorgy and Kuhlmann 1978; G. Meyer 1982; H. Nystrom 1979; Polsby 1984; M. Stein 1974; Zaltman, Duncan, and Holbeck 1973). Policy entrepreneurs are a crucial innovation factor, deserving separate considerations later.

Hard to handle is the question whether, in given situations, absence of good policy alternatives is a result of the objective nonexistence of such alternatives; or of cultural limitations on identifying such alternatives (e.g. propensities not to search for "technological shortcuts," Etzioni and Remp 1973); or of scarcity of policy creativity; or perhaps of bad luck. The issue of "open space for action" or, as already discussed, policy leeway is related, namely, the domains within which alternatives are meaningful because they may be feasible. As noted, static feasibility analysis is an insufficient way to handle this issue because of the need to enlarge policy leeway, which is tied to already-considered policy autonomy, so as to have scope for alternatives innovation. Hence, the need to understand from this additional perspective factors shaping policy leeway (Grottian and Murswieck 1974; Müller 1981) and to engage in policymaking directed at enlarging this space. Deliberate contraction of policy leeway, such as the proposal sometimes put forward in the United States to amend the Constitution so as to limit congressional budgeting freedom (Ellwood 1981; Wildavsky 1980), however explainable as preferring self-binding (Elster 1979) over succumbing to budget-increasing forces and pressures, is counterproductive, contradicting overriding needs to expand policy leeway and enlarge open spaces for alternatives innovation to face a period of shifting predicaments.

In the matter of policy leeway, again objective situations are hard to distinguish from subjective perceptions, with creativity constituting a leading way to overcome apparent limits.

Some incapacities in respect to policy-alternative innovation are similar to some incapacities hindering policy-paradigm reconsideration and policy-orthodoxies debunking, as already considered. In many respects, the most urgent policymaking-improvement needs are for innovations in policy paradigms and, especially, grand policies. These are inhibited by cultural limitations, organizational bondage to traditions, vested interests, and similar "closed-thinking" variables (Rokeach 1960). A small but illuminating illustration is provided by the inhibition on consideration of devaluation in the United Kingdom between 1964 and 1967 as a policy taboo, until reality shocks resulted in devaluation in a quite futile manner (Fry 1981: 63-64).

However difficult the improvement of policy creativity, this is a main need of adequate policymaking. Think tanks illustrate an invention in policymaking directed, in part, at the search for new policy alternatives (as well as at policy-paradigm reconsideration and at improvement of other mental-intellectual policymaking features. Dickson 1971; Dror 1980a; Dror 1984c; Enke 1967; Levien 1969; I. Marsh 1980; Ritchie 1971; Bruce Smith 1966; Slee Smith 1971). But, achievements till now, while impressive, are inadequate. Incapacities are too strong to be overcome by any single device. Further aspects of this matter are taken up later, when policy entrepreneurship is considered as a policymaking-quality specification.

Alternatives innovation is largely a matter for societal problem-handling abilities, even when the central minds of governments operate at their hypothetical best. Many variables shaping societal policy creativity are unknown and some additional ones are beyond deliberate intervention with available policy instruments. Open societies seem to have a greater potential for policy-alternatives innovation, with democracies enjoying here an advantage over nondemocracies.

It is interesting to note that many central minds of governments seem quite ignorant of policy alternatives known in other countries. In some policy domains, such as economics, new ideas are diffused rapidly; in disciplines less universal than theoretic economy and macroeconomic policies, the flow of ideas is much slower. Thus, the field study conducted by the author showed clearly that many senior policymakers, including professionals in domains such as health policy and administrative policy, are quite parochial in their knowledge. The main contribution of professional associations is to help in diffusion of experiences, with the Organization for Economic Cooperation and Development (OECD) fulfilling a major role in permitting accelerated diffusion of policy options among its member countries. Nevertheless, possibilities to increase policy alternatives by the relatively easy route of knowing the options considered in other countries are far from exhausted. Here, improvement is relatively easy, as contrasted with societal creativity, where justifiable operational prescriptions are hard to develop.

The policymaking-quality deficit identified by the analysis, well sustained by direct examination of policymaking realities, is one of great scarcity of innovative alternatives for handling adversity. From the perspective of the central minds of governments, this ties in with the lack of promising policy compasses as a major predicament, as discussed in chapter 2.

## Broad and Long-Term Perspectives

Close interdependencies among decisions as well as among target sectors and among predicaments require broad perspectives, going far beyond "coordination" (Siedentopf 1976) so as to control undesirable side effects and to achieve synergy. Not necessarily implied is "comprehensive planning" (Branch 1983), in the sense of detailed and finely tuned efforts to orchestrate simultaneously large sets of objects. Comprehensive planning is usually impossible, under adversity, because of indeterminacies, uncertainties, and rapid changes, which require robust policies focused on main goals, on the lines of the already-considered selective-radicalism policy principle. But "broadness" is necessary in considering predicaments and canvassing effects on wide domains and in checking possible interactions among main decisions. Unless care is taken to adopt broad perspectives, negative indirect and second-order effects can easily dominate results. The likelihood of individually considered minidecisions resulting in serious macroconsequences (analogous to "micromotives and macrobehaviour," Schelling 1978 and, with a broader perspective, Schelling 1984; as illustrated by "the tyranny of small decisions" in the environmental domain in Odum 1982; to be compared with R. Emerson 1983 in the social control area) once the illusionary secure haven of incrementalism is left behind is very dangerous.

The problem of unanticipated, and often unanticipative results, needs emphasis. The "gambling" view of policymaking proposed earlier as fitting most of policymaking under adversity makes undesired results a likely consequence of all policy options. Also, as policy gambling faces indeterminateness and ignorance, unanticipative results, including undesirable ones, are unavoidable even under hypothetically perfect policymaking.

A good set of illustrations of major policy problems caused by past policy is provided by the importation, or at least permitted immigration, of labor. Thus, within a longer-range perspective, the importaton of slaves from Africa to the United States had extremely potent and totally unanticipated consequences, whether "desirable" or "undesirable" depends on taste and on future evolvements beyond predictability. Within a short and conventional time frame are large migrations into the United Kingdom and the deliberate importation of labor into Germany and Switzerland, for instance, which have created difficult predicaments. At least some of these predicaments could have been predicted. But, even when some outcomes were predicted, such as racial tensions in the United Kingdom, the predictions were ignored as "taboo" (which is a matter quite different from considering the predictions on their merits and then deciding to accept possible adverse consequences of a free immigration policy for a generation or two because of more important humanitarian and liberal values).

Related issues will be further explored when the "fuzzy-betting" requisite and the unintended-consequences problem are taken up. At present, a double conclusion of the gambling view needs preliminary mention: (1) Maximum efforts to reduce unanticipated consequences are necessary, involving in part broad perspectives searching in advance large policy domains for possible impacts by considered alternatives; and (2) whatever is done, many unanticipated consequences are assured, making "comprehensive planning" an illusion, and requiring instead other modes for handling unanticipated and undesired consequences, such as accelerated learning, as discussed later.

Long-term perspectives are needed because of already-discussed policy-paradigm reconsideration needs and societal-architecture requisites, as well as the long minimum time needed for many policies to achieve effects. Inbuilt long lead times, as well as long implementation cycles, require policy time-horizons much longer than usual in practice (Emery and Trist 1972). Decisions with impacts on distant futures are especially vexing (Owen 1983).

At the same time, the contradiction between requirements for policy perspectives long in time because of minimum lead times and impact cycles, on one hand, and indeterminacy and uncertainty that push for shorter time-horizons with somewhat less ignorance, on the other hand, must be acknowledged. This contradiction poses a main intellectual dilemma for postulating optimal time perspectives in hypothetically best policymaking. Three considerations are relevant, namely: (1) value preferences in respect to different times in the future, (2) minimum and optimal policy cycles, from the perspective of impacts and lead times, and (3) various degrees of uncertainty and ignorance, often more extreme with longer time perspectives but not in any simple linear correlation with length of time and sometimes with more uncertainty in the medium range than in the longer range. Because of different optimal time perspectives stemming from these various considerations, there exists no overall "optimal" time perspective for policymaking, even if the policy issues under consideration are kept constant. All this on the theoretic level of policymaking at its best, showing that any simple idea of "perfect" policymaking is inherently doubtful.

Moving from modeling of policymaking at its best to policymaking realities, the need to increase time perspectives seems compelling—there being no danger that actual policymaking will move beyond preferable time perspectives as identified by any one of the above-mentioned considerations. This, because strong forces are at work to inhibit both broad and long-term perspectives. Thus:

- Broad and long-term perspectives are very demanding in respect to "policy sophistication," as discussed in the next specifications. In the absence of highly advanced mental-intellectual capacities, improvisation may be preferable to illusions of controlling complexity and predicting futures. Experience of failures with naive planning approaches has become in many countries a barrier to broad and long-term policy perspectives.
- A growing sense of turbulence and indeterminacy in relevant environments produces a sense of futility in striving for broad and long-term perspectives (rightly so, in the absence of policy sophistication).
- Consensus needs push toward reduced spans of attention, so as to minimize items requiring laborious bargaining and causing conflict.
- Much of policymaking is sectorialized, with strong forces supporting a kind of neofeudalism in dominating specific policy domains (on futility of the many counterefforts, see, for instance, Redford and Blissett 1981, ch. 8; Fain 1977, pt. 1).
- Electoral cycles, especially in democracies, dominate policymaking time perspectives (Tufte 1978).
- Turnovers in senior policymakers reduce long-term perspectives and consistency (Blondel 1980).

The last point illustrates some functional contradictions between different requisites of high-quality policymaking. Thus, to reconsider policy paradigms perhaps, to multiply options, and to increase learning, turnover of top policymakers is desirable, but to encourage long-term perspectives, stability in top policymakers is needed.

The Greek idea to overcome such contradictions through "mixed" governance is correct in principle, but does not provide much of a solution because it continues to beg the question, what mixes of which components can approximate the requisite. Thus, the "Whitehall Model," according to which career civil servants provide long-term perspectives, does not seem to work (C. Campbell and Szablowski 1979; Heclo and Wildavsky 1974; Brian Smith 1976); while the United States regular turnover of senior officials does not work either (Heclo 1977a).

Possibly, spacing of elections with longer intervals between them, as for instance under the Fifth Republic French Constitution, fits the needs of continuity cum innovation better, as may the Mexican constitutional provision for the turnover of politicians after a relatively long single term in office (Peter Smith 1979). Such constitutional arrangements illustrate possibilities and needs for redesigning main political institutions to meet the needs of high-quality policymaking, going far beyond the usual subjects of "administrative reforms," and even "policymaking-improvement," in their conventional meanings. The experience of Sri Lanka, which in 1978 adopted a Gaullist constitution (A. J. Wilson 1980), shows, however, that constitutions by themselves are a quite inadequate instrument for influencing policymaking quality. (See also Nwabueze 1982, on Nigeria.)

On a more limited scale, countries try to broaden and expand policy horizons through varieties of institutions, such as planning units, lookout units, and central policy staff units (Baehr and Wittrock 1981; C. Campbell 1983), and by using various naive and advanced forecasting methods (Armstrong 1978; Choucri and Robinson 1978, Harrel 1978; Helmer 1983; Maharidakis and Wheelwright 1982; Martino 1983; B. Schwartz, Svedin, and Wittrock 1982; Whiston 1979; psychological aspects are in part considered in Loye 1978). Many of these attempts fail and only a few achieve any impact on the currently discussed and related policymaking-quality requisites. The forces at work to abort longer-range and broader policy thinking in governments are well illustrated on a smaller scale in the early history of the State Department Policy Planning Staff in the United States (Kennan 1967, esp. 325-29; 464-70, to be compared to Bloomfield 1982, ch. 9. In 1983 the policy planning staff was again reformed, with a collegium-type five-member council at its head. The State Department outlook experience should be compared with the French setup, Samy Cohen 1982).

Another significant illustration of difficulties in moving in the direction of broader and longer-term perspectives is provided by the sorry history of budgeting reforms. In the abstract, multiyear budgeting, suitably adjusted to uncertainty (N. Caiden 1981; A. Robinson and Ysander 1981), should serve as a main instrument of broad and long-term perspectives for policymaking, but attempts in this direction have been mainly a failure (N. Caiden and Wildavsky 1974; Wildavsky 1975), testifying both to the inherent difficulties of this specification and to the strong barriers to its satisfaction. Most of the prescriptive literature in public budgeting (e.g. Premchand 1983; Rabin and Lynch 1983; Sweeny and Rachlin 1981), too, does not present any coherent and sophisticated proposals for making budgeting into a major tool for broadening and enlarging the time perspectives of policymaking.

Simple ideas for making policymaking more aware of the future (Bezold 1978; in part, Blum, Kocher, and Wittmann 1982) have, therefore, little merit, and more advanced proposals (Jouvenel 1967) have little chance of success, either. The idea that private initiatives without political support (Marien 1976; F. Tugwell 1973) can push policymaking into broader and longer-range perspectives has little factual support, though exceptions do exist, such as the educational effects of some of the work of the Club of Rome. It seems that changes in policymaking, including especially in the central minds of governments, are a precondition for more openness to such external inputs. This is also the conclusion of some studies by the author on impacts and nonimpacts of think tanks on policymaking and on the downgrading and closing down of some of the long-range outlook units in countries that have established such entities, such as the Swedish Secretariat for Futures Studies and the New Zealand Commission for the future.

Policymaking-quality deficits in the currently considered specification are quite clear-cut: strong tendencies to handle adversities in a piecemeal way and with a lot of ad-hocism, with policies being usually atomized and short time perspectives are the rule. This, also when obvious mismatches between policy time perspectives and the time cycles of the target phenomena are the result (as illustrated in Hansard Society 1979).

As already mentioned, these deficits need to be put into correct proportions by comparing them with the bigger policymaking errors of unsophisticated comprehensive and long-term policymaking. Under conditions of adversity, such as complexity and uncertainty, it is often better to improvise than to prepare plans based on totally mistaken assumptions and then to try to stick to them. Therefore, the specification of broad and long-range perspectives must be realized in tandem with high-quality handling of complexity and uncertainty, as considered in the next two specifications. But, first, some relationships between planning and broad and long-range perspectives deserve some attention in a brief excursus.

*Excursus on Planning*

Broad and long-term perspectives for policymaking under adversity are related to some of the meanings of the term *planning* and much of planning experience is relevant for the specification. Furthermore, modern planning theory does handle some of the problems of policymaking under adversity, as taken up in this book, sometimes more so than policy sciences literature (as illustrated by the First Israel-Canada Conference: Planning in an Age of Turbulance and Uncertainty, Jerusalem, July 2-5, 1984).

Despite reluctance to move into conceptual issues, a few observations are first in order on "planning" and its relations to "policymaking."

The first point is that in languages where no distinct verbal symbol exists for "policy," as distinct from politics (Heidenheimer 1983), the concept "planning" in general and "political planning" in particular overlap largely with the contents of the term *policymaking* in English. This, for instance, is the case in German (D. Frank 1976; Grube, Richter, and Thaysen 1976; Lendi and Linder 1979; Lompe 1971; Luhmann 1975; Naschold and Väth 1973; and many more).

A second point is that in business management much of the literature dealing with "planning" and, especially, "strategic planning" again focuses on what would largely be called "policymaking" in public policy writings (Ackoff 1970; Anthony 1965; Hussey 1974; Lorane and Vancil 1977; G.A. Steiner 1979).

Third, it is important to note the roles of the term *planning* as a political symbol, enjoying positive or negative evaluation, or cyclic movement between positive and negative attitudes, for instance in the United States (O. Graham 1976; Krueckeberg 1983; Pill 1979; D. Wilson 1980. Especially striking is the rise and decline of the National Resources Planning Board, see Clawson 1983).

A fourth point is that planning often refers to the distinct activity of preparing longer-range, multipurpose, comprehensive, rather detailed, and closely interdependent grids of decisions—often in the form of formalized "plans" for a number of years, such as the famous USSR five-year plans (W. Dill and Popov 1979). This was the case also in quite a number of developing countries that were trying "development planning" (W. Cook and Kuhn 1982; Waterson 1979).

Fifth, sometimes the term *planning* refers to a qualitative mode of decision preparation rather than to a type of decisions. Thus, one speaks about "policy planning," "decision planning," "surprise planning," and so on. Here, *planning* refers to careful preparation of decisions with a hint at usage of explicated methods (see the important discussion of relations between "planning" and "policy analysis" in Altermann and MacRea 1983).

Sixth, defense planning is especially closely related to policymaking, with "planning" in national defense matters being a main aspect of policymaking also in countries that avoid planning in other domains, such as the United States (e.g. see J. Collins 1982; Kronenberg 1982). Defense planning methods are important for policymaking improvement as a whole, overlapping what is often called "policy analysis" in the United States (e.g. Jennergren 1978), with defense problems having provided historically a main impetus to the advancement of modern policy analysis and policy planning methods, starting with operational research in the United Kingdom during World War II, and continuing with systems analysis and cost-effectiveness analysis as developed at the RAND Corporation, to recent work on advanced computer simulation of complex interactions (P. Davis and Winnefeld 1983; as further illustrated in Schwabe and Jamison 1982). In all these methods, complexity handling and longer-term perspectives constitute main aims. Historic experiences with the many failures of defense planning (e.g. Gooch 1974 and reevaluated in P. Davis 1984) also demonstrate the strength of policymaking incapacities.

Seventh, however conceptualized, parts of "planning," especially as referring to preparation of sets of interconnected, comprehensive, and longer-range decisions, constitute an important form of policymaking, related to the currently considered specification. Therefore, it is a mistake of many empiric studies on policymaking to neglect national planning, defense planning, sectorial planning, organizational planning, etc., even though strongly developed in Western democratic countries such as France and the Netherlands (Stephen Cohen 1975; Estrin and Holmes 1983; Hayward and Watson 1975; Herbet 1981. Much can also be learned from the failures of economic planning in the United Kingdom, see Lervez 1975). And prescriptive work on policymaking improvement should not neglect "planning" as an approach and a set of methods for preparing decision networks, including some treatments taking up features of adversity (e.g. Ansoff et al. 1982). Planning literature is very extensive and sometimes rich in quality (David Wilson 1979 is an outstanding bibliography). Better processing of that literature can add much to the understanding and improvement of policymaking. (In addition to the already-mentioned literature, Healey et al. Paris 1982 are also illuminating. Substantive contributions to be derived from planning literature for policy sciences require extensive treatment, beyond what is possible in this book. Lessons that can be drawn from planning failures are illustrative, e.g. P. Hall 1982.)

From the perspective of the comprehensive and long-range view specification under consideration here, the lessons of planning reinforce findings on strong incapacities. Thus, to pick up just two points from many lessons that can be drawn from planning experiences:

- In many Third World countries, planning decayed into detailed programming based on ill-considered paradigms, and contracted from a comprehensive ambition into macroeconomic modeling and some sectorial projects.
- In the communist countries, the situation is more complex because of the pervasive nature of "planning" and its many different forms (Ellman 1979). Handling of adversity through planning has clearly not worked in many communist countries, *inter alia,* because of awkward treatment of complexity and uncertainty, but communist planning has achieved some long-range and broad perspectives, partly thanks to the centralized

power structure, more so than because of planning, but partly thanks to planning.

With all such difficulties, planning in the sense of a broad, systematic longer-range approach to problems, without leading to detailed dirigisme may well constitute a preferable mode for parts of policymaking under adversity. The concept of "planning" in such a sense could have been used for the policymaking specification currently under consideration, but this was avoided because of the ambiguities of the term and its emotion-evoking effects. Nevertheless, planning in a clarified sense is a useful approach to policymaking under adversity, subsumed in this book under other specifications. (Still, or perhaps again, Shonfield 1965 is relevant because of adversity.)

## Complexity Handling

The "complexity-handling" specification introduces us to the first of two policymaking-sophistication requirements that are included in this set of policymaking-improvement needs. Complexity management can in part be supported by appropriate intuitive capacities, such as pattern recognition and Gestalt cognition, possessed in different degrees by various persons (Bastick 1982; Carroll 1979; Groot 1965; Mackinnon and Wearing 1980), but much more than such individual extrarational abilities is necessary. Suitable techniques, methods, units, and professionals, are needed (Baldwin 1975; La Porte 1975; Warfield 1976); and, much more difficult, what I propose to call "policymaking sophistication"—including appropriate cognitive maps, modes of thinking, ways of perception and apperception, and, hardest of all, fitting decision cultures in accord with appropriate policymaking philosophies—is needed.

The importance of complexity-handling capacities as a main policymaking requisite needs little elaboration: More and increasingly nonlinear interdependence among a larger number and variety of variables characterizes increasing areas of policy predicaments. This feature makes complexity-handling abilities an important determinant of policymaking quality as a whole. What does need emphasis is the strength of factors spoiling and preventing adequate complexity management (Dörner et al. 1983; Gomez, Malik, and Oeller 1975; G. Miller 1956; Mintzberg, Raisinghani, and Théorét 1976; Newell and Simon 1972; Suedfeld 1980).

Strong tendencies to simplify issues and see them as much more straightforward than they often are are disturbing. Glorification of the term *common sense*, which is often diametrically converse, as well as antagonistic, to the needs of complexity handling (in addition to being, as already mentioned, culture bound, Geertz 1983, ch. 4) illustrates the hold that simplistic, complexity-repressing ways of thinking have on politics, policymaking, and public culture.

Better complexity management is inhibited by the following factors, among others:

- Limitations of the human mind in comprehending complexity unless aided by specific tools, with scarce and not understood exceptions of surpassing pattern-recognition ability.
- Inbuilt features of organizational decisionmaking, requiring issue simplification.
- Needs of political dynamics for simplifying issues, so as to fit bargaining, communication, marketing, and mental makeups of politicians.
- Characteristics of mass media, pushing toward issue simplification.
- A different factor but a very important one: scarcity of appropriate complexity-handling knowledge and even greater dearth of suitable professionals.
- Another type of factor, of dominant importance: Tendencies toward oscillation between superficial practicalism and naive dogmatism as characterizing many policy-emcompassing cultures, illustrated in the above-mentioned glorification of *common sense* and by strong contemporary tendencies to escape from hard-to-penetrate complexities into resurrected policy theologies and political romanticism.
- Also to be taken into account is the growing complexity of government itself. Thus, the growth in size of government (Nutter 1978), the qualitative implications of "very big" government (Rose 1983b), and the complicated, nearly incomprehensible features of central policymaking processes such as budgeting (Greider 1982) impose on complexity-handling capacities beyond present and foreseeable maximum capacities.

Here, an important paradox of policymaking improvement is met: A strong, though not completely convincing, case can be made that, to handle the external complexity of policy predicaments, the central minds of governments must also be complex. Thus, it is interesting to consider application of the law of requisite variety from information theory (Ashby 1957, 206ff.) to policymaking, reformulating it from "only variety can destroy variety" to *only variety can handle variety.*

Leaving aside the problems of using such laws as applicable to policymaking, at least as analogues, the need for a complex central mind of government to handle adversity is based on broader grounds, as already considered and as brought out by the specifications of high-quality policymaking in this chapter. But, a complex policymaking process-system easily decays into harmful disorder, if not anarchy (in the sense of Sproull, Weiner, and Wolf 1978); or, alternatively, may require a complex meta-process-system to manage it.

As already mentioned, this book is not designed to take up the more technical issues of this subject, which lead, *inter alia*, into information theory and/or into some branches of evolution theory (dealing with the respective adaptability and survivability of more complex versus more simple organisms), with many problems on applicability to policymaking and to societal phenomena in general. Within the more limited domain of the concern of this book, the solution lies in breaking down the concept of "complexity," with the central mind of government needing high levels of internal variety and much internal sophistication to handle adversity with its complexities; but with the central mind of government simultaneously to be made compact and lean, with exclusion of unessential activities; and with a significant amount of internal "structured chaos" constituting a preferable feature of central minds of governments facing adversity—as further explored in chapter 9.

Deficits in complexity-management capacities produce distorted world images, fused with other policymaking weaknesses, such as in diagnostics; lead to ineffective and often counterproductive policies; and, more insidious but very significant, contribute much to what has been earlier called maze policy-behavior once main policymakers despair of making sense of complexity-produced perplexity.

All in all, with inadequate complexity-handling capacities, policymaking is seriously impaired in facing adversity, but to be noted is the apparent ability of human minds sometimes to cut through complexity and recognize patterns with the help of as yet ill-understood mental processes (as illustrated, on a lower level of decision making, by Daly and Mayor 1983). Figuratively, the modality of maze policy-behavior is not the worst way to face complexity, with much running around in an uncomprehended maze providing at least some chance of finding an exit. This conclusion may go beyond the legitimate uses of the "maze policy-behavior" construct, but it serves to indicate that complexity is not the most difficult feature being faced by human decision-making abilities. It seems that indeterminacy, and irreducible ignorance about the future is much harsher.

### Fuzzy-Gambling Sophistication

"Fuzzy-gambling sophistication" is the second of the two policymaking-sophistication specifications considered in this chapter. This concept, as already presented in chapter 4, refers to a quintessential feature of policymaking, namely choice between bundles of ill-defined and ill-definable uncertainties and ignorances (Loasby 1976), with the aim of influencing the probability of alternative possible futures.

The nature of policymaking under adversity as fuzzy gambling pervades and conditions, and often dominates, all features of policymaking reality and should shape all main improvement approaches. Nevertheless, this is a highly neglected perspective (but see I. Black 1983). Therefore, somewhat more detailed treatment is here justified, with full investigation to be undertaken in a separate book. (The treatment here borrows in parts from Dror 1983c).

## Models of Policymaking as Fuzzy Gambling

A good image for considering policymaking as fuzzy gambling is an unstable casino, where not playing is itself a game with high odds against the player; where the rules of the game, their mixes of chance and skill, and the payoffs change in unpredictable ways during the gambling itself; where unforeseeable forms of external "wild cards" may appear suddenly (such as a terrorist attack or the distribution of diamonds by prodigal millionaires); and where the health and life of oneself and one's loved ones may be at stake, sometimes without one's knowing it.

Moving to policy sciences terminology, pure-type "policymaking as extreme gambling" involves situations in which the dynamics shaping outcomes of decisions are unknowable and take the form of indeterminacy, discontinuities, and jumps. In such cases:

1. Outcomes cannot be predicted in terms of defined possibilities, not to speak of risk (in the technical sense of probability distributions).
2. Allocation of subjective probabilities is an act of delusion.
3. Nondecision or incremental decisions are futile as strategies for containing uncertainty, for repetition of the same act may bring about radically shifting results.
4. Values and goals themselves lose their constancy in decision making, *inter alia* because of unpredictable changes in contexts shaping priorities.
5. Better intelligence cannot do more than explicate ignorances, at best, even under the hypothetical assumption of "privileged witness" with full access to all information and realities. (On the concept, see Ayer 1982, 38.)
6. There is a high objective probability of low-probability events occurring frequently. In subjective terms, surprise dominates.

Moving from an extreme pure type to an intermediate model of policymaking as fuzzy gambling, main features of the construct include:

1. In part, outputs can be predicted in terms of risks and in terms of possibilities. In part, outputs will take the form of unpredictable configurations, with discontinuities and jumps.
2. In part, situations can be diagnosed as more in the direction of jumps or more in the direction of smooth continuity; in part, ignorance dominates, with no possibility to assess situations in advance as smooth or jumping.
3. Utility of subjective probabilities and decision-analysis methods based on them, constancy of values and goals, potentials of intelligence for containing and reducing ignorance, and so on depend on the situational mixes of uncertainties and on ignorance on this matter itself.
4. Low-probability events occur with changing frequency and surprise is endemic.

To be emphasized is the rooting of ignorance in reality itself, with indeterminacy, jump propensity, multiplicity of low-probability events, etc. being inbuilt in the dynamics of relevant processes, in any case as far as accessible to the human mind within its present capabilities.

Leaving aside various metaphysical problems posed by these constructs (for a pleasant introduction to some of them, see Eigen and Winkler 1981), it is sufficient to note here that the intermediate model fits contemporary thinking on various evolutionary and biological processes. The extreme construct is counterfactual, both to regularities inbuilt in the physical cosmos and to the pattern-creating *modus operandi* of the human brain. But, the extreme construct serves as an essential basis for clarification of the idea of policy gambling. *Inter alia*, it brings out the need for a concept package going beyond currently available terminology and notational symbols.

To build up a concept package adequate for handling policy gambling, verbal and notational symbols are needed as follows, in addition to available terminology such as certainty, risk, and uncertainty:

- A clear distinction is needed between two kinds of uncertainty: quantitative uncertainty, when the possibilities are known but without any probability distribution between them; and qualitative uncertainty, when the shape of future possibilities itself is unknown. The terms *quantitative uncertainty* and *qualitative uncertainty* can serve for this distinction.
- The term *mixed uncertainty* denotes situations in which some of the possibilities can be predicted but do not add up to a complete set, with other possibilities being qualitatively indeterminate.
- The term *volatile uncertainty* is suggested for situations in which possibilities can be expected to take the form of discontinuities and jumps. *Volatile quantitative uncertainty* and *volatile qualitative uncertainty* de-

note, respectively, potential jumps that can or cannot be sketched in advance.

- The term *ignorance* is suggested for situations in which predictability itself is unknown, there existing no base for defining the situation as risky, quantitatively or qualitatively uncertain, more or less volatile, and so on.

These and additional terms must be further developed. Also, additional mathematical and logical notations are needed to deal with such concepts, their combinations, and in-betweens. A number of logical problems must be worked out, such as the permissibility of combining in one probability distribution adding up to 1.0 some possibilities with specified probability, some in the form of qualitative characterization without probabilities, and a domain of qualitative uncertainty. And a revised calculus of ignorance, uncertainties, and risk-needs development, going beyond present probability logics.

All this, within the world of discourse and inquiry of decision making (in distinction, for instance, of the uses of probability as denoting the validity of inference). Present mathematical language, as used in the social sciences as a whole and policy sciences in particular, is inadequate for handling policy gambling: Smooth curves and simple probabilistics up to stochastics are inadequate and partly misleading. The theory of games is loaded with misleading assumptions. And fuzzy-set theory and catastrophe topology, as well as the emerging mathematics of chaos, are hard to apply even within their limited, mainly heuristic, potentials.

*Fits with Reality*

Even if the models of policymaking as fuzzy gambling were not more than a priori constructs, their working-out might provide additional languages and propositions of theoretic interest, but a strong claim can be made that actual policymaking circumstances partake increasingly of important elements of policy gambling. To illustrate domains of qualitative uncertainty and ignorance, it is enough to mention jumps in oil prices, the frequency of surprise events in the Middle East, and the unknown implications of persistent large-scale unemployment and of technologies for the future shapes of societies.

Exaggeration must be avoided: Many basic features of reality follow relatively smooth curves with much predictability within policy-relevant time spans, as illustrated by demographic data and main features of West-East relations, albeit structural features of reality can be shown to be unstable in part, with resulting indeterminacy in important facets including prediction of policy consequences. Historically, this is not new. Even during relatively stable situations such as the Middle Ages or Asian-mode-of-production societies, consequences of decisions were often qualitatively uncertain because of the very indeterminacy inbuilt in some main components of social dynamics within a decision-making minicontext, such as human life and behavior. But, at present, humanity is not in a period of relative stability but an epoch of transformation, as considered in chapter 2, and the homology of the intermediate policy-gambling model with significant parts of reality is pronounced. Therefore, the policy-gambling construct should be of some help in portraying reality, analyzing policymaking, and serving policymaking improvement.

*Fuzzy-Gambling Incapacities*

Under policy-gambling conditions, many aspects of policymaking must be changed. Thus, the concept of "news," as discussed for instance by Keynes (Keynes 1973, ch. 12) gets a new meaning, with "future news" becoming both more in demand and less available (Shackle 1972, 179-80), as well as often unacceptable because of its counterconventional characteristics; "future reconnaissance" is the maximum that can be done, "predictions" being often a dangerous illusion; policymaking, correctly seen, frequently partakes elements of "speculation"; the possibility that determined action may have under some conditions a better chance of imposing desired shapes on indeterminate futures than do hesitant and incremental decisions adds another consideration to the already-discussed critical-mass policy principle; and so on. Such requirements go far beyond currently available ideas in policy sciences and related disciplines, and their underlying worldviews. Even more, such requirements run counter to most of policymaking cultures and institutional doctrines. Furthermore, the requirements meet very strong and stubborn incapacities head on.

All the barriers to complexity management, as discussed earlier, also apply to fuzzy gambling, with many additions (Axelrod 1976; Benveniste 1977; J. Cohen 1960; Dörner et al. 1983; Fischhoff and Beyth 1975; Fischoff et al. 1981; J. Halliday and Fuller 1974; Hogarth 1980; Kirkpatrick 1975; Langer 1977; Nisbett and Ross 1980; Sienkiewicz 1979; Tversky and Kahneman 1973; Tversky and Kahneman 1981; Wallstein 1980; Warwick, with Mead and Read 1975; G. Wright 1984. Kahneman, Slovic, and Tversky 1982 is especially important; for a critique of some of the work see L. Cohen 1979. Some of the papers in R. Schwartz, in press, are quite different in being somewhat more optimistic about human thinking on uncertainty. Hogarth and Makridakis 1981 is an excellent summary of main studies and discussion of their significance for policymaking, under the term *planning*.) In particular:

- The human mind is often no good at handling uncertainty. Nothing comparable to good pattern recognition relieves the uniformity of error propensities apparently inbuilt in human behavior when facing uncertainty, unless—and often also when—judiciously following explicit approaches, which seem quite counterintuitive to the uninitiated. Thus, humans tend to an illusion of controlling chance events, which causes grievous decision errors. A number of studies indicate the ability of human decision makers to adjust decision styles to various conditions, such as uncertainty (e.g. Beach and Mitchell 1978; Christensen-Szalanski 1978; Christensen-Szalanski 1980; H. Weiss 1980). Still, most of the studies in decision psychology clearly show inherent weaknesses of human thinking when facing qualitative uncertainty and ignorance. Case studies of policymaking also reveal grave difficulties of decision makers in facing correctly qualitative uncertainty and ignorance.
- Political and organizational information processing stubbornly replaces objective uncertainty with subjective certainty. In addition, low-probability events tend to be ignored, even when they have very high potential impacts. Or, when low-probability events are considered, emotional reactions to their possible impacts sway attitudes. The already-discussed military intelligence failures provide much material on the organizational misapprehension of uncertainty situations and the incapacity to process correctly uncertainty information.
- Senior policymakers, with some exceptions, such as in the military, tend to resist perception of their decisions as fuzzy gambles. In this respect, they are definitely not "gambling professionals" who devote much effort to working out thinking to handle chance through the application of skilled strategies (as contrasted, for instance, with professional card players, see Hayano 1982, esp. ch. 3). In the consultative activities of the author, one of the major sources of conflict with senior policymakers has been their hostility to regarding themselves as fuzzy gamblers for high stakes. Even when the senior policymakers intellectually accepted this image, they resented it deeply. These findings well fit some studies in decision psychology on intolerance for ambiguity and uncertainty.
- Political culture supposes governments to know what they are doing and not to gamble with the fates of their nations, imposing facades of certainty even on central minds of governments who sometimes know better and giving a competitive advantage to the naives, who authentically fool themselves that they know for sure what they are doing. "Gambling with history" (Barrett 1983) is not accepted as a correct and unavoidable characterization of policymaking under adversity.
- Modern mass culture as a whole, especially in Western countries, seems to get more apprehensive about risks (Aharoni 1981; Douglas and Wildavsky 1982; Perrow 1984). Especially, dramatic very-low-probability contingencies seem to displace from consideration less dramatic contingencies with higher probabilities and with at least as harmful possible

outcomes (Wildavsky 1979a). Public opinion formation processes seem incapable of handling essential elements of decision making in the face of uncertainty, such as the distinction between estimating probabilities and judging their desirability or undesirability.

• Appropriate ideas on how to improve fuzzy gambling are very scarce (Holling 1980; Humphreys et al. 1983; Kunreuther 1978; Mack 1971; Raiffa 1968; Wang and Chang 1980). In particular, situations of qualitative uncertainty and ignorance are neglected in most of the quantitative uncertainty treatments (a partial exception is Shackle 1972). Methodological difficulties in handling fuzzy gambling encourage instead uncertainty-hiding techniques, such as subjective probability allocation (as in the Delphi Method, unusually carefully handled in Linstone and Turoff 1975), even when these are easily misused to build up delusions of knowledge, when explication of ignorances would be better. Institutional inventions for handling uncertainty (as illustrated historically by the development of maritime insurance, see Hodgson 1984; Spooner 1983) are as yet absent, with relevant functions of the "welfare state" and welfare policy being often incompletely realized and handled (e.g. N. Gilbert 1983; Rein 1983a).

In addition to its importance as a main requisite of high-quality policymaking, the fuzzy-gambling specification serves to bring out firm and infixed error propensities organic to core policymaking-system components. This, in respect to a specification's becoming increasingly crucial with growing indeterminacy as a dominant feature of adversity. Under more stable conditions, inherent incapacities to handle fuzzy gambling are less of a handicap. But, when conditions change and impose increasingly on fuzzy-gambling capacities, radical changes are needed in main qualities of policymaking to avoid dismal failures.

Policymaking-quality deficits in respect to fuzzy-gambling capacities take dismal forms: realities are misperceived; probabilities are allocated in very biased ways; uncertainties are repressed; chance is perceived as subject to control; refutational evidence is not looked for; and so on. When the weight of uncertainty and ignorance becomes finally realized in central minds of governments, serious forms of maze policy-behavior result, such as escape into policy theologies, fact denial, or recklessness. In such consequences, deficits in fuzzy-gambling qualities bring out the serious dangers of the inadequate sophistication of the central minds of governments and the unavoidable, grave policymaking errors stemming from them.

A·quotation from a treatment of "rubbish theory" may serve to sum up fundamental policymaking-quality issues brought out by the fuzzy-gambling sophistication requirement, including the contradiction between such requirements and basic features of policymaking as a cultural activity:

> Nature is essentially chaotic and continuous; culture is orderly and discrete. Thus nature continually threatens to break down the water-tight compartments which culture seeks to impose on it. Since natural compartments seldom, if ever, occur, it is likely that there will be some natural elements which are on the borderline between two cultural categories, no matter where that borderline is drawn. These borderline cases (if they are "visible") threaten to destroy the precarious order established by culture and so must be accorded special treatment by the culture bearers. Taboo behavior and pollution avoidances cluster about these borderline cases in all cultures [M. Thompson 1979,91].

To stretch "rubbish theory," there is little wonder that demands for fuzzy-gambling sophistication and their underlying perceptions of reality as uncertain and indeterminate are often regarded as "pollution" by both policymakers and policy analysts, to be categorized as "rubbish" and rejected accordingly.

### Excursus on Throwing Surprises at History

An extreme form of policy gambling is the throwing of surprises at history, in the sense of adopting a radically innovative and quite unexpected option. Related to other specifications discussed in this chapter, such as alternatives innovation and crisis decision making, an ability to throw surprises at history should be added to needed qualities of policymaking under adversity. As touched upon in chapter 5, when trends are ominous, then efforts to mutate them are preferable. Under such situations the throwing of surprises at history becomes a necessary policymaking mode. Similarly, when transient opportunities arise, the throwing of surprises at history may become a preferable, though less compelling, policymaking mode.

Despite the historic regularity of surprise policies being adopted from time to time, the long-standing recognition of surprise as one of the principles of war, and the prescriptive importance of making surprise moves in important situations, the subject has only recently been subjected to some more systematic studies (Axelrod 1979; Betts 1982; Dror 1975b; Handel 1981). Quite clearly, policymaking process-systems differ in their capacity to consider and sometimes adopt surprise options. Barriers to alternatives innovation and to fuzzy gambling as considered above and a broad tendency to try to avoid visible risks, as involved in surprise options, are shared by most central minds of governments (e.g. on the USSR, see Adomeit 1982). Policy entrepreneurs play an important role in initiating surprise policies and pushing them through, as illustrated by Kissinger in respect to China (Kissinger 1979, esp. ch. 18 and ch. 19). On a more systemic level, it seems that democracies have greater difficulties than authoritarian regimes in throwing surprises at history because of the needs for much power concentration, closed decision making, strict secrecy, and very centralized decision making.

If adversity becomes epochal and takes a shifting form, the ability to throw surprises at appropriate times may become an increasingly important policymaking specification. This applies to the domains of economic and social policies, *inter alia,* not less so than to external and security policies. This is a subject extending and making extreme the policy-gambling perspective, and is in need of much attention.

### Excursus on Unintended Consequences

The policy-gambling perspective serves to focus attention on a main problem of policymaking, clearly formulated by Robert Merton in 1936, namely, "unanticipated consequences of purposive social action" (Merton 1936). Herbert Simon has reiterated unintended consequences as one of the two most difficult issues in decision making (H. Simon 1978; H. Simon 1979b).

Aspects of the subject well treated in available literature (Boudon 1982; Sieber 1981) aside, the view proposed above of many policymaking realities as fuzzy-gambling situations adds a number of aspects to the issue of unintended consequences:

1. Policymaking objects and their relevant environments can be classified in terms of the nexus between intervention and outcome. In particular, unstable objects will react in less predictable modes, with more unexpectable consequences.
2. Especially interesting are so-called explosive situations (Shackle 1972, 384), in which intervention will trigger far-reaching consequences including surprises.
3. Early diagnosis of environments with strong propensities to produce unintended consequences can result in an expectation of unexpected consequences, permitting adoption of suitable policymaking modes, such as accelerated learning.
4. Given explosive situations, nonintervention often is not a way to reduce surprises because many situations will "explode" in any case. "Explosion containment and direction" and even "explosion utilization" may become a main goal of policymaking in respect to some such situations.
5. To relate this subject to the above-considered throwing of surprises at history, surprise policies aim at mutating trends and breaking undesired continuities. Unavoidably, surprise policies will therefore entail many and far-reaching unintended consequences.

In combination, the fuzzy-gambling specification together with the special case of throwing of surprises at history and the underlined problematics of unintended consequences form a main cluster of features of policymaking under adversity. This syndrome is radically different from the "incrementalism" cluster and its derivatives, being much more demanding in all respects. Hence, the crucial importance of fuzzy-gambling sophistication as a requisite of high-quality policymaking under adversity. Such sophistication is a precondition of adjusting main policymaking features to the needs of facing adversity, as well as for understanding better the realities underlying actual maze policy-behavior.

## Applied Social Sciences

The last decade or so has witnessed a vast quantitative growth in literature on applied social sciences as potential and actual important inputs into policymaking (Bulmer 1983; Charlesworth 1972; Cherns 1976; Cherns 1979; Covello 1980; C. Ferber and Kaufmann 1977; Horowitz 1971; Lazarsfeld and Reitz 1975; Mayer 1980; McCall and Weber 1983; Nagel 1975; OECD 1979a; Olsen and Micklin 1981; Podgorecki 1976; Rein 1976; Rein 1983b, passim; R. Rich 1981; C. Weiss 1980). A special case in point is social experimentation, proposed as a main aid to policymaking, as is "evaluation" (Bernstein and Freeman 1975; Fairweather and Tornatzky 1977; Larkey 1979; Patton 1975; Rivlin 1971; Rutman 1977; C. Weiss 1972; more critical are Alkin, Daillak, and White 1979; R. Ferber and Hirsch 1981). But, developments during the last decade have also clarified and sharpened some barriers to policy-relevant social scienes and to actual utilization of applied social sciences in policymaking (Badura 1976, passim; Bulmer 1982; Bruder 1980; N. Caplan, Morrison, and Stambaugh 1975; Deitchman 1976; Lindblom and Cohen 1979; L. Lynn 1978; Meister 1981; Rothschild 1982; Rule 1978; R. Scott and Shore 1979; C. Weiss 1977, passim), including:

- The social sciences have not made progress in understanding macrochange and rapid social transformation, and may be unable to do so (Boudon 1983).
- The social sciences have contributed a little, in the strict literary meaning of more but not much more than nothing, to the diagnosis and understanding of social problems, despite the proliferating literature going under that presumptuous name (one illustration will be enough, namely, Bourne and Levin 1983). On problems that have been worked on for many years, such as crime, the social sciences are still far from providing reliable diagnosis and understanding, not to speak of useful prescriptions (despite innovative efforts, such as J. Wilson 1983; see also Jacob 1984. On heroin, see J. Kaplan 1983).

- The social sciences have became increasingly involved in advocacy and social criticism, but without adding major insights or providing novel grand-policy alternatives, or usefully taking up main policy paradigms.
- The social sciences have progressed little beyond Western cultural assumptions and values, making applicability to other cultures doubtful. Also, policy cultures in some Third World countries are not congenial to social science utilization (Stifel, Davidson, and Coleman 1983).
- There exists no body of agreed "public knowledge" (Ziman 1968) in the social sciences on a policy-relevant level. The one discipline that approximated pseudoagreement were parts of economics, which got discredited by refusal of realities to be bound by positivistic economic assumptions, in addition to increasing disagreements in economics itself (e.g. for an unusual approach fitting well the needs of policymaking in the face of uncertainty, see B. Klein 1977).
- With some exceptions, such as in evaluation studies and social experimentation, few policy-oriented methods have been developed in the social sciences.
- In particular, the applied social sciences continue to be quite compartmentalized from prescriptive methodologies, precluding convergence with policy analysis and similar approaches in forms conducive to advancement of the social sciences in policy-relevant directions and their actual inputting into policymaking.
- The above weaknesses may well constitute manifest symptoms of deeper problems and characteristics, such as doubts among social scientists about appropriate forms and degrees of "engagement" with public issues (Schalk 1979); neglect of history and historic material, related to methodological fashions; and, perhaps, basic features of present social sciences assumptions and concepts, related to problems of underlying philosophy of science. Whatever the reasons may be, with the important exception of providing factual bases for some policy issues susceptible to empiric research, an overview of main social science publications of the last decade provides no "eureka" experiences to a seeker after major findings and ideas relevant to central themes of policymaking under adversity (though some social scientists serve as policy innovators, M. Young 1983).

This does not imply that, were such applied social science knowledge available, it would be rapidly accepted and utilized in policymaking. As can be learned from the fate of the substantive, though limited and sub-problem-oriented, social science knowledge that is available, its actual use in policymaking is limited and depends on peculiar and unusual circumstances. Thus, in the United States, the impact of some social science findings on very important policy issues occurred, thanks to judicial constitutional-political powers and the Brandeis Brief procedural device enabling the inputting of complex social science data into judicial considerations. Both these institutions are limited to the United States and have no functional equivalents in other countries.

The applied social sciences are an important requisite of high-quality policymaking, for only they can supply some of the knowledge essential for handling main policy predicaments. Here, inadequacies of contemporary scientific knowledge as essential policymaking infrastructure and as parts of the mental-intellectual qualities of minds of governments constitute a serious barrier to policymaking, different in important respects from other forms of incapacities considered in this chapter.

Some additional aspects of the applied social sciences as a requisite of high-quality policymaking under adversity are taken up, together with problematics of policy sciences, in the next chapter. Here, while reiterating that the social sciences have made important contributions to policymaking by factual findings and some contributions on a theoretic level, main policymaking-quality deficits resulting in parts from weaknesses of the applied social sciences can be summed up: lack of adequate understanding of main adversities and their underlying variables; scarcity of substantiated policy-paradigm reconsideration and policy-orthodoxy debunking, with some distinguished exceptions overshadowed by policy theologies having a stronghold in parts of the social sciences themselves; and absence of methodological contributions to policymaking under adversity, with single exceptions.

To balance the picture, progress in understanding the realities of policymaking itself should be mentioned, such as in decision psychology. Such progress will be considered in chapter 8, but belongs in part to the applied social sciences for policymaking, somewhat redressing the conclusion on their inadequacies, without reversing the finding as a whole.

## Effort Concentration

"Effort concentration" deals with levels of energy and strength of policymaking will necessary in policymaking under adversity, including their staying power, such as for realizing the earlier-considered policy principles of critical-mass and of active-up-to-powerful policies. In addition, the effort-concentration specification refers to the need to allocate priorities, such as indicated by the selective-radicalism policy principle.

Maze policy-behavior, as earlier considered, is characterized by policymaking enervation and debilitation, with short bursts of semiconvulsive activities. The specification of effort concentration puts converse requirements, namely, vigorous policymaking focused deliberately.

Levels of policymaking energy are difficult to define and nearly impossible to ascertain. The question of what is political or policymaking will as applied to the central policymaking process-system has no clear answers (thus D. Davidson 1980, ch. 2 which discusses "how is weakness of the will possible" is difficult to apply to collective minds of governments, and also to single rulers). And, the question whether policymaking will is a matter of accident and/or can be deliberately improved is hard to tackle. If the specification of effort concentration is expanded in its meaning so as to include acts of will to deny policymaking "drives" in favor of improved policymaking qualities, conceptual and operational difficulties are multiplied. Possible dependence of effort concentration on a few persons who hold key policymaking positions further introduces accidentalism and subjectivization into the treatment of this specification.

Other than a little literature on individual-psychological and -philosophical aspects of will, and some speculations on national aspiration levels as drive providers (D. McClelland 1961) and similar processes on organizational levels (Cyert and March 1963), and perhaps some material on relationships among subjective sense of efficaciousness, power, and drives, there is little in available knowledge that can be relied upon. And, application of the above ideas to minds of governments is too doubtful to be justified, even as a speculative conjecture. There exists no basis for trying to identify even tentatively relevant incapacities and for detailing present deficits. (For an attempt to explain some policy failures in terms of lack of political will, see P. Lodge and Blackstone 1982, to be contrasted with the treatment of the same subject by Boudon 1974.)

Despite such imponderables and protean materials, some starting points for exploration of the effort-concentration specification can be identified, such as:

- The concept of "central minds of government" must be disaggregated to examine the extent of internal frictions (in the sense of Clausewitz 1976, bk. 1, ch. 7. Clausewitz discussed the matter at greater length in his teaching material for the crown prince, surprisingly apparently not translated into English; see G. Dill 1980, 39-43). Relations between elected politicians and tenured civil servants, which can concentrate or dissipate policymaking will, are illustrative (Aberbach, Putnam, and Rockman 1981; Crossman 1975-77; Dogan 1975; Suleiman and Alba 1984).
- It is possible to achieve effort concentration through shared realistic visions, up to revolutionary fervor (as illustrated by Trotsky's action ideology, see Knei-Paz 1980). Integrated with a suitable model for government, very powerful effort concentration can be achieved, as illustrated by Lenin's ideas for organizing the Bolshevik revolutionary movement (for a fascinating discussion, deserving to be pondered by organization theory to overcome rather passive views of the potentials of organizations, see Lundquist 1982).

- Upbuilding the core "quarters" of the central minds of governments can help effort concentration, with concomitant costs in terms of overloads, implementation difficulties, and more (an important description of efforts in this direction is provided in C. Campbell 1983).
- Integrated training of the higher policymaking elites can increase effort concentration, as somewhat illustrated historically by the public-school tradition in the United Kingdom (R. Wilkinson 1964), and by the French National School of Administration (E.N.A.) nowadays (interesting to compare with the palace school of Muhammad the Conqueror, B. Miller 1941).
- Strong rulers can be a main factor in effort concentration, this constituting one of their principal contributions to policymaking under adversity.

These are only some pointers on an important subject, which reaches into the already-considered broader issues of the power bases of policymaking, to sets of advantages versus disadvantages of more or less effort concentration under various conditions, and to possible comparisons of various regime types in terms of their capacity to achieve effort concentrations in handling adversity.

The situation is even more complex than that: While it might seem reasonable to diagnose some countries as lacking effort concentration, this by no means is true in respect to all Western democracies, some of which pass through periods of quite pronounced policymaking will. In many of the nondemocratic countries, strong effort concentration can be found, sometimes too much, leading to a possible conjecture that there is a preferable range of effort concentration, varying with conditions; and that too much effort concentration is also harmful.

To construct any models of policymaking, the concept of effort concentration and its main component of policymaking will are essential. Without examination of such motive forces, policymaking cannot be understood (as well realized in Mackenzie 1975); and, without trying to analyze and, when necessary, improve such motive forces, upgrading of policymaking lacks a pivotal element.

Frustrations of the reader at being left with these observations on the importance of effort concentration as a specification of high-quality policymaking under adversity, without any further analysis and conjectures, are shared by the author. Lack of relevant concepts, data, and theories leaves the effort-concentration specification as a question mark and a challenge to research and thinking.

## Crisis Decision Making

The importance of effort concentration and some of its effects when pushed to an extreme, is in part brought out in crisis decision making.

Crisis decision making is a special mode of policymaking under adversity, of much importance in a number of countries and of critical potential importance to all. The more crises are prevalent or fateful, the more good crisis decision making becomes essential. Important and largely irreversible decisions are taken during crises. Therefore, much of ordinary policymaking can become futile, unless crisis decision making is designed to converge with policymaking as a whole and becomes integrated into it.

The specifications of crisis decision making need, in a number of countries, some broadening beyond their usual connotation of containing and reducing a crisis to status quo ante. In particular, when shifts in policies and policy paradigms and radical transformations in reality are needed, crisis instigation in the form of throwing of surprises at history, as already discussed, and crisis utilization to remold reality become important policymaking modes. To repeat some earlier observations in the present, somewhat different, context, crisis instigation is very risky, with high probabilities of many unanticipated and probably undesirable results (Dror 1975b). Special barriers in democracies to surprise policies, together with the dependence of surprise policies on the quality of single strong decision makers (Handel 1981), add to the problematics of crisis initiation and utilization. Nevertheless, conditions may require such policymaking to bend and reverse ominous trends and to utilize rapidly passing opportunities. In some countries, excellent crisis decision making in the thus broadened sense of the term constitutes therefore an especially important policymaking requisite.

Crisis decision making is a relatively well studied subject, behaviorally and prescriptively, including the psychology of individual decision under stress and strain (Coelho, Hamburg, and Adams 1974, ch. 8, 9; Cooper 1983; M. Hermann 1979; Holsti and George 1975; Janis and Mann 1977; M. Kaplan and Schwartz 1977; Schuler 1980); special effects of small groups working under crisis conditions (Minix 1982; Ridgeway 1983), such as "groupthink" (Janis 1982); and overall features of crisis decision making (Billings, Milburn, and Schaalman 1980; M. Brecher 1979; Frei 1979; Frei 1982; C. Herman 1972; M. Herman and Herman 1975; Holsti 1972; Oneal 1982; Smart and Stanbury 1978; Smart and Vertinsky 1977; Snyder and Diesing 1977; J. Stein and Tanter 1980; B.A. Turner 1976). Thanks to writings by actor-observers during the Cuba Bay of Pigs invasion and the missile crisis (Kennedy 1969; Schlesinger 1965; Sorensen 1966. Such writings were essential for sophisticated theoretic processing, such as Allison 1971. An interesting example of a different kind of crisis-manager memoirs is Kehrl 1973) and, much less so, other crises (e.g. H. Jordan 1982), some unusual inside data are available to serve as a calibration check on historic and case-study reconstruction and theoretic models. Nevertheless, caution is needed in relying on much of the theoretic and experiments-with-students-based literature, which clearly shows that the authors have never in their lives participated in a real high-level, crisis decision making incident. This is one of the matters in which acting-observing is essential as a source of reliable information.

Especially troublesome is the possibility that a very intense crisis may result in irrational behavior, caused by stress and strain, and that major crisis-management structures may make many unanticipated mistakes (D. Ball 1981; Bracker 1983; Hopple 1983; and, especially, Oneal 1983). This is in particular true for the extreme case of nuclear conflict, but applies also to lesser crises. Thus, limited available information on handling of economic crises provides a rather dismal picture. Also to be taken into account is that few countries make any effort to build up custom-designed processes and facilities for handling crises other than in the security domains and, sometimes, some repetitive kinds of mass emergencies. In the relatively advanced crisis-management systems for security emergencies, too, important components are scarcely prepared at all. Thus, senior politicians hardly partake in preparation for crisis decision making, with single individual exceptions, even though much of the onus in real crises is upon them. Visits by the author to crisis-management units in quite a number of countries did not impress him that much really sophisticated preparation for fateful policy gambling under extreme time pressure and in the face of surprises does take place. Overloads with current pressures; reluctance to "think on the unthinkable"; scarcity of suitable methods and professionals; anxiety about utilizing some relevant knowledge, such as in psychology— these are among the factors inhibiting adequate crisis decision making. Underlying incapacities may include the unavoidable overwhelming of "cold reasoning" by "hot" emotions and pressures under the impact of real crises. Many such problems are quite neglected in most of the studies on crisis management and are hardly accessible by the methods on which such studies are often based.

Crisis decision making is concentrated in all countries within small kernels of the minds of governments, which are kept well hidden from probing investigators. Evaluation of the quality of crisis decision making by results is also not easy. Thus, to take decision making under conditions of terror incidents: If a kidnapped person is released by successful application of force, this is a clear-cut success; but whether this was a matter of luck, or overall good antiterrorism policies and their implementation, and/or of high-quality crisis decision making is not always clear. More ambiguous are other outcomes, such as release of the victim as a result of giving in to terrorist demands; or murder of the victim because of nongiving in to terrorist demands. What here is success or failure of crisis decisionmaking? Also, more important, fateful crisis decision-making qualities must be evaluated before a crisis comes along to prevent hideous costs. Such evaluation is only partly possible, and requires extensive experimental running of cr'sis decision-making systems under controlled conditions, with full access to all data. It is not known what countries, if any, run such exercises in adequate forms, and the results of such endeavors are always kept highly secret.

Actual quality deficits of crisis decision making can be suspected as being very high, with all the error propensities mentioned above. But no direct evidence to refute or verify this conjecture is available, lack of information being more pronounced in respect to crisis decision-making realities than in regard to most of the other policymaking specifications considered in this chapter.

Subject to this caveat, studies on crisis decision making do provide important tentative and suggestive findings on the error propensities and incapacities inherent in the very situation of decision making under crisis conditions, such as: radical oversimplification of estimates of situations; wishful thinking on adopted options; locking on decisions, with escalating commitment in spite of negative feedback; substitution of group solidarity for achievement of task as group goals; shifts in risk propensities; fatigue phenomena; insidious swings between euphoria and depression; and more.

Crisis decisionmaking serves to illustrate the possibility to design operational improvement proposals on the basis of studies of incapacities. Thus, main improvement proposals (in addition to above-cited literature, for a different approach see Greene 1982), include: positive redundance and multiple advocacy, also under crisis conditions; running-in of crisis decision-making units; open-ended contingency planning; co-option of decision psychological advisors in crisis decision-making staffs; assurance of adequate communications and control facilities; real-time display of complex information in comprehensible formats; and more. But, when such improvements are attempted, additional improvement-inhibiting forces come to the fore. For instance, as mentioned above, in important crises senior politicians fulfill dominant roles. Therefore, running-in of crisis decision making requires participation of top politicians in some exercises. But, very soon, they refuse to do so (Mosher and Harr 1970): No politicians in their right senses put themselves voluntarily into situations where they are up for evaluation. Nevertheless, crisis decision making is a facet of policymaking under adversity for which useable improvement possibilities are available.

Ascertainment of actual deficits of crisis decision-making qualities poses a dilemma: On one hand, reliable indirect studies strongly identify a number of serious quality deficits inherent in crisis decision making, unless determined and sophisticated countermeasures are taken, and even if such

countermeasures are adopted; and, reliable studies on governmental behavior strongly indicate that no such determined and sophisticated efforts
to improve crisis decision making are likely to have been made. On the
other hand, direct evidence on present crisis decision-making qualities of
central policymaking process-systems is scarce.

## Strong, but Contained, Rulership

Moving squarely to the power-concentration dimension of high-quality
policymaking under adversity requirements, the specification that can best
bring out involved problematics poses strong, but contained, rulership as a
necessity. The fundamental antinomy confronted here can be briefly presented in a dialectic form.

Main thesis: Strong rulers (including, under some conditions, compact
collective ruler-teams) are necessary to achieve power concentrations and
political-will amplifications (and policy entrepreneurship as considered
later), as needed for policymaking under adversity. Policy packaging to
mobilize support, charismatic effects to overcome fragmentation and
shortcut alienation, mass-media utilization to appeal to public opinions
and remold them—these are some additional functions that strong rulers,
and often only strong rulers, can adequately fulfill. Providing inpetus, im-
pulse, and push for approximating high-quality policymaking as discussed
in this book (as well as for other requirements of effective governance),
again, depends largely on strong rulers. Therefore, the thesis.

Main antithesis: Rulers and rulership have strong inbuilt policymaking
incapacities, ranging from tendencies toward "rulerscraze," already noted
by Tactitus, in the sense of mental aberrations that can be looked at as
"occupational diseases," "occupational psychosis" as discussed by Dewey,
and "professional deformations" as discussed by Warnotte (Merton 1949,
153). These lead to accelerating decay of decision quality, with initial successes carrying the seeds of dismal failures, as a result of reinforcement of
self-confidence and of declining learning ability.

Some out of many typical incapacities and error propensities inbuilt in
rulership, within a statistical variance, seem to include:

- Distorted cognitive maps, especially in the direction of oversimplifica-
  tion and obsolescence.
- Consideration of only a narrow range of alternatives.
- Piecemeal approaches to issues, with much inconsistency.
- Irrelevant decision criteria, such as emotional support needs instead of
  issue handling, or idiosyncrasy.
- Oscillation between panic decision making and choice procrastination.

- Early "locking" on simple solutions, with rejection and repression of negative feedback and learning inputs.
- Ego hypertrophy, with loss of sense of proportion, up to "I-cannot-make-any-grave-mistake"delusions.

And many more. Such incapacities stem from interaction between rulers as human individuals and the special circumstances of rulership, being inherent in the role of rulership as an UR-component of governance, with many constants between different historic and contemporary regimes. Important variations between individuals and regimes do exist but do not reduce by much the fundamental inherent incapacities of rulers.

Synthesis, in the dialectic sense of bridging the thesis and antithesis, is very difficult. Plato applied his wisdom to this problem, without much applied or theoretic success. The unabated spectacle of nonsense and counterproductive decisions (including nondecisions) by rulers testifies to the stubborn unresolvability of this riddle posed to human governance-design ingenuity. The large literature dealing with rulers and rulership, descriptively and prescriptively, contains important leads and interesting findings and ideas, but no thread through the maze. (Recent writings in their diversity and disparate approaches, mainly in the United States but in some other countries as well—not including myth-shattering biographies, such as Caro 1982; Esbery 1980: and Greenstein 1982—are illustrated by Barger 1984; B. Buchanan 1978; J.Burns 1978; S. Cohen 1980; Cronin 1975; Cronin and Greenberg 1969; Edinger 1976; A. George 1980; C. Hardin 1974; Heclo 1977b; Heineman and Hessler 1980; M. Herman and Milburn 1977; Hess 1976; Hodgson 1980; R. Jackson and Roseberg 1982; Janus 1977; Knutson 1973; Meltsner 1981; Nash 1980; Neustadt 1980; Paige 1972; Paige 1977; Rejai and Phillips 1979; Robbins 1977; Rose and Suleiman 1980; Sanford 1981; Tucker 1981; R. Tugwell 1974; W. Williams 1980a; W. Williams 1981; and more.)

Possibilities of some progress in the direction of improving policymaking by influencing the performance of rulers in democracies in ways designed to reap benefits while containing costs and risks can, in part, be summed up as follows:

1. One main approach to handling the error propensities of rulers is to reduce the authority and functions of the latter. This is a main leitmotiv of the history of constitutionalism in general, and of democracy especially, albeit within the basic frame of Western democracy, for reasons already presented, further shackling of rulers is counterproductive because of essential tasks that can be adequately fulfilled only by rulers or with their active and often leading participation.

2. Democracy has gone quite far in reducing some of the error-producing features of rulership, such as symbols and paraphernalia (as compared, for instance, with the USSR; see C. Lane 1981). Further moves in this direction may, again, be counterproductive, impairing important capacities more than reducing incapacities.

3. Changes in the recruitment of persons to serve as rulers, so as to get personalities able to withstand error-producing features of rulership as an institution, are at present impossible for two reasons. (a) Not enough is known to identify "dangerous" personality characteristics of persons who consequently should not be permitted to reach rulership, assuming such universal findings are at all possible (which I doubt, despite J. Barber 1977). Particularly to be kept in mind is the possible correlation between some psychopathological tendencies and very positive abilities that may be essential for high-quality rulership under conditions of adversity (Lange-Eichbaum and Kurth 1967, to be compared with Simonton 1984). Lyon Mackenzie King provides an interesting and, relatively, mild illustration of this disturbing, but very real, possibility (Esbery 1980). And (b) the imposition of such restrictions on the right to be elected as ruler contradicts basic principles of democracy, as now understood. Surrogates proposed from time to time, such as to expose candidates better to the public, are very doubtful in their results because of mass media marketing techniques (M. Robinson and Sheehan 1983; Sabato 1981, ch. 3). Perhaps after bitter experiences, maybe in the future, the rules of democracy will change so as to permit some limitations on ruler selection, but this is far off.

4. Variations in terms of office, in collegial versus individual decision modes, and in forms of accountability and in removability illustrate constitutional changes that are, in principle, feasible within present democratic values. But (a) such proposals are far from proved effective; and (b) they are next to impossible to get approved, without a serious, dramatic, or prolonged crisis of governance and/or a "constitution-giving" ruler. This is an illustration of an area where good research and creative design may result in applied recommendations that have a chance to influence reality, though patience and persistence are essential.

5. Variations in the immediate support system of rulers are easier to do and potentially quite useful. Advisors are also an UR-component of government, accompanying rulers from their primordial beginnings (Goldhamer 1978). Developing, professionalizing, and institutionalizing advisory units for rulers is, therefore, a possible improvement avenue. It is based on the idea of binding oneself so as to reduce error propensities, or what I call "self-imposed metarationality" (well expressed in the Ulysses and the Sirens metaphor, Elster 1979; Schelling 1980). This is an ongoing endeavor in many democracies, as mentioned in chapter 3, though usually without adequate understanding of underlying issues.

Handling of rulership in nondemocracies poses even harder problems. In countries that aspire to engage in far-reaching societal transformation, intense needs for power concentration to succeed in difficult societal architecture require strong rulers, *inter alia.* But, in those very countries, dangers of misuse by rulers of their powers are particularly acute, because of absence of strong countervailing forces, weak traditions of self-restraint, and more.

The high-quality policymaking specification of strong, but contained, rulership brings out some fundamental problems of improving policymaking under adversity. Harmless measures have no chance of handling adversity, while possibly effective measures carry serious dangers of error and also evil. In the face of adversity risks are unavoidable, whatever is done or not done.

Realities of rulership differ radically among countries, depending on personalities not much less than on constitutional structures and actual power politics. Quality deficits vary, therefore, with different mixtures of inadequate strength of rulership and of inadequate containment of rulership. The pronounced error propensities of rulership, as considered above, and the very inadequate existence of possible arrangements to try to reduce some of the error propensities are universal.

One promising sign, mentioned in chapter 2, is a trend in some Western European democracies for the power of heads of governments to be augmented. According to the present specification, and my analysis of the needs of policymaking under adversity as a whole, this is a positive development contributing to reduction of a serious deficit in some countries, which might otherwise move toward dangerous power vacuums. In Western democracies there is little danger of strengthened heads of governments becoming too powerful (for a different view, see, for instance, Norton 1982, ch. 1). But the dangers of error propensitites and of consequent wrong policies being pushed by stronger rulers seem acute in a number of countries.

It should be added as a postscript that the ideal of "enlightened" rulers has not been proposed in this specification, and in the book as a whole, because of its ephemeral nature and relativistic contents. To take an extreme but illuminating example: In the opinion of one of the outstanding biographers of Adolf Hitler, if Hitler had been assassinated in 1938, "few would hesitate to call him one of the greatest German statesmen," with all his aggression, anti-Semitism, and so on being put aside. (Fest 1975, 9). There is no need to go so far to realize that judgment of a ruler as "enlightened," with the exception of extreme cases, is subjective and changes with time. Even within a given political culture, operational definition of *enlightenment* is impossible, other than in the form of a large, vague, and inconsistent shopping list. Therefore, the concept of "enlightened" rulers is eschewed in this book.

## Policy Entrepreneurship

Policy entrepreneurship combines a number of policymaking requirements in a particular form. Alternatives innovation and power concentration, together with "herestetics," in the sense of political strategy and creative adjustment skills (Riker 1984), leading to implementation breakthroughs—these characterize policy entrepreneurship in its purer forms.

The importance of entrepreneurship in the economic domains is fully recognized, at least since Schumpeter (Schumpeter 1952) and does receive some theoretic attention (e.g. Casson 1982; Kilby 1971; Meredith and Neck 1983; Silver 1983), even though remaining far from understood. In the public policy domain, entrepreneurship is an important phenomenon that is not difficult to identify when occurring. Illustrations picked at random include William Beveridge (J. Harris 1977), to be compared with Sir Edwin Chadwick (Finer 1952); Monnet (Monnet 1978), Moses (Caro 1975), Rickover (Polmar and Allen 1982), and Peccei (Peccei 1977; Peccei 1981)— to take just a few cases out of many. But, with some exceptional beginnings (E. Lewis 1980), no starting points for building a general theory of public policy entrepreneurship are available, and ministudies are also very scarce (Doig 1983).

A few of the relevant questions include:

- What is the interplay between personality, on one hand, and societal and cultural conditions, on the other hand, in bringing about policy entrepreneurship?
- In what measure is entrepreneurship determinative in bringing about policy innovations, or would similar innovations have been introduced in any case, with some changes in timing and details?
- What are the main relations between policy entrepreneurship and power, ranging from basically powerless innovators who achieve impact on realities through indirect influence, up to dictators who initiate and enforce very radical policies through their personal power and will?
- What are the possibilities, if any, to facilitate policy entrepreneurship when needed, such as for policymaking under adversity?

A glance at some historic material may permit the following speculative conjectures as a starting point for systematic work:

1. There is no assurance that a functional need for policy entrepreneurship will bring it about. Thus, comparison of Caesar and Augustus (Meier 1980b; Meier 1982) leads to the proposition that absence of an awareness of alternatives floating around in the political culture precludes, or at least delays, policy entrepreneurship's meeting predicaments, even if urgently needed. Comparison of Leon Blum and de Gaulle (Lacouture 1982; Ledwidge 1982) seems to support this speculative conjecture.

2. Some entrepreneurs have significant impacts on reality according to their idiosyncratic desires. An extreme illustration is Hitler. Although the Weimar Republic may have been doomed because of the economic situation and the nondemocratic preferences of most of the parties and the population at large, it was the personal initiatives of Hitler that imprinted Nazi Germany with its main features (Bullock 1964; W. Carr 1979; and Fest 1975; in addition to general literature on Nazi Germany cited elsewhere). The way in which Hitler brought about the "Final Solution" without ever giving orders in writing is relevant (Fleming 1982).

3. Much entrepreneurship accelerates and sets the details of policies that in any case would have been arrived at, such as the influence of Beveridge on national insurance in the United Kingdom. The policy of deterrence with the help of nuclear submarines would also probably have been arrived at, or some equivalent solution would have been developed, even if some years later, without Hyman Rickover.

4. Different actors can serve as policy entrepreneurs, in various combinations. Rulers and their advisors, other politicians, civil servants, priests, intellectuals, business executives, aristocrats, ideologues—these and other actors have served as policy entrepreneurs in various countries and at different periods. Some shifts in the relative importance of various groups of actors can be discerned in specific societies. Thus, in modern states, politicians seem to serve more as policy entrepreneurs than do civil servants (Aberbach, Putnam, and Rockman 1981), but no generalization on the level of a general theory can be made in the absence of suitable studies.

5. Some organizational structures have been explicitly designed to fulfill some roles of policy entrepreneurship, including in particular think tanks. But, keeping in mind the distinction between inventing a new policy alternative and engaging in the promotional and risk-taking activities characterizing entrepreneurship, one finds the performance of think tanks as policy entrepreneurs hard to evaluate.

6. Reasonable conjectures can be made about different regime types and different political cultures being more encouraging of policy entrepreneurship than others in relation to societal problem-handling capacity as a whole. Democracies may here enjoy a policymaking advantage over closed societies.

7. Under what conditions are developing countries able to produce policy entrepreneurship? is a very important and interesting question. If underdevelopment as such inhibits policy entrepreneurship, this constitutes another policy-incapacity vicious circle, with those societies most in need of policy entrepreneurship being least able to produce it. But there is no reason to assume that developing countries per se are handicapped in their ability to produce policy entrepreneurs, the political regime and the existence of some elites being perhaps more important, together with basic features of culture, than levels of socioeconomic development. With no relevant studies available, this question must be left open, including implications for possible measures to encourage policy entrepreneurship in developing countries. The success of some developing countries in rapid industrialization is relevant, as is the upsurge of grassroot entrepreneurship in Third World countries when permitted. But policy entrepreneurship is usually more constrained.

Such speculative conjectures leave the subject very much up in the air. In the absence of an understanding of the basic processes of policy entrepreneurship, and without empiric studies on the success of different organizational structures in bringing about policy entrepreneurship within government (in line with T. Peters and Waterman 1983, on excellence in business organizations) being available, policy entrepreneurship joins those specifications of high-quality policymaking under adversity that can be posed but not treated adequately. This is an additional subject put into the limelight by the needs of policymaking under adversity that needs in-depth study.

### Tragic Choice

The concept of "tragic choice" (Calabresi and Bobbitt 1979) well expresses a main requisite of policymaking that grows both more important and harder to meet with evolving policy predicaments. "Tragic choice" refers to the necessity to choose between the "unchooseable" and to allocate orders of priority and relative weights to values and goals all of which are absolute in themselves, at least in the eyes of many participants in policymaking. Needs for arbitrary decisions where indivisible costs must be imposed on particular and specified groups constitute a form of tragic choice. Location of nuclear waste illustrates such cases, as do some ethnic policies in the United States (Glazer 1983).

Tragic choice involves a number of policymaking dimensions, such as mental-intellectual dimensions in respect to developing and analyzing options; value dimensions in making the judgments; and power dimensions to be able at all to engage in effectuated tragic choice. Involved are interactions between ideas and pragmatism (Rebe et al. 1984) and main elements of "political judgment" (Beiner 1984).

Factors that increase the importance of tragic-choice improvement as a policymaking-quality specification in the face of adversity include: (a) the growing necessity for transincremental decisions, which pose and involve explicit choice among options that are highly sensitive to differential values and goals, and, therefore, are contingent upon tragic choice; (b) harsher scarcities, as illustrated in public expenditure squeezes and environmental constraints; and (c) more value disagreements, which pose more divisive tragic choice occasions and necessities.

At the same time, barriers to tragic choice are also on the increase, including:

- Expectations that more of everything will become available build up in many countries during prosperity because of political marketing competition and in relation to "revolutions in expectations," up to some version of what has been called "playboy democracy" (Ortlieb 1974).
- Intense value disagreements and disconsensus, with more single-goal action groups fighting militantly for what they believe in.
- In many democracies and also some nondemocracies, a spreading value that sacrifices and reductions must be agreed to by those involved, in addition to legitimate collective allocation decisions.
- Political fragmentation in many countries, as already discussed, requiring simultaneous satisfaction of many values and interests to build and maintain necessary coalitions.
- Absence of accepted and overriding values, goals, and codes, such as defying an enemy or a compact ideology, which provide agreed decision critera and tragic-choice legitimation.
- Hesitations to enforce duly approved decisions, and also to make decisions, against active resistance by minorities, as already discussed.

As a result, tragic choice runs into strong antinomies: To make policies more effective in achieving aimed-at impacts on reality, quite clear-cut value priorities are necessary. Furthermore, democratic values as well as most moral systems require such priorities to be determined consciously and publicly. But, to meet requisites of politics, such as coalition maintenance and conflict containment, tragic choices have to be avoided and diluted, or at least hidden and camouflaged.

There exists no "scientific" guide to tragic choice (despite attempts such as D.E. Bell, Keeney, and Raiffa 1977; Chankong and Jaimes 1983; Cochrane and Zeleny 1973; Dekema 1981; Keeney and Raiffa 1976; Rhodes 1980; H. Young, 1980; H. Young, Okada, and Hashimoto 1980; H.

Young, Okada, and Hashimoto 1981) other than explication of necessary value judgments, such as in the form of "scorecards" analyzing impacts and value consequences of different alternatives (Chesler and Goeller 1973, sec.2; Goeller et al. 1977; Goeller et al 1983). This adds to the political difficulties and the individual burdens of hard tragic choices (as illustrated by Tribe et al. 1976, still in too mild a form). It is necessary to take into account that tragic choice is a matter not only of deciding between different substantive goals and values but also of deciding between different risk distributions and different time preferences. All this is staggering mentally-intellectually, frightening morally, imposing psychologically, and prohibitive power-politically.

To sharpen the last point, three comments need adding:

1. Despite various attempts (e.g. Rokeach 1979), the sociopsychological and cultural natures of values are far from understood.
2. Various attempts to develop value-guides for decision making have failed operationally, in addition to always being themselves based on some particular axiological position. Thus, the idea to propose the "quality of life" concept as a tool for decision making (Environmental Protection Agency 1973) is a dismal failure (Springbourg 1981). The attempts to work out guidelines on what is a "just war," however interesting and worthwhile (e.g. Walzer 1977), also do not provide answers to tragic choices. Neither are broad value discourses, such as Rawls 1971 (a different example is Ackerman 1982), useful for actual policymaking (in addition to other problems, e.g. see Barry 1973).
3. Even when a government accepts a relatively clear value code, this does not significantly reduce the difficulties of tragic choices. This is well illustrated by the history of Catholic Church decisions (e.g. Böckenförde 1973; this is a very neglected subject, as is church governance as a whole in modern political science).

In countries with a shared sense of national mission or with dominant power concentrations, tragic choice is easier in its power-political aspects but still very difficult mentally-intellectually and, from an outsider's perspective, morally. When decisionmakers are true believers, their task subjectively is easier. These are limited situations, but the attractiveness of dogmas as "solving" tragic choice dilemmas must not be forgotten, the seeking of such compasses being a possible response to tragic choice impasses, as already mentioned.

In Western democracies and, to a lesser but still pronounced degree, in many nondemocracies, tragic-choice incapacities produce significant policymaking-quality deficits in the direction of nondecision, counterproductive compromises, harmful decision inconsistency, and some features of maze policy-behavior. Possible handicaps of democracies in handling tragic choice in comparison with nondemocracies can become a serious disadvantage if adversities impose harsher tragic-choices and if tragic-choice capacities of democracies are not improved significantly.

## Implementation Direction

Movement from the lofty heights of moral dilemmas to the more mundane issue of implementation may seem like a big drop, but both are integral to policymaking under adversity. However technical in some respects, implementation direction is important and its deficits are related to significant inbuilt incapacities of central policymaking process-systems.

When considering implementation, a distinction is necessary between the more administrative-organizational and the more public-political aspects of policy realization. These two are closely interactive and partly overlap but can analytically, in part, be handled separately. The present specification deals with "implementation," which refers mainly to the administrative-organizational aspects of policy realization. Political feasibility was considered in chapter 4 and in earlier specifications, and some additional aspects will be taken up later in this chapter.

Little needs to be said on the necessity of implementation direction. With the exception of declarative-symbolic policies and a few self-implementing ones, actual impacts of policymaking depend on implementation. Many studies (in addition to elsewhere cited ones, Larson 1980; Meehan 1979; Persson 1979; Ripley and Franklin 1982) demonstrate strong tendencies for policy spoilage and policy distortions during implementation, though the possibilities of policy-distorting implementation correcting policymaking mistakes are quite real and often ignored. The more policies are transincremental and the more policies deviate from accepted paradigms, the more serious are dangers of nonimplementation and of inappropriate implementation. Therefore, implementation direction constitutes an essential specification for policymaking under adversity and a precondition for achieving impacts with innovative policies (in addition to the importance of implementation monitoring for policy learning, as considered later).

Technically, implementation direction can take a number of forms. A necessary first step is suitable decision recording, nowadays preferably on a computer. Then, suitable instructions have to be given. Follow-up can include nominal confirmation of implementation by the agency in charge; specific and detailed reporting on implementation according to yardsticks; up to independent implementation checking and result monitoring. Antecedent to all this, implementation-feasibility consideration must be included within policymaking.

The finding of the survey by the author that the large majority of governments examined do not engage in meaningful implementation direction of main decisions by the central minds of governments, especially by heads of governments and cabinets, is relevant. Sometimes no usable systematic records of main decisions are kept; very seldom are decisions put on a computerized tracking program; even nominal implementation confirmation is an exception; and reliable implementation follow-up is practiced only in single countries. This situation calls for explanation. Principal factors at work inhibiting implementation direction by the central minds of governments include the following:

- Parceling of jurisdictions and power, implementation direction going beyond acceptable concentration of power and authority by the head of government and the cabinet as a collective.
- An atmosphere of enforced mutual trust, for instance between cabinet members, where implementation direction, and expecially follow-up, is regarded as infringing on accepted codes. It should be added that this is an agreed fiction, nonimplementation and misimplementation being well-recognized facts.
- In a number of countries, there is a lack of administrative skills and administrative discipline needed for implementation direction.
- Lack of desire to direct implementation, in part as a result of nonwillingness to face and handle nonimplementation and misimplementation.
- Tacit consensus that many decisions are not really expected to be implemented, being nominal in their real intent, despite formal appearance to the contrary.

The last factor is especially revealing, for it permits interpretation of lack of implementation direction as indicating a mode of decision making at very high levels that is not intended to have declared impacts on reality but to meet psychological and political needs, partly overlapping symbolic politics and policy theatre. How far are such decisions helpful in handling adversity, and when do they impair adversity handling by permitting indulgence in illusionary policymaking not intended for implementation? are questions in need of further research. Ambiguities about the degree to which a policy is really intended for implementation add to the dangers of such a decision mode at top levels of governments, especially when policy disagreements may increase misinterpretations on the implementation intents behind various innovative decisions. When policies not intended for implementation go beyond a certain proportion of all decisions, the whole seriousness of policymaking is impaired. Movement in such a direction was uncovered by the survey in a number of countries.

Resulting quality deficits can be summed up: Weaknesses of implementation direction impair policy impacts, especially when policies are innovative. Absence of implementation direction can reduce policymaking to nominal exercises not taken seriously by the participants and having no relation to governmental action. Some tendencies toward such a fundamental policymaking-quality deficit can be discerned in a number of countries.

The consideration of implementation feasibility within policymaking is a more complex matter. Tendencies in the literature to overplay implementation difficulties can easily combine with incrementalism tendencies in organizations and make implementation-feasibility mapping into a conservative process inhibiting necessary policy innovations. To be taken into account are, *inter alia*, the following considerations:

- "Implementation feasiblility" is a vague concept, with self-fulfilling and self-defying prophecy effects and similar diffuse factors playing hard-to-analyze roles.
- Implementaion feasibility is correlated with power concentration and rulership, as already discussed. In addition to such structural features, political skills (F.G. Bailey 1970; Bardach 1979; Riker 1984) play a large role, as clearly recognized by Machiavelli.
- Under turbulent conditions, as characterizing adversity, implementability is subject to change, including sudden and temporary shifts and "windows of opportunity."
- Implementability of policies must also be looked at within a fuzzy-gambling perpective, with ignorance and various forms of uncertainty surrounding implementation possibilities.
- Political cultures differ in taking a narrower or broader view of what can be done, ranging from very tradition-bound worldviews to regarding utopias as around the corner. While such worldviews are often detached from policymaking and policy-implementation realities, sometimes the latter are conditioned by a broader political culture.
- In Western democracies, curious mixes between narrow and broad views on policy implementability can be discerned, with jumps between optimistic and pessimistic moods conditioning policymaking.
- The mistaken tendency of implementation literature to emphasize failures needs reiteration. With few exceptions (e.g. Meltsner and Bellavita 1983), the mainstream of public policy literature ignores clear-cut cases of successful implementation (e.g. Koppes 1983), including such achievements as integration of women into jobs historically monopolized by men (a study on the Air Force Academy, Stiehm 1981, is striking).

Because policymaking under adversity requires policy innovations, a main need is to broaden implementation feasibility. Focused implementation direction, with powerful central minds of governments applying concentrated efforts to a limited number of issues, also according to the selective-radicalism policy principle, can significantly broaden the domains of implementability, but the transfiguration of implementation institution may be required. The latter is so important a specification of high-quality policymaking under adversity as to need some further examination.

## Transfiguration of Implementation Institutions

Implementation direction is an essential condition for achieving impacts on reality, especially by innovative policies. But, even when fully developed, implementation direction is sometimes insufficient to assure implementation in ways maximizing impact probabilities on reality in accordance with policy intentions. Often, the more innovative a policy, the less possible it is to get it implemented without transfiguration of implementation institutions. Therefore, transincremental policymaking, new options, and, especially, innovative societal architecture must include institutional redesigns of implementation structures as an integral policymaking specification.

Concomitantly, it is important to keep in mind the equifinal outputs, negative and positive, of a variety of institutional arrangements. Thus, it is quite possible to introduce a variety of structural changes in administrative agencies without achieving any real impact on main outputs, a phenomenon also related to the critical mass-change issue, discussed in chapter 5. Conversely, good policy implementation can be achieved through a variety of institutional arrangements.

Hindrances and incapacities to better consideration of implementation institution revamping are manifold, including both mental-intellectual and power-political ones.

Mentally-intellectually, no good institutional theories are available to serve as underpinnings for required transfigurations. Despite growing interest in organizational design and transformation (Beckhard and Harris 1977; Jay Galbraith 1977; Khandwalla 1978; Kilmann, Pondy, and Slevin 1976; Miles and Snow 1978; Mintzberg 1979a; Mintzberg 1983; Nystrom and Starbuck 1980 and 1981; Spray 1976) and continuous work on administrative reforms and change (Allison and Szanton 1976; G. Caiden 1969; G. Caiden and Seidenkopf 1982; Chapman and Greenaway 1980; Hammergren 1983; Leemans 1976; OECD 1980; Radian 1980, ch. 8; Steinberg 1979; Szanton 1981a; Weiss and Barton 1979), reliable knowledge on fitting public organizations to new policies is very scarce. The convergence of new policies with broader changes in the social, political, and economic ecology within which governmental institutions must operate makes the task even more difficult (Aldrich 1979), while outdating many past-based findings. Increasing interest in "implementation" within policy sciences is as yet of no help either, focusing more on adjusting policies to existing organizations or trying to motivate existing organizations to implement novel policies, rather than taking up more radical needs of organizational demolition (Kaufmann 1976) and transfiguration, in relation to transincremental policy innovations (Bardach 1977; Dunsire 1978; Edwards and Sharkansky 1978; Grindle 1980; Hargrove 1975; Pressman and Wildavsky 1973; James Thompson 1980; W. Williams 1980b; W. Williams 1982; Yaffee 1982; Hirschman 1965 is different and underutilized as a starting point for a revised theory of implementation institution transfiguration.)

Power-politically, the inertia of institutions, traditions (Shils 1981), and vested interests is so strong as to discourage and frighten off consideration of organizational and institutional transfiguration as essential for implementation of new policies. Thus, transformation of social policies is quite hopeless without shaking up welfare-delivery complexes. To agitate such hornet's nests by engaging in "constructive destruction" of administrative machineries is politically very expensive and dangerous. Therefore, impact-weak laws and policy declarations, together with minor reorganizations, are often, though not always, preferred to the Herculean (or Sisyphean? Elboim-Dror 1982) tasks of achieving real impacts through organizational transfiguration. Exceptions do occur, especially under pressure of changing conditions, as illustrated by the Tennessee Valley Authority in the United States (Hargrove and Conkin 1984). But exceptions are scarce.

In some Third World countries the situation is quite different, in part because of the absence of a highly developed administrative machinery and in part because of mistrust of such machineries by politicians (Honadle 1979; Honadle 1982). Often, special organizations are set up to look after the implementation of main policies, such as those related to accelerated development, sometimes successfully so (e.g. G. Lamb and Muller 1982). But, in many Third World countries the administrative infrastructure is inadequate for implementing complex societal architecture policies. Other approaches, such as mass mobilization, have been used in some Third World countries with a few successes but they also disappoint expectations rapidly.

It is a moot question, whether such implementation difficulties in many Third World countries are unavoidable, or could be overcome in part by adoption of better implementation strategies, including design of suitable implementation organizations. Efforts by Third World countries to develop administrative machineries fitting their specific needs may well have been inadequate (as have often been efforts to design political regimes fitting their special conditions and traditions together with accelerated development aspirations. Compare Apter and Doornbos 1965). Be that as it may, the finding about inadequacy of policy-implementation institutions in Third World countries is well supported by available evidence.

The policymaking-quality deficit of inadequate transfiguration and nova-design of implementation institutions is pronounced, with differences of degrees among countries. It seems reasonable to expect this deficit to become more manifest with continuous adversity, when innovative policies are increasingly developed by central minds of governments only to be frustrated by inadequate implementation, until implementation-institution transfiguration becomes an integral facet of policymaking under adversity, with invention of new forms of organizations fitting novel policies. Industrial policies in the United States are a good example, possible desires by the central mind of government to move in such direction being nonimplementable without quite some revamping of the machinery and staff of government (Schmuck 1983).

## Quality and Cohesion of Policy Elites

The subject of policy elites illustrates again a main set of barriers to meeting policymaking-quality requisites, namely, ideological taboos and political folklores. These have little to do with really reducing inequalities in society or achieving equity, but do prevent deliberate policy-elite development, leaving policy-elite qualities to self-recruitment and doubtful screening mechanisms.

The needs for policy elites with due qualifications and with some measures of cohesion can easily be derived from the requirements of high-quality policymaking under adversity as discussed up to now, without reconsidering elite theory as a whole and adjusting it to contemporary and emerging conditions (Bachrach 1967; Field and Higley 1980; Putnam 1976). To meet mental-intellectual requisites, policy elites need upgraded knowledge and abilities; and to meet power concentration requisites, policy elites must preserve and develop sufficient cohesion to permit compact policymaking. In addition, to permit policymaking autonomy, as discussed in chapter 4, in countries where significant societal architecture is needed, top policy elites should be partly detached from present realities, without losing touch with them—which adds up to a very difficult requisite.

Some countries do engage in cadre training or encourage it. An interesting illustration is provided by the Political Academies in Austria, run by the parties with public funds. Totalitiarian countries often presume to engage in cadre training, but this is usually more indoctrination in dogmas than preparation of high-quality policy elites (as illustrated in extreme form by the Nazi regime, Höhne 1978; Scholtz 1967; Scholtz 1973; Überhorst 1969; on East Germany see Ludz 1968).

The problem in Western democracies is difficult, with Jacksonian ideology the more accepted the less it fits increasingly complex realities. Changes in education, which in some countries reduce the elite-producing functions of schools and universities, are related. Relevant is the ongoing discussion in the Federal Republic of Germany on mass universities versus the need for elite universities. The latter are still rejected, with some exceptions, such as the private European Business School in Koblenz. Taboos inhibit frank consideration of the issue and the search for solutions meeting both equitable values and societal needs. Even relatively simple and harmless proposals, such as the setting up of national policy colleges for intensive upgrading of policy sophistication of mixed groups of elites (as done in some of the better defense colleges in a few countries in respect to defense policies), are often outside the domain of legitimate options.

Underlying are much harder questions about entrance into politics and public service and advancement channels. Politics in many countries seems to attract persons with problematic motivations and abilities. Thus, whatever little is known or surmised on the psychological profiles typical of politicians (Davies 1980; Greenstein 1970; Greenstein and Lerner 1971; M. Hermann with Milburn 1977; Iremonger 1970; Knutson 1974; Lasswell 1960; Robbins 1977) leaves little scope for much optimism.

Therefore, if spontaneous and unexpected processes cannot be expected to improve policy-elite qualities and if taboos continue to inhibit explicit action to improve policy elites, further depression in an important policy-quality-determining variable seems unavoidable.

Difficulties about deliberate action to improve the political parts of the policy elites are serious: Reliable knowledge on correlations between recruitment and career patterns on one hand and quality of policymaking on the other is not available; dangers to democracy of intervention with recruitment and career patterns of politicians are grave; consequences of interventions are hard to predict (as illustrated by the failures of many electoral reforms to achieve their aimed-at and expected results, Bogdanor and Butler 1982); and it is hard to see ways to make desirable changes politically feasible. Some things can be done, as illustrated in chapter 10, but improving the political parts of the policy elites is hardly the place to start policymaking upgrading.

The situation in respect to the civil service components of the policy elites is quite different. Here, ideology supports intense improvement efforts; taboos, while existing, are less intense; and some knowledge on which radical improvement of higher civil service elites can be based is available, as illustrated in quite a number of countries by interesting proposals, even if inadequate ones, made by many civil service reform commissions. Nevertheless, the survey by the author leads to the conclusion that no country has a civil service training and development scheme fitting the needs of policymaking under adversity. The French National School of Administration is the most advanced existing training institution for senior civil servants, but, till 1983 at least, the curricula did not fit the needs of policymaking under adversity. In most European countries, legal training continues to dominate among senior civil servants. The newly established European Institute of Public Administration, in Maastricht, Holland, initiates some needed innovations. In the United States, despite the Carter civil service reforms, not much has happened to upgrade the qualifications of senior civil servants and not much can happen as long as all top positions are reserved for short-term political appointees (Heclo 1977a) and the idea of an administrative elite is taboo; in the United Kingdom, nearly nothing of the Fulton Commission recommendations has remained; and so on. Resistance by established civil servants; lack of understanding of needs for a different kind of civil service policy-professional on the part of politicians, combined with apprehensions about a new class of "technocrats"; public hostility to civil servants in a number of countries; and preoccupation of public administration studies with other issues—these are among the factors explaining lack of significant improvements in the civil service components of policy elites in the highly developed Western democracies as well as Japan. In most Third World countries the situation is worse, lack of resources and absence of clear ideas on desirable features of senior civil servants adding to the causes of grossly inadequate improvement efforts. Export by the highly developed countries to the Third World of inappropriate models for civil service training and of outdated "experts" adds to the barriers.

Growing groups of various specialists in government do not compensate for the weaknesses of main policy elites. Thus, the expanding numbers and power of economists in governments (Coats 1981) help with some kinds of issues but do not significantly upgrade the qualities of policymaking under adversity as a whole, especially in view of the failings of modern economics as mentioned in chapter 2.

Moving from the internal staffs of central minds of governments to policymaking infrastructure leads into the roles of intellectuals and their functions in politics and policymaking (Alatas 1977; Aron 1962; Brym 1980; Debray 1979; Gouldner 1979; Oren 1984; Schalk 1979; Shils 1972. An interesting case study is Keren 1983; also relevant is M. Young 1983.).

Especially significant is the type going under the term of "policy intellectual" and related groupings. Prescriptively, intellectuals have crucial functions to fulfill in policymaking under adversity, such as alternatives innovation, policy entrepreneurship, policy knowledge production, and enlightenment of public opinion. Factually, such functions are fulfilled to some extent, especially in open societies—again, providing the latter with a relative advantage. Until suitable studies are available, evaluation of the points of strength and weakness in the contributions of intellectuals to policymaking under adversity in various countries and types of regimes is impossible. *Inter alia,* the question whether present and emerging features of adversity may enhance suitable contributions by intellectuals, by stimulating innovative policy thinking, or may depress such contributions, by pushing intellectuals into policy theologies, is important but cannot be answered. Developments in both directions are visible, but not much more can be said at present on this very important matter. Neither does the sociology of knowledge provide a basis for considering possible ways to encourage innovative thinking by policy intellectuals in already open societies. Even relatively simple issues are quite opaque, such as the advantages versus the disadvantages of policy intellectuals' having more access to central minds of governments.

The next question is the even broader and more important one, namely, what is the distribution of the scarcest of all of social resources, namely highly capable persons, among different activities? Does an adequate quota of such persons enter policymaking and policy-influencing positions? And how can the entrance of such persons into policymaking and policy-influencing positions be influenced, if desirable, without disproportional costs?

This leads into questions of elite recruitment, elite self-images, elite values, elite cultures, elite identifications, etc. Good studies are available on parts of the subject (Czudnowski 1975; Eliassen and Pedersen 1978; Putnam 1976), some pertinent issues are covered by the University of Michigan Comparative Elites Project (summed up mainly in Aberback, Putnam, and Rockman 1981; specific country studies are illustrated by Eldersveld, Kooiman, and Tak 1981), but most such issues are shrouded in ignorance. Thus, during interviews with top-level policymakers as well as policy intellectuals, in the United Kingdom, the opinion was expressed that the higher civil service draws too high a proportion of the best-endowed and -educated persons, leaving industry short of capable candidates (a view also expressed by Denis Healey in H. Young and Sloman 1983). But, in Japan, there is tough competition by the best students to get into the civil service via the Tokyo University Law School, without any adverse results for industry occurring. Contrariwise, in the United States, business seems to draw a large proportion of "the best," sometimes recruited later for short terms of office in government. In brief, the situation is diverse and unclear; and the question itself may well need reformulation. Still, the problem of distribution of persons with diverse capabilities among careers, including various components of policy elites, is a serious one, deserving more attention. In addition to the above-mentioned universal underpreparation, if not mispreparation, of senior civil servants, especially •disturbing is the widespread opinion that politics draws many persons of doubtful quality as policymakers and that the advancement of politicians is mainly determined by criteria having little to do with skills and knowledge relevant to policymaking.

An esoteric, but potentially significant, question is whether persons with special capabilities for policymaking under adversity exist, comparable to great chess masters or calculation prodigies (S.B. Smith 1983). And, if such persons exist, is there any way to draw them into suitable policymaking positions? Present knowledge does not even permit conceptualization of such possible special talents, but in principle these questions need attention.

In a number of countries, including some Third World countries especially in need of high-quality policymaking, additional problematics include lack of interest by the policy elites in the long-range advancement of their countries, sometimes with moral corruption; inadequate stock of educated human resources for producing and maintaining a minimally qualified policy elite; and brain drain of such large dimensions as to deplete policy elites of essential components. Far-reaching indoctrinization of policy elites with various nonsensible policy theologies in some countries illustrates additional factors ruining policymaking capacities.

However looked at, serious deficits in policy elites seem to emerge, with important differences among various societies and regime types. Some ways to try and perhaps to reduce such policy elite inadequacies include:

- Acceleration of policy-elite turnover, with changes in bases of recruitment. This can also take, in part, the special form of introducing new types of professionals into policymaking positions.
- Resocialization of crucial elements of policymaking elites, through special "training" institutes.
- Strengthen elected or appointed politicians who reflect cultures different from that of most of the traditional policy elites.
- Shocks that drive policymaking elites out of their frames of appreciation, usually as a result of overwhelming events, can provide opportunities for elite reshaping.
- Transfer of parts of policymaking to other entities, controlled by different cultures, such as through regionalization.

• Change of large parts of the policy elite, usually in conjunction with social power transformations in periods of revolutions.

Such possibilities transgress in the main the scope of this book, however broad. They illustrate the overlap between the study of policymaking and overall societal issues, and the need to enlarge the perspectives and interests of policymaking improvement in the direction of governance redesign, as considered later in this chapter. Some operational proposals for building up elites as a way to improve policymaking under adversity are presented in chapter 10.

### Enlightened Policy Publics

Available data on public opinion do not show that the public is always wrong. Neither has the *vox populi vox Dei* assumption empiric support. On one hand, changes in public values (Inglehart 1977a; Klages and Kmieciak 1979), however difficult to measure (Handy 1970), show adjustment capacities and progress potentials of public opinion. On the other hand, studies also indicate serious weaknesses in public processing of news (Graber 1984) and judgment on complex issues. Analysis of direct democracy experiences provides little support for optimism (Butler and Ranney 1978; Ranney 1981; Troitzsch 1979). Even under ideal commune conditions, opinion formation demonstrates disturbing features (Zablocki 1980). In many countries, tendencies toward populism and mass behavior persist (Broch 1979; Canetti 1960; Canovan 1981; Connuff 1982; Ortega y Gasset 1932; on the related interplay among sports, culture, and politics, see Cantelon and Gruneau 1982). Historic studies on mass support and mass bases for "irrational" politics cast further doubts on currently widespread optimistic views on public opinion and popular movements (Collingwood 1947; Linz and Stepan 1978; Mosse 1975; Talmon 1952; Talmon 1960; Talmon 1981; still provocative is W. Reich 1946). In particular, impacts of "harsh situations" (Preisl and Mohler 1979) on public opinion raise serious problems, especially in an epoch of nuclear *Angst* and long-term economic troubles. Exaggeration must be avoided, and some of the attacks on mass culture should be recognized as biased (for balanced evaluation in historic contexts, see Barrows 1981; Brantlinger 1984). But, still, findings on the policy quality of public attitudes, argumentations, and opinion are as a whole quite problematic—especially on complex and agitating issues, such as those characterizing adversity. Hence my aphorism that, unless the capacities of publics to comprehend policy issues improve, the impacts of publics on policymaking will either decrease or often (but not always) have effects for the worse.

Not surprisingly, the progress of democracy has often been tied in with hopes for an enlightened citizenry, through mass schooling, mass media, etc. (Brennan 1981; Janowitz 1983; Mannheim 1950; Mannheim 1951a), but, as yet, mass schooling is not automatically producing mass policy enlightenment (Allard and Rokkan 1970), to understate the matter. Mass-media coverage of news hardly helps (W. Adams 1982, to be compared with the situation in Yugoslavia [G. Robinson 1977], which was quite untypical for nondemocracies). Other diverse efforts in this direction are illustrated by the injection of readable policy studies into public debates (such as Green Books in the United Kingdom) and the establishment of semi-independent policy research organizations to contribute diverse and more objective inputs into public opinion formation, such as the Dutch Scientific Council for Government Policy and the New Zealand Planning Commission, not to speak of various other bodies (as illustrated in the United States by the Commission on Critical Choices for Americans [1976]).

Improving the policy opinions of the public is a difficult matter, inhibited by many factors. Thus:

- Despite years of research, the basic dynamics of public opinion formation are not clear, may differ among cultures, and may or may not be changing significantly with modern mass media (T. Cook et al. 1983; Elgin 1982; Liebert and Schwartzberg 1977; Milavsky et al. 1983; National Institute of Mental Health 1982; Pearl 1982; Phelan 1980; Ranney 1983; D. Roberts and Bachen 1981; M. Robinson and Sheehan 1983; Tannenbaum and Kostrick 1983) and social transformation (Noelle-Neumann 1980; Weissberg 1976). To take a relatively simple policy-related illustration: Public opinion on science seems to be jumpy and hard to rationalize (Markovits and Deutsch 1980; Jon Miller 1983).
- Not only are no reliable ways known to "enlighten" the public but potential tools can easily be misused for symbol manipulation, propaganda, and political marketing (C. Elder and Cobb 1983; Freedman and Freedman 1975; Goodin 1980; Nimmo and Combs 1982). Related is the serious problem of media monopoly, also in the United States (Bagdikian 1983).
- Ideological differences of opinion make distinctions between "enlightenment" and "propaganda" difficult to maintain and, in part, politically unacceptable.
- Some inbuilt features of politics may have negative impacts on public opinion qualities, such as political competition for a growing floating vote with help of advanced public relations and "political marketing" techniques and a new breed of political consultants (Sabato 1982) in

democracies; and, much worse, support-recruitment engineering in nondemocracies.

- The very subject of "enlightening" the public is taboo, especially in democracies, as if it insults the sovereign voters and as if it undermines essential democratic myth (which may be a real danger, although sophisticated democratic ideology is based on the right of participation and political self-determination, and not on assumptions about the wisdom of the populace).

- There is very little knowledge available on improving policy opinions of the public. Thus, experience with political enlightenment through mass media is rudimentary (Schultheiss 1976); uses of social studies at schools for preparing future citizens better to fulfill their roles are far from promising (Hartmann 1980; Heater 1981; Mehlinger and Davis, 1981; Merelman 1984, ch. 5); and systematic work on presentation of complex issues in easier, comprehensible formats is inconclusive (Fisher 1984; Wainer 1981). Whether new communication technologies, home computers, and similar advances may change the situation, as supposed by some (e.g. Hiltz and Turoff 1978; Servan-Schreiber 1974; Servan-Schreiber 1981, passim), and whether new types of material may get rid of widespread biases in citizen preparation (Hudson Institute 1983a, Hudson Institute 1983b; Kahn 1983) are open questions.

The very least that can be said on quality-deficits of policy publics is that optimistic opinions on "the vision of the people" as problem solvers (Wolfe 1977) and on the growing political capacity of individuals (Somjee 1982) are premature. Therefore, policy publics cannot be relied upon to serve adequately as a suitable infrastructure for policymaking under adversity and to compensate for the policymaking weaknesses of minds of governments.

These findings apply to all modes of influence by public opinion on policymaking, such as impact of opinion polls on politicians; direct contacts between politicians and electors; various forms of opinion expression in the mass media, demonstrations, and other forms of street action; and, more complex and more crucial, aggregation of public opinion into electoral behavior (with all the problems well considered in positive political theory and collective-choice theorems, as conveniently summed up in Blair and Pollak 1983, and put into a striking and taboo-shattering form by Riker 1982).

Serious conclusions stem from this picture. At the very least, minds of governments face urgent needs to help to upgrade policy enlightenment of policy publics, with unavoidable related dangers of misuse and misdirection. In a number of countries, minds of governments must gear themselves to handle adverse impacts of policy publics on policymaking quality, such as mass tendencies toward policy theologies and fanaticism, as already mentioned several times. Countries with relatively enlightened policy publics must be careful not to project their realities on some other countries, where quite different situations may prevail.

*Inter alia*, growing adversity and consequent policymaking needs may require various steps in respect to policy publics and their roles in policymaking, in ascending order of severity:

1. Greater efforts to enlighten public opinion on complex policy issues are essential.
2. The functions of top politicians in educating the public and enlightening the public, rather than in reflecting public opinion and executing current public preferences, need augmentation.
3. The autonomy of the central minds of governments from current opinions of policy publics needs strengthening, in line with Edmund Burke's view of the mission of elected politicians to act according to their best opinion, subject to accountability on election day. This, instead of populistic conceptions that elected politicians should try to reflect on a current basis the changing "will of the people," as widespread in U.S. parlance.
4. Various forms of participatory democracy and direct democracy have to be reconsidered (e.g. Sewell and Coppock 1977) to preserve political democracy as a viable form of regime that can handle harsh adversities.
5. Some components of the central minds of governments and units working for it need isolation from policy publics, as earlier illustrated with the example of central banks, constitutional courts, and think tanks.
6. In special cases, carefully monitored and time-limited emergency regimes should permit necessary policymaking and policy enforcement against current public preferences, subject to later judgment by the voters.
7. Forms of public opinion expression that may intimidate policymakers and that are not integral to political democracy may have to be contained, such as direct action in its more aggressive forms.
8. The dependence of viable democracy on reasonably informed and enlighted policy publics needs acknowledgment, with the conclusion that quite a number of Third World countries may not be able to maintain effective democratic regimes in the Western sense for a generation or two (which is a quite different matter from respecting basic human rights and moving toward adjusted modes of quasi democracy).

Even more severe problems are posed by the possibility that public ignorance about some important policies may be beneficial in the longer run, such as by gaining passive agreement from present generations to serve as guinea pigs for various technological innovations that will benefit future generations but would be inhibited if the present policy publics were fully aware of the possible side effects from which they may suffer (Hirschman 1982b, 59; to be contrasted with Nelkin and Pollak 1981 and, differently, T. Williams 1982). A new public philosophy may be necessary to handle adequately such issues (Sullivan 1982), leading into domains far beyond the scope of this book.

The above points move squarely into the politics of adversity, raising very painful issues beyond the scope of this book. But the problems posed by gaps between some main features of policy publics on one hand and requirements of high-quality policymaking under adversity on the other must be cognized.

All the observations above need reconsideration in light of policy-thinking pluralism as necessary for high-quality policymaking under adversity. This, in addition to all the value issues and tragic choices involved in balancing various versions of democratic theory (Pennock 1979) with needs of policymaking performance in terms of handling adversity (as well illustrated, in the relatively congenial context of the United States, by Yates 1982).

### Pluralism in Policy Thinking

Positive redundancy, multiple advocacy, and other forms of pluralism, within some limits to preserve basic values on one hand and the ability to act on the other hand, are an essential requisite of policymaking quality, as fully recognized by early proponents of freedom of opinion and expression (Spinner 1974). Analysis of inbuilt incapacities of main components of policymaking process-systems further reinforces the case for pluralism in policy thinking, as a chief way to counterbalance limitations through mutual complementarity, supplementarity, bias diversity, and error offsetting. Thus, the opinion that policy paradigm innovations are very difficult within establishments, depending often on an infrastructure of policy-thinking pluralism, is historically demonstrated and analytically supported.

Policy-thinking pluralism and its inputting into policymaking runs into many barriers, inhibiting its scope and reducing its beneficial effects. In authoritarian countries, pluralistic policy thinking is repressed, causing a major inbuilt policy botcher. In countries with intensely held policy theologies, these serve as blinders that reduce significantly the scope of policy-thinking pluralism. In democracies, commonly held opinions and shared assumptions also serve as blindfolds. On a more technical level, lack of access to information (Galnoor 1977; Robertson 1982; Rowat 1979), non-availability of resources, scarcity of institutionalized supports for "free thinkers," and a too-tight informal net of interconnections with the establishment illustrate factors that reduce policy-thinking pluralism.

Underlying policy-thinking pluralism are more fundamental features of social creativity and of desire and ability by innovators to work on policy-relevant material, tying in policy-thinking pluralism with policy entrepreneurship. These are little-understood phenomena, hard to encourage and easy to impede. Pluralistic policy research institutionalization (Coleman 1982, 168-71) may be of help.

A special form of policy-thinking pluralism is represented by deliberate positive redundancy within the establishment itself. Illustrations of such arrangements include government-supported think tanks, professional equipment for legislatures, party research organizations (Ramsden 1980), and special control agencies working on policymaking evaluation and effectiveness audit. Absence of such units assures reduced policy-thinking pluralism, though presence of such units is by itself no guarantee of such meaningful thinking. Resistance to intraestablishment policy-thinking pluralism is intense, as evidenced by the relative scarcity of such units and the hard going of those that exist. Causes for resistance range from "practical" skepticism about such arrangements to desire to preserve monopolies on information, option development, and policy influence.

The question can be posed whether policy-thinking pluralism can go too far, with overloads of ideas, mixed with various forms of noise, reducing its utility for policymaking. There are few indicators of such a danger, in either historic situations or in present or foreseeable ones. Quite different is the problem of necessary limits on legitimate policy-thinking pluralism also in democracies, with ideas endangering basic values and undermining fundamental morals perhaps to be restrained. The principle to control some forms of behavior but to leave all public thinking and expressions of opinions free cannot always provide a complete solution. Thus, democracies face the problem of what to do with antidemocratic, discriminatory, and fanatic views once those start to get some support instead of being esoteric opinions held by isolated individuals. These are marginal situations at present, but such dilemmas may become more acute with continuing adversity and with possible emergence of more radical response patterns to policymaking inadequacies.

To move from such problems to summing up deficits in respect to policy-thinking pluralism, no estimation of broad validity can be made: The situation is widely different among countries and regime types. Policy-thinking pluralism is a specification of high-quality policymaking under adversity where democracies enjoy a significant advantage (though different forms of pluralism operate in the USSR, see Solomon 1983). At the same time, the present paucity of promising policy alternatives for handling adversity may indicate inadequacies in policy-thinking pluralism also in democracies, with few ideas being available on how to make pluralism produce needed policy ideas innovations.

## Rapid Policy Learning

Little needs saying to justify the policymaking-quality specification of "rapid policy learning." Accelerated transformation in problems combines with weaknesses in policymaking and high costs of policy mistakes to make rapid policy learning a must. Furthermore, in the face of irreducible uncertainty and ignorance, rapid learning of unfolding realities constitutes a main preferable policymaking mode. Hence, the crucial importance of policy-learning capacities as a main determinant of policymaking achievements. It is not an overstatement to regard most present policies as temporary and increasingly obsolescent (Bennis and Slater 1968) and to require movement toward an "experimental society" (Haworth 1960; see also Rondinelli 1983).

Beginnings only exist of a policy learning theory enmeshed with broader processes of learning organizations (Rome and Rome 1971), learning governments and learning societies (Bogart 1980; Deutsch 1975; E. Dunn 1971; Michael 1973; Schon 1971). The need for policy learning is universally admitted on a verbal level, but reality looks quite different.

It is perhaps too harsh to state that actual policy learning takes place, if at all, as a tortuous process, dispersed in nonlearning and mislearning. But, well-supported studies do indicate strong counterlearning forces at work, such as: dissonance reduction (Aronson 1976; Wicklung and Brehm 1976); preservation of cognitive map consistency (Fischhoff and Beyth 1975); escalating commitment to earlier-chosen policies (Staw 1976; Staw and Fox 1977); misprocessing of the past (March and Olsen 1975; Fischhoff 1974; Fuchser 1983; E. May 1972); various organizational dynamics (Dery 1982; Dery 1983); and more (Wildavsky 1979b, ch. 9). Difficulties in learning as brought out in case studies, such as on the histories of military planning (Gooch 1974) and on actual result evaluation practicies (Wholley et al. 1970), reinforce conclusions on the existence of strong barriers to policy learning (Kaufman 1973).

Policy learning is closely related to the subject of policy memory (a metaphorically stimulating discussion of human memory is provided in Klatzky 1980). The history of archives, as revealed by archeological findings, testifies to the essentiality of institutional memories as a component of government from the early emergence of the state. In China, highly developed institutions were in charge of institutionalized memories, partly for learning purposes (Wu 1970). But memories must be selective and, unavoidably, biased, with impaired learning potentials. For instance, dramatic events may dominate memories of the past (analogous to "flashbulb memories" on the individual level, R. Brown and Kulik 1977), compounding the inherent problems of learning from history (Fischhoff 1974). A striking modern illustration is the Vietnam war: Not only are studies drawing serious lessons from the Vietnam war scarce, despite the large literature on the subject (exceptional are Summers 1982, and W. Thompson and Frizzell 1977), but traumatic effects seem to influence significant aspects of U.S. policymaking in modes that cannot be characterized as other than very distorted and have little to do with "cold learning."

The study of the author uncovered serious weaknesses of institutional memories of central minds of governments on more mundane levels: Archives are seldom kept in formats useful for utilization in future policymaking; computers are not yet utilized to build up new types of institutional policy memories; personnel policies often prevent the building up of adequate accumulated memories, such as by too-rapid rotation and changeover, as dramatically illustrated in the White House staff; and main policy events are seldom analyzed systematically for the drawing of lessons for the future.

An additional perspective on policy-learning difficulties is gained by putting it into the context of policy cycles (J.V. May and Wildavsky 1978), rigidity of participants in policy circuits (Richardson 1982, 180), policy succession processes (Hogwood and Peters 1982), and policy termination issues (Behn 1978; Brewer 1978; de Leon 1978). Policy learning is directed at terminating goal-nonachieving policies (whether explicit goals or latent goals, this is another matter) and at intervening with the "natural" life cycle of policies, by accelerating succession of promising policies and speedy policy revisions. All this runs head on into incapacities, counter forces, and resistances at every step of a tortuous way. Very large critical masses are, therefore, essential for improving policy learning.

To be mentioned are attempts to improve policy learning through institutionalization of periodic policy reconsideration, such as in U.S. "sunset" legislation; and through special "evaluation" methodologies and setups (Glass 1980; Grumm 1975; Patton 1975; R. Perloff, Perloff and Sussna 1976; Rossi, Freeman, and Wright 1979; Rutman 1977; C. Weiss 1972). An additional step leads into social experimentation, as an attempt to establish structured situations for accelerated policy learning (Hellstern and Wollmann 1983; Fairweather and Tornatzky 1977; R. Ferber and Hirsch 1981; Rivlin 1971; Rondinelli 1983). Various other proposals abound in literature (Argyris 1982; Argyris and Schon 1978; Argyris and Schon 1983) and in some practice. The Netherlands, for instance, has taken some steps in the direction of becoming an "experimenting state"

(Hoogewerf 1978). But, most of reality looks quite different: Serious attempts in governments to draw policy lessons from even obvious failures are a scarcity. (An interesting exception is Neustadt and Fineberg 1983, originally done for the U.S. Department of Health, Education, and Welfare; but see Silverstein 1982. A Polish communist panel report mentioned in Dan Fischer 1983 is interesting.) Usually, rapid policy learning is distinguished by its scarcity, if not absence.

To understand more the difficulties of rapid policy learning, an inbuilt logical-philosophical problem must be added: Assuming ultrachange, lessons drawn from the past are inapplicable to the future. Under less extreme assumptions still, policy learning must take some time, especially because many policies require long periods to show any results. Therefore, change short of rapid ultrachange suffices to make lessons obsolete by the time they can be distilled. Viewed in such a light, the saying that armies are better prepared for the last war as a result of learning from it reflects a hard-to-avoid situation. Gearing policymaking to unpredictable futures cannot be aided much by learning from the past substantive lessons on particular policies but only by drawing from such past experiences nomographic conclusions that can be applied to the future and by learning to improve policymaking in the face of uncertainty, including by accelerating learning itself.

Within the above perspective, evaluation studies are problematic because the dynamics underlying the past experiences are themselves perhaps changing. Thus, conclusions on a negative income tax drawn from experiments during a period of full employment are very doubtful as a basis for policymaking in a period of large unemployment, unless validated theories can be derived that also apply to radically different conditions—which is asking for too much from present states of knowledge in social sciences. Evaluation studies and similar accelerated learning methods may be useful for showing what will not work and for debunking policy paradigms, which constitute very important lessons. But, positive policy lessons are hard to draw in an epoch of change. This conclusion must be applied with care in different policy domains, depending on the dynamics of phenomena. In many domains, some substantive policy learning is possible, but underlying assumptions on stability of relevant processes need checking.

Learning poses even harder problems under conditions of fuzzy gambling, when one and the same policy may, as a result of chance factors, produce quite different results, even when conditions are stable. Basic assumptions of both simple determinism and of stable regularities underlie contemporary thinking on learning, especially in the context of policymaking. Such worldviews fit large parts of the physical cosmos, permitting the development of modern science. But with rapid and nonsmooth change characterizing large parts of policy domains, a quite different worldview is appropriate for policymaking, including policy learning. One of the main challenges facing a useful philosophy of knowledge for policymaking, as discussed earlier in this chapter, is to develop a policy-learning theory taking full cognizance of ultrachange and fuzzy-gambling realities. Many difficulties of governmental learning are similar to those of diagnostics, as a closely related process, such as organizational propensities, human psychological characteristics, and cultural blinders (partly explored in Etheredge 1984), but underlying philosophy of knowledge difficulties are more fundamental and must be handled before institutional learning difficulties can effectively be taken on. In combination, inherent policy-learning difficulties are very formidable in all respects.

Such consideration leads to a need for more advanced approaches to policy learning, which, in turn, depend on unavailable sophistication in minds of governments, and on equally scarce knowledge and modes of thinking within relevant disciplines of knowledge.

The emerging deficit estimation differentiates between policy learning of the ordinary form which assumes sufficient stability and simple causality to permit the drawing of substantive lessons from conventional learning, and policy learning of a dynamic form, which assumes rapid change and part indeterminacy, which permits learning only via theoretic generalizations and sophisticated processing. Ordinary policy learning is weak, with some variation among countries and policy domains and with some useful learning going on, often outside the policymaking process-system. Advanced learning, as described above, is nearly nonexistent and its preconditions, in terms of knowledge and inference modes, have not been adequately worked out.

### Metapolicymaking and Governance Redesign

The existence of large quality deficits, as partly examined in this chapter, makes policymaking improvememt an essential precondition for deliberate and success-potent handling of adversity. Metapolicymaking engages in policymaking on policymaking, including efforts to upgrade policymaking qualities. In many respects, high-quality metapolicymaking is the main mode for building up needed capacities of policymaking under adversity, though other factors, such as autonomous infrastructure advancements, can also play an important role.

Such metapolicymaking is difficult. Metapolicymaking serves as an additional illustration of a policy-inadequacy vicious circle: When policymaking is of low quality, high-grade metapolicymaking is needed the most; but under such conditions, high-grade metapolicymaking is quite unlikely to take place. This closed loop is only one of the incapacities hindering high-quality metapolicymaking and often preventing it. Other incapacities and barriers include, for instance:

- Ideological and power-political resistances to improving central minds of governments, which are disliked, rejected on ideological grounds, or regarded as hostile to interests and traditions.
- Hostility to improvement of policymaking within the machinery of government, for reasons of bureaucratic politics (Rosat 1981), civil service traditions, and bona fide doubts about proposed changes.
- Most important of all, lack of interest in and also active resistance to metapolicymaking on the central minds of governments by top decision makers themselves. Multiple causes bring about such lack of support for improvement, such as: apprehensions about power consequences and personal burdens of improvements; doubts up to skepticism about many improvement proposals and their intellectual bases; fear that inadequacies may be revealed; sensitivities to political costs; unwillingness to accept self-bindings involved in many of the improvements; allocation of priority to panacea, such as "privatization"; and more. It is very difficult and often impossible to introduce significant improvements into central minds of governments without support by top decision makers. Therefore, there would be little hope for the whole endeavor but for the empiric fact that some openings for improvements are provided, partly by accidents of personal interests of top decision makers and increasingly by the growing sense of top decision makers that they need help to handle adversity.
- Scarcity of knowledge and ideas that can serve metapolicymaking is an additional incapacity; as is absence of infrastructure and of necessary resources in a number of countries, especially in the Third World.

Metapolicymaking is further complicated by its overlap with governance redesign. It is possible to introduce significant improvements into the central minds of governments without touching upon governance as a whole, including politics; and such improvements are often preferable but, very soon, overlaps between policymaking and governance redesign and close interactions between them begin to appear. Thus:

1. Improving the central minds of governments without upgrading other main components of governance may introduce undesirable power shifts and distortions. For instance, impacts on the functions of legislatures must not be neglected (Mezey 1979; Joel Smith and Musolf 1979), parallel upgrading being often preferable for the capacity to govern as a whole and also for policymaking under adversity.
2. Upgrading of policymaking infrastructure is often essential, and this frequently involves intervention with main components of governance, such as policy elites and policy publics.

3. Value problems involved in metapolicymaking, such as pattern-values versus output-values priorities, closely link metapolicymaking to political ideology and political culture.

4. Vice versa, governance-redesign attempts not undertaken primarily to improve policymaking under adversity in general and upgrade the performance of the central minds of governments in particular often have significant implications for the latter (e.g. Rieselbach 1978). Therefore, in all governance redesign endeavors, metapolicymaking considerations should receive due attention.

5. Close affinities in problematics and methods between metapolicymaking and governance redesign permit much mutual learning and provide strong arguments for their study to be integrated.

6. Experiences with and thinking about governance redesign provide important inputs into metapolicymaking methods and implementation strategies (Apter 1973, 118-46; Benz 1979; Crotty 1977; Germann 1975; Janowitz 1976; Janowitz 1978; Kochen and Deutsch 1980; H. Perloff 1971; Ranney 1976; Stewart 1975). This holds true, in different form, for organizational and systems redesign approaches, which sometimes provide knowledge relevant for governance redesign and metapolicymaking (Ackoff 1974; Butack and Negmandhi 1977; Jay Galbraith 1977; Kilmann 1977; Kilmann et al. 1976; Mintzberg 1980, as fully elaborated in Mintzberg 1983; Sutherland 1975; D. Thomas et al. 1972). Concomitantly, experiences with metapolicymaking provide important inputs into governance redesign.

On these accounts, metapolicymaking cannot and should not be divorced from governance redesign. There are differences in emphasis and focus between them, with metapolicymaking concentrating on the central policymaking process-system, on facets of the machinery of governance salient for policymaking and policy implementation, and on dimensions and institutions of governance as a whole and of society and culture at large, which interact closely with central policymaking and influence the quality of the latter. A broad approach to governance redesign may adopt quite different perspectives, often regarding the central minds of governments as secondary in importance within governance redesign directed at achieving various goals, such as increased democratic participation. Indeed, within some governance redesign objectives in a number of countries, weakening central policymaking may be preferable. But, whatever may be the significance of central minds of governments and their improvement within various approaches to governance redesign, within endeavors to improve the central minds of governments metapolicymaking must move into governance redesign.

A broad conclusion of the examination in this book is that improvement of the central minds of governments is a priority need for possibly adequate societal handling of adversity. It follows that within comprehensive governance-redesign approaches, too, metapolicymaking should receive priority, with special attention to be given to improvement of the central minds of governments. Hence, this book can serve also as a portal into governance redesign in the face of adversity as a whole. This is true for the book as representing an approach and dealing with a central concern of governance redesign, namely, the central policymaking process-system. Some of the following parts of the book apply largely to governance redesign as a whole. Thus, chapter 9 develops an approach to policymaking redesign that fits, with few adjustments, governance redesign as a whole. The improvement recommendations presented in chapter 10 cluster around metapolicymaking but move selectively into governance redesign, as far as essential for upgrading central minds of governments.

As recognized through this book, policymaking is only one dimension of societal problem-handling capacities, though a critical one. Therefore, approaches to upgrading societal problem-handling capacities independent from the quality of the central mind of government are often useful, and may sometimes be preferable to upgrading the central mind of government. To examine such possibilities it is necessary to move beyond the scope of this book, into a general theory of societal command and control—an endeavor for which little basis exists in present social science knowledge. But, some aspects of societal problem-handling capacities can be examined from the perspective of policymaking, as done in this chapter in respect to alternative innovation, policy entrepreneurship, policy publics, and policy-thinking pluralism. Here, metapolicymaking must move beyond governance redesign into societal architecture to build up the infrastructure essential for bettering performance of the central mind of government.

To return from the desirable to the existing, deficits in metapolicymaking and governance redesign are large. Few countries are cheerful about their policymaking and governance abilities and quite some experimentation with some innovations does go on, as surveyed in part in chapter 3. Interests in constitutional reforms, are also on the increase, partly in the direction of upgrading policymaking. (A comprehensive comparative study of constitutional reforms, both historic and presently under consideration is urgently needed. Interesting country studies or comparative studies of reform on specific institutions proposals are available, as illustrated by Benz 1979; Hicks 1979; and Norton 1982. The few comprehensive treatments are illustrated by McWhinney 1981.) Very few central governments are equipped for coherent thinking on metapolicymaking and governance redesign, sometimes using special commissions for such purposes (as illustrated by U.K. Royal Commission on The Constitution

1973, the report of which typically was outdated when published). Even when an interest in metapolicymaking and governance redesign appears in the central minds of governments, or is forced upon them, the quality of metapolicymaking and governance redesign is usually quite low. There exist counterexamples, showing that high metapolicymaking quality and governance-redesign quality are not absolutely impossible. Thus, the Consitution of the Fifth French Republic is in many respects well fitted for facing adversity. Whether such high-quality metapolicymaking and governance redesign can appear only after castastrophe, or whether lesser amounts of adversity may suffice, and/or whether they are mainly a matter of personal accidents is uncertain.

## Aggregate Conclusions

Without reiterating the main incapacities and quality deficits brought out in relation to the twenty-one specifications of high-quality policymaking under adversity examined in this chapter, a number of robust conclusions seem justified:

1. It is possible to specify some of the features of high-quality policymaking under adversity. Different classifications are possible, but the twenty-one specifications discussed in this chapter do illustrate some main features of high-quality policymaking requirements under adversity.
2. Each one of the specifications confronts incapacities, which are in part inbuilt in the materials and components out of which central policymaking process-systems are made.
3. Another main type of incapacity takes the form of vicious spirals and closed loops, with a number of incapacities and quality deficits reinforcing each other, and with improvements presupposing situations the very absence of which makes the improvement necessary.
4. Many incapacities are shared by all central minds of governments, being in the main common to all contemporary forms of governments and to many historic forms of governments.
5. Some incapacities are specific to different forms of contemporary regimes and societies, such as democracies, communist countries, and developing countries.
6. Incapacities are latent under many conditions, not being evoked when demands upon policymaking are low. Under adversity, policymaking reveals many deficits largely caused by underlying incapacities.
7. Direct examination of policymaking qualities reveals many deficits as a matter of fact, whether those are explained by currently understood incapacities or not.
8. Systematic improvement efforts need more in-depth understanding of policymaking deficits to take up deeply rooted incapacities and to over-

come fundamental quality deficits. Tinkering has little chance to overcome inherent incapacities and to achieve the specifications of policymaking qualities needed under adversity.

The last point brings us to the next chapter, examining policy sciences as
a main body of knowledge for understanding and improving policymaking.

# 8

# Needed Breakthroughs in Policy Sciences

## Breakthroughs Are Required

Advancement of policy sciences assumes many names—applied systems analysis, public policy, policy studies, policy analysis, and even "social engineering" in Japan—all of which constitute both a symptom of efforts toward policymaking improvement and a main condition for meaningful policymaking improvement. About fifteen years ago, it seemed that policy sciences moved into a taking-off stage. Since then, much has happened in policy sciences: Five major professional journals directly devoted to policy sciences have been established; *Policy Studies Review Annual* has been published since 1977 (vol.8 is now published by Transaction); various book series are devoted to policy sciences (e.g. Nagel 1984b); a large number of textbooks fully focusing on policy sciences have been published; essential disciplinary pillars of policy sciences have progressed, such as decision psychology, organization theory, large-systems modeling and applied sociology; professional associations have been set up; and, most important of all, a distinct species of policy sciences teaching programs has thrived at a number of universities, including some excellent ones. Most of these activities are located in the United States, but diffusion is taking place to other countries such as the Philippines and Japan, with growing interests in policy sciences, in one version or another, spreading (often under other names, e.g. Bayraktar et al. 1979). In many respects, policy sciences perspectives have infiltrated much further, as evidenced by the policymaking frame of many textbooks in political science (C. Anderson 1977; Aranson 1981; Lovell 1970; W. Mitchell 1971; Sharkansky 1975; Sharkansky and Meter 1975; Wendzel 1981a; Wendzel 1981b). Traces of a policy sciences orientation, whether intended or not, can also be discerned in a new crop of "how-to-make-decisions" handbooks (Ackoff 1978; Behn and Vaupel 1982; Cornell 1980; Kepner and Tregoe 1981; Wheeler and Janis 1980).

Detailed analysis and evaluation of policy sciences activities and problematics (as partly attempted in S. Hansen 1983; Heclo 1972; Higgot 1980; Finifter 1983; Jann 1983; Kruse 1979; Mead 1983; Portis 1982; Pross 1982;

Rhodes 1979; Simeon 1976), however needed, goes beyond the scope of this book. A much longer time perspective is needed for such a task (compare an evaluation of nineteenth-century political science, Collini et al. 1984). But policy sciences is not only a part of the human endeavor to increase knowledge and understanding but also an essential infrastructure for policymaking under adversity and a crucial input into metapolicymaking and some parts of governance redesign. (It also fulfills social functions needing analysis on lines of MacRea 1976.) Therefore, high-quality policy sciences is an essential requisite of adequate policymaking under adversity. Examination of policy sciences from such an angle is integral to the main subject of this book, completing and partly revising earlier and separate treatments (Dror 1971a; Dror 1971b; Dror 1983a, esp. new introduction; Dror 1983d; Dror 1984a; Lasswell 1971).

Shunning self-serving exercises of complimenting the achievements of an interdiscipline in which one is personally closely involved, I shall limit my positive evaluation to underlining activities as mentioned above and acknowledging much progress reflected in diverse literature, as in part built upon in this book. In view of the slow rhythm of scientific progress and the inherent difficulties of policy sciences in subject matter and aims, its advance during a relatively very short time has been remarkable.

At the same time, contemporary policy sciences suffers from a number of afflictions, all the more serious because these may reflect dominant trends rather than passing childhood diseases. The history of other disappointments with new disciplines after promising beginnings serves as a warning. Operations research, for instance, began as a very promising systematic and partly scientific approach to complex problems, only to become at many, though not all, universities and in much application a set of mathematical techniques of narrow, though useful, utility. Strategic studies also rapidly exhausted themselves (see Lyons and Morton 1965; not much have been achieved since then). Another useful warning is provided by some "sorcery" tendencies in social sciences (Andreski 1972), which can easily imbrue policy sciences.

Instead of presenting a list of weaknesses of contemporary policy sciences, it is more positive to consider briefly fourteen main required breakthroughs. Many of these have already been indirectly identified in earlier chapters, especially during examination of policymaking-quality specifications. Focused consideration of needed breakthroughs, with a somewhat different clustering and nomenclature, will provide an operational approach to the advancement of policy sciences as necessary for policymaking under adversity. The following treatment is based on a study of main literature, including major texts on policymaking realities (such as, to cite again some central books and add a few to the list: J. Anderson 1983; J.

Anderson et al. 1978; Ballard 1981; Bauer and Gergen 1968; Beyme and Schmidt forthcoming; Bresnick 1982; Castles et. al. 1976; D. Davis 1972; Derthick 1979; Dye 1984; Frohick 1979; H. Gardner 1982; R. Goodin 1982; Gunther 1980; Gwyn and Edwards 1975; R. Hall and Quinn, 1980; Higgins 1983; Hofferbert 1974; C. Jones 1977; S. Leach and Stewart 1982; Lehmbruch and Schmitter 1982; Lindblom 1968; Lineberry 1977; Liske et al. 1975; McGrew and Wilson 1982; J. Mitchell and Mitchell 1969; Montgomery 1974; R. Nelson 1983; G. Peters 1982; Pollitt 1979; Ranney 1968; Rourke 1984; Sharpe and Newton 1984; Steiner and Dorff 1980; Valenta and Potter 1984; and Wade 1972), and principal texts on prescriptive approaches, such as policy analysis, planning, and systems approaches (such as, to pick some recent better examples, in addition to literature cited elsewhere in this book: R. Baker, Michaels and Preston 1975; Bardach and Kagan 1982; Bozeman 1979; Brewer and de Leon 1983; Carley 1980; P. Checkland 1981; Churchman 1982; Clarkson 1982; Diesing 1982; Dubnick and Bardes 1983; W. Dunn 1981; *Harvard Business Review* 1983; Hogwood and Gunn 1984; House 1982; Lave 1981; Krone 1980; MacRea and Wilde 1979; Majone and Quade 1980; Meltsner 1976; Monti 1982; Mood 1983; Nagel 1980; Nagel 1983a; Nagel 1984a; Paris and Reynolds 1983; Quade 1982; Quade and Miser 1984; Stokey and Zeckhauser 1978; Wildavsky 1979b). In addition, the treatment in this chapter is based on partial acquantiance with ongoing research and writings, as reflected in the chief periodicals and case studies and at conferences, as well as personal meetings, and on close observation of the evolution of some of the main public policy teaching programs (see also P. Bell 1981 and underlying Ford Foundation evaluation material; Coplin 1978; Crecine 1982; L. Lynn 1980. Analogous are some planning teaching programs, e.g. see Center for Human Settlements 1984).

## Provide Philosophic and Intellectual Underpinning for Policymaking and for Policy Sciences

Both policymaking and policy sciences need philosophic and intellectual underpinnings, which are partly separate and partly overlap.

The primary subjects to be taken up within a philosophy for policymaking have been considered in chapter 7. Potentials of human decisions in the gray area between necessity and chance; different meanings of "rationality"; various bases of policymaking improvement; policymaking potentials under different social conditions; philosophy of knowledge and of Weltanschauung for policymaking—these illustrate subjects to be added to main policy sciences concerns.

Policy sciences must pay more attention to the fundamental problems of policy sciences itself to have a chance to move ahead. Underlying assumptions, philosophies of knowledge, and ideas on social functions of policy sciences need explication and reconsideration. Pragmatism is inadequate for handling the problems of policy sciences, which involve fundamental issues of epistemology, axiology, social roles, professional reflection-in-action (Schon 1983), and more; while policy sciences is sufficiently different from social sciences in general to make reliance on the underlying intellectual bases of the latter, as far as at all developed (Habermas 1982), inappropriate. Hence, the need for self-awareness and focused attention to advancement of the foundations of policy sciences itself.( Relevant issues are discussed in Michalos 1978.)

Awareness of inbuilt limitations of main concepts and methods, such as value biases inbuilt in most systems concepts (Boguslaw 1981; Boguslaw 1982; Habermas and Luhmann 1971; Hoos 1983; Greven 1974), is another essential input into policy sciences, to be provided by due attention to philosophic issues and underpinnings.

To return to the idea of policy gambling, it can serve to illustrate necessary and far-reaching revisions and innovations in the philosophic underpinnings of policy sciences, and of policymaking philosophies as supplied by appropriate policy sciences breakthroughs. Renaissance attempts to conceptualize and "manage" overwhelming transformations with the help of an innovative concept package of "fortuna," "occasione," and "virtue," as already mentioned, illustrate efforts in the past by very intelligent thinkers to face turbulence. Looking over policy sciences literature, one cannot easily discern obviously superior ideas for handling fuzzy-gambling situations. With the exception of various versions of "decision analysis" and similar methods, all of which depend on allocation of subjective probability (Raiffa 1968, as applied to policy analysis in Stokey and Zeckhauser 1978, Ch. 7,12) and some endeavors in the direction of creative search for futuribles, such as in the form of scenario writing (Builder 1983), nearly no concepts, findings, models, and ideas useful for handling policy gambling are available. At the same time, existing methods become rapidly useless, if not counterproductive if pushed beyond the domains of quantitative uncertainty. Adjustment of policy sciences, to conditions of qualitative uncertainty, volatile uncertainty, and ignorance is all the more urgent as quite a number of main ideas may have to be revised to fit such conditions. To repeat just one example: evaluation studies and social experimentation become problematic, with learning from past experiences for future situations assuming degrees of stability increasingly absent in reality.

Implications of a policy-gambling perspective for needed innovations in the underlying philosophy of policy sciences, as well as methodologies as taken up later in this chapter, include:

1. Thorough understanding of the concept of probability, its history (Hacking 1975), its relations to causality (Burks 1977), its operational uses (DeFinetti 1975, passim) and its relations to decision making (Shackle 1972) is a must. This, with expansions into qualitative uncertainty, ignorance, indeterminacy, surprise-prone situations, and so on, as already mentioned.

2. The evolvement of actual policies and their consequences has to be considered within a fuzzy-gambling perspective, with explicit consideration of uncertainties inbuilt in relevant realities, of ways in which such uncertainties were handled, and of impacts on actual policy consequences. *Inter alia*:
   - The theoretic schemata for studying policymaking reality need reconsideration, with a more realistic view of inherent uncertainties and the importance of chance elements.
   - Policymaking case studies should, consequently, devote attention to relevant indeterminacies, chance elements, and uncertainty-handling behaviors.
   - Additional frameworks are needed for considering policy implementation, such as the functions of implementation in handling uncertainty and adjusting decisions to the transition from conjectures on futures to past events inherent in the passage of time.

3. The policymaking behavior of main actors has to be reconsidered as "gambling." Some work on organizational behavior and group dynamics has been moving in such a direction, but very slowly and inadequately. Recent relevant work in decision-making psychology has not been utilized in policy sciences, despite many interesting findings on behavior under uncertainty. In particular, growing understanding of human-error propensities when facing uncertainty can add much to understanding inherent policymaking incapacities of main governmental institutions, adding important dimensions to empiric theories of policymaking.

4. As already indicated, thinking on evaluation needs revision to fit a gambling view of policymaking. In fuzzy-gambling situations it is impossible to draw conclusions on the quality of policymaking from its results, and similar policies under comparable conditions may have quite divergent consequences.

5. Basic decision modes, as well developed in conventional policy studies literature, need reconsideration. Thus, the very concept of "incrementalism" loses its meanings in fuzzy-gambling situations—when doing the same may be one of the worst gambling options. So-called strategic-planning approaches are also quite obsolescent in ignoring the challenges of uncertainty and ignorance (with important implications also for strategic direction in business, as described in Donaldson and Lorsch 1983).

6. Moving to prescriptive methodologies, the whole arsenal of methods of "preferizing" decisions under uncertainty needs reevaluation, as already mentioned. Heuristic approaches to improving policy gambling

need development, to take over from decision analysis and expected-value approaches with very limited domains of applicability. *Inter alia,* the whole economic foundations of prescriptive approaches must be subjected to critical reexamination (as done by some economists, e.g. Shackle 1972; and B. Klein 1977).

7. Debugging emerges as a main mode for improving decision making, with reduction of main errors in handling uncertainty going hand in hand with heuristic strategies for policy gambling.

As a foundation for progress in such directions, the basic epistemological and philosophy-of-knowledge assumptions underlying policy sciences need revision. Thus, a view of reality as between chance and necessity with much indeterminacy should condition inference from facts and search for prescriptive conjectures. Concomitantly, as already mentioned, limited expectations from better intelligence as inherently incapable of reducing much of uncertainty throw a different perspective on historic intelligence errors and limit hopes for reducing them in the future, illustrating implications of a policy-gambling perspective.

A policy-gambling perspective of policymaking leads into *terra incognita.* Enough can be precognized to make strenuous exploration of that terrain worthwhile. But quite some retooling of modes of thinking by policy scholars and policy professions and of their disciplinary knowledge is required for moving forward in the proposed directions. This well illustrates the depth and broadness of policy-science breakthroughs needed, for all of which novel philosophic and intellectual underpinnings are essential. The gambling perspective is only one illustration of needed reconsiderations of philosophic and intellectual underpinnings. Other illustrations are provided by the need for expanded views of rationality, necessities for a novel axiology, and so on as discussed in chapter 7. Here, the policy-gambling illustration should serve somewhat to concretize the policy-sciences innovations needed to meet salient specifications of high-quality policymaking under adversity.

### Add Historic and Comparative Perspectives

As often noted, few if any are the policy issues that can be comprehended within thin slices of time. Even less can policymaking be understood and improved within a narrow contemporary world of inquiry. To perceive patterns and understand present and emerging realities, a historic perspective is often essential and always useful (as illustrated for concrete policy issues in Knorr 1976).

Relevant time bits may be relatively short or encompass centuries, depending on issues and their natural life cycles. But, imminentism is always an inadequate basis for policy sciences. Hence, the recommendation to strengthen the temporal dimension so as to consider problems within their historic settings. Work attempted at the Applied History/Social Science program at Carnegie-Mellon University illustrates some needed approaches as well as their dangers (Levinson and Fallon 1981), though still very narrow. Special care must be taken not to dilute history and fall into many waiting traps (D. Fischer 1970; on the neglect of historic dimensions in modern social sciences, see Zaret 1980).

Comparative perspectives serve somewhat different, complementary, needs. For many policy issues, comparative material is a partial substitute for impossible experimentation, providing a wealth of experiences on which to base improved analysis. Comparative perspectives may also stimulate the elusive alternative-invention and option-design dimensions of policy sciences, at least by inputting a wealth of ideas from other jurisdictions. On a more general level, balance perception of issues is aided by the background of multiple countries (e.g. Leichter 1979).

Substantive knowledge of comparative experiences in select issue domains and familiarity with sources of comparative data as well as comparative analysis methods are, therefore, essential. Some beginnings have been made (Ashford 1978; Dogan and Pelassy 1984; Godwin 1975; Heclo 1974; Heidenheimer, Heclo, and Adams 1983; McDaniel 1978; Rose 1973; Sidjansku 1973; and literature quoted earlier). But, as a whole, policy sciences is still quite parochial in its works. This does not imply underrating of the difficulties of comparative work (as discussed on the much easier level of organization comparison, by Lammers and Hickson 1979; Mohan 1979; K. Roberts 1970; relevant is Brislin 1983). But, till now, attempts at systematic comparison as a base for policy sciences, including policy analysis of specific issues, are scarce and often weak.

Needs for broad comparative and historic perspectives are multiplied when understanding and improvement of policymaking and central minds of governments, up to governance redesign, are to be taken up. Thus, comparative examination of the policymaking performance of different regimes and of various countries within the same regime type is essential to arrive at supportable conjectures concerning preferable features for policymaking under adversity. (Andreski 1965 illustrates some possible approaches, as does Holt and Turner 1970. Richardson 1982 illustrates useful but too narrow attempts in needed directions. Schematic treatments even by excellent scholars are difficult; see Sundquist 1978.)

Cross-cultural investigations are very demanding, but, without them, crucial features of present reality are hard to discern, policy paradigms are difficult to explicate and review, grand policy innovation is too narrow, and improvement of central minds of governments lacks necessary vistas.

In combination, historic and comparative perspectives are needed for taking a broad view of policy and policymaking issues and analyzing them within appropriate contexts. To move in this direction, broad perspectives, as well as technical skills, are necessary. Therefore, advanced policy sciences professionals need reading knowledge in at least one major foreign language and should spend parts of their career in a culture other than their own.

## Handle Policymaking Actuality Realistically

In-depth understanding and comprehending of policymaking actuality are a precondition of policy sciences in all its diversity. The existential nature of policymaking and its complex mix of variance, field-dependant features, and constants make this a difficult endeavor. Fashions in relevant disciplines make the task even more demanding. Thus, neglect of irrational behavior, mass politics, and hate in large parts of U.S. political science combines with "rational" images of politics (Rogowski 1978) and with public-choice schools (Mueller 1979), associated with overfixation on economic approaches to policymaking (Havemen and Margolis 1977; Willett 1976). Serious biases in much of the treatment of politics as a main dimension of policymaking realities (Self 1975) often result. Schismatic conflicts of opinions in social sciences between, say, neo-Marxist and system-conservative approaches add and further distort policymaking-reality treatments.

Equally serious are other forms of simplistic treatment of politics in policy sciences works, including by outstanding authors. Thus, to regard political constraints as sometimes ignorable while technological constraints should always be taken into account (Ackoff 1978,72) and to enumerate politics among the "enemies" of the systems approach (Churchman 1979) testify to something very wrong in some regions of policy sciences.

While often handled incorrectly, the importance of politics in policymaking is at least usually acknowledged. The situation on the realities of individual and group behavior as dominating policymaking is worse. Good literature in decision psychology is increasingly available (as illustrated, in addition to literature already cited in this book, for instance, by J. Erikson and Jones 1978; Hogarth 1980; Jungermann and Zeeuw 1977; M.Kaplan and Schwartz 1977; Kozielsecki 1982; Sjobert et al. 1980; and Slovic et al. 1977), and some progress is taking place in relevant parts of group psychology (as reflected in Janis 1982 and by Brandstatter et al. 1978; Brandstatter et al. 1982; and Zander 1979). Parts of such literature are reflected in political science publications (e.g. Cotter 1974; Cotter 1975) but still are ignored in most political science texts. In policy sciences, neglect of decision psychology in the main body of literature serves as a troubling indicator of the "reality-distance" characterizing much of policy sciences, and as a major omission hurting policy sciences in all its dimensions.

A similar case could be made about work in organization theory, which is recognized as important in many policy sciences writings and then curiously left aside when broad descriptive theories are developed and prescriptive methods are taken up. The dichotomy in much of organization theory itself between low-grade "practical" writings and high-quality theories on a very abstract level and hard to transform into prescriptive approaches (as illustrated, to add some examples to already-cited literature, by Arrow 1974; England et al. 1981; and March 1978. Different and unusual in combining high theoretic sophistication with application potentials are, for instance, March 1965; Mintzberg 1983; H. Simon 1976a; H. Simon 1976b; H. Simon 1977; and H. Simon 1979b) contributes to nonintegration of organization theory into much of policy sciences. (As does some surprising lack of familiarity by a number of policy sciences scholars with writings in organization theory, as far as one can judge from their publications.) Shared biases in nearly all of present organization theory, such as neglect of committed, goal-focused, and innovative governmental organizations and of the realities of top-level decisionmaking, further add to difficulties.

No single view of policymaking can do justice to all its existential variety and complexity, but much more can be and needs to be done to move toward more realistic perspectives, before reaching the perhaps unknowable. Policymaking under adversity surely requires policy sciences knowledge that fits policymaking realities instead of addressing itself to never-never lands. It may well be that policy scientists should spend a couple of years inside governments, to gain subjective realistic knowledge far beyond the reaches of present research methods and professional literature.

## Seek Grand Theories

There are four main, and partly overlapping, approaches to the study of policymaking. None of them, nor all of them in combination, "solve" the study difficulties inherent in the very nature of policymaking as an existential feature of society and a dimension of historic processes. Each one of these four approaches has some utility, however, and, in combination, they can move forward on the endless (not infinite!) road of trying to understand and improve policymaking as an aspect of human collective life.

The first approach is reductionism. It tries to dissect policymaking reality till arriving at its most elementary particles and underlying forces. In a naive reductionistic approach, understanding of elemenary particles and underlying forces is expected to yield a master key to understanding policymaking as a whole. In an advanced version of the reductionistic approach, it is recognized that the understanding of elements and underlying forces does not add up to the understanding of higher levels of structure-process (R.Collins 1981). Instead, knowledge of the elements and underlying forces is regarded as a partial contribution to knowledge about policymaking as a whole. Illustrations of reductionist approaches relevant to the study of policymaking include: psychology, such as behaviorism (Skinner 1971; Skinner 1974; Skinner 1978) or other schools (Eberlein and Kondratowitz 1977), including some of already-considered decision psychology; sociobiology (Barash 1977; Sahlins 1976; E. Wilson 1975; E. Wilson 1978); and economic materialism (Wright 1978). Economizing behavior can also serve as a reductionistic approach (Becker 1976; Leibenstein 1976; different, but very relevant, is Downs 1967) when regarded as more than a "science of the artificial" (H. Simon 1981).

The second approach is decomposition. In it, policymaking segments are identified and studied. In distinction from reductionism, the effort here is directed not at arriving at elementary particles and underlying forces but at those policymaking segments in which the researcher is interested, which are significant for some theory, and which are susceptible to research methods accepted by the relevant community of scholars as "scientific" and fitting the criteria of "public knowledge" (Ziman 1968). Most empirical studies adopt this approach (as illustrated in many of the cited works on policymaking and in Greenstein and Polsby 1975, vol. 6, chs. 2-5,7. A good case-study illustration of this approach is Moharir 1979).

The third approach is holistic. In it, some scheme with internal logical and/or functional consistency and with some theoretic claim is applied to policymaking as a whole, yielding some systematic information, regularities, and insights. These schemes can be positivistic, pure-type constructs of different forms, or theoretic-analytic in nature. Well-known illustrations include: cybernetics (Stafford Beer 1966; Stafford Beer 1981; Deutsch 1969, as further advanced and applied in Galnoor 1982; Geyer and Zouwen 1978, passim; Steinbrunner 1974); input-output approaches (Dye 1966; Easton 1965; Sharkansky 1970); market and other economic models (Dahl and Lindblom 1953; Lindblom 1965; Lindblom 1977); collective choice theory (Mueller 1979; Olson 1971; Wade and Curry 1970) bureaucratic-politics and other pure-type or mixed decision structures (surveyed in Rosat 1981); and more. This does not imply that holistic approaches must start with procrustean schemata to be applied to policymaking. While this also happens, an iterative process of movement between concept packages and policymaking reality is often practiced. But, at the end, every holistic approach to policymaking must rely on some theoretic system to handle the potentially endless features of relevant realities.

The fourth approach looks at policymaking as part of larger, encompassing process-systems up to overall theories of sociopolitical processes and systems (e.g. Boulding 1978; Khokshkish 1979; A. Wiener 1978). Such theories must be institution oriented, to be relevant for policy sciences, rather than of the Parsons-type grand theories (but Max Weber repays reprocessing within a policy sciences perspective, starting with his sociology of the state [Weber 1966]).

All four approaches permit progress and can be much further advanced. Thus, better psychological knowledge provides knowledge on policymaking particles, feeding also into studies of policymaking segments and into holistic approaches. Study of segments can become broader and more reliable with the help of combinational methods and comparative perspectives (a good illustration is Bunce 1981). More advanced holistic approaches can provide overall understanding of main policymaking facets, while also supplying frameworks and hypotheses for other study approaches. And examination of policymaking within encompassing process-systems is essential for understanding its functions and forms as a facet of historical-societal processes.

A promising possibility is to apply additional schemata and theoretic systems to the study of policymaking. Thus, work in systems theory (James Miller 1978, as discussed in Book Review Symposium 1980), on purposeful systems (Ackoff and Emery 1972; Churchman 1971), on positive political theory (Riker and Ordeshook 1973; with adjustments, Snyder and Diesing 1977), and, earlier but underutilized, in medical sciences (Rothschuh 1965) may provide interesting possibilities for additional holistic approaches to the study of policymaking. Other holistic schemes may come along and be useful for policy sciences.

These four main approaches to studying policymaking, working in combination and with additional ones, permit significant progress in policy sciences. But more is needed: A general theory of policymaking in the broadest senses of that term is required, with both empiric generalizations and prescriptive dimensions.

No one overarching and dominating theory can encompass all of policymaking, different starting points, and concerns resulting in various grand theories. For instance, the idea of a general theory of societal command and control, as mentioned several times in this book, can serve as one approach to developing a grand theory of policymaking. Other approaches are useful for bringing out different aspects of existential policymaking realities, such as broad-gauged historic investigations of the evolution of main policymaking patterns and institutions.

At present, no grand theories of policymaking are available, other than application to policymaking of holistic approaches, as mentioned above. Holistic approaches as existing at present can help to build up policymaking grand theories but are inadequate for serving in their stead. Dogma-based presumptions at grand-theories, such as neo-Marxian ones, are useless and misleading, although these too sometimes include valuable elements, for instance, examination of inbuilt limits of specific policymaking settings such as capitalism, and critique of overoptimistic views of policymaking autonomy.

## Policy-Paradigm Critique

Policy sciences must be kept separate from ideological criticism of social realities however important, such as the Frankfurter school and other attempts at value-based and ideological reconsideration of society (Berg 1981; Crocker 1982; Geuss 1981; Held 1980; Marković 1974; McCarthy 1978; John Thompson and Held 1982; Vedung 1976). At the same time, policy-paradigm critique, as discussed in chapter 7, is a main subject for policy sciences. This, in turn, requires careful attention to relations between policy sciences and values as well as between theory and practice (T. Ball 1977; Habermas 1971).

Borders between policy-paradigm critique on one hand and social critique on the other hand will remain in debate and vague, which is not an impediment as long as some distinction is preserved. For advancing policy sciences, it is often better to err in the direction of moving into social critique than to restrain policy-paradigm review and debunking, which are an especially important part of policy sciences for handling policymaking under adversity.

## Take Up Grand-Policy Innovation

Closely related to grand-theory neglect, but analytically distinct from it, is the tendency of prescriptive parts of policy sciences, such as "policy analysis" in one of its main meanings, to concentrate on delimited and decomposable issues. This is understandable and has many advantages: Narrow policy issues are easier to comprehend and analyze, and most methods available at present fit only constricted problems. Nevertheless, policy sciences must take up grand-policy innovation because of the actual need for innovative grand policies to handle overwhelming policy predicaments, as explored in this book. Unless policy sciences does so, it remains largely irrelevant to real-life needs. Worse, policy sciences that shies from grand policy can easily do more harm than good by increasing rigidities in policymaking and, thus, reducing chances of adequate responses to adversity.

## Move into Metapolicymaking, up to Governance Redesign

One step beyond grand policies lies metapolicymaking. In proposing a move into metapolicymaking, the emphasis is on policymaking improvement as a main area in need of policy sciences breakthroughs. As already considered in chapter 7, if present features of policymaking process-systems are taken as static or as susceptible only to incremental change, there is little hope for essential improvements. With inherent incapacities taken into account, movement in the direction of meeting essential policymaking-quality requisites, as discussed in this book, depends largely on trans-incremental reforms of policymaking process-systems. Hence, the importance of appropriate study of policymaking systems and of design of metapolicymaking proposals. At present, such work does proceed on policymaking segments. Thus, some studies deal with information supports for decision making (Fick and Sprague 1981; Hussain and Hussain 1981; Keen and Morton 1978; Mowitz 1980; Sproull and Larkey 1983); with specific processes, such as planning (Mayntz and Scharpf 1973); with select institutions, such as presidential advisory systems (A. George 1980; R. Porter 1980; also relevant is Szanton 1981b), or public commissions (Chapman 1973; Lompe, Rass, and Rehfeld 1981; Tutchings 1979); with select principles, such as positive redundancy (Landau 1969); and so on, but such studies are not well integrated into the main body of policy sciences literature. More serious, comprehensive work in the direction of meta-policymaking-theory and overall policymaking process-system improvement is nearly nonexistent. (For an unusual recognition of the need to work in such directions, see Ranney 1976.)

Comprehensive policy sciences work on metapolicymaking requires, inter alia, evaluation of the overall policymaking process-system. This on lines suggested in this book and elsewhere (Dror 1983a), and/or through other approaches, such as application of network analysis (Laumann and Pappi 1976) to governmental policymaking as a whole, leading to evaluation and improvement proposals (unusual in some relevant respects is Kriesi 1980, combined with Germann 1975). Holistic studies and designs of policymaking process-systems overlap with governance redesign, up to consideration of far-reaching governance revisions (Lester Brown 1981; Diem and Neisser 1969; Lindberg 1976; R. Tugwell 1974). This also applies to particular institutions. Thus, in U.S. context, redesign of the presidency involves main issues of governance as well as of policymaking (C. Hardin 1974). The tasks of policy sciences in this respect can be somewhat circumscribed by putting policymaking into the focus of investigation and improvement, but some movement into governance redesign is necessary for high-quality policymaking under adversity and, consequently, in policy sciences.

The need to overcome some extreme promarket biases in parts of U.S.-based policy sciences must be mentioned, as it hinders appropriate concerns with policymaking-improvement within the context of very active governments. Policymaking studies do bring out many weaknesses of governments often inherent in their very nature, but comparison of actual governmental performance with the hypothetical advantages of pure-market models and/or particular features of some Western democracies at a particular period can be misleading for purposes of nomographic generalizations and universal prescriptions. (Some misleading conclusions are illustrated by Zeckhauser and Leebaert 1983.)

However audacious the endeavor and however difficult, movement into metapolicy up to governance redesign is essential, both to complete the theoretic edifice of policy sciences and to fulfill its applied missions. The next breakthrough desideratum continues to deal with this need in a different form.

## Consider Policymaking-Improvement Approaches

A main task of policy sciences is to contribute to policymaking improvement. Therefore, in addition to the provision of underlying understanding and substantive improvement proposals, the problems of improvement approaches need attention. This, all the more because most of the literature on administrative reforms is of limited relevance to policymaking improvement (G. Caiden 1969; G. Caiden and Seidenkopf 1982; Chapman and Greenaway 1980; Leemans 1976; OECD 1980; Szanton 1981a). A broad approach to various forms and modalities of "reforms" is required (D. Campbell 1969; Greiffenhagen 1978; Krockow 1976), as well as a search for appropriate intervention modes (Argyris 1971; Revans 1982; Susman and Evered 1978), planned change approaches (Golembiewski 1979; Mayer, Moroney, and Morris 1976; Zaltman and Duncan 1977), and institution-building models (Thomas et al. 1972).

Underlying problems of improvement principles, reform strategies, and improvement recommendations pose serious methodological issues of movement from empiric knowledge and theories on one hand to prescriptive endeavors on the other hand. Alternative logics of improvement approaches, such as "preferization" and debugging, must serve as central concerns of policy sciences, converging with other policy sciences requirements as considered in this chapter.

While some starting points for such concerns do exist, meaningful policymaking-improvements approaches as such are a quite ignored subject in contemporary policy sciences. Some ideas in this matter are presented in the next chapters, further illustrating the scope of this issue and its calling for attention.

## Work on Inputting into Policymaking

Closely related to some reform approaches but deserving separate attention is the need to improve inputting of policy sciences knowledge into policymaking reality. Some of the barriers to doing so are shared with applied social sciences as a whole (Scott and Shore 1979; Stifel et al. 1983), but some problems are unique, for policy sciences deals in part with more sensitive issues of the very decision-making process itself. Inputting of policy sciences into the central minds of governments is an especially difficult and essential matter. A related special problem is how to convey a very complex analysis to busy policymakers without undue oversimplification, with a consequent need for novel display communication techniques. (E.g. Waller 1982. New forms of geometric presentations illustrate novel possibilities [Abraham and Shaw 1983; Fisher 1984; Holden 1983], especially in combination with powerful graphic interactive computer systems; Winston 1975.) Power implications of policy sciences knowledge and consequent resistance to its inputting, add to the complexities of issues (still worth pondering is Merton 1949, ch. 6). Within a somewhat different perspective, the cluster of problems relating to roles and functions of policy scientists working in government are tangent to this subject and require reconsideration. This is an area in which progress has been slow (Goldwin 1980; Meltsner 1976, Szanton 1981b), needing all the more breakthroughs.

A main form of inputting policy sciences into policymaking and metapolicymaking is through preparing policy sciences professionals and through training in parts of policy sciences knowledge of other personnel active in minds of governments and in policy influencing as a whole. This is so important a subject as to deserve separate consideration, toward the end of this chapter.

## Enlarge Disciplinary Bases

A real jump is needed in the disciplinary bases of the core of policy sciences. This requirement follows the desiderata of policy sciences discussed above: decision psychology, defense intelligence studies, systems engineering, organization theory, parts of business management, sociology, historic approaches—these illustrate bases that need adding to policy sciences to meet its conspectus, as proposed here (as well as in Dror 1971a). The necessity for much enlarged disciplinary bases is further exposed by the methodological needs of policy sciences as following, which require much broader foundations than those currently prevalent. Also needed are multiple ways of learning and knowing (Mitroff and Kilmann 1981), to permit inclusion of appropriate tacit knowledge and clinical skills within an enlarged disciplinary base.

Needs go beyond a broader disciplinary base, into interdisciplinarity. Ways to advance toward interdisciplinarity need to serve as significant concerns of policy sciences. Thus, it may well be advisable to motivate and push policy sciences professionals to learn a "counterdiscipline" to their main one, such as sociology and psychology to be taken up by policy scientists with a background in economic and quantitative approaches, and the converse; and some studies in history and social archeology, for instance, being advisable for all policy sciences professionals. This matter has direct application to the public-policy teaching programs, which tend to be much too narrow in the range of subjects that all students must take.

An illustration of neglected additional needed disciplinary bases for policy sciences is law. Legislation is a main mode of policymaking and laws are a main constraint on policies as well as a main policy instrument (Dror 1971b, pt. 5; Rose 1982; Rose 1983c). In a number of countries and especially the United States, courts are also a main policymaking institution, with select but important interactions with central policymaking process-systems. Many of the policies needed for handling adversity do involve legislation and much interaction with courts. Therefore, some overlap and much interdependence exists between policymaking and law, as was recognized by Roscoe Pound, who spoke in 1907 about law in the context of "social engineering" (Pound 1907). It follows that attention to legislation and law in policy sciences is needed but much neglected in practice (despite a few teaching programs enabling combined study of law and public policy, but without much integration. On parallel neglects in law schools see Stevens 1983).

In the many countries where administrative law is highly developed and legal training is the main road to senior government positions, integration of suitable parts of jurisprudence, legislation, and law into policy sciences (and of parts of policy sciences into law curricula, which in some European countries are somewhat broader in scope than those in the United States and the United Kingdom) is a precondition for the latter's achieving standing and impact within the foreseeable future.

Apropos the broadening of the disciplinary bases of policy sciences, mutual benefits for all involved disciplines should be mentioned. More attention to policymaking realities and needs can well provide additional stimuli and agenda for a number of disciplines, helping in their advancement. To take an example, though decision psychology has been mentioned several times as rich in knowledge relevant to policymaking, still a policy sciences perspective reveals serious weaknesses in decision psychology. Thus, the reliability of experiments with students for drawing conclusions in respect to quite different decision contexts, as in the central minds of governments, is quite doubtful. At least, much calibration is essential and more focused attention by decision psychology to top-level decision making in the real world is needed. Progress in such directions is important for advancing decision psychology as a discipline or sub-discipline, and is essential for needed contributions by decision psychology to policy sciences.

Comparable conclusions stem from examination of other disciplines from the perspective of policy sciences: While policy sciences can and need draw on many disciplines, the latter reveal many inadequacies when evaluated in terms of the needs of policymaking understanding and improvement. Therefore, increased interface and mutual learning between various social science and other disciplines on one hand and policy sciences on the other hand are of benefit to all involved domains of study and knowledge.

The question of what institutional arrangements may be necessary for permitting fruitful interaction between policy sciences and other disciplines is different. The fact that some disciplines, such as sociology, are also quite isolated from policy sciences in think tanks and in special public policy faculties, shows that institutional innovations are needed to achieve the necessary interaction and cross-fertilization. Awareness in policy sciences of the need to build up its disciplinary basis is a first and essential step before such institutionalization issues can be taken up.

### Develop Multidimensional Methods, Methodologies, and Techniques

All specifications for policymaking under adversity and for policy sciences breakthroughs, as well as other needs of policymaking under adversity as discussed in the book, have direct implications for needed enlargements and inventions in methods, methodologies, and techniques. This applies to all facets of policy sciences: Empiric research needs additional tools to arrive at reliable data on policymaking, and additional modes of understanding to arrive at comprehension of policymaking. Theory building needs a variety of concept packages, model formats, pure-type constructs, and innovative languages. Transition from the empiric-theoretic modality to the prescriptive modality needs additional foundations, such as constructs of various forms of rationality, goal-seeking and other ideal and preferable models; and systematic debugging and reality-critical methods. And, new methods, methodologies, and techniques are needed to develop operational recommendations for policymaking improvements, as considered in the next chapters.

To meet such needs, additional methods, methodologies, and techniques on line with currently available ones, while needed too, are not enough. Rather, new dimensions must be added, in the direction of heuristic approaches, applied philosophy (e.g. in respect to value analysis), historic processes consideration, subjective knowledge distillation (partly, but not necessarily mainly, in combination with quantitative processing, as discussed in Hopple and Kuhlman 1981), *Gedankenexperiments,* and so on (Mintzberg 1979b; Mitroff and Kilmann 1981. Strictly to be rejected are attempts to apply to social sciences "scientific" methods that are inapplicable to many of the natural sciences themselves, as proposed by Papineau 1979).

This does not imply that currently available methods should be discounted and that their further development is superfluous. Social experimentation methodology (T. Cook and Campbell 1979; Ferber and Hirsch 1981; McKenna 1980; Nachmias 1979; R. Perloff et al. 1976; Wortman 1983; and other already-quoted literature), simulation and model building (Bremer 1977; Carbonell 1978; K. Clark et al. 1975; Graubard and Builder 1980; Meadows, Richardson, and Bruckman 1982; Rivett 1980), some branches of formal decision theory (Basu 1980; Keeney and Raiffa 1976; McGuire and Radner 1972; Plott 1976; esoteric but stimulating is Brams 1983), and combined approaches (Goeller et al. 1983) illustrate a few out of many methods, methodologies, and tools now being worked on that need further development and that can make rich contributions to the advancement of policy sciences, but present orientations must not become a Procustean bed stifling needed multidimensionality. In particular, quantitative methods and economics-based approaches, however essential, are unable to satisfy many of the requisites of policymaking under adversity and of necessary breakthroughs in policy sciences.

The substantial body of high-quality policy analysis practice available in a number of countries is based on skills and craftsmanship beyond explicated methods, methodologies, and techniques. This not only demonstrates that progress is possible but also provides one of several avenues for advancing methods, namely the better distilling of knowledge from clinical experience. Successful policy-improvement practitioners have an important role to fulfill in building up policy sciences and helping with needed breakthroughs. To realize potential cross-fertilization, most policy scientists should move between teaching, theoretic and empiric research, and applied work; and outstanding policy-analysis practitioners should be active in policy sciences research.

## Avoid Dilution

The needs of policy sciences are immense; therefore, it is all the more necessary to concentrate on main tasks and avoid dilution with subjects and interests that are not essential for the core concerns of policy sciences. A good case in point is "implementation." While implementability direction and implementation-institution reconsiderations are essential for policymaking improvement, details of implementation belong to management and administration. This is not a trivial matter of taste, but is important for preserving the quintessential profile of policy sciences and for concentrating scarce intellectual resources on the most pressing subjects. Misdirection of policy sciences and its dilution in its present, still chrysalid, phase may yet ruin the whole endeavor.

## Intensify and Upgrade Teaching and Training

Preparation of high-quality advanced professionals in policy sciences to fill key positions in the minds of governments and in policymaking in general, together with conveyance of main policy sciences approaches to top decision makers and policy shapers as a whole, is a main mode of increased contributions of policy sciences to policymaking under adversity and a precondition for such contributions.

Although, as already mentioned, there is a proliferation of public policy teaching in the United States with some diffusion to other countries, still the situation is very unsatisfactory. Thus:

- Even the better public policy schools in the United States fall short of needs, such as considered in this chapter and book. In particular, quantitative and economic approaches often overdominate; social sciences, history, decision psychology, and law are often neglected; grand policies and metapolicymaking receive inadequate consideration; comprehensive historic and comparative perspectives are sorely missing; philosophic foundations for policymaking and for policy sciences receive scant attention; and so on.
- With a few partial exceptions, public policy teaching is very underdeveloped and usually nonexistent in other countries. When some relevant teaching under other titles, such as planning and systems analysis, is taken into account, Europe is still clearly lacking any adequate public policy programs. In the Third World there is very little going on in policy sciences, despite some interest. In the communist countries there seems to exist nothing comparable.

- In no country, including the United States, do suitable courses and institutes exist to convey needed policy sciences knowledge to various groups of policymakers and policy influencers, such as senior officials, rising politicians, mass media commentators, military officers, and so on.

The teaching and training tasks of policy sciences are mentioned here among required policy sciences breakthroughs because of their crucial importance for putting required knowledge into policymaking under adversity. But expanded and improved policy sciences teaching depends upon policy sciences itself progressing greatly, such as on lines considered in this chapter. More diffusion of currently limited knowledge cannot be of much help in policymaking under adversity, and is of little use for handling critical problems facing the central minds of governments.

### Adopt Tough Stances

The tasks of policy sciences, as sketched anew in this chapter and the book as a whole, are most demanding. This is not the result of personal predilection but stems from the nature of policy predicaments, from inbuilt policy spoilers, and from stubborn needs of policymaking improvements. Mild efforts will bear scant fruits.

Tough stances provide the only hope for policy sciences achievements. This applies to all facets of the endeavor. Thus:

- Moral toughness is needed to adopt the necessary stances of clinical concern (to borrow from medical ethics) for studying, analyzing, and prescribing "coldly" on human anguish, human futures, and human hopes. Even more, moral toughness is necessary for the difficult mixture of enthusiasm and stoicism needed for the nearly impossible missions of policy sciences. Thinking about the unthinkable, analyzing the terrible, prescribing the unpalatable, and trying the nearly impossible—all these features of policy sciences require moral toughness.
- Intellectual and mental top capacities (a term much broader than I.Q. but including the latter in its conventional meanings) are essential for handling the scientific and professional contents of policy sciences advancement. Policy sciences in no way constitutes some new kind of *arcana imperii* (i.e. secret knowledge of rulers). Popularized versions to improve the capacity of citizens to consider complex issues are possible and desirable (Dolbeare 1982, passim; Edmunds 1978; P. Hill et al. 1979; MacRea and Wilde 1978), but for advancing policy sciences as an interdiscipline and for usefully applying it to policymaking under adversity—top intellectual and mental capacities are hardly enough.

Some university programs in policy sciences and some policy sciences publications achieve high levels, but a number of university programs and policy sciences publications are substandard. The facts that policy sciences is fashionable and that it lacks a crystallized community of scholars who can preserve standards permit and invite misuses of policy sciences titles as flags of convenience for many ill-conceived, ignorant, and irrelevant activities. Unless standards are raised and guarded, policy sciences may still decay into a fashion and fad, without lasting contributions to knowledge, to policymaking under adversity, and to societal steering abilities.

Systematic reevaluations of policy sciences achievements and weaknesses are needed (in part, analogous to Daniel Bell 1982). A good "Encylopaedia of Policy Ignorance" (analogous to Duncan and Weston-Smith 1977) could be very stimulating. Consideration of conditions favoring major advances in policy sciences and in policymaking is urgent (analogous to Deutsch, Platt, and Sanghaas 1971, reconsidered at a conference in June 1982, see Deutsch, Platt, and Markovits 1984). Such examinations will arrive at improved lists of required breakthroughs in policy sciences, as well as in recommendations on how to bring those about. But breakthroughs are surely essential in policy sciences, and they are also feasible.

The difficulties of required breakthroughs, and of all policy sciences endeavors beyond the microlevel, must be fully recognized. The fact that some outstanding thinkers and researchers, who contributed much to policy sciences, deviated at some phases of their life cycles into quasi-mystic writings and into poetic modes of paraprofessional expression, provides material for speculation on frustrations awaiting policy scientists and on dangerous "escapes" that may seduce them. (E.g.,see Stafford Beer 1975; Friedmann 1979; Jantch 1975. For a positive evaluation of such modes of "knowledge" see Richard Brown 1977.) Some important truths about existential processes, such as policymaking, may be best expressed in literary forms; nevertheless, such modes of cognition should be kept strictly controlled in scientific and professional endeavors. Semimystical approaches that provide psychological escapes from depressing realities are to be rejected completely.

Warnings against escape into semimysticism may seem out of place here, but quite a number of opinions found in some writings by distinguished policy researchers and thinkers are hard to distinguish from semimysticism. Sudden jumps into believing in spontaneous transformations of human behavior as providing a way out of dismal futures are a relatively mild and quite widespread form of escape into semimagic assumptions in writings by some policy sciences professionals also. Such responses to very disturbing conclusions of analysis are understandable in human terms and are sometimes honorable morally, but they are completely destructive of the basic philosophy and mission of policy sciences. (A good exercise is to try and apply Crawshaw-Williams 1947 to policy sciences.)

Strong frustrations and much anguish are inherent in the subject matter of policy sciences endeavors. Conditions of adversity further aggravate the often painful conclusions of responsible policy sciences research and analysis. All the more then, is toughness called for as an essential ingredient of policy sciences breakthrough endeavors.

Comparisons between governance and politics on one hand and business corporations on the other hand are more misleading than enlightening. Widespread assumptions in some countries that government has a lot to learn from market organizations ignore fundamental differences. Subject to such reservations, studies on the impact of new and improved professionals on the emergence of modern corporations (Chandler 1977; Noble 1977) suggest possibilities to upgrade policymaking under adversity with the help of the injection of new types of professionals and knowledge. Such hopes and ambitions are limited by the basic nature of policymaking as a power-dependent and power-allocating process, by the crucial importance of transscientific processes in policymaking, and more. Nevertheless, a new breed of policy scientists and a new generation of policy sciences knowledge can provide a chance to improve policymaking somewhat and may be essential for upgrading policymaking under adversity. Certainly, the absence of such professionals and knowledge forecloses some promising avenues for policymaking improvement. Maximum efforts to advance policy sciences, inter alia in the direction of the presented breakthrough directions, are therefore a major policymaking-improvement requisite, strategy, and prescription.

One of the results of the failure of medieval medicine in handling the Black Death in Europe was complete discreditation of accepted medical knowledge and the laying of foundations for modern medicine (Gottfried 1983, ch. 6). The social sciences are in a much more complex situation, and present and foreseeable adversities are far from a plague pandemic. Nevertheless, with luck, the inadequacies of social sciences in general, and policy sciences in particular, as an aid in handling adversity may help to displace inappropriate assumptions and approaches and accelerate construction of radically better ones. There is no assurance that this will happen, with antiscientism perhaps becoming stronger instead, or policy theologies rushing in a new age of orthodoxy. Possibly, the difficulties of the problems transgress far beyond maximum human capacities in their present state, but intensive efforts to build up policy sciences and striving for breakthroughs in it do constitute one of the best bets available, to humanity in general and to policy scholars and policy professionals in particular.

# 9

# Approaches to Policymaking Redesign

## Scope of Endeavor

A main finding of this book is that central minds of governments find themselves increasingly in *aporie*, in the earlier explained sense of being in situations with no way out. Adversities pose challenges beyond the capacity of present policymaking process-systems and also beyond the capacity of societal problem-handling processes. While catastrophe is not a high-probability result of present and foreseen *aporie*, costs in terms of contemporary values can be very high. Therefore, policymaking improvement is a main need. Without policymaking improvement adversities will not necessarily become worse, for they may dissipate without the benefits of human invention because of their internal dynamics or other societal processes. But, within the world of inquiry of this book, policymaking improvement and, especially, upgrading of central policymaking process-systems, emerge as one of the better bets in human endeavors to influence futures in desired directions through collective deliberate interventions.

There is no guarantee of success. As already discussed, even the best of policymaking achieves at its utmost changes in the probabilities of events and trends. Under adversity, realistic expectations from better policymaking are limited to some reduction of catastrophe risks, some amelioration of human suffering, some achievement of a few aspirations, and continuous buildup of conditions and resources that may permit mutations for the better in human conditions through forces other than conscious collective choice. Under favorable conditions and in combination with suitable societal variables, improved policymaking may also help advance realistic visions, but this cannot be assured; is partly independent from the quality of policymaking; and positive effects can be outweighed by instances where more effective policymaking serves forces of darkness.

Such guesstimation of maximum benefits from policymaking improvement may be unexciting to many. Assuming commitment to bettering the human condition (which is only one of many possible personal life projects from which one can choose), alternatives to policymaking improvement include, on one side, prophecy, revolution, utopia design, and charismatic leadership, and, on the other side, brain research, genetic engineering, psychopharmacology, and similar branches of science that may change the psychogenetic profile of so-called *Homo sapiens* and mutate humankind into a different universe of potentials, and other branches of science, which may change human existence.

This book adopts the stance of clinging stubbornly to the tasks of policymaking improvement. While recognizing the limits of policymaking improvement within currently envisaged possibilities, such improvement is regarded as of pivotal importance: Achievement of the maximum possible in policymaking improvement may be a minimum for worthwhile survival and value-achievement chances, and a sine qua non for other forces to have a chance to transmutate human conditions. Hope that accelerated change may produce conditions permitting high-quality policymaking to achieve positive aspirations, and fear that less than excellent policymaking may carry a growing probability of very negative results combine to increase the pivotal importance of hoped-for returns from stubborn commitment to policymaking improvement. To these considerations one may add a moral feeling that it is up to humanity to try to use its reasoning capacities to increase collective abilities to influence futures, without foreclosing free choice by future generations on their lives and values. Doing the best to improve policymaking qualities is thus also part of a moral endeavor, if underlying axiological assumptions are accepted. It is possible that breakthroughs in artificial intelligence, or impacts on human decision makers of interaction from a young age with computers, or chemical augmentation of human brain powers, or some other intervening factor will significantly upgrade policymaking quality, much more so than policymaking process-system redesign. But, till such a jump occurs, it is up to humanity as a whole, and policy scientists in particular, to do their limited best to improve policymaking under adversity.

To serve this mission, a bridge must be built between the more theoretic parts of this book and concrete recommendations for policymaking improvement. Specific prescriptions must be tailor-made to concrete circumstances and idiosyncratic occasions. Nevertheless, general guidelines for policymaking improvement can be derived and improvement approaches can be designed on a middle range of operationalization to fit in principle a large set of conditions and to serve as a basis for detailed custom fitting.

The position that improvement of the central minds of governments is a worthwhile attempt goes in tandem with findings on the difficulties of such efforts. In particular, built-in policymaking incapacities constitute a strong barrier to improvement, together with scarcities of improvement resources, lack of adequate knowledge, noninterest in improvement in the central

minds of governments, and additional improvement hindrances. Therefore, policymaking improvement requires much effort and needs deliberate
methodological guidelines, substantive principles, and reform strategies,
within an overall policymaking-redesign approach.

In the present chapter, some main dimensions of a systematic approach
to policymaking redesign are developed, with the next chapter presenting
some specific policymaking-improvement recommendations. Treatment
in this chapter focuses on the improvement of policymaking, but most of
the presented approach can be applied to governance redesign as a whole,
with some adjustments.

As indicated in the last chapter and further elaborated in the next sec-
tion, little work has been done to develop systematic approaches to governance and policymaking redesign. The proposed approach is all the more
conjectural, being provisional and introductory to a complex and important subject, to be further considered at other opportunities.

## Knowledge for Policymaking Redesign

In view of the difficulties of the subject, more detailed looking at relevant
knowledge may be a useful redundancy, adding to earlier remarks in chapter 8.

Interest in governance redesign has a long history, going back to Plato,
who, in *The Republic* and *Laws*, worked out two pure-type solutions to
central problems of governance that are fully relevant today. The major
founders of modern social sciences have shown applied interest in restructuring governments, as illustrated by Max Weber (Weber 1971, 448ff.).
Nevertheless, knowledge on and for governance redesign in general
(Blondel 1982, introduction) and policymaking redesign in particular is
poor.

Processing of the dispersed literature that might be relevant to policymaking redesign provides many pieces but no way for combining them
into meaningful redesign mosaics. Relevant literature can, in part, be divided into the following main categories, with a few illustrations cited in
each one:

- Literature dealing directly with governance reforms, usually emphasizing the process (G. Caiden 1969; G. Caiden and Seidenkopf 1982; Chapman and Greenaway 1980; Crotty 1977; C. Gilbert 1983; Hammergren
  1983; Leemans 1976; Radian 1980, Ch. 8).
- Writings presenting general approaches to governance design, up to a
  quasi-philosophic position. The writings of Hayek (e.g. Hayek 1979; see

the discussion in E. Butler 1983, to be compared with Albert 1972) well illustrate such literature.

- Literature dealing with particular governance processes and evaluating them, with implications for redesign, as in respect to federalism (Samuel Beer 1977; Breton and Scott 1978; Hicks 1979; Forsyth 1982; P. King 1982); referenda (Butler and Ranney 1978; Ranney 1981; Troitzsch 1979); court reform (Feeley 1983); party reform (Harmel and Janda 1982; Polsby 1983b; Shafer 1983); civil service reforms (Bruce Smith 1984).

- Literature proposing a broader set of improvements, on the basis of careful analysis focused on some dimension of governance (Kochen and Deutsch 1980; D. Yates 1982, ch. 7. Crozier 1982; Dahl 1982, passim. illustrate the stronghold of incrementalism here, too).

- A growing literature that proposes various changes in governance, mainly in a normative stance, such as more citizen participation (Kweit and Kweit 1981; T. Williams 1982); increasing reliance on capitalistic markets (Novak 1982); reduced hierarchy (Thayer 1981; P. Ward 1981); growing "democratization" (Joshua Cohen and Rogers 1983; Mansbridge 1980; M. Margolis 1979;) and so on—without any reasonable feasibility testing and without confrontation with the constants of the materials out of which human institutions are built. More realistic, while still imaginative, treatments do exist (e.g. Michael Taylor 1982) but are overshadowed in this genre by calls for "more passion" as a basis for governance redesign (W. Scott 1983).

- Literature on the very theory of reform processes in a broad sense, applicable also to governance redesign (mainly in German, Greiffenhagen 1978; Krockow 1976; Schulenberg 1976).

- Large amounts of government documents, commission reports, constitutional deliberations, and similar materials dealing with concrete governance and policymaking redesign and reform attempts in particular countries at specific occasions (Benz 1979; Committee on the General Structure of the Netherlands Government Services 1980; Commonwealth of Australia 1983; IIAS Study Group 1983; Lipsey 1982; Stewart 1975; Swedish Commission on Public Policy Planning 1979; U.K. Committee 1968). Growing interest in governmental management by the World Bank (World Bank 1983, pt. 2) and by OECD is relevant, with many pertinent internal working papers (also in the public administration division of the United Nations).

- Large amounts of salient materials and ideas dispersed in political science, public law, public administration, and public policy literature not directly focused on governance and policymaking improvement.

- An even larger literature dealing with policymaking process-systems components, such as mass behavior, group dynamics, organizational processes, interorganizational dynamics, and political culture, up to impact of infrastructure, global situations, and other exogenous variables on governance and policymaking. Also relevant is literature dealing with uses and nonuses of various types of knowledge in governance (Bulmer 1982; Kochen 1975; Scott and Shore 1979) and in societal problem-handling (Boulding and Senesh 1984). And more.

Despite this wealth of raw material and studies, processing of available publications reveals serious lacunas. Thus:

1. There is very little integrative processing of historic and comparative experiences into a general theory of governance and policymaking re-design. Some initial attempts in this direction have been made on a limited contemporary-comparative basis (e.g. in public administration, Heady 1979, passim; and on government, Blondel 1982, passim), but without adequate integration of rich historic-comparative material.
2. No comprehensive collection, analysis, and evaluation of inventions in governance are available (despite some beginnings in Deutsch, Platt, and Senghaas 1971). Especially striking is the absence of systematic surveys, analyses, and evaluations of the many contemporary attempts of governance improvement, from which much can be learned (partial exceptions include Baehr and Wittrock 1981; and C. Campbell 1983, on higher levels of policymaking. Broad studies of governance changes are needed, as illustrated in respect to elections by Bogdanor and Butler 1982).
3. Few systematic evaluation of constitution-writing experiences, historic and contemporary, is available; some relevant work is in its beginning (as illustrated by the American Enterprise Institute meeting on constitution-writing experiences, September 1983; the few comprehensive studies are illustrated by McWhinney 1981).
4. Treatments of particular problems and presentation of specific improvement proposals sometimes reach high levels of "practical" sense, and sometimes also theoretic sophistication, but with very few exceptions, available knowledge on main features of utilized materials, such as human-behavior propensities, is not adequately and explicitly taken into account. Good illustrations of this weakness are provided by the very large literature on the U.S. presidency, with the vast majority of treatments ignoring many of the inherent incapacities and built-in problems in favor of formal and nominal processes and structures (e.g. compare A. George 1980 with Shogan 1982).
5. No overall design approach to governance and policymaking improvment has been developed.

To this should be added that, as far as could be found out, few courses and no university programs focus on governance and policymaking re-design, nor could many broad and integrative research projects on this subject be identified. Some exceptions do exist, such as the project on legislatures at the State University of New York at Albany; the Research Group on Guidance, Control and Performance Evaluation in the Public Sector that worked during 1981-82 at the Bielefeld University Center for Interdisciplinary Research, Germany; a new project on revising the U.S. Constitution at the Brookings Institution; and more. But, despite occasional calls for work on that subject (e.g. Ranney 1976), ongoing endeavors are very minor compared to the scientific and applied importance of governance and policymaking redesign.

As a result, with single exceptions (e.g. Apter and Doornbos 1965, Germann 1975; R. Tugwell 1974), narrow perspectives dominate approaches to governance and policymaking improvement; and the scarcity of underlying knowledge, theories, and systematic approaches usually results in superficial "practicalism" (not to be miscalled "pragmatism," which is quite different). Tinkering with governance and policymaking realities rather than dealing with systematic evaluation and redesign characterizes the vast majority of proposals, most of the rest being dogmatic in one direction or another, with a few distinguished exceptions.

This state-of-the-art-and-knowledge poverty constitutes a main barrier to policymaking-improvement. A quite different barrier, but often a more difficult one that impedes both useful research and actual policymaking improvements, is posed by the dilemmas surrounding pattern-values versus output-values as conflicting goals and criteria for policymaking redesign.

## Pattern-Values versus Output-Values

Evaluation of present policymaking process-systems and approaches to policymaking redesign can be dominated by various mixes of two main value categories, namely pattern-values and output-values, as already considered in a different context in chapter 5.

Applied to the present context, pattern-values relate directly to the main patterns and institutions of policymaking, such as structures, processes, and staffing. Participation, representation, transparency—these illustrate widely accepted relevant pattern-values.

Output-values relate to values to be achieved through policymaking outputs, in a broad sense of the term. Law and order, stable economic growth, equity, social security, and—differently—accountability for results—these are some output-values expected from policymaking in Western democracies and other countries.

This rudimentary distinction needs much refinement. Thus, efforts to assure survival of a specific type of regime fuse desire to maintain pattern-values and to continue benefits of output-values. In respect to output-values, distinction between outputs directly meeting values and outputs building up capacities to meet undefined values in the future is necessary. Care must be taken to include broad impacts of policymaking, such as societal architecture, within the rather narrow concept of "output," used here for convenience despite its problematics. Choice between risks and time preferences fuse output-values with some pattern-values and more.

Despite many such and other oversimplifications, analytic distinction between pattern-values and output-values is essential for considering policymaking-redesign needs and proposals going beyond the "bureaucracy versus democracy" (Etzioni-Halevy 1983) and the "democracy" versus efficiency (D.Yates 1982) dilemmas. In particular, the distinction serves to pose choices when advancement of pattern-values and achievement of output-values contradict one another. Debates on freedom of information in respect to intelligence services serve as a typical illustration. The more extreme case of possible need for additional nondemocratic enclaves within democracies to meet economic problems and assure survival of democracy in a harsher world (Brecht 1978; Shonfield 1982) poses truly tragic choices.

Interrelations between pattern-values and output-values are intense, because improvement of policymaking effectiveness—that is, upgrading of its output-values productivity—usually proceeds through reconsidering policymaking patterns that have some supposed causal effects on output values increases (March 1978; H. Simon 1976a; the detailed investigation of procedural reform on policy-outcomes in Caldwell 1982 is important). Logically, three main types of relationships are possible:

1. Positive correlation, in the sense that increasing achievement of both, pattern-values and goal-values, goes together. Thus, it may be that progress in antidiscrimination policies requiring minorities to occupy main policymaking positions will increase policy quality by stimulating creativity by new staffs. Or, in some opinions, more participation may simultaneously satisfy an expanded-democracy pattern-value and make policymaking better informed and, therefore, more effective in terms of output-values.
2. Negative correlation, when achieving a pattern-value has a cost in terms of output-values, and vice versa. Thus, increased participation may impair policy quality because of ignorance becoming more influential, or local interests gaining veto power over broad national goal achievement.
3. Insensitivity—many administrative improvements, for instance, making no difference to pattern-values; and, some pattern-values, such as reduced distance between ruler and citizens, having in some countries no real impact on governance performance in terms of output-values.

Alternatives that increase satisfaction of both pattern-values and output-values are dominant and should be eagerly sought. Insensitivity is a second-best situation, but it seems that often negative correlations prevail. Thus, increasing "democratization" beyond a certain point may well entail serious costs in policymaking output-values (Löwental 1979, 172-96).

The above concepts and analysis do entail at least three methodological rules for policymaking-redesign endeavors:

1. Dominant improvements, increasing both pattern-values and output-value productivity, should be searched for intensively. If this fails, then improvements that increase pattern-values or output-values, without costs to output-values or pattern-values, respectively, should be looked for.
2. All improvement proposals should be tested for sensitivity in terms of main pattern-value and output-value benefits/costs, so as to pose clarified choices to legitimate value judges. Predominance of uncertainties in such analyses shifts choice to uncertainty-facing strategies but does not change the nature of the issue or impair the need for sensitivity-testing, qualitative costing, and responsible value judgment.
3. In trying to improve policymaking, one should strictly reject fixation on any particular pattern-value or output-value in all professional endeavors, even within advocacy stances. Costs in terms of other types of values may be very high and, therefore, must be considered carefully.

Assuming that there exists a wide range of pattern-values and output-values that one would like to increase, an efficient (though not always logically or morally compelling) approach may be to start with those more in need of betterment. Thus, when policymaking outputs are more or less regarded as satisfactory, efforts can concentrate on upgrading pattern-values, and vice versa. This requires ascertainment of main pattern-values and output-values required from policymaking and appraisal of their actual degrees of achievement, with efforts concentrating on output-value or pattern-value upgrading, accordingly.

To return to an argument presented in chapter 5, examination of adversity in this book leads to the conclusion that, once basic human rights are assured, priority must be given to handling ominous predicaments. This conclusion applies with particular force to policymaking improvement in Western democracies. In Western democracies, main process-values of political democratic ideology are already realized in policymaking patterns, while adversities can cause grievous harm and perhaps endanger the future of democracy itself unless policymaking outputs much improve. Hence, the overall recommendation that in Western democracies priority should be given to output-values in improving policymaking.

The above conclusion is all the more important in light of the continuous priority being given in much of discourse in Western democracies to changing policymaking modes so as to satisfy additional pattern-values. The final choice of priorities is a matter of value judgment, but some considerations should be taken into account, in addition to the main point made above on the imperatives of handling harsher predicaments:

- Care must be taken to select a sophisticated version of democratic theory as a guide for value judgment. The availability of a range of versions of democracy in the Western sense should be recognized, providing a broad rage of policymaking-pattern alternatives that can satisfy the main body of values shared by different versions of democratic theory, though not all of them. (For a comprehensive coverage of main democratic theories, see Pennock 1979, to be supplemented with the different perspectives of Plamenatz 1973.)
- Whatever one's value preferences and readings of situational imperatives may be, care must be taken to avoid the fallacy of seeing dominant solutions where none exist. Early versions of the human relations school (e.g. McGregor 1960) well illustrate tendencies to escape from value dilemmas by believing that some solutions that provide more of all values do exist, in that case of both worker satisfaction and productivity. Similarly, while there do exist some policymaking-improvement possibilities that under some conditions may supply both more pattern-values and more output-values, optimistic views that significantly more satisfaction of pattern-values often goes together with much upgrading of output-values in policymaking improvement have little factual basis under conditions of adversity. (For such views, in respect to the technical operations research level, see Hildebrandt 1979; and in respect to the broad policymaking level, see Sowell 1980).
- Possible indirect correlations between policymaking patterns and policymaking output-value upgrading must be added to the analysis. Thus, legitimation of policymaking in the eyes of some groups may be important for implementation. In such a case, changes in policymaking patterns that increase legitimation are a part of improving the value-output production of policymaking, in addition to the possible appeal of such changes in terms of pattern-values. Here too care must be taken not to neglect costs in terms of other aspects of policymaking outputs.

Thus, getting more acceptance for a wrong policy, in the sense of one's mishandling main adversities, may sometimes be much worse under conditions of adversity than enforcing a policy in the face of a recalcitrant and militant small minority. Maximizing consensus is not necessarily a principal feature of good policymaking, in terms of pattern-values or in terms of output-values, especially not under adversity. Neither is consensus maximization a basic norm of democratic ideology, once a government has been duly approved and continues to rule according to the constitutional laws and within basic norms of political democracy.

As emphasized several times, the proposed priorities to be given to output-values in improving policymaking under adversity apply to Western democracies where main democratic values are realized. Application to nondemocracies is another matter. Beyond categoric value priorities to be given to basic human rights, value judgments must take into account the particular conditions of various countries. A priori conclusions that Western values fully apply to countries with quite different traditions, conditions, and aspirations have no convincing basis.

Whatever one's views and judgments may be, issues of pattern-values and output-values are cardinal to policymaking redesign and need explicit exposition, analysis, and choice.

## A Systematic Approach to Policymaking Redesign

Underdevelopment of studies on and for policymaking redesign makes it all the more necessary to try to evolve at least a rudimentary systematic approach, despite the hazards of doing so without an adequate research infrastructure. To move somewhat in this direction, some phases of a systematic approach to policymaking redesign are sketched out. Then, a few substantive principles and strategies for policymaking redesign are proposed.

A systematic approach to policymaking redesign involves eight main phases, each one of which requires appropriate objective and subjective knowledge, methods, supports, interfaces with various features of reality, and more. Overlaps and iteration are the rule, rather than the analytic tidiness of theoretic distinctions.

### Research

The processing of historic and comparative experiences with policymaking-improvement attempts; survey and adaptation of relevant findings in multiple disciplinary studies, such as psychology, organizational research, anthropology, political sociology, political science, and systems theory; stocktaking of innovations in policymaking, their causes and effects; and evolvement of general theories on these phenomena and on reforms in general, including subsubjects such as intervention theory (Argyris 1971)—these are among the tasks of basic research in relation to policymaking improvement and governance redesign. Without such studies, essential underpinnings for a systematic approach are missing.

A different, but essential, component of necessary research is study of relevant values, especially pattern-values. On the more abstract level, this overlaps political philosophy and is relatively well covered, but more operational approaches are underdeveloped.

Also essential is wide searching for ideas on policymaking redesign, including in unconventional places, such as writings by politicians and officials up to science fiction and "alternative" literature. Needless to say, careful processing of the multitude of commission reports, government documents, and similar sources of "practical" proposals for policymaking improvement is essential too.

*Design*

The research phase poses a number of interesting methodological issues, such as reprocessing of historic material with modern concept packages, with all related dangers of misinterpretations and fallacious conclusions (D.H. Fischer 1970). But, in principle, research belongs to the body of well-developed science. The situation is quite different in respect to design.

In design, jumps are made between empiric findings and empiric theory on one side, and prescriptive inventions on the other. Eased by reliance on available experiences and stimulated by the surveying and processing of historic and comparative improvement attempts, nevertheless a different dimension is added. This is true for the relatively easier, but still very difficult, task of applying an improvement well tested in one country to another. The challenges of inventing new ideas for redesigning policymaking are on a different level, altogether depending on ill-understood creativity. Here, application of the little available knowledge and proposals for encouraging creative design (E. Alexander 1979; E. Alexander 1982) to the domain of policymaking redesign reflects the little that can at present be recommended.

*Analysis*

The task of analyzing main design proposals brings us back to more "normal" scientific and policy analysis endeavors, but lack of adequate theories on policymaking process-systems and their interfaces with social, technological, economic, and other factors, as well as unpredictable changes in the dynamics of such phenomena, make prediction of consequences of transincremental changes in policymaking very difficult. Field dependence of relevant dynamics hinders transfer of lessons of experience between countries. Therefore, the best of analysis will leave much ignorance and uncertainty in respect to innovative policymaking redesigns.

*Integral Application Study*

Research, design, and analysis can, and largely should, proceed without intense relation to the particular needs of a country in a given situation. The next phases of operationalization, experimentation, support recruitment, and institutionalization can, in the main, proceed only within concrete contexts of particular countries and regime types. This is not a sharp and absolute distinction, for research, design, and analysis can, in part, proceed within an actual application-oriented track; and problems of operationalization can, and should in part, be considered within a theoretic perspective and in relation to broad clusters of conditions, including historic and hypothetic, and even imaginary, ones.

Nevertheless, the present "integral-application-study" phase constitutes somewhat of a watershed between more universal and more country-specific endeavors. This phase is concerned with choice of a bundle of policymaking redesign proposals to be actually applied in a particular country, subject to iterative reconsideration.

To take into account the affinity of this phase to concrete redesign proposals and their particular features, it is more convenient to consider it in details later, just before some examples of concrete redesign proposals are presented.

*Operationalization*

Operationalization, approximately in the sense of the "development" and "engineering" phases of technological research and development, includes elaboration of concrete proposals for introducing a redesign into a particular governance. Here, attention must be paid to details, such as necessary legal instruments, establishment orders, staffing, physical equipment, interlocking into communication networks, working methods, organizational structures, etc. An open-ended approach is necessary to permit adjustment by learning, but too-vague proposals may easily be distorted during adoption and implementation, bringing about quite different results than intended in the design.

*Experimentation*

In human affairs no "pilot testing" is possible. On some policies, social experimentation may be possible, with all its ambiguities and uncertainties (Fairweather and Tornatzky 1977; R. Ferber and Hirsch 1981), but this is impossible, with few exceptions, with policymaking redesign. Even if nominally a "trial" is proposed, the very effects of its being known as a "trial" often will distort results completely (the so-called Hawthorne effect); therefore, often surrogate experimentation is necessary, from *Gedankenexperi-*

*ment,* through simulation, up to reevaluation by knowledgeable experts and reprocessing of relevant experiences of other countries as a kind of ex-post-factum experiment approximation.

Difficulties with experimentation and pilot testing make all the more necessary an "experimental attitude" after a redesign is put into practice. The principle of "reform as experiments" (D. Campbell 1969; Rondinelli 1983) applies here with special force. Careful monitoring, with periodic systematic reevaluation, is necessary. Parts of this process may have to be very carefully handled to avoid an air of "provisionality" surrounding the redesign, which may well ruin it.

*Support Recruitment*

The need for support recruitment needs little argumentation, care to be taken instead not to overdo this element. To be noted, in respect to many governance redesigns, is their dependence on sustained top-level support (Boston 1980; changes introduced in the Canadian Privy Council Office and related units following the 1984 change of prime ministers further demonstrate this point). Standard advice to have the potential clients involved in preparatory phases is often counterproductive in policymaking redesign, where this may mobilize more resistance than support. Often, policymaking redesigns involving central minds of governments have to be enforced against departmental ministries and civil servants, for instance. Public interest and support can be helpful but is effective in respect to some forms of policymaking redesign only. Sometimes support be civil servants is crucial (Gremion 1979), but the will of top politicians is the preeminent factor in making a policymaking redesign feasible, within the constraints of a given society as a whole.

All this does not imply that support recruitment is anything less than very important. Indeed, design of novel strategies to gain support, such as interbranch informal cooperation (Cannon and Likins 1981), may be very desirable. But, essential policymaking improvements are too consequential to be abandoned to veto by narrow interest groups and traditional organizational forces.

*Institutionalization*

A main feature of "implementation" in respect to policymaking redesigns is institutionalization, in the sense of becoming an integral part of the governance process-system according to the rules of a country. In many countries this requires legal instruments, establishment tables, promulgation formalities, and more. Informal arrangements do work for a small number of policymaking redesigns. Provisional institutionalization is very appropriate in some countries, used in such a way as to try out new policymaking designs, as illustrated in the interesting history of the Netherlands Scientific Council for Government Policy, established first in 1972 by a provisional royal decree and put on a permanent legal basis in 1976. But, in principle, the core of implementation in respect to policymaking redesigns is institutionalization.

The above-mentioned elements include iterative monitoring, evaluation, constant learning and improvement, and so forth, with care to be taken to avoid too-rapid revisions before a new design has had a chance to prove itself as either a success or a failure. Supplementary facets of a systematic approach to policymaking redesign are brought out later. Here, the eight elements, as presented above, suffice to provide some taste of attempts to build up a systematic approach to policymaking redesign that is applicable also to governance redesign as a whole.

The somewhat nominal and formal features of the design elements presented above leave open more important issues of substantive contents as well as of strategies. These are taken up next, moving more into the contents of policymaking redesign, though not yet presenting specific improvement proposals.

### Principles and Strategies for Policymaking Redesign

Twenty-two main principles and strategies for policymaking redesign under adversity, dealing with different redesign dimensions, are presented here. For more advanced treatment, it is necessary to differentiate between principles, which deal with substantive ideas to serve as guides for redesign, and strategies, which deal with ways to make redesigns more feasible. But at the present underdeveloped, if not zero-developed, state of approaches to governance and policymaking redesign such distinctions are over-refined. Some overlaps and close interfaces between redesign principles and redesign strategies further justify mixed consideration within the limited world of inquiry of this book.

#### Taboos Must Be Broken

There is little chance for significant policymaking redesign if all taboos are respected. Multiple ritualistic anomies sanctify so many institutions and processes and overload them with such amounts of paraphernalia as to reduce the scope of open movement for policymaking redesign too much—unless taboos are broken through. A simple illustration is provided by the need for politicians, once elected, to engage in further studies. There is nothing standing between the legitimation of politicians in democracies through elections and a possible statutory requirement, or at least positive incentives, directed at getting politicians during suitable phases of their careers to engage in some systematic study. Or, to take up an even harder problem, the motivation to enter politics needs attention. After all, unless politics draws some of "the best," however defined, there is no chance for upgrading the personal attributes of senior politicians, as a main factor determining policymaking qualities. Therefore, encouragement of highly capable persons to enter politics may be useful and, in some countries, essential. There is nothing in such an idea to impair chief democratic values, other than some simplistic versions of Jacksonian thinking. Indeed, the whole issue of upgrading the qualities of policymaking elites, as already considered, is repressed by antielitism taboos, which must be broken through.

Various forms of *Angst* can conveniently be considered as related to taboos, even though somewhat different in nature. A good illustration is provided in some countries by apprehensions about a "computer state" (Burnham 1983) as a kind of "1984" threat, and these inhibit some very promising avenues for improving policymaking.

Hence, the principle to break taboos as far as necessary for arriving at significant policymaking redesigns. How to implement taboo-breaking proposals is another question, but if thinking on taboo-breaking proposals is inhibited, problems of marketing, adoption, and implementation are not reached at all. Possibilities to implement taboo-breaking ideas in part without going through formal adoption procedures, for instance through private and public nongovernmental initiatives, add to the importance of developing useful redesigns, even if they contradict taboos.

## Limits of the Material Should Be Carefully Considered

The basic materials out of which policymaking process-systems are made are, in the main, given for the foreseeable future: human beings within open-ended roles; group processes; various types of organizations; publics in different forms; and so on. The malleability of these materials is limited, though far from small. The limits of malleability are not really known, traditionalists seeing malleability as smaller and reformers seeing it as larger.

Even with the admission of such ignorances, which inhibit operationalization of the principle to take carefully into account limits of the material when engaging in policymaking redesign, nevertheless this is a cardinal guideline. In particular, it excludes many far-reaching proposals for policymaking transformation that are based on unwarranted assumptions of freedom in molding human behavior and the dynamics of human institutions, as already discussed.

The concept of policymaking incapabilities, as developed in chapter 6, poses some of the main rigidities facing policymaking redesign. Putting aside possibilities to augment human mental abilities far beyond the perspectives of psychology, as historically evolving (Donnelly 1983), leaving open the question whether large steps forward in human comprehension may occur (Hawkins 1983), and not entering the debate in anthropology on the plasticity of human institutions (e.g. compare D. Freeman 1983, debunking Margaret Mead's classical optimistic study of Samoa, with Hames and Vickers 1983, illustrating human adjustment capacities under Amazonian conditions), one can illustrate some relevant points to be taken into account as follows, supplementing relevant discourse in chapter 6:

1.  While it is doubtful whether at present and in the foreseeable future human intelligence can be increased significantly (Brim and Kagan 1980; Detterman and Sternberg 1982; Sternberg 1982), human decision making can be somewhat improved by suitable training and "decision engineering" (Isen and Patrick 1983; Jungermann 1980; Sjobert 1982; Bolt and Newman 1980 is overoptimistic; and differently, Maxwell 1983).
2.  Group decision making and organizational decision behavior can be somewhat upgraded (Janis 1982; K. Greene 1982; Mason and Mitroff 1981.)
3.  Political culture illustrates a much more difficult material, the dynamics of which are hard to influence (also relevant is organization culture, see Jelinek, Smircich, and Hirsch 1983). Thus, overinfluence by Western patterns of government may have imposed governmental systems not really fitting local traditions in quite a number of Third World countries (L. Beer 1979), with some main characteristics of various cultures not being comprehended by Western political science. For example, Indian politics cannot really be understood and improved without considering its embedment in a deeply rooted conception of *Homo hierarchicus* (Dumont 1981; together with Dumont 1979 and 1983, for sharper understanding of such cultural and historical differences and their importance for policymaking improvement).

Such conjectures bring out the problematics of trying to improve the performance of central minds of governments, given the rigidities of the principal materials out of which they are composed. Recombination of materials, invention of "composite materials," and intensive efforts to upgrade the performance of given materials, together with the restructuring of situations and tasks so as to fall more into the domains of capacities than of incapacities—these are main redesign directives resulting from a realistic view of the elasticity-limits of human institutions. The fact that these limits are not known for certain and that transcendental assumptions very soon enter the picture and shape our perceptions of the potentials of humans and human institutions makes care all the more necessary. However hard to operationalize, the principle to take carefully into account the limits of the materials is a prime and often neglected imperative of policymaking redesign.

## Latent Functions Must Be Taken into Account

Policymaking institutions fulfill many latent functions (Merton 1949, ch. 1; see also Gross 1964, pt. 5, esp. ch. 19, where he discusses the "matrix of purposes"). Therefore, improvements that focus on manifest functions only will have many unexpected consequences, in part both undesirable and preventable. The tendency in many countries to follow a rather formalistic approach to organizational reforms further aggravates the propensity to ignore latent functions. Taboos concerning some of the important latent functions fulfilled by policymaking institutions, such as party-political benefits, further hinder explicit consideration of latent functions during improvement endeavors. Hence the theoretical and practical importance of this principle. It also illustrates the necessity to locate parts of the improvement thinking and analysis within compartmentalized units, where taboos can be openly handled without uncontrolled and counterproductive leakages. (This is another illustration of a possible conflict between pattern-values, in this case "open" government, and output-values—policymaking-improvement).

## Political Feasibility Requires Aggressive Handling

The importance and problematics of the principle to consider the limits of the materials are further illustrated by the issue of the political feasibility of policymaking redesign proposals, with "political feasibility" looked upon as analogous to a dynamic composite "material" essential for redesign realization.

The rigidity and elasticity of the political feasibility of policymaking redesigns vary between countries, but some universal factors can be mentioned, as guidance for application to specific contexts.

1. Historically speaking, what was regarded as impossible at one time often became possible at another time, often within the same main paradigms of the system. Revolutionary situations further loosen up political feasibility limits, though outcomes are different from intentions and visions (Eisenstadt 1978).
2. The widespread feeling of uneasiness and inadequacies in governance may result in entrenchment but often broaden domains of feasibility. This is illustrated by reforms in governance during the last twenty years or so, many of which would have been regarded "nonfeasible" earlier.

3. The feasibility of policymaking redesign proposals varies with passing opportunities, interest of power holders, marketing skills, public fashions, and additional variables.
4. All in all, growing failures in policymaking enlarge the domain of political feasibility for redesigns. This, primarily if top decisionmakers think that the redesigns may help them in their missions impossible.
5. Time frames needed for introducing significant improvements into governance and policymaking may be long. Thus, the idea of a general staff in the military took a long time to develop (Goerlitz 1961; for an early picture, see S. Wilkinson 1895. Difficulties to adopt the idea in the United States are well discussed in O. Nelson 1946). Since then the matter has been raised several times, but neither has it been resolved nor fully implemented even now, including in the United States. Fifty to one hundred years is a quite reasonable time for a significant innovation in government to crystallize, build up support, and be institutionalized, with ups and downs. Therefore, shorter perspectives on administrative reforms may well lead to wrong conclusions, with conflicts between administrative rhetoric and rigid realpolitik dominating the immediate scenery, hiding longer-range processes (J.G. March and Olsen 1983 requires, therefore, reconsideration). Such a time frame may not meet immediate adversity-handling needs and should not reduce efforts to achieve rapid improvements, but, nevertheless, too short a political-feasibility horizon leads to wrong conclusions.
6. The effects of self-fulfilling prophecies may be very strong in the domains of political feasibility, providing an optimistic stance with more chance of impact than an overpessimistic one.
7. The already-considered role of policy entrepreneurs is especially important in changing and enlarging the domains of political feasibility.
8. The importance of rulers in increasing the feasibility of policymaking redesigns deserves reemphasis. Quite a number of improvement proposals do not impinge upon large and rigid societal interests but are in the main endogenous to the machinery or government. Here, too, resistances are often strong, but support of rulers can often enlarge the domain of feasibility.
9. Policy intellectuals, including scholars, can influence the political feasibility domain of policymaking redesigns too, especially in the longer run.

All in all, I tend to the conclusion that political feasibility may be larger than assumed in much of professional literature, though far from approaching the utopias or dystopias of the proponents of politics metamorphosis—this in line with the general examination of policymaking-impact potentials in chapter 4, and within a gambling view of feasibility. As a practical principle, the emerging recommendation is, to assume during most of the redesign preparation phases more political feasibility in the longer run than current situations justify—this within the basic paradigms of the existing system. In the few cases where thinking on policymaking redesign takes place within revolutionary planning, constraints can be relaxed somewhat more, but still the principle of realistically taking into account the limits of the basic materials remains fully in force.

Some of the following principles and strategies are oriented in part toward problems of political feasibility, further working out a few of the points made above.

*Build Extensively, but Not Exclusively, on Available Experiences*

To increase reliability of design proposals, to improve political feasibility, and to shortcut through difficult phases of invention and development, available experiences should, as far as possible, be utilized. The success story of the transfer of a major innovation in governance, namely, the British civil service systems, from China via the British Indian trading companies to the United Kingdom more than one hundred years ago (Têng 1942-1943), and then in part to the United States (Titlow 1978), is a striking illustration of diffusion of experiences accompanied with adjustment and acculturation.

The extensive survey of contemporary experiences with policymaking improvements on which this book is partly based resulted, *inter alia*, in three main findings:

First, a very large number of interesting improvements have been tried out in various countries in a widely dispersed way, as partly enumerated in chapter 3. This provides a wealth of experiences on which redesign proposals can in part be based.

Second, there is an amazing ignorance about such experiments, attempts, and experiences. Not only, as already mentioned, is little comprehensive literature available, but persons in charge of specific innovations in policymaking in one country are often unfamiliar with directly comparable attempts in other countries, and units looking for policymaking and governance improvement are often ignorant about similar interests in other countries, other than on technical subjects or on ideas that become fashionable and diffuse rapidly for a limited time. This is true also among countries used to intense cooperation in many domains. Special setups for exchanges of experience on policymaking and governance improvements are just in their beginning and some earlier attempts vanished without leaving traces.

The second finding should be tempered by some cases of incorrect shared learning and indiscriminate imitation. Diffusion of new budgeting techniques illustrates waves of enthusiasm, followed by disappointment, passing over many countries. This was the case with Planning-Programming-Budgeting-Systems (PPBS) and, on lesser a scale, with zero-based Budgeting.

A third main finding of the survey is that there are many pressing needs for policymaking redesign not met by any presently attempted improvement. Further, most actual improvement attempts are partial and lacking in important ingredients. Therefore, available experience cannot serve as an exclusive base for upgrading policymaking under adversity. Many inventions and much innovation are essential. The already-mentioned scarcity of novel ideas in social fiction literature (including social science fiction, e.g. Polsby 1982) makes innovative thinking all the more essential.

Preferable mixes of experience-based proposals and original proposals depend on needs. It must also be taken into account that when a country is distinguished by many unique features in politics, government, and main facets of policymaking, transfer of experiences to it is very difficult. An improvement that may work well under some conditions may have radically different results when planted in other soils.

Subject to such circumstances, the advantages of building upon available experiences make it preferable to start with redesigns that have been tried out in comparable form under related conditions. At the same time, a set of redesign proposals should also include a number of innovative recommendations, to take up urgent needs on which no experiences are avilable. If no relevant experiences exist, then no choice remains other than to concentrate on innovations based on partial analogues with comparable attempts elsewhere, or in the past.

*Redesign Should Focus on Most Urgent Needs*

In distinction from incremental improvement efforts that can proceed on a wide front, policymaking redesign efforts have such great attendant difficulties that they should concentrate on the most urgent needs. According to the analysis of this book, once preconditions of governance stability and minimum functioning capacity are satisfied, and basic human rights are assured, the cardinal task of governance for which redesign is urgently necessary is policymaking under adversity by the central minds of governments. Within that domain, priorities vary among countries depending on their situations and predicaments.

It is important to underline the need to fit redesigns to conditions of adversity, with associated changes in order of priority, as illustrated earlier in respect to the growing importance of output-values. Clinging to ideas and conceptions that perhaps may have been appropriate under better conditions but that fail to meet adversity is a main failing of much current thinking on policymaking improvement. The policy principles for handling adversity, as considered in chapter 5, serve as an essential link between substantive needs of handling adversity and needed redesigns in the central minds of governments, so as to enable the latter to perform better in terms of producing and implementing appropriate policies.

*Selective Radicalism Constitutes the Preferable Strategy*

Given an order of priority, a fundamental dilemma in preferable redesign strategies is reached, as already considered in chapter 6 in respect to policies. On one hand, incremental changes have little chance of meaningful impact on policymaking under adversity, being far below the minimum-change threshold of such a resilient and tradition-bound process-system as the central minds of governments. On the other hand, radical transformation of many aspects and facets of policymaking all at once and in close interaction is nonfeasible under all but revolutionary conditions and entails huge transition costs.

Selective radicalism provides a way out of the dilemma. Its main features deserve here repetition and supplementation, applied to policymaking:

1. Selection of a small number of variables that have broad-spectrum significant impacts on policymaking quality as a whole, and on priority domains in particular, directly and by diffusion.
2. Radical changes in the selected variables, so as to achieve large upgrading in their performance.
3. A modular approach, with each change in every variable standing as far as possible by itself, but with careful attention to essential interdependencies and with efforts to aggregate a number of such changes in a synergistic way.
4. Some of the radical changes may be introduced not for their direct effects but because they open the way for other redesigns of major usefulness, such as by loosening up some parts of the central minds of governments.

The selective-radicalism strategy goes beyond policymaking redesign, constituting, as discussed in chapter 5, a major recommended approach for intervention theory as a whole, including the substantive tasks of policies such as societal architecture. In respect to policymaking redesign, selective radicalism constitutes a main key to achieving impacts within constrained feasibility domains and with limited resources, in ways containing transformation and transition costs. Success of the selective-radicalism strategy depends on the correct selection of variables to be changed and on sufficiently radical changes being made in them.

As mentioned above, each policymaking component change made within a selective-radicalism strategy should, as far as possible, be useful and viable by itself. At a maximum, selective radicalism should not involve more than four to five modules that are to be changed synchronously. Longer-range and more comprehensive reforms can be planned in the form of multiple phases of modular selective radicalism, in open-ended sequence, and with each phase standing by itself. The modular approach is especially important as bridging immediate improvements and long-range policymaking-redesigns, permitting open-ended comprehensive reforms to proceed through successive phases of selective radicalism.

The selective-radicalism-cum-modular-approach change strategy may well be optimal under many circumstances for policymaking improvement, as well as for administrative reforms and governance redesign as a whole. Lack of such a strategy is a major cause of many failures of governmental improvement efforts, even though seldom recognized as such. (In addition to already-cited administrative reform literature, a comprehensive effort by the U.S. General Accounting Office to analyze failures of government-wide management-improvement efforts misses, too, the absence of a suitable selective-radicalism or alternative deliberate strategy as a main cause of lack of success. See U.S. General Accounting Office 1983.)

*Avoid Simple Schemata and Models*

As already pointed out several times, correct understanding of the modalities of policymaking process-systems depends on avoidance of simplistic schemata and models, behaviorally and prescriptively. Both mechanical and biological analogues are largely misleading, but the latter at least brings out the complexity, multiplicity, redundancy, substitutability, multicircuity, changeability, and similar "existential" features of the central minds of governments. It is enough to mention the main dimensions of formal structures, individuals, group processes, interfaces with multiple environments, and cultural variables to demonstrate the multiplicity of variant processes that in changing interactions constitute the policymaking process-system in action. To take a different and more analytic cut at the matter, a swift look at the facets considered in chapter 7, as embedded in limited potentials of various materials considered in chapter 6, suffices to bring out the variety of complex processes involved in policymaking from an analytic perspective, ranging from cognition, to value search and goal selection, up to creativity; with even more protean processes, such as energy generation and will crystallization, differentially conditioning and interacting with all components of policymaking.

A number of implications important for the concerns of this book emerge from such a multivaried view of policymaking:

1. Although disaggregation and decomposition are essential for scientific investigation of policymaking, the limits of such proceedings should be

recognized. A major weakness of most available empiric and theoretic treatments of policymaking reality (as, in part, conveniently summed up in Dye 1984) is their fixation on limited aspects of policymaking, without adequate efforts to put segmented views into a broader holistic perspective.

2. Prescriptive treatments suffer from two sets of limitations stemming from segmented and partial views of policymaking. One set of prescriptive approaches starts with too narrow a view of the potentials of policymaking and consequently overconstrains improvement possibilities as being subjugated to "satisficing," "incrementalism," "bounded rationality," etc. A second set of prescriptive approaches operates with much-too-narrow models of "rationality" as guides for policymaking improvement, ignoring *inter alia* the crucial importance of extrarational processes, such as goal search, value judgment, and alternative invention.

3. Instead, a much more complex and holistic view of policymaking should serve as framework for segmented research and improvement approaches. Presently available computer languages do not permit adequate modeling of policymaking as a whole. In particular, so-called expert systems (B.G. Buchanan 1982; and, as an illustration for many relatively advanced approaches, Konopasek and Jayaraman 1984) are of very limited use for our needs. Additional computer metalanguages are needed to model policymaking appropriately (as well as to serve as a tool for policymaking on complex issues). But presently available languages permit some beginnings, also using complex graphics, at least qualitatively and indicatively. This, as already mentioned, cannot be attempted in this book, but should be kept in mind as a worthwhile project. The image of such a presentation of a more adequate holistic view of policymaking can serve to put partial endeavors into correct proportions. More advanced segmented views of policymaking can then be developed, such as "dialectic-systems" models (Mitroff, Quinton, and Mason 1983), and additional designs taken, for instance, from artificial intelligence literature (Barr and Feigenbaum 1981-82; Kent 1981), up to philosophy-of-the-mind speculations (Hofstadter 1979; Hofstadter, forthcoming), and the insidious effect on improvement approaches of human likings for decorative order (as explored in a very different context in Gombrich 1983) can be countervailed.

4. Concerning approaches to policymaking redesign, operational implications of a view of policymaking as a very complex mixture between patterned chaos and kaleidoscopic cosmos leads to a number of additional implications:

- A large range of potential improvement avenues exists, directed at different facets of policymaking.
- Quite a number of different approaches may be equifinal in their impacts of policymaking, providing a choice that increases chances

for feasibility of at least some improvements oriented toward priority issues.

- Prediction of consequences of improvement proposals is doubtful, with many unexpected results being assured. Hence, the need to approach metapolicymaking within the fuzzy-betting perspective applying to all of policymaking.
- A set of substantive metapolicymaking principles is much superior to formal models as guides for policymaking improvement, though advanced models can be of heuristic help in deriving some such principles.

The next few sections present a number of policymaking improvement principles, illustrating the above point and guided by it. These substantive metapolicymaking principles should be evaluated within a holistic perspective as proposed, even if the latter cannot be made concrete in the form of a detailed comprehensive model. Within available literature, the already-mentioned philosophic works on the mind and artificial intelligence by Douglas R. Hofstadter (1979; forthcoming) provide a good introduction to broad contemplation of the policymaking process-systems, in particular as an antidote to simplistic models that abound in political science, economics, and operations research and that misguide much of contemporary policy sciences.

## Avoid Dogmas and Slogans

The study of the author diagnosed many senior policymakers to be captivated by dogmas and slogans whenever policymaking-improvement was discussed. Impressionistic content analysis of offical pronouncements on the subject, too, brings out similar dogmas and slogans as conditioning many actual policymaking-improvement efforts. Some such dogmas and slogans have also infiltrated into parts of policy sciences literature. Sometimes it is difficult to distinguish between dogmas and slogans on one hand, which should be rejected as guides for policymaking redesign, and ideologies, which serve as legitimate value compasses, on the other hand. Nevertheless, some dogmas and slogans can quite clearly be identified as being shared by many countries and characterizing some groupings of states:

1. In many countries, reducing the size of the civil service together with the cutting of public expenditures, has become a main goal of administrative reforms, indiscriminately applied. This, in part, is more a dogma and slogan than a correct line of endeavors. Intense efforts to reduce the size of the civil service, while often desirable, frequently sap all available energy, leaving more important upgradings of policymak-

ing capacities defaulted. Also, in situations of much unemployment, adverse social and political consequences of reducing the functions of the civil service as an employment provider must be taken into account, however anathematic such thinking may be to traditional budgeters and narrow "efficiency experts." In our context, efforts to reduce civil services must not hinder upbuilding the central minds of governments, even when this entails additional staffs.

2. Formal structures, with neat organizational charts and logically formal division of labor between ministries and agencies, preoccupy some countries. These usually do not produce significant results.

3. Changes in legal instruments, in civil service acts, and in formal regulations also preoccupy some countries. These have little effect, unless integrated into a broader approach, with attention to staff qualifications, to incentive systems, and to organizational cultures, *inter alia*.

4. Search for consensus, at least in the civil service, dominates in some countries' improvement efforts. This, as already discussed, is an error. While efforts to gain support and consensus for administrative improvements are essential, determined will, strong power concentrations, and active involvement of top politicians are cardinal. Changes necessary for improving policymaking should be introduced and enforced, even in the absence of consensus and in the face of opposition and conflict.

5. In some Western democracies, views that the size of government should be reduced are based on the assumption that private organizations perform better and that "privatization" will result in more efficiency. In the United States this position is especially strong, even being presented as a "lesson from policy research" (as in some contributions to Zeckhauser and Leebaert 1983). As distinct from an ideological position that government should do less, irrespective of efficiency and effectiveness considerations, dogmatic views on relative advantages and disadvantages of governmental organizations and market organizations should be rejected as guides to policymaking improvement. "Smaller is beautiful" and, even more so, "smaller is more effective" and "private is more efficient" are slogans and dogmas, not a universally valid finding of reliable research. Nor, of course, is a reverse dogma and slogan more acceptable. The relative benefits and costs of having different tasks undertaken by various institutions have to be carefully considered in specific contexts, not presupposed axiomatically (see, e.g. Shonfield 1984).

6. An exaggerated view of the effectiveness of adversary procedures characterizes some thinking about policymaking improvement in a number of countries, as illustrated by the "Science Court" proposal (Kantrowitz 1968; for an interesting German discussion, see Dierkes and Thienen 1977). When the idea of adversary procedures becomes a dogma, rather than a tentative improvement principle to be applied with care, it becomes quite counterproductive.

These six illustrations of dogmas and slogans to be avoided in policymaking redesign also serve as a warning in respect to the principles for policymaking improvement that are presented in the next few sections. These principles are intended to serve as tentative guidelines and search patterns, not as new dogmas and slogans.

*Institutionalize Effort Allocation*

A main problem of policymaking under adversity, as already discussed, is misallocation of attention, with large parts of policymaking resources going to relatively minor issues, and critical choices not receiving adequate attention and effort. The interviews by the author clearly brought out, for example, that the time budgets of main policymakers and policy advisors are contorted, with large amounts of time and energy going to relatively unimportant matters. This fact was often recognized by respondents and was brought up at their initiative; they blamed rigid institutional features for imposing loads of trivial matters on them. Therefore, institutionalization of better effort allocation constitutes a recommended principle of policymaking redesign.

A first need is to relieve the central minds of governments of unessential matters, which consume disproportional amounts of policymaking resources. Typical is the fact that the offices of heads of governments are often loaded with many unessential functions, such as civil service management, adjudication of minor budgeting disagreements, detailed supervision of intelligence agencies, and more. Transfer of unessential functions to executive agencies outside the central mind of government is, therefore, a concrete guideline for policymaking improvement.

A second need is to establish a special track for critical issues, with units devoted to their handling and with procedures assuring due attention to them. The tendency for acute concerns to drive out of circulation fundamental but not burning issues makes this guideline all the more important.

*Assurance of Integrative Perspective*

This principle illustrates the derivation of guidelines for policymaking redesign from the quality specifications, as elaborated in chapter 7. Related to the tension between centrifugal and centripetal forces and their various combinations in governments (e.g. Samuel Beer 1977) and the antinomy between departmental concerns on one side and realities of interdependencies and interactions on the other side, policymaking realities in most countries tend to be weak in integrative perspectives. However much this may be recognized on the verbal level, segmenting forces are so strong as to prevent adequate integrative perspectives in the absence of special setups directed at assuring the latter. In fact, search for more integrative perspectives underlies many attempts at policymaking improvement, as surveyed in chapter 3, but failures still outweigh success. Therefore, the importance of this policymaking redesign principle.

### Islands of Excellence Are a Schema for Much of Redesign

A main principle for policymaking redesign is the proposition to proceed, in part, by setting up islands of excellence to engage in main phases and tasks of policymaking under adversity in and for central minds of governments.

Islands of excellence, as a main feature of policymaking redesign, should meet a number of not-easy requirements, such as: critical size; study autonomy; adequate access to information; sufficient time to work on main issues; ability to engage in iconoclasm; ways to input their products into actual policymaking; and power protection against takeovers and destruction by regular government establishments. At present some think tanks, as well as a few staffs near top policymakers, are the main prevailing illustration of islands of excellence as parts of policymaking process-systems and of their infrastructure. Their achievements as well as problematics (Dror 1964) illustrate possibilities of broader use of the principle of islands of excellence as a design schema for policymaking improvement, as well as some of the involved difficulties.

### Positive Redundancy Is a Useful Construction Principle

The idea of positive redundancy (Landau 1969) is another important substantive principle for policymaking redesign. Controlled overlaps, competition in thinking and in parts of implementation, multiplicity in crucial facets of policymaking under adversity, special devil's advocate units—these are among the more important construction principles for policymaking redesign.

Related is the issue of countervaillance, (C. Campbell 1983, passim), which well illustrates the quantitative dimensions of the redesign principles handled in this book on a qualitative level. Too much countervaillance can produce stalemate, ruining policymaking under adversity, as partly illustrated by Congress-presidency relations in the United States (A. King 1983; Sundquist 1981, to be contrasted with the situation in France, W. Andrews 1982). Too little countervailing impairs policymaking, by preventing adequate "second looks" and pluralism in consideration of issues. Therefore, while positive redundancy, countervailing, some adversary processes, etc. are useful principles for reconstructing policymaking process-systems, this is a matter of degrees. In some domains more of redundancy and countervailing is needed, while in other cases they might better be reduced.

*Debugging Is a Main Principle for Improving Policymaking*

Three basic approaches for improving policymaking process-systems can be useful, to be followed in various combinations: to construct an optimal model and then to try to change reality so as to move in the direction of that model; to conceptualize preferable complex images, or sophisticated preferable multimodels, to serve as guides for redesign; and to identify major weaknesses in the present performance of the process-system and to look for debugging interventions.

This book as a whole combines the second and the third approaches, which epistemologically are related because of the dependence of identification of weaknesses on underlying tacit ideas of preferable situations. For the applied purposes of policymaking redesign, the third approach is especially important, with incapacities and, in particular, error propensities serving as main targets for improvement endeavors. Therefore, on the level of principles for policymaking redesign, error reduction through debugging is important. This principle also serves as a middle ground between widespread actual tinkering with policymaking, based on directly perceived weaknesses, and more systematic approaches such as advocated in this book.

Further, to realize the importance of the debugging approach, it should be noted that much of the hope for improving policymaking under adversity is based on the prevalence of many and often obvious weaknesses in actual policymaking (as brought out, for instance, in Malek 1978). If policymaking weaknesses were all complex and their improvement depended on the availability of very sophisticated and advanced methods and designs, then the present weaknesses of policy sciences and related knowledge, as discussed in chapter 8, might have precluded policymaking improvement. But, paradoxically, the very starkness of actual policymaking weaknesses provide concrete opportunities for meaningful improvements, often through a combination between debugging and application of preferable models. (Some concrete possibilities for debugging on the level of individual decision making, illustrated in Cosier 1978 and Lichtenstein and Fischoff 1980, further clarify this principle, though on a micro-level).

*Introduce and Strengthen Debunking, Iconoclasm, and Heterodoxy*

A further-reaching substantive principle for improving the central minds of governments, again related directly to specifications discussed in chapter 7, is the need for debunking, iconoclasm, and heterodoxy in and near the central policymaking process-system. Counterconventional and still credible inputs into policymaking under adversity are needed to push innovative options, to advance policy-paradigm reconsideration, to overcome the ballast of outdated institutions and traditions, to confront policy theologies, and more. Therefore, introduction and reinforcement of debunking, iconoclasm, and heterodoxy into the central minds of governments is another main redesign principle.

## Introduce Additional Types of Knowledge

Policymaking under adversity requires types and qualities of knowledge beyond those available in society as a whole and far beyond those in use in most governments. The recruitment of higher-quality persons into policymaking positions and the upgrading of knowledge by available policymaking staffs, together with encouragement of the production of suitable knowledge, its inputting into policymaking, and its correct utilization by central minds of governments, are, therefore, an additional substantive principle for policymaking redesign.

## Aim at Some Shortcuts

When needs are urgent, as in policymaking improvement, shortcuts must be sought, with high discounts for delayed results. Also, without some quick and visible results, change feasibility goes down and alterations in conditions may overturn hopes for the future. In particular, political support essential for policymaking improvement dissipates rapidly if not maintained and reinforced by some quick results. Beyond such tactical considerations, there is an overriding need for urgent breakthroughs in policymaking quality to handle pressing adversities and to try to prevent adversity aggravations. An improvement module set should therefore include some components providing rapid improvements and some oriented toward longer-range achievements.

## Devote Attention to Infrastructure Advancement

The search for shortcuts must be balanced with advancement of infrastructure for better policymaking. Establishment of think tanks for in-depth consideration of problems; investments in the understanding of policy by citizens, starting in kindergarten; and better policy sciences research and teaching—these illustrate possibilities and needs for infrastructure advancement as a main policymaking-improvement strategy, in conjunction with shortcuts. True, infrastructure advancement takes much time, but without it possibilities for policymaking improvement will remain low in the foreseeable future.

## Prepare Good Redesign Ideas, Even if Not Immediately Practical

Feasibility changes with time, and some ideas need an extended period to ripen and gain acceptance. The already-mentioned history of general staffs is enlightening as an example (Goerlitz 1981). Mainly invented in the eighteenth century in Germany (Wilkinson 1985), it took a long time for general staffs to be set up in other countries (O. Nelson 1946); and some, such as the United States, still lack one. Some important proposals for improving the minds of governments can be viewed as applications of the general staff idea to policymaking as a whole. Interestingly and typically, also in military regimes as in some Latin American countries, it takes a long time to build up general staffs for the central minds of governments, and often this is done by incorrect and simplistic application of conventional military patterns, which long since required significant changes in the military itself.

Another interesting illustration of the longer-range impact of governance redesign ideas is provided by the proposal of Bertrand de Jouvenel to set up forums to surmise alternative futures (Jouvenel 1967). This idea directly influenced establishment of the Commission on the Year 2000 in the United States, followed by comparable endeavors in other countries. Also, the idea was partly realized, though not too successfully, in a number of countries: the National Goal Research Staff in the White House (closed down after producing a weak report), the Swedish Secretariat for Futures Studies (downgraded), and the New Zealand Commission for the Future (closed down after provoking the government by one of its reports).

Because of such time requirements, overattachment to immediate feasibility is shortsighted. Parts of policymaking-redesign work can and should develop and float ideas with no apparent chances for realization in the short future. This is not a dispensation from the constraints of the materials, which must always be considered, but short-range feasibility considerations should not bind all of policymaking-improvement thinking and efforts.

Introduction of policymaking improvements depends on passing opportunities of support, entrepreneurship, crises, and personal accidents. Therefore, good ideas for policymaking improvement must be readied and necessary resources, such as professionals, must be prepared to utilize temporary openings. Concomitantly, elasticity is necessary to draw and adjust from a repertoire of improvement proposals those that fit into the slot provided by changing circumstances.

*Careful Marketing*

Policymaking improvement is confronted by many barriers, ranging from tradition and habits to resistance by power holders, who are apprehensive about shifts in power topography consequent upon all changes in policymaking, never mind technological and procedural facades. Hindrances to every and all administrative and political reforms are multiplied in respect to policymaking improvements because of the power intensity of their field and its subjection to fervent conflicts. Suspicions, if not fears, of top policymakers engendered by the intellectual demands with which policy improvements are imbued and by the political costs of most of them add to the obstacles.

In quite a number of countries, proposals to improve policymaking run into serious additional difficulties, already mentioned, because of efforts to cut public expenditure. The facts that some main redesigns are essential precisely to enable governments to handle the dangers of economic decline, and that the small monetary costs of policymaking-improvements are negligible in comparison with its potential benefits if at least partly successful help little. This subject is worthy of another Parkinson's Law.

Such adverse circumstances can be overcome only by the combined effects of diverse variables, such as widespread frustrations about present policymaking, active policymaking-improvement entrepreneurs, and interested powerful policymakers. The history of many policymaking-improvement attempts testified, as already mentioned, to the essentiality of sustained support by top authority wielders (Boston 1980; W. William 1971).

Occasion utilization and preparation of a diverse menu of improvement ideas to fit changing tastes is therefore a "must." Just as imperative is careful marketing, with constant efforts to push the cause of policymaking improvement. Expedient marketing is necessary to prepare the ground for policymaking improvement, to support ongoing improvements, and to ward off destruction of institutionalized improvements.

## Build Up a Capacity for Policymaking Redesign

A main and semi-final principle and strategy to be mentioned again here is to build up a capacity on the metalevel, to engage in redesigning policymaking. Parts of such a capacity are more academic and parts are more professional-political, probably to be located in distinct loci—such as universities, institutes for advanced study, think tanks, on one hand, and suitable special units such as "machinery of government" overseeing staffs, inside governments, on the other—with close interfaces. Often existing capacities can be built upon, but sometimes starting anew is less difficult.

## Keep Aspirations at an Appropriate Level

When all is said and done, there are strict limits to possibilities for improving policymaking. Indeed, the double findings on the need for fargoing upgradings of policymaking under adversity on one hand, and on inherent limits to policymaking-improvement possibilities on the other—

constitute a main antinomy and internal tension as brought out by the present volume.

My position, as reflected throughout the book, is that policymaking can be improved and that the importance of policymaking makes even limited improvements, as long as they go beyond useless incrementalism, a very worthy endeavor. This position is further reinforced by the concrete improvement proposals in the text chapter, which at least serve to demonstrate the possibility to design feasible and useful policymaking improvement recommendations.

But recognition of the limitation of possible policymaking improvements requires translation into the principle of keeping aspirations at an appropriate level: if too high, disappointment would follow and inhibit possible improvements; if too low, inadequate efforts to improve policymaking would be the result. This applies to the collective levels of policymakers and policy improvers alike. On the personal level of policy scientists the derived recommendation is to adopt a stance of stoic enthusiasm: without enthusiasm, nothing can be achieved; without some stoicism, frustrations will be overwhelming.

Additional principles and strategies for policymaking redesign can be evolved, *inter alia*, on the basis of the specifications considered in chapter 7, historic experiences, and varieties of theoretic knowledge. The above twenty-two items illustrate various aspects of a systematic approach to policymaking and governance redesign, but are far from an exhaustive list of relevant principles and strategies.

### Integrated Country Application Study

During consideration of the phases of a systematic approach to policymaking redesign, earlier in this chapter, the integrated application study phase was mentioned, but left for consideration at the end of the chapter, just before concrete illustrations of redesign proposals are presented in the next one. Necessarily, the prescriptive recommendations proposed in the next chapter are on a middle range of generality, needing detailed application to particular countries. Therefore, some exploration of the nature and contents of integrated country application studies serves as an antecedent to presentation of the prescription recommendations, and winds up our consideration of approaches to policymaking redesign.

Comprehensive, overall policymaking redesign has been rejected, as explained earlier, as inappropriate for most countries. Instead, a selective-radicalism strategy was proposed, concentrating on priority needs, and proceeding modularly. Given such an overall stance, application of policymaking redesign in specific polities should be based on an integrated approach, so as to pick a preferable mix of redesign proposals that "preferizes," if not maximizes, positive impact probabilities, within a qualitative cost/risk/benefit guesstimation.

To move in such a direction, an integrated application study is proposed, including five prime heuristic phases. These are interdependent and are to be pursued iteratively, and in constant interaction with the other phases of the systematic approach to policymaking redesign, as discussed in this chapter.

## Identification of Main Capacity Deficits

Capacities for policymaking under adversity should be evaluated, in relation to predicaments, so as to identify main capacity deficits. This is nearly never done systematically (Kriesi 1980 illustrates an unusual part-exception), though segmental surveys and evaluations can be found in various scholarly books, commission reports, and special investigations. Improved methods for engaging in comprehensive capacity-deficit evaluation, with methodologies for more exact examination of particular incapacities, need to be developed. At the present state of the art, surveys on a guesstimation level together with in-depth studies of selected facets are possible, to provide at least a broad perspective for selection of policymaking redesigns to be given priority. But as already mentioned, on a pragmatic level many policymaking deficiencies are glaringly obvious once perception is sensitized to look for them.

## Improvement Feasibility-Domain Mapping

Improvement feasibility-domains should be mapped within the concrete situations of the country and in respect to its more serious policymaking-quality deficits. Earlier considered problems of conservative and radical biases appear here in a concrete context, perhaps sharpened by intense partisan politics. As indicated before, an often useful rule of thumb may be to expand feasibility domains beyond what looks easy and not to hesitate to include among the proposals some that are sure to have tough going.

## Evaluation of Redesign Proposals in Terms of Contributions to Overcoming Policymaking Quality Deficits and Impacts on Main Pattern-Values

After preliminary screening, a variety of redesign proposals should be evaluated in terms of their potential contributions to reducing main policymaking-quality deficits. Also, probable implications of the various redesign proposals for pattern-values need evaluation. Needless to say, if some redesign proposals promise both—large contributions to improving glaring policymaking quality-deficits and achievements of additional significant pattern-values—such redesign proposals dominate, assuming they also fit into feasibility domains, as mapped within the earlier-discussed stage.

If the set of considered redesign proposals includes some that greatly contribute to reducing main quality-deficits without satisfying more pattern-values, but without impairing main pattern-values seriously, and if such proposals are not clearly beyond optimistic feasibility domains, these proposals are good candidates for a set of preferable proposals. This, on condition that incrementalism is contained. Small increments of improvement are usually not a useful mode of policymaking redesign, even if sometimes cost effective. The danger of small improvements' displacing more painful efforts needed to arrive at significant improvements is serious. Therefore, special efforts to contain low-aspiration "satisficing" and "incrementalism" are in order.

If no proposals that meet the criteria above are identified, further search should be engaged in, as considered earlier in the research and design phases of the systematic approach to policymaking redesign. If such search fails, constraints should be relaxed. Thus, redesign proposals that contribute significantly to policymaking outputs but impair important pattern-values do pose tragic choices, as mentioned earlier. The choices should be identified and brought to decision by the legitimate value judges.

Estimation of the relevance of particular redesign proposals to various requisites of policymaking under adversity should not pose difficulties that are too serious, especially if the analytic phase of the proffered systematic approach to policymaking redesign gets sufficient attention. Thus, to take a few preview illustrations from the improvement recommendations presented in the next chapter:

- Policy-professional islands of excellence near rulers can contribute much to complexity and uncertainty sophistication and to integrative perspectives. They, usually, are too overloaded to add much to long-term perspectives, and they do not contribute to consensus and participation or to realistic vision.
- Institutionalization of public-opinion enlightenment on policy issues can add somewhat to consensus and participation and a little to complexity and uncertainty sophistication, but not to policy innovation or implementation direction.
- National policy colleges can add to complexity and uncertainty sophistication, to consensus and participation, and, sometimes, to policy innovation. If not accompanied by undesirable indoctrination, which ruins the very idea, they do not add to power concentration. And so on.

Such evaluation of some redesign-proposals shows areas where all presented redesign ideas are inadequate. Thus, none of the recommendations developed in the next chapter meet the realistic-vision specification. This indicates an area where more creative inventions are called for.

*Interdependence Testing*

The preliminary basket of redesign modules passing through the screenings and selections above needs to be tested for internal interdependence. In particular, interactions that are essential for effectiveness must be accommodated; synergistic mutual reinforcements should get preferential treatment; and mutually contradictory redesigns should not be included in the same set of modules.

To give two illustrations from the redesign proposals to be presented: (1) Some kind of professional teaching program in relevant knowledge, often on a crash basis, is essential to staff-proposed policy-professional positions with suitable professionals (all the more so as imported personnel cannot be utilized for sensitive positions). (2) Think tanks have little direct effects on decisions of central minds of governments unless inside policy-professional advisory units are sufficiently developed to serve as channels and liaison.

*Reevaluation in Terms of Principles and Strategies*
*for Policymaking Redesign*

An additional test to which baskets of provisional redesign proposals should be subjected is their reevaluation in terms of the principles and strategies for policymaking redesign developed earlier in this chapter. This reevaluation should be applied not only to each redesign proposal itself but to the set of modules as a whole. Thus: (1) Strengthened rulers with many advisory supports may impair the positive redundancy principle, unless balanced by advisory services for legislatures or parties, for instance. (2) Inclusion of more than four to six redesign proposals in a concrete action program may deviate from the selective-radicalism principle. (3) Care should be taken to include in the action program a majority of redesign proposals supported by experience relevant to the country, if it all possible. And so on.

Heuristically viewed, iteratively applied, and constantly to be reconsidered in light of specific local conditions, the above stages should produce a tentative list of redesign prescriptions preliminarily fitted to the particular circumstances of a country. These serve as inputs into operationalization, experimentation, support recruitment, and institutionalization, as considered earlier, always with iterative reconsideration.

## Hedging against Failure

An important conclusion from consideration of the strength of inherent incapacities is that success in redesigning policymaking under adversity cannot be taken for granted. Far from it: The difficulties of the tasks of handling adversity may be beyond all doable, and perhaps also largely beyond currently conceivable, proposals for policymaking redesign. Therefore, and because of the limits of policymaking even at its best, as considered in chapter 4, thought should also be given to building up the capacity of societies and governance to absorb painful failures, up to catastrophe.

Regretfully doubtful, as already examined, are opinions that reduced dependence on governance and increased insensitivity of societal institutions to governance inadequacies (Gershuny 1978a) may provide a way to respond adequately to threatening predicaments while going around inherent incapacities of governance. These views ignore incapacities of other societal problem-handling systems' processes and institutions that are no less fundamental, as well as crucial functions of states in handling adversity, for which no substitutes are available. All the more pressing, therefore, is the question, what policymaking and government redesigns and what societal rearrangements, directed at reducing the consequences of adversity-handling failures, should be added to active efforts to improve policymaking capacities to engage successfully in the handling of adversity? In actual redesign attempts, both lines of redesign endeavors should be pursued concurrently, with priority to proposals that simultaneously help in both directions.

Systematic exploration of policymaking redesigns (and, even more so, of substantive policy issues) to reduce failure costs is an endeavor quite different from the main concerns of this book, involving, for instance, preparations for sustained policymaking under catastrophe, as distinct from short-crisis decision making. Such issues of policymaking redesign cannot be taken up without redesigning governance as a whole to fit completely different circumstances.

Arrangements for emergency regimes, on the lines of "constitutional dictatorships," enter the picture here, with special attention to economic breakdowns, energy shortages, ethnic riots, large-scale civil disobedience, and similar possibilities, in addition to classical security dangers and natural calamities. The probability of such occurrences increases with some adversities. Extreme historic cases, such as outbreak of the English Civil War (Fletcher 1983) and of the Spanish Civil War (Preston 1983) are illuminating, without necessarily expecting such contingencies in most democracies (for a contary view, see Peikoff 1982).

Policymaking, with all the improvements that perhaps may occur, cannot be relied upon to prevent breakdowns of normal situations. Therefore, preparations for emergency regimes, including and going far beyond augmented crisis decision making and combined with building up spare resources for emergency use and recuperation are an essential supplement to efforts at improving policymaking. In some countries that lack workable constitutional provisions for national emergency situations, such as the United States, appropriate constitutional revisions may be a priority item, though one hard to take up unless and until bitter learning from harsh experience does take place. Establishment of the U.S. Emergency Management Agency illustrates steps in the right direction, though inadequate ones.

The specter of serious failures in handling adversity leads to subjects beyond the scope of this book, but its helps to put proposals for policymaking improvement, as taken up in the next chapter, into due perspective: they are not guarantees against catastrophes, though they do somewhat improve the odds of policy gambling.

# 10

# Recommendations for Policymaking Improvement

## Introduction

Policymaking under adversity has little chance of success unless significant redesigns are introduced into the central minds of governments, into the broader policymaking process-system, into governance as a whole, and into societal problem-handling capacities viewed comprehensively. The above statement is a major conclusion of this book. Matters could be left with that conclusion, as supplemented with the proposed approach to policymaking redesign presented in chapter 9, but this would leave the idea of policymaking improvement somewhat in the air and would ignore urgent needs of policy sciences as well as of the real world of policymaking. Therefore, the risky task of moving on to concrete recommendations for policymaking improvement is taken on. In evaluating the recommendations presented in this chapter, one should keep in mind a number of considerations:

1. The improvement recommendations deal directly, with one exception, with central minds of governments, as the main subject to which this book is devoted, but other policymaking redesigns may be more important under various conditions. Thus, in the United States relations between the presidency and the Congress may need redesign more urgently than the White House itself; in quite a number of countries participatory pluralism, carefully handled (Olsen 1982), may deserve priority also in terms of policymaking-output improvement; in the United States and some other countries, the policymaking roles of the courts deserve and require some redesign (different aspects of this important subject are discussed by J. Bell 1983; Birky 1983; Carp and Rowland 1983; Neely 1983; and M.C. Porter and G.A. Tarr 1982; to be rejected for our purposes is legal positivism, e.g. H. Hart 1983).
2. The improvement recommendations are developed on a middle range of generality. Much more detailed elaboration is possible and often

279

desirable before country application is taken up. The level of middle-range generality chosen here, however, does permit sufficient concreteness to clarify the operational contents of the proposals and to serve as starting points for detailed country application, while fitting a wide range of circumstances.

3. Most of the proposals are applicable to Western democracies, with due adjustments. To illustrate specific needs of different regime types and societal conditions, one proposal is oriented specifically toward Third World countries. Some of the proposals also fit communist countries, but the scarcity of reliable information on their central policymaking process-systems requires caution.

4. The recommendations have been selected from a larger set so as to reflect and illustrate different possibilities to improve the capacities of the central minds of governments to engage in policymaking under adversity. Still, many additional approaches are not brought out by the nine selected proposals. Some neglected possibilities can be derived easily from the specifications of high-quality policymaking, as discussed in chapter 7, but there are additional avenues to improvement, such as: far-reaching computerization of information storing and processing, to serve the central minds of governments (as only partly discussed in literature, e.g. Hoaglin et al. 1982; Horton and Marchand 1982); attention to bettering the performance of middle-rank officials, whose aggregate effects on policymaking are very substantial (as considered in the business context in Grove 1983; and Kanter 1983); and efforts to encourage an innovative climate (Allen and Kraft 1982) with dispersed creative groups (as discussed in respect to outstanding business corporations in Peters and Waterman 1983. In principle, transfer of ideas from business corporations to government is a doubtful matter, although it has been supported for quite some time, e.g. A. White 1901. Also, as already pointed out, market organizations are not necessarily more efficient and effective than government organizations; nevertheless, mutual learning is possible, such as in the domains mentioned just now). Adjustment of budgeting to fuzzy-gambling conditions (N. Caiden 1981; A. Robinson and Ysander 1981) poses another important improvement avenue. Therefore, the scope for improving policymaking under adversity is much larger than indicated by the selected nine proposals, but they do present some main and most promising possibilities. This, in line with the selective-radicalism strategy and related principles, as considered in chapter 9.

5. The recommendations are in the main based on available experiences and constitute in my opinion strong prescriptive conjectures. At the same time, the recommendations deviate from the standard proposals made in most of the literature so as not to repeat what is already public knowledge; and to try to develop proposals fitting the needs of policymaking under adversity, as explored throughout this book.

6. An additional consideration in selecting the improvement proposals was to avoid ideas that need lengthy technical treatment. Thus, intelligence services in most countries need much revamping to meet diagnostics needs, and policy analysis and policy planning methods have to be revised to fit conditions of fuzzy gambling, but to go beyond the comments made in chapters 7 and 8 and to present middle-range generality proposals on such subjects requires lengthy and technical discourse, out of place in this book.

The recommendations serve in the aggregate to bring out possibilities for improving policymaking under adversity, quite independent from the merits or demerits of one or another prescription and the desirability of including some other and additional proposals in the list. (For a different list and earlier treatments see Dror 1983e; Dror 1984f.)

### Recommendation 1: Establish Policy Planning and Policy Analysis Units Near Heads of Governments

The idea underlying this proposal is to build up islands of professional excellence near main decisionmaking loci, to provide holistic and innovative analysis as an aid to top-level decisionmaking. Endeavors in such a direction can take a variety of forms to fit divergent conditions, such as party research organizations, professional staffs to parliamentary committees, and more. Without going into details—even though these can make or break units as proposed—and leaving exploration of many relevant issues to other occasions (Dror 1984d), I can sum up the essence of the proposal as follows:

1. Such a unit should be composed of fifteen to twenty-five professionals, partly from within government and partly recruited from the outside for a period of four to six years.
2. Staff members should have diverse academic backgrounds and different life experiences.
3. Modern policy sciences should constitute the basic shared approach.
4. The principal function of the unit is to provide a comprehensive and professional perspective for evaluating major current decision issues, with special attention to the more critical ones. Early identification of emerging momentous choices and initiation of appropriate staff work on watershed decisions is a main task. The unit should also work on setting governmental priorities in some relation to budgeting, help with crisis management, and engage in a variety of special activities, such as preparation of important negotiations.
5. The unit is no substitute for any function fulfilled by regular departments, but (a) reconsiders agenda setting; (b) provides a second look; (c)

reviews options from a broader and longer-range perspective; (d) pays special attention to interfaces between different decisions; and (e) initiates in-depth studies as needed.

6. The unit should introduce some heterodoxy into the central mind of government, though real iconoclasm is usually impossible near a head of government.

7. The client of the unit is the head of government and, sometimes, the cabinet as a whole. Close access to the client and relations of confidence with him are an essential prerequisite of success.

It would be misleading to present this proposal without taking up some of the obstacles on the way to its realization. A few of the obstacles and proposed ways for tackling them include:

- Suitable individuals to staff such a unit may be hard to find in some countries, but, taking into account the small numbers involved, intensive search should uncover at least a number of such persons. Intensive crash training can help, as discussed later in this chapter.
- Friction will be generated with ministers and departments, but, if some care is taken, the friction can be molded into "constructive conflict"— with competition resulting in the upgrading of decisionmaking as a whole. Indeed, a major desirable spin-off of a central policy planning and policy analysis unit is to stimulate heads of departments to improve their own staffs. This should be encouraged, subject to keeping ministerial advisory staffs lean and professional.
- The office of the head of government may become complex and cumbersome. This is a danger that should be handled by eliminating from that office all activities that are not essential for its main functions. Also, a loose structure with much informal cooperation among all parts of the office should be encouraged.
- In some countries, the head of government may seem to augment his power and increase his staff while public expenditure as a whole is cut. (Compare Weller 1983 with G. Jones 1983). This can be a real problem, but one that can be handled by frank and clear explanation of the importance of improving momentous choices and the cost effectiveness of having staffs to help to improve such decisions. Straightforward presentation on such lines may well constitute a winning strategy for overcoming difficulties in "public understanding." Parallel support for a research staff to serve the head of the opposition has in some cases proved to be a good strategy to recruit support, while also justified in terms of upgrading national decision making as a whole.
- In some countries leaks are very disturbing, inhibiting the kind of free thinking without which staffs as proposed are useless. Public clarification of the role of the staff in bringing up unconventional ideas and explanation of the difference between explorative staff papers and gov-

ernmental policies may help. Ways to prevent leaks need careful consideration.

- The staff may become irrelevant to real decisions. To ward off such a danger, the staff must be integrated into the decision flow. At the same time, overinvolvement of the unit in current politicking and trivial pressing issues must be avoided. Concomitantly, decision-preparation processes need adjustments. In particular, very important decision issues must be recognized as such in advance and be prepared and handled quite differently from routine decisions (cf. Dror 1984b; Krieger, forthcoming).
- Last, but most important of all, the head of government may not like the mental discipline necessary for working with such a unit, or may feel so sure of himself as not to regard professional help as necessary. There is no remedy for such quite-frequent situations other than to try to make a convincing case for policy planning and policy analysis units, to reach future heads of governments while they are still able to learn, to strengthen existing units so they can survive periods of doubts, and to have operational proposals ready when an interested head of government comes along.

In addition to such general obstacles, different countries have specific barriers against maintaining adequate policy planning and policy analysis units in the core of the central minds of governments. Thus, in the United States, despite intense attention to White House organization and many experiments with it (as well discussed in J. Hart 1984, for instance), it continues to suffer from a number of cardinal weaknesses, including the absence of professionals serving in the higher White House staff (as distinct from the large Executive Office of the President and, especially, the Office of Management and Budget) for an extended period, and thus accumulating experience and knowledge; and the displacement of longer-range and in-depth policy thinking by current pressures and, especially, the complexities of relations with Congress. In the United Kingdom, to take another example, the decision, in June 1983, by the prime minister to close down the Central Policy Review Staff, which approximated some though not all of the specifications of a policy planning and policy analysis unit as discussed in this chapter, demonstrates the survival difficulties of such units even after years of useful though limited work.

More striking than any list of difficulties is the finding, on the basis of visits by the author to the offices of more than thirty heads of governments, that most of them had no professional staff whatsoever other than a few personal advisors, and some civil servants on secondment, serving as liaison with the main departments. Even though many heads of governments get some aid from party offices and other nongovernmental sources, still the scarcity of policy planning and policy analysis units and the weaknesses of most of those that do exist demonstrate the underequipment of central minds of governments for facing adversity.

It may be worthwhile to underline the unambiguous finding of the author's study that the most highly developed offices of heads of governments that are accessible to study, such as the White House in the United States, the Cabinet Office in the United Kingdom, the Privy Council Office in Canada, the Department of the Prime Minister and Cabinet in Australia, the Office of the President of France, and the Office of the Chancellor in the Federal Republic of Germany, have no unit adequately approximating the proposed policy planning and policy analysis unit. This fact must not be forgotten under the impression of the large number of persons working in these offices, sometimes including highly qualified professionals and doing useful, but inadequate, staff studies. It is the actual weakness of present central minds of governments, as illustrated by the absence of policy planning and policy analysis units, that provides openings for substantive though limited improvements in policymaking under adversity, even with relatively simple improvement proposals, illustrating the general observation on these lines made earlier.

Although these and other obstacles and problems are present (see also Boston 1980; and C. Campbell 1983, esp. pt. 1), still the proposal to build up professional policy planning and policy analysis units near heads of governments is cardinal for upgrading capacities to handle momentous choices. Other modes of improving the central mind of government often depend on the existence of a good policy planning and policy analysis unit near the head of government. Thus, think tanks as discussed next have little chance to contribute directly to momentous choices without such a unit's serving as a link into top-level decision making.

### Recommendation 2: Set up and Advance Think Tanks for In-depth Work on Main Policy and Policymaking Issues

Handling of adversity requires more than can be delivered by a policy planning and policy analysis unit near a head of government, even if operating very well. In-depth analysis of very complex issues, design of radically innovative options, iconoclasm in respect to dearly held policy paradigms—these and other requirements for handling adversity well require some detachment from current issues, some distance from the main arenas of politics, and rather massive investments of multidisciplinary and policy sciences knowledge. Therefore, think tanks (in the sense of policy research, design, and analysis organizations, as mentioned in chapter 3) working for the central mind of government are needed, in addition to the proposed policy planning and policy analysis units and as an essential complement to them.

The principal features of a minimum think tank to help a central mind of government in policymaking under adversity can be summarized as follows:

1. Critical mass of a minimum of twenty to thirty high-quality staff members from a diversity of disciplines, investing large amounts of time in teams to study a small number of momentous policy issues.
2. Autonomy in reformulating issues, doubting accepted policy paradigms, and questioning conventional policy "wisdom." This, with due respect to the basic values of the government but without being bound by ritualistic dogmas, a priori assumptions, formal doctrines and policy orthodoxies.
3. Freedom in designing and evaluating options, including counterconventional ones, subject to explicit sensitivity testing to alternative values and maintenance of high professional standards.
4. Direct channels to top-level decision making, including the head of government, the cabinet, and the main ministers—usually through senior advisors of the decision makers but with a right to present chief findings and recommendations directly.

The fourth specification illustrates shortcomings of existing think tanks from the perspective of aiding central minds of governments to handle adversities. Most existing think tanks have no direct relations with the top echelons of government, working for individual ministries on middle-level issues, or for the public at large.

As illustrated in chapter 3, a number of think tanks do exist principally but not only in the United States. Most countries are distinguished by the complete absence of such entities or equifunctional substitutes. Most existing think tanks, including those in the United States, are far from fulfilling their appropriate roles in improving policymaking. Reasons for their inadequacies are external and internal, such as lack of demand for in-depth work on crucial policy issues and unbalanced methodological equipment, respectively. In those respects, the advancement of think tanks to fulfill appropriate functions is a quite radical recommendation, even for the United States, where think tanks are widespread.

It may be relevant to present in condensed table form some findings on the weaknesses of think tank contributions in relation to some specification of high-quality policymaking under adversity (see Table 1).

To overcome such weaknesses, think tanks must be established in the many countries that have none, and existing think tanks require much upgrading in their performance. Thus:

## TABLE 1
### Main Weaknesses of Think Tank Contributions to Policymaking[1]

| Policymaking Requisite[2] | Main Weaknesses of Think Tank Contributions |
| --- | --- |
| Policy-paradigm reconsideration, policy-orthodoxy debunking, heterodoxity, and iconoclasm | Done only in limited domains |
| Diagnostics of fundamental problems and their causes | Problems posed pragmatically and causes not deeply sought |
| Policy agenda setting | Little work on these lines, problem formulations mainly taken as given, with marginal changes |
| Alternatives innovation | Mostly incremental, with few radically new alternatives posed |
| Broad and long-term perspectives | Interface between main issues hardly considered, with comprehensive approaches being an exception; time spans considered usually quite short |
| Uncertainty handling | Naive and confined to refined techniques based on subjective probabilities; nearly no debunking of human errors; little policy-gambling sophistication |
| Crisis management | Little work on this subject |
| Implementation direction | Despite much talk little penetrating work |
| Rapid policy learning | Limited evaluation methods and interesting social experimentation |
| Grand-policy innovation | Little work on macroproblem levels and few grand-policy innovations |
| Metapolicymaking and governance redesign | Only on single elements of policymaking and public administration; only few comprehensive works on constitutional reforms |

1. This table is aggregated from the material on think tanks collected by the author. It fits the large majority of think tanks most of the time, but there are some striking exceptions. (Adjusted from Dror 1984c.)
2. Taken from chapter 7.

1. The disciplinary composition of the staff must be diversified. If a think tank is primarily staffed by economists and decision scientists, and some physical scientists, social scientists should be added; and the converse. Probably in neither case does the staff include any historians or philosophers, and surely no literati. Some of those should be recruited.

2. Strenuous and stubborn efforts to push toward interdisciplinary work are essential for attaining high-quality performance. To do so, more is required than setting up work teams for specific projects composed of staff members coming from different disciplines; the teams must really work as integrated groups, not subdivide their tasks according to disciplines. A broadly gauged conception of policy sciences may serve as a shared open-ended framework for all think tank work. Workshops and annual seminars for professional staff members are a good way to advance think tank capacities and to encourage interdisciplinarity.

3. A principal way to advance think tank capacities, especially in the methodological domain and in the direction of interdisciplinarity, is to push staff members to familiarize themselves with the modes of thinking and central ideas of a "counterdiscipline," that is, a discipline different in basic paradigms and worldviews from their own. Thus, economists should be pushed to absorb some psychology or history, and historians should learn the fundamental schemata of decision sciences. Staff members should also be encouraged to gain a sophisticated understanding of policymaking realities within a macroview of society as a whole, and to broaden their worldviews and professional perspectives by spending some time in governments, working in another country, moving between more theoretic and more applied studies, and so on.

4. Finding and developing supradisciplinary individuals is a prime necessity, with such persons to serve as intellectual leaders and professional symbols of identification for all think tank professionals.

5. Some think tanks resources should be devoted to what can be looked at as "venture projects," namely, studies that have no defined client and that may even be disliked by major clients but that develop new policy ideas and advance think tanks capacities. Select grand-policy issues and metapolicymaking issues are good candidates for venture projects. Most staff should participate from time to time in some such research projects.

6. Special attention should be paid to addressing rulers, as far as possible directly and through their senior advisors; if this is impossible, through surrogate channels, such as the mass media. Rulers are not only an essential support for think tanks but are of cardinal importance in policymaking; therefore, contributing to their decisions is a main mode of significantly inputting think tank studies into actual policymaking. Also, trying to look at problems from the perspective of

rulers adds an important dimension to all think tank work, as well as forcing think tank staffs to understand policymaking realities better.

7. Efforts to build up innovative methodologies and overcome methodological narrowness, as discussed in chapter 8, are a leading imperative. Thus, social science methods and prescriptive methodologies must be brought together and fused into a comprehensive prescriptive approach with its appropriate philosophy of knowledge bases; debugging of main decision errors, based in part on decision psychology, should supplement optimization and "preferization" models; historic perspectives and comparative knowledge should serve as contexts for study of contemporary policy problems; heuristic approaches should displace much of present decision analysis in handling radical uncertainty and ignorance; heterodoxy, iconoclasm, counterconventional thinking and creativity need encouragement through structured situations; and so on.

8. In addition to the steps mentioned above, such as expanding the knowledge of staff members, recommended activities to advance approaches and methodologies include, for instance:

   • Efforts to explicate methodologies actually used in studies, with recognition that "soft" and heuristic approaches are a legitimate family of methods and approaches, to be recognized as such. In particular, outstanding staff members should be encouraged and pushed to explicate their practical wisdom as far as possible. Getting them to write methodological appendixes to main studies, to teach in special workshops, to run staff seminars, and to prepare learned papers on soft methodological issues may help.

   • Resouces should be devoted to focused work on methodology, in conjunction with substantive policy projects and as separate projects, within the venture activities mentioned above.

   • Appointment of a suitable staff member, who has the qualities for advancing methodological paradigms on his own and for motivating others to do so, as a "chief scientist" may be convenient.

9. Special attention must be devoted to better diffusion of the work of think tanks. The running of short courses and workshops, for policymakers as well as for professionals, to present think tank findings and to share methodologies and ways of thinking may be especially attractive. If not yet done, improved publication formats with special executive versions for busy policymakers should be introduced. If a think tank is active in improving the level of public debate on policy issues, better utilization of mass media, such as presentation of complex issues on television, is a prime candidate for additional efforts. If a think tank does much work for government, and probably in all cases, an exemplary briefing room that permits multimedia presentation of complex studies to professionally unsophisticated clienteles should often receive priority.

10. Systematic and comprehensive evaluation of the activities, achievements, and problems of a think tank is a must. Retreats of staff members to reevaluate think tank activities; having one or two senior staff members do a periodic evaluation study; encouraging doctoral dissertations written on a think tank; and inviting full-scale confidential evaluations of activities of a think tank as a whole by outside experts—these, in ascending order of difficulty and usefulness, are some ways to go about self-evaluation. The better keeping of records and real-time collection of data that may be useful for evaluation should be institutionalized.

11. Cooperation between think tanks opens up interesting possibilities for mutual learning and shared endeavors; the present weaknesses of communication between principal think tanks constitute quite an omission. A preliminary meeting of some heads of think tanks at OECD in April 1981 demonstrated strong interest in building up cooperation and much potential for shared activities, such as:

    • Systematic exchange of publications and information on major ongoing studies.
    • Shared staff-development activities, ranging from reciprocal study visits to one-year attachments, up to common workshops, seminars, and training activities.
    • Shared working teams on subjects of common interest, such as methodology advancement and study-diffusion modes, as already started in the United States. In some cases, partnerships in working on specific policy projects might be attractive.
    • Mutual exchange of experience between heads of think tanks on management problems, staff development, marketing, communication, and more.
    • Shared publications, such as collections of policy study cases, books on the operation of think tanks, state-of-the-art volumes, and more.

Beyond such specific activities is the overall need to build up the self-image of think tanks and to appreciate better the unique missions of think tanks, through mutual discourse and shared thinking.

All the activities recommended above, as well as additional ones that can in part be derived from the need to counteract think tank weaknesses as presented in part in Table 1, should be integrated into an open-ended and elastic capacity-development strategy. Working out such a strategy provides an opportunity to reconsider the leading features of think tanks, to challenge some basic assumptions (Mason and Mitroff 1981), and to stimulate the staff to engage in fresh thinking.

Elaboration and presentation of relatively detailed specific improvement proposals in respect to think tanks serves not only to work out a recommendation very important for upgrading policymaking under adversity but to highlight an interesting omission in most of political science literature: Although think tanks have been around for more than thirty years (Dickson 1971; Saunders 1966; Bruce Smith 1966), most texts on government ignore this important policy-influencing institution; and the growing literature on needed governance reforms hardly ever mentions the need to upgrade the performance of think tanks (mistaken treatments are illustrated by Guttman and Willner 1976). All the more, then, the importance of think tanks for policymaking under adversity and the need for important changes in think tanks to permit them to fulfill cardinal functions in upgrading policymaking under adversity should be emphasized.

### Recommendation 3: Establish Independent State-of-the-Nation and Policy Audit

A variety of integrated or dispersed institutional arrangements can meet this recommendation, depending on circumstances. But, in the absence of special independent institutions in charge of collecting data, composing comprehensive state-of-the-nation estimations, preparing factual surveys on main issues, and engaging in systematic audit of policy results, including policy inquests, an essential basis for diagnostics, agenda setting, policy opinions enlightenment, policy thinking pluralism and policy learning is missing. Highly developed countries have some setups moving slowly in the proposed direction, such as state comptrollers in various forms and the General Accounting Office of the United States. Still, much information is missing. Policy audit is in its infancy everywhere.

Suitable arrangements can include, for instance:

- Restructured central statistical offices, with strengthened independence, data-collection authority, and diversified interdisciplinary staffs.
- Expanded roles for state comptroller offices, with due changes in professional qualifications of staffs.
- Statutory policy evaluation institutionalization, with safeguards for the work to be done by independent research organization.
- Think tanks to undertake parts of the job, such as preparing state-of-the-nation estimations (as illustrated, on a multination basis, by the Organization for Economic Cooperation and Development, OECD, *inter alia* in the economic domain).

Other possibilities exist. But, in whatever mixes, institutionalized state-of-the-nation estimations and policy audits are important modules of a policymaking-improvement strategy.

## Recommendation 4: Cadre Development

Jacksonian ideology seems to be increasingly accepted in some (though not all) democracies and also nondemocracies the less it fits growing complexity. Slowly increasing knowledge on self-selection of politicians and on typical career channels of top decision makers does little to relax apprehensions that a hiatus exists between needed and actual profiles of most top policymakers within a statistical variance and with differences among countries. Relevant questions, in part already mentioned, are: What percentage of "the best" (a multidimensional concept) moves into politics and government service? What initial and trained capacities and incapacities do policymakers bring to their positions? What about the qualities of the broader strata of policy influentials? And, how far do various interaction modes, such as bargaining, reinforce better or worse features of the participants? These are crucial for evaluating policymaking reality and searching for ways to improve it.

To take up the easier part first, despite years of experience and thinking, many countries recruit their top civil servants and prepare them in ways very inadequate for their important functions in policymaking under adversity. Even countries with relatively very advanced approaches to selection and preparation of top civil servants lag behind changing needs more and more. This also applies to foreign service staffs, proposals for the improvement of which (Allison and Szanton 1976, passim; Bacchus 1983) have very little impact. In the Third World, hardly any countries have arrived at the suitable innovative approaches needed to prepare top officials in ways meeting the countries' special needs and conditions.

The broader question of elite preparation is more sensitive ideologically and politically. Accepting a functional "performance" approach to elites and open-ended multidimensional criteria for its delimitation, some countries nevertheless repress the term and many other countries distort approaches to it, which do not help to achieve equity or equality and to reduce political poverty. Rather, power and privilege aggregate according to other criteria, while the positive functions of high-quality elites go unfulfilled. Frank recognition of the essential functions of a diversity of elites in societies under adversity together with efforts to reshape elites so as to meet changing values can provide much better results.

Most sensitive of all is the taboo on recruitment, advancement, and continuous upgrading of politicians. Strongly resisted by present politicians is consideration of possible steps to improve the qualities of these amateurish professionals, even though much could be done without overturning basic conventions.

To illustrate concrete proposals for some facets of cadre development, let me mention briefly a few doable prescriptions.

### Prescription in Respect to Senior Civil Servants

- Recognize the special needs for "superofficials," and establish an explicit policy for their recruitment and continuous development.
- Academic background is, in principle, a must, to be focused on relevant subjects, broadly considered. Also necessary is intense postentry training, preferably on an extended basis, such as in France, but with a program better fitting policymaking-under-adversity needs, within an overall and multidimensional policy sciences perspective. Six-month crash programs of intensive study can serve as a temporary substitute till full-scale, postentry professional training can be institutionalized. This subject well illustrates the strength of inertia; many highly developed countries still stick to outdated traditional-content training for their senior officials.
- Turnover and rotation are essential, inter alia to prevent closed minds.
- Continuous learning must be institutionalized, say, an average of two weeks a year and six months every six years as a minimum.

### Prescriptions in Respect to Elites

This subject goes beyond the subject of this paper, though it is salient for it, especially in respect to societal problem-handling capacities and human infrastructure for better policymaking. Relevant ideas include, for instance: special attention to the very gifted children through intensive enrichment programs (Passow 1979); elite universities, or elite programs at mass universities; special institutes for advanced study and research, and similar enclaves for creativity; arrangements encouraging elite rotation; and more.

Most important is the frank facing of the need for elites, never mind under what terminology, with due attention to basic values.

### Prescriptions in Respect to Politicians

- Provide opportunities and incentives for politicians to engage in continuous studies such as sabbatic leaves from elected positions.
- Finance cadre-training activities by parties (as done, for instance, in the Political Academies in Austria).
- Develop intensive workshops for senior politicians on main policy issues and on policymaking as a whole.
- Search for mechanisms to intervene in political recruitment dynamics, which in any case seems to be in flux in many countries (Eliassen and Pederson 1978, for instance). Steps to accelerate turnover and withdrawal from politics, such as by providing alternative positions and even

by legal provisions (as in Mexico, P. Smith 1979), illustrate possible ways to proceed.

Intensive preoccupation with the presidential selection process in the United States illustrates interesting work on the subject (e.g. Ceaser 1982; Cronin 1982), though statistical considerations throw doubts on the correlation between specific selection procedures and personal qualities as president, which are a difficult matter to specify and change with conditions, as already mentioned.

Admittedly, all these suggestions are of limited impact. If serious breakdowns in capacity to govern occur, more radical steps may become necessary and feasible, such as the obligatory participation of politicians, after due election, in learning opportunities, such as the national policy college presented in the next recommendation. Infrastructure improvement may also help, such as by providing attractive and useful academic programs to be self-selected by persons wishing to move into politics (as illustrated by the Harvard University combined law and public policy program). In Third World countries tougher measures may be indicated for the accelerated growth of a committed and qualified cadre for societal architecture. In any case, present taboos must be overcome.

## Recommendation 5: Open a National Policy College

Given persons with high-level experience, it is possible to acquire salient knowledge and to build up relevant policy knowledge by participating in intensive, suitably structured learning experiences. The proposal to set up national policy colleges is oriented toward providing such experiences for senior policymakers, including those who do or may in the future occupy main positions in the central mind of government.

Principal features of a national policy college are brought out by the following specifications:

1. Intensive study periods of three weeks to six months.
2. Participants to include mixture of senior policymakers and policy influentials, as well as candidates for such positions, from different groups, such as politicians, civil servants, military officers, corporate directors, labor leaders, scholars and intellectuals, professional policy advisors, and more.
3. Active study methods with a combination between knowledge inputs, exposure to modern policy planning and policy analysis methods, and application to concrete complex policy issues. About half the time to be devoted to structured learning via multiple teaching methods and half to group projects and individual assignments.

4. Extensive use of special learning methods, ranging from traditional lectures to individual computer programs, with emphasis on active methods, such as policy gaming and crisis exercises—all this based on specially prepared teaching materials adjusted to the particular characteristics of the participants.
5. Total immersion, with sixteen hours of structured activities a day.
6. Special attention to advancing capacities to handle complexity, uncertainty, and ultrachange by developing sophistication and advancing modes of thinking, not techniques.
7. Strict intellectual discipline, with emphasis on critical rationality, heterodoxy, and iconoclasm in respect to policy theologies, and search for innovative policy ideas. Value issues and interest conflicts to be handled clinically.
8. Different study periods can focus on particular policy domains and be oriented toward various mixes of participants, including shorter workshops for top-level policymakers, but the preceeding specifications apply to all activities of a national policy college.

Building up a national policy college as proposed above is not an easy task. A core faculty of about ten outstanding persons combining academic distinction with extensive policy experience is essential. A lead time of at least one year after the core faculty is assembled is required for preparation of teaching materials and detailed study programs. A suitable physical facility is also essential. Sufficient resources for an initial period of five years should be assured to give the idea of a national policy college a fair trial.

The idea of a national policy college seems so obvious that the question why nearly no such colleges exist outside the domains of national security, is justified. A number of obstacles face the establishment of a national policy college, starting with taboos on acknowledging the need of senior policymakers to learn continuously, up to the ideological controversies and political suspicions that may surround the establishment of such a college. In quite a number of countries, the already-mentioned antielitistic ideologies constitute an additional strong barrier. On a more mundane level, a number of policymakers with whom the author discussed the idea explained its unacceptability by fear that potential participants be exposed at the college to intellectual challenges beyond their capacities, with subsequent serious damage to their careers.

Despite those hindrances and others, national policy colleges can make significant contributions to upgrading policymaking under adversity, while also helping to build up consensus on major issues, including secondary agreement, that is agreement on what one disagrees and why, which is another main need of handling adversity.

## Recommendation 6: In Third World Countries, the Military Should Be Involved in National Policymaking

This recommendation illustrates the special needs of many Third World countries. It has a double basis: (1) The military, as a highly organized force, can be very helpful in policymaking, including implementation, under adversity; and (2) in any case, in many Third World countries, the military plays an active role in public life. Preparing the military for participating productively may help to channel its activities into desirable directions and, in case a military regime takes over, prepare it to do a better job.

The awkwardness of this recommendation, in a number of countries, can be overcome through adjusting the ways of getting the military involved in policymaking to local values and realities. But engaging, for instance, in societal architecture under adversity on one hand and having an army on the other hand without many bridges between them is in many Third World countries both wasteful and asking for trouble. Appropriate studies in military staff colleges, integrating the military into the avantgarde with careful safeguards, and utilizing the army as a task force for specific societal architecture missions—these illustrate operational contents of this recommendation that fit some Third World countries.

Some parts of this recommendation may also be relevant to some Western democracies and have significance for communist countries.

## Recommendation 7: Grass-Roots Activities Should Be Encouraged and Given Scope for Autonomous Unfolding

Most of the recommendations selected for this chapter deal with the central minds of governments, which unavoidably carry the main burden of policymaking under adversity. This, not because such a situation is "beautiful" but because it is necessary for effective societal steering. Unless accompanied by authentic and autonomous grass-roots initiatives, however, central policymaking may both fail in essential respects and get out of hand. Intensive grass-roots activities are not only often desirable value-wise but frequently essential to handle delicate social realities, to meet local conditions, to involve people better, and to assure a counterweight to overcentralization and bureaucratization.

This recommendation applies differently to Western democracies and to Third World countries (Foster 1980). In Western democracies, many forms of grass-roots activities are highly developed and enjoy much support. Therefore, the question is less one of supporting them than of due integration into handling adversity—which is not always a simple and straightfoward matter. In Third World countries, the problem is much more diffi-cult, with strains between traditional local structures and central governance. The needs of agriculture (World Bank 1982) well demonstrate the necessity for innovative integration between central societal architec-ture and grass-roots autonomous participation.

The allocation of additional functions to local and regional authorities can conveniently be mentioned here as a possible approach to improve operations of central minds of governments by decreasing some of their decision loads. But care must be taken; it is not true that the more func-tions are devolved, the easier the tasks of central minds of governments . Coordination may become so difficult, especially under conditions of ad-versity, as to result in a net added burden on central minds of governments. (R. Eschenburg 1977 provides useful criteria; the subject is dealt with in Samuel Beer 1977; Kochen and Deutsch 1980; Scharpf et al. 1976; and Scharpf et al. 1977; on related difficulties of local government reforms see Dearlove 1979).

### Recommendation 8: Promote Citizen Policy Enlightenment

With minor exceptions, such as some school teaching, a few think tanks working for the public at large, a few high-quality newspapers, and some public broadcasting and television programs, little is done to enlighten the public on policy matters other than by partisan and establishment inter-ests. Intensive action to improve public policy enlightenment is an impor-tant requisite of policymaking quality, especially in democracies; this clearly follows consideration of incapacities of populations, in chapter 6.

Some of the earlier-considered proposals also operate partly in the direc-tion of citizen policy enlightenment, such as national policy colleges and some kinds of think tanks, but much more is needed. Provisions in the necessary direction can include:

- Establishment and support of think tanks working for the public at large.
- Public financing for party research and training activities.
- Utilization of the display potentials of color television to analyze com-plex issues in ways improving public comprehension.
- Investment in preparation of future citizen, ranging from building up abilities to think in terms of uncertainty from kindergarten on, up to courses on national problems for all high school and college students.
- On the metapolicymaking level, establishment of special research in-stitutes to study the public's policy understanding and to develop and pilot test ways for improving the public's policy enlightenment. Thus, possibilities to combine entertainment with enlightenment may provide

important avenues in need of research (the psychology of video games is relevant, for instance,_as explored in Loftus and Loftus 1983).

The dangers of "mind control" associated with concentrated activities to "enlighten the masses" constitute a weighty counterargument to the proposals mentioned above. Between the dangers of providing governments with more effective means to influence public opinion on one hand, and media monopolies (Bagdikian 1983) on the other hand, no easy solution exists to the need to upgrade the information and thinking of policy publics, without impairing thinking autonomy and opinion pluralism. This may well become a most critical issue of democracy, all the more so under the pressures of adversity, with little signs around of a new psychological "apprenticeship" of populations (Agulhon 1983) solving the problem. The above-presented proposals for citizen policy enlightenment are, therefore, very tentative and should be reconsidered within the broader problematics of public opinion in democracies in the modern media age.

### Recommendation 9: Periodic Constitutional Revisions Should Take Place

The recommendations presented in this paper do not in the main move into the constitutional revisions needed to adjust some major regime features to requisites of policymaking under adversity. Such a possibility exists, as evidenced by differences in performance of the same countries brought about, in part, by changes in significant constitutional provisions; and, as evidenced more tentatively, because of comparison problematics, by considering differences in performance between countries similar in many respects but with diverse constitutional regimes (though matters are more complex, as illustrated by comparison of France and the United Kingdom in Ashford 1982; see also Hayward and Watson 1975).

Constitutional setups that work fine under one set of conditions may work inadequately under quite different sets of conditions. Because circumstances are changing radically in important respects, reevaluation and reconsideration of constitutional regime features that may have worked fine in the past are in order, especially in polities where governance performance in respect to adversity is increasingly inadequate because of constitutional features.

Within Western democracies, some of the constitutional provisions that may require reconsideration include, for instance:

- Authority of the head of government, as already discussed, with possible movement toward semipresidential government (Duverger 1980).
- Frequency of elections, to reduce impacts of electoral cycles.

- Division of functions between central government and regional authorities.
- Public initiatives and referenda.
- Electoral system, such as to reduce weight of pivotal small groups.
- Arrangements for emergency regimes (Peisl and Mohler 1979).
- And more.

In Third World countries, needs are much more urgent. Often, constitutions were adopted following for the most part the constitutional provisions of colonial countries with completely different traditions, conditions, and tasks (Gifford and Louis 1983). Thus, the special aims of high-aspiration Third World countries were not taken into account and not given due constitutional expression (Apter 1973). Even if the countries have values similar to those of Western liberal democracy (which is not self-evident), fundamental social differences, radically dissimilar political traditions (e.g. Dumont 1981), and quite disparate tasks require constitutional setups other than those that evolved slowly in Western democracies.

Exploration of substantive issues, such as those illustrated above, aside, at least two general recommendations seem justified. The main one is that periodic constitutional revisions should take place to provide a structured opportunity for reconsideration of such issues as mentioned above, and for constitutional adjustments, as needed and approved.

This recommendation does not apply equally to all countries. Countries where loose constitutions permit easy evolvement and adjustment, and countries in which constitutional provisions seem not to impair governance capacities, or countries in which constitutional revisions are a cultural-political impossibility are excepted from the recommendation. But, many countries remain to which the recommendation applies, and their number may be growing in the future. The preferable form for considering constitutional revisions depends on the constitutional norms and political realities of diverse countries.

The second recommendation is to give to policymaking-improvement considerations much weight when a constitution is up for revision, whatever the triggering factors may have been. The revision of the Canadian Constitution in the 1980s illustrates a missed passing opportunity to use constitutional revisions, brought about by quite other causes, for trying to introduce policymaking-upgrading provisions. (Available material leaves open the question whether this was a case of default and lack of attention to policymaking-improvement needs, or whether the political difficulties of the constitutional revision made it impossible to use this opportunity for additional effects. See S. Beck and Bernier 1983; Davenport and Leach 1982; and R. Leach 1983—all of which do not permit a reliable answer to the above question.)

The matter of constitutional revisions brings us again to the overlaps and interfaces between policymaking, politics, and society—and rightly so. As repeatedly emphasized throughout the book, policymaking, politics, and societal problem handling are closely interwoven. To make the subject matter somewhat manageable, this book focused on a part of the relevant configurations, namely, the central minds of governments, but the much broader scope of interaction between society and adversities must be underlined. This, in turn, raises many possibilities to try to improve the facing of adversity by changes in features of society and politics other than central minds of governments. Nevertheless, the latter are very significant and may sometimes shape the fate of nations.

Intense efforts to improve the performance of central minds of governments are justified and, indeed, urgently needed. This, in turn, requires inter alia better understanding of the problematics of policymaking under adversity within its broad setting and improvement approaches based on such understanding. To provide some help with such endeavors is the very aim of the present book.

# References

Aberbach, Joel D., Robert D. Putnam, and Bert A. Rockman. 1981. *Bureaucrats and Politicians in Western Democracies.* Cambridge: Harvard University Press.

Abernathy, William J., Kim B. Clark, and Alan M. Kantrow. 1983. *Industrial Renaissance: Producing a Competitive Future for America.* New York: Basic Books.

Abraham, David. 1981. *The Collapse of the Weimar Republic: Political Economy and Crisis.* Princeton: Princeton University Press.

Abraham, Ralph H., and Christopher D. Shaw. 1983. *Dynamics—The Geometry of Behavior.* Part 1, *Periodic Behavior.* Santa Cruz, CA: Aerial Press.

Abrahamian, Ervand. 1982. *Iran Between Two Revolutions.* Princeton: Princeton University Press.

Ackerman, Bruce A. 1980. *Social Justice in the Liberal State.* New Haven: Yale University Press.

Ackoff, Russell L. 1970. *A Concept of Corporate Planning.* New York: Wiley.

——. 1974. *Redesigning the Future. A Systems Approach to Societal Problems.* New York: Wiley.

——.1978. *The Art of Problem Solving.* New York: Wiley.

Ackoff, Russell L., and Fred E. Emery. 1972. *On Purposeful Systems.* Chicago: Aldine-Atherton.

Adams, Robert M. 1983. *Decadent Societies.* San Francisco: North Point Press.

Adams, William C., ed. 1982. *Television Coverage of International Affairs.* Norwood, NJ: Ablex.

Adkins, Bruce M., ed. 1984. *Man and Technology.* Discoveries International Symposium, The Fellowship of Engineering. Newmarket, UK: Cambridge Information & Research Service.

Adomeit, Hannes. 1982. *Soviet Risk-Taking and Crisis Behavior: A Theoretic and Empirical Analysis.* London: Allen & Unwin.

Agarwala, P.N., ed. 1982. *The New International Economic Order: An Overview.* New York: Pergamon.

Agranat Report. 1974. *Commission of Inquiry—Yom Kippur War: Partial Report.* Submitted April 2, 1974. English translation, *Jerusalem Journal of International Relations* 4, no.1 1979: 70-90.

Agulhon, Maurice. 1983. *The Republican Experiment, 1848-1852.* Cambridge: Cambridge University Press.

Aharoni, Yair. 1981. *The No-Risk Society.* Chatham, NJ: Chatham House.

Ajami, Fouad. 1981. *The Arab Predicament: Arab Political Thought and Practice Since 1967.* Cambridge: Cambridge University Press.

Alatas, Syed Hussein. 1977. *Intellectuals in Developing Societies.* London: Cass.

Alba, Victor. 1978. *Transition in Spain: From Franco to Democracy.* New Brunswick, NJ: Transaction.

Albert, Hans. 1972. *Ökonomische Ideologie und Politische Theorie: Das Ökonomische Argument in der Ordnungspolitischen Debatte.* 2d ed. Göttingen: Otto Schwartz.

————. 1978. *Traktat über Rationale Praxis.* Tübingen: J.C.B. Mohr.

————. 1980. 4th ed. *Traktat über Kritische Vernunft.* Tübingen: J.C.B. Mohr.

Aldrich, Howard E. 1979. *Organizations and Enviroment.* Englewood Cliffs, NJ: Prentice-Hall.

Alexander, Ernest R. 1979. "The Design of Alternatives in Organizational Contexts: A Pilot Study." *Administrative Science Quarterly* 24 (September): 382-404.

————. 1982. "Design in the Decision-Making Process." *Policy Sciences* 14 (June): 279-92.

Alexander, Peter, and Roger Gill, ed. 1984. *Utopias.* London: Duckworth.

Alkin, Marvin C., Richard Daillak, and Peter White. 1979. *Using Evaluations: Does Evaluation Make a Difference?* Beverly Hills, CA: Sage.

Allard, Erik, and Stein Rokkan. 1970. *Mass Politics: Studies in Political Sociology.* New York: Free Press.

Allen, Robert F., and Charlotte Kraft. 1982. *The Organizational Unconscious: How to Create the Corporate Culture You Want and Need.* Englewood Cliffs, NJ: Prentice-Hall.

Allison, Graham T. 1971. *Essence of Decision.* Boston: Little, Brown.

Allison, Graham, and Peter Szanton. 1976. *Remaking Foreign Policy: The Organizational Connection.* New York: Basic Books.

Almond, Gabriel A., Scott C. Flanagan, and Robert J. Mundt, eds. 1973. *Crisis, Choice, and Change: Historical Studies of Political Development.* Boston: Little, Brown.

Almond, Gabriel A., and G. Bingham Powell, Jr. 1983. *Comparative Political Systems: Process and Policy.* 3d ed. rev. Boston: Little, Brown.

Almond, Gabriel, and Sidney Verba. 1963. *The Civic Culture: Political Attitudes and Democracy in Five Nations.* Princeton: Princeton University Press.

————. eds. 1980. *The Civic Culture Revisited.* Boston: Little, Brown.

Alon, Hanan. 1980. *Countering Palestinian Terrorism in Israel: Toward a Policy Analysis of Countermeasures.* N-1567-FF. Santa Monica, CA: Rand Corporation.

Alston, Richard M. 1983. *The Individual vs. the Public Interest: Political Ideology and National Forest Policy.* Boulder, CO: Westview.

Alt, James E. 1979. *The Politics of Economic Decline: Economic Management and Political Behavior in Britain Since 1964.* Cambridge: Cambridge University Press.

Altermann, Rachelle, and Duncan MacRae, Jr. 1983. "Planning and Policy Analysis: Converging or Diverging Trends?" *Journal of the American Planning Association* 49 (Spring): 200-15.

Amarshu, Azeem, et al. 1979. *Development and Dependency: The Political Economy of Papua New Guinea.* Oxford: Oxford University Press.

Amin, Sahir, Giovanni Arrighi, André Gunder Frank, and Immanuel Wallerstein. 1982. *Dynamics of Global Crisis.* London: Macmillan.

Amman, Ronald, and Julian Cooper, eds. 1982. *Industrial Innovation in the Soviet Union.* New Haven: Yale University Press.

Anderson, Charles W. 1977. *Statecraft: An Introduction to Political Choice and Judgment.* New York: Wiley.

Anderson, James E. 1983. *Public Policy Making.* Rev. ed. New York: Holt, Rinehart & Winston.

Anderson, James E., David W. Brady, and Charles Bullock 1978. *Public Policy and Politics in America.* North Scituate, MA: Duxbury.

Andreski, Stanislav. 1965. *The Uses of Comparative Sociology.* Berkeley and Los Angeles: University of California Press.

_____. 1972. *Social Sciences as Sorcery.* New York: St. Martin's Press.

Andrews, Frank M., and Stephen B. Withey. 1976. *Social Indicators of Well-Being: Americans' Perception of Life Quality.* New York: Plenum Press.

Andrews, William G. 1982. *Presidential Government in Gaullist France: A Study in Executive-Legislative Relations, 1958-1974.* Albany: State University of New York Press.

Anscombe, G.E.M. 1966. *Intention.* Ithaca, NY: Cornell University Press.

_____. 1981. *Metaphysics and the Philosophy of Mind.* Vol. 2, *Collected Philosophical Papers.* Minneapolis: University of Minnesota Press.

Ansoff, H. Igor, Aart Bosman, and Peter M. Storm, eds. 1982.*Understanding and Managing Strategic Change.* New York: North-Holland.

Anthony, Robert N. 1965. *Planning and Control Systems: A Framework for Analysis.* Boston: Harvard University Graduate School of Business.

Anton, T. 1980. *Administered Politics: Elite Political Culture in Sweden.* Boston: Martinus Nijhoff.

Appel, Willa. 1983. *Cults in America: Programmed for Paradise.* New York: Holt, Rinehart & Winston.

Apter, David E. 1965. *The Politics of Modernization.* Chicago: University of Chicago Press.

_____. 1973. *Political Change: Collected Essays.* London: Cass.

Apter, David E., and Martin R. Doornbos. 1965. "Development and the Political Process: A Plan for a Constitution." In *The Politics of Modernization,* edited by David E. Apter. Chicago: University of Chicago Press.

Aranson, Peter H. 1981. *American Government: Strategy and Choice.* Cambridge, MA: Winthrop.

Arendt, Hannah. 1965. *On Revolution.* New York: Viking.

Argyris, Chris. 1971. *Intervention Theory and Method: Behavioral Sciences View.* Reading, MA: Addison-Wesley.

_____. 1982. *Reasoning, Learning, and Action.* San Francisco: Jossey-Bass.

Argyris, Chris, and Donald A. Schon. 1978. *Organizational Learning: A Theory of Action Perspective.* Reading, MA: Addison-Wesley.

Argyris C., and Donald A. Schon, eds. 1983. *Organizational Learning.* Special issue, *Journal of Management Studies* 20 (January).

Arieti, Silvano 1976. *Creativity: The Magic Synthesis*. New York: Basic Books.

Armstrong, J.S. 1978. *Long Range Forecasting*. New York: Wiley.

Aron, Raymond. 1961. *Introduction to the Philosophy of History*. London: Weidenfeld & Nicolson. Published in French in 1938.

———. 1962. *The Opium of the Intellectuals*. New York: Norton. Published in French in 1957.

Aronson, Elliot. 1972. *The Social Animal*. San Francisco: Freeman.

Arora, Ramesh K., G.B. Sharman, Hoshiar Singh, and Meena Sogani, eds. 1978. *The Indian Administrative System: Essays in Honour of Zlavddin Khan*. New Delhi: Associated Publishing House.

Arrow, Kenneth J. 1974. *The Limits of Organizations*. New York: Norton.

Ascher, William, and William H. Overholt. 1983. *Strategic Planning and Forecasting: Political Risk and Economic Opportunity*. New York: Wiley.

Ashby, W. Ross. 1957. *An Introduction to Cybernetics*. New York: Wiley.

Ashford, Douglas E. 1978. *Comparing Public Policies: New Concepts and Methods*. Beverly Hills, CA: Sage.

———. 1981. *Policy and Politics in Britain: The Limits of Consensus*. Oxford: Blackwell.

———. 1982. *British Dogmatism and French Pragmatism: Central-Local Policymaking in the Welfare State*. London: Allen & Unwin.

Attfield, Robin. 1983. *The Ethics of Environmental Concern*. Oxford: Blackwell.

Avasthi, A., and Ramesh K. Arora, eds. 1978. *Bureaucracy and Development: Indian Perspectives*. New Delhi: Associated Publishing House.

Axelrod, Robert, ed. 1976. *Structure of Decision*. Princeton: Princeton University Press.

———. 1979. "The Rational Timing of Surprise." *World Politics* 31: 228-46.

Aya, Rod. 1979. "Theories of Revolution Reconsidered: Contrasting Models of Collective Violence." *Theory and Society* 8 (July): 39-99.

Ayer, A.J. 1982. *Philosophy in the Twentieth Century*. New York: Random House.

Ayres, Robert L. 1983. *Banking and the Poor: The World Bank and World Poverty*. Cambridge: MIT Press.

Babbage, Ross. 1980. *Rethinking Australia's Defence*. St. Lucia: University of Queensland Press.

Bacchus, William J. 1983. *Staffing for Foreign Affairs: Personnel Systems for the 1980's and 1990's*. Princeton: Princeton University Press.

Bachrach, Peter. 1967. *The Theory of Democratic Elitism*. Boston: Little, Brown.

Backer, John H. 1978. *The Decision to Divide Germany*. Durham, NC: Duke University Press.

Bacon, Robert, and Walter Eltis. 1978. *Britain's Economic Problem: Too Few Producers*. 2d ed. London: Macmillan.

Badcock, C.R. 1983. *Madness and Modernity*. Oxford: Blackwell.

Badie, Bertrand, and Pierre Birnbaum 1983. *The Sociology of the State*. Chicago: University of Chicago Press. Translated from the French.

Badura, Bernhard, ed. 1976. *Seminar: Angewandte Sozialforschung: Studien Über Voraussetzungen und Bedingungen der Produktion, Diffusion und Verwertung Sozialwissenschaftlichen Wissens*. Frankfurt am Main: Suhrkamp.

Baehr, Peter R., and Bjorn Wittrock. 1981. *Policy Analysis and Policy Innovation: Patterns Problems and Potentials*. Beverly Hills, CA: Sage.

Bagdikian, Ben H. 1983. *The Media Monopoly*. Boston: Beacon.

Bailey, Anne M., and Joseph R. Llobera, eds. 1981. *The Asian Mode of Production: Science and Politics*. London: Routledge & Kegan Paul.

Bailey, Derek. 1981. *Improvisation: Its Nature and Practice in Music*. Ashbourne, United Kingdom: Moorland.

Bailey, F.G. 1970. *Stratagems and Spoils: A Social Anthropology of Politics*. Oxford: Blackwell.

Baker, David. 1982. *The Shape of Wars to Come*. New York: Stein & Day.

Baker, Robert F., Richard M. Michaels, and Everett S. Preston. 1975. *Public Policy Development: Linking the Technical and Political Processes*. New York: Wiley.

Baldwin, Maynard M., ed. 1975. *Portraits of Complexity: Application of Systems Methodologies to Societal Problems*. Columbus, OH: Battelle Memorial Institute.

Ball, Desmond. 1981. *Can Nuclear War Be Controlled?* Adelphi Paper No. 169. London: International Institute for Strategic Studies.

Ball, Terrence, ed. 1977. *Political Theory and Practice: New Perspectives*. Minneapolis: University of Minnesota Press.

Ballard, J.A., ed. 1981. *Policy-Making in a New State: Papua New Guinea, 1972-77*. St. Lucia: University of Queensland Press.

Banting, Keith G. 1979. *Poverty, Politics and Policy: Britain in the 1960s*. London: Macmillan.

Barash, David P. 1977. *Sociobiology and Behavior*. New York: Elsevier.

Barber, Bernard. 1983. *The Logic and Limits of Trust*. New Brunswick, NJ: Rutgers University Press.

Barber, James D. 1977. *The Presidential Character: Predicting Performance in the White House*. 2d ed. Englewood Cliffs, NJ: Prentice-Hall.

Bardach, Eugene. 1977. *The Implementation Game*. Cambridge: MIT Press.

_____. 1979. *The Skill Factor in Politics: Repealing The Mental Commitment Laws in California*. Berkeley and Los Angeles: University of California Press.

Bardach, E., and R.A. Kagan, eds. 1982. *Social Regulation: Strategies for Reform*. San Francisco: Institute for Contemporary Studies.

Barger, Harold M. 1984. *The Impossible Presidency: Illusions and Realities of Executive Power*. Glenview, IL: Scott, Foresman.

Barkan, Joel D., and John J. Okumo, eds. 1983. *Politics and Public Policy in Kenya and Tanzania*. Rev. ed. New York: Praeger.

Barker, Michael, ed. 1982. *Rebuilding America's Infrastructure: An Agenda for the 1980s*. Durham, NC: Duke University Press.

Barnes, Samuel H., Max Kaase, et al. 1979. *Political Action: Mass Participation in Five Western Democracies*. Beverly Hills, CA: Sage.

Barr, Avron, and Edward A. Feigenbaum, eds. 1981-82. *The Handbook of Artificial Intelligence*. 3 vols. Stanford, CA: Heuristech Press.

Barrett, Laurence I. 1983. *Gambling with History: Reagan in the White House*. New York: Doubleday.

Barron, Frank, and David M. Harrington. 1981. "Creativity, Intelligence and Personality." *Annual Review of Psychology* 32: 439-79.

Barrows, Susanna. 1981. *Distorting Mirrors: Visions of the Crowd in Late Nineteenth-Century France.* New Haven: Yale University Press.

Barry, Brian. 1973. *The Liberal Theory of Justice: A Critical Examination of the Principal Doctrines in a Theory of Justice by John Rawls.* Oxford: Clarendon.

――――. ed. 1976. *Power and Political Theory: Some European Perspectives.* New York: Wiley.

Barry, Brian, and Russell Hardin, eds. 1982. *Rational Man and Irrational Society?: An Introduction and Sourcebook.* Beverly Hills, CA: Sage.

Bartley, William Warren, III. 1962. *The Retreat to Commitment.* New York: Knopf.

Bass, Bernard M. 1983. *Organizational Decision Making.* Homewood, IL: Irwin.

Bastick, Tony. 1982. *Intuition: How We Think and Act.* New York: Wiley.

Basu, Kaushik. 1980. *Revealed Preference of Government.* New York: Cambridge University Press.

Bauer, Peter T. 1981. *Equality, the Third World and Economic Delusion.* Cambridge: Harvard University Press.

――――. 1983. *Reality and Rhetoric: Studies in the Economics of Development.* Cambridge: Harvard University Press.

Bauer, Raymond A., ed. 1966. *Social Indicators.* Cambridge: MIT Press.

Bauer, Raymond A., and Kenneth Gergen, eds. 1968. *The Study of Policy Formation.* New York: Free Press.

Bauer, Raymond A., Ithiel de Sola Pool, and Lewis Anthony Dexter. 1972. *American Business and Public Policy: the Politics of Foreign Trade.* 2d ed. Chicago: Aldine.

Baughan, Michalina, Martin Kolinsky, and Peta Sheriff. 1980. *Social Change in France.* NY: St. Martin's Press.

Baumann, Zygmunt. 1978. *Hermeneutics and Social Sciences.* New York: Columbia University Press.

Bayraktar, B.A., H. Müller-Merbach, J.E. Roberts, and M.G. Simpson, eds. 1979. *Education in Systems Science.* London: Taylor & Francis.

Beach, Lee Roy, and Terence R. Mitchell. 1978. "A Contingency Model for the Selection of Decision Strategies." *Academy of Management Review* 3 (January): 439-49.

Beaufré, André 1974. *Strategy for Tomorrow.* New York: Crane, Russak. Translated from the French.

Beck, Carl, and Carmelo Meso-Lago, eds. 1975. *Comparative Socialist Systems: Essays on Politics and Economics.* Pittsburgh, PA: Pittsburgh University Press.

Beck, Stanley M., and Ivan Bernier, eds. 1983. *Canada and the New Constitution: The Unfinished Agenda.* 2 vols. Montreal: Institute for Research on Public Policy.

Becker, Gary. 1976. *The Economic Approach to Human Behavior.* Chicago: University of Chicago Press.

Beckhard, Richard, and Reuben Harris. 1977. *Organizational Transitions: Managing Complex Change.* Reading, MA: Addison-Wesley.

Beer, Lawrence Ward. 1979. *Constitutionalism in Asia: Asian Views of the American Influence*. Berkeley and Los Angeles: University of California Press.

Beer, Samuel H. 1977. "Political Overload and Federalism." *Polity* 10 (Fall): 5-17.

———. 1982. *Britain Against Itself: The Political Contradictions of Collectivism*. New York: Norton.

Beer, Stafford. 1966. *Decision and Control: The Meaning of Operational Research and Management Cybernetics*. London: Wiley.

———. 1975. *Platform for Change*. New York: Wiley.

———. 1981. *Brain of the Firm*. 2d ed. London: Wiley.

Behn, R.D. 1978. "How to Terminate a Public Policy: A Dozen Hints for the Would-Be-Terminator." *Policy Sciences* 4: 393-413.

Behn, Robert D., and James W. Vaupel. 1982. *Quick Analysis for Busy Decision Makers*. New York: Basic Books.

Beier, Ulli. 1980. *Voices of Independence: New Black Writings from Papua New Guinea*. St. Lucia: University of Queensland Press.

Beiner, Ronald. 1984. *Political Judgment*. Chicago: University of Chicago Press.

Bell, Bowyer J. 1976. *On Revolt: Strategies of National Liberation*. Cambridge: Harvard University Press.

———. 1978. *A Time of Terror: How Democratic Societies Respond to Revolutionary Violence*. New York: Basic Books.

Bell, Daniel. 1973. *The Coming of the Post-Industrial Society*. New York: Penguin.

———. 1979. *The Cultural Contradictions of Capitalism*. 2d ed. London: Heinemann.

———. 1982. *The Social Sciences Since the Second World War*. New Brunswick, NJ: Transaction. First published in two parts, 1980 and 1981.

Bell, Daniel, and Irving Kristol, eds. 1981. *The Crisis of Economic Theory*. New York: Basic Books.

Bell, D.E., R.L. Keeney, and H. Raiffa, eds. 1977. *Conflicting Objectives in Decisions*. New York: Wiley.

Bell, John. 1983. *Policy Arguments in Judicial Decisions*. Oxford: Clarendon.

Bell, Peter D. 1981. *Graduate Training Programs in Public Policy Supported by the Ford Foundation*. New York: Ford Foundation.

Beloff, Max 1962. *The Age of Absolutism, 1660-1815,* London: Hutchinson.

Bendersky, Joseph W. 1983. *Carl Schmitt, Theorist for the Reich*. Princeton: Princeton University Press.

Bendix, Reinhard, ed. 1968. *State and Society: A Reader in Comparative Political Sociology*. Berkeley and Los Angeles: University of California Press.

Benello, C.G., and D. Roassopoulos. 1971. *The Case for Participatory Democracy*. New York: Grossman.

Benjamin, Roger. 1980. *The Limits of Politics: Collective Goods and Political Change in Postindustrial Societies*. Chicago: University of Chicago Press.

Benn, S.I., and G.W. Mortimore, eds. 1976. *Rationality and the Social Sciences: Contributions to the Philosophy and Methodology of the Social Sciences*. London: Routledge & Kegan Paul.

Bennett, Lance W., ed. 1983. *The Politics of Illusion*. New York: Longman.

Bennis, Warren. G., and Philip E. Slater. 1968. *The Temporary Society.* New York: Harper & Row.

Bentley, Michael. 1977. *The Liberal Mind, 1914-1929.* Cambridge: Cambridge University Press.

Benveniste, Guy B. 1977. *Bureaucracy.* San Francisco: Boyd & Fraser.

Benz, Wolfgang. 1979. *Bewegt von der Hoffnung Aller Deutschen: Zur Geschichte des Grundgesetzes Entwürfe und Diskussionen 1941-1949.* Munich: Deutscher Taschenbuch Verlag.

Berg, Axel van den. 1981. "Critical Theory: Is There Still Hope?" *American Journal of Sociology* 86: 449ff.

Bergenholtz, Henning. 1979. *Das Wortfeld "Angst": Eine Lexikographische Untersuchung mit Vorschlägen für ein grosses interdisziplinäres Wörterbuch der deutschen Sprache.* Stuttgart: Klett.

Berger, P.L., and T. Luckmann. 1980. *Die Gesellschaftliche Konstruktion der Wirklichkeit: Eine Theorie der Wissenssoziologie.* Frankfurt am Main: Fischer Taschenbücher. Earlier edition translated into English: *The Social Construction of Reality.* New York: Doubleday, 1966.

Berger, Suzanne, ed. 1981. *Organizing Interests in Western Europe: Pluralism, Corporatism and the Transformation of Politics.* Cambridge: Cambridge University Press.

Bergesen, Albert, ed. 1980. *Studies of the Modern World System.* New York: Academic Press.

Bergson, Abram. 1978. *Productivity and the Social System—The USSR and the West.* Cambridge: Harvard University Press.

Bermback, Udo, ed. 1973. *Theorie und Praxis der Direkten Demokratie.* Opladen: Westdeutscher.

Bernard, Harold. 1981. *The Greenhouse Effect.* New York: Harper & Row. First published 1980.

Bernard, Thomas. 1983. *The Consensus-Conflict Debate: Form and Content in Social Theories.* New York: Columbia University Press.

Bernstein, Ilene N., and Howard E. Freeman. 1975. *Academic and Entrepreneurial Research: The Consequences of Diversity in Federal Evaluation Studies.* New York: Russell Sage Foundation.

Bertsch, Gary K., ed. 1982. *Global Policy Studies.* Beverly Hills, CA: Sage.

Best, Michael H., and William E. Connolly. 1982. *The Politicized Economy.* 2d ed. Lexington, MA: Heath.

Bettelheim, Bruno. 1983. *Freud and Man's Soul.* New York: Knopf.

Bettman, J.R. 1979. *An Information Processing Theory of Consumer Choice.* Reading, MA: Addison-Wesley.

Betts, Richard K. 1978. "Analysis, War, and Decision: Why Intelligence Failures are Inevitable." *World Politics.* 31 (October): 61-89.

_____. 1980. "Intelligence for Policymaking." *Washington Quarterly* 3 (Summer): 118-29.

_____. 1982. *Surprise Attack: Lessons for Defense Planning.* Washington, DC: Brookings Institution.

Beyme, Klaus von, and Manfred G. Schmidt, eds. 1982. *Policy Making in the Federal Republic of Germany.* London: Hants, Gower.

Bezold, Clement, ed. 1978. *Anticipatory Democracy: People in the Politics of the Future.* New York: Random House.

Billings, Robert S., Thomas W. Milburn, and Mary Lou Schaalman 1980. "A Model of Crisis Perception: A Theoretic and Empiric Analysis." *Administrative Science Quarterly* 25 (June): 300-316.

Billington, James H. 1980. *Fire in the Minds of Men.* New York: Basic Books.

Binder, Leonard, et al. 1971. *Crisis and Sequences in Political Development.* Princeton: Princeton University Press.

Binstock, Robert H., and Ethel Shanas, eds. 1976. *Handbook of Aging and the Social Sciences,* New York: Van Nostrand Reinhold.

Binswanger, Hans P., and Vernon W. Ruttan, et al. 1978. *Induced Innovation: Technology, Institutions, and Development.* Baltimore, MD: Johns Hopkins University Press.

Birky, Robert H. 1983. *The Court and Public Policy.* Washington, DC: Congressional Quarterly Press.

Birnbaum, Pierre. 1982. *The Height of Power: An Essay on the Power Elite in France.* Chicago, IL: University of Chicago Press.

Black, Cyril E., ed. 1975. *The Modernization of Japan and Russia.* New York: Free Press.

Black, Cyril E., and John P. Burke. 1983. "Organizational Participation and Public Policy." *World Politics* 35 (April): 393-425.

Black, Ian Donald. 1983. *A Gambling Style of Government: The Establishment of Chartered Company Rule in Sabeh, 1878-1915.* Oxford: Oxford University Press.

Blackaby, Frank, ed. 1979. *De-industrialization.* National Institute of Economic and Social Research, Economic Policy Papers 2. London: Heinemann.

Blainey, Geoffrey. 1966. *The Tyranny of Distance: How Distance Shaped Australia's History.* Melbourne: Sun Books.

Blair, Douglas H., and Robert A. Pollak. 1983. "Rational Collective Choice." *Scientific American* 249 (August): 88-95.

Blaney III, and Harry Clay. 1979. *Global Challenges: A World at Risk.* New York: Watts.

Blank, Robert H. 1984. *Redefining Human Life: Reproductive Technologies and Social Policy.* Boulder, CO: Westview.

Blits, Jan H. 1983. *The End of the Ancient Republic: Essays on Julius Caesar.* Durham, NC: Carolina Academic Press.

Bloch, Arthur. 1977. *Murphy's Law: And Other Reasons Why Things Go Wrong.* Los Angeles: Price Stern.

———. 1980. *Murphy's Law Book Two: More Reasons Why Things Go Wrong.* Los Angeles: Price Stern.

———. 1982. *Murphy's Law Book Three: And Other Reasons Why Things Continue to Go Wrong.* Los Angeles: Price Stern.

Blondel, Jean. 1980. *World Leaders: Heads of Government in the Postwar Period.* Beverly Hills, CA: Sage.

_____. 1982. *The Organization of Governments: A Comparative Analysis of Governmental Structures.* Beverly Hills, CA: Sage.

Bloodsworth, Dennis. 1982. *The Messiah and the Mandarins: The Paradox of Mao's China.* London: Weidenfeld & Nicolson.

Bloomfield, Lincoln P. 1982. *The Foreign Policy Process: A Modern Primer.* Englewood Cliffs, NJ: Prentice-Hall.

Bluestone, Barry, and Bennett Harrison. 1982. *The Deindustrialization of America: Plant Closings, Community Abandonment, and the Dismantling of Basic Industry.* New York: Basic Books.

Blum, Andreas, Gerhard Kocher, and Walter Wittmann, eds. 1982. *Die Zukunftstauglichkeit der Schweizerischen Entscheidungsstrukturen.* Diessenhogen: Verlag Rügger.

Bobrow, B. Davis, Steven Chan, and Johan A. Kringer. 1979. *Understanding Foreign Policy Decisions: The Chinese Case.* New York: Free Press.

Böckenförde, Ernst-Wolfgang. 1973. *Kirchlicher Auftrag und politische Entscheidung.* Freiburg: Rombach.

_____. 1976, *Staat, Gesellschaft, Freiheit: Studien zur Staatstheorie und zum Verfassungsrecht.* Frankfurt am Main: Suhrkamp.

Bogart, Dodd H. 1980. "Feedback, Feedforward, and Feedwithin: Strategic Information in Systems." *Behavioral Science* 25: 237-49.

Bogdanor, Vernon, and David Butler, eds. 1983. *Democracy and Elections: Electoral Systems and Their Political Consequences.* Cambridge: Cambridge University Press.

Boguslaw, Robert. 1981. *The New Utopians: A Study of Systems Design and Social Change.* Enl. ed. New York: Irvington.

_____. 1982. *Systems Analysis and Social Planning: Human Problems of Post-Industrial Society.* New York: Irvington.

Bohret, Carl. 1971. "Effizienz der Exekutive als Argument gegen Demokratisierung?" In *Politische Vierteljahresschrift, Probleme der Demokratie Heute.* Opladen: Westdeutscher.

Bois, Guy. 1984. *The Crisis of Feudalism: Economy and Society in Eastern Normandy, c 1300-1550.* Cambridge: Cambridge University Press. Translated from French.

Boli-Bennett, John. 1979. "The Ideology of Expanding State Authority in National Constitutions, 1870-1970." In *National Development and the World System.* Edited by J. Meyer and M. Hanna. Chicago: University of Chicago Press.

Böll, Heinrich. 1982. *The Safety Net.* New York: Knopf. Published in German in 1979.

Bölling, Klaus. 1982. *Die letzten 30 Tage des Kanzlers Helmut Schmidt: Ein Tagebuch.* Reinbek bei Hamburg: Rowohlt.

Bolt Beranek and Newman, Inc. 1980. *Project Intelligence: The Development of Procedures to Enhance Thinking Skills, Final Report, Phase I.* Prepared for Harvard University. Submitted to Ministry for the Development of Human Intelligence, Republic of Venezuela, Cambridge: Harvard University.

Boltho, Andrea, ed. 1982. *The European Economy: Growth and Crisis.* Oxford: Oxford University Press.

Bonnell, Victoria E. 1980. "The Use of Theory, Concepts and Comparison in Historical Sociology." *Comparative Studies in Society and History* 22: 156-73.

Book Review Symposium. 1980. "Living Systems." *Behavioral Science* 25: 33-87.

Booth, David, and Bernardo Sorj, eds. 1983. *Military Reformism and Social Classes: The Peruvian Experience, 1968-80.* New York: St. Martin's Press.

Borchardt, Knut. 1982. *Wachstum, Krisen, Handlungsspielräume der Wirtschaftspolitik.* Göttingen: Vandenhoeck & Ruprecht.

Bornstein, Stephen, David Held, and Joel Krieger, ed. 1984. *The State in Capitalist Europe: A Case Book.* London: Allen & Unwin.

Boserup, Ester. 1982. *Population and Technological Change: A Study of Long-Term Trends.* Chicago: University of Chicago Press.

Boston, Jonathan G. 1980. "High Level Advisory Groups in Central Government: A Comparative Study of the Origins, Structure and Activities of the Australian Priorities Review Staff and the New Zealand Prime Minister's Advisory Group." Master's thesis, University of Canterbury, New Zealand.

Boswell, Jonathan S. 1983. *Business Policies in the Making: Three Steel Companies Compared.* London: Allen & Unwin.

Boudon, Raymond. 1974. *Education, Opportunity, and Social Inequality: Changing Prospects in Western Society.* New York: Wiley. Published in French in 1973.

_____. 1981. *The Logic of Social Action: An Introduction to Sociological Analysis.* London: Routledge & Kegan Paul. Published in French in 1979.

_____. 1982. *The Unintended Consequences of Social Action.* London: Macmillan.

_____. 1983. "Why Theories of Social Change Fail: Some Methodological Thoughts." *Public Opinion Quarterly* 47: 143-60.

Boulding, Kenneth. 1978. *Ecodynamics: A New Theory of Societal Evolution.* Beverly Hills, CA: Sage.

Boulding, Kenneth E., and Lawrence Senesh, eds. 1984. *The Optimum Utilization of Knowledge: Making Knowledge Serve Human Betterment.* Boulder, CO: Westview.

Bourne, Richard, and Jack Levin. 1983. *Social Problems: Causes, Consequences and Interventions.* St. Paul, MN: West.

Bowles, Samuel, David Gordon, and Thomas E. Weisskopf. 1983. *Beyond the Waste Land: A Democratic Alternative to Economic Decline.* New York: Doubleday, Anchor.

Bowyer, Barton J. 1982. *Cheating: Deception in War and Magic, Games and Sports, Sex and Religion, Business and Con Games, Politics and Espionage, Art and Science.* New York: St. Martin's Press.

Boyer, Paul. 1978. *Urban Masses and Moral Order in America, 1820-1920.* Cambridge: Harvard University Press.

Bozeman, Barry. 1979. *Public Management and Policy Analysis.* New York: St. Martin's Press.

Bracher, Karl Dietrich. 1978. *Die Auflösung der Weimarer Republik.* Königstein am Taunus: Atheneum.

_____. 1980. *Die Deutsche Diktatur: Entstehung—Struktur—Folgen des Nationalsozialismus.* Rev. ed. Frankfurt am Main: Ullstein.

———. 1982. *Zeit der Ideologien: Eine Geschichte Politischen Denkens im 20. Jahrhundert.* Stuttgart: Deutsche Verlags-Anstalt.

Bracker, Paul. 1983. *The Command and Control of Nuclear Forces.* New Haven: Yale University Press.

Bradley, Ian. 1980. *The Optimists: Themes and Personalities in Victorian Liberalism.* London: Faber and Faber.

Braibanti, Ralph, and Joseph J. Spengler, eds. 1963. *Administration and Economic Development in India.* Durham, NC: Duke University Press.

Brams, Steven. 1983. *God, Power and Game Theory.* New York: Springer-Verlag.

Branch, Melville C. 1983. *Comprehenive Planning: General Theory and Principles.* Pacific Palisades, CA: Palisades.

Brandstatter, Hermann, James H. Davies, and Heinz Schuler. 1978. *Dynamics of Group Decisions.* Beverly Hills, CA: Sage.

Brandstatter, Herman, James H. Davies, and Gisela Stocker-Kreichgauer. 1982. *Group Decision Making.* New York: Academic Press.

Brandt Commission. 1983. *Common Crisis: North South Cooperation for World Recovery.* Cambridge: MIT Press.

Brandt, Willy, et al. 1980. *North-South: A Programme for Survival—Report of the Independent Commission on International Development Issues.* Cambridge: MIT Press.

Brantlinger, Patrick. 1984. *Bread and Circuses: Theories of Mass Culture as Social Decay.* Ithaca, NY: Cornell University Press.

Braybrooke, David, and Charles E. Lindblom. 1963. *A Strategy of Decision.* New York: Free Press.

Brecher, Charles, and Raymond D. Horton, eds. 1983. *Setting Municipal Priorities, 1984.* New York: Columbia University Press.

Brecher, Michael, ed. 1979, *Studies in Crisis Behavior.* New Brunswick, NJ: Transaction.

Brecht, Arnold. 1978. *Kann die Demokratie Überleben? Die Herausforderungen der Zukunft und die Regierungsformen der Gegenwart.* Stuttgart: Deutsche Verlags-Anstalt.

Breisach, Ernst. 1983 *Historiography: Ancient, Medieval and Modern.* Chicago: University of Chicago Press.

Bremer, Stuart A. 1977. *Simulated Worlds: A Computer Model of National Decision-Making.* Princeton: Princeton University Press.

Brenna, E.J.T. 1975. *Education for National Efficiency: The Contribution of Sidney and Beatrice Webb.* London: Athlone.

Brennan, Tom. 1981. *Political Education and Democracy.* Cambridge: Cambridge University Press.

Breslauer, George W. 1982. *Khrushchev and Brezhnev as Leaders: Building Authority in Soviet Politics.* London: Allen & Unwin.

Bresnick, David. 1982. *Public Organizations and Policy: An Experiential Approach to Public Policy and Its Execution.* Glenview, IL: Scott, Foresman.

Bressand, Albert. 1983. "Mastering the 'worldeconomy.'" *Foreign Affairs* 61 (Spring): 745-72.

Breton, Albert, and Anthony Scott. 1978. *The Economic Constitution of Federal States.* Toronto: University of Toronto Press.

Breton, Albert, and Ronald Wintrobe. 1982. *The Logic of Bureaucratic Conduct: An Economic Analysis of Competition, Exchange, and Efficiency in Private and Public Organizations.* Cambridge: Cambridge University Press.

Bretzke, Wolf-Rüdiger. 1980. *Der Problembezug von Entscheidungsmodellen.* Tübingen: J. C. B. Mohr.

Brewer, Garry D. 1978. "Termination: Hard Choices, Harder Questions." *Public Administration Review* 38: 338-44.

Brewer, Garry D., and Ronald D. Brunner, eds. 1975. *Policy Development and Change: A Policy Approach.* New York: Free Press.

Brewer, Garry D., and Peter de Leon. 1983. *The Foundations of Policy Analysis.* Homewood, IL: Dorsey Press.

Brim, Orville G., Jr., and Jerome Kagan, eds. 1980. *Constancy and Change in Human Development.* Cambridge: Harvard University Press.

Brislin, Richard W. 1983. "Cross-Cultural Research in Psychology." In *Annual Review of Psychology, Vol. 34,* edited by Mark R. Rosenzweig and Lyman W. Porter. Palo Alto, CA: Annual Reviews.

Brittan, Samuel. 1975, "The Economic Contradictions of Democracy." *British Journal of Political Science* 5: 129-59.

———. 1979. *The Economic Consequences of Democracy.* London: Holmes & Meier.

Broad, C.D. 1978. *Kant: An Introduction,* Cambridge: Cambridge University Press.

Broch, Herman. 1979. *Massenwahntheorie: Beiträge zu einer Psychologie der Politik.* Frankfurt am Main: Suhrkamp.

Broszat, M. 1969. *Der Staat Hitlers: Grundlegung und Entwicklung Seiner Inneren Verfassung.* Munich: Deutscher Taschenbuch Verlag. Translated into English: *The Hitler State: The Foundation and Development of the Internal Structure of the Third Reich.* New York: Longman. 1981.

Brown, Colin. 1984. *Black and White Britain.* Policy Studies Institute Report. London: Heinemann.

Brown, Harold I. 1978. "On Being Rational." *American Philosophical Quarterly* 15 (October): 241-48.

Brown, Lawrence D. 1983. *New Policies, New Politics: Government's Response to Government's Growth.* Washington, DC: Brookings Institution.

Brown, Lester R. 1981. *Building a Sustainable Society.* New York: Norton, for Worldwatch Institute.

Brown, Lester R., and Erik P. Eckholm. 1974. *By Bread Alone.* New York: Praeger.

Brown, Lester R., et al., eds. 1984. *State of the World 1984.* New York: Norton.

Brown, Richard H. 1977. *A Poetic for Sociology: Toward a Logic of Discovery for the Human Sciences.* Cambridge: Cambridge University Press.

Brown, Roger, and James Kulik. 1977. "Flashbulb Memories." *Cognition* 5 (March): 73-99.

Brown, Stephen I. 1983. *The Art of Problem Posing.* Philadelphia: Franklin Institute.

Bruce-Gardyne, Jock. 1974. *What Happened to the Quiet Revolution?* London: Knight.

Bruder, Wolfgang. 1980. *Sozialwissenschaften und Politikberatung: Zur Nutzung Sozialwissenschaftlicher Information in der Ministerialorganisation.* Opladen: Westdeutscher.

Brunsson, Nils. 1982. "The Irrationality of Action and Action Rationality: Decisions, Ideologies and Organizational Action." *Journal of Management Studies* 19: 29-44.

Brym, R.J. 1980. *Intellectuals and Politics.* London: Allen & Unwin.

Buchanan, B.G. 1982. "New Research on Expert Systems." *Machine Intelligence* 10: 269-99.

Buchanan, Bruce. 1978. *The Presidential Experience: What the Office Does to the Man.* Englewood Cliffs, NJ: Prentice-Hall.

Buchanan, James M., and Richard E. Wagner. 1977. *Democracy in Deficit: The Political Legacy of Lord Keynes.* New York: Academic Press.

Buchheim, Hans. 1967. *Anatomie des SS-Staates.* Vol. 1, *Die SS—das Herrschaftsinstrument; Befehl und Gehorsam.* Munich: Deutscher Taschenbuch Verlag.

Builder, Carl H. 1983. *Towards a Calculus of Scenarios.* N-1855-DNA. Santa Monica, CA: Rand Corporation.

Bull, Hedley. 1977. *The Anarchical Society: A Study of Order in World Politics.* London: Macmillan.

Bullock, Alan. 1964. *Hitler: A Study in Tyranny.* Rev. ed. New York: Harper and Row.

Bulmer, Martin. 1982. *The Uses of Social Research: Social Investigation in Public Policy-Making.* London: Allen & Unwin.

———, ed. 1983. "Social Science and Policymaking: The Use of Research in Government Commissions." *American Behavioral Scientist* 26 (May/June). Special issue.

Bunce, Valerie. 1981. *Do New Leaders Make a Difference? Executive Succession and Public Policy under Capitalism and Socialism.* Princeton: Princeton University Press.

Burg, Steven L. 1983. *Conflict and Cohesion in Socialist Yugoslavia: Political Decision Making Since 1966.* Princeton: Princeton University Press.

Burk, Kathleen, ed. 1982. *War and the State: The Transformation of British Government, 1914-1919.* London: Allen & Unwin.

Burke, T.E. 1983. *The Philosophy of Popper.* Manchester, United Kingdom: Manchester University Press.

Burks, Arthur W. 1977. *Cause, Chance and Reason: An Inquiry into the Nature of Scientific Evidence.* Chicago: University of Chicago Press.

Burnham, David. 1983. *The Rise of the Computer State.* New York: Random House.

Burns, Elizabeth. 1972. *Theatricality: A Study of Convention in the Theatre and in Social Life.* London: Longman.

Burns, James MacGregor. 1978. *Leadership.* New York: Harper & Row.

Burns, Tom, and George M. Stalker. 1961. *The Management of Innovation.* London: Tavistock.

Butack, Elber H., and Anant R. Negandhi, eds. 1977. *Organizational Design: Theoretic Perspectives and Empiric Findings.* Kent, OH: Kent State University Press.

Butler, David, and Austin Ranney, eds. 1978. *Referendums: A Comparative Study of Practice and Theory.* Washington, DC: American Enterprise Institute.

Butler, Eamonn. 1983. *Hayek: His Contribution to the Political and Economic Thought of Our Time.* London: Temple Smith.

Butz, William P., et al. 1982. *Demographic Challenges in America's Future.* R-2911-RC. Santa Monica, CA: Rand Corporation.

Caiden, Gerald. 1969. *Administrative Reform.* Chicago: Aldine.

Caiden, Gerald, and H. Seidenkopf, eds. 1982. *Strategies for Administrative Reform.* Lexington, MA: Heath.

Caiden, Naomi. 1981. "Public Budgeting Amidst Uncertainty and Instability." *Public Budgeting and Finance* (Spring): 6-19.

Caiden, Naomi, and Aaron Wildavsky. 1974. *Planning and Budgeting in Poor Countries.* New York: Wiley.

Cairncross, Frances, ed. 1981. *Changing Perceptions of Economic Policy.* London: Methuen.

Calabresi, Guido, and Philip Bobbitt. 1979. *Tragic Choice.* New York: Norton.

Caldwell, Lynton K. 1982. *Science and the National Environmental Policy Act: Redirecting Policy Through Procedural Reform.* University: University of Alabama Press.

Calhoun, Richard B. 1978. *In Search of the New Old. Redefining Old Age in America, 1945-1970.* New York: Elsevier.

Callahan, Daniel, and Bruce Jennings, eds. 1983. *Ethics, the Social Sciences, and Policy Analysis.* New York: Plenum Press.

Calleo, David P. 1982. *The Imperious Economy.* Cambridge: Harvard University Press.

Cameron, Kim S., and David A. Whetten, eds. 1983. *Organizational Effectiveness: A Comparison of Multiple Models.* New York: Academic Press.

Camilleri, A. Joseph. 1976. *Civilization in Crisis: Human Prospects in a Changing World.* Cambridge: Cambridge University Press.

Campbell, Colin. 1983. *Governments Under Stress: Political Executives and Key Bureaucrats in Washington, London, and Ottawa.* Toronto: University of Toronto Press.

Campbell, Colin, and George J. Szablowski. 1979. *The Super-Bureaucrats: Structure and Behavior in Central Agencies.* Toronto: Macmillan.

Campbell, Donald T. 1969. "Reforms as Experiments." *American Psychologist* 24: 409-29.

Campbell, John Creighton. 1977. *Contemporary Japanese Budget Politics.* Berkeley and Los Angeles: University of California Press.

Canan, James. 1982. *War in Space.* New York: Harper & Row.

Canetti, Elias. 1960. *Masse und Macht.* Düsseldorf: Claassen Verlag. Republished, Fischer Taschenbuch Verlag, 1980. English translation: *Crowds and Power,* 1973, Harmondsworth, United Kingdom: Penguin.

Cannon, Mark W., and Warren I. Likins. 1981. "Interbranch Cooperation in Improving the Administration of Justice: A Major Innovation." *Washington and Lee Law Review* 38 (Winter): 1-20.

Canovan, Margaret. 1981. *Populism.* New York: Harcourt Brace Jovanovich.

Cantelon, H., and R. Gruneau, eds. 1982. *Sport, Culture, and the Modern State.* Toronto: University of Toronto Press.

Caplan, Arthur L., ed. 1979. *The Sociobiology Debate.* New York: Harper & Row.

Caplan, Jane. 1974. "The Civil Servant in the Third Reich." Deposited thesis, Bodleian Library, Oxford University.

———. 1978. "Bureaucracy, Politics and the National Socialist State." In *The Shaping of the Nazi State,* edited by Peter D. Stachura. London: Croom Helm.

Caplan, Nathan. 1976. "Factors Associated with Knowledge Use among Federal Executives." *Policy Studies Journal* 4, 3: 229-34.

Caplan, Nathan, Andrea Morrison, and Roger J. Stambaugh. 1975. *The Uses of Social Science Knowledge in Policy Decisions at the National Level.* Ann Arbor, MI: Institute for Social Research.

Carbonell, J.G., Jr. 1978. "Politics: Automated Ideological Reasoning." *Cognitive Science* 2: 27-51.

Carley, Michael. 1980. *Rational Techniques in Policy Analysis.* London: Heinemann.

Carnoy, Martin, et al. 1983. *A New Social Contract: The Economy and Government after Reagan.* New York: Harper & Row.

———. 1984. *The State and Political Theory.* Princeton: Princeton University Press.

Caro, Robert A. 1975. *The Power Broker: Robert Moses and the Fall of New York.* New York, Random House.

———. 1982. *The Path to Power: The Years of Lyndon Johnson.* New York: Knopf.

Carp, Robert A., and C.K. Rowland. 1983. *Policymaking and Politics in the Federal District Courts.* Knoxville: University of Tennessee Press.

Carr, Raymond. 1982. *Spain: 1808-1975.* 2d ed. Oxford: Oxford University Press.

Carr, Raymond, and J.P. Fusi Aizpurua. 1979. *Spain, Dictatorship to Democracy.* London: Allen & Unwin.

Carr, William. 1979. *Hitler: A Study in Personality and Politics.* New York: St. Martin's Press.

Carroll, John B. 1979. "Individual Differences in Cognitive Abilities." *Annual Review of Psychology* 30: 603-40.

Carter, Charles, and John Pinder. 1982. *Policies for a Constrained Economy.* London: Heinemann.

Carter, Gwendolen M. 1980. *Which Way Is South Africa Going?* Bloomington: Indiana University Press.

Casals, Felipe Garcia. 1980. *The Syncretic Society.* White Plains, NY: M.E. Sharpe.

Casson, Mark. 1982. *The Entrepreneur: An Economic Theory.* Totowa, NJ: Barnes & Noble.

Castles, Francis G. 1981. "How Does Politics Matter?" *European Journal of Political Research* 9: 119-32.

———, ed. 1982. *The Impact of Parties: Politics and Policies in Democratic Capitalistic States.* Beverly Hills, CA: Sage.

Castles, Francis G., D.J. Murray, C.J. Pollitt, and D.C. Potter, eds. 1976. *Decisions, Organizations and Society.* Harmondsworth, United Kingdom: Penguin.

Castles, Frances G., and R. D. McKinlay. 1979. "Does Politics Matter? An Analysis of Public Welfare Commitment in Advanced Democratic States." *European Journal of Political Research* 7: 169-86.

Ceaser, James W. 1982. *Reforming the Reform: A Critical Analysis of the Presidential Selection Process.* Cambridge, MA: Ballinger.

Cell, John W. 1983. *The Highest Stage of White Supremacy: The Origins of Segregation in South Africa and the American South.* Cambridge: Cambridge University Press.

Centre for Human Settlements. 1984. *Along the North/South Axis: Sharing Responsibilities and Roles for Training in Planning and Development.* Vancouver, Canada: University of British Columbia, Centre for Human Settlements.

Cerny, Philip G. 1980. *The Politics of Grandeur: Ideological Aspects of de Gaulle's Foreign Policy.* Cambridge: Cambridge University Press.

Cerny, P.G., and M.A. Schain, eds. 1980. *French Politics and Public Policy.* London: Pinter.

Chaliand, Gerard. 1977. *Revolution in the Third World: Myths and Prospects.* New York: Viking.

Chandler, Alfred D., Jr. 1977. *The Visible Hand: The Managerial Revolution in American Business.* Cambridge: Harvard University Press.

Chankong, Vira, and Yacov Y. Jaimes. 1983. *Multiobjective Decision Making.* New York: North-Holland.

Chapman, Richard, ed. 1973. *The Role of Commissions in Policy Making.* London: Allen & Unwin.

Chapman, Richard, and J.R. Greenaway. 1980. *The Dynamics of Administrative Reform.* London: Croom Helm.

Charlesworth, James C., ed. 1972. *Integration of the Social Sciences through Policy Analysis.* Philadelphia: American Academy of Political and Social Science.

Chazan, Naomi. 1983. *An Anatomy of Ghanaian Politics: Managing Political Recession, 1959-1982.* Boulder, CO: Westview.

Checkland, P. 1981. *Systems Thinking, Systems Practice.* London: Wiley.

Checkland, Sydney. 1983. *British Public Policy, 1776-1939: An Economic, Social and Political Perspective.* Cambridge: Cambridge University Press.

Cherns, Albert, ed. 1976. *Sociotechnics.* London: Malaby Press.

———. 1979. *Using the Social Sciences.* London: Routledge & Kegan Paul.

Chesler, L.G., and A.B.F. Goeller. 1973. *The STAR Methodology for Short-Haul Transportation Impact Assessment.* R-1359-DOT. Santa Monica, CA: Rand Corporation.

Chester, D.N., ed. 1951. *Lessons of the British War Economy.* Cambridge; Cambridge University Press.

Childe, V. Gordon. 1981. *Man Makes Himself.* Atlantic Highlands, NJ: Humanities Press.

Childs, Marquis W. 1980, *Sweden: The Middle Way on Trial.* New Haven: Yale University Press.

Choate, Pat, and Susan Walter. 1983. *America in Ruins: The Decaying Infrastructure.* Durham, NC: Duke University Press.

Chomsky, Noam, and Edward S. Herman. 1979. *The Political Economy of Human Rights.* Vol. 1, *The Washington Connection and Third World Fascism.* Vol. 2, *After the Cataclysm: Postwar Indochina and the Reconstruction of Imperial Ideology.* Nottingham, United Kingdom: Spokesman.

Choucri, Nazli, and Thomas W. Robinson, eds. 1978. *Forecasting in International Relations.* San Fransicso: Freeman.

Christensen-Szalanski, Jay J.J. 1978. "Problem Solving Strategies: A Selection Mechanism, Some Implications and Some Data." *Organizational Behavior and Human Performance* 22: 307-23.

———. 1980. "A Further Examiniation of the Selection of Problem-Solving Strategies: The Effects of Deadlines and Analytic Attitudes." *Organizational Behavior and Human Performance* 25: 107-22.

Chu, Godwin C., and Francis L.K. Hsu, eds. 1983. *China's New Social Fabric.* London: Routledge & Kegan Paul.

Chubb, John E. 1983. *Interest Groups and the Bureaucracy: The Politics of Energy.* Stanford: Stanford University Press.

Chubin, Daryl E., and Kenneth E. Studer. 1978. "The Politics of Cancer." *Theory and Society* 6 (July): 55-74.

Churchman, C. West. 1971. *Design of Inquiring Systems.* New York: Basic Books.

———. 1979. *The Systems Approach and Its Enemies.* New York: Basic Books.

———. 1982. *The Systems Approach: Revised and Updated.* New York: Dell.

CIA. 1982. *USSR Measures of Economic Growth and Development, 1950-1980.* Prepared for the Joint Economic Committee. Washington DC: U.S. Congress.

Clapham, Christopher. 1979. *Foreign Policy Making in Developing Countries.* New York: Praeger.

———, ed. 1982. *Private Patronage and Public Power: Political Clientelism in the Modern State.* London: Pinter.

Clapham, Christopher, and William Wallace, eds. 1977. *Foreign Policy Making in Developing States: A Comparative Approach.* Westmead, United Kingdom: Saxon House.

Clark, Gordon L., and Michael Dear. 1984. *State Apparatus: Structure and Language of Legitimation.* London: Allen & Unwin.

Clark, Grahame 1970. *Aspects of Prehistory.* Chicago: University of Chicago Press.

———. 1983. *The Identity of Man.* London: Methuen.

Clark, K., and S. Cole, with R. Curnow and M. Hopkins. 1975. *Global Simulation Models: A Comparative Study.* New York: Wiley

Clark, William. 1984. *Cataclysm: The North-South Conflict of 1987.* London: Sidgwick & Jackson.

Clarkson, Albert. 1982. *Toward Effective Strategic Analysis: New Applications of Information Technology.* Boulder, CO: Westview.

Clausewitz, Karl von. 1976. *On War.* Princeton, NJ: Princeton University Press. Original edition published in German in 1832-34.

Clawson, Marion. 1983. *New Deal Planning: The National Resources Planning Board.* Baltimore: Johns Hopkins University Press.

Cline, William. 1983. *International Debt and the Stability of the World Economy.* Boston: MIT Press.

Cline, William R., ed. 1979. *Policy Alternatives for a New International Economic Order: An Economic Analysis.* New York: Praeger.

Clube, Victor, and Bill Napier. 1982. *The Cosmic Serpent: A Catastrophist View of Earth History.* London: Faber & Faber.

Coate, Roger A. 1982. *Global Issue Regimes.* New York: Praeger.

Coats, A.W., ed. 1981. *Economists in Government: An International Comparative Study.* Durham, NC: Duke University Press.

Cobb, R.W., and C.D. Elder. 1983. *Participation in American Politics: The Dynamics of Agenda-Building.* Rev. ed. Baltimore: Johns Hopkins University Press.

Cobb, Roger, Jennie-Keith Ross, and Marc Howard Ross. 1976. "Agenda Building as a Comparative Political Process." *American Political Science Review* 70 (March): 126-38.

Cochrane, James L., and Milan Zeleny, eds. 1973. *Multiple Criteria Decision Making,* Columbia: University of South Carolina Press.

Cockerell, Michael, Peter Hennessy, and David Walker. 1984. *Sources Close to the Prime Minister: Inside the Hidden World of the News Manipulators.* London: Macmillan.

Cocks, Paul, Robert V. Daniels, and Nancy Whittier Heer, eds. 1976. *The Dynamics of Soviet Politics.* Cambridge: Harvard University Press.

Coelho, George V., David A. Hamburg, and John Adams, eds. 1974. *Coping and Adaptation.* New York: Basic Books.

Cohan, A.S. 1975. *Theories of Revolutions: An Introduction.* New York: Halsted Press.

Cohen, J. 1960. *Chance, Skill, and Luck: The Psychology of Guessing and Gambling.* Baltimore: Penguin Books.

Cohen, Joshua, and Joel Rogers. 1983. *On Democracy: Towards a Transformation of American Society.* New York: Penguin.

Cohen, L. Jonathan. 1977. *The Probable and the Provable.* Oxford: Clarendon Press.

———. 1979. "On the Psychology of Prediction: Whose Is the Fallacy?" *Cognition* 7: 385-407.

Cohen, Michael D., James G. March, and Johan P. Olsen. 1972. "A Garbage Can Model of Organizational Choice." *Administrative Science Quarterly* 17 (March): 1-25.

Cohen, Norman. 1970. *The Pursuit of the Millennium: Revolutionary Messianism in Medieval and Reformation Europe and Its Bearing on Modern Totalitarian Movements.* Rev. ed. Oxford: Oxford University Press.

Cohen, Samy 1980. *Les Conseillers du Président: De Charles de Gaulle à Valéry Giscard d'Estaing.* Paris: Presses Universitaires de France.

———. 1982. "Prospective et politique étranger: Le Centre d'Analyse et de Prévision du Ministère des Relations Extérieures." *Revue Française de science politique* 32: 1055-76.

Cohen, Stephen S. 1975. *Modern Capitalist Planning: The French Model.* Berkeley and Los Angeles: University of California Press.

Cole, H.S.D., et al. 1973. *Thinking about the Future: A Critique of the Limits to Growth.* London: Chatto & Windus, for Sussex University Press.

Coleman, James J. 1982. *The Asymmetric Society.* Syracuse: Syracuse University Press.

Collier, D., ed. 1980. *The New Authoritarianism in Latin America.* Princeton: Princeton University Press.

Collingridge, David. 1982. *Critical Decision Making: A New Theory of Social Choice.* London: Pinter.

Collingwood, R.G. 1947. *The New Leviathan: Or Man, Society, Civilization and Barbarism.* Oxford: Oxford University Press. First edition 1942.

Collini, Stefan, Donald Winch, and John Burrow. 1984. *The Noble Science of Politics: A Study in Nineteenth-Century Intellectual History.* Cambridge: Cambridge University Press.

Collins, John M. 1982. *U.S. Defense Planning: A Critique.* Boulder, CO: Westview.

Collins, Randall. 1981. "On the Microfoundations of Macrosociology." *American Journal of Sociology* 86: 948-1014.

Combs, James E. 1980. *Dimensions of Political Drama.* Santa Monica, CA: Goodyear.

Commission on Critical Choices for Americans. 1976. *Report.* 16 vols. Lexington, MA: Lexington Books.

Commission of the European Communities. 1984. *Eurofutures: The Challenges of Innovation: The FAST Report.* London: Butterworths.

Committee on the General Structure of the Netherlands Government Services. 1980. *Third Report: Research Results, Analysis and Pointers for Solutions.* The Hague. Private distribution. Translated from the Dutch.

Commonwealth of Australia. 1983. *Reforming the Australian Public Service.* Canberra: Commonwealth Government Printer.

Connuff, M. ed., 1982. *Latin American Populism in Comparative Perspective.* Albuquerque: University of New Mexico Press.

Conrad, J., ed. 1980. *Society, Technology and Risk.* London: Academic Press.

Constantinides, George C. 1983. *Intelligence and Espionage: An Analytical Bibliography.* Boulder, CO: Westview.

Cook, Thomas, and Donald Campbell. 1979. *Quasi-Experimentation: Design and Analysis for Field Experimentation.* Chicago: Rand McNally.

Cook, Thomas D., Deborah A. Kendziersky, and Stephen V. Thomas. 1983. "The Implicit Assumptions of Television Research: An Analysis of the 1982 NIMH Report on *Television and Behavior.*" *Public Opinion Quarterly* 47 (Summer): 161-201.

Cook, W. D., and T. E. Kuhn, eds. 1982. *Planning Processes in Developing Countries: Techniques and Achievements.* Amsterdam: North-Holland.

Cooper, C.L., ed. 1983. *Stress Research: Issues for the Eighties.* Chichester, United Kingdom: Wiley.

Coplin, William, ed. 1978. *Teaching Policy Studies: What and How.* Lexington, MA: Heath.

Corgett, Michael. 1982. *Political Tolerance in America: Freedom and Equality in Public Attitudes.* New York: Longman.

Cornell, Alexander H. 1980. *The Decision-Maker's Handbook.* Englewood Cliffs, NJ: Prentice-Hall.

Cornford, James, ed. 1975. *The Failure of the State: On the Distribution of Political and Economic Power in Europe.* London: Croom Helm.

Corning, Peter A. 1983. *The Synergism Hypothesis: A Theory of Progressive Evolution.* New York: McGraw-Hill.

Cornish, Edward, ed. 1984. *Global Solutions: Innovative Approaches to World Problems.* Washington, DC: World Future Society.

Cornuelle, Richard. 1983. *Healing America.* Putnam.

Cosier, Richard A. 1978. "The Effects of Three Potential Aids for Making Strategic Decisions on Prediction Accuracy." *Organizational Behavior and Human Performance* 22: 295-306.

Cotgrove, Stephen. 1982. *Catastrophe or Cornucopia: The Environment, Politics and the Future.* New York: Wiley.

Cotter, Cornelius P., ed. 1974. *Political Science Annual, An International Review,* vol. 5. Indianapolis, IN: Bobbs-Merrill.

———, ed. 1975. *Political Science Annual, An International Review,* vol. 6. Indianapolis, IN: Bobbs-Merrill.

Coulam, Robert F. 1977. *Illusion of Choice: The F-111 and the Problem of Weapons Acquisition Reform.* Princeton: Princeton University Press.

Coulam, Robert F., and Richard A. Smith, eds. 1984. *Advances in Information Processing in Organizations.* Greenwich, CT: JAI Press.

Coultner, Jeff. 1983. *Rethinking Cognitive Theory.* New York: St. Martin's Press.

Covello, Vincent T., ed. 1980. *Poverty and Public Policy: An Evaluation of Social Science Research.* Cambridge, MA: Schenkman.

———. 1983. "The Perception of Technological Risks—A Literature Review." *Technological Forecasting and Social Change* 23 (August): 285-98.

Cox, A., ed. 1981. *Policy, Politics and Economic Recession in West Germany.* London: Macmillan.

Cragg, John G., and Burton G. Malkiel. 1982. *Expectation and the Structure of Share Prices.* Chicago: University of Chicago Press.

Cranach, Mario von, and Rom Harré, eds. 1982. *The Analysis of Action: Recent Theoretic and Empiric Advances.* Cambridge: Cambridge University Press.

Cranach, Mario von, et al. 1982. *Goal-Directed Action.* New York: Academic Press. Translated from the German.

Crankshaw, Edward. 1981. *Bismarck.* New York: Viking.

Crawshay-Williams, Rupert. 1947. *The Comforts of Unreason: A Study of the Motives behing Irrational Thought.* London: Kegan Paul.

Crecine, J.P., ed. 1982. *New Educational Programs in Public Policy: The First Decade.* Research in Public Policy Analysis and Management, Supplement 1. Greenwich, CT: JAI Press.

Crewe, I., B. Särlvik, and J. Alt. 1977. "Partisan Dealignment in Britain, 1964-74." *British Journal of Political Science* 7, no. 2: 371-89.

Crocker, David A. 1982. *Praxis and Democratic Socialism: The Critical Social Theory of Markovic and Stojanovic.* Atlantic Highlands, NJ: Humanities Press.

Cronin, Thomas E. 1975. *The State of the Presidency.* Boston: Little, Brown.

———, ed. 1982. *Rethinking the Presidency.* Boston: Little, Brown.

Cronin, Thomas E., and Sanford D. Greenberg, eds. 1969. *The Presidential Advisory System.* New York: Harper & Row.

Crossman, Richard. 1972. *Inside View: Three Lectures on Prime Ministerial Government.* London: Cape.

———. 1975-77. *The Diaries of a Cabinet Minister.* 3 vols. London: Hamilton.

Crotty, William J. 1977. *Political Reform and the American Experiment.* New York: Crowell.

Crouch, Colin, ed. 1979. *State and Economy in Contemporary Capitalism.* London: Croom Helm.

Crouch, Colin, and Alessandro Pizzorno, eds. 1978. *The Resurgence of Class Conflict in Western Europe Since 1968.* Vol. 1, *National Studies.* Vol. 2, *Comparative Analysis.* New York: Holmes & Meier.

Crozier, Michel. 1973. *The Stalled Society.* New York: Viking. First published in French in 1970.

———. 1982. *A Strategy for Change: The Future of French Society.* Cambridge: MIT Press. First published in French in 1979.

Crozier, Michel, and Erhard Friedberg. 1980. *Actors and Systems.* Chicago: University of Chicago Press. First published in French in 1977.

Crozier, Michel, Samuel P. Huntington, and Joji Watanuki. 1975. *The Crisis of Democracy: Report on the Governability of Democracies to the Trilateral Commission.* New York: New York University Press. First published in French in 1977.

Crystal, Stephen. 1982. *America's Old Age Crisis: Public Policy and the Two Worlds of Aging.* New York: Knopf.

Cuny, Frederich C. 1983. *Disaster and Development.* Oxford: Oxford University Press.

Currie, L. 1981. *The Role of Economic Advisers in Developing Countries.* Westport, CO: Greenwood.

Curtis, Richard K. 1982. *Evolution or Extinction: The Choice Before Us—A Systems Approach to the Study of the Future.* Elmsford, NY: Pergamon.

Cuthbertson, Gilbert Morris. 1975. *Political Myth and Epic.* Lansing: Michigan State University Press.

Cyert, Richard, and James G. March. 1963. *A Behavioral Theory of the Firm.* Englewood Cliffs, NJ: Prentice-Hall.

Czudnowski, Moshe. 1975. "Political Recruitment." In *Handbook of Political Science,* vol. 2, edited by F. Greenstein and N. Polsby. Reading, MA: Addison-Wesley.

———, ed. 1982. *Does Who Governs Matter?* De Kalb: Northern Illinois University Press.

Daalder, Hans. 1963. *Cabinet Reform in Britain, 1914-1963.* Stanford, CA: Stanford University Press.

_____. 1974. *Politisering en lijdelijkheid in de Nederlandse politick.* Assen: Van Gorcum.

_____. 1979. "The Netherlands." In *Political Parties in the European Community,* edited by S. Honig. London: Allen & Unwin.

Daalder, Hans, and Edward Shils, eds. 1982. *Universities, Politicians, and Bureaucrats: Europe and the United States.* Cambridge: Cambridge University Press.

Dahl, Robert A. 1967. *Pluralist Democracy in the United States.* Chicago: Rand McNally.

_____. 1982. *Dilemmas of Pluralistic Democracy: Autonomy vs. Control.* New Haven: Yale University Press.

Dahl, Robert A., and Charles Lindblom. 1953. *Politics, Economics, and Welfare.* New York: Harper & Row.

Dahrendorf, Ralf. 1980. *Life Chances: Approaches to Social and Political Theory.* Chicago: University of Chicago Press.

_____, ed. 1982a. *Europe's Economy in Crisis.* London: Weidenfeld & Nicolson.

_____. 1982b. *On Britain.* London: BBC.

Dale, Richard, and Richard Mattione. 1983. *Managing Global Debt.* Washington, DC: Brookings Institution.

Daly, George G., and Thomas H. Mayor. 1983. "Reason and Rationality During Energy Crises." *Journal of Political Economy* 91, no. 1: 168-81.

Darwall, Stephen L. 1983. *Impartial Reason.* Ithaca, NY: Cornell University Press.

Davenport, Paul, and Richard H. Leach, eds. 1982. "Canadian Constitution, 1982." *Law and Contemporary Problems* 45 (Autumn).

Davidson, Donald. 1980. *Essays on Actions and Events.* Oxford: Clarendon.

Davidson, Frank P. 1983. *Macro: Neoindustrializing America and the World.* New York: Morrow.

Davidson, James West, and Mark Hamilton Lytle. 1982. *After the Fact: The Art of Historical Detection.* New York: Knopf.

Davies, Alan F. 1980. *Skills, Outlooks and Passions: A Psychoanalytical Contribution to the Study of Politics.* Cambridge: Cambridge University Press.

Davies D. R., and R. Parasuraman. 1982. *The Psychology of Vigilance.* New York: Academic Press.

Davies, Phil, and Dermot Walsh. 1983. *Alcohol Problems and Alcohol Control in Europe.* London: Croom Helm.

Davis, David Howard. 1972. *How the Bureacracy Makes Foreign Policy: An Exchange Analysis.* Lexington, MA: Heath.

Davis, Glenn. 1977. *Childhood and History in America.* New York: Psychohistory Press.

Davis, J. Morton. 1983. *How to Make America Work Again.* New York: Crown.

Davis, Paul K. 1984. *Rand's Experience in Applying Artificial Intelligence Techniques to Strategic-Level Military-Political War Gaming.* P-6977. Santa Monica, CA: Rand Corporation.

Davis, Paul K., and James A. Winnefeld. 1983. *The Rand Strategy Assessment Center: An Overview and Interim Conclusions about Utility and Development Options.* R-2945-DNA. Santa Monica, CA: Rand Corporation.

Davis, Vincent, ed. 1980. *The Post-Imperial Presidency*. New Brunswick, NJ: Transaction.

Dawkins, Richard. 1984. *The Extended Phenotype*. Oxford: Oxford University Press.

Dearlove, John. 1979. *The Reorganization of British Local Government: Old Orthodoxies and a Political Perspective*. Cambridge: Cambridge University Press.

Debray, Régis. 1979. *Le Pouvoir Intellectuel en France*. Paris: Edition Ramsay.

DeFinetti, Bruno. 1975.*Theory of Probability,* 3 vols. New York: Wiley. First published in Italian in 1970.

DeFleur, Melvin L., ed. 1983. *Social Problems in American Society*. Boston: Houghton Mifflin.

Deitchman, Seymour J. 1976. *The Best-Laid Schemes: A Tale of Social Research and Bureaucrats*. Cambridge: MIT Press.

Dekema, Jan D. 1981. "Incommensurability and Judgment." *Theory and Society* 10 (July): 521-46.

Delamaide, Darrell. 1984. *Debt Shock: The Full Story of the World Credit Crisis*. New York: Doubleday.

deLeon, Peter 1978. "Public Policy Termination: An End and a Beginning." *Policy Analysis* 4: 369-92.

Deleuze, Gilles, and Felix Guattari. 1977. *Anti-Oedipus: Capitalism and Schizophrenia*. New York: Viking.

Demandt, Alexander. 1978. *Metaphern für Geschichte: Sprachbilder und Gleichnisse im Historisch-Politischen Denken*. Munich: C.H. Beck.

Demerath, N.J., III, and Richard A. Peterson. 1967. *System, Change, and Conflict: A Reader in Contemporary Sociological Theory and the Debate over Functionalism*. New York: Free Press.

Dempster, M.A.H., and Aaron Wildavsky. 1979. "On Change: Or, There is No Magic Size for an Increment." *Political Studies* 27, no. 3: 371-89.

d'Encausse, Helene Carrere. 1981. *Decline of an Empire: The Soviet Socialist Republic in Revolt*. Slough, United Kingdom: Newsweek Book.

Denitch, B., ed. 1979. *Legitimation of Regimes*. Beverly Hills, CA: Sage.

Dennett, Daniel. 1980. *Brainstorms: Philosophical Essays on Mind and Psychology*. Cambridge: MIT Press.

Derthick, Martha. 1979. *Policymaking for Social Security*. Washington, DC: Brookings Institution.

Dery, David. 1982. "Erring and Learning: An Organizational Analysis." *Accounting, Organizations. and Society* 7, no. 3: 217-23.

———. 1983. "Decision-making, Problem-solving and Organizational learning." *Omega* 11, no. 4: 321-28.

Detterman, D.K., and R.J. Sternberg, eds. 1982. *How and How Much Can Intelligence Be Increased?*. Norwood, NY: Ablex.

Dettling, Warnfried, ed. 1976. *Macht der Verbände—Ohnmacht der Demokratie? Beitrage zur Theorie und Politik der Verbände*. Munich: Gunter Olzog.

Deutsch, Karl W. 1969. *The Nerves of Government*. New York: Free Press.

_____. 1975. "On the Learning Capacity of Large Political Systems." In *Information for Action: From Knowledge to Wisdom,* edited by Manfred Kochen. New York: Academic Press.

_____. 1981. "The Crisis of the State." *Government and Opposition* 16 (Summer): 331-43. Earlier enlarged version, under the title "Functions and Transformations of the State: Notes Toward a General Theory." Berlin: Institute for Comparative Social Research, Wissenschaftszentrum Berlin, September 1980.

Deutsch, Karl, John Platt, and Andrei Markovits. 1984. *Advances in the Social Sciences Since 1900.* Cambridge, MA: Abt Books.

Deutsch, Karl W., John Platt, and Dieter Senghaas. 1971. "Conditions Favouring Major Advances in Social Science." *Science.* 171 (February 5): 450-59.

Diamond, Cora, and Jenny Teichman, eds. 1980. *Intention and Intentionality: Essays for G. F. M. Anscombe.* Ithaca, NY: Cornell University Press.

Dickson, Paul. 1971. *Think Tanks.* New York. Atheneum.

_____. 1978. *The Official Rule.* New York: Delacorte.

Didsbury, Howard F., Jr., ed. 1984. *Creating a Global Agenda: Assessments, Solutions, and Action Plans.* Washington, DC: World Future Society.

Diem, Peter, and Heinrich Neisser. 1969. *Zeit zur Reform: Parteireform Parlamentsreform Demokratieform.* Vienna: Kurt Wedl.

Dierkes, Meinolf, and Volker von Thienen. 1977. "Science Court—Ein Ausweg aus der Krise? Mittler zwischen Wissenschaft, Politik und Gesellschaft." *Wirtschaft Und Wissenschaft* 4: 1-14.

Dierkes, Meinolf, Sam Edwards, and Rob Coppock. 1980. *Technological Risk: Its Perception and Handling in the European Community.* Cambridge, MA: Oelgeschlager, Gunn & Hain.

Diesing, Paul. 1962. *Reason in Society: Five Types of Decisions and Their Social Conditions.* Urbana: University of Illinois Press.

_____. 1982. *Science and Ideology in the Policy Sciences.* Hawthorne, NY: Aldine.

Diesner, Hans-Joachim. 1982. *The Great Migration.* Maryknoll, NY: Orbis.

Dietz, Henry A. 1980. *Poverty and Problem-Solving under Military-Rule: The Urban Poor in Lima, Peru.* Austin: University of Texas Press.

Diggins, John P., and Mash E. Kann, eds. 1982. *the Problem of Authority in America.* Philadelphia: Temple University Press.

Dill, Günther, ed. 1980. *Clausewitz in Perspektive: Materialien zu Carl von Clausewitz: Vom Kriege.* Frankfurt am Main: Ullstein.

Dill, W. R., and G. Kh. Popov, eds. 1979. *Organization for Forecasting and Planning: Experience in the Soviet Union and the United States.* IIASA Series. New York: Wiley.

Dilnot, A.W., J.A. Kay, and C.N. Morris. 1984. *The Reform of Social Security.* Oxford: Oxford University Press.

Dixon, Norman. 1976. *On the Psychology of Military Incompetence.* New York: Basic Books.

Dobel, J. Patrick. 1978. "The Corruption of a State." *American Political Science Review* 72: 958-73.

Dogan, Mattei, ed. 1975. *The Mandarins of Western Europe: The Political Role of Top Civil Servants.* New York: Halsted Press.

Dogan, Mattei, and Dominique Pelassy. 1984. *How to Compare Nations: Strategies in Comparative Politics.* Chatham, NJ: Chatham House.

Doig, Jameson W. 1983. "Entrepreneurial Leadership in the 'Independent' Government Organization: Experience at American Public Authorities and Their Country Cousins." Paper presented at the annual meeting of the American Political Science Association, Chicago.

Dokumentation des BDI/IW-Symposium. 1980. *Strukturberichterstattung: Ein Informationsinstrument der Wirtschaftspolitik?.* Oberländer Ufer: Deutscher Instituts-Verlag.

Dolbeare, Kenneth M. 1982. *American Public Policy: A Citizen's Guide.* New York: McGraw-Hill.

Donagan, A. 1962. *The Late Philosophy of R.G. Collingwood.* Oxford: Clarendon.

Donaldson, Gordon, and Jay W. Lorsch. 1983. *Decision Making at the Top: The Shaping of Strategic Direction.* New York: Basic Books.

Donelan, Michael, ed. 1978. *The Reason of State.* London: Allen & Unwin.

Donnelly, Michael. 1983. *Managing the Mind.* New York: Methuen.

Dörner, Dietrich, Heinz W. Kreuzig, Franz Rheither, and Thea Stäudel, eds. 1983. *Lohhausen: Vom Umgang mit Unbestimmtheit und Komplexität.* Bern: Verlag Hans Huber.

Doughty, Martin. 1983. *Merchant Shipping and War: A Study in Defense Planning in Twentieth-Century Britain.* London: Royal Historical Society.

Douglas, Mary, and Aaron Wildavsky. 1982. *Risk and Culture: An Essay on the Selection of Technological and Environmental Dangers.* Berkeley and Los Angeles: University of California Press.

Downs, Anthony. 1967. *Inside Bureaucracy.* Boston: Little, Brown.

――――. 1972. "Up and Down with Ecology—The 'Issue-Attention Cycle.'" *Public Interest* 28 (Summer): 38-50.

Downs, George W., Jr. 1976. *Bureaucracy, Innovation and Public Policy.* Lexington, MA: Heath.

Downs, George W., Jr., and Lawrence B. Mohr. 1976. "Conceptual Issues in the Study of Innovation." *Administrative Science Quarterly* 21 (December): 700-714.

Drewnowski, Jan, ed. 1983. *Crisis in the East European Economy: The Spread of the Polish Disease.* London: Croom Helm.

Dror, Yehezkel. 1971a. *Design for Policy Sciences.* New York: Elsevier.

――――. 1971b. *Ventures in Policy Sciences: Concepts and Applications.* New York: Elsevier.

――――. 1975a. "Some Fundamental Philosophical, Psychological and Intellectual Assumptions of Future Studies." In *The Future as an Academic Discipline,* edited by C. H. Waddington. New York: Elsevier.

――――. 1975b. "How to Spring Surprises on History." Paper prepared for symposium, When Patterns Change: Turning Points in International Politics,

Leonard Davis Institute for International Relations, Hebrew University of Jerusalem, April 7 to 9.

_____. 1980a. "Think Tanks: A New Invention in Government." In *Making Bureaucracy Work*, edited by Carol H. Weiss and Allen H. Barton. Beverly Hills, CA: Sage.

_____. 1980b. *Crazy States: A Counterconventional Strategic Problem*. Updated ed. Millwood, NY: Kraus Reprint.

_____. 1983a. *Public Policymaking Reexamined*. 2d ed., with a new introduction. New Brunswick, NJ: Transaction.

_____. 1983b. "Terrorism as a Challenge to the Democratic Capacity to Govern." In *Terrorism, Legitimacy and Power: The Consequences of Political Violence*, edited by Martha Crenshaw. Middletown, CT: Wesleyan University Press.

_____. 1983c. "Policy-Gambling: A Preliminary Exploration." *Policy Studies Journal* 12 (September): 9-13.

_____. 1983d. "New Advances in Public Policy Teaching." *Journal of Policy Analysis and Management* 2 (Spring): 449-54.

_____. 1983e. "Governance Redesign for Handling the Future." In *The Future of Politics: Governance, Movements and World Order*, edited by William Page. London: Pinter.

_____. 1984a. "On Becoming More of a Policy Scientist." *Policy Studies Review* 4: 13-21.

_____. 1984b. "Facing Momentous Choices." *International Review of Administrative Sciences* 50: 97-106.

_____. 1984c. "Required Breakthroughs in Think Tanks." *Policy Sciences* 16: 199-225.

_____. 1984d, "Policy Analysis for Advising Rulers." In *Rethinking the Process of Operations Research*, edited by Rolfe Tomlinson and Istvan Kiss. Oxford: Pergamon.

_____. 1984e. "Thinking on Grand Issues." *Technological Forecasting and Social Change* 26: 135-43.

_____. 1984f. "Governance Redesign for Societal Architecture." *World Future Society Bulletin* 18: 17-24.

_____. 1985. *Advanced Aids for Top Decisionmaking: An Action Approach*. Paris: OECD, forthcoming.

_____. (in work) *On the Incapacity to Govern*.

Dubnick, Melvin J., and Barbara A. Bardes. 1983. *Thinking about Public Policy: A Problem-Solving Approach*. New York: Wiley.

Duignan, Peter, and Alvin Rabushka, eds. 1980. *The United States in the 1980's*. Stanford, CA: Hoover Institution.

Duijn, Alec. 1983. *The Long Wave in Economic Life*. London: Allen & Unwin.

Dumont, Louis. 1979. *From Mandeville to Marx: The Genesis and Triumph of Economic Ideology*. Chicago: University of Chicago Press. Translated from the French.

_____. 1981. *Homo Hierarchicus: The Caste System and Its Implications*. Rev. ed. Chicago: University of Chicago Press.

_____. 1983. *Essais sur l'individualisme.* Paris: Seuil.

Duncan, Ronald, and Miranda Weston-Smith. 1977. *The Encyclopaedia of Ignorance: Everything You Ever Want to Know about the Unknown.* Oxford: Pergamon.

Dunn, Edgar S., Jr. 1971. *Economic and Social Development: A Process of Social Learning.* Baltimore: Johns Hopkins University Press.

Dunn, John. 1972. *Modern Revolutions: An Introduction to the Analysis of a Political Phenomenon.* Cambridge: Cambridge University Press.

Dunn, Stephen P. 1982. *The Fall and Rise of the Asiatic Mode of Production.* London: Routledge & Kegan Paul.

Dunn, William N. 1981. *Public Policy Analysis: An Introduction.* Englewood Cliffs, NJ: Prentice-Hall.

Dunnette, Marvin D., ed. 1976. *Handbook of Industrial and Organizational Psychology.* Chicago: Rand McNally.

Dunsire, Andrew. 1978. *Implementation in a Bureaucracy.* New York: St. Martin's Press.

Duvall, Raymond D., and John R. Freeman. 1983. "The Techno-Bureaucratic Elite and the Entrepreneurial State in Dependent Industrialization." *American Political Science Review* 77: 569-87.

Duverger, Maurice. 1980, "A New Political System Model: Semi-Presidential Government." *European Journal of Political Research* 8: 165-87.

Dwarkadas, R. 1958. *The Role of Higher Civil Service in India.* Bombay: Popular Book Depot.

Dye, Thomas R. 1966. *Politics, Economics and the Public: Policy Outcomes in the American States.* Chicago: Rand McNally.

_____. 1984. *Understanding Public Policy.* 5th ed. Englewood Cliffs, NJ: Prentice-Hall.

Dyson, Kenneth H.F. 1980. *The State Tradition in Western Europe: A Study of an Idea and Institution.* Oxford: M. Robertson.

Easton, David. 1965. *A System Analysis of Political Life.* New York: Wiley.

_____. 1976. "Theoretic Approaches to Political Support." *Canadian Journal of Political Science* 9 no. 3: 431-48.

Eberlein, Gerald, and Hans-Joachim von Kondratowitz, eds. 1977. *Psychologie statt Soziologie? Zur Reduzierbarkeit sozialer Strukturen auf Verhalten.* Frankfurt am Main: Campus.

Eby, Charles. 1982. *Performance Norms in Non-Market Organizations: An Exploratory Survey.* N-1830-Yale. Santa Monica, CA: Rand Corporation.

Eckstein, Susan. 1977. *The Poverty of Revolution: The State and the Urban Poor in Mexico.* Princeton: Princeton University Press.

Edelman, M. 1971. *Politics as Symbolic Action: Mass Arousal and Quiescence.* Chicago: Markham.

Edinger, Lewis J., ed. 1976. *Political Leadership in Industrialized Societies: Studies in Comparative Analysis.* Huntington, NY: Krieger.

Edmunds, Stahrl W. 1978. *Alternative U.S. Futures: A Policy Analysis of Individual Choices in a Political Economy.* Santa Monica, CA: Goodyear.

Edwards, George C., III, and Ira Sharkansky. 1978. *The Policy Predicament: Making and Implementing Public Policy*. San Francisco: Freeman.

Efron, Edith. 1984. *The Apocalyptics: The Political Manipulation of Environmental Science*. New York: Simon & Schuster.

Eigen, Manfred, and Ruthild Winkler. 1981. *Laws of the Game: How the Principles of Nature Govern Chance*. New York: Knopf. Translated from the German.

Eisenstadt, N. Shmuel. 1963. *The Political Systems of Empires: The Rise and Fall of the Historic Bureaucratic Societies*. New York: Free Press.

_____. 1966. *Modernization: Protest and Change*. Englewood Cliffs, NJ: Prentice-Hall.

_____. 1978. *Revolution and the Transformation of Societies*. New York: Free Press.

Eisenstein, Elizabeth L. 1979. *The Printing Press as the Agent of Change*. Cambridge: Cambridge University Press.

EIU. 1984. *The Major European Economies, 1984-1990*. Economic Intelligence Unit, Special Report No. 173. London: The Economist.

Elboim-Dror, Rachel. 1982. "Israel: Sysyphean Reform Cycles." In *Strategies for Administrative Reform*, edited by G. Caiden and H. Seidenkopf. Lexington, MA: Heath.

Elder, Charles, and Roger W. Cobb. 1983. *The Political Uses of Symbols*. New York: Longman.

Elder, Neil, Alastair H. Thomas, and David Apter. 1982. *The Consensual Democracies? The Government and Politics of the Scandinavian States*. London: M. Robertson.

Eldersveld, Samuel Z., Jan Kooiman, and Theo van der Tak. 1981. *Elite Images of Dutch Politics: Accommodation and Conflict*. Ann Arbor: University of Michigan Press.

Elgin, Duane. 1982. *Television and Democracy at the Crossroads: A Report on Changing Public Attitudes*. Research Report No. 1. Menlo Park, CA: Citizens for Video Democracy.

Elias, Norbert. 1977. *The Civilizing Process*. Vol. 1, *The Development of Manners*. New York: Pantheon. Translated from the German.

Eliassen, Kjell A., and Mogens N. Pedersen. 1978. "Professionalization of Legislatures: Long-Term Change in Political Recruitment in Denmark and Norway." *Comparative Studies in Society and History* 20: 286-318.

Elliot, J.H. 1984. *Richelieu and Olivares*. Cambridge: Cambridge University Press.

Ellis, Adrian, and Krishan Kumar, eds. 1983. *Dilemmas of Liberal Democracies: Studies in Fred Hirsch's Social Limits to Growth*. London: Chapman & Hall.

Ellman, M. 1979. *Socialist Planning*. Cambridge: Cambridge University Press.

Ellwood, John William. 1981. "Making and Enforcing Federal Spending Limitations: Issues and Options." *Public Budgeting and Finance* 1 (Spring): 28-42.

_____, ed. 1982. *Reductions in U. S. Domestic Spending: How They Affect State and Local Governments*. New Brunswick, NJ: Transaction.

Elstein, Arthur S., et al. 1978. *Medical Problem Solving: An Analysis of Clinical Reasoning*. Cambridge: Harvard University Press.

Elster, Jon. 1978. *Logic and Society: Contradictions and Possible Worlds*. New York: Wiley.

_____. 1979. *Ulysses and the Sirens: Studies in Rationality and Irrationality.* Cambridge: Cambridge University Press.

_____. 1983. *Explaining Technical Change: A Case Study in the Philosophy of Science.* Cambridge: Cambridge University Press.

_____. 1983. *Sour Grapes: Studies in the Subversion of Rationality.* Cambridge: Cambridge University Press.

Emerson, Robert M. 1983. "Holistic Effects in Social Control Decision-Making." *Law and Society Review* 17, no. 3: 425-55.

Emery, F.E., and E.L. Trist. 1972. *Towards a Social Ecology: Contextual Appreciation of the Future in the Present.* London: Plenum Press.

England, George W., Anant R. Negandhi, and Bernard Wilpert. 1981. *The Functioning of Complex Organizations.* Cambridge, MA: Oelgeschlager, Gunn & Hain.

Enke, Stephen. 1967. *Think Tanks for Better Government.* Santa Monica, CA: Tempo Corporation.

Environmental Protection Agency. 1973. *The Quality of Life Concept: A Potential New Tool for Decision-Makers.* Washington, DC: Environmental Protection Agency, Office of Research and Monitoring, Environmental Studies Division.

Eppler, Erhard. 1981. *Wege aus der Gefahr.* Reinbek bei Hamburg: Rowohlt.

Erdmann, Karl Dietrich, and Hagen Schulze, eds. 1980. *Weimar: Selbstpreisgabe einer Demokratie: Eine Bilanz Heute.* Düsseldorf: Droste Verlag.

Erikson, Erik H. 1975. *Life History and the Historical Moment: Diverse Presentations.* New York: Norton.

Erickson, James R., and Marie Riess Jones. 1978. "Thinking." *Annual Review of Psychology* 29: 61-90.

Esbery, E. Joy. 1980. *Knight of the Holy Spirit: A Study of William Lyon Mackenzie King.* Toronto: University of Toronto Press.

Eschenburg, Rolf. 1977. *Der Ökonomische Ansatz zu einer Theorie der Verfassung: Die Entwicklung einer liberalen Verfassung im Spannungsverhältnis zwischen Produktivität und Effektivität der Kooperation.* Tübingen: J.C.B. Mohr.

Eschenburg, Theodor. 1976. *Über Autorität.* Rev. ed. Frankfurt am Main: Suhrkamp.

Esman, Milton J., ed. 1977. *Ethnic Conflict in the Western World.* Ithaca, NY: Cornell University Press.

Estrin, Saul, and Peter Holmes. 1983. *French Planning in Theory and Practice.* London: Allen & Unwin.

Etheredge, Lloyd S. 1984. *Can Governments Learn?* Elmsford, NY: Pergamon.

Etzioni, Amitai. 1968. *The Active Society: A Theory of Societal and Political Processes.* New York: Free Press.

_____. 1982. *An Immodest Agenda: Rebuilding America Before the 21st Century. Our Economic, Ethical, Personal and Political Options for the Next Two Decades.* New York: McGraw-Hill.

Etzioni, Amitai, and Richard Remp. 1973. *Technological Shortcuts to Social Change.* New York: Russell Sage Foundation.

Etzioni-Halevy, Eva. 1983. *Bureaucracy and Democracy: A Political Dilemma.* London: Routledge & Kegan Paul.

Evans, Ernest. 1979. *Calling a Truce to Terror: The American Response to International Terrorism.* Westport, CT: Greenwood Press.

Eversley, David, and Wolfgang Köllmann, eds. 1982. *Population Change and Social Planning: Social and Economic Implications of the Recent Decline in Fertility in the United Kingdom and the Federal Republic of Germany.* London: Edward Arnold.

Faber, Karl-George, and Christian Meier, eds. 1978. *Historische Prozesse.* Munich: Deutscher Taschenbuch Verlag.

Fain, Tyrus G., et al. 1977. *Federal Reorganization: The Executive Branch.* Public Documents Series. New York: Bowker.

Fairweather, George W., and Louis G. Tornatzky. 1977. *Experimental Methods for Social Policy Research.* New York: Pergamon.

Falco, Maria J., ed. 1979. *Through the Looking Glass: Epistemology and the Conduct of Inquiry, An Anthology.* Lanham, MD: University Press of America.

Falk, Richard A. 1975. *A Study of Future Worlds.* New York: Free Press.

Fallows, James. 1981. *National Defense.* New York: Random House.

Fawcett, Edmund, and Tony Thomas. 1982. *The American Condition.* New York: Harper & Row.

Feeley, Malcolm M. 1983. *Court Reform on Trial: Why Simple Solutions Fail.* New York: Basic Books.

Feigenbaum, Edward A., and Pamela McCorduck. 1984. *The Fifth Generation: Artificial Intelligence and Japan's Computer Challenge to the World.* Rev. ed., London: Pan Books.

Feinberg, Richard E. 1983. *The Intemperate Zone: The Third World Challenge to U.S. Foreign Policy.* New York: Norton.

Feinberg, Walter, ed. 1978. *Equality and Social Policy.* Urbana: University of Illinois Press.

Femia, Joseph V. 1981. *Gramsci's Political Thought: Hegemony, Consciousness, and the Revolutionary Process.* Oxford: Oxford University Press.

Ferber, Christian von, and Franz-Xaver Kaufmann, eds. 1977. *Soziologie und Sozialpolitik.* Opladen: Westdeutscher.

Ferber, Robert, and Werner Z. Hirsch. 1981. *Social Experimentation and Economic Policy.* Cambridge: Cambridge University Press.

Ferns, H.S. 1978. *The Disease of Government.* New York: St. Martin's Press.

Feshbach, Murray. 1982. "Between the Lines of the 1979 Soviet Census." *Problems of Communism* 31 (January/February): 27-37.

Fest, Joachim C. 1975. *Hitler.* New York: Vintage Books. Translated from the German.

Festinger, Leon. 1983. *The Human Legacy.* New York: Columbia University Press.

Fick, G., and R.H. Sprague, Jr., eds. 1981. *Decision Support Systems: Issues and Challenges.* IIASA Volume. Oxford: Pergamon.

Field, G. Lowell, and John Higley. 1980. *Elitism.* London: Routledge & Kegan Paul.

Fijalkowski, Jürgen. 1958. *Die Wendung zum Führerstaat: Ideologische Komponenten in der Politischen Philosophie Carl Schmitts.* Cologne: Westdeutscher.

Findley, Carter V. 1980. *Bureaucratic Reform in the Ottoman Empire: The Sublime Porte, 1789-1922*. Princeton: Princeton University Press.

Finer, S.E. [1952] 1970. *The Life and Times of Sir Edwin Chadwick*. Reprint. New York: Barnes & Noble.

Finifter, Ada W., ed. 1983. *Political Science: The State of the Discipline*. Washington, DC: American Political Science Association.

Finlay, David J., Ole R. Holsti, and Richard R. Fagen. 1967. *Enemies in Politics*. Chicago: Rand McNally.

Finley, M.I. 1983. *Politics in the Ancient World*. Cambridge: Cambridge University Press.

Fischer, Dan. 1983. "Draft Report by Communist Panel Blames Polish Leaders for Crisis." *International Herald Tribune*, 19 January, 1, 2.

Fischer, David Hackett. 1970. *Historians' Fallacies: Toward a Logic of Historical Thought*. New York: Harper & Row.

Fischer, Frank. 1980. *Politics, Values, and Public Policy: The Problem of Methodology*. Boulder, CO: Westview.

Fischer, Heinz, ed. 1977. *Das Politische System Österreichs*. 2d ed. Vienna: Europaverlag.

Fischer, Wolfram. 1968. *Deutsche Wirtschaftspolitik 1918-1945*. Opladen: C.W. Leske.

Fischhoff, B. 1974. "Aspects of Historical Judgment." Ph.D. diss., Hebrew University of Jerusalem.

Fischhoff, Baruch, and Ruth Beyth. 1975. "I Knew It Would Happen—Remembering Probabilities of Once Future Things." *Organizational Behavior and Human Performance* 13: 1-16.

Fischhoff, B., et al. 1981. *Acceptable Risk*. Cambridge: Cambridge University Press.

Fisher, Howard. 1984. *Mapping Information*. Cambridge, MA: Abt Books.

Fishman, Joshua A. 1972. *The Sociology of Language: An Interdisciplinary Social Science Approach to Language in Society*. Rowley, MA: Newbury House.

Flathman, Richard E. 1980. *The Practice of Political Authority: Authority and the Authoritative*. Chicago: University of Chicago Press.

Fleming, Gerald. 1982. *Hitler und die Endlösung: Es ist des Führers Wunsch*. Munich: Limes.

Fletcher, A.J. 1983. *The Outbreak of English Civil War*. London: Edward Arnold.

Flickinger, Richard. 1983. "The Comparative Politics of Agenda Setting: The Emergence of Consumer Protection as a Public Policy Issue in Britain and the United States." *Policy Studies Review* 2 (February): 429-44.

Floher, H. 1980. *Possible Climatic Consequences of a Man-Made Global Warming*. RR-80-30. Laxenburg, Austria: International Institute for Applied Systems Analysis.

Flora, Peter, and A.J. Heidenheimer, eds. 1980. *The Development of Welfare States in Europe and America*. New Brunswick, NJ: Transaction.

Forrester, Jay W. 1969. *Urban Dynamics*. Cambridge, MA: MIT Press.

Forstmeier, Friedrich, and Hans-Erich Volkmann, eds. 1975. *Wirtschaft und Rüstung am Vorabend des Zweiten Weltkrieges*. Düsseldorf: Droste Verlag.

Forstmeier, Friedrich, and Hans-Erich Volkmann, eds. 1977. *Kriegswirtschaft und Rüstung, 1939-1945*. Düsseldorf: Droste Verlag.

Forsyth, Murray. 1982. *Unions of States: The Theory and Practice of Confederation*. Leicester, United Kingdom: Leicester University Press.

Foster, C. F. 1980. *Comparative Public Policy and Citizen Participation*. New York: Pergamon.

Foucault, Michel. 1976. *The Archaeology of Knowledge*, New York: Harper & Row. Translated from the French.

Francis, Arthur, Jeremy Turk, and Paul Willman, eds. 1982. *Power, Efficiency and Institutions: A Critical Appraisal of the 'Markets and Hierarchies' Paradigm*. London: Heinemann.

Frank, André Gunder. 1980. *Crisis: In the Third World*. New York: Holmes & Meier.

————. 1981. *Crisis: In the World Economy*. New York: Holmes & Meier.

Frank, Dietrich. 1976. *Politische Planung im Spannungsverhältnis zwischen Regierung und Parlament*. Meisenheim an Glan: Anton Hain.

Frankel, Boris. 1979. "On the State of the State: Marxist Theories of the State after Leninism." *Theory and Society* 7 (January-March): 199-242.

Frankel, Glenn. 1984. "The Afrikaners: A Tribe Divided." *International Herald Tribune*, 7-10 August.

Frankfort, Henri. 1958. *Kingship and the Gods: A Study of Ancient Near Eastern Religions as the Integration of Society and Nature*. Chicago: University of Chicago Press. Phoenix ed., with new preface, 1978.

Frankfurt, Harry G. 1971. "Freedom of the Will and the Concept of a Person." *Journal of Philosophy* 68: 5-20.

Franks, The Lord, Chairman. 1982. *Falkland Islands Review: Report of a Committee of Privy Counsellors*. Cmnd. 8787. London: Her Majesty's Stationery Office.

Franqui, Carlos. 1980. *Diary of the Cuban Revolution*. New York: Viking.

Fratianni, M., and F. Soinelli. 1982. "The Growth of Government in Italy: Evidence from 1861 to 1979." *Public Choice* 32, no. 2: 221-44.

Freedman, Anne E., and P.E. Freedman. 1975. *The Psychology of Political Control*. New York: St. Martin's Press.

Freedman, James O. 1978. *Crisis and Legitimacy: The Administrative Process and American Government*. Cambridge: Cambridge University Press.

Freeman, Christopher, ed. 1983. *Long Waves in the World Economy*. Borough Green, United Kingdom: Butterworth.

Freeman, C., and M. Jahoda, eds. 1978. *World Futures: The Great Debate*. London: M. Robertson.

Freeman, Derek. 1983. *Margaret Mead and Samoa: The Making and Unmaking of an Anthropological Myth*. Cambridge: Harvard University Press.

Frei, D. 1979. *International Crises and Crisis Management*. Farnborough, United Kingdom: Saxon House.

Frei, Daniel, ed. 1982. *Managing International Crises*. Beverly Hills, CA: Sage.

French, David. 1982. *British Economic and Strategic Planning, 1905-1915*. London: Allen & Unwin.

French, Richard D. 1980. *How Ottawa Decides: Planning and Industrial Policy-Making, 1968-1980*. Toronto: James Lorimer, for the Canadian Institute for Economic Policy.

Friedmann, John. 1979. *The Good Society: A Primer for Social Practice*. Cambridge: Harvard University Press.

Friedrichs, Gunter, and Adam Schaff, eds. 1982. *Microelectronics and Society: For Better or for Worse*. A report to the Club of Rome. Elmsford, NY: Pergamon.

Fritsch, Bruno. 1981. *Wir werden Überleben: Orientierungen und Hoffnungen in Schwieriger Zeit*. Munich: Olzog.

Fritschler, A. Lee. 1983. *Smoking and Politics: Policymaking and the Federal Bureaucracy*. 3d ed. Englewood Cliffs, NJ: Prentice-Hall.

Frohick, Fred M. 1979. *Public Policy: Scope and Logic*. Englewood Cliffs, NJ: Prentice-Hall.

Fry, Geoffrey Kingdon. 1969. *Statesmen in Disguise: The Changing of the Administrative Class of the British Home Civil Service, 1853-1966*. London: Macmillan.

_____. 1979. *The Growth of Government: The Development of Ideas about the Role of the State and the Machinery and Functions of Government in Britain since 1780*. London: Cass.

_____. 1981. *The Administrative 'Revolution' in Whitehall*. London: Croom Helm.

Fuchser, Larry William. 1983. *Neville Chamberlain and Appeasement: A Study in the Politics of History*. New York: Norton.

Fuller, R. Buckminster. 1978. *Operating Manual for Spaceship Earth*. New York: Dutton.

Galbraith, Jay R. 1977. *Organization Design*. Reading, MA: Addison-Wesley.

Galbraith, John Kenneth. 1979. *The Nature of Mass Poverty*. Cambridge: Harvard University Press.

_____. 1983. *The Anatomy of Power*. Boston: Houghton Mifflin.

Gall, John. 1975. *Systemantics: How Systems Work and Especially How They Fail*. New York: Quadrangle.

Gall, Lothar. 1980. *Bismarck Der Weisse Revolutionär*, Frankfurt am Main: Verlag Ullstein.

Galnoor, Itzhak, ed. 1977. *Government Secrecy in Democracies*. New York: Harper.

_____. 1982. *Steering the Polity: Communication and Politics in Israel*. Beverly Hills, CA: Sage.

Galtung, Johan. 1980. *The True Worlds*. New York: Institute for World Order.

Gardner, H. Stephen. 1982. *Soviet Foreign Trade: The Decision Process*. Hingham, MA: Kluwer.

Gardner, Howard. 1982. *Art, Mind and Brain: A Cognitive Approach to Creativity*. New York: Basic Books.

_____. 1983. *Frames of Mind: The Theory of Multiple Intelligences*. New York: Basic Books.

Gardner, John. 1982. *Chinese Politics and the Succession to Mao*. London: Macmillan.

Garraty, John A. 1978. *Unemployment in History: Economic Thought and Public Policy*. New York: Harper & Row.

Garthoff, Raymond L. 1984. *Intelligence Assessment and Policymaking: A Decision Point in the Kennedy Administration*. Washington, DC: Brookings Institution.

Gaxotte, Pierre. 1973. *Friedrich der Grosse*. Rev. ed. Frankfurt am Main: Verlag Ullstein. Translated from the French.

Geertz, Clifford. 1980. *Negara: The Theatre State in Nineteenth-Century Bali*. Princeton: Princeton University Press.

_____. 1983. *Local Knowledge: Further Essays in Interpretive Anthropology*. New York: Basic Books.

Geist, B., ed. 1981. *State Audit: Developments in Public Accountability*. London: Macmillan.

Gelb, Leslie H., with Richard Betts. 1979. *The Irony of Vietnam: The System Worked*. Washington, DC: Brookings Institution.

Gellner, Ernest. 1974. *Legitimation and Belief*. Cambridge: Cambridge University Press.

_____. 1979. *Spectacles and Predicaments: Essays in Social Theory*, edited by I.C. Jarvie and J. Agassi. Cambridge: Cambridge University Press.

_____. 1983. *Nations and Nationalism*. Oxford: Blackwell.

_____. 1983. "Stagnation Without Salvation: Review of Stephen P. Dunn, *The Fall and Rise of the Asian Mode of Production*." *Times Literary Supplement*, no. 4163 (14 January): 27-28.

Gelman, Harry. 1981. *The Politburo's Management of Its American Problem*. R-2707-NA. Santa Monica, CA: Rand Corporation.

Gentner, D., and A. L. Stevens. 1983. *Mental Models: Cognitive Science*. Hillsdale, NJ: Erlbaum.

George, Alexander L. 1980. *Presidential Decisionmaking in Foreign Policy: The Effective Use of Information and Advice*. Boulder, CO: Westview.

George, S.A. 1984. *Politics and Policy in the European Community*. Oxford: Oxford University Press.

Germann, Raimund E. 1975. *Politische Innovation und Verfassungsreform: Ein Beitrag zur schweizerischen Diskussion Über die Totalrevision der Bundesverfassungs*. St. Galler Studien zur Politikwissenschaft. Bern: Paul Haupt.

Gershuny, Jonathan I. 1978. "Policymaking Rationality: A Reformulation," *Policy Sciences* 9: 295-316.

_____.1979. *After Industrial Society: The Emerging Self-service Economy*. Atlantic Highlands, NJ: Humanities Press.

Gershuny, Jonathan I., and I.D. Miles. 1983. *The New Service Economy: The Transformation of Employment in Industrial Societies*. London: Pinter.

Geuss, Raymond. 1981. *The Idea of a Critical Theory: Habermas and the Frankfurt School*. Cambridge: Cambridge University Press.

Geyer, R. Felix, and Johannes van der Zouwen, eds. 1978. *Sociocybernetics: An Actor-Oriented Social Systems Approach*. 2 vols. Boston: Martinus Nijhoff.

Geze, François, Yves Lacoste, and Alfredo Valladao. 1982. *World View 1983: What the Press and Television Have Not Told You about the Year's Mega-Issues*. New York: Pantheon. Adapted from the French.

Gibney, Frank. 1983. *Miracle by Design: The Real Reasons Behind Japan's Economic Success.* New York: Times Book.

Gifford, Prosser, and W.M. Roger Louis, eds. 1983. *the Transfer of Power in Africa: Decolonization, 1940-1960.* New Haven: Yale University Press.

Gilbert, Charles E., ed. 1983. *Implementing Governmental Change.* Special issue, *Annals of the American Academy of Political and Social Sciences* 466 (March).

Gilbert, Felix. 1965. *Machiavelli and Guicciardini: Politics and History in Sixteenth-Century Florence.* Princeton: Princeton University Press.

———. ed. 1975. *The Historic Essays of Otto Hintze.* New York: Oxford University Press.

———. 1977. *History: Choice and Commitment.* Cambridge: Harvard University Press.

Gilbert, Neil. 1983. *Capitalism and the Welfare State.* New Haven: Yale University Press.

Gilder, George. 1981. *Wealth and Poverty.* New York: Basic Books.

Giliomee, Hermann. 1982. *The Parting of the Ways: South African Politics, 1976-1982.* Cape Town: D. Philip.

Glass, Gene V. 1980. "Evaluation Research." *Annual Review of Psychology* 31: 211-28.

Glazer, Nathan. 1983. *Ethnic Dilemmas, 1964-1982.* Cambridge: Harvard University Press.

Glotz, Peter. 1982. *Die Beweglichkeit des Tankers: Die Sozialdemokratie zwischen Staat und neuen sozialen Bewegungen.* Munich: C. Bertelsmann.

Glucksmann, André. 1984. *Philosophie der abschreckung.* Translated from French. Stuttgart: Deutsche Verlags-Anstalt.

Godson, Roy, ed. 1980. *Intelligence Requirements for the 1980s: Analysis and Estimates.* Washington, DC: National Strategy Information Center, and New Brunswick, NJ: Transaction.

Godwin, P. Kenneth, ed. 1975. *Comparative Policy Analysis.* Lexington, MA: Lexington Books.

Goebel, Julius. 1982. *The Struggle for the Falkland Islands: A Study in Legal and Diplomatic History.* New Haven: Yale University Press. First published 1927.

Goeller, B.F., et al. 1977. *Protecting an Estuary from Floods: A Policy Analysis of the Oosterschelde.* Vol. 1, *Summary Report.* R-2121/1-NETH. Santa Monica, CA: Rand Corporation.

———. 1983. *Policy Analysis of Water Management in the Netherlands.* Vol. 1, *Summary Report.* R-2500/1-NETH. Santa Monica, CA: Rand Corporation.

Goerlitz, Walter. 1961. *The German General Staff, 1657-1945.* New York: Praeger.

Goerner, E.A., ed. 1971. *Democracy in Crisis: New Challenges to Constitutional Democracy in the Atlantic Area.* Notre Dame: University of Notre Dame Press.

Goldhamer, Herbert. 1978. *The Adviser.* New York: Elsevier.

Goldman, Marshall I. 1983. *U.S.S.R. in Crisis: The Failure of an Economic System.* New York: Norton.

Goldsmith, William M. 1974. *The Growth of Presidential Power: A Documented History.* Vol. 1, *The Formative Years.* Vol. 2, *Decline and Resurgence.* Vol. 3, *Triumph and Reappraisal.* New York: Bowker.

Goldthorpe, John H., ed. 1984. *Order and Conflict in Contemporary Capitalism: Studies in the Political Economy of West European Nations.* Oxford: Oxford University Press.

Goldwin, Robert A., ed. 1980. *Bureaucrats, Policy Analysis, Statesman: Who Leads?.* Washington, DC: American Enterprise Institute.

Golembiewski, Robert T. 1979. *Approaches to Planned Change.* Part 2, *Macro-Level Interventions and Change-Agent Strategies.* New York: Dekker.

Gombrich, E.H. 1983. *The Sense of Order: A Study in the Psychology of Decorative Art.* Ithaca, NY: Cornell University Press.

Gomez, Peter, Fredmund Malik, and Karl-Heinz Oeller. 1975. *Systemmethodik: Grundlagen einer Methodik zur Erforschung und Gestaltung komplexer soziotechnischer Systeme.* 2 vols. Bern: Verlag Paul Haupt.

Gooch, John. 1974. *The Plans of War.* London: Routledge & Kegan Paul.

Gooch, John, and Amos Perlmutter, eds. 1982. *Military Deception and Strategic Surprise.* London: Cass.

Goode, William J. 1978. *The Celebration of Heroes: Prestige as a Control System.* Berkeley and Los Angeles: University of California Press.

Goodin, E. Robert. 1980. *Manipulatory Politics.* New Haven: Yale University Press.

———. 1982. *Political Theory and Public Policy.* Chicago: University of Chicago Press.

Goodman, Paul S., and Johannes M. Pennings, eds. 1977. *New Perspectives on Organizational Effectiveness.* San Francisco: Jossey-Bass.

Goodwin, Barbara, and Keith Taylor. 1982. *The Politics of Utopia: A Study in Theory and Practice.* London: Hutchinson.

Gorman, Stephen M., ed. 1982. *Post-Revolutionary Peru: The Politics of Transformation.* Boulder, CO: Westview.

Gottfried, Robert S. 1983. *The Black Death: Natural and Human Disaster in Medieval Europe.* New York: Free Press.

Gouldner, Alvin W. 1979. *The Future of Intellectuals and the Rise of the New Class.* London: Macmillan.

Gowing, Margaret, assisted by Lorna Arnold. 1974. *Independence and Deterrence: Britain and Atomic Energy, 1945-1952.* Vol. 1, *Policy Making.* London: Macmillan.

Graber, Doris A. 1984. *Processing the News: How People Tame the Information Tide.* New York: Longman.

Graebner, William. 1980. *A History of Retirement: The Meaning and Function of an American Institution, 1885-1978.* New Haven: Yale University Press.

Grafton, Carl, and Anne Permaloff. 1983. "Budgeting Reforms in Perspective." In *Handbook on Public Budgeting and Financial Management,* edited by Jack Rabin and Thomas D. Lynch. New York: Dekker.

Graham, A.K. and P.M. Senge. 1980. "A Long-Wave Hypothesis on Innovation." *Technological Forecasting and Social Change* 17: 283-311.

Graham, George A. 1960. *America's Capacity to Govern: Some Preliminary Thoughts for Prospective Administrators.* University: University of Alabama Press.

Graham, Otil L., Jr. 1976. *Towards a Planned Society: From Roosevelt to Nixon.* New York: Oxford University Press.

Grainger, Alan. 1983. *Desertification.* London: Earthscan, for International Institute for Environment and Development.

Grainger, L., and J. Gibson. 1981. *Coal Utilization: Technology, Economics, and Policy.* London: Graham & Trotman.

Granovetter, Mark. 1979. "The Idea of 'Advancement' in Theories of Social Evolution and Development." *American Journal of Sociology* 85: 489-515.

Grant, George F. 1979. *Development Administration: Concepts, Goals, Methods.* Madison: University of Wisconsin Press.

Grant, Wyn. 1982. *The Political Economy of Industrial Policy.* London: Butterworth.

Graubard, M.H., and C.H. Builder. 1980. *Rand's Strategic Assessment Center: An Overview of the Concept.* N-1583-DNA. Santa Monica, CA: Rand Corporation.

Graubard, Stephen R., ed. 1981. *The State.* New York: Norton.

Grauhan, Rolf Richard, and Rudolf Hickel, eds. 1978. *Krise des Steuerstaates? Wiedersprüche, Perspektiven, Ausweichstrategien.* Opladen: Westdeutscher.

Gray, Andrew, and Bill Jenkins. 1982. "Policy Analysis in British Central Government: The Experience of PAR." *Public Administration* 60 (Winter): 429-50.

Greenberger, Martin, et al. 1983. *Caught Unawares: The Energy Decade in Retrospect.* Cambridge, MA: Ballinger.

Greenblatt, Sidney L., Richard W. Wilson, and Amy Auerbacher Wilson, eds. 1981. *Organizational Behavior in Chinese Society.* New York: Praeger.

Greene, Kenyon D., De. 1982. *The Adaptive Organization: Anticipation and Management in Crisis.* New York: Wiley.

Greene, Thomas H. 1983. *Comparative Revolutionary Movements: Search for Theory and Justice.* 2d ed. Englewood Cliffs, NJ: Prentice-Hall.

Greenleaf, W.H. 1983. *The British Political Tradition.* Vol. 1, *The Rise of Collectivism.* London: Methuen.

Greenstein, Fred I. 1970. *Personality and Politics.* Chicago: Markham.

———. 1982. *The Hidden-Hand Presidency. Eisenhower as Leader.* New York: Basic Books.

Greenstein, Fred I., and M. Lerner, eds. 1971. *A Sourcebook for the Study of Personality and Politics.* Chicago: Markham.

Greenstein, F., and N. Polsby, eds. 1975. *Handbook of Political Science.* 9 Vols. Vol. 6, *Policies and Policymaking.* Reading, MA: Addison-Wesley.

Greenstone, J. David, ed. 1982. *Public Values and Private Power in American Politics.* Chicago: University of Chicago Press.

Greider, William. 1982. *The Education of David Stockman and Other Americans.* New York: Dutton.

Greiffenhagen, Martin, ed. 1973. *Demokratisierung in Staat und Gesellschaft.* Munich: R. Piper.

_____, ed. 1978. *Zur Theorie der Reform: Entwurfe und Strategien.* Karlsruhe: C.F. Müller.

Gremion, Catherine. 1979. *Profession: Décideurs pouvoir des hauts fonctionnaires et réforme de l'état.* Paris: Gaulhier-Villars.

Greven, Michael Th. 1974. *Systemtheorie und Gesellschaftsanalyse: Kritik der Werte und Erkenntnismöglichkeiten in Gesellschaftsmodellen der kybernetischen Systemtheorie.* Darmstadt: Luchterhand.

Grew, Raymond, ed. 1978. *Crisis of Political Development in Europe and the United States.* Princeton: Princeton University Press.

Grindle, Merilee S. 1977. *Bureaucrats, Politicians and Peasants in Mexico: A Study in Public Policy.* Berkeley and Los Angeles: University of California Press.

_____, ed. 1980. *Politics and Policy Implementation in the Third World.* Rev. ed., 1983. Princeton: Princeton University Press.

Groot, Adriaan D., de. 1965. *Thought and Choice in Chess.* The Hague: Mouton.

Gross, Bertram. 1964. *The Managing of Organizations: The Administrative Struggle.* 2 vols. New York: Free Press.

_____, ed. 1964. *Social Intelligence for America's Future.* Boston: Allyn & Bacon.

_____. 1982. *Friendly Fascism: The New Face of Power in America.* Boston, MA: South End Press. Supplemented edition. First published 1980.

Grossman, Michael Baruch, and Martha Joynt Kumat. 1981. *Portraying the President: The White House and the News Media.* Baltimore: Johns Hopkins University Press.

Grottian, Peter, and Axel Murswieck, eds. 1974. *Handlungsspielraüme der Staatsadministration: Beiträge zur Politologisch-Soziologischen Verwaltungsforschung.* Hamburg: Hoffmann & Campe.

Grove, Andrew S. 1983. *High Output Management.* New York: Random House.

Grube, Frank, Gerhard Richter, and Uwe Thaysen. 1976. *Politische Planung in Parteien und Parlamentsfraktionen.* Göttingen: Schwartz.

Gruhl, Herbert. 1975. *Ein Planet wird geplündert: Die Schreckensbilanz unserer Politik.* Frankfurt: Fischer.

Grumm, John G. 1975. "The Analysis of Policy Impact." In *Handbook of Political Science.* Vol. 6, *Policies and Policymaking,* edited by F. Greenstein and N. Polsby. Reading, MA: Addison-Wesley.

Guha, Ashok S. 1982. *An Evolutionary View of Economic Growth.* Oxford: Oxford University Press.

Guillemard, A.M., ed. 1983. *Old Age and the Welfare State.* Beverly Hills, CA: Sage.

Guldimann, Tim. 1976. *Die Grenzen des Wohlfahrtsstaates: Am Beispiel Schwedens und der Bundesrepublik.* Munich: C.H. Beck.

Gunther, Richard. 1980. *Public Policy in a No-Party State: Spanish Planning and Budgeting in the Twilight of the Franquist Era.* Berkeley and Los Angeles: University of California Press.

Gurr, Ted. 1970. *Why Men Rebel.* Princeton: Princeton University Press.

Gustafsson, G., and J.J. Richardson. 1979. "Concepts of Rationality and the Policy Process." *European Journal of Political Research* 7, no. 4: 415-36.

Guttman, Daniel, and Barry Willner. 1976. *The Shadow Government: The Government's Multibillion-Dollar Giveaway of Its Decision-making Powers to Private*

*Management Consultants, "Experts," and Think Tanks.* New York: Pantheon.

Gwyn, William B., and George C. Edwards III, eds. 1975. *Perspectives on Public Policy-Making.* Vol. 15, Tulane Studies in Political Science. New Orleans: Tulane University.

Gyorgy, Andrew, and James A. Kuhlman, eds. 1978. *Innovation in Communist Systems.* Boulder, CO: Westview.

Haas, Ernst B. 1983. "Regime Decay: Conflict Management and International Organizations, 1945-1981." *International Organization* 37 (Spring): 189-256.

Habermas, Jürgen. 1971. *Theory und Praxis: Sozialphilosophische Studien.* Frankfurt am Main: Suhrkamp.

––––––. 1976. *Legitimation Crisis.* London: Heinemann.

––––––. 1982. *Zur Logik der Sozialwissenschaften.* Frankfurt am Main: Suhrkamp

––––––. 1984. *The Theory of Communicative Action.* Vol. 1: *Reason and the Rationalization of Society.* London: Heinemann.

Habermas, Jürgen, and Niklas Luhmann. 1971. *Theorie der Gesellschaft oder Sozialtechnologie—Was leistet die Systemforschung?.* Frankfurt am Main: Suhrkamp.

Hackett, John. 1982. *The Third World War: The Untold Story.* 2d ed. New York: Macmillan.

Hacking, Ian. 1975. *The Emergence of Probability,* New York: Cambridge University Press.

Haendel, Dan. 1977. *The Process of Priority Formulation: U.S. Foreign Policy in the Indo-Paskistani War of 1971.* Boulder, CO: Westview.

Häfele, Wolf. 1981. *Energy in a Finite World: Paths to a Sustainable Future.* IIASA volume. Cambridge, MA: Ballinger.

Hagopian, Mark N. 1974. *The Phenomenon of Revolution.* New York: Dodd, Mead.

Hall, Peter. 1982. *Great Planning Disasters.* Supp. ed. Berkeley and Los Angeles: University of California Press.

Hall, Richard H., and Robert E. Quinn, eds. 1980. *Organizational Theory and Public Policy.* Beverly Hills, CA: Sage Publications.

Hall, Roger I. 1976. "A System Pathology of an Organization: The Rise and Fall of the Saturday Evening Post." *Administrative Science Quarterly* 21: 185-211.

––––––. 1981. "Decisionmaking in a Complex Organization." In *The Functioning of Complex Organizations,* edited by George W. England, Anant R. Negandhi, and Bernard Wilpert. Cambridge, MA: Oelgeschlager, Gunn & Hain.

Halliday, Jon, and Peter Fuller, eds. 1974. *The Psychology of Gambling.* New York: Penguin.

Halliday, M.A.K. 1978. *Language as Social Semiotic: The Social Interpretation of Language and Meaning.* Baltimore, MD: University Park Press.

Hallowell, John H., ed. 1976. *Prospects for Constitutional Democracy: Essays in Honor of R. Taylor Cole.* Durham, NC: Duke University Press.

Halsey, A.H. 1978. *Change in British Society.* Oxford: Oxford University Press.

Hames, R.B., and W.T. Vickers, eds. 1983. *Adaptive Responses of Native Amazonians.* New York: Academic Press.

Hamilton, Nora. 1983. *The Limits of State Autonomy: Post-Revolutionary Mexico.* Princeton: Princeton University Press.

Hammack, David C. 1982. *Power and Society: Greater New York at the Turn of the Century.* New York: Russell Sage Foundation.

Hammergren, L.A. 1983. *Development and the Politics of Administrative Reform: Lessons from Latin America.* Boulder, CO: Westview.

Handel, I. Michael. 1981. *The Diplomacy of Surprise: Hitler, Nixon, Sadat.* Cambridge: Harvard University Center for International Affairs.

Handy, Charles. 1984. *The Future of Work.* Oxford: Blackwell.

Handy, Rollo. 1970. *The Measurement of Values: Behavioral Science and Philosophical Approaches,* St. Louis, MO: Warren H. Green.

Hanf, Kenneth, and Fritz W. Scharpf, eds. 1978. *Interorganizational Policy Making: Limits to Coordination and Central Control.* Beverly Hills, CA: Sage.

Hansard Society. 1979. *Politics and Industry—the Great Mismatch.* London: Hansard Society.

Hansen, Roger D. 1979. *Beyond the North-South Stalemate.* New York: McGraw-Hill.

Hansen, Susan B. 1983. "Public Policy Analysis: Some Recent Developments and Current Problems." *Policy Studies Journal* 12 (September): 14-42.

Haraszti, Eva H. 1983. *The Invaders: Hitler Occupies the Rhineland.* Budapest: Akademiai Kiado.

Hardin, Charles M. 1974. *Presidential Power and Accountability: Towards a New Constitution.* Chicago: University of Chicago Press.

Hardin, Russell. 1983. *Collective Action.* Baltimore: Johns Hopkins University Press.

Harding,. Harry. 1981. *Organizing China: The Problem of Bureaucracy, 1949-1976.* Stanford: Stanford University Press.

Harding, Neil. 1984. *The State in Socialist Society.* London: Macmillan.

Hargrove, Erwin. 1975. *The Missing Link: The Study of the Implementation of Social Policy.* Washington, DC: Urban Institute.

Hargrove, Erwin, and Paul K. Conkin, eds. 1984. *TVA: Fifty Years of Grass-Roots Bureaucracy..* Champaign: University of Illinois Press.

Harmel, Robert, and Kenneth Janda 1982. *Parties and Their Environments: Limits to Reform?* New York: Longman.

Harrel, Allen T. 1978. *New Methods in Social Science Research: Policy Sciences and Futures Research.* New York: Praeger.

Harrington, Michael. 1983. *The Politics at God's Funeral: The Spiritual Crisis of Western Civilization.* New York: Holt, Rinehart & Winston.

Harris, José. 1977. *William Beveridge: A Biography.* Oxford: Clarendon.

Harris, Marvin. 1977. *Cannibals and Kings: The Origins of Culture.* New York: Vintage.

Harrison, Brian. 1982. *Peaceable Kingdom: Stability and Change in Modern Britain.* Oxford: Clarendon.

Harrison, Reginald J. 1980. *Pluralism and Corporatism: The Political Evolution of Modern Democracies.* London: Allen & Unwin.

Harrison, Ross, ed. 1983. *Rational Action: Studies in Philosophy and Social Science*. Cambridge: Cambridge University Press.

Hart, H.L.A. 1984. *Essays in Jurisprudence and Philosophy*. Oxford: Clarendon.

Hart, John. 1984. *The Presidential Branch*. Elmsford, NY: Pergamon.

Hartmann, Klaus Dieter, ed. 1980. *Politische Bildung und Politische Psychologie*. Munich: Wilhelm Fink.

Hartwig, Richard. 1978. "Rationality and the Problems of Administrative Theory." *Public Administration* 56 (Summer): 159-79.

Harvard Business Review. 1983. *Using Logical Techniques for Making Better Decisions*. New York: Wiley.

Harvard Nuclear Study Group, Albert Carnesale, et al. 1983. *Living with Nuclear Weapons*. Cambridge: Harvard University Press.

Hastings, Max, and Simon Jenkins. 1982. *The Battle for the Falklands*. New York: Norton.

Haveman, Robert H., and Julius Margolis, eds. 1977. *Public Expenditure Analysis*. 2d ed. Chicago: Rand McNally.

Hawker, Geoffrey, R.F.J. Smith, and Patrick Weller. 1979. *Politics and Policy in Australia*. St. Lucia: University of Queensland Press.

Hawkins, Gerald S. 1983. *Mindsteps to the Cosmos.* New York: Harper & Row.

Haworth, Lawrence. 1960. "The Experimental Society. Dewey and Jordan." *Ethics* 71 (October): 27-40.

Hawrylyshyn, Bohdan. 1980. *Road Maps to the Future: Towards More Effective Societies*. A Report to the Club of Rome. New York: Pergamon.

Hayano, David M. 1982. *Poker Faces: The Life and Work of Professional Card Players*. Berkeley and Los Angeles: University of California Press.

Hayek, F.A. 1979. *Law, Legislation and Liberty*. Vol 3, *The Political Order of a Free People*. Chicago: University of Chicago Press.

Hays, Samuel P. 1980. *American Political History as Social Analysis*. Knoxville: University of Tennessee Press.

Hayward, Jack. 1974. "National Aptitudes for Planning in Britain, France and Italy." *Government and Opposition*. no. 4: 397-410.

———. 1976. "Institutional Inertia and Political Impetus in France and Britain." *European Journal of Political Research* 4: 342-59.

———. 1982. "Mobilising Private Interests in the Service of Public Ambitions: The Salient Element in the Dual French Policy Style?" In *Policy Styles in Western Europe*, edited by Jeremy Richardson. London: Allen & Unwin.

Hayward, Jack, and R.N. Berki, eds. 1979. *State and Society in Contemporary Europe*. Oxford: Martin Robertson.

Hayward Jack, and Michael Watson, eds. 1975. *Planning, Politics and Public Policy: The British, French and Italian Experience*. Cambridge: Cambridge University Press.

Heady, Ferrel. 1979. *Public Administration: A Comparative Perspective*. Rev. 2d ed. New York: Marcel Dekker.

Healey, P., G. McDougall, and M.J. Thomas, eds. 1983. *Planning Theory: Prospects for the 1980s*. Selected papers from a conference held in Oxford, 2-4 April 1981. Oxford: Pergamon.

Heater, Derek, and Judith A. Gillespie, eds. 1981. *Political Education in Flux.* Beverly Hills, CA: Sage.

Heatherly, Charles L. 1981. *Mandate for Leadership: Policy Management in a Conservative Administration.* Washington, DC: Heritage Foundation.

Heclo, Hugh. 1972. "Review Article: Policy Analysis," *British Journal of Political Science* 2: 83-108.

———. 1974. *Modern Social Politics in Britain and Sweden: From Relief to Income Maintenance.* New Haven: Yale University Press.

———. 1977a. *A Government of Strangers: Executive Politics in Washington.* Washington, DC: Brookings Institution.

———. 1977b. *Studying the Presidency: A Report to the Ford Foundation.* New York: Ford Foundation.

Heclo, Hugh, and Aaron Wildavsky. 1974. *The Private Governance of Public Money.* London: Macmillan.

Heeman, David A. 1983. *The Re-United States of America: An Action Agenda for Improving Business, Government and Labor Relations.* Reading, MA: Addison-Wesley.

Heidenheimer, Arnold J. 1983. "Politics, Policy and Police as Concepts in the Western Languages or: Why are the 'Kontis' Deprived?" Paper presented at the annual meeting of the American Political Science Association, Chicago.

Heidenheimer, Arnold J., Hugh Heclo, and Carolyn Teich Adams. 1983. *Comparative Public Policy: The Politics of Social Choice in Europe and America.* 2d ed. New York: St. Martin's Press.

Heidorn, Joachim. 1982. *Legitimität und Regierbarkeit: Studien zu den Legitimitätstheorien von Max Weber, Niklas Luhmann, Jürgen Habermas und der Unregierbarkeitsforschung.* Berlin: Duncker & Humblot.

Heilbroner, Robert L. 1963. *The Great Ascent.* New York: Harper & Row.

———. 1975. *An Inquiry into the Human Prospect.* New York: Norton.

———. 1978. *Beyond Boom and Crash.* New York: Norton.

Heineman, Ben W., Jr., and Curtis A. Hessler. 1980. *Memorandum for the President: A Strategic Approach to Domestic Affairs in the 1980s.* New York: Random House.

Hekman, Susan J. 1983. *Weber: The Ideal Type and Contemporary Social Theory.* Notre Dame, IL: University of Notre Dame Press.

Held, D. 1980. *Introduction to Critical Theory: Horkheimer to Habermas.* London: Hutchinson.

Hellman, Judith Adler. 1983. *Mexico in Crisis.* 2d ed. New York: Holmes & Meier.

Hellstern, Gerd-Michael, and Hellmut Wollmann, eds. 1983. *Experimentelle Politik—Reformstrohfeuer oder Lernstrategie: Bestandsaufnahme und Evaluierung.* Opladen: Westdeutscher.

Helmer, Olaf. 1983. *Looking Forward: A Guide to Futures Research.* Beverly Hills, CA: Sage.

Henderson, Gail E., and Myron S. Cohen. 1984. *The Chinese Hospital: A Socialist Work Unit.* New Haven: Yale Unviersity Press.

Henderson, P.D. 1977. "Two British Errors: Their Probable Size and Some Possible Lessons." *Oxford Economic Papers*, n.s. 29: 159-205.

Hennen, Manfred. 1976. *Krise der Rationalität—Dilemma der Soziologie: Zur Kritischen Rezeption Max Webers*, Stuttgart: Ferdinand Enke.

Hennis, Wilhelm, Peter Graf Kielmansegg, and Ulrich Matz, eds. 1977, 1979. *Regierbarkeit: Studien zu Ihrer Problematisierung*, vols. 1,2. Stuttgart: Klett-Cotta.

Henshel, Richard L. 1982. "The Boundary of The Self-Fulfilling Prophecy and the Dilemma of Social Prediction." *British Journal of Sociology* 33 (December): 511-28.

Herbet, Mikkan E. 1981. "Politics, Planning and Capitalism: National Economic Planning in France and Britain." *Political Studies* 29 no. 4: 497-516.

Herf, Jeffrey. 1981. "Reactionary Modernism: Some Ideological Origins of the Primacy of Politics in the Third Reich." *Theory and Society* 10 (November): 805-32.

Hermann, Charles F., ed. 1972. *International Crises: Insights from Behaviorial Research*. New York: Free Press

Hermann, Margaret G. 1979. "Indicators of Stress in Policymakers During Foreign Policy Crises." *Political Psychology* 1 (Spring): 27-46.

Hermann, Margaret G., and Charles F. Hermann. 1975. "Maintaining the Quality of Decision Making in Foreign Policy Crisis: A Proposal." Paper presented at the International Conference on Psychological Stress and Adjustment in Time of War and Peace, Tel Aviv, Israel, 6-10 January.

Hermann, Margaret G., with Thomas W. Milburn, eds. 1977. *A Psychological Examination of Political Leaders*. New York: Free Press.

Herzog, Chaim. 1982. *The Arab-Israel Wars*. New York: Random House.

Hess, Stephen. 1976. *Organizing the Presidency*. Washington, DC: Brookings Institution.

Hewstone, Miles, ed. 1983. *Attribution Theory: Social and Functional Extensions*. Oxford: Blackwell.

Hibbs, Douglas A., Jr., and Henrik Jess Madsen. 1981. "Public Reactions to the Growth of Taxation and Government Expenditure." *World Politics* 33, no. 3: 413-35.

Hicks, John. 1974. *The Crisis in Keynesian Economics*. New York: Basic Books.

Hicks, Ursula K. 1979. *Federalism: Failure and Success: A Comparative Study*. New York: Oxford University Press.

Higgins, Joan, et al. 1983. *Government and Urban Poverty: Inside the Policy-Making Process*. Oxford: Blackwell.

Higgott, Richard A. 1980. "From Modernization Theory to Public Policy: Continuity and Change in the Political Science of Political Development". *Studies in Comparative International Development* 15, no. 4: 26-58.

Higley, J., G.L. Field, and K. Groholt. 1976. *Elite Structure and Ideology*. New York: Columbia University Press.

Hildebrand, Klaus. 1980. *Das Dritte Reich*. 2d ed. Munich: R. Oldenbourg.

Hildebrandt, Steen. 1979. " From Manipulation to Participation in the Operations Research Process." In *Operational Research '78*, edited by K.B. Haley. Amsterdam: North-Holland.

Hill, Dilys M. 1978. "Political Ambiguity and Policy: The Case of Welfare." *Social and Economic Administration* 12 (Summer): 89-119.

Hill, Percy H. et al. 1979. *Making Decisions: A Multidisciplinary Introduction.* Reading, MA: Addison-Wesley.

Hiltz, Starr Roxanne, and Murray Turoff. 1978. *The Network Nation: Human Communication via Computer.* Reading, MA: Addison-Wesley.

Himmelweit, Hilde T., Patrick Humphreys, Marianne Jaeger, and Michael Katz. 1981. *How Voters Decide: A Longitudinal Study of Political Attitudes and Voting Extended Over Fifteen Years.* London: Academic Press.

Hinsley, F.H. 1979. *British Intelligence in the Second World War: Its Influence on Strategic Operations.* London: Her Majesty's Stationery Office.

Hintze, Otto. 1964. *Soziologie und Geschichte: Gesammelte Abhandlungen zur Soziologie, Politik und Theorie der Geschichte.* Göttingen: Vandenhoeck & Ruprecht.

_____. 1967. *Regierung und Verwaltung: Gesammelte Abhandlungen zur Staat-Recht und Sozialgeschichte Preussens.* Göttingen: Vandenhoeck & Ruprecht.

_____. 1970. *Staat und Verfassung: Gesammelte Abhandlungen zur Allgemeinen Verfassungsgeschichte.* Göttingen: Vandenhoeck & Ruprecht.

Hirsch, Fred. 1976. *Social Limits to Growth.* Cambridge: Harvard University Press.

Hirsch, Fred, and John H. Goldthorpe, eds. 1978. *The Political Economy of Inflation.* Cambridge: Harvard University Press.

Hirschman, Albert O. 1958. *The Strategy of Economic Development.* New Haven: Yale University Press.

_____. 1965. *Journeys Towards Progress.* Garden City, NY: Doubleday Anchor.

_____. 1967. *Development Projects Observed.* Washington, DC: Brookings Institution.

_____. 1970. *Exit, Voice, and Loyalty: Responses to Decline in Firms, Organizations, and States.* Cambridge: Harvard University Press.

_____. 1981a. *Essays in Trespassing: Economics to Politics and Beyond.* Cambridge: Cambridge University Press.

_____. 1981b. *Shifting Involvement: Private Interest and Public Action.* Oxford: M. Robertson.

Hoaglin, David C., et al. 1982. *Data for Decisions: Information Strategies for Policymakers.* New York: Abt Books.

Hodgson, Godfrey. 1980. *All Things to All Men: The False Promise of the Modern American Presidency.* New York: Simon & Schuster.

_____. 1984. *Lloyd's of London: A Reputation at Risk.* London: Allen Lane.

Hofferbert, Richard I. 1974. *The Study of Public Policy.* Indianapolis, IN: Bobbs-Merrill.

Hofheinz, Roy, Jr., and Kent E. Calder. 1982. *The Eastasia Edge.* New York: Basic Books.

Hofstadter, Douglas R. 1979. *Godel, Escher, Bach: An Eternal Golden Braid.* New York: Basic Books.

_____. (forthcoming). *Artificial Intelligence: Subcognition as Computation.*

Hofstadter, Douglas R., and Daniel Dennett. 1981. *The Mind's I: Fantasies and Reflections on Self and Soul.* New York: Basic Books.

Hogarth, Robin M. 1980. *Judgment and Choice: The Psychology of Decision.* Chichester, United Kingdom: Wiley.

Hogarth, Robin M., and Spyros Makridakis. 1981. "Forecasting and Planning: An Evaluation." *Management Science* 27 (February): 115-38.

Hogwood, Brian W., and Guy B. Peters. 1982. "The Dynamics of Policy Change: Policy Sucession." *Policy Sciences* 14 (June): 225-45.

Hogwood, Brian W., and Lewis A. Gunn. 1984. *Policy Analysis for the Real World.* Oxford: Oxford University Press.

Höhne, Heinz. 1978. *Der Orden unter dem Toteskopf: Dir Geschichte der SS.* Munich: Goldmann.

———. 1983. *Die Machtergreifung: Deutschlands Weg in die Hitler-Diktatur.* Hamburg: Rowohlt.

Holden, Alan. 1983. *Orderly Tangles: Cloverleafs, Gordian Knots, and Regular Polylinks.* New York: Columbia University Press.

Holling, C.S., ed. 1980. *Adaptive Environmental Assessment and Management.* IIASA volume. New York: Wiley.

Holmes, Leslie. 1981. *The Withering away of the State? Party and State under Communism.* Beverly Hills, CA: Sage.

Holsti, Ole R. 1972. *Crisis Escalation War.* Montreal: McGill-Queen's University Press.

Holsti, Ole R., and Alexander L. George. 1975. "The Effects of Stress on the Performance of Foreign Policy-Makers." *Political Science Annual* 6: 255-319.

Holt, Robert, and John Turner, eds. 1970. *The Methodology of Comparative Research,* New York: Free Press.

Holwill, Richard N. 1983. *Agenda '83.* Washington, DC: Heritage Foundation.

Homann, Karl. 1980. *Die Interdependenz von Zielen and Mitteln.* Tübingen: J.C.B. Mohr.

Honadle, George. 1982. "Development Administration in the Eighties: New Agendas or Old Perspectives?" *Public Administration Review* 42: 174-79.

Honadle, George, and Rudi Lauss, eds. 1979. *International Development Administration: Implementation Analysis for Development Projects.* New York: Praeger.

Hood, Christopher, and Maurice Wright, eds. 1981. *Big Government in Hard Times.* Oxford: M. Robertson.

Hoogerwerf, A. 1978. "The 'Experimenting' State." *Planning and Development in the Netherlands* 10, no. 1: 3-20.

Hook, Sidney. 1943. *The Hero in History: A Study in Limitation and Possibility.* New York: Day.

Hoos, Ida R. 1983. *Systems Analysis in Public Policy: A Critique.* Rev. ed. Berkeley and Los Angeles: University of California Press.

Höpfl, Harro. 1982. *The Christian Polity of John Calvin.* Cambridge: Cambridge University Press.

Hopple, Gerald W., and Stephen J. Andriole, eds. 1983. *National Security Crisis Forecasting and Management.* Boulder, CO: Westview.

Hopple, Gerald W., and James A. Kuhlman. 1981. *Expert-Generated Data: Applications in International Affairs.* Boulder, CO: Westview.

Irving Louis Horowitz. 1982. *Beyond Empire and Revolution: Militarization and Consolidation in the Third World.* New York: Oxford University Press.

_____. 1983. "The Routinization of Terrorism and Its Unanticipated Consequences." In *Terrorism, Legitimacy, and Power: The Consequences of Political Violence,* edited by Martha Crenshaw. Middletown, CT: Wesleyan University Press.

_____. ed. 1971. *The Uses and Abuses of Social Science.* New Brunswick, NJ: Transaction.

Horton, F.W., and D.A. Marchand, eds. 1982. *Information Management in Public Administration: An Introduction and Resource Guide to Government in the Information Age.* Washington, DC: Information Resources Press.

Horwitch, Mel. 1982. *Clipped Wings: The Story of the American SST Conflict.* Cambridge: MIT Press.

House, Peter W. 1982. *The Art of Public Policy Analysis.* Beverly Hills, CA: Sage Publications.

Howard, J.H. 1983. "Perspectives on 'Overloaded Government': Issues in the Meaning and Measurement of 'Government Presence.'" Background paper for annual conference, Royal Australian Institute of Public Administration. Hobart, Australia.

Howard, Roy J. 1983. *Three Faces of Hermeneutics: An Introduction to Current Theories of Understanding.* Berkeley and Los Angeles: University of California Press.

Howorth, Jolyan, and Philipp G. Cerny, eds. 1981. *Elites in France: Origins, Reproduction and Power.* London: Pinter.

Howson, S., and D. Winch. 1977. *The Economic Advisory Council, 1930-39: A Study in Economic Advice During Depression and Recovery.* Cambridge: Cambridge University Press.

Hsu, Francis L.K. 1983. *Rugged Individualism Reconsidered: Essays in Psychological Anthropology.* Knoxville: University of Tennessee Press.

Hudson Institute. 1983a. *Visions of the Future: Program Summary.* Croton-on-Hudson, NY: Hudson Institute.

_____. 1983b. *Visions of the Future: Materials.* Croton-on-Hudson, NY: Hudson Institute.

Hughes, Thomas L. 1976. *The Fate of Facts in a World of Men: Foreign Policy and Intelligence-Making.* New York: Foreign Policy Association.

Hull, John A. 1981. *Diagnosis of Our Time.* London: Heinemann.

Humphrey, Nicholas. 1983. *Consciousness Regained.* Oxford: Oxford University Press.

Humphreys, P., O. Svenson, and A. Vari, eds. 1983. *Analysing and Aiding Decision Processes.* Amsterdam: North-Holland.

Hunter, D.J. 1980. *Coping with Uncertainty: Policy and Politics in the National Health Service.* Chichester, United Kingdom: Wiley.

Huntington, Samuel P. 1969. *Political Order in Changing Societies.* New Haven: Yale University Press.

_____. 1974. "Postindustrial Politics: How Benign Will It Be?" *Comparative Politics* 6 January: 163-91.

———. 1981. *American Politics: The Promise of Disharmony.* Cambridge: Harvard University Press, Belknap Press.

Hussain, D., and K. Hussain. 1981. *Information Processing Systems for Management.* Homewood, IL: Richard D. Irwin.

Hussey, David. 1974. *Corporative Planning: Theory and Practice.* New York: Pergamon.

Hutchison, T.W. 1979. *Knowledge and Ignorance in Economics.* Chicago: University of Chicago Press.

IIAS Study Group. 1983. *Policy Formulating Processes of Central Government: Discussion Draft of Final Report.* Brussels: International Institute of Administrative Sciences.

IISS. 1983. *Defence and Consensus: The Domestic Aspects of Western Security,* 3 parts. Adelphi Papers, 182, 183, 184. London: International Institute for Strategic Studies.

Illich, Ivan. 1973. *Tools for Conviviality.* London: Caldar and Boyars.

———. 1982. *Genus.* New York: Plenum Press.

Inbar, Michael. 1979. *Routine Decision Making: The Future of Bureaucracy.* Beverly Hills, CA: Sage.

Independent Commission on Disarmament and Security Issues. (Olaf Palme, chairperson) 1982. *Common Security.* London: Pan Books.

Inglehart, Ronald. 1977a. *The Silent Revolution: Changing Values and Political Styles Among Western Publics.* Princeton: Princeton Universtiy Press.

———, ed. 1977b. *Policy Problems of Advanced Industrial Society,* Special issue, *Comparative Political Studies* 10 (October)

Institute of Social Studies. 1979. *Development of Societies: The Next Twenty-Five Years.* Boston: Martinus Nijhoff.

International Energy Agency. 1982. *World Energy Outlook.* Paris: OECD.

Inwagen, Peter, van. 1983. *An Essay on Free Will.* Oxford: Oxford University Press.

Ion, D.C. 1980. *Availability of World Energy Resources.* London: Graham & Trotman.

Ionescu, Ghita, ed. 1973. *Between Sovereignty and Integration.* New York: Halsted Press.

———. 1975. *Centrepetal Politics: Government and the New Centres of Power.* London: Hart-Davis, MacGibbon.

Iremonger, Lucille. 1970. *The Fierce Chariot: A Study of British Prime Ministers and the Search for Love.* London: Secker & Warburg.

Isen, Alice M., and Robert Patrick. 1983. "The Effect of Positive Feelings on Risk Taking: When the Chips are Down." *Organizational Behavior and Human Performance* 31 (April): 194-202.

Isensee, Josef, and Hans Meyer. 1979. *Zur Regierbarkeit Der Parlamentarischen Demokratie.* Cologne: Grote.

Isnard, C.A., and E.C. Zeeman. 1976. "Some Models from Catastrophe Theory in the Social Sciences." In *The Use of Models in the Social Sciences,* edited by Lyndhurst Collins. Boulder, CO: Westview.

Jackson, P.M. 1981. *Government Policy Initiatives, 1979-1980: Some Studies in Public Administration.* London: Royal Institute of Public Administration.

Jackson, Robert H., and Carl G. Roseberg. 1982. *Personal Rule in Black Africa: Prince, Autocrat, Prophet, Tyrant.* Berkeley and Los Angeles: University of California Press.

Jacob, Herbert. 1984. *The Frustration of Policy: Responses to Crime by American Cities.* Boston: Little, Brown.

Jamshidi, Mohammad. 1983. *Large-Scale Systems: Modeling and Control.* New York: North-Holland.

Jänicke, Martin, ed. 1973a. *Politische Systemskrisen.* Colone: Kiepenheuer & Witsch.

_____, ed. 1973b. *Herrschaft und Krise: Beitrage zur politik-wissenschaftlichen Krisenforschung.* Opladen: Westdeutscher.

Janis, Irving L. 1982. *Groupthink: Psychological Studies of Policy Decisions and Fiascoes.* Rev. ed. Boston: Houghton Mifflin.

Janis, Irving L., and Leon Mann. 1977. *Decision Making: A Psychological Analysis of Conflict, Choice, and Commitment.* New York: Free Press.

Jann, Werner. 1983. *Der Policy-Ansatz: Ein Überblick über Entwicklungen in der Bundesrepublik Deutschland und in den USA.* Speyer: Hoschschule fuer Verwaltungswissenschaften, Arbeitsheft 45.

Janoska-Bendl, Judith. 1965. *Methodologische Aspekte des Idealtypus: Max Weber und die Soziologie der Geschichte.* Berlin: Duncker & Humbolt.

Janowitz, Morris. 1976. *Social Control and the Welfare State.* New York: Elsevier.

_____. 1977. *Military Institutions and Coercion in the Developing Nations.* Chicago: University of Chicago Press.

_____. 1978. *The Last Half-Century: Social Change and Politics in America.* Chicago: University of Chicago Press.

_____. 1983. *The Reconstruction of Patriotism: Education for Civic Consciousness.* Chicago: University of Chicago Press.

Jantsch, Erich. 1975. *Design for Evolution: Self-Organization and Planning in the Life of Human Systems.* New York: Braziller.

Janus, Sam, Barbara Bess, and Carol Saltus. 1977. *A Sexual Profile of Men in Power.* Englewood Cliffs, NJ: Prentice-Hall.

Janvry, Alain de. 1983. *The Agrarian Question and Reformism in Latin America.* Baltimore: Johns Hopkins University Press.

Jarvis, R. 1975. *Perception and Misperception in International Relations.* Princeton: Princeton University Press.

Jasper, Karl. 1960. *Psychologie der Weltanschauungen.* 2d ed. Berlin: Springer. First published 1922.

Jeffery, K. and P. Hennesey. 1983. *States of Emergency: British Governments and Strikebreaking since 1919.* London: Routledge & Kegan Paul.

Jeffrey, Richard C. 1983. *The Logic of Decision.* 2d ed. Chicago: University of Chicago Press.

Jelinek, Mariam, Londa Smircich, and Paul Hirsch, eds. 1983. *Organizational Culture.* Special issue, *Administrative Science Quarterly* 28 (September).

Jenkins, Clive, and Barrie Sherman. 1979. *The Collapse of Work.* London: Methuen.

Jennergren, C.G., ed. 1978. *Trends in Planning.* Stockholm: Swedish National Defense Research Institute.

Jensen, A. 1969. "How Much Can We Boost IQ and Scholastic Achievement?" *Harvard Education Review* 39, no. 1: 1-123.

Jodice, David H., Charles Lewis Taylor, and Karl W. Deutsch. 1980. *Cumulation in Social Science Data Archiving: A Study of the Impact of the Two World Handbooks of Political and Social Indicators.* Königstein/Ts.: Verlag Anton Hain.

Johannesson, Jan, and Günther Schmid. 1980. "The Development of Labour Market Policy in Sweden and Germany: Competing or Convergent Models to Combat Unemployment?" *European Journal of Political Research* 387-406.

Johnson, Brian. 1979. *The Secret War.* New York: Methuen.

Johnson, Chalmers. 1982. *MITI and the Japanese Miracle: The Growth of Industrial Policy, 1925-1975.* Stanford: Stanford University Press.

Johnson, Franklyn A. 1980. *Defense by Ministry: The British Ministry of Defense, 1944-1974.* New York: Holmes & Meier.

Johnson, Paul. 1983. *A History of the Modern World from 1917 to the 1980s.* London: Weidenfeld & Nicolson.

Johnson-Laird, P.N., and P.C. Wason, eds. 1977. *Thinking: Readings in Cognitive Science.* Cambridge: Cambridge University Press.

Jones, Charles O. 1977. *An Introduction to the Study of Public Policy.* 2nd ed. North Scituate, MA: Duxbury.

Jones, Edward E., et al. 1972. *Attribution: Perceiving the Causes of Behavior.* Morristown, NJ: General Learning Press.

Jones, E. Thomas. 1980. *Options for the Future: A Comparative Analysis of Policy-Oriented Forecasts.* New York: Praeger.

Jones, G.W. 1983. "Prime Ministers' Departments Really Create Problems: A Rejoinder to Patrick Weller." *Public Administration* 61 Spring: 79-84.

Jones, R.V. 1978. *Most Secret War: British Scientific Intelligence 1939-1945.* London: Hamish Hamilton.

Jonsson, C., ed. 1982. *Cognitive Dynamics and International Politics.* London: Pinter.

Jordan, A.G., and J. Richardson. 1979. *Governing Under Pressure: The Policy Process in a Post-Parliamentary Democracy.* London: M. Robertson.

Jordan, Amos A., and William J. Taylor, Jr. 1981. *American National Security.* Baltimore: Johns Hopkins University Press.

Jordon, Bill. 1982. *Mass Unemployment and the Future of Britain.* Oxford: Blackwell.

Jordon, Hamilton. 1982. *Crisis: The Last Year of the Carter Presidency.* New York: Putnam.

*Journal of Interdisciplinary History.* 1980, *History and Climate: Interdisciplinary Explorations* (special issue) 10 (Spring).

Jouvenel, Bertrand de. 1967. *The Art of Conjecture.* New York: Basic Books. Translated from the French.

Jungermann, Helmut. 1980. "Speculations about Decision-Theoretic Aids for Personal Decision Making." *Acta Psychologica* 45: 7-34.

Jungermann, Helmut, and Gerard De Zeeuw, eds. 1977. *Decision Making and Change in Human Affairs: Proceedings of the Fifth Research Conference on Subjective Probability, Utility and Decision Making, Darmstadt, 1-4 September 1975.* Dortrecht, Holland: D. Reidel.

Juviler, Peter H., and Henry W. Morton, eds. 1967. *Soviet Policy-Making.* New York: Praeger.

Kahn, Herman. 1982. *The Coming Boom.* New York: Simon & Schuster.

_____. 1983. "Kahn: Schools Cheat Kids by Painting Grim Picture of the Future." *American School Board Journal,* January, 31-33.

Kahn, Herman, W. Brown, L. Martel. 1976. *The Next 200 Years.* New York: Morrow.

Kahn, Herman, and Thomas Pepper. 1978. *The Japanese Challenge: The Success and Failure of Economic Success.* New York: Harper & Row.

Kahn, Herman, and Thomas Pepper. 1980. *Will She Be Right? The Future of Australia.* St. Lucia: University of Queensland Press.

Kahn, Herman, with the Hudson Institute. 1979. *World Economic Development: 1979 and Beyond.* Boulder, CO: Westview.

Kahnemann, Daniel, Paul Slovic, and Amos Tversky, eds. 1982. *Judgement under Uncertainty: Heuristics and Biases.* Cambridge: Cambridge University Press.

Kanter, Rosabeth Moss. 1983. *The Change Masters: Innovation for Productivity in the American Corporation.* New York: Simon & Schuster.

Kantrowitz, Arthur. 1968. "Proposal for an Institution for Scientific Judgment." *Science* 156 (May): 763ff.

Kaplan, John. 1983. *The Hardest Drug: Heroin and Public Policy.* Chicago: University of Chicago Press.

Kaplan, Martin F., and Steven Schwartz, eds. 1977. *Human Judgement and Decision Processes in Applied Settings.* New York: Academic Press.

Katz, M.B. 1983. *Poverty and Policy in American History: Studies in Social Discontinuity.* New York: Academic Press.

Kaufman, Edy. 1979. *Uruguay in Transition from Civilian to Military Rule.* New Brunswick, NJ: Transaction Books.

Kaufman, H. 1973. *Administrative Feedback,* Washington, DC: Brookings Institution.

_____. 1976. *Are Government Organizations Immortal?* Washington, DC: Brookings Institution.

Kavanagh, Dennis, ed. 1982. *The Politics of the Labour Party.* London: Allen & Unwin.

Keddie, Nikki R., and Richard Yann 1981. *Roots of Revolution: An Interpretive History of Modern Iran.* New Haven: Yale University Press.

Keegan, William. 1984. *Mrs. Thatcher's Economic Experiment.* London: Penguin.

Keegan, William, and R. Pennant-Rea. 1979. *Who Runs the Economy?: Control and Influence in British Economic Policy.* Houndslow, United Kingdom: M.P. Smith.

Keen, Peter G.W., and Michael S. Scott Morton. 1978. *Decision Support Systems: An Organizational Perspective.* Reading, MA: Addison-Wesley.

Keeney, Ralph L., and Howard Raiffa. 1976. *Decisions with Multiple Objectives: Preferences and Value Tradeoffs*. New York: Wiley.

Kehrl, Hans. 1973. *Krisenmanager im Dritten Reich: 6 Jahre Frieden—6 Jahre Krieg, Erinnerungen*. Düsseldorf: Droste.

Kelley, Aileen, and Mikhail Bakunin. 1983. *A Study in the Psychology and Politics of Utopianism*. Oxford: Oxford University Press.

Kelley, Donald R. 1982. *The Beginning of Ideology: Consciousness and Society in the French Reformation*. Cambridge: Cambridge University Press.

Kelley, Harold H., and John L. Michela. 1980. "Attribution Theory and Research." *Annual Review of Psychology* 31: 457-501.

Kelley, Jonathan, and Herbert S. Klein. 1982. *Revolution and the Rebirth of Inequality*. Berkeley and Los Angeles: University of California Press.

Kelso, William Alton. 1979. *American Democratic Theory: Pluralism and Its Critics*. Westport, CT: Greenwood Press.

Kennan, George F. 1967. *Memoirs, 1925-1950*. Boston: Little, Brown.

———. 1982. *The Nuclear Delusion: Soviet-American Relations in the Atomic Age*. New York: Pantheon.

Kennedy, R.F. 1969. *Thirteen Days*. New York: Norton.

Kent, Ernest W. 1981. *The Brain of Men and Machines*. Peterborough, NH: Byte/McGraw-Hill.

Kepner, C.H., and B.J. Tregoe. 1981. *The New Rational Manager*. London: John Martins.

Keren, Michael. 1983. *Ben-Gurion and the Intellectuals: Power, Knowledge, Charisma*. Bekalk, IL: Northern Illinois University Press.

Kerr, Clark. 1983. *The Future of Industrial Societies? Convergence or Continuing Diversity?* Cambridge: Harvard University Press.

Kevenhörster, Paul. 1974. *Das Rätesystem als Instrument zur Kontrolle Politischer und Wirtschaftlicher Macht*. Opladen: Westdeutscher.

Keynes, John M. 1973. *The Collected Writings. Vol. 7, The General Theory of Employment, Interest and Money*. Cambridge: Cambridge University Press. First published 1935.

Khandwalla, Pradip, N. 1978. *The Design of Organizations*. New York: Harcourt Brace Jovanovich.

Khoshkish, A. 1979. *The Socio-Political Complex: An Interdisciplinary Approach to Political Life*. New York: Pergamon.

Kickert, Walter J.M. 1978. *Fuzzy Theories of Decision Making*. Boston: Martinus Nijhoff.

———. 1980. *Organization of Decision Making*. Amsterdam: North-Holland.

Kielmansegg, Peter Graf. 1976. *Legitimationsprobleme Politischer Systeme*. Politische Vierteljahresschrift, Sonderheft 7. Opladen: Westdeutscher.

———. 1977. *Volkssouveränität: Eine Untersuchung der Bedingungen demokratischer Legitimatät*. Stuttgart: Ernst Klett.

Kiernan, V.G. 1982. *State and Society in Europe, 1550-1650*. Oxford: Blackwell.

Kiewiet, D. Roderick. 1983. *Macroeconomics and Micropolitics*. Chicago: University of Chicago Press.

Kilby, P., ed. 1971. *Entrepreneurship and Economic Development*. New York: Free Press.

Kilmann, Ralph. 1977. *Social Systems Design: Normative Theory and the MAPS Design Technology*. New York: Elsevier.

Kilmann, Ralph H., Louis R. Pondy, and Dennis P. Slevin, eds. 1976. *The Management of Organization Design*. Vol. 1, *Strategies and Implementation*. Vol. 2, *Research and Methodology*. New York: North-Holland.

Kindleberger, Charles P. 1973. *The World in Depression, 1929-1939*. Berkeley and Los Angeles: University of California Press.

_____. 1984. *A Financial History of Western Europe*. London: Allen & Unwin.

King, Anthony, ed. 1976. *Why Is Britain Becoming Harder to Govern?* London: BBC.

_____, ed. 1978. *The New American Political System*. Washington, DC: American Enterprise Institute.

_____, ed. 1983. *Both Ends of the Avenue: The Presidency, the Executive Branch, and Congress in the 1980s*. Washington, DC: American Enterprise Institute.

King, Gail Buchwalter, and Peter N. Stearns. 1981. "The Retirement Experience as a Policy Factor: An Applied History Approach." *Journal of Social History* 14 (Summer): 589-625.

King, Preston. 1982. *Federalism and Federation*. London: Croom Helm.

Kingdon, John M. 1984. *Agendas, Alternatives and Public Policy*. Boston: Little, Brown.

Kingross, Lord. 1978. *Ataturk: A Biography of Mustafa Kemal, Father of Modern Turkey*. New York: Morrow. First published 1964.

Kirkpatrick, Samuel A. 1975. "Psychological Views of Decison-Making." In *Political Science Annual* 6: 30-112 (Indianapolis, IN: Bobbs-Merrill). Edited by C.P. Cotter.

Kirlin, John J. 1982. *The Political Economy of Fiscal Limits*. Lexington, MA: Heath.

Kissinger, Henry A. 1979. *White House Years*. Boston: Little, Brown.

_____. 1984. "Solving the Debt Crisis: What's Needed Is Statesmanship." *International Herald Tribune* (25 June): 5.

Klages, Helmut, and Peter Kmiecieak, eds. 1979. *Wertwandel und Gesellschaftlicher Wandel*. Frankfurt: Campus.

Klatzky, Roberta L. 1980. *Human Memory: Structures and Processes*. 2 ed. San Francisco: Freeman.

Klein, Burton H. 1977. *Dynamic Economics*. Cambridge: Harvard University Press.

Klein, Rudolf. 1983. *The Politics of the National Health Service*. London: Longman.

Klion N., and S. Waterman, eds. 1983. *Pluralism and Political Geography: People, Territory and State*. London: Croom Helm.

Knei-Paz, Baruch. 1980. *The Social and Political Thought of Leon Trotsky*. Oxford: Oxford University Press.

_____. 1984. "Ideas, Political Intentions and Historic Consequences—The Case of the Russian Revolution."

Knopp, Guido, and Bernot Wiegmann, ed. 1983. *Warum habt ihr Hitler nicht verhindert? Fragen an Mächtige und Ohnmächtige.* Frankfurt am Main: Fischer.

Knorr, Klaus, ed., 1976. *Historic Dimensions of National Security Problems.* Lawrence: University Press of Kansas.

Knutson, Jeanne, ed. 1973. *Handbook of Political Psychology.* San Francisco: Jossey-Bass.

Kobrin, Stephen J. 1982. *Managing Political Risk Assessment: Strategic Response to Environmental Change.* Berkeley and Los Angeles: University of California Press.

Kochen, Manfred, ed. 1975. *Information for Action: From Knowledge to Wisdom.* New York: Academic Press.

Kochen, Manfred, and Karl W. Deutsch. 1980. *Decentralization: Sketches Towards a Rational Theory.* Cambridge, MA: Oelgeschlager, Gunn & Hain.

Koertge, Noretta. 1979. "The Methodological Status of Popper's Rationality Principle." *Theory and Decision* 10: 83-95.

Köhler, Peter A., and Hans F. Zacher, with Martin Partington, eds. 1982. *The Evolution of Social Insurance, 1881-1981: Studies of Germany, France, Great Britain, Austria and Switzerland.* London: Pinter.

Kondratieff, Nikolai D. 1936. "The Long Waves in Economic Life." *Review of Economics and Statistics* 17 (November): 105-15.

Konner, Melvin. 1982. *The Tangled Wing: Biological Constraints on the Human Spirit..* New York: Holt, Rinehart & Winston.

Konopasek, Milos, and Sundaresan Yayaraman. 1984. "Expert Systems for Personal Computers: The T.K. Solver Approach." *Byte* 9 (May): 137-56.

Koppes, Clayton R. 1983. *JPL and the American Space Program: A History of the Jet Propulsion Laboratory.* New Haven CT: Yale University Press.

Kornberg, Allan, ed. 1973. *Legislatures in Comparative Perspective.* New York: McKay.

Kornberg, Allan, and Harold D. Clarke, eds. 1983. *Political Support in Canada: The Crisis Years.* Durham, NC: Duke University Press.

Korner, Stephan, ed. 1974. *Practical Reason.* New Haven: Yale University Press.

Kosslyn, Stephen M. 1983. *Ghosts in the Mind's Machine: How We Create and Use Pictures in Our Brains.* New York: Norton.

Kotharu, Rajni. 1974. *Footsteps into the Future: Diagnosis of the Present World and Design for an Alternative.* Amsterdam: North-Holland.

Kozielsecki, Josef. 1982. *Psychological Decision Theory.* Dortrecht, Holland: D. Reidel. First Published in Polish in 1975.

Kraft, Michael E., and Mark Schneider, ed. 1978. *Population Policy Analysis: Issues in American Politics.* New Brunswick, NJ: Transaction.

Kramer, Daniel C. 1972. *Participatory Democracy: Developing Ideas of the Political Left.* Cambridge, MA: Schenkman.

Kramnick, Isaac, ed. 1979. *Is Britain Dying?* Ithaca, NY: Cornell University Press.

Krasner, Stephen D. 1978. *Defending the National Interest: Raw Materials Investments and U.S. Foreign Policy.* Princeton: Princeton University Press.

_____, ed. 1983. *International Regimes.* Ithaca, NY: Cornell University Press. First published as *International Organization*, vol. 36 (Spring 1982).

Krieger, Martin H. 1981. *Advice and Planning.* Philadelphia: Temple University Press.

_____. Forthcoming. *Big Decisions and a Culture of Decision Making.*

Kriesi, Hanspeter. 1980. *Entscheidungstrukturen und Entscheidungsprozesse in der Schweizer Politik.* Frankfurt am Main: Campus.

Krockow, Christian Graf von. 1976. *Reform als Politisches Prinzip.* Munich: R. Piper.

Krone, Robert. 1980. *Systems Analysis and Policy Sciences.* New York: Wiley.

Kronenberg, Philip S., ed. 1982. *Planning U.S. Security: Defense Policy in the Eighties.* New York: Pergamon.

Krueckeberg, Donald A., ed. 1983. *Introduction to Planning History in the United States.* New Brunswick, NJ: Rutgers University Press.

Kruse, David S. 1979. *Policy Studies: An Overview of the Contemporary Enterprise.* Private distribution.

Kuhn, Reinhard. 1976. *The Demon of Noontide: Ennui in Western Literature.* Princeton: Princeton University Press.

Kuhn, Thomas S. 1970. *The Stucture of Scientific Revolutions.* 2d ed. Chicago: University of Chicago Press.

_____. 1977. *The Essential Tension: Selected Studies in Scientific Traditions and Change.* Chicago: University of Chicago Press.

Kuisel, Richard F. 1981. *Capitalism and the State in Modern France: Renovation and Economic Management in the Twentieth Century.* Cambridge: Cambridge University Press.

Kumar, Krishan. 1978. *Prophecy and Progress: The Sociology of Industrial and Post-Industrial Society.* New York: Penguin.

Kunreuther, H. 1978. *Diaster Insurance Protection: Public Policy Lessons.* New York: Wiley.

Kupperman, Robert, and Darrell Trent, eds. 1979. *Terrorism: Threat, Reality, Response.* Stanford: Hoover Institution.

Kweit, Mary Grisez, and Robert W. Kweit. 1981. *Implementing Citizen Participation in a Bureaucratic Society: A Contingency Approach.* New York: Praeger.

Laboratory of Comparative Human Cognition. 1979. "What's Cultural about Cross-Cultural Cognitive Psychology?" *Annual Review of Psychology* 30: 145-72.

Lacouture, Jean. 1982. *Léon Blum.* New York: Holmes and Meier. Translated from the French.

Lakoff, George, and Mark Johnson. 1980. *Metaphors We Live By.* Chicago University of Chicago Press.

Lall, Arthur. 1981. *The Emergence of Modern India.* New York: Columbia University Press.

Lamb, David. 1982. *The Africans.* New York: Random House.

Lamb, Geoffrey, and Linda Muller. 1982. *Control, Accountability, and Incentives in a Successful Development Institution: The Kenya Tea Development Authority.* Staff Working Paper No. 550. Washington, DC: World Bank.

Lamb, H.H. 1982. *Climate, History and the Modern World.* London: Methuen.

Lammers, Cornelis J., and David J. Hickson, eds. 1979. *Organizations Alike and Unlike: International Studies in the Sociology of Organizations.* London: Routledge & Kegan Paul.

Lammers, William W. 1983. *Public Policy and the Aging.* Washington, DC: Congressional Quarterly Press.

Lampton, David M. 1977. *The Politics of Medicine in China: The Policy Process, 1949-1977.* Boulder, CO: Westview.

Landau, Martin. 1969. "Redundancy, Rationality and the Problem of Duplication and Overlap." *Public Administration Review* 29 (July-August): 346-58.

Landes, David S. 1969. *The Unbound Prometheus: Technological Change and Industrial Development in Western Europe from 1750 to the Present.* Cambridge: Cambridge University Press.

Lane, Christel. 1981. *The Rites of Rulers: Ritual in Industrial Society: The Soviet Case.* Cambridge: Cambridge University Press.

Lane, Robert E. 1978. "Markets and the Satisfaction of Human Wants" *Journal of Economic Issues* 12 (December): 799-827.

Lange, Peter, George Ross, and Maurizio Vannicelli. 1982. *Unions, Change and Crisis: French and Italian Union Strategy and the Political Economy, 1945-1980.* London: Allen & Unwin.

Lange-Eichbaum, Wilhelm, and Wolfram Kurth. 1967. *Genie Irrsinn and Ruhm: Genie-Mythus und Pathographie des Genies.* 6th ed. Munich: Ernest Reinhardt. Reprinted 1979. First published 1927.

Langer, Ellen J. 1977. "The Psychology of Chance." *Journal for the Theory of Social Behavior* 7, no. 2: 185-207.

Langton, John. 1979. "Darwinism and the Behavioral Theory of Sociocultural Evolution: An Analysis." *American Journal of Sociology* 85, no. 2: 288-309.

Lanir, Zvi. 1983. *Fundamental Surprise: The National Intelligence Crisis.* Tel Aviv: Kibbutz Meuchad. In Hebrew.

La Porte, R. Todd, ed. 1975. *Organized Social Complexity: Challenge to Politics and Policy.* Princeton: Princeton University Press.

Laqueur, Walter. 1976. *A History of Zionism.* New York: Schocken Books. First published 1972.

Larkey, Patrick D. 1979. *Evaluating Public Programs: The Impact of General Revenue Shaping on Municipal Government.* Princeton: Princeton University Press.

Larson, J.S. 1980. *Why Government Programs Fail: Improving Policy Implementation.* New York: Praeger.

Lasswell, Harold. 1960. *Psychopathology and Politics.* 2d ed. New York: Viking.

——. 1971. *A Preview of Policy Sciences.* New York: Elsevier.

——. 1975. "Research in Policy Analysis: The Intelligence and Appraisal Functions." In *Handbook of Political Science.* Vol. 6, *Policies and Policymaking,* edited by F. Greenstein and N. Polsby: Reading, MA: Addison-Wesley.

Laszlo, Erwin. 1977a. *Goals in a Global Community.* New York: Pergamon.

Laszlo, Erwin, et al., eds. 1977b. *Goals for Mankind: A Report to the Club of Rome on the New Horizons of Global Community.* New York: Dutton.

_____. 1983. *Systems Science and World Order: Selected Studies.* Oxford: Pergamon.

Latham, Earl. 1965. *The Group Basis of Politics.* New York: Octagon.

Laufer, Heinz. 1962. *Das Kriterium Politischen Handelns: eine Studie zur Freund-Feind-Doktrin von Carl Schmitt auf der Grundlage der Aristotelischen Theorie der Politik. Zugleich ein Beitrag zur Methodologie der Politischen Wissenschaften.* Munich: Institut für Politische Wissenschaften der Universität München.

Laumann, Edward O., and Franz V. Pappi. 1976. *Networks of Collective Action: A Perspective on Community Influence Systems.* New York: Academic Press.

Lauterbach, Albert. 1974. *Psychological Challenges to Modernization.* New York: Elsevier.

Lave, Lester B. 1981. *The Strategy of Social Regulation: Decision Frameworks for Policy.* Washington, DC: Brookings Institution.

Lazarsfeld, Paul F., and Jeffrey G. Reitz. 1975. *An Introduction to Applied Sociology.* New York: Elsevier.

Leach, Richard H., ed. 1983. *Canada's New Constitution.* Durham, NC: Duke University Press.

Leach, Steve, and John Stewart, eds. 1982. *Approaches to Public Policy.* Birmingham Institute of Local Government Studies. London: Allen & Unwin.

Ledwidge, Bernard. 1982. *De Gaulle.* London: Weidenfeld & Nicolson.

Leemans, Arne F., ed. 1976. *The Management of Change in Government.* The Hague: Martinus Nijhoff.

Lehmbruch, Gerhard, and Phillippe C. Schmitter, eds. 1982. *Patterns of Corporatist Policy-Making.* Beverly Hills, CA: Sage.

Lehner, Franz. 1979. *Grenzen des Regierens: Eine Studie zur Regierungsproblematik Hochindustrialisierter Demokratien.* Königstein/Ts.: Athenaum.

Leibenstein, Harvey. 1976. *Beyond Economic Man: A New Foundation for Microeconomics.* Cambridge: Harvard University Press.

Leichter, Howard M. 1979. *A Comparative Approach to Policy Analysis: Health Care Policy in Four Nations.* Cambridge: Cambridge University Press.

_____. 1983. "The Patterns and Origins of Policy Diffusion: The Case of the Commonwealth." *Comparative Politics* 15 (January): 223-34.

Lenczowski, George C., ed. 1978. *Iran under the Pahlavis.* Stanford, CA: Hoover Institution Press.

Lendi, Martin, and Wolf Linder, eds. 1979. *Politische Planung in Theorie und Praxis: Ein Kolloquium des Instituts für Orts-, Regional- und Landesplanung der ETH Zürich.* Bern: Verlag Paul Haupt.

Lenhardt, Geso, ed. 1979. *Der Hilflose Sozialstaat: Jugendarbeitslosigkeit und Politik.* Frankfurt am Main: Suhrkamp.

Lenk, Hans, ed. 1977-1981. *Handlungstheorien Interdisziplinär.* Vol. 1: *Handlungslogik, formale und spachwissenschaftliche Handlungstheorien* 1980. Vol. 2: *Handlungserklärungen und philosophische Handlungsinterpretation* (Part 1, 1978; Part 2, 1979). Vol. 3: *Verhaltenswissenschaftliche und psychol-*

*ogische Handlungstheorien.* (Part 1, 1981). Vol. 4: *Sozialwissenschaftliche Handlungtheorien und spezielle systemwissenschaftliche Ansätze.* (1977). Munich: Wilhelm Fink.

Leontief, Wassily, et al. 1977. *The Future of World Economy: A United Nations Study.* New York: Oxford University Press.

Leontief, Wassily, and Faye Duchin. 1983. *Military Spending: Facts and Figures, Worldwise Implications and Future Outlook.* Oxford: Oxford University Press.

Lerner, Allen W. 1976. *The Politics of Decision Making: Strategy, Cooperation, and Conflict.* Beverly Hills, CA: Sage.

Leruez, Jacques. 1975. *Economic Planning and Politics in Britain.* London: M. Robertson. Translated from the French.

Leveson, Irving, and Jimmy W. Wheeler, eds. 1980. *Western Economies in Transition: Structural Change and Adjustment Policies in Industrial Countries.* Boulder, CO: Westview.

Levien, Roger E. 1969. *Independent Policy Analysis Organizations—A Major Social Invention.* P-4231. Santa Monica, CA: Rand Corporation.

Levine, Michael E., and Charles R. Plott. 1977. "Agenda Influence and Its Implications." *Virginia Law Review* 63 (May): 561-604.

Levine, Robert A. 1981. "Program Evaluation and Policy Analysis in Western Nations: An Overview." In *Evaluation Research and Practice: Comparative and International Perspectives,* edited by Robert A. Levine and Marian A. Solomon. Beverly Hills, CA: Sage.

Levinson, Sue, and Marc Fallon, eds. 1981. *Applied History.* Special issue, *Journal of Social History* 14 (Summer).

Levitan, A. Sara, and Robert Taggart. 1976. *The Promise of Greatness.* Cambridge: Harvard University Press.

Levy, S. Jay, and David A. Levy. 1983. *Profits and the Future of American Society: A Dramatic New Perspective on Capitalism.* New York: Harper & Row.

Lewin, Leonard C. (psued.) 1967. *Report from Iron Mountain on the Possibility and Desirability of Peace.* New York: Dell.

Lewin, Ronald. 1978. *Ultra Goes to War.* London: Hutchinson.

Lewis, Alan. 1982. *The Psychology of Taxation.* London: M. Robertson.

Lewis, Bernard. 1968. *The Emergence of Modern Turkey.* 2d ed. Oxford: Oxford University Press.

Lewis, Eugene. 1980. *Public Entrepreneurship: Towards a Theory of Bureaucratic Political Power—The Organizational Lives of Hyman Rickover, J. Edgar Hoover and Robert Moses.* Bloomington: Indiana University Press.

Lewis-Beck, Michael S. 1979. "Some Economic Effects of Revolutions: Models, Measurements, and the Cuban Evidence." *American Journal of Sociology* 84, no. 5: 1127-49.

Lewontin, R.C. and Peter Rose. 1984. *Not in Our Genes.* New York: Pantheon.

Lichtenstein, Sarah, and Baruch Fischoff. 1980. "Training for Calibration." *Organizational Behavior and Human Performance* 26: 149-71.

Lieberam, Ekkehard. 1977. *Krise der Regierbarkeit—ein neues Thema Bürgerlicher Staatsideologie.* Frankfurt am Main: Verlag Marxistische Blätter.

Lieberman, Jethro K. 1983. *The Litigious Society.* New York: Basic Books.

Liebert, Robert M., and Neala S. Schwartzberg. 1977. "Effects of Mass Media." *Annual Review of Psychology* 28: 141-73.

Light, Paul C. 1983. *The President's Agenda: Domestic Policy Choice from Kennedy to Carter, with Notes on Ronald Reagan.* Supplemented ed. Baltimore: Johns Hopkins University Press.

Lijphart, Arend. 1966. *The Trauma of Decolonization: The Dutch and West New Guinea.* New Haven: Yale University Press.

_____. 1968. *The Politics of Accommodation: Pluralism and Democracy in the Netherlands.* Berkeley and Los Angeles: University of California Press.

_____. 1977 *Democracy in Plural Societies: A Comparative Exploration.* New Haven: Yale University Press.

Lind, Robert C., et al. 1982. *Discounting for Time and Risk in Energy Policy.* Baltimore: Johns Hopkins University Press.

Lindberg, Leon N. 1976. *Politics and the Future of Industrial Society.* New York: McKay.

Lindberg, Leon N., Robert Alford, Colin Crouch, and Claus Offe, eds. 1975. *Stress and Contradiction in Modern Capitalism: Public Policy and the Theory of the State.* Lexington, MA: Heath.

Lindblom, Charles E. 1965. *The Intelligence of Democracy.* New York: Free Press.

_____. 1968. *The Policy-Making Process.* Englewood Cliffs, NJ: Prentice-Hall.

_____. 1977. *Politics and Markets: The World's Political-Economic Systems.* New York: Basic Books.

_____. 1979. "Still Muddling, Not Yet Through." *Public Administration Review* 39 (November/December): 517-26.

Lindblom, Charles E., and David K. Cohen. 1979. *Useable Knowledge: Social Science and Social Problem Solving.* New Haven: Yale University Press.

Lindenberg, Marc, and Benjamin Crosby. 1981. *Managing Development: The Political Dimension.* West Hartford, CT: Kumarian Press.

Lineberry, Robert L. 1977. *American Public Policy: What Government Does and What Difference It Makes.* New York: Harper & Row.

Linstone, Herald A., and Murray Turoff. 1975. *The Delphi Method: Techniques and Applications.* Reading, MA: Addison-Wesley.

Linstone, Herald A., et al. 1984. *Multiple Perspectives for Decision Making: Bridging the Gap Between Analysis and Action.* New York: Elsevier.

Linz, J. Juan, and Alfred Stepan, eds. 1978. *The Breakdown of Democratic Regimes.* Baltimore: Johns Hopkins University Press.

Lipset, Martin, and William Schneider. 1983. *The Confidence Gap: Business, Labor and Government in the Public Mind.* New York: Free Press.

Lipsey, David, ed. 1982. *Making Government Work.* Fabian Tract 480. London: Fabian Society.

Liske, Craig, William Loehr, and John McCamant, eds. 1975. *Comparative Public Policy: Issues, Theories, and Methods.* New York: Wiley.

Lloyd, Howell A. 1983. *The State, France and the Sixteenth Century.* London: Allen & Unwin.

Loasby, Brian J. 1976. *Choice, Complexity and Ignorance: An Inquiry into Economic Theory and the Practice of Decisionmaking.* Cambridge: Cambridge University Press.

Lockyer, Roger. 1982. "Long Live the Kings!" *Times Higher Education Supplement,* 24, December 1982, p. 14.

Lodge, Juliet, ed. 1981. *Terrorism: A Challenge to the State.* New York: St. Martin's Press.

Lodge, Paul, and Tessa Blackstone. 1982. *Educational Policy and Educational Inequality.* London: M. Robertson.

Loftus, Geoffrey R., and Elizabeth F. Loftus. 1983. *Mind at Play: The Psychology of Video Games.* New York: Basic Books.

Lompe, Klaus. 1971. *Gesellschaftspolitik und Planung: Probleme Politischer Planung in der Sozialstaatlichen Demokratie.* Freiburg: Rombach.

Lompe, Klaus, Hans Heinrich Rass, and Dieter Rehfeld. 1981.—*Enquête-Kommissionen und Royal Commissions: Beispiele Wissenschaftlicher Politikberatung in der Bundesrepublik Deutschland und in Grossbritannien, mit einem Beitrag zur Paritatischen Kommission in Österreich.* Göttingen: Vandenhoeck & Ruprecht.

Lopreato, Joseph. 1984. *Human Nature and Biocultural Evolution.* Boston: Allen & Unwin.

Lorane, Peter, and Richard F. Vancil, eds. 1977. *Strategic Planning Systems.* Englewood Cliffs, NJ: Prentice-Hall.

Loup, Jacques. 1982. *Can the Third World Survive?* Baltimore: Johns Hopkins University Press. First published in French in 1980.

Lovell, John P. 1970. *Foreign Policy in Perspective: Strategy, Adaption, Decision Making,* Hinsdale, IL: Dryden.

Lowe, Philip, and Jane Goyder. 1983. *Environmental Groups in Politics.* London: Allen & Unwin.

Lowenhardt, John. 1981. *Decision Making in Soviet Politics.* New York: St. Martin's Press.

Löwenthal, Richard. 1979. *Gesellschaftswandel und Kulturkrise: Zukunftsprobleme der Westlichen Demokratien.* Frankfurt am Main: Fischer.

Lowi, Theodore J. 1979. *The End of Liberalism: The Second Republic of the United States.* 2d ed. New York: Norton.

Loye, David. 1978. *The Knowable Future: A Psychology of Forecasting and Prophecy.* New York: Wiley.

Ludlow, Peter. 1982. *The Making of the European Monetary System.* London: Butterworth.

Ludz, Peter C. 1972. *The Changing Party Elite in East Germany.* Cambridge: MIT. Press. Translated from the German.

Luhmann, Niklas. 1968. *Zweckbegriff und Systemrationalität: Über die Funktion von Zwecken in Sozialen Systemen.* Tübingen: J.C.B. Mohr. Reprint, Frankfurt am Main: Suhrkamp, 1977.

———. 1975. *Politische Planung: Aufsätze von Politik und Verwaltung.* 2d ed. Opladen: Westdeutscher.

_____. 1978. "Temporalization of Complexity." In *Sociocybernetics,* vol. 2, edited by R.F. Geyer and J. van der Zouwen.

Lumsden, Charles J., and Edward O. Wilson. 1981. *Genes, Mind, and Culture: The Coevolutionary Process.* Cambridge: Harvard University Press.

_____. 1983. *Promethean Fire: Reflections on the Origin of Mind.* Cambridge: Harvard University Press.

Lundquist, Lennart. 1980. *The Hare and the Tortoise: Clean Air Policies in the United States and Sweden.* Ann Arbor: University of Michigan Press.

_____. 1982. *The Party and the Masses: An Interorganizational Analysis of Lenin's Model for the Bolshevik Revolutionary Movement.* New York: Transnational.

Luttwak, Edward N. 1977. *The Grand Strategy of the Roman Empire: From the First Century A.D. to the Third.* Baltimore: Johns Hopkins University Press.

_____. 1983. *The Grand Strategy of the Soviet Union.* New York: St. Martin's Press.

Lyles, Marjorie A., and Ian I. Mitroff. 1980. "Organizational Problem Formulation: An Empirical Study." *Administrative Science Quarterly* 25 (March): 102-119.

Lynn, Jonathan, and Antony Jay. 1981-83. *Yes Minister: The Diaries of a Cabinet Minister by the Rt. Hon. James Hacker MP.* 3 vols. London: BBC.

Lynn, Laurence E., Jr., ed. 1978. *Knowledge and Policy: The Uncertain Connection.* Study Project on Social Research and Development, vol.5. Washington, DC: National Academy of Sciences.

Lynn, Laurence E., Jr. 1980. *Designing Public Policy: A Casebook on the Role of Policy Analysis.* Santa Monica, CA: Goodyear.

Lynn, Laurence E., Jr., and David deF. Whitman. 1981. *The President as Policymaker: Jimmy Carter and Welfare Reform.* Philadelphia: Temple University Press.

Lyons, Gene M., and Louis Morton. 1965. *Schools for Strategy: Education and Research in National Security Affairs.* New York: Praeger.

Macarov, David. 1980. *Work and Welfare: The Unholy Alliance.* Beverly Hills, CA: Sage.

MacCrimmon, Kenneth R., and Ronald N. Taylor. 1976. "Decision Making and Problem Solving." In *Handbook of Industrial and Organizational Psychology,* edited by Marvin D. Dunnette. Chicago: Rand McNally.

MacFarquhar, Roderick. 1983. *The Origins of the Cultural Revolution.* vol. 2, *The Great Leap Forward, 1958-1960.* Oxford: Oxford University Press.

Machan, Tibor R. 1980. "Rational Choice and Public Affairs." *Theory and Decision* 12: 229-58.

Mack, P. Ruth. 1971. *Planning on Uncertainty: Decision Making in Business and Government Administration.* New York: Wiley.

Mackenzie, W.J.M. 1975. *Power, Violence, Decision.* Harmondsworth, United Kingdom: Penguin.

Mackinnon, Andrew J., and Alexander J. Wearing. 1980. "Complexity and Decision Making." *Behavioral Science* 25: 285-96.

_____. 1982. "Decision-Making in Dynamic Environments." Paper submitted at First International Conference on Foundations of Utility and Risk Theory, Oslo, 21-26 June.

Mackintosh, John F. 1981. *The British Cabinet*. 3d ed. London: Methuen.

MacMullen, Ramsey. 1976. *Roman Government's Response to Crisis, A.D. 235-337.* New Haven: Yale University Press.

MacRae, Duncan, Jr. 1976. *The Social Functions of Social Sciences.* New Haven: Yale University Press.

MacRae, Duncan, Jr., and James A. Wilde. 1978. *Policy Analysis for the Citizen.* North Scituate, MA: Duxbury.

———. 1979. *Policy Analysis for Public Decisions.* North Scituate, MA: Duxbury.

Maddison, Angus. 1983. *Phases of Capitalist Development.* Oxford: Oxford University Press.

Madigan, Carol Orsag, and Ann Elwood. 1984. *Brainstorms and Thunderbolts: How Creative Genius Works.* New York: Macmillan.

Magaziner, Ira C., and Robert B. Reich. 1983. *Minding America's Business: The Decline and Rise of the American Economy.* New York: Vintage.

Maharidakis, Spyros, and Steven C. Wheelwright, eds. 1982. *A Handbook for Forecasting: A Manager's Guide.* New York: Wiley.

Majone, Giandomenico, and Edward S. Quade, eds. 1980. *Pitfalls of Analysis.* IIASA volume. New York: Wiley.

Malek, F.V. 1978. *Washington's Hidden Tragedy: The Failure to Make Government Work.* London: Collier-Macmillan.

Malettke, Klaus, ed. 1980. *Ämterkäuflichkeit: Aspekte Sozialer Mobilität im Europäischen Vergleich (17. Und 18. Jahrhundert).* Berlin: Colloquium.

Mandel, Robert. 1978. *Perception, Decision Making and Conflict.* Lanham, MD: University Press of America.

Mannheim, Karl. 1950. *Freedom, Power and Democratic Planning.* New York: Oxford University Press.

———. 1951a. *Man and Society in an Age of Reconstruction.* London: Routledge & Kegan Paul.

———. 1951b. *Diagnosis of Our Time.* London: Routledge & Kegan Paul.

Manning, Roberta Thompson. 1983. *The Crisis of the Old Order in Russia: Gentry and Government.* Princeton: Princeton University Press.

Mansbridge, Jane J. 1980. *Beyond Adversary Democracy.* Supplemented ed. Chicago: University of Chicago Press.

Manuel, Frank E., and Fritzie P. Manuel. 1979. *Utopian Thought in the Western World.* Cambridge: Harvard University Press.

Maravall, José. 1982. *The Transition to Democracy in Spain.* London: Croom Helm.

March, D., and W. Grant. 1977. "Tripartism: Reality or Myth?" *Government and Opposition.* 12, no. 2: 194-211.

March, James G. 1976. *Ambiguity and Choice in Organizations.* Oslo: Universitetsforlaget.

———. 1978. "Bounded Rationality, Ambiguity, and the Engineering of Choice." *Bell Journal of Economics* 9 (Autumn): 587-608.

———. 1983. "Organizing Political Life: What Administrative Reorganization Tells Us about Government." *American Political Science Review.* 77 (June): 281-96.

March, James G., ed. 1965. *Handbook of Organizations.* Chicago: Rand McNally.

March, James G., and Johan P. Olsen. 1975. "The Uncertainty of the Past: Organizational Learning Under Ambiguity." *European Journal of Political Research.* 3: 147-71.

Marchetti, Cesare. 1980. "Society as a Learning System: Discovery, Invention, and Innovation Cycles Revisited." *Technological Forecasting and Social Change* 18: 267-82.

Margolis, Howard. 1982. *Selfishness, Altruism and Rationality: A Theory of Social Choice.* Cambridge: Cambridge University Press.

_____. (in work). *Logic, Interest and Cognition* (tentative title).

_____. (Forthcoming). *Political Capital* (tentative title).

Margolis, M. 1979. *Viable Democracy.* Harmondsworth, United Kingdom: Penguin.

Marien, Michael. 1976. *Societal Directions and Alternatives.* LaFayette, NY: Information for Policy Design.

_____. 1980. *Future Survey Annual 1979.* Washington, DC: World Future Society.

_____. 1982. *Future Survey Annual 1980.* Washington, DC: World Future Society.

_____. 1983. *Future Survey Annual 1981-82.* Washington, DC: World Future Society.

Marković, Mihailo. 1974. *From Affluence to Praxis: Philosophy and Social Criticism.* Ann Arbor: University of Michigan Press.

Markovits, Andrei S., and Karl W. Deutsch, eds. 1980. *Fear of Science—Trust in Science: Conditions for Change in the Climate of Opinion.* Cambridge, MA: Oelgeschlager, Gunn & Hain.

Marsh, Alan. 1977. *Protest and Political Consciousness.* Beverly Hills, CA: Sage.

Marsh, Ian. 1980. *An Australian Think Tank?* Kensington: New South Wales University Press.

Marsh, Peter, ed. 1979. *The Conscience of the Victorian State.* Syracuse: Syracuse University Press.

Martino, Joseph P. 1983. *Technological Forecasting for Decision Making.* 2d ed. New York: Elsevier.

Martinussen, Willy. 1977. *The Distant Democracy: Social Inequality, Political Resources and Political Influence in Norway.* London: Wiley.

Marx, Leo. 1964. *The Machine in the Garden: Technology and the Pastoral Ideal in America.* London: Oxford University Press.

Mason, Richard O., and Ian I. Mitroff. 1981. *Challenging Strategic Planning Assumptions: Theory, Cases and Techniques.* New York: Wiley.

Matlin, Margaret, and David Stang. 1978. *The Pollyanna Principle: Selectivity in Language, Memory, and Thought.* Cambridge, MA: Schenkman.

Matzeratz, Horst, and Heinrich Volkmann. 1977. "Modernisierungstheorie und Nationalsozialismus." In *Theorien in der Praxis des Historikers: Forschungsbeispiele und ihre Diskussion.* Edited by Jürgen Kocha. Göttingen: Vanderhoeck & Ruprecht.

Matzner, Egon. 1982. *Der Wohlfahrtsstaat von Morgen: Entwurf Eines Zeitgemässen Musters Staatlicher Interventionen.* Frankfurt: Campus.

Maxwell, William, ed. 1983. *Thinking: The Expanding Frontier.* Philadelphia: Franklin Institute.

May, Ernest R. 1972. *"Lessons" of the Past: The Uses and Misuses of History in American Foreign Policy.* New York: Oxford University Press.

May, J.V., and A. Wildavsky, eds. 1978. *The Policy Cycle,* Beverly Hills, CA: Sage.

Mayer, R. Robert. 1980. *The Design of Social Policy Research.* Englewood Cliffs, NJ: Prentice-Hall.

Mayer, Robert, Robert Moroney, and Robert Morris, eds. 1976. *Centrally Planned Change: A Reexamination of Theory and Practice.* Urbana: University of Illinois Press.

Mayntz, Renate, and Fritz Scharpf, eds. 1973. *Planungsorganisation: Die Diskussion um die Reform Von Regierung und Verwaltung des Bundes.* Munich: R. Piper.

Mazuri, Ali A. 1972. *Cultural Engineering and Nation Building in East Africa.* Evanston, IL: Northwestern University Press.

McCall, George J., and George H. Weber. 1983. *Social Science and Public Policy: The Roles of Academic Disciplines in Policy Analysis.* Port Washington, NY: Associated Faculty Press.

McCann, Joseph E. 1983. "Diagnosing Organizational Decision." *Sloan Management Review* 24 (Winter): 3-16.

McCarthy, Thomas. 1978. *The Critical Theory of Jürgen Habermas.* Cambridge: MIT Press.

McClelland, David. 1961. *The Achieving Society.* New York: D. Van Nostrand.

McClelland, Peter P., and Alan L. Magdovitz. 1981. *Crisis in the Making: The Political Economy of New York State Since 1945.* Cambridge: Cambridge University Press.

McClintock, Cynthia, and Abraham F. Lowenthal. 1983. *The Peruvian Experiment Reconsidered.* Princeton: Princeton University Press.

McCloskey, Donald N. 1983. "The Rhetoric of Economics." *Economic Literature* 21 (June): 481-517.

McClosky, Herbert, and Alida Brill. 1983. *Dimensions of Tolerance: What Americans Believe about Civil Liberties.* New York: Russell Sage Foundation.

McDaniel, Timothy. 1978. "Meaning and Comparative Concepts." *Theory and Society* 6 (July): 93-117.

McGinn, Colin. 1983. *The Subjective View: Secondary Qualities and Indexical Thought.* Oxford: Oxford University Press.

McGregor, Douglas. 1960. *Human Side of Enterprise.* New York: McGraw-Hill.

McGrew, G., and M.J. Wilson, eds. 1982. *Decision Making: Approaches and Analysis.* Manchester, United Kingdom: Manchester University Press.

McGuire, C.B., and Roy Radner, eds. 1972. *Decision and Organization: A Volume in Honor of Jacob Marschak.* Amsterdam: North-Holland.

McHale, Magda Cordell. 1981. *Ominous Trends and Valid Hopes: A Comparison of Five World Reports.* Minneapolis: University of Minnesota, Hubert H. Humphrey Institute of Public Affairs.

McKenna, Christopher. 1980. *Quantitative Methods for Public Decision Making.* New York: McGraw-Hill.

McKenzie, Richard B. 1982. *The Limits of Economic Science*. Hingham, MA: Kluwer.

McNeill, William H. 1977. *Plagues and People*. New York: Doubleday.

_____. 1982. *The Pursuit of Power: Technology, Armed Force and Society Since A.D. 1000*. Chicago: University of Chicago Press.

McQuaid, Kim. 1982. *Big Business and Presidential Power: From Ford to Reagan*. New York: Morrow.

McSeveney, Samuel. 1972. *The Politics of Depression: Behavior in the Northeast 1893-1896*. Oxford: Oxford University Press.

McWhinney, Edward. 1981. *Constitution-Making: Principles, Process, Practice*. Toronto: University of Toronto Press.

Mead, Lawrence M. 1983. "Policy Studies and Political Science." Chicago: Annual Meeting of the American Political Science Association.

Meade, J. 1973. "The Inheritance of Inequalities: Some Biological, Demographic, Social and Economic Factors." *Proceedings of the British Academy* 59 (December): 1-29.

Meadows, Dennis L., et al. 1972. *The Limits to Growth*. New York: New American Library.

Meadows, Donella, J. Richardson, and G. Bruckmann. 1982. *Groping in the Dark: The First Decade of Global Modelling*. New York: Wiley.

Medley, Richard, ed., 1982. *The Politics of Inflation: A Comparative Analysis*. New York: Pergamon.

Meehan, E.J. 1979. *The Quality of Federal Policymaking: Programmed Failure in Public Housing*. Columbia: University of Missouri Press.

Mehlinger, Howard D., and O.L. Davis, Jr. 1981. *The Social Studies*. Eightieth Yearbook of the National Society for the Study of Education. Chicago: University of Chicago Press.

Meier, Christian. 1980a. *Res Publica Amissa: Eine Studie zur Verfassung und Geschichte der Späten Römischen Republik*. Frankfurt am Main: Suhrkamp.

_____. 1980b. *Die Ohnmacht des Allmächtigen Dictators Caesar*. Frankfurt am Main: Suhrkamp.

_____. 1980c. *Die Entstehung des Politischen bei den Griechen*. Frankfurt am Main: Suhrkamp.

_____. 1982. *Caesar*. Berlin: Severin & Siedler.

Meinecke, Friedrich. 1957. *Machiavellism: The Doctrine of Raison D'Etat and Its Place in Modern History*. New Haven: Yale University Press. Translated from the German. First published 1924.

_____. 1965. *Die Entstehung des Historismus*. 2d ed Stuttgart: Koehler. First published 1936.

Meister, D. 1981. *Behavioral Research and Government Policy: Civilian and Military R & D*. New York: Pergamon.

Meltsner, Arnold J. 1976. *Policy Analysis in the Bureaucracy*. Berkeley and Los Angeles: University of California Press.

_____. 1981. *Politics and the Oval Office*. San Francisco: Institute for Contemporary Studies.

Meltsner, Arnold J., and Christopher Bellavita. 1983. *The Policy Organization.* Beverly Hills, CA: Sage.

Mendel, Arthur P., and Michael Bakunin. 1983. *Roots of Apocalypse.* Eastbourne, United Kingdom: Holt-Saunders.

Mendlovitz, Saul H., ed. 1975. *On The Creation of a Just World Order: Preferred Worlds for the 1990's.* Amsterdam: North-Holland.

Mensch, G. 1979. *Stalemate in Technology.* Cambridge, MA: Ballinger. First published in German in 1975.

Meredith, G., R. Nelson, and P. Neck. 1983. *The Practice of Entrepreneurship.* Geneva: ILO.

Merelman, Richard. 1984. *Making Something of Ourselves.* Berkeley and Los Angeles: University of California Press.

Merritt, Richard L., ed. 1980. *Studies in Systems Transformation.* Special issue, *International Political Science Review* 1 (January).

Merton, Robert. 1936. "The Unanticipated Consequences of Purposive Social Action." *American Sociological Review* 1: 894-904.

————. 1949. *Social Theory and Social Structure: Towards the Codification of Theory and Research.* Glencoe, IL: Free Press.

Meyer, Gerd. 1982. *Strukturinterne und umstrukturierende Neuerungen Dargestellt am Beispiel der Forschung: Konflikt und Versohnung der Prinzipien der Demokratie, der Rationalitat und der Kreativitat bei der Entstehung und der Beurteilung von Neuerungen.* Vol. 1: *Entwurf der Theorie.* Bern: Peter Lang.

Meyer, John W., and Michael T. Hannan. 1979. *National Development and the World System: Educational, Economic, and Political Change.* Chicago: University of Chicago Press.

Mezey, Michael L. 1979. *Comparative Legislatures.* Durham, NC: Duke University Press.

Michael, N. Donald. 1973. *On Learning to Plan—and Planning to Learn: The Social Psychology of Changing Toward Future-Responsive Societal Learning.* San Francisco: Jossey-Bass.

Michalos, Alex C. 1978. *Foundations of Decision-Making.* Ottawa: Canadian Library of Philosophy.

Michels, Robert. 1962. *Political Parties: A Study of the Oligarchical Tendencies of Modern Democracy.* New York: Collier. First published in Italian.

Middlemas, Keith. 1979. *Politics in Industrial Society: The Experience of the British System Since 1911.* London: André Deutsch.

Milavksy, Ronald J., et al. 1983. *Television and Aggression: A Panel Study.* New York: Academic Press.

Miles, Raymond E., and Charles C. Snow. 1978. *Organizational Strategy, Structure, and Process.* New York: McGraw-Hill.

Miles, Robert H. 1980. *Macro Organizational Behavior.* Santa Monica, CA: Goodyear.

Miliband, Ralph. 1982. *Capitalist Democracy in Britain.* Oxford: Oxford University Press.

Millar, Fergus. 1977. *The Emperor in the Roman World (31 B.C.-A.D. 337)*. London: Duckworth.

Miller, Arthur. 1983. "Is Confidence Rebounding?" *Public Opinion* 6 (June/July): 16-20.

Miller, Arthur H. 1974. "Political Issues and Trust in Government: 1964-1970." *American Political Science Review* 68 (September): 951-72; Comment and Rejoinder, pp. 973-1001.

Miller, Barnette. 1941. *The Palace School of Muhammad the Conqueror*. Cambridge: Harvard University Press. Reprint, New York: Arno Press, 1973.

Miller, G.A. 1956. "The Magic Number Seven, Plus or Minus Two: Some Limits on Our Capacity to Process Information." *Psychological Review* 63: 81-97.

Miller, James Grier. 1978. *Living Systems*. New York: McGraw-Hill.

Miller, Jon D. 1983. *The American People and Science Policy: The Role of Public Attitudes in the Policy Process*. Elmsford, NY: Pergamon.

Miller, Stuart Creighton. 1982. *"Benevolent Assimilation": The American Conquest of the Philippines, 1899-1903*. New Haven: Yale University Press.

Miller, S.M., and Donald Tomaskovic-Devey. 1983. *Recapitalizing America*. London: Routledge & Kegan Paul.

Miners, N.J. 1975. *The Government and Politics of Hong Kong*. Hong Kong: Oxford University Press.

Minix, Dean A. 1982. *Small Groups and Foreign Policy Decision-Making*. Lanham, MD: University Press of America.

Mintzberg, Henry. 1979a. *The Structuring of Organizations: A Synthesis of Research*. Englewood Cliffs, NJ: Prentice-Hall.

———. 1979b. "Beyond Implementation: An Analysis of the Resistance to Policy Analysis." In *Operational Research '78*, edited by K.B. Haley. Amsterdam: North-Holland.

———. 1980. "Structure in 5's: A Synthesis of the Research on Organizational Design." *Management Science*, March, 322-41.

———. 1983. *Structure in Fives: Designing Effective Organizations*. Englewood Cliffs, NJ: Prentice-Hall.

Mintzberg, Henry, Duru Raisinghani, and André Théorét. 1976. "The Structure of 'Unstructured' Decision Processes." *Administrative Science Quarterly* 21 (June): 246-75.

Misra, B.B. 1970. *The Administrative History of India, 1834-1947*. Oxford: Oxford University Press.

Mitchell, Arnold. 1983. *The Nine American Lifestyles: Who We Are and Where We Are Going*. New York: Macmillan.

Mitchell, Joyce M., and William C. Mitchell. 1969. *Political Analysis and Public Policy*. Chicago: Rand McNally.

Mitchell, Otis C. 1983. *Hitler Over Germany: The Establishment of the Nazi Dictatorship (1918-1934)*. Philadelphia: Institute for the Study of Human Issues.

Mitchell, Terence R. 1979. "Organizational Behavior." *Annual Review of Psychology* 30: 243-81.

Mitchell, William C. 1971. *Public Choice in America: An Introduction to American Government.* Chicago: Markham.

Mitroff, Ian I., and Ralph H. Kilmann. 1981. "The Four-Fold Way of Knowing: The Varieties of Social Science Experience." *Theory and Society* 10 (March): 227-48.

Mitroff, Ian I., Harold Quinton, and Richard O. Mason. 1983. "Beyond Contradictions and Consistency: A Design for a Dialectic Policy System." *Theory and Decision* 15 (June): 107-120.

Mitroff, Ian, Richard O. Mason, and Vincent P. Barabba. 1983. *The 1980 Census: Policymaking Amid Turbulence.* Lexington, MA: Lexington Books.

Modelski, George. 1978. "The Long Cycle of Global Politics and the Nation-State." *Comparative Studies in Society and History* 20: 214-35.

Moerings, Martin. 1983. "Protest in the Netherlands: Developments in a Pillarised Society." *Contemporary Crises* 7 (April): 95-112.

Moffitt, Michael. 1984. *The World's Money: International Banking from Bretton Woods to the Brink of Insolvency.* San Mateo, CA: Joseph.

Mohan, Raj P., ed. 1979. *Management and Complex Organizations in Comparative Perspective.* Westport, CT: Greenwood Press.

Moharir, V.V. 1979. *Process of Public Policy-Making in the Netherlands: A Case Study of the Dutch Government's Policy for Closing Down the Coal Mines in South Limburg, 1965-1975.* The Hague: Institute of Social Studies.

Mohr, Lawrence B. 1982. *Explaining Organization Behavior.* San Francisco: Jossey-Bass.

Moise, Edwin E. 1983. *Land Reform in China and North Vietnam: Consolidating the Revolution at Village Level.* Chapel Hill: University of North Carolina Press.

Mommsen, H. 1966. *Beamtentum im Dritten Reich: Mit ausgewählten Quellen zur nationalsozialistischen Beamtenpolitik.* Stuttgart: Deutsche Verlags-Anstalt.

Mommsen, W.J., with Wolfgang Mock, eds. 1981. *The Emergence of the Welfare State in Britain and Germany.* London: Croom Helm.

Monnet, Jean. 1978. *Erinnerungen Eines Europäers.* Munich: Carl Hanser. Translated from the French.

Monod, Jacques. 1972. *Chance and Necessity.* New York: Random House.

Montagu, Ewan. 1979. *Beyond Top Secret Ultra.* London: Lorgi.

Montgomery, John D. 1957. *Forced to Be Free: The Artificial Revolution in Germany and Japan.* Chicago: University of Chicago Press.

———. 1974. *Technology and Civic Life: Making and Implementing Development Decisions.* Cambridge: MIT Press.

Montgomery, John D., Harold D. Lasswell, and Joel S. Migdal, eds. 1979. *Patterns of Policy: Comparative and Longitudinal Studies of Population Events.* New Brunswick, NJ: Transaction.

Monti, Joseph. 1982. *Ethics and Public Policy: Conditions of Public Moral Discourse.* Lanham, MD: University Press of America.

Mood, Alexander M. 1983. *Introduction to Policy Analysis.* New York: North-Holland.

Morch, Michael K., and Louis R. Pondy. 1977. "Book Review of March and Olson." *Administrative Science Quarterly*, 22 (1977): 351-62.

Morgan, K., ed. 1982. *The Falklands Campaign: A Digest of Debates in the House of Commons, 2 April to 15 April 1982.* London: Her Majesty's Stationery Office.

Morgan, Roger, and Stefano Silvestri, eds. 1982. *Moderates and Conservatives in Western Europe.* London: Heinemann.

Morishima, Michio. 1982. *Why Has Japan "Succeeded"? Western Technology and the Japanese Ethos.* Cambridge: Cambridge University Press.

Morse, Ronald A., ed. 1983. *The Limits of Reform in China.* Boulder, CO: Westview.

Mosher, Frederick. 1979. *The GAO: The Quest for Accountability in American Government.* Boulder, CO: Westview.

Mosher, Frederick C., and John E. Harr. 1970. *Programming Systems and Foreign Affairs Leadership: An Attempted Innovation.* New York: Oxford University Press.

Mosse, George L. 1975. *The Nationalization of the Masses: Political Symbolism and Mass Movements in Germany from the Napoleonic Wars Through the Third Reich.* New York: Fertig.

Mowitz, Robert J. 1980. *The Design of Public Decision Systems.* Baltimore: University Park Press.

Mueller, Dennis C. 1979. *Public Choice.* Cambridge: Cambridge University Press.

———, ed. 1983. *The Political Economy of Growth.* New Haven: Yale University Press.

Mühlmann, Wilhelm E., ed. 1964. *Chiliasmus und Nativismus: Studien zur Psychologie, Soziologie und historischen Kasuistik der Umsturzbewegungen.* Berlin: Dietrich Reimer.

Mulcahy, Kevin V., and C. Richard Swaim. 1982. *Public Policy and the Arts.* Boulder, CO: Westview.

Muller, Edward N. 1979. *Aggressive Political Participation.* Princeton: Princeton University Press.

Muller, Edward N., and Thomas O. Jukam. 1983. "Discontent and Aggressive Political Participation." *British Journal of Political Science* 13, part 2 (April): 159-80.

Müller, Georg. 1981 *Gouvernmentale Handlungsspierlraüme und die Mobilität von Nationen.* Zurich: Zentralstelle der Studentenschaft.

Murdock, William W. 1983. *The Poverty of Nations: The Political Economy of Hunger and Population.* Baltimore: Johns Hopkins University Press.

Murswieck, Axel. 1975. *Regierungsreform durch Planungsorganisation: Eine Empirische Untersuchung im Bereich der Bundesregierung.* Opladen: Westdeutscher.

Nachmias, David. 1979. *Public Policy Evaluation: Approaches and Methods.* New York: St. Martin's Press.

Nagel, Stuart S., ed. 1975. *Policy Studies and the Social Sciences.* Lexington, MA: Heath.

_____, ed. 1980. *Improving Policy Analysis.* Beverly Hills, CA: Sage.

_____, ed. 1983a. *Encyclopedia of Policy Studies.* New York: Dekker.

_____, ed. 1983b. *Basic Literature in Policy Studies: A Comprehensive Bibliography.* Greenwich, CT: JAI Press.

_____. 1984a. *Public Policy: Goals, Means, and Methods.* New York: St. Martin's Press.

_____, gen. ed. 1984b. *Public Policy Studies: A Multi-Volume Treatise,* 8 vols. Greenwich, CT: JAI Press.

Naisbitt, John. 1983. *Megatrends: Ten New Directions Transforming Our Lives.* Updated ed. New York: Warner.

Nalimov, V.V. 1982. *Realms of the Unconscious: The Enchanted Frontier.* Philadelphia: ISI Press. Translated from the Russian.

Narr, Wolf-Dieter, ed. 1975. *Politik und Ökonomie: Autonome Handlungsmöglichkeiten des Politischen Systems.* Sonderheft 6 des Politischen Vierteljahresschrift. Opladen: Westdeutscher.

Narr, Wolf-Dieter, and Claus Offe, eds. 1975. *Wohlfahrtsstaat und Massenloyalitat.* Cologne: Kiepenheuer & Witsch.

Naschold, Frieder and Werner Väth, eds. 1973. *Politische Planungssysteme.* Opladen: Westdeutscher.

Nash, Bradley D. et al. 1980. *Organizing and Staffing the Presidency.* New York: Center for the Study of the Presidency.

National Institute of Mental Health. 1982. *Television and Behavior: The Years of Scientific Progress and Implications for the Eighties,* edited by D. Pearl, L. Bonthilet, and J. Lazar. Rockville, MD: NIMH.

Nee, V., and D. Mozingo eds. 1983. *State and Society in Contemporary China.* Ithaca, NY: Cornell University Press.

Neely, Richard 1983. *Why Courts Don't Work.* New York: McGraw-Hill.

Nelkin D. 1978. *Technological Decisions and Democracy: European Experiments in Public Participation.* Beverly Hills, CA: Sage.

Nelkin, Dorothy, and Michael Pollak. 1981. *The Atom Besieged: Extraparliamentary Dissent in France and Germany.* Cambridge: MIT Press.

Nelson, Otto C., Jr. 1946. *National Security and the General Staff.* Washington, DC: Infantry Journal Press.

Nelson, Richard., and Sidney G. Winter. 1983. *An Evolutionary Theory of Economic Change.* Cambridge: Harvard University Press.

Nelson, Robert H. 1983. *The Making of Federal Coal Policy.* Durham, NC: Duke University Press.

Netherlands Scientific Council for Government Policy. 1980. *Place and Future of Industry in The Netherlands.* The Hague: Wetenschappelijke Raad voor her Regieringsbeleid.

_____. 1983. *A Reappraisal of Welfare Policy.* The Hague: Scientific Council for Government Policy. Summary of report published in Dutch in 1982.

Neustadt, Richard E. 1970. *Alliance Politics.* New York: Columbia University Press.

_____. 1980. *Presidential Power: The Politics of Leadership from FDR to Carter.* New York: Wiley. First edition 1960.

Neustadt, Richard, and Harvey Fineberg. 1983. *The Epidemic That Never Was: Policy-Making and the Swine Flu Affair.* New York: Vintage. Earlier version 1976.

New Zealand Planning Council. 1979. *The Welfare State? Social Policy in the 1980's.* Wellington: New Zealand Planning Council.

Newell, A., and H.A. Simon. 1972. *Human Problem Solving.* Englewood Cliffs, NJ: Prentice-Hall.

Nimmo, Dan, and James E. Combs. 1982. *Mediated Political Realities.* New York: Longman.

NIRA. 1979. *Japan Toward the 21st Century.* Tokyo: National Institute for Research Advancement.

Nisbet, Robert A. 1969. *Social Change and History: Aspects of the Western Theory of Development.* Oxford: Oxford University Press.

———. 1980. *History of the Idea of Progress.* New York: Basic Books.

Nisbett, Richard, and Lee Ross. 1980. *Human Inference: Strategies and Shortcomings of Social Judgement..* Englewood Cliffs, NJ: Prentice-Hall.

Nishi, Toshio. 1982. *Unconditional Democracy: Education and Politics in Occupied Japan, 1945-1952.* Stanford, CA: Hoover Institution.

Noack, Paul. 1981. *Ist die Demokratie noch Regierbar?* Munich: List.

Noble, David F. 1977. *America by Design: Science, Technology, and the Rise of Corporate Capitalism,* New York: Knopf.

Noelle-Neumann, Elisabeth. 1980. *Die Schweigespirale: Öffentliche Meinung—und Soziale Haut.* Munich: R. Piper.

Nolutshungu, Sam C. 1982. *Changing South Africa: Political Considerations.* Manchester, United Kingdom: Manchester University Press.

Nordlinger, Eric A. 1981. *On the Autonomy of the Democratic State.* Cambridge: Harvard University Press.

Norton, Philip. 1982. *The Constitution in Flux.* Oxford: M. Robertson.

Novak, Michael. 1982. *The Spirit of Democratic Capitalism.* New York: Simon & Schuster.

Nove, Alec. 1983. *The Economics of Feasible Socialism.* London: Allen & Unwin.

Nozick, Robert. 1974. *Anarchy, State and Utopia.* New York: Basic Books.

Nussbaum, Bruce. 1983. *The World after Oil: The Shifting Axis of Power and Wealth.* New York: Simon & Schuster.

Nutter, G. Warren. 1978. *Growth of Government in the West.* Washington, DC: American Enterprise Institute.

Nwabueze, B.O. 1982. *The Presidential Constitution of Nigeria.* New York: St. Martin's Press.

Nystrom, Harry. 1979. *Creativity and Innovation.* Somerset, NJ: Wiley.

Nystrom, Paul C., and William H. Starbuck, eds. 1980 and 1981. *Handbook of Organizational Design.* Vol. 1, *Adapting Organizations to Their Environments.* Vol. 2 (1981), *Remodeling Organizations and Their Environments.* Oxford: Oxford University Press.

Öberndorfer, Dieter, and Wolfgang Jäger, eds. 1975. *Die Neue Elite: Eine Kritik der Kritischen Demokratietheorie.* Freiburg: Rombach.

Obler, Jeffrey, Jürg Steiner, and Guido Dierick. 1977. *Decision-Making in Smaller Democracies: The Consociational "Burden".* Beverly Hills, CA: Sage.

O'Connor, James. 1973. *The Fiscal Crisis of the State.* New York: St. Martin's Press.

———. 1984. *Accumulation Crisis.* Oxford: Blackwell.

O'Driscoll, Gerald, and Mario Rizzo. 1983. *The Economics of Time and Ignorance.* New York: Columbia University Press.

Odum, William E. 1982. "Environmental Degradation and the Tyranny of Small Decisions." *BioScience* 32 (October): 728-29.

OECD 1976. *Measuring Social Well-Being: A Progress Report on the Development of Social Indicators.* Paris: OECD.

———. 1979a. *Social Sciences in Policymaking.* Paris: OECD.

———. 1979b. *Interfutures: Facing the Future—Mastering the Probable and Managing the Unpredictable.* Paris: OECD.

———. 1980. *Strategies for Change and Reform in Public Management.* Paris: OECD.

———. 1981a. *The Welfare State in Crisis.* Paris: OECD.

———. 1981b. *Integrated Social Policy: A Review of the Austrian Experience.* Paris: OECD.

———. 1983. *Positive Adjustment Policies: Managing Structural Change.* Paris: OECD.

Offe, Claus. 1972. *Strukturprobleme des kapitalistischen Staates: Aufsätze zur Politischen Soziologie.* Frankfurt am Main: Suhrkamp.

Office of Management and Budget. 1974. *Social Indicators.* Washington, DC: Government Printing Office.

Ogden, Charles, and Ivor A. Richards. 1938. *The Meaning of Meaning.* New York: Harcourt Brace Jovanovich. Reprint, 1959.

Oliver, Frederick S. 1931. *The Endless Adventure: Personalities and Practical Politics in Eighteenth-Century England.* Boston: Houghton Mifflin.

Olsen, Marvin E. 1982. *Participatory Pluralism: Political Participation and Influence in the United States and Sweden.* Chicago: Nelson-Hall.

Olsen, Marvin E. and Michael Micklin, eds. 1981. *Handbook of Applied Sociology: Frontiers of Contemporary Research.* New York: Praeger.

Olson, Laura Katz. 1982. *The Political Economy of Aging: The State, Private Power, and Social Welfare.* New York: Columbia University Press.

Olson, Mancur L., Jr. 1971. *Logic of Collective Action: Public Goods and the Theory of Groups.* Cambridge: Harvard University Press.

———. 1982. *The Rise and Decline of Nations: Economic Growth, Stagflation, and Social Rigidities.* New Haven: Yale University Press.

Olson, Mancur, Jr., and Hans H. Landsberg, eds. 1973. *The No-Growth Society.* New York: Norton.

Omer, Salima M. 1983. *Institution Building and Comprehensive Social Development.* Lanham, MD: University Press of America.

Oneal, John R. 1982. *Foreign Policy Making in Times of Crisis.* Columbus, OH: Ohio State University Press.

Oneal, John R. 1983. "The Appropriateness of the Rational Actor Model in the Study of Crisis Decision Making." Paper presented at the annual meeting of the American Political Science Association, Chicago.

Ophuls, William. 1977. *Ecology and the Politics of Scarcity: Prologue to a Political Theory of the Steady State.* San Francisco: Freeman.

Oren, Nissan, ed. 1984. *Intellectuals in Politics.* Jerusalem: Magnes.

Orlovsky, T. Daniel. 1981. *The Limits of Reform: The Ministry of Internal Affairs in Imperial Russia, 1802-1818.* Cambridge: Harvard University Press.

Ortega y Gassett, José. 1932. *The Revolt of the Masses.* New York: Norton.

Ortlieb, Heniz-Dietrich. 1974. *Vom Volkskapitalismus zur Playboy-Demokratie.* Zürich: Edition Interfrom AG.

Orwell, George. 1954. *Nineteen Eighty-Four.* London: Penguin.

Osborne, Thomas R. 1983. *A Grande Ecole for the Grands Corps: The Recruitment and Training of the French Administrative Elite in the Nineteenth and Twentieth Century.* New York: Columbia University Press.

Osgood, Charles E., William H. May, and Murray S. Miron. 1975. *Cross-Cultural Universals of Affective Meaning.* Urbana: University of Illinois Press.

Osterfeld, David. 1983. *Freedom, Society and the State: An Investigation into the Possibility of Society without Government.* Lanham, MD: University Press of America.

Owen, David, Saburo Okita, and Zbigniew Brzezinski. 1984. "Democracy Must Work." *International Herald Tribune.* 9 April 1984. Trilateral Commission Report.

Owen, P.A. 1983. "Decisions That Influence Outcomes in the Distant Future." *IEEE Transactions on Systems, Man, and Cybernetics* 13 (January-February): 1-10.

Oxford Analytica. 1984. *America in Perspective.* Oxford: Oxford Analytica.

Ozbudun, Ergun, and Ali Kazancigil. 1982. *Ataturk: Founder of a Modern State.* Hamden, CT: Shoe String Press.

Ozment, Steven. 1980. *The Age of Reform, 1250-1550: An Intellectual and Religious History of Late Medieval and Reformation Europe.* New Haven: Yale University Press.

Paddison, Ronan. 1983. *The Fragmented State: The Political Geography of Power.* New York: St. Martin's Press.

Padgett, John F. 1980. "Managing Garbage Can Hierarchies." *Administrative Science Quarterly* 25: 583-604.

Page, Benjamin I. 1983. *Who Gets What from Government.* Berkeley and Los Angeles: University of California Press.

Paige, Glenn, D., ed. 1972. *Political Leadership.* New York: Free Press.

———. 1977. *The Scientific Study of Political Leadership.* New York: Free Press.

Palmer, Bruce Jr., ed. 1976. *Grand Strategy for the 1980s.* Washington, DC: American Enterprise Institute.

Palmer, John L., and Isabel V. Sawhill, eds. 1982. *The Reagan Experiment: An Examination of Economic and Social Policies under the Reagan Administration.* Washington, DC: Urban Institute Press.

Papineau, David. 1979. *For Science in the Social Sciences*. New York: St. Martin's Press.

Parfit, Derek. 1983. *Reasons and Persons*. Oxford: Oxford University Press.

Parikh, Kirit, and Ferenc Rabár, eds. 1981. *Food for All in a Sustainable World: The IIASA Food and Agriculture Program*. SR-81-2. Laxenburg, Austria: International Institute for Applied Systems Analysis.

Paris, Chris, ed. 1982. *Critical Readings in Planning Theory*. New York: Pergamon.

Paris, David C., and James F. Reynolds. 1983. *The Logic of Policy Inquiry*. New York: Longman.

Parkinson, C. Northcote. 1980. *Parkinson: The Law*. Boston: Houghton Miffflin.

Passingham, R.T. 1983. *The Human Primate*. San Francisco: Freeman.

Passow, Harry A. 1979. *The Gifted and the Talented: Their Education and Development*. The 78th Yearbook of the National Society for the Study of Education, pt. 1. Chicago: University of Chicago Press.

Patton, Michael Q. 1975. *Alternative Evaluation Research Paradigm*. Grand Forks: University of North Dakota.

Pauker, J. Guy. 1977. *Military Implications of a Possible World Order Crisis in the 1980s*. R-2003-AF. Santa Monica, CA: Rand Corporation.

Paulson, Ronald. 1983. *Representations of Revolutions (1789-1820)*. New Haven: Yale University Press.

Peacock, Alan. 1979. *The Economic Analysis of Government: And Related Themes*. New York: St. Martin's Press.

Pearl, David. 1982. *Television and Behavior*. Washington, DC: U.S. Department of Health and Human Services.

Pears, David. 1984. *Motivated Irrationality*. New York: Oxford University Press.

Peccei, Aurelio. 1977. *The Human Quality*. Oxford: Pergamon.

_____. 1981. *One Hundred Pages for the Future: Reflections of the President of the Club of Rome*. New York: Pergamon.

Pechmann, Joseph A., ed. 1983. *Setting National Priorities: The 1984 Budget*. Washington, DC: Brookings Institution.

Peikoff, Leonard. 1982. *The Ominous Parallels: The End of Freedom in America*. New York: Stein & Day.

Pempel, T.J., ed. 1977. *Policymaking in Contemporary Japan*. Ithaca, NY: Cornell University Press.

_____. 1978. *Patterns of Japanese Policymaking: Experiences from Higher Education*. Boulder, CO: Westview.

_____. 1982. *Policy and Politics in Japan: Creative Conservatism*. Philadelphia: Temple University Press.

Pennock, J. Roland. 1979. *Democratic Political Theory*. Princeton: Princeton University Press.

Perkins, D.N. 1981. *The Mind's Best Work: A New Psychology of Creative Thinking*. Cambridge: Harvard University Press.

Perlmutter, Amos. 1981. *Modern Authoritarianism: A Comparative Institutional Analysis*. New Haven: Yale University Press.

Perloff, Harvey S., ed. 1971. *The Future of the U.S. Government: Toward the Year 2000*. Englewood Cliffs, NJ: Prentice-Hall.

Perloff, Robert, Evelyn Perloff, and Edward Sussna. 1976. "Program Evaluation." *Annual Review of Psychology* 27: 569-94.

Perrow, Charles. 1977. "Review of March and Olsen." *Contemporary Sociology* (May): 294-98.

_____. 1984. *Normal Accidents: Living with High-Risk Technologies.* New York: Basic Books.

Perry, Marvin. 1982. *Arnold Toynbee and the Crisis of the West.* Lanham, MD: University Press of America.

Persson, B., ed. 1979. *Surviving Failures: Patterns and Causes of Project Mismanagement.* Stockholm: Almqvist & Wiksell.

Pertschuk, Michael. 1982. *Revolt Against Regulation: The Rise and Pause of the Consumer Movement.* Berkeley and Los Angeles: University of California Press.

Peter, Laurence J., and Raymond Hull. 1969. *Peter Principle: Why Things Always Go Wrong.* New York: Morrow.

Peters, Guy B. 1982. *American Public Policy: Process and Performance.* New York: Watts.

Peters, Thomas J., and Robert H. Waterman, Jr. 1983. *In Search of Excellence: Lessons from America's Best-Run Companies.* New York: Harper & Row.

Peterson, Steven A. 1983. "Why Policies Don't Work: A Biocognitive Perspective." Paper prepared for annual meeting of the American Political Science Association, Chicago.

Pettigrew, Andrew M. 1973. *The Politics of Organizational Decision Making.* New York: Tavistock.

Pfalzgraff, Robert L., Jr., Uri Ra'anan, and Wasser H. Milberg, eds. 1981. *Intelligence Policy and National Security.* London: Macmillan.

Pfister, Oskar. 1944. *Das Christentum und die Angst: Eine religionspsychologische, historische und religionshygienische Untersuchung.* Zürich: Artemis-Verlag.

Phelan, M. John. 1980. *Disenchantement: Meaning and Morality in the Media.* New York: Hastings House.

Phillips, Kevin. 1982. *Post-Conservative America: People, Politics, and Ideology in a Time of Crisis.* New York: Random House.

Phillipson, Chris. 1982. *Capitalism and the Construction of Old Age.* London: Macmillan.

Pill, Juri. 1979. *Planning and Politics.* Cambridge: MIT Press.

Pinder, John. 1982. *National Industrial Strategies and the World Economy.* London: Croom Helm.

Pitkin, Walter B. 1932. *A Short Introduction to the History of Human Stupidity.* New York: Simon & Schuster.

Plamenatz, John. 1973. *Democracy and Illusion: An Examination of Certain Aspects of Modern Democratic Theory.* London: Longman.

Plechanow, J. W. 1977. *Über die Rolle der Persönlichkeit in der Geschichte.* Frankfurt: Verlag Marxistische Blätter. Translated from the Russian.

Plessner, Helmuth. 1931. *Macht und Menschliche Natur: Ein Versuch zur Anthropoligie der Geschichtlichen Weltansicht.* Berlin: Juncker & Dünnhaupt.

Pletsch, Carl E. 1981. "The Three Worlds, or the Division of Social Scientific Labor circa 1950-1975." *Comparative Studies in Society and History* 23: 565-90.

Plott, Charles R. 1976. "Axiomatic Social Choice Theory: An Overview and Interpretation." *American Journal of Political Science* 20 (August): 511-96.

Plott, Charles R. and Michael E. Levine. 1978. "A Model of Agenda Influence on Committee Decisions." *American Economic Review* 68, no. 1: 146-60.

Pocock, J.G.A. 1971. *Politics, Language and Time: Essays on Political Thought and History.* New York: Atheneum.

———. 1975. *The Machiavellian Moment: Florentine Political Thought and the Atlantic Republic Tradition.* Princeton: Princeton University Press.

Podgorecki, Adam. 1976. *Practical Social Sciences.* London: Routledge & Kegan Paul.

Poggi, Gianfranco. 1978. *The Development of the Modern State: A Sociological Introduction.* Stanford: Stanford University Press.

Polanyi, Michael. 1974. *Personal Knowledge Towards a Post-Critical Philosophy.* Chicago: University of Chicago Press.

Policy Studies Institute. 1980. *Japanese Industrial Policy.* Report No. 585. London: Policy Studies Institute.

Pollard, Sidney. 1981. *The Wasting of the British Economy: British Economic Policy, 1945 to the Present.* London: Croom Helm.

Pollitt, Christopher. 1980. "Rationalizing the Machinery of Government: The Conservatives, 1970-1974." *Political Studies* 208, no. 1: 84-98.

Pollitt, Christopher, et al., eds. 1979. *Public Policy in Theory and Practice.* Mill Road, United Kingdom: Hodder & Stoughton.

Polmar, Norman, and Thomas B. Allen. 1982. *Rickover.* New York: Simon & Schuster.

Polsby, Nelson W., ed. 1982. *What if . . .? Explorations in Social Science Fiction.* Lexington, MA: Lewis.

———. 1983a. "Tanks But Not Tanks." *Public Opinion* 6 (April/May): 14-16, 58-59.

———. 1983b. *Consequences of Party Reform.* Oxford: Oxford University Press.

———. 1984. *Political Innovation in America: The Politics of Policy Initiation.* New Haven: Yale University Press.

Popper, Karl R. 1961. *The Poverty of Historicism.* London: Routledge & Kegan Paul. First published 1957.

———. 1966. *Of Clouds and Clocks: An Approach to the Problem of Rationality and the Freedom of Man.* St. Louis, MO: Washington University.

———. 1967. "La Rationalite et le statut du principe de rationalite." In *Les Fondements Philosophiques des Systemes Economiques,* edited by Emil M. Claassen. Paris: Payot.

———. 1972a. *Objective Knowledge: An Evolutionary Approach.* Oxford: Oxford University Press.

———. 1972b. *Logic of Scientific Discovery.* New York: Harper & Row.

———. 1972c. *Conjectures and Refutations: The Growth of Scientific Knowledge.* 4th ed. London: Routledge & Kegan Paul.

———. 1982. *The Open Universe: An Argument for Indeterminism,* edited by W.W. Bartley. London: Hutchinson.

Porter, Bernard. 1983. *Britain, Europe and the World, 1850-1982: Delusions of Grandeur*. London: Allen & Unwin.

Porter, Mary Cornelia, and G. Alan Tarr, eds. 1982. *State Supreme Courts: Policymakers in the Federal System*. Westport, CO: Greenwood Press.

Porter, Roger B. 1980. *Presidential Decision Making: The Economic Policy Board*. Cambridge: Cambridge University Press.

Portis, Edward B., and Dwight F. Davis. 1982. "Policy Analysis and Scientific Ossification." *PS* 15 (Fall): 593-99.

Potter, David M. 1954. *People of Plenty: Economic Abundance and the American Character*. Chicago: University of Chicago Press.

Pound, Roscoe. 1907. "The Need of a Sociological Jurisprudence." *The Green Bag* 19: 607ff.

Powell, G. Bingham, Jr. 1982. *Contemporary Democracies: Participation, Stability and Violence*. Cambridge: Harvard University Press.

Prados, John. 1982. *The Soviet Estimate: U.S. Intelligence Analysis and Russian Military Strength*. New York: Dial.

Pratt, Henry J. 1976. *The Gray Lobby*. Chicago: University of Chicago Press.

Preisl, Anton, and Armin Mohler, eds. 1979. *Der Ernstfall*. Frankfurt am Main: Propylaen.

Premack, David, and Ann James Premack. 1983. *The Mind of an Ape*. New York: Norton.

Premchand, A. 1983. *Government Budgeting and Expenditure Controls*. Washington, DC: International Monetary Fund.

Pressman, Jeffrey L., and Aaron Wildavsky. 1973. *Implementation*. Berkeley and Los Angeles: University of California Press.

Preston, Paul. 1983. *The Coming of the Spanish Civil War: Reform, Reaction and Revolution in the Second Republic*. London: Methuen.

Prince, M.J. 1983. *Policy Advice and Organizational Survival: Policy Planning and Research Units in British Government*. Aldershot, United Kingdom: Gower.

Privy Council Office. 1981. *The Policy and Expenditure Management System*. Ottawa: Privy Council Office.

Pross, A.P. 1982. "From System to Serendipity: The Practice and Study of Public Policy in the Trudeau Years." *Canadian Public Administration* 25 (Winter): 520-44.

Przeworski, Adam, and Henry Teune. 1970. *The Logic of Comparative Social Inquiry*. New York: Wiley.

Punnett, R.M. 1977. *The Prime Minister in Canadian Government and Politics*. Toronto: Macmillan.

Putnam, Robert D. 1973. *The Beliefs of Politicians: Ideology, Conflict, and Democracy in Britain and Italy*. New Haven: Yale University Press.

———. 1976. *The Comparative Study of Political Elites*. Englewood Cliffs, NJ: Prentice-Hall.

Putten, Jan van. 1982. "Policy Styles in the Netherlands: Negotiation and Conflict." In *Policy Styles in Western Europe*, edited by Jeremy Richardson. London: Allen & Unwin.

Quade, Edward. 1982. *Analysis for Public Decisions.* Rev. ed. New York: Elsevier.

Quade, Edward S., and Hugh J. Miser, eds. 1985. *Handbook of Systems Analysis: Overview of Uses, Procedures, Applications, and Practice.* New York: Elsevier.

Quandt, William B. 1982. *Saudi Arabia in the 1980s: Foreign Policy, Security and Oil.* London: Blackwell.

Ra'anan, Uri, ed. 1980. *Ethnic Resurgence in Modern Democratic States: A Multidisciplinary Approach to Human Resources and Conflict.* New York: Pergamon.

Rabin, Jack, and Thomas D. Lynch, eds. 1983. *Handbook of Public Budgeting and Financial Management.* New York: Dekker.

Rabinow, Paul, and William M. Sullivan, ed. 1979. *Interpretive Social Science: A Reader.* Berkeley and Los Angeles: University of California Press.

Rabushka, Alvin, and Pauline Ryan. 1982. *The Tax Revolt.* Stanford: Hoover Institution.

Radian, Alex 1980. *Resource Mobilization in Poor Countries: Implementing Tax Policies.* New Brunswick, NJ: Transaction.

Raeff, Marc. 1983. *The Well-Ordered Police State: Social and Institutional Change Through Law in the Germanies and Russia, 1600-1800.* New Haven: Yale University Press.

Raiffa, Howard. 1968. *Decision Analysis.* Reading, MA: Addison-Wesley.

Rajecki, D.W., ed. 1983. *Comparing Behavior: Studying Man Studying Animals.* Hillsdale, NJ: Erlbaum.

Ramo, Simon. 1983. *What's Wrong with Our Technological Society—And How to Fix It.* New York: McGraw-Hill.

Ramsay, Robert. 1983. *The Corsican Time-Bomb.* Manchester, United Kingdom: Manchester University Press.

Ramsden, John. 1980. *The Making of Conservative Party Policy: The Conservative Research Department Since 1929.* London: Longman.

Ranney, Austin, ed. 1968. *Political Science and Public Policy.* Chicago: Markham.

———. 1976. "'The Divine Science': Political Engineering in American Culture." *American Political Science Review* 70 (March): 140-48.

———, ed. 1981. *The Referendum Device.* Washington, DC: American Enterprise Institute.

———. 1983. *Channels of Power: The Impact of Television on American Politics.* New York: Basic Books.

Rawls, John. 1971. *A Theory of Justice.* Cambridge: Harvard University Press.

Rea, Desmond, ed. 1982. *Political Co-operation in Divided Societies: A Series of Papers Relevant to the Conflict in Northern Island.* London: Gill and Macmillan.

Rebe, Bernd, Klaus Lompe, and Rudolf von Thadden, eds. 1984. *Idee und Pragmatick in der Politischen Entscheidung: Alfred Kubel zum 75. Geburtstag.* Berlin: Verlag Neue Gesellschaft.

Redford, Emmette S., and Marlan Blissett. 1981. *Organizing the Executive Branch: The Johnson Presidency.* Chicago: University of Chicago Press.

Reich, Robert B. 1983. *The Next American Frontier.* New York: Times Books.

Reich, Wilhelm. 1946. *The Mass Psychology of Fascism*. Translated from German. New York: Orgone Institute.

Rein, Martin. 1976. *Social Science and Public Policy*. Harmondsworth, United Kingdom: Penguin.

———. 1983a. *Social Policy: Issues of Choice and Change*. Abr. ed., 1970 version. New York: Sharpe.

———. 1983b. *From Policy to Practice*. New York: Sharpe.

Rejai, Mostafa, with Kay Phillips. 1979. *Leaders of Revolutions*. Beverly Hills, CA: Sage.

Renshon, Stanley A. 1977. "Temporal Orientations and Political Life: The Psychology of Political Impatience." *British Journal of Political Science* 7, pt. 2 (April): 262-72.

Rettig, Richard A. 1977. *Cancer Crusade: The Story of the National Cancer Act of 1971*. Princeton: Princeton University Press.

Revans, Regina W. 1982. *The Origins and Growth of Action Learning*. Bromley, United Kingdom: Chatwell-Brath.

Rhoads, Steven E. 1980. *Valuing Life: Public Policy Dilemmas*. Boulder, CO: Westview.

Rhodes, R.A. 1979. *Public Administration and Policy Analysis: Recent Developments in Britain and America*. Farnborough, United Kingdom: Saxon House.

Rich, Paul B. 1984. *White Power and the Liberal Conscience: Radical Segregation and South Africa Liberalism, 1921-60*. Manchester, United Kingdom: Manchester University Press.

Rich, Robert F. 1981. *The Power of Social Science Information and Public Policymaking: The Case of the Continuous National Survey*. San Francisco: Jossey-Bass.

Richardson, Jeremy, ed. 1982. *Policy Styles in Western Europe*. London: Allen & Unwin.

Ridgeway, Cecilia L. 1983. *The Dynamics of Small Groups*. New York: St. Martin's Press.

Rieselbach, Leroy N., ed. 1978. *Legislative Reform: The Policy Impact*. Lexington, MA: Lexington Books.

Riker, William H. 1982. *Liberalism against Populism: A Confrontation between the Theory of Democracy and the Theory of Social Choice*. San Francisco: Freeman.

———. 1984. "The Heresthetics of Constitution-Making: The Presidency in 1787, with Comments on Determinism and Rational Choice". *American Political Science Review* (March): 1-16.

Riker, William H., and Peter C. Ordeshook. 1973. *An Introduction to Positive Political Theory*. Englewood Cliffs, NJ: Prentice-Hall.

Riklin, Alois, and Ronald Kley. 1982. Quoted in Harry Trimborn, "Increasing Apathy in Swiss Elections May Point to Overdose of Democracy." *International Herald Tribune*, 12 January 1983.

Ripley, Randall, and Grace A. Franklin. 1982. *Bureaucracy and Policy Implementation*. Homewood, IL: Dorsey Press.

Ritchie, Ronald S. 1971. *An Institute for Research on Public Policy*. Ottawa: Information Canada.

Ritter, Gerhard. 1969-73. *The Sword and the Scepter: The Problem of Militarism in Germany*. 4 vols. Baltimore, MD: University of Miami Press. Translated from the German.

Rivera, Joseph de. 1968. *The Psychological Dimension of Foreign Policy*. Columbus, OH: Charles E. Merrill.

Rivett, Patrick. 1980. *Model Building for Decision Analysis*. New York: Wiley.

Rivlin, Alice. 1971. *Systematic Thinking for Social Action*. Washington, DC: Brookings Institution.

Robbins, R.S., ed. 1977. *Psychopathology and Political Leadership*. New Orleans: Tulane University Press.

Roberts, Donald F., and Christine M. Bachen. 1981. "Mass Communication Effects." *Annual Review of Psychology* 32: 307-56.

Roberts, Karlene H. 1970. "On Looking at an Elephant: An Evaluation of Cross-Cultural Research Related to Organizations." *Psychological Bulletin* 74 (November): 327-50.

Robertson, K.G. 1982. *Public Secrets: A Study in the Development of Government Secrecy*. London: Macmillan.

Robey, John S. 1984. *Public Policy Analysis: Annotated Bibliography*. Frankfurt am Main: Gerland.

Robinson, A., and B.-C. Ysander. 1981. *Flexibility in Budget Policy: The Changing Problems and Requirements of Public Budgeting*. Working Paper No. 50. Stockholm: Industrial Institute for Economic and Social Research.

Robinson, Gertrude Joch. 1977. *Tito's Maverick Media: The Politics of Mass Communication in Yugoslavia*. Urbana: University of Illinois Press.

Robinson, Michael J., and Margaret A. Sheehan. 1983. *Over the Wire and on TV: CBS and UPI in Campaign '80*. New York: Russell Sage Foundation.

Rock, Irvin. 1975. *The Logic of Perception*. New York: Macmillan.

Roebuck, Janet. 1979. "When Does 'Old Age' Begin?: The Evolution of the English Definition." *Journal of Social History* 12 (Spring): 416-28.

Roemer, John E. 1982. *A General Theory of Exploitation and Class*. Cambridge: Harvard University Press.

Rogger, Hans. 1984. *Russia in the Age of Modernisation and Revolution 1881-1917*. London: Longman.

Rogowski, Ronald. 1974. *Rational Legitimacy: A Theory of Political Support*. Princeton: Princeton University Press.

———. 1978. "Rationalistic Theories of Politics: A Midterm Report." *World Politics* 30 (January): 296-323.

Rohety, James M., ed. 1980, *Defense Policy Formation: Towards Comparative Analysis*. Durham, NC: Carolina Academic Press.

Rokeach, Milton. 1960. *Open and Closed Mind*. New York: Basic Books.

———. 1973. *The Nature of Human Values*. New York: Free Press.

———. 1979. *Understanding Human Values: Individual and Societal*. New York: Free Press.

Rokkan, S., and D.W. Urwin, eds. 1982. *The Politics of Territorial Identity: Studies in European Regionalism.* Beverly Hills, CA: Sage.

Romasco, Albert U. 1983. *The Politics of Recovery: Roosevelt's New Deal.* New York: Oxford University Press.

Rome, Beatrice K., and Sydney C. Rome. 1971. *Organizational Growth through Decision Making: A Computer-Based Experiment in Educative Method.* New York: Elsevier.

Rondinelli, D.A. 1983. *Development Projects as Policy Experiments: An Adaptive Approach to Development Administration.* London: Methuen.

Roosevelt, Elliot. 1983. *The Conservators.* New York: Arbor House.

Röpke, Jochen. 1977. *Die Strategie der Innovation: Eine systemtheoretische Untersuchung der Interaktion von Individuum, Organisation und Markt im Neuerungsprozess.* Tübingen: J.C.B. Mohr.

Rorty, Amelie. 1980. "Self-Deception, Akrasia, and Irrationality." *Social Science Information* 19: 905-22.

Rosa, Jean-Jacques, ed. 1982. *The World Crisis in Social Security.* Paris: Bonnel.

Rosat, Jerel A. 1981. "Developing a Systematic Decision-Making Framework: Bureaucratic Politics in Perspective." *World Politics* 30: 234-52.

Rose, Richard. 1973. "Comparing Public Policy: An Overview." *European Journal of Political Research* 1: 67-94.

_____. 1976. "On the Priorities of Government: A Developmental Analysis of Public Policies." *European Journal of Political Research* 4: 247-89.

_____, ed. 1980. *Challenge to Governance: Studies in Overloaded Politics.* Beverly Hills, CA: Sage.

_____. 1981. "What If Anything Is Wrong with Big Government." *Journal of Public Policy* 1, pt. 1 (February): 5-36.

_____. 1982. *The Role of Laws in Comparative Perspective.* Glasgow: Centre for the Study of Public Policy, University of Strathclyde.

_____. 1983a. *Getting By in Three Economies.* Glasgow: Centre for the Study of Policy, University of Strathclyde.

_____. 1983b. *Understanding Big Government.* Beverly Hills, CA: Sage.

_____. 1983c. *Under What Circumstances Is Statute Law a Resource of Public Policy.* Oxford: SSRC Centre for Socio-Legal Studies.

Rose, Richard, and Guy Peters. 1978. *Can Government Go Bankrupt?* London: Macmillan.

Rose, Richard, and Ezra N. Suleiman, eds. 1980. *Presidents and Prime Ministers.* Washington, DC: American Enterprise Institute.

Rosser, J.B., and A.R. Turquette. 1977. *Many-Valued Logics.* Westport, CT: Greenwood Press. First published 1952.

Rossi, Peter, Howard Freeman, and Sonia Wright. 1979. *Evaluation: A Systematic Approach.* Beverly Hills, CA: Sage.

Rossi, Peter H., et al. 1983. *Natural Hazards and Public Choice: The State and Local Politics of Hazard Mitigation.* New York: Academic Press.

Rostow, W.W. 1978. *The World Economy: History and Prospects.* Austin: University of Texas Press.

_____. 1982. *The Division of Europe After World War II.* Farnborough, United Kingdom: Gower.

_____. 1983. *The Barbaric Counter-Revolution: Cause and Cure.* Austin: University of Texas Press.

Rotberg, Robert I. 1980. *Suffer the Future: Policy Choices in Southern Africa.* Cambridge: Harvard University Press.

Rothchild, S. Donald, and Robert L. Curry, Jr. 1978. *Scarcity, Choice, and Public Policy in Middle Africa.* Berkeley and Los Angeles: University of California Press.

Rothschild, Lord. 1982. *An Enquiry into the Social Science Research Council.* Cmnd 8554. London: Her Majesty's Stationery Office.

Rothschuh, Karl E. 1965. *Prinzipien der Medizin: Ein Wegweiser durch die Medizin.* Munich: Urban & Schwarzenberg.

Rothschuh, Karl E., ed. 1975. *Was ist Krankheit? Erscheinung, Erklärung, Sinngebung.* Darmstadt: Wissenschaftliche Buchgesellschaft.

Rourke, Francis E. 1984. *Bureaucracy, Politics and Public Policy.* 3d ed. Boston: Little, Brown.

Rousseas, Stephen. 1979. *Capitalism and Catastrophe: A Critical Appraisal of the Limits to Capitalism.* Cambridge: Cambridge University Press.

Rowat, D.C., ed. 1979. *Administrative Secrecy in Developed Countries.* London: Macmillan.

Ruin, Olof. 1982. "Sweden in the 1970s: Policy-Making Becoming More Difficult." In *Policy Styles in Western Europe*, edited by Jeremy Richardson. London: Allen & Unwin.

Rule, James B. 1978. *Insight and Social Betterment.* New York: Oxford University Press.

Ruse, Michael. 1974. "Cultural Evolution." *Theory and Decision* 5: 413-40.

Rush, Michael. 1984. *The Cabinet and Policy Formation.* Essex, United Kingdom: Longman.

Russell, Bertrand. 1948. *Human Knowledge: Its Scope and Limits.* New York: Simon & Schuster.

Rüstow, Alexander. 1981. *Freedom and Domination: A Historical Critique of Civilization.* Princeton: Princeton University Press. Abridged translation from German original: *Ortsbestimmung der Gegenwart.* 3 vols. Stuttgart: Eugen Rentsche, 1950, 1952, 1957.

Rutman, Leonard, ed. 1977. *Evaluation Research Methods: A Basic Guide.* Beverly Hills, CA: Sage.

Sabato, Larry J. 1982. *The Rise of Political Consultants: New Ways of Winning Elections.* New York: Basic Books.

Sacks, Sheldon, ed. 1979. *On Metaphor.* Chicago: University of Chicago Press.

Sahlins, Marshall. 1976. *The Use and Abuse of Biology: An Anthropological Critique of Sociobiology.* Ann Arbor: University of Michigan Press.

Salk, Jonas. 1983. *Anatomy of Reality: The Merging of Intuition and Reason.* New York: Columbia University Press.

Salk, Jonas, and Jonathan Salk. 1981. *World Population and Human Value: A New Reality.* New York: Harper & Row.

Salmon, J.H.M. 1975. *Society in Crisis: France in the Sixteenth Century.* New York: St. Martin's Press.

Samoff, Joel. 1979. "The Bureaucracy and the Bourgeoisie: Decentralization and Class Structure in Tanzania." *Comparative Studies in Society and History* 21: 30-62.

Sampton, Anthony. 1983. *The Changing Anatomy of Britain.* New York: Random House.

Sandel, Michael J. 1982. *Liberalism and the Limits of Justice.* Cambridge: Cambridge University Press.

Sanders, David. 1981. *Patterns of Political Instability.* London: Macmillan.

Sanders, Ralph. 1973. *The Politics of Defense Analysis.* New York: Dunellen.

Sanford, Terry. 1981. *A Danger of Democracy: The Presidential Nominating Process.* Boulder, CO: Westview.

Sargeaunt, H.A., and Geoffrey West. 1942. *Grand Strategy: The Search for Victory.* London: Jonathan Cape.

Sarkisyanz, Emanuel. 1955. *Russland und der Messianismus des Orients: Sendungsbewusstsein und politischer Chiliasmus des Ostens.* Tübingen: J.C.B. Mohr.

Sathyamurthy, T.V. 1982. *Nationalism in the Contemporary World: Political and Sociological Perspectives.* Totowa, NJ: Rowman & Allanheld.

Saunders, Charles B., Jr. 1966. *Brookings Institution: A Fifty-Year History.* Washington, DC: Brookings Institution.

Schalk, L. David. 1979. *The Spectrum of Political Engagement.* Princeton: Princeton University Press.

Schank, R.C., and R.P. Abelson. 1977. *Scripts, Plans, Goals, and Understanding.* Hillsdale, NJ: Lawrence Erlbaum.

Schapera, Isaac. 1970. *Tribal Innovators: Tswana Chiefs and Social Change, 1795-1940.* London: Athlone Press.

Scharpf, Fritz W. 1981. *The Political Economy of Inflation and Unemployment in Western Europe: An Outline.* ISSN Br. 0720-4914. Berlin: International Institute of Management, Wissenschaftszentrum Berlin.

Scharpf, Fritz W., Bernd Reissert, and Fritz Schnabel. 1976. *Politikverflechtung: Theorie und Empirie des kooperativen Föderalismus in der Bundesrepublik.* Kronberg/Ts.: Athenäum.

_____. 1977. *Politikverflechtung II: Kritik und Berichte aus der Praxis.* Kronberg/Ts.: Athenäum.

Scheler, Max. 1974. *Die Stellung des Menschen im Kosmos.* Rev. ed. Munich: Nymphenberger Verlagshandlung. First published 1927.

Schell, Jonathan. 1982. *The Fate of the Earth,* New York: Knopf.

Schelling, Thomas C. 1978. *Micromotives and Macrobehavior.* New York: Norton.

_____. 1980. "The Intimate Contest for Self-Command." *Public Interest,* no. 60 (Summer): 94-118.

_____. 1984. *Choice and Consequence.* Cambridge, MA: Harvard University Press.

Schelsky, Helmut. 1965. *Auf der Suche nach Wirklichkeit: Gesammelte Aufsatze.* Düsseldorf: Eugen Diederichs.

———. 1984. *Politik und Publizität*. Stuttgart: Seewald.

Schick, Frederic. 1983. *Having Reasons: An Essay on Rationality and Sociality*. Princeton: Princeton University Press.

Schilpp, P.A., ed. 1974. *The Philosophy of Karl Popper*. La Salle, IL: Open Court.

Schlesinger, Arthur M. 1949. *Paths to the Present*. New York: Macmillan.

Schlesinger, A.M., Jr., 1965. *A Thousand Days: John F. Kennedy in the White House*. Boston: Houghton Mifflin.

Schmidt, Joachim K.H.W., ed. 1975. *Planvolle Steuerung Gesellschaftlichen Handelns: Grundlegende Beiträge zur Gesellschafttechnik und Gesellschaftsarchitektur*. Opladen: Westdeutscher.

Schmidt, Peter, ed. 1976. *Innovation: Diffusion von Neuerungen im Sozialen Bereich*. Hamburg: Hoffmann & Campe.

Schmitt, Carl. 1963. *Der Begriff des Politischen*. Berlin: Duncker & Humblot. Shorter version first published 1927.

———. 1954. *Gespräch Über die Macht und den Zugang zum Machthaber*. Pfullingen: Günther Neske.

———. 1970. *Politische Theologie II: Die Legende von der Erledigung jeder Politischen Theologie*. Berlin: Duncker & Humblot.

———. 1975. *Theorie der Partisanen: Zwischenbemerkung zum Begriff des Politischen*. 2d ed. Berlin: Duncker & Humblot.

———. 1979. *Politische Theologie: Vier Kapital zur Lehre von der Souveränität*. Berlin: Duncker & Humblot. Reprint of 2d ed., 1934.

———. 1982. *Politische Romantik*. Berlin: Duncker & Humblot. Reprint of 2d ed., 1925.

Schmitter, Philippe C., ed. 1977. *Corporatism and Policy-Making in Contemporary Western Europe*. Special issue, *Comparative Political Studies* 10 (April).

———. 1981. "Interest Intermediation and Regime Governability in Contemporary Western Europe and North America." In *Organizing Interests in Western Europe: Pluralism, Corporatism and the Transformation of Politics*, edited by Suzanne Berger. Cambridge: Cambridge University Press.

Schmuck, Peter H. 1983. "Industrial Policy's Obstacles." *New York Times*, 6 September, A23.

Schmukler, Nathan, and Edward Marcus, eds. 1983. *Inflation Through the Ages: Economic, Social, Psychological and Historical Aspects*. New York: Columbia University Press.

Scholtz, Harald. 1967, "Die 'NS-Ordensburgen'." *Vierteljahreshefte Für Zeitgeschichte* 15: 269-98.

———. 1973. *NS-Ausleseschulen: Internatschulen als Herrschaftsmittel des Führerstaates*. Göttingen: Vandenhoeck & Ruprecht.

Schon, Donald A. 1971. *Beyond the Stable State: Public and Private Learning in a Changing Society*. London: Temple Smith.

———. 1983. *The Reflective Practitioner: How Professionals Think in Action*. New York: Basic Books.

Schram, Glenn N. 1982. *Toward a Response to the American Crisis*. Lanham, MD: University Press of America.

Schulenberg, Wolfgang, ed. 1976. *Reform in der Demokratie: Theoretische Ansätze—Konkrete Erfahrungen—Politische Konsequenzen.* Hamburg: Hoffmann & Campe.

Schuler, Randall S. 1980. "Definition and Conceptualization of Stress in Organizations." *Organizational Behavior and Human Performance* 25: 184-215.

Schulman, Paul R. 1980. *Large-Scale Policy Making.* New York: Elsevier.

Schultheiss, Franklin. 1976. "Politische Bildung durch Massenmedien-Experimente und Erfahrungen." In Schulenberg, op. cit., pp. 247-58.

Schulz, James. 1979. *The Economics of Aging* 3d ed. Belmont, CA: Wadworth.

Schulze, Hagen. 1982. *Weimar: Deutschland, 1917-1933.* Berlin: Severin & Siedler.

Schumacher, E.F. 1973. *Small Is Beautiful: A Study of Economics as If People Mattered.* New York: Harper & Row.

Schumpeter, Joseph. 1952. *Capitalism, Socialism and Democracy.* London: Allen & Unwin.

Schurmann, Franz. 1968. *Ideology and Organization in Communist China.* Rev. ed. Berkeley and Los Angeles: University of California Press.

Schwabe, William, and Lewis M. Jamison. 1982. *A Rule-Based Policy-Level Model of Nonsuperpower Behavior in Strategic Conflicts.* R-2962-DNA. Santa Monica, CA: Rand Corporation.

Schwarz, Brita, Uno Svedin, and Bjorn Wittrock. 1982. *Methods in Futures Studies: Problems and Applications.* Boulder, CO: Westview.

Schwartz, J.E. 1980. "Exploring a New Role in Policy Making: The British House of Commons." *American Political Science Review* 74, no. 1: 23-36.

Schwarz, John E. 1983. *America's Hidden Success: A Reassessment of Twenty Years of Public Policy.* New York: Norton.

Schwartz, R.W., ed. 1983. *Decision Making under Uncertainty.* Amsterdam: North-Holland.

Schweitzer, Avraham. 1984. *Upheavals.* Tel Aviv: Zmora, Bitan. In Hebrew.

Scott, Robert A., and Arnold R. Shore. 1979. *Why Sociology Does Not Apply? A Study of the Use of Sociology in Public Policy.* New York: Elsevier.

Scott, William G. 1983. "Administrative Reform: The Revolutionary Renewal of America." *Public Administration Review* 43 (March/April): 182-90.

Searle, G.R. 1971. *The Quest for National Efficiency: A Study in British Politics and Political Thought, 1899-1914.* Berkeley and Los Angeles: University of California Press.

Searle, John R. 1983. *Intensionality: An Essay in the Philosophy of Mind.* Cambridge: Cambridge University Press.

Sears, David O., and Jack Citrin. 1982. *Tax Revolt: Something for Nothing in California.* Cambridge: Harvard University Press.

Sebeok, Thomas A. 1976. *Contributions to the Theory of Signs.* Bloomington: Indiana University Press.

Seidman, Edward, ed. 1983. *Handbook of Social Intervention.* Beverly Hills, CA: Sage.

Sekora, John. 1977. *Luxury: The Concept in Western Thought, Eden to Smollett.* Baltimore: Johns Hopkins University Press.

Self, Peter. 1975. *Econocrats and the Policy Process: The Politics and Philosophy of Cost-Benefit Analysis.* London: Macmillan.

Seliger, Martin. 1976. *Ideology and Politics.* London: Allen & Unwin.

Servan-Schreiber, Jean-Jacques. 1974. *The Power to Inform.* New York: McGraw-Hill. Translated from the French.

_____. 1981. *The World Challenge: OPEC and the New World Order.* New York: Simon & Schuster. Translated from the French.

Service, Elman. 1971. *Primitive Social Organization: An Evolutionary Process.* New York: Random House.

_____. 1975. *Origins of the State and Civilization: The Process of Cultural Evolution.* New York: Norton.

Sewell, W.R.D., and J.T. Coppock, eds. 1977. *Public Participation in Planning.* London: Wiley.

Shackle, G.L.S. 1952. *Expectation in Economics.* Cambridge: Cambridge University Press.

_____. 1961. *Decision, Order, and Time in Human Affairs.* Cambridge: Cambridge University Press.

_____. 1972. *Epistemics and Economics: A Critique of Economic Doctrines.* Cambridge: Cambridge University Press.

Shafer, Byron E. 1983. *Quiet Revolution: The Struggle for the Democratic Party and the Shaping of Post-Reform Politics.* New York: Russell Sage Foundation.

Sharkansky, Ira, ed. 1970. *Policy Analysis in Political Science.* Chicago: Markham.

_____. 1975. *Public Administration.* Chicago: Rand McNally.

Sharkansky, Ira, and Donald Van Meter. 1975. *Policy and Politics in American Governments.* New York: McGraw-Hill.

Sharpe, L.J., and K. Newton. 1984. *Does Politics Matter? The Determinants of Public Policy.* Oxford: Oxford University Press.

Sheehan, N., et al. 1971. *The Pentagon Papers as Published by the New York Times.* New York: Bantam.

Sheikh, A.A., ed. 1983. *Imagery: Current Theory, Research and Application.* New York: Wiley.

Sheldon, Eleanor B., and Wilbert E. Moore, eds. 1968. *Indicators of Social Change: Concepts and Measurement.* New York: Russell Sage Foundation.

Shils, Edward. 1972. *The Intelligence and the Power and Other Essays.* Chicago: University of Chicago Press.

_____. 1981. *Tradition.* London: Faber and Faber.

Shoesmith, D.J., and T.J. Smiley. 1978. *Multi-conclusion Logic.* Cambridge, United Kingdom: Cambridge University Press.

Shogan, Robert. 1982. *None of the Above: Why Presidents Fail—And What Can Be Done About It.* New York: New American Library.

Shonfield, Andrew. 1965. *Modern Capitalism: The Changing Balance of Public and Private Power.* Oxford: Oxford University Press.

_____. 1982. *The Use of Public Power.* Edited by Zuzanna Shonfield. Oxford: Oxford University Press.

_____. 1984. *In Defence of the Mixed Economy.* Edited by Zuzanna Shonfield. Oxford: Oxford University Press.

Shope, Robert K. 1983. *The Analysis of Knowing: A Decade of Research.* Princeton: Princeton University Press.

Sidjansku, Dusan 1973. *Political Decision-Making Processes: Studies in National, Comparative and International Politics.* New York: Elsevier.

Sieber, Sam D. 1981. *Fatal Remedies: The Ironies of Social Intervention.* New York: Plenum Press.

Siedentopf, Heinrich, ed. 1976. *Regierungspolitik und Koordination.* Berlin: Duncker & Humblot.

Sienkiewicz, Stanley. 1979. "Observations on the Impact of Uncertainty in Strategic Analysis." *World Politics* 32: 90-110.

Silver, Morris. 1983. *Enterprise and the Scope of the Firm.* Oxford: Blackwell.

Silverman, Dan P. 1982. *Reconstructing Europe after the Great War,* Cambridge: Harvard University Press.

Silverstein, Arthur M. 1982. *Pure Politics and Impure Science: The Swine Flu Affair.* Baltimore: Johns Hopkins University Press.

Simeon, Richard. 1976. "Studying Public Policy." *Canadian Journal of Political Science* 9 no. 4: 548-80.

Simes, Dimitri, ed. 1977. *Nationalities and Nationalism in the USSR: A Soviet Dilemma.* Washington, DC: Center for Strategic and International Studies, Georgetown University.

Simon, Herbert A. 1976a. "From Substantive to Procedural Rationality." In *Method and Appraisal in Economics,* edited by Spiro J. Latsis. Cambridge: Cambridge University Press.

———. 1976b. *Administrative Behavior.* 3d ed. New York: Free Press.

———. 1977. *The New Science of Management Decision.* Rev. ed. Englewood Cliffs, NJ: Prentice-Hall.

———. 1978. "Rationality as Process and as Product of Thought." *American Economic Review* 68 (May): 1-16.

———. 1979a. "Information Processing Models of Cognition." *Annual Review of Psychology* 30: 363-96.

———. 1979b. "Rational Decision Making in Business Organizations." *American Economic Review* 69, no. 4: 493-513.

———. 1981. *The Sciences of the Artificial.* Rev. ed. Cambridge: MIT Press.

———. 1982. *Models of Bounded Rationality.* Vol. 1, *Economic Analysis and Public Policy.* Vol. 2, *Behavioral Economics and Business Organization.* Cambridge: MIT Press.

——— 1983. *Reason in Human Affairs.* Stanford: Stanford University Press.

Simon, L. Julian. 1980. *The Ultimate Resource.* London: M. Robertson.

Simonton, Dean Keith. 1984. *Genius, Creativity, and Leadership.* Cambridge: Harvard University Press.

Siu-Kai, Lau. 1983. *Society and Politics in Hong Kong.* New York: St. Martin's Press.

Sjobert, L. 1982. "Aided and Unaided Decision Making—Improving Intuitive Judgment." *Journal of Forecasting* 1 (October-December): 349-64.

Sjobert, L., T. Tyszka, and J.A. Wise, eds. 1980. *Human Decision Making.* 2 vols. Bodafors, Sweden: Doxa.

Skinner, B.F. 1971. *Beyond Freedom and Dignity.* New York: Knopf.

———. 1974. *About Behaviorism.* New York: Knopf.

———. 1978. *Reflections on Behaviorism and Society.* Englewood Cliffs, NJ: Prentice-Hall.

Skirbekk, Gunnard, ed. 1983. *Praxeology: An Anthology.* Oslo: Universitetsforlaget.

Skocpol, Theda. 1979. *States and Social Revolutions: A Comparative Analysis of France, Russia, and China.* Cambridge: Cambridge University Press.

Skowronek, Stephen. 1982. *Building a New American State: The Expansion of National Administrative Capacities, 1877-1920.* Cambridge: Cambridge University Press.

Slabbert, F. van Zul, and David Welsh. 1979. *South Africa's Options.* London: Collings.

Slack, Walter H. 1982. *The Surplus Species: Need Man Prevail?* Lanham, MD: University Press of America.

Sloma, Richard. 1983. *No-nonsense Government.* Briarcliff Manor, NY: Stein & Day.

Slovic, Paul, Baruch Fischhoff, and Sara Lichtenstein. 1977. "Behavioral Decision Theory." *Annual Review of Psychology* 28: 1-39.

Smart, C.F., and W.T. Stanbury, eds. 1978. *Studies on Crisis Management.* Institute for Research on Public Policy volume. Toronto: Butterworth.

Smart, Carolyne, and Ilan Vertinsky. 1977. "Designs for Crisis Decision Units." *Administrative Science Quarterly* 22 (December): 640-57.

Smith, Brian. 1976. *Policy Making in British Government: An Analysis of Power and Rationality.* London: M. Robertson.

Smith, Bruce L.R. 1966. *The RAND Corporation: Case Study of a Nonprofit Advisory Corporation.* Cambridge: Harvard University Press.

———, ed. 1984. *The Higher Civil Service in Europe and Canada: Lessons for the United States.* Washington, DC: Brookings Institution.

Smith, David M. 1982. *Where the Grass Is Greener: Living in an Unequal World.* Baltimore: Johns Hopkins University Press.

Smith, Geoffrey, and Nelson W. Polsby. 1981. *British Government and Its Discontents.* New York: Basic Books.

Smith, Gordon B., ed. 1980. *Public Policy and Administration in the Soviet Union.* New York: Praeger.

Smith, Joel, and Lloyd D. Musolf, eds. 1979. *Legislatures in Development.* Durham, NC: Duke University Press.

Smith, Jonathan Z. 1982. *Imagining Religion: From Babylon to Jonestown.* Chicago: University of Chicago Press.

Smith, Peter H. 1979. *Labyrinths of Power: Political Recruitment in Twentieth-Century Mexico.* Princeton: Princeton University Press.

Smith, P.J. Slee. 1971. *Think Tanks and Problem Solving.* London: Business Books.

Smith, Steven B. 1983. *The Great Mental Calculators: The Psychology, Methods, and Lives of Calculating Prodigies, Past and Present.* New York: Columbia University Press.

Smith, Trevor 1979. *The Politics of the Corporate Economy.* Oxford: M. Robertson.

Snyder, Glenn H., and Paul Diesing. 1977. *Conflict Among Nations: Bargaining, Decision Making, and System Structure in International Crises.* Princeton: Princeton University Press.

Social Science Research Council. 1983. *The Council's Program in Social Indicators.* Special issue of *Items* 37 (December): 73-101.

Solo, Robert A. 1982. *The Positive State.* Cincinnati, OH: South-West.

Solomon, Susan Gross, ed. 1983. *Pluralism in the Soviet Union: Essays in Honour of H. Gordon Shilling.* New York: St. Martin's Press

Somare, Michael. 1975. *Sana: An Autobiography.* Port Moresby, Papua New Guinea: Niugini Press.

Somjee, A.H. 1982. *Political Capacity in Developing Societies.* London: Macmillan.

Sorensen, T.C. 1966. *Kennedy.* New York: Harper & Row.

Sorokin, Pitirim A. 1942. *Man and Society in Calamity: The Effects of War, Revolution, Famine, Pestilence Upon Human Mind, Behavior, Social Organization and Cultural Life.* New York: Dutton. Reprint, Westport, CT: Greenwood Press, 1968.

Sowell, Thomas. 1980. *Knowledge and Decisions.* New York: Basic Books.

———. 1983. *The Economics and Politics of Race: An International Perspective.* New York: Morrow.

Sperry, Roger. 1983. *Science and Moral Priority: The Merging of Mind, Brain and Values.* Oxford: Blackwell.

Spinner, Helmut. 1974. *Pluralismus als Erkenntnismodell.* Frankfurt am Main: Suhrkamp.

———. 1978. *Popper und die Politik.* Vol. 1, *Geschlossenheitsproblem.* Berlin: J.H.W. Dietz.

———. 1982. *Popper und die Politik.* Vol. 2, *Ist der Kritische Rationalismus am Ende? Auf der Suche nach den Verlorenene Masstäben des Kritischen Rationalismus—für eine Offene Sozialphilosophie und Kritische Sozialwissenschaft.* Weinhem: Beltz.

Spooner, Frank C. 1983. *Risks at Sea: Amsterdam Insurance and Maritime Europe, 1766-1780.* Cambridge: Cambridge University Press.

Spray, Lee S., ed. 1976. *Organizational Effectiveness: Theory, Research and Application.* Kent, OH: Kent State University Press.

Springborg, Patricia. 1981. *The Problem of Human Needs and the Critique of Civilisation.* London: Allen & Unwin.

Sproull, Lee S., Stephen Weiner, and David Wolf. 1978. *Organizing an Anarchy: Belief, Bureaucracy, and Politics in the National Institute of Education.* Chicago: University of Chicago Press.

Sproull, Lee S., and Patrick D. Larkey, eds. 1983. *Advances in Information Processing in Organizations.* Greenwich, CT: JAI Press.

Stacey, F. 1975. *British Government, 1966-1975. Years of Reform.* Oxford: Oxford University Press.

Stachura, Peter D., ed. 1978. *The Shaping of the Nazi State.* London: Croom Helm.

———, ed. 1983. *The Nazi Machtergreifung.* London: Allen & Unwin.

Stanley, Steven M. 1981. *The New Evolutionary Timetable: Fossils, Genes and the Origin of Species.* New York: Basic Books.

Starbuck, William H. 1982. "Congealing Oil: Inventing Ideologies to Justify Acting Ideologies Out." *Journal of Management Studies* 19: 3-28.

Starr, Chester G. 1982. *The Roman Empire, 27 B.C.-A.D. 476: A Study in Survival.* Oxford: Oxford University Press.

Starr, Paul. 1982. *The Social Transformation of American Medicine.* New York: Basic Books.

Staveley, E.S. 1972. *Greek and Roman Voting and Elections.* Ithaca, NY: Cornell University Press.

Stavrianos, L.S. 1976. *The Promise of the Coming Dark Age.* San Francisco: Freeman.

Staw, Barry M. 1976. "Knee-Deep in the Big Muddy: A Study of Escalating Commitment to a Chosen Course of Action." *Organizational Behavior and Human Performance* 16: 27-44.

Staw, Barry M., and Frederick V. Fox. 1977. "Escalation: The Determinants of Commitment to a Chosen Course of Action." *Human Relations* 30, no. 5: 431-50.

Stein, Janice Gross, and Raymond Tanter. 1980. *Rational Decision-Making: Israel's Security Choices, 1967.* Columbus: Ohio State University Press.

Stein, Morris I. 1974. *Stimulating Creativity.* New York: Academic Press.

Steinberg, Rudolf. 1979. *Politik und Verwaltungsorganisation: Zur Reform der Regierungs- und Verwaltungsorganisation Unter Besonderer Berücksichtigung der Obersten Bundesbehörden in den Vereiningten Staaten von Amerika.* Baden-Baden: Nomos Verlagsgesellschaft.

Steinbrunner, John D. 1974. *The Cybernetic Theory of Decision.* Princeton: Princeton University Press.

Steiner, George. 1975. *After Babel: Aspects of Language and Translation.* New York: Oxford University Press.

Steiner, George A. 1979. *Strategic Planning.* New York: Free Press.

Steiner, John M. 1975. *Power Politics and Social Change in National Socialist Germany: A Process of Escalation into Mass Destruction.* The Hague: Mouton.

Steiner, Jörg, and Robert Dorff. 1980. *A Theory of Political Decision Modes: Interparty Decision Making in Switzerland.* Chapel Hill: University of North Carolina Press.

Stemmer, Nathan. 1983. *The Roots of Knowledge.* New York: St. Martin's Press.

Stepan, Alfred. 1978. *The State and Society: Peru in Comparative Perspective.* Princeton: Princeton University Press.

Stern, Fritz. 1961. *The Politics of Cultural Despair: A Study in the Rise of the German Ideology.* Berkeley and Los Angeles: University of California Press.

Sternberg, R.J., ed. 1982. *Advances in the Psychology of Human Intelligence*, vol. 1. Hillsdale, NJ: Erlbaum.

Sternheimer, Stephan. 1980. "Administration for Development: The Emerging Bureaucratic Elite, 1920-1930." In *Russian Officialdom: The Bureaucratization of Russian Society from the Seventeenth to the Twentieth Century*, edited by Walter McKenzie Pinter and Don Karl Rowney. Chapel Hill: University of North Carolina Press.

Stevens, Robert. 1983. *Law School: Legal Education in America from the 1950s to the 1980s.* Chapel Hill: University of North Carolina Press.

Stewart, William H., Jr. 1975. *The Alabama Constitutional Commission: A Pragmatic Approach to Constitutional Revision.* University: University of Alabama Press.

Stiehm, Judith Hicks. 1981. *Bring Me Men and Women: Mandated Change at the U.S. Air Force Academy.* Berkeley and Los Angeles: University of California Press.

Stifel, Laurence D., Ralph K. Davidson, and James S. Coleman, eds. 1983. *Social Sciences and Public Policy in the Developing World.* Lexington, MA: D.C. Heath.

Stigler, George J. 1983. *The Economist as Preacher and Other Essays.* Chicago: University of Chicago Press.

Stokey, Edith, and Richard Zeckhauser. 1978. *A Primer for Policy Analysis.* New York: Norton.

Study Commission on U.S. Policy Towards Southern Africa. 1981. *South Africa: Time Running Out.* Berkeley and Los Angeles: University of California Press and Foreign Policy Study Foundation.

Sudnow, David. 1979. *Talk's Body: A Mediation Between Two Keyboards.* New York: Knopf.

_____. 1981. *Ways of the Hand: The Organization of Improvised Conduct.* New York: Wiley.

Suedfeld, Peter. 1980. *Restricted Environmental Stimulation: Research and Clinical Application.* New York: Wiley.

Suleiman, Ezra. N. 1974. *Politics, Power, and Bureaucracy in France.* Princeton: Princeton University Press.

_____. 1978. *Elites in French Society: The Politics of Survival.* Princeton: Princeton University Press.

Suleiman, Ezra N., and Carlos Alba, eds. 1984. *Higher Civil Servants in the Policy-Making Process.* New York: Holmes and Meier.

Sullivan, John L., James Piereson, and George E. Marcus. 1982. *Political Tolerance and American Democracy.* Chicago: University of Chicago Press.

Sullivan, William M. 1982. *Reconstructing Public Philosophy.* Berkeley and Los Angeles: University of California Press.

Summers, Harry G., Jr. 1982. *On Strategy: A Critical Analysis of the Vietnam War.* Novato, CA: Presido Press.

Sundquist, James L. 1978. "A Comparison of Policy-Making Capacity in the United States and Five European Countries: The Case of Population Distribution." In *Population Policy Analysis: Issues in American Politics,* edited by Michael E. Kraft and Mark Schneider, Lexington, MA: Lexington Books.

_____. 1980. "The Crisis of Competence in Government." In *Setting National Priorities: Agenda for the 1980s,* edited by Joseph A. Pechman. Washington, DC: Brookings Institution.

_____. 1981. *The Decline and Resurgence of Congress.* Washington, DC: Brookings Institution.

Susman, Gerald I., and Roger D. Evered. 1978. "An Assessment of the Scientific Merits of Action Research." *Administrative Science Quarterly* 23 (December) 582-603.

Sutherland, John W. 1975. *Systems: Analysis, Administration and Architecture.* New York: Van Nostrand Reinhold.

———. 1978. *Societal Systems: Methodology, Modelling and Management.* New York: Elsevier.

Swain, Marshall. 1981. *Reason and Knowledge.* Ithaca, NY: Cornell University Press.

Swanson, Carl P. 1983. *Ever-Expanding Horizons: The Dual Information Sources of Human Evolution.* Amherst: University of Massachusetts Press.

Swedish Government Commission on Public Policy Planning. 1979. *Policy Innovation Through Policy Reappraisal: Summary of a Report by the Swedish Commission on Public Policy Planning.* Summary of SOU 1979: 61, Förnyelse genom omprövning. Stockholm: Private distribution.

Sweeny, H.W. Allen, and Robert Rachlin, eds. 1981. *Handbook of Budgeting.* New York: Wiley.

Sylvan, Donald, and Steve Chan, eds. 1984. *Foreign Policy Decision Making: Perception, Cognition and Artificial Intelligence.* New York: Praeger.

Szanton, Peter, ed. 1981a. *Federal Reorganizations: What Have We Learned?* Chatham, NJ: Chatham House.

———. 1981b. *Not Well Advised.* New York: Russell Sage Foundation.

Talmon, J.T. 1952. *The Origins of Totalitarian Democracy.* London: Secker & Warburg.

———. 1960. *Political Messianism: The Romantic Phase.* London: Secker & Warburg.

———. 1981. *The Myth of the Nation and the Vision of Revolution: The Origins of Ideological Polarisation in the Twentieth Century.* London: Secker & Warburg.

Tannenbaum, Percy H., and Leslie J. Kostrich. 1983. *Turned-On Television and Turned-Off Voters: Policy Options for Election Projections.* Beverly Hills, CA: Sage.

Tarschys, Daniel. 1982. *Curbing Public Expenditure: A Survey of Current Trends.* Working paper. Paris: OECD/TECO.

Tauberman, Paul. 1978. "What We Learn from Estimating the Genetic Contribution to Inequality in Earnings: Reply." *American Economic Review* 68, no. 5: 970-76.

Taylor, Charles Lewis, ed. 1980. *Indicator Systems for Political, Economic, and Social Analysis.* Cambridge, MA: Oelgeschlager, Gunn & Hain.

———, ed. 1983. *Why Governments Grow: Measuring Public Sector Size.* Beverly Hills, CA: Sage.

Taylor, Charles Lewis, and David A. Jodice. 1983. *World Handbook of Political and Social Indicators.* Vol. 1, *Cross-National Attributes and Rates of Change.* Vol. 2, *Political Protest and Government Change.* 3d. ed. New Haven: Yale University Press.

Taylor, Donald W. 1965. "Decision Making and Problem Solving." In *Handbook of Organizations,* edited by James G. March. Chicago: Rand McNally.

Taylor, Marcia Wicker. 1978. *A Computer Simulation of Innovative Decision-Making in Organizations.* Lanham, MD: University Press of America.

Taylor, Michael. 1982. *Community, Anarchy and Liberty.* Cambridge: Cambridge University Press.

Taylor, Peter. 1984. *Smoke Ring: The Politics of Tobacco.* London: Bodley Head.

Teng, Ssu-Yü. 1942-43. "Chinese Influence on the Western Examination System." *Harvard Journal of Asian Studies.* 7: 267-312.

Thane, Pat, ed. 1978. *The Origins of British Social Policy.* London: Croom Helm.

Thayer, Frederick C. 1981. *An End to Hierarchy and Competition: Administration in the Post-Affluent World.* 2d ed. New York: Watts.

Theophanous, Andrew. 1983. *Australian Democracy in Crisis: A New Theoretic Introduction to Australian Politics.* Oxford: Oxford University Press.

Theory and Society. 1979. *State and Revolution,* special issue, Vol. 7, No. 1 and 2, January-March, pp. 1-272.

Thirlwall, A.P., ed. 1982. *Keynes as a Policy Adviser: The Fifth Keynes Seminar Held at the University of Kent at Canterbury, 1980.* London: Macmillan.

Thomas, D. Woods, et al., eds. 1972. *Institution Building: A Model for Applied Social Change.* Cambridge, MA: Schenkman.

Thomas, George M., and John W. Meyer. 1980. "Regime Changes and State Power in an Intensifying World-State-System." In *Studies of the Modern World System,* edited by Albert Bergesen. New York: Academic Press.

Thomas, Keith. 1983. *Man and the Natural World: Changing Attitudes in England, 1500-1800.* London: Allen Lane.

Thompson, James Clay. 1980. *Rolling Thunder: Understanding Policy and Program Failure.* Chapel Hill: University of North Carolina Press.

Thompson, John B. 1981. *Critical Hermeneutics: A Study of the Thought of Paul Ricoeur and Jürgen Habermas.* Cambridge: Cambridge University Press.

Thompson, John B., and D. Held, eds. 1982. *Habermas: Critical Debates.* Cambridge: MIT Press.

Thompson, Leonard, and Andrew Prior. 1982. *South African Politics.* New Haven: Yale University Press.

Thompson, Michael. 1979. *Rubbish Theory: The Creation and Destruction of Value.* Oxford: Oxford University Press.

Thompson, Scott W., and Donaldson D. Frizzell, eds. 1977. *The Lessons of Vietnam.* New York: Crane, Russak.

Thornhill, W., ed., 1975. *The Modernization of British Government.* London: Pitman.

Thurow, Lester C. 1980. *The Zero-Sum Society: Distribution and the Possibilities for Economic Change.* New York: Basic Books.

———. 1983. *Dangerous Currents: The State of the Economy.* New York: Random House.

Tinbergen, Jan. 1981. "Benelux: Unity in Diversity—A Pattern for Europe?", In *Europe's Economy in Crisis,* edited by Ralf Dahrendorf. London: Weidenfeld and Nicolson.

Tinbergen, Jan, Antony J. Dolman, and Jan van Ettinger. 1976. *RIO: Reshaping the International Order—A Report to the Club of Rome.* New York: Dutton.

Tisdell, C.A. 1981. *Science and Technology Policy: Priorities of Governments.* London: Chapman & Hall.

Titlow, Richard E. 1978. *Americans Import Merit: Origins of the U.S. Civil Service System and the Influence of the British Model.* Lanham, MD: University Press of America.

Tivey, L. 1978. *The Politics of the Firm.* Oxford: M. Robertson.

Toffler, Alvin. 1981. *The Third Wave.* New York: Bantam. First published by Morrow in 1980.

———. 1983. *Preview and Premises.* New York: Morrow.

Toulmain, Stephen, Richard Rieke, and Allan Janik. 1979. *An Introduction to Reasoning.* London: Collier Macmillan.

Touraine, Alain, et al. 1983. *Anti-Nuclear Protest: The Opposition to Nuclear Energy in France.* Cambridge: Cambridge University Press.

Treasury Board of Canada. 1980. *Guide to the Policy and Expenditure Management System.* Ottawa: Ministry of Supply and Services.

Trezise, Philip H. 1982. *Industry Vitalization: Toward a National Industrial Policy.* New York: Pergamon.

Tribe, Laurence H. 1972. "Policy Science: Analysis or Ideology." *Philosophy and Public Affairs* 2 (Fall): 66-110.

Tribe, L.H., C.S. Schelling, and J. Voss, eds. 1976. *When Values Conflict.* Cambridge, MA: Ballinger.

Trimberger, Ellen Kay. 1978. *Revolution from Above: Military Bureaucrats and Development in Japan, Turkey, Egypt and Peru.* New Brunswick, NJ: Transaction.

Triska, Jan, and Paul Cocks, eds. 1977. *Political Development in Eastern Europe.* New York: Praeger.

Troeltsch, Ernst. 1977. *Der Historismus und seine Probleme.* Aalen: Scientia. First published 1922.

Troitzsch, Klaus G. 1979. *Volksbegehren und Volksentscheid: Eine vergleichende Analyse direktdemokratischer Verfassungsinstitutionen unter besonderer Berücksichtigung der Bundesrepublik Deutschland und der Schweiz.* Meidenheim am Glan: Anton Hein.

Troyer, Ronald, and Gerald Markle. 1983. *Cigarettes: The Battle over Smoking.* New Brunswick, NJ: Rutgers University Press.

Truman, David. 1951. *The Governmental Process.* New York: Knopf.

Trunk, Isaiah. 1972. *Judenrat: The Jewish Councils in Eastern Europe under Nazi Occupation.* New York: Macmillan.

Tuchman, Barbara W. 1984. *The March of Folly: From Troy to Vietnam,* New York: Knopf.

Tucker, Robert C. 1981. *Politics as Leadership,* Columbia: University of Missouri Press.

Tufte, Edward R. 1978. *Political Control of the Economy.* Princeton: Princeton University Press.

Tugwell, Franklin, ed. 1973. *Search from Alternatives: Public Policy and the Study of the Future.* Cambridge, MA: Winthrop.

Tugwell, Rexford G. 1974. *The Emerging Constitution.* New York: Harper & Row.

Tullock, Gordon. 1970. *Private Wants, Public Means: An Economic Analysis of the Desirable Scope of Government.* New York: Basic Books.

Tuma, Elias H. 1979. "Agrarian Reform in Historical Perspective Revisited." *Comparative Studies in Society and History* 21: 3-29.

Turkle, Sherry. 1984. *The Second Self: Computers and the Human Spirit.* New York: Simon & Schuster.

Turner, Barry A. 1976. "The Organizational and Interorganizational Development of Disasters." *Administrative Science Quarterly* 21 (September): 378-97.

Turner, Barry, and Gunilla Nordquist. 1982. *The Other European Community: Integration and Co-operation in Nordic Europe.* London: Weidenfeld & Nicolson.

Turner, C.F., and E. Krauss. 1978. "Fallible Indicators of the Subjective State of the Nation." *American Psychologist* 33: 456-70.

Turner, J. 1980. *Lloyd George's Secretariat.* Cambridge: Cambridge University Press.

Turner, Stephen R. 1983. "Weber on Action." *American Sociological Review* 48 (August): 506-19.

Tutchings, Terrence R. 1979. *Rhetoric and Reality: Presidential Commissions and the Making of Public Policy.* Boulder, CO: Westview.

Tversky, Amos, and Daniel Kahneman. 1973. "Availability: A Heuristic for Judging Frequency and Probability." *Cognitive Psychology* 5: 207-232.

_____. 1981. "The Framing of Decisions and the Psychology of Choice." *Science* 211 (30 January): 453-58.

Überhorst, Host, ed. 1969. *Elite für die Diktatur: Die Nationalpolitischen Eziehungsanstalten 1933-1945—Ein Dokumentarbericht.* Düsseldorf: Droste Verlag.

United Kingdom Committee. 1968. *The Civil Service.* Vol. 1, *Report of the Committee 1966-1968.* London: Her Majesty's Stationery Office.

United Kingdom Government. 1970. *The Reorganization of Central Government.* Cmnd 4506. London: Her Majesty's Stationery Office.

United Kingdom Royal Commission on the Constitution. 1973. *Royal Commission on the Constitution 1969-1972.* Vol. 1, *Report.* Vol. 2, *Memorandum of Dissent.* London: Her Majesty's Stationery Office.

United Nations Committee for Development Planning. 1982. *World Economic Recovery and International and Financial Cooperation.* New York: United Nations.

U.S. Council on Environmental Quality and the Department of State. 1980. *The Global 2000 Report to the President: Entering the Twenty-First Century.* Washington, DC: Government Printing Office.

U.S. Department of Health, Education, and Welfare. 1969. *Toward A Social Report.* Washington, DC: Government Printing Office.

U.S. General Accounting Office. 1983. *Selected Government-Wide Management Improvement Efforts—1970 to 1980.* GAO/GGD-83-69. Washington, DC: General Accounting Office.

Useem, Michael. 1983. *The Inner Circle: Large Corporations and the Rise of Business Political Activity in the U.S. and U.K.* Oxford: Oxford University Press.

Usher, Dan. 1981. *The Economic Prerequisite to Democracy.* Oxford: Blackwell.

Vaizey, John. 1983. *The Squandered Peace: The World, 1945-1975.* London: Hodder & Stoughton.

Valenta, Jiri, and William Potter, eds. 1984. *Soviet Decision Making for National Security.* London: Allen & Unwin.

Vasquez, John A., and Richard W. Mansback. 1983. "The Issue Cycle: Conceptualizing Long-Term Global Political Change." *International Organization* 37 (Spring): 257-79.

Vedung, Evert. 1976. "The Comparative Method and its Neighbours." In *Power and Political Theory: Some European Perspectives,* edited by Brian Barry. New York: Wiley.

Verba, Sidney, Norman H. Nie, and Jae-on Kim. 1978. *Participation and Political Equality: A Seven-Nation Comparison.* Cambridge: Cambridge University Press.

Vernon, Richard. 1976. "The 'Great Society' and the 'Open Society': Liberalism in Hayek and Popper." *Canadian Journal of Political Science* 9, no. 2: 261-76.

Verrier, Anthony. 1983. *Through the Looking Glass: British Foreign Policy in an Age of Illusion.* London: Cape.

Vickers, Geoffrey. 1973. *Making Institutions Work,* London: Associated Business Programmes.

Vilmar, Fritz. 1973. *Strategien der Demokratisierung.* Band I: *Theorie der Praxis.* Band II. *Modelle und Kämpfe der Praxis.* Darmstadt: Herman Luchterhand.

Voegelin, Eric. 1952. *The New Science of Politics.* Chicago: University of Chicago Press.

Vogel, Ezra F., ed. 1975. *Modern Japanese Organization and Decision Making.* Tokyo: Tuttle.

Vogel, Ezra F. 1979. *Japan as Number One.* Cambridge: Harvard University Press.

Vovelle, Michel. 1984. *The Fall of the French Monarchy.* Cambridge: Cambridge University Press. Translated from the French.

Wade, Larry L. 1972. *The Elements of Public Policy.* Columbus, OH: Merrill.

Wade, Larry L. and Curry, R.L. 1970. *A Logic of Public Policy: Aspects of Political Economy.* Belmont, CA:Wadsworth.

Wade, Nicholas. 1982. *The Art and Science of Visual Illusions.* London: Routledge & Kegan Paul.

Wagar, W. Warren. 1983. *Terminal Visions: The Literature of Last Things.* Bloomington: Indiana University Press.

Wainer, Howard. 1981. "Graphical Data Analysis." *Annual Review of Psychology* 32: 191-241.

Waldo, Dwight. 1983. *The Administrative State.* 2d ed. New York: Holmes & Meier.

Walker, Jack L. 1977. "Setting the Agenda in the U.S. Senate: A Theory of Problem Selection." *British Journal of Political Science* 7, part 4 (October): 423-45.

Walker, Stephen. 1983. *Animal Thought.* London: Routledge & Kegan Paul.

Waller, Robert J. 1982. "Complexity and the Boundaries of Human Policy Making." *International Yearbook of General Systems* 9: 1-11.

Wallerstein, Immanuel. 1974. *The Modern World-System.* Vol.1, *Capitalist Agriculture and The Origins of the European World Economy in the Sixteenth Century.* New York: Academic Press.

_____. 1980. *The Modern World System.* Vol.2, *Mercantilism and the Consolidation of the European Economy, 1600-1750.* New York: Academic Press.

Wallstein, T., ed. 1980. *Cognitive Processes in Choice and Decision Behavior.* Hillsdale, NJ: Erlbaum.

Walter, Edward. 1981. *The Immorality of Limiting Growth.* Albany: State University of New York Press.

Walters, Ronald G. 1978. *American Reformers, 1815-1860.* New York: Hill & Wang.

Walzer, Michael. 1977. *Just and Unjust Wars: A Moral Argument with Historical Illustrations.* New York: Basic Books.

Wang, Paul P., and S.K. Chang, eds. 1980. *Fuzzy Sets: Theory and Applications to Policy Analysis and Information Systems.* New York: Plenum Press.

Ward, Barbara, and René Dubos. 1983. *Only One Earth: The Care and Maintenance of a Small Planet.* New York: Norton.

Ward, Paul Von. 1981. *Dismantling the Pyramid: Government . . . By the People. . . .* Washington, DC: Delphi Press.

Warfield, N. Johan. 1976. *Societal Systems: Planning, Policy and Complexity.* New York: Wiley.

Warner, Malcolm. 1977. *Organizational Choice and Constraint.* Lexington, MA: Heath.

Warren, Ronald L. 1977. *Social Change and Human Purpose: Towards Understanding and Action.* Chicago: Rand McNally.

Warwick, Donald P., in collaboration with M. Mead and T. Read. 1975. *A Theory of Public Bureucracy: Politics, Personality and Organization in the State Department.* Cambridge: Harvard University Press.

Wason, P.C.,and P.N. Johnson-Laird. 1972. *Psychology of Reasoning: Structure and Content.* Cambridge: Harvard University Press.

Waterkamp, Rainer.1974. *Politische Leitung und Systemveränderung: Zum Problemlösungsprozess durch Planungs- und Informationssysteme.* Cologne: Europäische Verlagsanstalt.

Waterston, Albert. 1979. *Development Planning: Lessons of Experience.* Baltimore: Johns Hopkins University Press.

Watkins, John W.N. 1970. "Imperfect Rationality." In *Explanations in the Behavioral Sciences,* edited by Robert Borger and Frank Cioffi. Cambridge: Cambridge University Press.

_____. 1975. "Three Views Concerning Human Freedom." In *Nature and Conduct,* edited by R.S. Peters. London: Macmillan.

_____. 1978. *Freiheit und Entscheidung.* Tübingen: J.C.B. Mohr. Translated from the English.

Weaver, David H., et al. 1981. *Media Agenda-Setting in a Presidential Election.* New York: Praeger.

Webb, James E. 1969. *Space-Age Management.* New York: McGraw-Hill.

Weber, Max. 1966. *Staatssoziologie.* Berlin: Duncker & Humblot. Supplemented special.

_____ . 1971. *Gesammelte politische Schriften.* 3d rev. ed. Tübingen: J.C.B. Mohr print from Max Weber, *Wirtschaft und Gesellschaft,* 5th rev. ed. pt. 8, pp. 815-68. Tübingen: J.C.B. Mohr, 1980.

Weick, Karl E. 1979. *The Social Psychology of Organizing.* 2d ed. Reading, MA: Addison-Wesley.

Weinstein, Donald, and Rudolph M. Bell. 1982. *Saints and Society: The Two Worlds of Western Christendom, 1000-1700.* Chicago: University of Chicago Press.

Weiss, Carol H. 1972. *Evaluation Research.* Englewood Cliffs, NJ: Prentice-Hall.

――――. ed. 1977. *Using Social Research in Public Policy Making.* Lexington, MA: Heath.

――――. 1980. *Social Science Research in Decision-Making.* New York: Columbia University Press.

Weiss, Carol H., and Allen H. Barton, eds. 1979. *Bureaucratic Maladies and Remedies.* Special issue, *American Behavioral Scientist* 22 (May/June).

Weiss, Howard M. 1980. "The Utility of Humility: Self-Esteem, Information Search, and Problem-Solving Efficiency." *Organizational Behavior and Human Performance* 25: 216-23.

Weissberg, Robert. 1976. *Public Opinion and Popular Government.* Englewood Cliffs, NJ: Prentice-Hall.

Weizsäcker, Carl Friedrich von. 1976. *Wege in der Gefahr: Eine Studie Über Wirtschaft, Gesellschaft und Kriegsverhütung,* Munich: Hansen.

Welch, Susan, and Robert Miewald, eds. 1983. *Scarce Natural Resources: The Challenge to Public Policymaking.* Beverly Hills, CA: Sage.

Weller, Patrick. 1983. "Do Prime Ministers' Departments Really Create Problems?". *Public Administration* 61 (Spring): 59-78.

Wendzel, Robert L. 1981a. *International Relations: A Policymaker Focus.* New York: Wiley.

――――. 1981b. *International Politics: Policymakers and Policymaking.* New York: Wiley.

Wenk, Edward, Jr. 1979. *Margins for Survival: Overcoming Political Limits in Steering Technology.* Oxford: Pergamon.

Wertheim, W.F. 1974. *Evolution and Revolution: The Rising Waves of Emancipation.* Baltimore: Penguin.

Westmeyer, Hans. 1972. *Logik der Diagnostik: Grundlagen Einer Normativen Diagnostik.* Stuttgart: Kohlhammer.

Wettenhall, Roger L. 1975. *Bushfire Disaster: An Australian Community in Crisis.* Sydney, Australia: Angus & Robertson.

Whaley, Barton. 1969. *Stratagem: Deception and Surprise in War.* Cambridge: MIT Center for International Studies.

――――. 1973. *Codeword Barbarossa.* Cambridge: MIT Press.

Wheeler, Daniel D., and Irving L. Janis. 1980. *A Practical Guide for Making Decision—New Ways to Improve Your Decisions about: Your Job, Your Love Life, Your Health, Your Finances, Other Personal or Business Choices.* New York: Free Press.

Whiston, Tom, ed. 1979. *The Uses and Abuses of Forecasting.* A Science Policy Research Unit, Sussex, book. London: Macmillan.

White, Arnold. 1901. *Efficiency and Empire.* London: Methuen. Republished by Harvester, 1973; edited by G.R. Searle.

White, Gilbert F., ed. 1974. *Natural Hazards: Local, National, Global.* New York: Oxford University Press.

Wholley, Joseph, et al. 1970. *Federal Evaluation Policy: Analyzing the Effects of Public Programs.* Washington, DC: Urban Institute.

Wicklung, Robert A., and Jack W. Brehm. 1976. *Perspectives on Cognitive Dissonance.* Hillsdale, NJ: Erlbaum.

Wiener, A. 1978. *Magnificent Myth: Pattern of Control in Post-Industrial Society.* New York: Pergamon.

Wiener, Martin J. 1980. *English Culture and the Decline of the Industrial Spirit, 1850-1980.* New York: Cambridge University Press.

Wieseltier, Leon. 1983. *Nuclear War, Nuclear Peace.* New York: Holt, Rinehart & Winston.

Wilber, Charles K., and Kenneth P. Jameson. 1983. *An Inquiry into the Poverty of Economics.* Notre Dame: University of Notre Dame Press.

Wilcox, Leslie D., et al. 1974. *Social Indicators and Societal Monitoring: An Annotated Bibliography.* New York: Elsevier.

Wildavsky, Aaron. 1975. *Budgeting: A Comparative Theory of the Budgetary Process.* Boston: Little, Brown.

_____. 1979a. "No Risk Is the Highest Risk of All." *American Scientist* 67 (January-February): 32-37.

_____. 1979b. *Speaking Truth to Power: The Art and Craft of Policy Analysis.* Boston: Little, Brown. London: Macmillan, 1980; with a postscript.

_____. 1980. *How to Limit Goverment Spending.* Berkeley and Los Angeles: University of California Press.

Wilensky, Harold L. 1967. *Organizational Intelligence.* New York: Basic Books.

_____. 1975. *The Welfare State and Equality: Structural and Ideological Roots of Public Policy.* Berkeley and Los Angeles: University of California Press.

_____. 1976. *The "New Corporatism": Centralization and the Welfare State,* Beverly Hills, CA: Sage.

Wilkinson, Rupert. 1964. *Gentlemanly Power: British Leadership and the Public School Tradition—A Comparative Study in the Making of Rulers.* Oxford: Oxford University Press.

Wilkinson, Spenser. 1895. *The Brain of an Army: A Popular Account of the German General Staff.* Reprint. Carlisle Barracks, PA: U.S. Army War College, 1983.

Will, George F. 1983. *Statecraft as Soulcraft: What Government Does.* New York: Simon & Schuster.

Willett, Thomas D., ed. 1976. *The Economic Approach to Public Policy.* Ithaca, NY: Cornell University Press.

Williams, John, Eric Dunning, and Patrick Murphy. 1984. *Hooligans Abroad: The Behavior and Control of English Fans in Continental Europe.* London: Routledge & Kegan Paul.

Williams, Trevor A. 1982. *Learning to Manage Our Future: The Participative Redesign of Societies in Turbulent Transition.* New York: Wiley.

Williams, Walter. 1971. *Social Policy Research and Analysis.* New York: Elsevier.

———. 1980a. *Domestic Program Policy Analysis: Some Observations on Its Practice at the Top of the Government in the U.S. and the U.K.*. Seattle: Institute of Governmental Research, University of Washington.

———. 1980b. *The Implementation Perspective*, Berkeley and Los Angeles: University of California Press.

———. 1981. *Strangers and Brothers: The Dilemma of Organizing and Staffing the American Presidency*. Seattle: Institute of Governmental Research, University of Washington.

———. 1983. *Reagan: The First Two Years*. Public Policy Paper No. 18. Seattle: Institute for Public Policy and Management, University of Washington.

Williams, Walter, et al. 1982. *Studying Implementation: Methodological and Administrative Issues*. Chatham, NJ: Chatham House.

Williamson, Oliver E. 1975. *Markets and Hierarchies—Analysis and Antitrust Implications: A Study in the Economics of International Organizations*. New York: Free Press.

Willner, Ann Ruth. 1983. *The Spellbinders: Charismatic Political Leadership*. New Haven: Yale University Press.

Wilson, A. Jeyaratnam. 1980. *The Gaullist System in Asia: The Constitution of Sri Lanka (1978)*. London: Macmillan.

Wilson, Bryan, R., ed. 1970. *Rationality*, Oxford: Blackwell.

Wilson, David E. 1979. *National Planning in the United States: An Annotated Bilbliography*. Boulder, CO: Westview.

———. 1980. *The National Planning Idea in U.S. Public Policy: Five Alternative Approaches*. Boulder, CO: Westview.

Wilson, Dorothy. 1979. *The Welfare State in Sweden*, London: Heinemann.

Wilson, Edward O. 1975. *Sociobiology: The New Synthesis*. Cambridge: Harvard University Press.

———. 1978. *On Human Nature*. Cambridge: Harvard University Press.

Wilson, James Q. 1983. *Thinking about Crime*. Rev. ed. New York: Basic Books.

Wimbush, S. Enders, and Alex Alexiev. 1982. *The Ethnic Factor in the Soviet Armed Forces*. Santa Monica, CA: Rand Corporation.

Winston, P., ed. 1975. *The Psychology of Computer Vision*. New York: McGraw-Hill.

Wittfogel, A. Karl. 1957. *Oriental Despotism: A Comparative Study of Total Power*. New Haven: Yale University Press.

Wittrock, Bjorn, ed. 1983. *Governance in Crisis*. Special issue, *Policy Sciences* 15 (April).

Wohlstetter, Albert. 1964. "The Analysis and Design of Conflict Systems." In *Analysis for Military Decisions*, edited by Edward S. Quade. Amsterdam: North-Holland.

Wohlstetter, Roberta. 1962. *Pearl Harbor: Warning and Decision*. Stanford: Stanford University Press.

———. 1979. "The Pleasures of Self-Deception." *Washington Quarterly* 2 (Autumn): 54-64.

Wolf, Charles W., Jr. 1979. "A Theory of Nonmarket Failure: Framework for Implementation Analysis." *Journal of Law and Economics* 22 (April): 107-39.

Wolfe, Alan. 1977. *The Limits of Legitimacy: Political Contradictions of Contemporary Capitalism*. New York: Free Press.

———. 1981. *America's Impasse: The Rise and Fall of the Politics of Growth*. New York: Pantheon.

Wood, John Cunningham. 1983. *British Economists and the Empire, 1860-1914*. London: Croom Helm.

Woodcock, Alexander, and Monte Davis. 1980. *Catastrophe Theory*, New York: Dutton.

Woodside, K. 1982. "The Tax Revolt in International Perspective—Britain, Canada, and the United States." In *Comparative Social Research*, vol. 5, edited by R.F. Tomasson. Greenwich, CT: JAI Press.

World Bank. 1982. *World Development Report 1982*. Oxford: Oxford University Press.

———. 1983. *World Development Report 1983*. Oxford: Oxford University Press.

———. 1984. *World Development Report 1984*. Oxford: Oxford University Press.

World Meteorological Organization. 1978. *World Climate Conference*. Geneva: World Meteorological Organization.

Wortman, Paul M. 1983. "Evaluation Research: A Methodological Perspective," *Annual Review of Psychology, Vol. 34*. Edited by Mark R. Rosenzweig and Lyman W. Porter. Palo Alto, CA: Annual Reviews.

Wriggins, Howard W. 1969. *The Rulers' Imperative: Strategies for Political Survival in Asia and Africa*. New York: Columbia University Press.

Wright, Erik Olin. 1978. *Class, Crisis and the State*. London: New Left Books.

Wright, George. 1984. *Behavioral Decision Theory: An Introduction*. London: Penguin.

Wright, James D. 1976. *The Dissent of the Governed: Alienation and Democracy in America*. New York: Academic Press.

Wright, Maurice, ed. 1980. *Public Spending Decision: Growth and Restraint in the 1970s*. London: Allen & Unwin.

Wrong, Dennis. 1979. *Power: Its Forms, Bases, and Uses*. New York: Harper & Row.

Wu, Silas H.L. 1970. *Communication and Imperial Control in China: Evolution of the Palace Memorial System, 1693-1735*. Cambridge: Harvard University Press.

Wynne, George, ed. 1983. *Cutback Management*. Learning from Abroad Series, vol. 6. New Brunswick, NJ: Transaction Books.

Yaffee, Steven Lewis. 1982. *Prohibitive Policy: Implementing the Federal Endangered Species Act*. Cambridge: MIT Press.

Yanvey, George. 1983. *The Urge to Mobilize: Agrarian Reform in Russia, 1861-1930*. Urbana: University of Illinois Press.

Yarmolinsky, Adam, and Gregory D. Foster. 1983. *Paradoxes of Power: The Military Establishment in the Eighties*. Bloomington: University of Indiana Press.

Yates, Brock. 1983. *The Decline and Fall of the American Automobile Industry*. New York: Empire Books.

Yates, Douglas. 1977. *The Ungovernable City.* Cambridge: MIT Press.

———. 1982. *Bureaucratic Democracy: The Search for Democracy and Efficiency in American Government.* Cambridge: Harvard University Press.

Yavetz, Zvi. 1969. *Plebs and Princepts.* Oxford: Clarendon.

———. 1983. *Julius Caesar and His Public Image.* London: Thames & Hodson. Translated from the German.

Yergin, Daniel, and Martin Hillenbrand, eds. 1982. *Global Insecurity: A Strategy for Energy and Economic Renewal.* Boston: Houghton Mifflin.

Young, Hugo, and Anne Sloman. 1983. *But, Chancellor.* London: BBC.

Young, Michael. 1983. *Social Scientist as Innovator.* Cambridge, MA: Abt Books.

Young, Peyton H. 1980. *Cost Allocation and Demand Revelation in Public Enterprises.* WP-80-130. Laxenburg, Austria: IIASA.

Young, Peyton H., N. Okada, and T. Hashimoto. 1980. *Cost Allocation in Water Resources Development—A Case Study of Sweden.* RR-80-32. Laxenburg, Austria: IIASA.

———. 1981. *Sharing Costs Fairly: A Practical Introduction to Cooperative Game Theory.* Executive Report 5. Laxenburg, Austria: IIASA.

Young, Robert J. 1978. *In Command of France: French Foreign Policy and Military Planning, 1933-1940.* Cambridge: Harvard University Press.

Zablocki, Benjamin. 1980. *Alienation and Charisma: A Study of Contemporary American Communes.* New York: Free Press.

Zagorin, Perez. 1982. *Rebels and Rulers.* Vol. 1, *Society, States and Early Revolution.* Vol. 2, *Provincial Rebellion.* Cambridge: Cambridge University Press.

Zaltman, Gerald, and Robert Duncan. 1977. *Strategies for Planned Change.* New York: Wiley.

Zaltman, Gerald, Robert Duncan, and Jonny Holbeck. 1973. *Innovations and Organizations.* New York: Wiley.

Zander, Alvin. 1979. "The Psychology of Group Processes." *Annual Review of Psychology* 30: 417-51.

Zapf, Wolfgang. 1975. "Systems of Social Indicators: Current Approaches and Problems." *International Social Science Journal* 27, no. 3: 479-98.

Zaret, David. 1980. "From Weber to Parsons and Schutz: The Eclipse of History in Modern Social Theory." *American Journal of Sociology* 85, no. 5: 1180-1201.

Zeckhauser, Richard J., and Derek Leebaert, eds. 1983. *What Role for Government? Lessons from Policy Research.* Durham, NC: Duke University Press.

Ziegler, Philip. 1969. *The Black Death: A Study of the Plague in Fourteenth-Century Europe.* New York: Day.

Ziman, J.M. 1968. *Public Knowledge: An Essay Concerning the Social Dimensions of Science.* Cambridge: Cambridge University Press.

Zimmermann, Ekkart. 1979. "Crisis and Crisis Outcome: Towards a New Synthetic Approach." *European Journal of Political Research* 7: 67-115.

Zinberg, Dorothy, ed. 1983. *Uncertain Power: The Struggle for a National Energy Policy.* Elmsford, NY: Pergamon.

# Reference Index

**403**

Aronson, Elliot (1972), 209

Arora, Ramesh K.: with Avasthi (1978), 92; with Sharman, Singh, and Sogani (1978), 92

Arrighi, Giovanni (with Amin, Frank, and Wallerstein, 1982), 47

Arrow, Kenneth J. (1974), 227

Ascher, William (with Overholt, 1983), 34

Ashby, W. Ross (1957), 166

Ashford, Douglas E.: (1978), 225; (1981), 16; (1982), 297

Attfield, Robin (1983), 125

Avasthi, A. (with Arora, 1978), 92

Axelrod, Robert: (1976), 151, 171; (1979), 174

Aya, Rod (1979), 96

Ayer, A.J. (1982), 168

Ayres, Robert L. (1983), 33


Babbage, Ross (1980), 13

Bacchus, William J. (1983), 291

Bachen, Christine M. (with Roberts, 1981), 204

Bachrach, Peter (1967), 198

Backer, John H. (1978), 76

Bacon, Robert (with Eltis, 1978), 18, 153

Badcock, C.R. (1983), 125

Badie, Bertrand (with Birnbaum, 1983), 86

Badura, Bernhard (1976), 176

Baehr, Peter R. (with Wittrock, 1981), 60, 161, 245

Bagdikian, Ben H. (1983), 204, 297

Bailey, Anne M. (with Llobeta, 1981), 40

Bailey, Derek (1981), 57

Bailey, F.G. (1970), 195

Baker, David (1982), 24

Baker, Robert E. (with Michaels and Preston, 1975), 221

Bakunin, Michael: with Kelley (1983), 42; with Mendel (1983), 42

Baldwin, Maynard M. (1975), 165

Ball, Desmond (1981), 182

Ball, Terrence (1977), 230

Ballard, J.A. (1981), 9, 14, 221

Banting, Keith G. (1979), 91

Barabba, Vincent P. (with Mitroff and Mason, 1983), 48

Barash, David P. (1977), 228

Barber, Bernard (1983), 28

Barber, James D. (1977), 186

Bardach, Eugene: (1977), 128, 197; (1979), 195; with Kagan (1982), 221

Bardes, Barbara A. (with Dubnick, 1983), 221

Barger, Harold M. (1984), 185

Barkan, Joel D. (with Okumo, 1983), 9

Barker, Michael (1982), 65

Barnes, Samuel H. (with Kaase et al., 1979), 29, 30

Barr, Avron (with Feigenbaum, 1981-82), 263

Barrett, Laurence I. (1983), 172

Barron, Frank (with Harrington, 1981), 155

Barrows, Susanna (1981), 203

Barry, Brian: (1973), 192; (1976) 88; with Hardin (1982), 121

Bartley, William Warren (1962), 146

Barton, Allan H. (with Weiss, 1979), 196

Bass, Bernard M. (1983), 145

Bastick, Tony (1982), 122, 165

Basu, Kaushik (1980), 236

Bauer, Peter T. (1981), 24; (1983), 33

Bauer, Raymond A.: (1966), 150; with Gergen (1968), 221; with Pool and Dexter (1972), 88

Baughan, Michalina (with Kolinsky and Sheriff, 1980), 77

Baumann, Zygmunt (1978), 142

Bayraktar, B.A. (with Müller-Merbach, Roberts, and Simpson, 1979), 219

Beach, Lee Roy (with Mitchell, 1978), 172

Beaufré, André (1974), 102

Beck, Carl (with Meso-Lago, 1975), 9

Beck, Stanley, M. (with Bernier, 1983), 298

Becker, Gary (1976), 228

Beckhard, Richard (with Harris, 1977), 196

Beer, Lawrence Ward (1979), 256

Beer, Samuel H.: (1977), 244, 266, 296; (1982), 16

Beer, Stafford (1966), 121, 228; (1975), 121, 239; (1981), 4, 121, 228

Behn, Robert D.: (1978), 210; with Vaupel (1982), 219

Beier, Ulli (1980), 14

Beiner, Ronald (1984), 191

Bell, Bowyer J. (1976), 47, 96

Bell, D.E. (with Keeney and Raiffa, 1977), 191

Bell, Daniel: (1973), 41; (1978), 32; (1982), 7, 239; with Kristol (1981), 33

Wilson, Richard W. (with Greenblatt and A.A. Wilson, 1981), 9
Wimbush, S. Enders (with Alexiev, 1982), 15
Winch, Donald: with Howson (1977), 49; with Collini and Burrow (1984), 220
Winkler, Rutheld (with Eigen, 1981), 169
Winnefeld, James A. (with Davis, 1983), 164
Winston, P. (1975), 233
Winter, Sidney G. (with Nelson, 1983), 135
Withey, Stephen B. (with Andrews, 1976), 150
Wintrobe, Ronald (with Breton, 1982), 145
Wise, J.A. (with Sjobert and Tyszka, 1980), 226
Wittfogel, A. Karl (1957), 36
Wittmann, Walter (with Blum and Kocher, 1982), 162
Wittrock, Bjorn: (1983), 26; with Baehr (1981), 60, 161, 245; with Schwartz and Svedin (1982), 161
Wohlstetter, Albert (1964), 144
Wohlstetter, Roberta: (1962), 149; (1979), 149
Wolf, Charles W. (1979), 83
Wolf, David (with Sproull and Weiner, 1978), 167
Wolfe, Alan: (1977), 32, 88, 118, 205; (1981), 32, 65
Wollmann, Hellmut (with Hellstern, 1983), 210
Wood, John Cunningham (1983), 34
Woodcock, Alexander (with Monte Davis, 1980), 43
Woodside, K. (1982), 30
World Bank: (1982), 24, 296; (1983), 24, 244; (1984), 25
World Meteorological Organization (1978), 25
Wortman, Paul M. (1983), 236
Wriggins, Howard W. (1969), 126
Wright, Erik Olin (1978), 228
Wright, George (1984), 171
Wright, James D. (1976), 26
Wright, Maurice: (1980), 23; with Hood (1981), 2, 57
Wright, Sonia (with Rossi and Freeman, 1979), 210

Wrong, Dennis (1979), 30
Wu, Silas J.L. (1970), 209
Wynne, George (1983), 49


Yaffee, Steven Lewis (1982), 197
Yann, Richard (with Keddie, 1981), 88
Yanvey, George (1983), 112
Yarmolinsky, Adam (with Foster, 1983), 93
Yates, Brock (1983), 48, 49
Yates, Douglas: (1977), 26, 94; (1982), 127, 207, 244, 247
Yavetz, Zvi: (1969), 36; (1983), 28
Yayaraman, Sundaressan (with Konopasek, 1984), 263
Yergin, Daniel (with Hillenbrand, 1982), 24
Young, Hugo (with Sloman, 1983), 201
Young, Michael (1983), 177, 200
Young, Peyton H.: with Okada and Hashimoto (1980), 80, 191; with Okada and Hashimoto (1981), 80, 192
Young, Robert J. (1978), 144
Ysander, B.-C. (with Robinson, 1981), 161, 280


Zablocki, Benjamin (1980), 203
Zacher, Hans F. (with Kohler and Partington, 1982), 90
Zagorin, Perez (1982), 95
Zaltman, Gerald: with Duncan and Holbeck (1973), 156; with Duncan (1977), 104, 232
Zander, Alvin (1979), 226
Zapf, Wolfgang (1975), 150
Zaret, David (1980), 225
Zeckhauser, Richard J.: with Stokey (1978), 221, 222; with Leebaert (1983), 232, 265
Zeeman, E.C. (with Isnard, 1976), 43
Zeeuw, Gerard de (with Jungerman, 1977), 226
Zeleny, Milan (with Cochrane, 1973), 191
Ziegler, Philip (1969), 48
Ziman, J.M. (1968), 11, 20, 177, 228
Zimmerman, Ekkart (1979), 3
Zinberg, Dorothy (1983), 93
Zouwen, Johannes van der (with Geyer, 1978), 228

# Subject Index